Books by Stanley Kimmel

Crucifixion
Leaves on the Water
The Kingdom of Smoke
The Mad Booths of Maryland
Mr. Lincoln's Washington
Mr. Davis's Richmond

THE MAD BOOTHS OF MARYLAND

Junius Brutus Booth, Sr., as Richard III. Etching after a drawing by Rouse. *(Courtesy of the Harvard Theatre Collection)*

THE MAD BOOTHS
OF MARYLAND

BY
STANLEY KIMMEL

SECOND REVISED AND ENLARGED EDITION
WITH 83 ILLUSTRATIONS

DOVER PUBLICATIONS, INC.
NEW YORK

Copyright © 1940 by the Bobbs-Merrill Company; Copyright © renewed 1967 by Stanley Kimmel
Copyright © 1969 by Stanley Kimmel
All rights reserved under Pan American and International Copyright Conventions.

Published in Canada by General Publishing Company, Ltd., 30 Lesmill Road, Don Mills, Toronto, Ontario.
Published in the United Kingdom by Constable and Company, Ltd., 10 Orange Street, London WC 2.

This Dover edition, first published in 1969, is a revised and enlarged republication of the work originally published by The Bobbs-Merrill Company, Indianapolis and New York, in 1940. Ten of the original 11 illustrations reappear in this edition, while 73 have been added. The present edition also contains six supplementary articles and a new foreword by the author.

T 73 19186

Standard Book Number: 486-22231-4
Library of Congress Catalog Card Number: 69-19162

Manufactured in the United States of America
Dover Publications, Inc.
180 Varick Street
New York, N. Y. 10014

*To my devoted wife, Elsie,
who has helped me weather
many storms*

FOREWORD
TO THE DOVER EDITION

The Mad Booths of Maryland was the first biography of that tragic family to give a full account of the elder Booth's matrimonial affairs; the true story of the original birthplace of eight of the ten Booth children and the disappearance of the house; the career of the oldest son, Junius Brutus Booth, Jr., who became one of the noted theatrical managers of the time; Edwin Booth's early days in California; the violent dislike of his sister, Asia, for Mary Devlin, Edwin's first wife, and her opposition to their marriage.

The biography also was the first to give a full report on John Parker of the Washington Metropolitan Police Force, who failed to guard President Lincoln at Ford's Theatre on the night of the assassination, and on the route actually taken out of the city by John Wilkes Booth and David E. Herold after the crime.

To this first edition of more than 200,000 words has now been added, in the form of corrections and revisions of the text, new evidence concerning John Wilkes Booth's common-law wife and children, and other information from heretofore unpublished documents and family letters. Six new Supplements, including excerpts from articles by the present writer which appeared during the intervening years, add to the information in the previous work.

Many of the illustrations in this edition (much more numerous than in the first edition) have never before been published. Among these are photographs of the country through which Booth and Herold traveled, and the places where they found shelter, on their flight southward, including the Tom Jones cabin before it was remodeled into a modern dwelling, and the Garrett house (then about to fall in ruins), where Booth died.

Also in this category of special interest are photographs of Ann Hall, "Mammy" at the Booth farm; of Rosalie Booth, the eldest daughter; and of Dr. Joseph Adrian Booth, youngest of the sons living at the time of their brother's mad act. A copy of the latter photograph was in the War Department file incorrectly marked as a portrait of David E. Herold until identified by the present writer (see p. 336). There is also a photograph of "Tudor Hall," the last Maryland home of the Booths, which is still standing, and occupied, on the farm they once owned in Harford County.

For permission to reprint sections of my articles that first appeared in their publications, I am grateful to Mr. Edwin Tribble, Sunday Editor of the Washington *Star*; Mr. Kenneth W. Harter, Night Managing Editor of the Washington *Post*; and Mr. Robb Sagendorph, President of *Yankee* Magazine, Dublin, N.H.

For certain additional material and photographs, I am indebted to Mr. Richard Merrifield and his daughter Miss Gail Merrifield, descendants of John Wilkes Booth; Mr. Louis A. Rachow, Librarian, The Players; Mr. Paul Myers, Curator of the Theatre Collection, New York Public Library, and his First Assistant, Miss Dorothy Swerdlove.

New York City, S. K.
February 12, 1969.

FOREWORD
to the First Edition

In October, 1934, I first visited the farm near Belair, Maryland, where the Booth family had lived. I was a resident of Washington at the time, and an interest in the legends surrounding John Wilkes Booth prompted my visit. The same interest led me in November to retrace the route over which he escaped from Ford's Theatre to Garrett's farm in Virginia where he died. On this trip I photographed all places having any connection with the man who had killed Lincoln.

That was the beginning of a search that has gone on more or less continuously until today, and that has resulted in this chronicle of the Booth family. My initial research was solely on John Wilkes Booth, in the voluminous government archives dealing with the Lincoln assassination, and in the surviving people who could contribute their items of recollection about the characters involved in that tragedy. I succeeded in bringing to light a number of new facts pertaining to the Booths and to the assassination, which were incorporated in a series of articles in the Washington *Star* in 1936.

I was now too deep in the Booth family to stop. I had early come to realize that the motives for the assassination lay far back in the life of John Wilkes Booth, and that in turn his life could be understood only as a part of the story of the remarkable family of which he was a member. However important Wilkes' act of madness might be in American history, it was but an event in the drama of a family that dominated the American stage for more than seventy years.

At the outset of this larger task, an old actor who had known Edwin Booth called my attention to the fact that several other writers in the past had attempted to tell the story of the Maryland Booths, and had given up in despair when they found themselves in such a maze of fact and fiction that they were unable to distinguish between the two. For the Booths were a family of extraordinary clannishness; and because of the scandal of the elder Booth's flight to America, they balked at nothing to hide their family history from contemporaries. At the same time, they were a family of actors in a period when a recognized American actor toured the theatrical circuits constantly and was always before the public. It was a rare occasion when a quorum of the Booth family could be found in the same spot. The major problems of this book have been to disentangle the facts from the family and theatrical legends, and to tell concurrently the stories of family members who were frequently separated by many states, if not by continents and oceans.

For the most part, my chronology of the theatrical careers of the Booths has been based on a study of contemporary newspaper notices and reviews. Contradictory accounts and dates, as well as other controversial matters, I have discussed in the Comments. All quotations relative to the conspiracy, unless otherwise indicated, are from official records such as Ben Pitman's *Assassination of President Lincoln and the Trial of the Conspirators* and *Trial of John Surratt*.

I wish to thank the Honorable Harry H. Woodring, Secretary of War, for permission to include the various government documents in this work. For theatrical reviews, I am indebted to practically all librarians in the principal cities of the United States, several in England, and those of Honolulu, Sydney and Melbourne, Australia. Special acknowledgment is due Mr. Louis H. Dielman, Librarian, and Mr. Samuel E. Lafferty, of the Peabody Institute, Baltimore; Mr. Macgill James, Director, and Miss Margery Whyte, Secretary, of the Municipal Museum in that city; Mr. George Freedley, Librarian in Charge of the Theatre Collection, and his assistants, and Mr. Louis H. Fox, Chief of the Newspaper Division, New York City Public Library; Miss May Davenport Seymour, Curator of the Theatre and Music Collection of the Museum of the City of New York; and *Variety* for the generous use of their New York *Clipper* files. I am also indebted to Mr. H. S. Parsons, Chief of the Periodical Division, Library of Congress, for facilitating my work there; the late Mr. Edwin B. Pitts, Chief Clerk, Judge Advocate's Office, Washington, D. C. who gave me access to all documents and relics in his care having to do with Lincoln's assassination and the trial of the conspirators; his successor, Mr. Joseph L. Lyons, who aided in checking important material; Mr. George E. Mierke, File Clerk of the Washington Metropolitan Police, for the

FOREWORD TO THE FIRST EDITION

records of John Parker; Miss Mabel R. Gillis, State Librarian, Sacramento, California, whose kindness in answering a flow of letters westward made possible a complete account of the Booths in California; Miss Helen Menken, the well-known actress, who placed at my disposal her collection of Booth letters once belonging to Asia Booth Clarke; Dr. Douglas S. Freeman, Miss Susan B. Harrison, House Regent of the Confederate Museum, Miss Helen McCormack, Director of the Valentine Museum, and Miss Martha Martin, in charge of the Edgar Allen Poe Shrine, Richmond, Virginia, all of whom were most helpful and supplied me with much interesting material relating to the elder Booth, Edwin, and John Wilkes; and to a long list of others who have answered requests for information.

S. K.

New York City,
February 12, 1940.

CONTENTS

BOOK ONE
A MAD TRAGEDIAN
13–92

BOOK TWO
THE BROTHERS
93–145

BOOK THREE
CONFLICT
147–212

BOOK FOUR
CATASTROPHE
213–264

BOOK FIVE
A CHILD OF TRAGEDY
265–334

COMMENTS
335–384

SUPPLEMENTS
385–400

INDEX
401–418

ILLUSTRATIONS

Junius Brutus Booth, Sr., as Richard III   *Frontispiece*

on or following page

Junius Brutus Booth, Sr.	14
First home of the Booths in Harford County, Md.	38
Booth family tree	38
Mary Ann Holmes	38
The elder Booth and three of his sons	38
Asia Booth Clarke	38
Rosalie Ann Booth	38
Ann Hall, servant of the Booths	38
Dr. Joseph Adrian Booth	38
The elder Booth before his nose was broken	72
Tudor Hall, the Booth home	72
The elder Booth at fifty-three and Edwin at sixteen	72
Junius Brutus Booth, Jr.	94
Young Edwin Booth	108
Laura Keene	108
Edwin Booth at twenty-four	108
Edwin Forrest	108
Agnes Booth, wife of Junius Brutus Booth, Jr.	132
John Sleeper Clarke, husband of Asia Booth	132
Mary Devlin, Edwin Booth's first wife	146
Rare photograph of John Wilkes Booth	148
Ford's Theatre	172
Ford's poster advertising his new theatre	172
Original painting of John Wilkes Booth	172
John Thompson Ford, owner of Ford's Theatre	172
David E. Herold, John Wilkes Booth's accomplice	172
Samuel Arnold, one of the conspirators	186
Michael O'Laughlin, one of the conspirators	186
George A. Atzerodt, one of the conspirators	186
Edward Spangler, one of the conspirators	186
Mrs. Mary Surratt	194
Dr. Samuel Mudd	194
Anna Surratt	194
John Surratt	194
Lewis Paine (Powell), one of the conspirators	202
Telegram from John Wilkes Booth to O'Laughlin	202
Lincoln's second inaugural	202

11

ILLUSTRATIONS

The old National Hotel	202
Title page of a song dedicated to John Wilkes Booth	214
Handbills for the performance at which Lincoln was shot	220
The Treasury Guard flag	220
The escape route: (1) The old Navy Yard Bridge	230
The escape route: (2) Lloyd's tavern	230
The escape route: (3) The village of T. B.	230
The escape route: (4) Road to the Mudd house	230
The escape route: (5) The Mudd house	230
The escape route: (6) Path leading away from Mudd house	230
The escape route: (7) Approach to Zachiah Swamp	230
The escape route: (8) The Cox house	236
The escape route: (9) Mary Swan	236
The escape route: (10) The Jones cabin	236
The escape route: (11) Stream below Dent's Meadow	236
The escape route: (12) Shore of the Potomac	236
The escape route: (13) Nanjemoy Stores	236
The escape route: (14) Point of crossing Potomac	240
The escape route: (15) Gambo Creek	240
The escape route: (16) The Quesenberry house	240
The escape route: (17) Quesenberry slave quarters	240
The escape route: (18) Road to the Stewart house	246
The escape route: (19) Rear of the Stewart house	246
The escape route: (20) Front of the Stewart house	246
The escape route: (21) Cabin similar to the Lucas cabin	246
The escape route: (22) Ferry landing at Port Conway	246
The escape route: (23) The Garrett house	246
Bessie Hale, John Wilkes Booth's fiancée	258
Col. La Fayette Curry Baker	258
Booth's body brought back to Washington	258
Edwin Booth	266
Edwin Booth with his daughter Edwina and his second wife, Mary McVicker	276
Booth's Theatre in New York	276
Henry Irving	304
Asia Booth Clarke in 1884	304
Mary Ann Booth in her old age	304
Edwin Booth in 1890	330
Edwin Booth statue in Gramercy Park	330
Letter about Joseph A. Booth photograph	336
Excerpt from letter about John Wilkes Booth's family	386
Izola Martha Mills D'Arcy, Wilkes' common-law wife	388
Ogarita Booth, daughter of Izola and John Wilkes Booth	388

BOOK ONE
A MAD TRAGEDIAN

Junius Brutus Booth, Sr.

CHAPTER I

On a murky day in September, 1813, Richard Booth, a handsome barrister attired in the robes of his profession, took his stand in a London court. He was tall, dark-complexioned, with a flashing eye that defied any question of his respectability. For fifty years he had lived on British soil without a scandal involving his honor and now that honor was in jeopardy. In a stern voice he proclaimed that he was there to defend his son, Junius Brutus Booth, the youth awaiting trial.

A young woman, Elizabeth Walters, of uncertain virtue, formerly in Richard's employ, had sworn to have borne a child by Junius. The defendant declined to answer the charge, but his father spoke at considerable length in his behalf. He said that while living as a servant in his house, Miss Walters had permitted men to sleep there with her all night. This had not been discovered until she had left his service. He quoted extracts from some old acts of Parliament tending to show the illegality of detaining his son upon the evidence of such a woman.

Miss Walters then declared that Junius had offered her a sum of money to swear that the child was his father's, but that she had rejected the offer. The defense failed to impress the court and Junius was ordered to present sufficient sureties to the officers that the child should not become a burden to the parish. He did so and the case was closed.

Though seventeen years of age, Junius was less than average height and slenderly built. His large and expressive features, the straight nose and thin lips of his aristocratic face, framed by a disordered mass of lustrous black hair, claimed immediate attention. One hardly noticed the slightly bowed legs that might have made a less arresting person seem ridiculous. He was not an industrious scholar, but he was quick to learn, and particularly adept in acquiring languages. His knowledge of Greek and Latin pleased his father, who was a great admirer of the classics. However, the compelling magnetism of Junius' dark eyes often led him into romances which interrupted much of his study.

On this day one of these digressions was responsible for his arraignment at the bar. It was not the first (nor was it to be the last) of young Booth's illicit amours to harass Richard. Once before he had been forced to pay a sum of money to a frail nymph when she accused Junius of that "deed of darkness which her situation could no longer conceal."

Richard himself had spent a somewhat irregular youth, but no slanderous escapades had fallen under the prying eyes of the law courts. He had been a vigorous young man, possessed of a spirited idealism which he was determined to shape into reality. At the age of twenty he and his cousin, John Brevitt, imbued with a love of freedom, ran away from England, bent upon reaching the shores of North America and joining the Colonial troops then fighting for independence.

The two young men went to France where they consulted agents for the Congress of America and were informed that they would be unable to secure appointments in the Provincial Service without first obtaining a letter of recommendation from some English gentleman interested in the cause of Liberty abroad. The desire to proceed quickly led the young cousins to dispatch a letter to the celebrated agitator John Wilkes of Westminster, London. This stormy petrel, who had left his wife and kept open house for young men possessing more wit than morals, was a distant relative. They reminded him of their relationship, boasted of their flight from England, and asked that he send them credentials to promote their adventures in the New World.

Unfortunately Wilkes was not sympathetic, for, instead of granting their request, he immediately forwarded the letter to Richard's father, John Booth, a Jewish silversmith whose ancestors had been exiled from Portugal because of their radical political views. In London the refugees had continued their trade and free-thinking, and John had married Wilkes' cousin Elizabeth. Richard's veneration for his mother's famous kinsman prompted him at a later date to suggest the name of John Wilkes for one of his grandchildren.

John Booth was incensed by his son's antics, and with Wilkes' assistance succeeded in having Richard arrested in France and conveyed back to England. John Brevitt was more fortunate and escaped the fate of his cousin. Eventually he arrived in North America, fought the Redcoats, received a captain's commission in Washington's army, married a Quakeress, and helped to swell the ranks of the Sons and Daughters of the American Revolution.

What lay ahead of Richard when he was brought home again, he did not know nor care, but some day he, too, would reach America! Next time no one would be consulted—no one would have an inkling of what he planned to do; he would just pack up and go! His suspicion that the old man's plans for his immediate future would not be to his liking proved to be true. John Booth's firm grasp was like a prisoner's chain. He put a law book into the hand of his rebellious son and bellowed that he must prepare himself to be something more than cannon fodder. Richard obeyed reluctantly; he even acceded to the parental ultimatum by settling down to married life with a young woman having the appropriate family name of Game. Two sons were born to them, Junius Brutus, father of the Maryland Booths, and Algernon Sydney, of whom little is known. The mother died at the birth of a daughter Jane, leaving the three children in the hands of an easy-going, unambitious father.[1]

Richard's practice never prospered too brilliantly, yet he made enough money to live in comfort, buy the Greek and Latin classics he loved to read, and cater to the fashion of the day. In any crowd he was easily recognized by the exceptionally wide lace that fringed his coat and set off his swarthy features to advantage. Through all his apparent acquiescence in this mode of living, he never forgot the budding Republic across the sea and made himself unpopular by insisting that his callers uncover their heads and bow in reverence before a portrait of George Washington which looked down from the wall of his Queen Street quarters in Bloomsbury.

As years passed he began spending more of his time in a near-by tavern sipping his toddy, and his children were left to their own fancies. It was this freedom that had given Junius the opportunity to entangle himself with the frail nymph and Elizabeth Walters. Notwithstanding Richard's apparent neglect, he had been observant of his son's lack of purpose. Between Junius' indiscretions the father had attempted to direct the boy's inclinations from romantic pleasures to profitable work. He had endeavored to apprentice him, first to a printer, then to an architect, and finally to a sculptor. Of all these, Junius wanted most to be a sculptor. The amount Richard was required to pay for his son's tutelage in any one of these professions was more than he could afford, so Junius signed as a midshipman on the brig, *Boxer*, bound for the Mediterranean.

England was again at war with the United States, and before the *Boxer* sailed, its commander, Blyth, was ordered to change its course and proceed to America. Just as the brig was about to depart, Junius was hauled off by the summons to appear in a London court to answer the charges of Elizabeth Walters, and the *Boxer* left without him.[2] Richard was then ignorant of the narrow margin by which his son had missed being at odds with the country which Richard had termed "the grand desideratum of all men." Even had he known, it is doubtful that he would have thanked Miss Walters. When her case was settled, Richard placed Junius in his office to take down his ponderous legal dictations, to study law, and thus earn some of the money paid out for him. This procedure was almost identical with that of John Booth with Richard, although it was not instigated by similar incidents, nor did it produce the same results.

Junius was consumed with an intense desire for adventure and a vent for the creative ability that was bursting within him. Alert and impulsive, his inventive mind chafed at the redundance of legal declamations. He felt he was destined for fame and distinction if he could but find the medium of expressing himself. His attendance of *Othello* at Covent Garden was the deciding factor.

On this, his first visit to the theatre, his quick response to dramatic values was shown in his asking the man seated beside him if Iago would not be hanged in the last act. After he entered his father's office he not only went regularly to the theatre but also read every play he could obtain, and found in the world of make-believe the very outlet for which he had thirsted. He studied a part and then watched every gesture, listened to every intonation of the player in that rôle upon the stage. In his mind he enacted his favorite characters over and over, and often became so enthralled by them that he could not extricate himself from their shadowy clutches. Richard wondered what such strange actions indicated, but he did not deny his son the paltry sum needed for this new interest so long as it kept him out of mischief. Unconsciously, Junius was preparing himself for an event which was to sweep him on to achievements greater than he visioned in his daily dreams.

One of the plays he enjoyed most was Shakespeare's *Richard III*, a favorite with the great bombastic actors, as it gave them a chance to display their talent for swashbuckling oratory to advantage and to reap both money and applause. Junius saw such renowned performers as the Kembles, and grew familiar with the famous rôles of Shakespeare and other popular playwrights. His visits at home became less frequent, and while again out of parental reach and discipline, he made the acquaintance of a few actors who were able to give him the opportunity for which he had been longing.

It was in the fall of 1813 that seventeen-year-old Junius first appeared in the comedy of *John Bull* at a temporary theatre in a London cowhouse on Pancras Street. Here, a curtain of many-colored patches of cloth, no footlights, few and meagre props including an old street lamp and some dilapidated pieces of furniture, a crudely painted backdrop having an exterior scene on one side and an interior scene on the other, served as settings for a variety of plays. Costumes were such as poor aspirants to theatrical fame could beg, steal or buy. The dim candlelight failed to conceal the curve in Junius' legs which once caused bawdy ridicule and loud laughter to mingle with the applause that greeted his initial efforts. This occurred one evening when he appeared as the Duke of Buckingham in *Richard III* and the occupant of a front seat remarked, "Ah, ah, you'd be a pretty fellow to stop a pig." [3] There was little to intimate to Junius that his career would rival those of the most celebrated tragedians.

Young Booth's determination to be an actor displeased his father, so he left home and joined a suburban company under the management of Penley and Jonas, at Peckham, where stage effects and properties were more abundant. His salary was only one pound a week, but this engagement marked the beginning of his professional activity in the theatre. It opened on December 13, 1813, with *The Honeymoon*, in which Booth appeared as Campillo. Then he played with their company at Deptford. For a brief period after the first of the New Year, illness forced him to return home. Upon his recovery he again skipped away with Penley and Jonas' troupe of strolling players who, in May of 1814, arrived in Amsterdam.

The quaint houses with large wooden chimneys, the streets dimly lighted by lamps suspended from ropes swung from one dwelling to another, the drawbridges, lifted by boys and old women for barges to pass under, were all described by Booth in his diary. The English Theatre in which they appeared was commodious and had a painted drop-scene in place of a curtain, but it was awkward to reach the stage as entrances had to be made from above it. Their repertoire included plays such as *Travelers Benighted, Of Age To-morrow, Matrimony*, and the popular bills of Shakespeare's *Hamlet, Richard III*, and *The Merchant of Venice*. They often tossed for the lion's share of the receipts on a designated night which was dubbed a benefit for the fortunate winner. After playing this engagement the troupe went to Antwerp, where the churches filled Booth with such reverence that he was tempted to remain away from the theatre that first evening.

Their journey from Antwerp to Brussels by overland coach passed through a part of the country devastated by the war. Napoleon, having abdicated and retired to Elba, was to emerge for continued hostilities which would end with the battle of Waterloo and St. Helena. Lord Wellington was then in Brussels; hotels were crowded with army officers, pimps, and scavengers profiting from war, and members of the troupe were forced to search for lodgings elsewhere. While knocking at private doors, Booth reached the comfortable home of

Madame Delannoy, who offered him shelter during his sojourn in the city. Madame was the mother of three daughters, the youngest Adelaide, lingering on the verge of spinsterhood. Although none of the young women was beautiful, Adelaide had a pleasing manner and was well-educated. Booth saw her and felt that he was under the right roof. He had no intention of being lonely in this land of exiled Englishmen, shattered demi-reps, and retired swindlers. That this attractive young woman was four years older than Junius did not deter him from making overtures to her. He admired her spirited character and she, in turn, was undoubtedly fascinated by the glamour of his theatrical life. It was not long before they became friendly, and he was calling her Adelaide. What followed was a private matter; even Madame Delannoy did not know.

Since the troupe appeared before small houses, their earnings did not support the number of actors required for the parts, and Booth was often called upon to double in the bills. Penley, of course, took all the title rôles, but Booth was considered the most competent member of the troupe, and after Penley, had his choice of parts. In Brussels, however, he occasionally alternated with Penley in star rôles and was given credit for the perfection of his performances. Among the group of theatrical aspirants there were the Chapman brothers, Samuel and William, who later became members of the famous Chapman family of showboat days on the Ohio and Mississippi rivers.

At the close of the Brussels engagement, Booth left with more baggage than he had upon his arrival—taking Adelaide and her belongings with him. Madame Delannoy did not discover her daughter's departure until she had gone beyond recalling. As he trouped about the country with his stolen prize, Booth's conscience—or the recollection of his experience in an English court—began to haunt him, and he decided to write to Madame Delannoy, requesting her consent to their marriage. His letter was sent from Ostend four months after the flight from Brussels.

Madame Delannoy's answer contained some conditions: she would approve of the union if Booth would give up the stage, return to Brussels, and accept a position more stable than acting. She was shrewd enough to add that she would obtain such a position for him. In replying to her proposal, Booth wrote: "I would like to know how much the place is worth." This was merely an evasion; he had no intention of returning to Brussels. When he posted the letter he knew it was time to leave Ostend.

A few days later, he and Adelaide arrived by packet at Gravesend, England. Not having a passport for his companion, he was obliged to take her to the Alien Office, where he was fortunate in finding a friend who vouched for them with the commissioners. From there they continued on to London.

As Booth's funds were low, they went to his father's home. The old man asked them a few questions and, getting more information than he wanted, flew into a tantrum. He told the lovers to find employment and to legalize their passion. Adelaide was quartered in the house, and Richard kept an eye on his son. During the day, Adelaide trudged from shop to shop hoping to get a position, while her Lothario besieged theatrical managers for a trial night. In time, she found work in a millinery store, and young Booth secured a minor part at Covent Garden Theatre. Sally Booth, leading lady of the company, requested him to add an *e* to his family name so that no one would presume they were related.

When the youthful lovers had saved a few coins, his father hustled them off to the presiding curate in the parish of St. George, who married them on May 8, 1815. As they could not afford to risk the possibility of Adelaide being dismissed by her employer, their wedding remained a secret in the neighborhood. Adelaide, however, hastened to send word of it to her mother and to promise another marriage ceremony "by a Catholic priest when our finances are better." But this was more than she was ever able to maneuver.

Within the first two years after their marriage, a child was born to them and baptized Emilie, but she died while an infant. During this period Booth journeyed in and out of London, playing subordinate rôles there and in the provinces. Then, suddenly, one night at Brighton, he was tossed into an unprecedented theatrical career when he substituted for the celebrated actor Edmund Kean (who had not arrived from London) as Sir Giles Overreach, in *A New Way To Pay Old Debts*. He exhibited such extraordinary talent and ability that many in the astonished audience, having seen Kean in the same character, regarded Booth as his equal.

Kean was known for his lightning-like flashes of interpretation, but here was a younger actor who gave his spectators a panorama of all the emotions in Nature. He was not only the quick dash of fire across the sky—he was also the thunder, the wind and the rain, and the sun breaking through the clouds. Within him were all joys and sorrows— he could draw them to the surface of his being and portray them as an artist painting a canvas before their very eyes. His performance lifted other actors into the proper perspective, giving the play a new and deeper meaning. He had no rules, he followed no traditions, but he made his character think and feel and come alive, largely by the superb control of his voice. When, as Sir Giles, he struck his scabbard and cried, "Do I wear my sword for fashion!", then raised his right arm, exclaiming, "Or is this arm shrunk up or withered!"—when, at the moment of his mad challenge to Lord Lovell, he dashed from the stage to reappear suddenly and ask, with livid lips and chilling voice, "Are you pale?"—the effect he produced froze his audience to their seats. His rendition of this famous rôle was so much a part of him that no one was ever able to imitate it with like results.[4]

News of his success reached London. Lord Erskine, the Honorable Mrs. Chambers, and several other influential persons were impressed by these reports and prevailed upon Harris, manager of Covent Garden Theatre, to secure Booth for an immediate engagement. Harris wrote to Booth, but the letter passed him on his way to London. Upon his arrival there, February 11, 1817, he was amazed to see playbills announcing him in the title rôle of *Richard III* at Covent Garden the following night. Booth went to rehearsal the next morning and was received with cool indifference by the other actors, who looked on him as a young upstart making himself ridiculous by trying to usurp the eminent position of Edmund Kean, actually risking one of Kean's best parts. In spite of the awkward situation, Booth went ahead with his performance.

Even at this early date, he played *Richard III* much the same as in later years. His opening scenes were given in a moderate tempo so that he could sway his audience by his fiery outbursts as the tragedy progressed. With his magical, dynamic voice, he wooed Lady Anne, kneeling in mock humility at her feet. After his remorseful dream in the tent, he arose from his couch to rush downstage like one gone mad, until the clearing of his mind was signaled by his utterance, "Richard is himself again." The combat scene of the last act was one of savage fury. Never had the crook'd-back tyrant Richard fought so gallantly. Booth sprang at his adversary as if to cut him down with one blow, but failing, carried on the fight while the audience arose and wildly cheered him. Richard's scorn of all danger, his will to triumph over Richmond, echoed in the agonizing cry of his defeat:

> The vast renown thou hast acquir'd
> In conquering Richard, does afflict him more
> Than e'en his body's parting with his soul.

Again Booth was compared with Kean, who was then playing at the Drury Lane on alternate nights (a custom followed by many great stars), and realized that he had a serious rival in the handsome young actor. The celebrated tragedian had a host of ardent followers, yet Booth had undermined his support and had captivated a dangerous share of zealous admirers. Kean had been reigning supreme in London and jealous of his proud position in the theatrical world, began scheming to disqualify this pretender to his throne. He decided to get Booth under his control by making him an offer for their joint engagement; then he would put the young rascal in his place by giving him the difficult rôle of Iago to his Othello.

The applause of the most brilliant and critical audience of the day dazzled Booth. Congratulated by great men, sought after by managers, he had no experience to help him choose the wisest course. His father had not attended his performance and took little interest in his new-found fame. A second appearance, as Richard, at Covent Garden increased the plaudits ringing in young Booth's ears, so he set a higher value on his acting and demanded better terms from Harris. Delay in settling the matter, however, gave Kean the chance to suggest that Booth sign an agreement with the management of Drury Lane to play counter-parts with him. Such an opportunity to perform with the most renowned actor of the time was not to be turned down. Young and pulsing with ambition, Booth made the obvious choice. He was too inexperienced to realize that Kean had trapped him into a contract which would be detrimental to his advancement.

Shortly after his brilliant introduction at Covent Garden, he left without warning and was announced to appear with Kean at Drury Lane. They opened February twentieth, with Kean as Othello and Booth as Iago. From the moment they were on the stage until the final drop of the curtain, Kean took every possible advantage of Booth. He tossed him aside, clipped his lines, and tried in every way to confuse him. Booth was caught, but he stood his ground and gave a fair performance. It was not a triumph for him—nor was it for Kean. What occurred warned each man of the other, and they planned accordingly.

Overnight Drury Lane became the center of theatrical interest. The rivalry between Kean and Booth, the new discovery, was the talk of the town. Newspapers were filled with stories and critical opinions. Since Booth was receiving more than his share of publicity and flattering attention, Kean concluded to have him put down once and for all by assigning him only minor rôles, so that his youthful rival would be unable to measure his strength adequately against him. But Booth was not so easy to manage.

No change was made for February twenty-second, the alternate night of his engagement at Drury Lane, as he was scheduled to repeat Iago to Kean's Othello. The house was packed with fashionables who had paid the fantastic sum of a guinea a seat. Excitement was intense. Everyone had made a choice, and was ready to shower his favorite with wild applause. Then the manager stepped before the curtain, announcing that Mr. Booth was ill and would not appear. This snapped the tension of the audience and they broke into uncontrolled confusion.

The next morning posters throughout the city told of Booth's return to Covent Garden under a three-year contract, and informed the bewildered public that he would perform *Richard III* early the following week. The management of Drury Lane promptly posted placards denouncing Booth for violating his engagement with them, and from then on a bitter animosity developed between the supporters of the two theatres. The Covent Garden curtain went up before an audience crowded to suffocation. But from Booth's first appearance, he was greeted with such an outburst of groans and hisses that not a word could be heard from the stage throughout the entire play. Kean's enthusiasts had filled the house with the intention of causing as much disorder as possible, to give the impression that Booth was a miserable failure.

London was vibrant with excitement over the affair, but Booth was calm. He published an apology for leaving Drury Lane and continued playing at Covent Garden. The first few evenings he was heckled and tormented by Kean's followers, but, finally, his persistence was rewarded by the tumultuous applause of friends. From that time opposition dwindled. Kean's champions found it useless to go further, and Booth's admirers thronged to see their young hero night after night. Kean now found himself in a dangerous light as the instigator of these disturbances and published a statement repudiating all responsibility for the vehement hostility to his rival. However, a short engagement they played together at Drury Lane, in August of 1820, also was unmarked by any evidence of friendliness.

Following Booth's return to Covent Garden, money flowed into his coffers so plentifully that Adelaide was released from trimming hats, and he began the collection of a theatrical wardrobe noted for its accuracy in every detail. He became intimate with many famed actors, one of whom, Charles Kemble, supported him in a production of *Cymbeline*. The handsome young man who had shown such defiance and magnificent ability was in great demand for social functions, and the numerous invitations he and Adelaide received were gratefully accepted. Booth wrote to his mother-in-law, boasting of his earnings, and later, as proof of his affluence, sent Adelaide home to visit her while he toured the provinces. In several cities the ovation given him after his final exit was so deafening that it was impossible to continue and the performance was abruptly closed. He expected to make a fortune from his work and became impatient with his theatrical career when his wealth did not materialize as rapidly as he had hoped. "Unless I am more successful this season, I shall quit the stage and enter the army," he wrote to Adelaide.

Booth cannot be blamed for this slight discouragement. He had worked so earnestly to attain success that failure to achieve an objective beyond his reach threw him off balance. Adelaide answered and urged him to be sure that he preferred a military life to that of the theatre before he made a definite change. Fortunately, he did not yield to this eccentric impulse, and upon her return to London, he was again being applauded by the multitudes at Covent Garden. The success of this engagement plunged him decisively into his tempestuous career in the world of make-believe.

Yet for all the good judgment and determined character that Booth had shown in the first weeks of his London success, he had an erratic streak of impetuosity which, when controlled, made him an undisputed genius, but when unleashed, led him to the edge of madness. His emotional instability was manifested by an escapade that took place in the manufacturing town of Manchester on one of his early jaunts to the provinces.

A large audience greeted him, and he realized that failure to please them would endanger his future in that locality. At every appearance on the stage he made an effort to increase their applause; still all the tricks he used to win them over were of no avail. At last, he reached that part of the play in which a fight occurred, and the fury within him caused by the apathy of the spectators was vented upon the poor actor playing the opposing part. He gave him an overdose of what Kean had given Iago at Drury Lane. As Booth boxed him about the stage, the audience broke into shouts and cheers. The more he belabored the man, the louder grew the applause. His antagonist was yelling with pain, but Booth kept on until he had knocked him out. Then he sat down in a chair, leaned his panting body toward the pit, his face depicting the most bitter contempt, and exclaimed: "What do you think of that, you low-lived button-makers?" A few seconds later, Booth was fleeing from the theatre with a mob at his heels, who so threatened him that he was forced to leave the city.

This incident was similar to many such freakish displays of Booth's temperament at a later date, but just now he did not allow himself to indulge perniciously in them. On the contrary, his grasp of rôles showed uncanny clarity of thought. The gifts that the young actor had so strikingly displayed on that historic evening in Brighton were not superficial endowments. He went from peak to peak, thrilling audiences with his astounding voice, playing upon it like an instrument, and throwing a transcendent light on one part after another. Flights of rhetoric were popular in his day, but more than mere waving of arms and thundering phrases, his gestures were as eloquent as his inflections, rendering his listeners breathless. He had an intuitive sense of cumulative effect in characterization and could direct and control the motivation of a play purely by the modulation of his voice. The emotional strain of such interpretation was exacting to a degree, but with few exceptions, he maintained an astonishing level of excellence during these early years.

Mr. and Mrs. Junius Brutus Booth were now being toasted and fêted all over London. Adelaide was popular for her ready wit and fascinating foreign accent, and Junius was the lion of the hour. They went everywhere together when he was in town and were much admired as an attractive, happily married couple. On January 21, 1819, they had a son and named him Richard Junius.[5] Adelaide was overjoyed. Her husband was away much of the time, rehearsing and playing, and now she would not feel so lonely.

The following year Booth's natural aptitude for the drama and his strong healthy constitution took him to the highest pinnacle of his youthful endeavors. The Lord Chamberlain had prohibited the presentation of *King Lear* during the last part of the Regency in George III's time, feeling that Lear's madness was too delicate a subject and too pertinent to the English monarch's current condition. On the death of the King, however, the ban was lifted, and Booth prepared to play Lear on alternate nights for several weeks, beginning April 13, 1820, at Covent Garden.

In the cast were Charles Kemble, W. C. Macready, and Sally Booth. It was the young actor's crowning performance. He seemed to penetrate Lear's madness as if he himself had suffered the same tortures of the mind. "The white beard; the nose in profile, keen as the curve of a falchion; the ringing utterance of the names, 'Regan,' 'Goneril;' the close-pent-up passion, striving for expression; the kingly energy; the affecting recognition of Cordelia in the last act,"[6]—were masterpieces of likeness and the emotions that swayed the baffled mind and heart of the deposed and abandoned old sovereign.

Booth's Lear was a triumph. Even the critics who favored Kean reluctantly admitted that the younger man's impersonation was subtler and more moving.

At this time Booth also played at the Cobourg Theatre in East London. But soon he packed his costumes, told his family good-by, and sailed for Amsterdam, Holland, where he appeared in the English Theatre. There he displayed another of those peculiarities that were to beset his later life.

Thomas Flynn, a London actor, was also a member of this company. He was a jovial Irishman with a plump face, dark eyes, a long narrow nose, sensitive mouth and compressed lips, crowned by an abundance of dark curly hair. The two men were seen together so much that soon they were known as "the inseparables."

In Amsterdam, the Prince of Orange, hearing of Booth's superlative performances, commanded him to appear as Macbeth that he might see him in that character. On the designated night, however, Booth could not be found, and the manager asked Flynn to make further search for him. Several days passed, and Booth's disappearance was still a mystery. It was feared that he had fallen into the canal and drowned or that he had met with some other fatal accident. One afternoon, as Flynn was playing billiards in a tavern, he thought he heard Booth's voice in an adjoining barroom, and hastened there to find his friend surrounded by beautiful Dutch girls. He informed Booth of the anxiety he had caused by his actions, and the displeasure of his royal highness when he failed to appear as commanded. Booth replied that he regretted having disappointed those concerned, and was then preparing to apologize to the Prince in the native tongue by perfecting his Dutch in a method different from that taught in textbooks. Booth needed more than Adelaide's charms to bind him with fidelity. Another date was announced for the command performance, and the young actor's Macbeth so delighted the Prince that he forgave his lack of courtesy and presented him with a sum of money.

By autumn of 1820, Booth was back in London, adding more laurels to his crown at Drury Lane, where he again appeared with Kean and had the support of noted actors. With him as Cassius, in a production of *Julius Caesar*, were James W. Wallack as Brutus, and John Cooper as Marc Antony, the initial appearance of each one in his part. Then at the moment that Booth seemed destined for great success and the realization of his most cherished ambitions, he was caught by the dark loveliness of a girl peddling flowers from the Bow Street Market surrounding Covent Theatre. Her name was Mary Ann Holmes.

Booth was twenty-four, and Mary Ann six years younger. She was his equal in height and had an attractively rounded figure. Her full generous mouth, soft brown eyes, and regular features in the pale oval face with its halo of glossy black curls, were a blend of almost

Latin beauty. Her home was at Reading with a widowed mother, but employment in London required her to live in the English capital.

It had not been necessary for him to introduce himself when he spoke to her at a flower stand in the market—she recognized him at once as the handsome young actor who was being acclaimed by all London. He had taken her hand in his and it seemed he must have done so before, yet it was their first meeting. His compliment to her, his melodious voice, the appeal in his eyes, all overpowered her, and she felt drawn toward him by some uncontrollable force.

Did she often visit the theatre, he asked her. Not often, was her reply, though she had seen him in *King Lear* and could hardly believe now that *he* was actually that poor little old man on the stage. She laughed and felt the pressure of his hand as he asked, "When will you have a day to spend with me?" He waited, but she turned away. "Tomorrow?" This audacious young actor was urging "tomorrow!" Her answer came before she knew she was whispering, "Yes—tomorrow."

A moment later he had gone—people were passing and flowers had to be sold. But reverberating like some chord of music above the roar, she could hear that word, "tomorrow!"

Booth continued his domestic life with Adelaide, seeing his flower girl only at intervals. He became an actor at home as well as on the stage. However, a wife and child, and a father who would not tolerate such philandering, made this double rôle perilous. Soon, Booth planned with Mary Ann to get away from London to some place where they would not be recognized. Under the pretext of another tour, he packed his theatrical wardrobe and sailed to France with his flower girl.

To contend that Mary Ann Holmes did not know of Adelaide would be absurd. Mr. and Mrs. Junius Brutus Booth had gone about socially a great deal, and the tragedian was too prominent in London to escape public interest in his personal and domestic affairs. But it is certain that Adelaide did not know of her youthful rival.

Perhaps Booth at first intended this voyage to be no more than an interlude in his life, but constant association with Mary Ann deepened his love for her, and they stopped longer than he had proposed at Calais and Boulogne.

Upon their arrival in London, Mary Ann returned to her quarters and Booth went home to Adelaide and his son. Neither she nor his father had any idea of what had occurred. Adelaide's presence made Booth feel that he could not live without the other charmer. She had been more responsive to his moods during the short time he had known her than Adelaide had been in all the seven years they had spent together. Unlike his over-active wife, Mary Ann possessed a depth of understanding and a poised serenity far beyond her age. The passion he felt for her did not pass like his other infatuations, for the realization of Mary Ann's endowments enslaved and tormented him day and night. The situation in which he was placed now became more difficult to endure than before, and he asked Mary Ann to accompany him to Deal, a summer resort on the North Sea not far from Dover. Again the trusting Adelaide heard Booth's alibi of another theatrical engagement. It was fortunate that, to complete the illusion, he took the usual clothing and costumes with him. Although he did not then know it, he was to be away a long time.

At Deal, Booth purchased a piebald pony named Peacock that had attracted his fancy, and galloped about like a young knight. But the danger of meeting friends at such a place was apparent, and he decided to take Mary Ann on another voyage. With Peacock in tow, they boarded a sailing vessel bound for the West Indies and due to stop over at Funchal, a port on the Island of Madeira off the coast of Portugal.

They arrived late in April, 1821, and were enthralled by the striking grandeur of rugged peaks towering above deep ravines and abundant vineyards. Rooms were engaged at a small inn, and Peacock was given a stall in a stable. Each day Booth rode him up and down a narrow street in the port while groups of natives admired the hearty little animal. Only mules and oxen were used on the island, and a piebald pony was something of an oddity. While he was there, Booth had many offers for Peacock, but refused to part with him.

Once Booth tasted the native wines, the island became a paradise, and with Mary Ann in his arms, he forgot the fame he had won, and the family he had left in England. Here they celebrated his twenty-fifth birthday, on May first, and visited the Carmelite Convent, built high above the town. On the trip up the steep mountain side, Mary Ann was carried in a palanquin on the shoulders of natives. As the Angelus bells sounded for prayer, they set their burden gently down and bowed in reverence. Booth crossed himself and fervently joined the natives, but they were not so amazed as Mary Ann, who had never seen him in such a devout attitude.

One evening, as the young couple sat on the veranda of the little inn, Booth held a half-filled wineglass in his hand and related what he had learned of the wonderful process by which it was made. Mary Ann listened patiently, waiting for him to finish, for she too had something to say. They hardly noticed the islanders sauntering toward the harbor until Booth, putting down his glass to look in the direction they were taking, saw a great clipper ship, with an overhanging bow and tall raking masts, lying off the port. It was the *Two Brothers*.

"Where's she bound?" he called out to several men who were passing.

"For the States," one answered. "She's putting in here for cargo." Booth's silence as he gazed seaward gave Mary an opportunity to speak.

It was then she told him she was going to have a child.

Her confession did not startle Booth as she had expected. She was unaware that he had been placed in similar situations even before he had taken his marriage vows. But the father of Elizabeth Walters' bastard was not a man to hesitate under any circumstances. He came to decisions quickly and acted on them. He knew if they should return to London there would come a time when Mary could no longer continue as a flower girl in the public market without her condition being noticed. Neither could she go home and face her mother's wrath. He had endured such ordeals with his father, and did not care now to plead for Adelaide's forgiveness if the secret should be discovered. The way out of their dilemma was as clear to Booth as a stride across an unobstructed stage.

He told Mary Ann that all his life he had looked at a portrait of George Washington, and listened to his father expound the benefits to be derived from living in that great Republic across the sea. Often he had thought of going there; and, since it now offered more inducements than even his father had included in his eulogies, and since Providence had placed within their reach the very means of accomplishing that purpose, he suggested that they sail to the United States. There he could take care of her and plan for the future. Would she go with him?

It was hardly necessary for the young actor to ask. From the day they met, Mary Ann had been willing to follow him anywhere. He prevailed on the captain of the *Two Brothers* to allow them passage, and, again with Peacock in tow, they went aboard. As there were no accommodations other than for the crew, the captain generously gave up his cabin to the handsome young man and the winsome girl whom he supposed to be his wife.

Once under way Booth began to face the problem that lay before him. He did not have enough funds to support two people, even on a short visit to the United States, and so he would have to secure engagements in American theatres when he arrived. Yet this would not be a simple matter, as most of the actors trouping through the Atlantic states were English people who knew of his marriage to Adelaide and might ask for explanations about Mary Ann. Edmund Kean and several other well-known stars had preceded him and were then playing in eastern cities. If his old rival ever discovered his philandering, Booth knew he would make the most of it! Any one of a dozen Britishers who had known him intimately in London might return there before he sailed back and tell his wife about seeing him abroad with a charming girl as his constant companion! The only solution was to play in smaller American cities, hoping to avoid his countrymen, make enough money to cover expenses, attend to Mary Ann's needs, and get home to England, quickly and quietly, as soon as it was at all possible.

But such a plan was soon discarded. In the New World their romance was to continue. From this time until Booth's death no other woman ever attracted the great tragedian.

Almost half a century later, Asia Booth Clarke, in her books of discretions, stated that her father, Junius Brutus Booth, married Mary Ann Holmes at the home of the Honorable Mrs. Chambers in London, on January 18, 1821, before they departed for the United States.[7] On this occasion, Asia continued, Mrs. Chambers presented the young bride with the jewels Booth afterward used in his Richard's crown. Such a marriage could not possibly have taken place, but since ten children were born to them, of whom Asia was one, she insisted for the sake of legitimacy that there had been a wedding in England.

Few lines have been written about this London flower girl who became the mother of the Maryland Booths. Notwithstanding the facts here related, all the evidence of those who knew her indicates that she was a woman of intelligence and character. She bore the many vicissitudes in her life heroically, and in the story of this unfortunate family, she stands above the tragic scene, helpless, silent, uncomplaining. But as she sailed from the island of Madeira with Junius Brutus Booth, a young actor already famous, she thought only of the happiness that she found in his companionship, and was confident that her trust in him would never be shaken.

CHAPTER II

On June 30, 1821, after a voyage of forty-four days, the young couple landed at Norfolk, Virginia.[8] A crinkled manifest recently found in the archives of the Bureau of Immigration reveals that they listed themselves as actors. Booth immediately sent word of his whereabouts to Adelaide and assured her that he would forward money to her whenever possible. He added that his sudden decision to sail to the United States was due to some trouble he had had with English managers. What excuse Mary Ann sent her mother is not known, but from subsequent events we can believe she informed her of a marriage.

Charles Gilfert was then manager of the Richmond Theatre, and Booth's fame made it easy to arrange with him for his American début in that southern city. July sixth was agreed upon, and the announcements that he would appear as Richard III were posted. An hour before curtain time, the house was crammed from pit to gallery. Booth had not fully recovered from his long voyage and during the first three acts of the play his performance was so tame that Gilfert became suspicious of his identity, believing himself to be the victim of an impostor. But in the fourth act Booth strode into so glamorous a portrayal of the crook'd-back tyrant that the audience, critics, and Gilfert were enraptured, and when the curtain went down he was booked for a return engagement.

Booth's next appearance was in Petersburg, where he opened in the same bill. On the morning of the date announced for this engagement, he did not show up for rehearsal, and the company was compelled to go through the lines of the play without him until "a small man that looked to be a well-grown boy of about sixteen years of age came running up the stairs, wearing a round-about jacket and a cheap straw hat, both covered with dust, and inquired for the stage-manager." Members of the company were astonished when they discovered the young fellow's name was Booth and heard him say "he had been late for the stage-coach that left Richmond early in the morning, and that he soon after started on foot, and had walked all the way—twenty-five miles!"[9] Evidently Peacock was taking a holiday.

After this performance Booth returned to Richmond, finished his engagement there, then reappeared in Petersburg, playing Sir Edward Mortimer, in *The Iron Chest*. It was during this rendition that his acting so affected Noah M. Ludlow, a member of the cast, that he was unable to continue and only recovered his self-possession when Booth said, in an undertone, "Go on—go on." With money in his pockets, Booth took Mary Ann to a near-by roadside inn presuming it a safe retreat in which to shelter her while he was on tour. Her condition was now beginning to be noticeable and added to the complications of having her travel with him. But the inn turned out to be a favorite with English actors playing in the South, and a meeting with the distinguished tragedian Thomas Cooper, who was also a guest, warned Booth that this was not the place he was seeking.

In September he played another engagement in Richmond, adding to his purse and laurels, and then went on to New York. What became of Mary Ann during the next three months is not definitely known. As her confinement came within this period it is not very probable that she traveled north with Booth. Apparently he took Mary Ann to Charleston and left her there, intending to return in time to be with her at the birth of their child.

The New York that Booth first saw in 1821 clustered about the Battery and its surrounding streets where flimsy frame houses served as homes or shops for a population of over one hundred thousand people. Cobblestones and red bricks formed winding lanes that turned the lower end of the island into a maze through which no stranger could find his way. Private carriages were seldom seen, for the city was so compact that there was no need for them. "Citizens" walked, or took one of several omnibuses which tossed them about with no regard for their anatomies. With the exception of the theatre, there were few places of amusement other than the taverns where men sat in clouds of thick smoke, gulping brandy and shouting at the tops of their voices. Social life after dark was limited to family gatherings or an occasional quilting party which ended with the serving of some homemade delicacy and cider or a whisky punch. Inns were haunted by a variety of bugs, and had not a semblance of comfort. If the night were cold, and the traveler had an extra coin, he could rent a warming pan for his bed. Dress and customs reminded Booth of England, but the polished elegance of Old World towns was missing. One of his countrymen remarked that New York then "was beyond the pale of metropolitan possibilities."

At the theatre, Shakespeare was most in favor, varied with Goldsmith, Sheridan, and other playwrights on alternating nights. This demand for classical drama made matters easy for the managers who avoided all risk of novelty by catering to the popular taste. The English custom of benefit nights for stars, however, curtailed a manager's profits by withholding all or a part of the receipts. These benefits were usually given on the last night of a short engagement or at least once a week if a star were playing over a longer period.

The Park Theatre where Booth opened with a performance of *Richard III* on October fifth of that year, was in Park Row, one of the busy districts of the city. It was here that the manager, Edmund Simpson, introduced nearly all the distinguished English actors of the period, Charles and Fanny Kemble, George Cooke, Edmund Kean, James Wallack, and many others. The interior of the theatre was illuminated by flickering candles and tallow dips, while on the stage the uncertain flare of an oil lamp sent out a narrow beam known as the focus, which each actor strove to capture for himself. This somewhat modified the entire effect of a production. A performance often amounted to no more than a contest of strategy among the players for the focus spot. Kean, who had made his New York début before Booth arrived, was congratulated by a friend on his remarkable performance as Othello at this theatre, where, it seems, he had difficulties with another Iago. "I thought you were really going to choke Iago in earnest," the friend observed, to which Kean replied, "In earnest? I should think so! Hang the fellow, he was trying to keep me out of the focus!"[10] In spite of such disadvantages, New York was captivated by Booth's performance. Critics reported that he made his first favorable impression in the wooing scene with Lady Anne, and that, in the contest with Richmond, he was loudly applauded, and fell amid cries of "Bravo! Bravo!" from all parts of the house. At the close of the engagement he took a benefit and cleared twelve hundred dollars. He was deeply touched by the warmth of his reception, and when asked to speak to his delighted audience, his manner was so modest and gracious that it served only to raise him higher in their esteem. "Few actors have been better received," commented the *Evening Post.* "His histrionic abilities exceeded all expectations and he fully maintained his reputation as a great tragedian." With shouts and huzzahs echoing in his ears, Booth continued his tour and, on November first, made his Baltimore début in the same bill, and created another furore.

At this time there was little native theatrical talent in the United States. The American theatre relied solely on visiting English stars to bring life to the popular drama. When Booth eventually came into the lamplight in the larger towns, it was only natural that his style of acting should be again compared to Kean's. Critical opinion shows that Booth was considered a worthy rival and not only equaled Kean in his interpretations but often added original touches that greatly enhanced his performance.

At intervals Booth wrote to Adelaide, transmitting money for her support and little Richard's, giving them reason to believe he would return to them in time. But, following a triumphal engagement in Charleston, the event occurred which was destined ultimately to separate him forever from Adelaide. In that city, on December 22, 1821, a first child was born to Mary Ann Holmes and named Junius Brutus Booth, Jr. As Booth was announced to appear elsewhere on that date, it is unlikely that he was able to be present, as he had planned, at the birth of his namesake.[11]

Early in the next year Booth surprised his friends by applying for the position of lighthouse-keeper on Cape Hatteras. The birth of Junius, and the necessity of keeping mother and child away from the prying interest of English actors traveling over the theatrical circuit of the States, was responsible for this otherwise eccentric notion. Booth was determined to prevent any knowledge of Mary Ann and little Junius from reaching those who might know of Adelaide and their son Richard. He made notes of what was required to live at such a place, the salary he would receive, the fact that no taxes were paid, and he implored a collector of customs to intercede with the government for him. Theatrical managers, not wishing to lose so profitable an asset, whispered into the ear of the customs collector, and Booth did not get the job. Unintentionally, they probably performed a great service to mariners. A friend of Booth's said later it would have been better to put out the light than to leave him in charge of it. Thwarted in this whim, he went back to the theatre and on May 6, 1822, began his first Boston engagement, as Richard III, before an appreciative audience. His benefit night in *Hamlet* netted him eight hundred dollars. A portion of all receipts from such sources was carefully tucked away for the purpose of buying a home in the United States when he could afford it.

By summer he had returned to a temporary shelter for Mary Ann and the baby in Baltimore. Now that he had come before the public in the largest American cities, it meant that he must often run into friends from England, and whether he remained permanently in the United States or not, he could hardly risk the coveted social position he had gained in London by the disclosure of a family in America. Absolute isolation was imperative. Baltimore was midway between northern and southern engagements and made a convenient headquarters in the summertime when the theatre was inactive. So Booth began a search for some inaccessible retreat in Maryland. While exploring the wooded region of Harford County, about twenty-five miles north of Baltimore near Belair, he discovered a vacant log house on the farm of Elijah Rogers. It consisted of four rooms, a kitchen, and a loft. Booth rented it immediately.

His motive for removing Mary Ann and their child to this wilderness was said to have been the need to escape from yellow fever, then raging in Baltimore, but the same danger of discovery that had influenced his dream of a lighthouse domicile really determined his choice. There were places other than snake-infested forests to live in if Booth wished merely to escape yellow fever.

The privacy of this shelter was guarded by three large dogs; and pony Peacock's adventures were just beginning. With Mary Ann and little Junius safely ensconced, Booth galloped off with a pack of costumes for some near-by appearance or carted his trunk to a Baltimore steamer or overland coach if engagements took him to distant parts of the country. Until now the natural exuberance of youth had supplied him with boundless energy, but the physical strain of his acting and the worry of providing for two families began to tell on the young man, and he started to indulge in an excess of drinking while on tour. Although his appearances were later affected by an increasing weakness in this direction, there is no indication that the excellence of his acting was impaired at this time. His failure to draw large audiences in Philadelphia following his début in *Richard III* on February 17, 1823, was due to the prior engagement of Charles Mathews, a popular English comedian, who had played to full houses and temporarily absorbed the funds and interest of the theatre-going public.

Far across the Atlantic, Adelaide and her son had drifted back and forth between the home of old Richard in London and her mother's in Brussels. Mail was slow in those days and she could not hope to hear from Booth in America more than every two months. Her confidence in his promise to return was not shaken by his delay in doing so, nor did his long absence arouse suspicion of some other affiliation. That Booth managed to keep her from following him to the United States for over twenty-five years is amazing. The visit he paid her in England, the letters he wrote, and money he sent, were probably for the purpose of keeping her in constant expectancy of their reunion so that she would not become curious and investigate his affairs. Her reliance in his integrity was not shared by his father, who by this time must have sensed why his son had failed to return within a reasonable period.

The situation the old gentleman was in by the summer of 1822 made it necessary for Adelaide and her child to take up living quarters elsewhere while in London.

Richard Booth was then having trouble with his daughter Jane. A young good-for-nothing named Jimmy Mitchell had been bringing his goat around to Richard's house and milking it of the quantity Richard wished to purchase. Periodically, he blacked the boots of the proud old gentleman and scoured the knives in his kitchen. By means of his backdoor entrée, Jimmy became acquainted with Jane and persuaded her to marry him.

Richard's legal practice was still not a flourishing source of income. His daughter's marriage to an upstart irritated him to the point of distraction, and when he heard of Junius' retreat in the New World, he knew that the time had come to fulfill his lifelong desire to live in a republic. He decided to get away from the smell of Jimmy's goat and pack off to America. Without warning, he moved them all out of his house, sold his property, and suddenly disappeared from London. The possibility that those he wished to leave behind might insist on accompanying him was sufficient cause for his secrecy. Late in 1822, the scholarly old man arrived at the Rogers farm with little more than a load of classical literature and the clothes of an English gentleman, his snow-white hair wrapped in a queue. This fashionable attire caused Harford County citizens to look on him as something of a freak, but he remained there, and a year later, on July fifth, was present at the birth of Mary Ann's second child, Rosalie. If Richard had intended to censure this union, he was silenced by Mary Ann's imperturbable common sense and understanding affection for his son.

In 1824, Junius, having accumulated a sufficient sum of money, decided to settle permanently in that section of Maryland. He approached Dr. Richard W. Hall, who lived in the community, about the purchase of one hundred and fifty acres of densely wooded land adjoining the Rogers property. As Booth was an alien and could not hold landed property in the United States in perpetuity, it was leased to him for a period of one thousand years, at a rental of one cent, payable annually, if lawfully demanded on the premises.[12]

He then bought the log house in which his family were living on the Rogers place and moved it across several fields to his newly acquired acreage. "This proceeding caused great wonderment among the villagers, as every available man, ox, and horse, that could be hired, were in requisition. Much time and money were expended in this undertaking, but its successful accomplishment stamped the owner as a master mind, and the more fiercely the winter storms raged and the summer tornadoes swept by, the more wise did he appear to those who had predicted the quick demolition of the taut little cabin."[13] When the log house had been anchored, the raising of more American Booths began. Eight of the ten children were born on that site, and all but one of them in the log house.[14]

The only exit from this retreat was a crooked and narrow pathway, leading to a coach road about a quarter of a mile off. Once a week the post boy tossed papers and letters over a gate at the main highway and sometimes on moonlight nights it became the free hunting ground for sportsmen and their baying hounds. Otherwise it was devoid of human beings.

Since there was little or no theatrical activity in the summer, Booth decided to turn over his acreage to farming. This would supply the family with food and milk and if well-managed could be the source of a marketable surplus. Not only that, but by working on the land himself, he could build up strength and vitality to pursue his profession in the winter months. The admirable plan of being a farmer in the summer and an actor in the winter proved so successful that Booth followed this pattern of life to the end of his days in Maryland.

Shortly after settling on the farm, Booth hired a slave from Dr. Elijah Bond at Belair. The slave was a giant Negro named Joe, jet black and boasting descent from a Madagascan prince. When Richard went to town on some family errand Joe accompanied him, following at his heels as he shuffled about the streets. The sight of the strange pair brought shopkeepers to their windows and made villagers nudge one another. Eventually Joe married Ann Hall, a young colored woman in the neighborhood, and brought her to the Booth home, where she became the genial "mammy" of the household.[15]

Booth put all hands to work. The cabin was plastered, then whitewashed, and its small, square window frames and broad, plain shutters were painted red. A cherry-shoot was planted near the door and grew to be a favorite shade tree for family gatherings on warm afternoons. Ground was cleared, a vineyard planted, and an orchard laid out. Stables were erected, horses and cows purchased, a dairy built, and a near-by spring, in which an enormous green bullfrog croaked, was ornamented with a granite ledge and steps. Booth subscribed to a weekly magazine on farming which hung on a file with his playbills. In an old notebook he jotted down items concerning the tilling of the soil and the acting of great dramas. The Booth library now consisted of a varied number of subjects and included the works of such authors as Shelley, Keats, Racine, Tasso, Dante, and Shakespeare. A few engravings adorned the side wall of the parlor, furnished in the roughest

The first home of the Booths in Harford County, Maryland. The center portion of this dwelling was the original log cabin. Exterior alterations and additions were made after it was moved to Booth's farm. In this house, and on this site, eight of ten children, including Edwin and John Wilkes, were born. The family of Mr. Patrick Henry King (tenants of Tudor Hall at the time of Lincoln's assassination) appear in the foreground with several visitors. (*From a copy of the original in possession of the author; courtesy of the Washington 'Sunday Star'*)

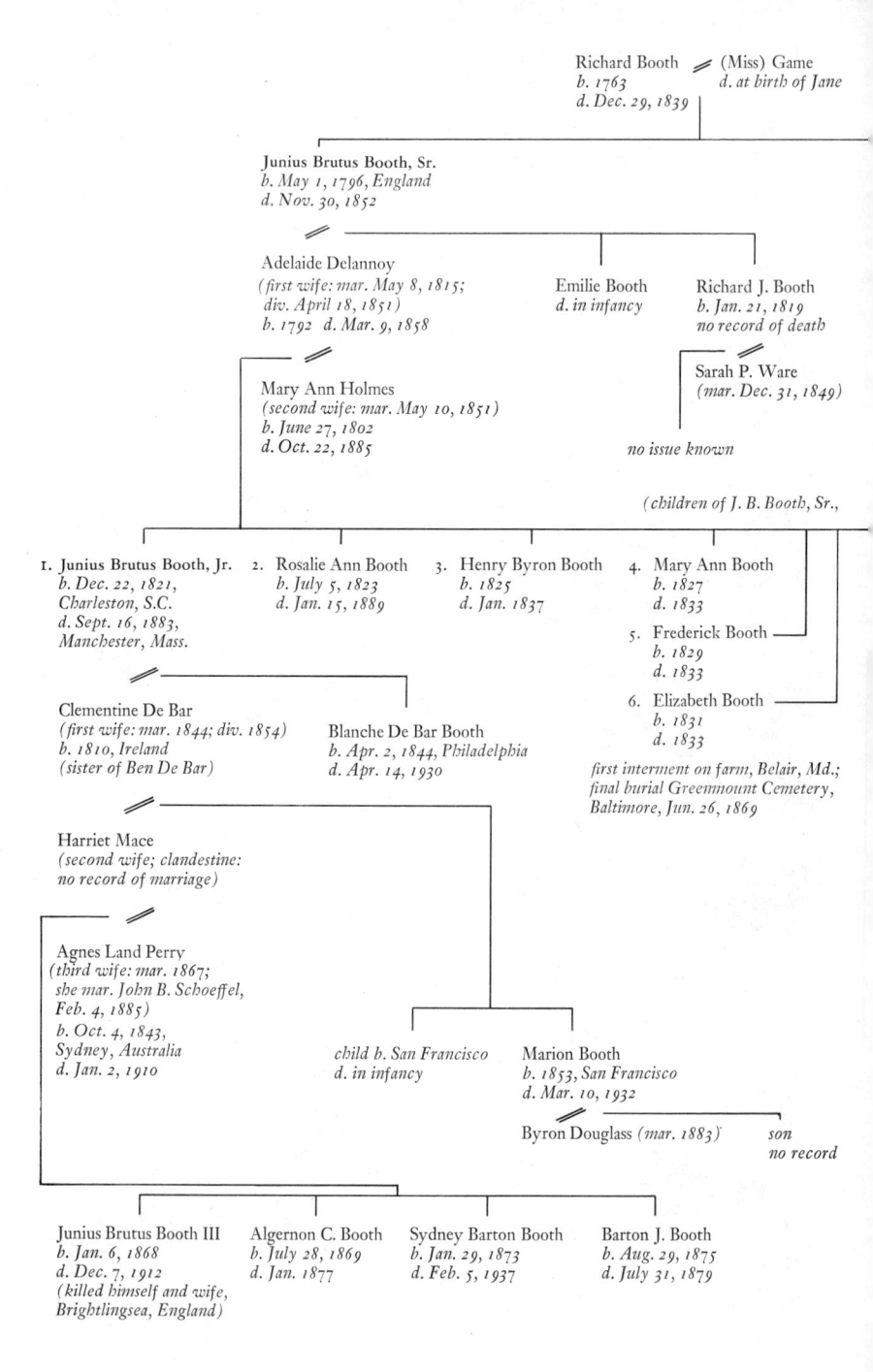

Richard Booth ⚯ (Miss) Game
b. 1763   d. at birth of Jane
d. Dec. 29, 1839

Junius Brutus Booth, Sr.
b. May 1, 1796, England
d. Nov. 30, 1852

⚯

Adelaide Delannoy
(first wife: mar. May 8, 1815;
div. April 18, 1851)
b. 1792 d. Mar. 9, 1858

Emilie Booth
d. in infancy

Richard J. Booth
b. Jan. 21, 1819
no record of death

⚯

Mary Ann Holmes
(second wife: mar. May 10, 1851)
b. June 27, 1802
d. Oct. 22, 1885

Sarah P. Ware
(mar. Dec. 31, 1849)

no issue known

(children of J. B. Booth, Sr.,

1. Junius Brutus Booth, Jr.
b. Dec. 22, 1821,
Charleston, S.C.
d. Sept. 16, 1883,
Manchester, Mass.

2. Rosalie Ann Booth
b. July 5, 1823
d. Jan. 15, 1889

3. Henry Byron Booth
b. 1825
d. Jan. 1837

4. Mary Ann Booth
b. 1827
d. 1833

5. Frederick Booth
b. 1829
d. 1833

6. Elizabeth Booth
b. 1831
d. 1833

first interment on farm, Belair, Md.;
final burial Greenmount Cemetery,
Baltimore, Jun. 26, 1869

⚯

Clementine De Bar
(first wife: mar. 1844; div. 1854)
b. 1810, Ireland
(sister of Ben De Bar)

Blanche De Bar Booth
b. Apr. 2, 1844, Philadelphia
d. Apr. 14, 1930

⚯

Harriet Mace
(second wife; clandestine:
no record of marriage)

⚯

Agnes Land Perry
(third wife: mar. 1867;
she mar. John B. Schoeffel,
Feb. 4, 1885)
b. Oct. 4, 1843,
Sydney, Australia
d. Jan. 2, 1910

child b. San Francisco
d. in infancy

Marion Booth
b. 1853, San Francisco
d. Mar. 10, 1932

Byron Douglass (mar. 1883)   son
                              no record

Junius Brutus Booth III
b. Jan. 6, 1868
d. Dec. 7, 1912
(killed himself and wife,
Brightlingsea, England)

Algernon C. Booth
b. July 28, 1869
d. Jan. 1877

Sydney Barton Booth
b. Jan. 29, 1873
d. Feb. 5, 1937

Barton J. Booth
b. Aug. 29, 1875
d. July 31, 1879

Algernon Sydney Booth
no record

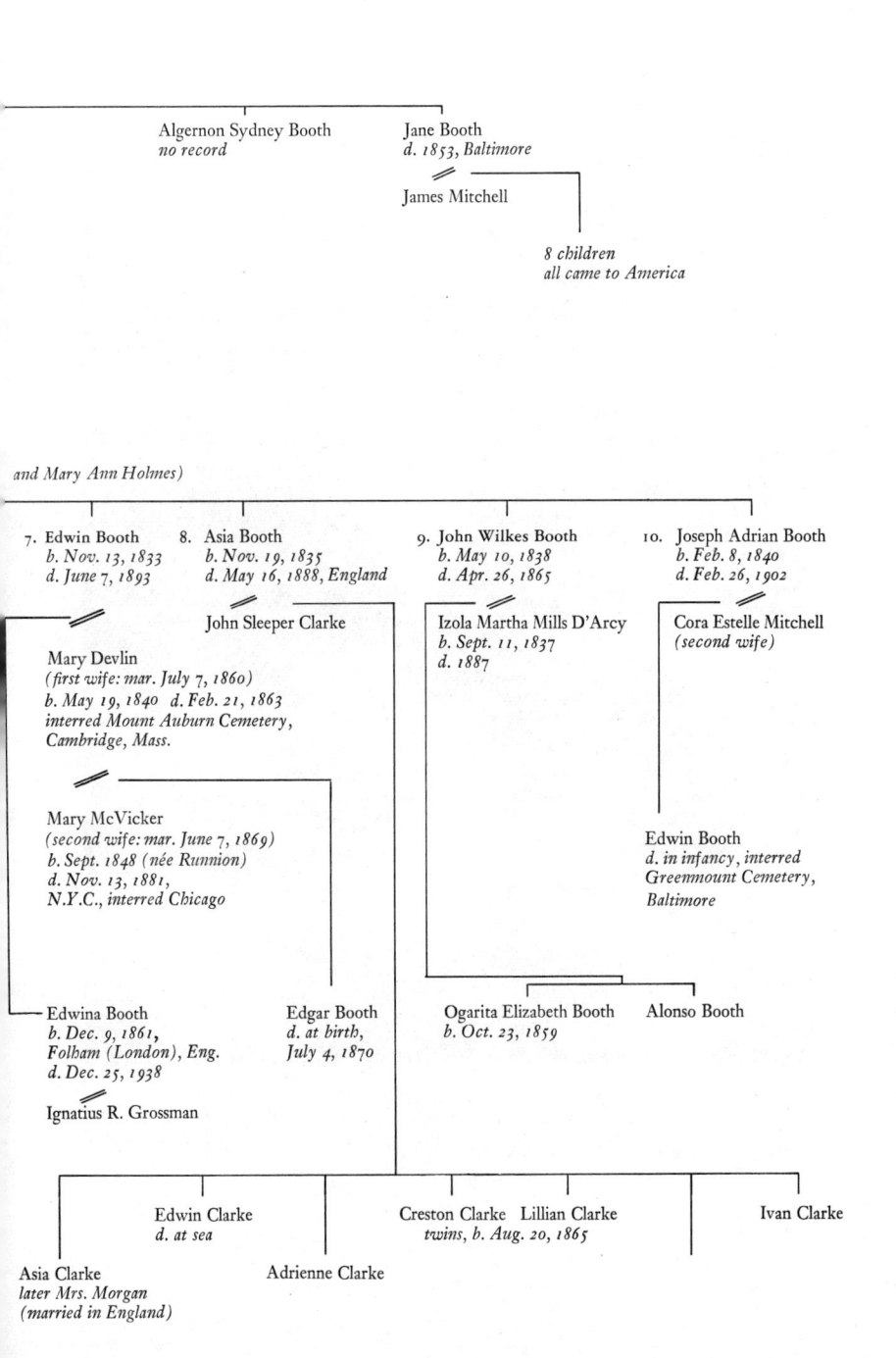

Jane Booth
d. 1853, Baltimore
= James Mitchell

*8 children
all came to America*

and Mary Ann Holmes)

7. Edwin Booth
   *b. Nov. 13, 1833
   d. June 7, 1893*

8. Asia Booth
   *b. Nov. 19, 1835
   d. May 16, 1888, England*
   = John Sleeper Clarke

9. John Wilkes Booth
   *b. May 10, 1838
   d. Apr. 26, 1865*
   Izola Martha Mills D'Arcy
   *b. Sept. 11, 1837
   d. 1887*

10. Joseph Adrian Booth
    *b. Feb. 8, 1840
    d. Feb. 26, 1902*
    Cora Estelle Mitchell
    (second wife)

Mary Devlin
*(first wife: mar. July 7, 1860)
b. May 19, 1840 d. Feb. 21, 1863
interred Mount Auburn Cemetery,
Cambridge, Mass.*

=

Mary McVicker
*(second wife: mar. June 7, 1869)
b. Sept. 1848 (née Runnion)
d. Nov. 13, 1881,
N.Y.C., interred Chicago*

Edwin Booth
*d. in infancy, interred
Greenmount Cemetery,
Baltimore*

Edwina Booth
*b. Dec. 9, 1861,
Folham (London), Eng.
d. Dec. 25, 1938*
= Ignatius R. Grossman

Edgar Booth
*d. at birth,
July 4, 1870*

Ogarita Elizabeth Booth
b. Oct. 23, 1859

Alonso Booth

Asia Clarke
*later Mrs. Morgan
(married in England)*

Edwin Clarke
d. at sea

Adrienne Clarke

Creston Clarke   Lillian Clarke
twins, b. Aug. 20, 1865

Ivan Clarke

Mary Ann Holmes, mother of the Maryland Booths; from a Brady daguerreotype. *(Courtesy of the Handy Studios, Washington, D.C.)*

The elder Booth    Junius Brutus, Jr.

Edwin Thomas    John Wilkes

The elder Booth and three of his sons. *(Original photographs from the collection of the author)*

Asia Booth Clarke, shortly before her departure for England. *(Albert Davis Collection)*

Rosalie Ann Booth, as depicted in the Baltimore *American* of July 12, 1896.

Ann Hall, servant of the Booths. (*Original photograph from the collection of the author*)

Dr. Joseph Adrian Booth, younger brother of Edwin and John Wilkes. *(War Department, Office of the Judge Advocate General, 1940)*

manner, and a round Dutch oven cooked meals which were served on heavy pewter platters. Booth was far from Piccadilly.

Their life at the farm was quiet and unmolested. After the babies had been put to bed, the evenings were spent beside the open fire. Booth was hard at work writing a play for Mr. and Mrs. Henry Wallack. Mary Ann mended his theatrical wardrobe or fashioned a new cloak for some historical character, and old Richard was buried in his study of the *Aeneid*, which he believed could be translated and adapted to the stage to great advantage. They were the complete example of a tranquil, cultured family and seldom visited their neighbors or took part in community affairs.

Whenever it became necessary for Booth to leave the farm and attend to business matters or theatrical engagements, he put the supervision of the Negroes in his father's hands. But Richard, for all his aristocratic gentility, had the same deplorable weakness that his son was so apt to indulge in when away from home. Instead of caring for Junius' interests in his absence, the old man would slip away, leaving the Negroes to their own devices and their petty thieveries while he enjoyed himself at a local tavern. Booth would come home and upbraid his wayward father for getting intoxicated and careless of important affairs, then dash off on a bibulous tour himself. The irony of it was that father and son never enjoyed each other's company on these alcoholic bouts but solemnly stood over each other with dreadful warnings about the evils of drink.[16]

Sternly enforced rules governed this household. Members were prohibited from eating any animal food; flowers were not to be picked, nor trees cut down; all wild creatures of the woods were to be left to their willful ways. "Tell Junius not to go opossum hunting, or setting rabbit traps, but to let the poor devils live," Booth was to write later on to his father. "Cruelty is the offspring of idleness of mind and beastly ignorance, and, in children, should be repressed and not encouraged, as is too often the case, by unthinking beings who surround them. A thief, who takes property from another, has it in his power, should he repent, to make restoration; but the robber of life never can give back what he has wantonly and sacrilegiously taken from beings perhaps innocent, and equally capable of enjoying pleasures or suffering torture with himself. The ideas of Pythagoras I have adopted; and as respects our accountability to animals hereafter, nothing that man can preach can make me believe to the contrary. 'Every death its own avenger breeds.' " Booth went so far with Pythagoras that he would not allow his stock to be branded—until many sheep and hogs had been stolen and he was forced to put his mark on them for identification.

Once, in traveling through the Midwest, he was assigned a seat in the dining room of a river steamboat opposite a devout Quaker. Booth's fluent and expressive conversation gained the admiration of the Quaker, who, seeing no meat on his plate, offered to serve him.

"Friend, shall I not help thee to the breast of this chicken?" he asked.

"No, I thank you, friend," answered Booth.

"Shall I not cut thee a slice of ham?" suggested the Quaker.

"No, friend, not any," said the tragedian, smiling.

The Quaker then insisted, "Thee must take a piece of mutton; thy plate is empty."

His entreaties were beginning to irritate Booth and he decided to startle him into silence. "Friend," he exclaimed, "I never eat any flesh but human flesh, and I prefer that raw!"

The dumbfounded Quaker moved to another table.

While working in the fields Booth went about in his bare feet, grubbing the soil and sowing the seed. His diligence was often spoken of by the neighbors. However, too many obligations at home and in the theatre continued to overtax him mentally and physically and he sought more of the stimulant he had counseled his father to reject. His appearances in beer saloons and oyster cellars became more frequent, and his reputation for singing "Billy Taylor" and drinking all the pothouse pedants under the table increased. Whatever Mary Ann's concern may have been over this laxity, and similar lapses at home, she never allowed it to cause any unpleasantness between them.

The pride of his stable, pony Peacock, developed an uncanny sense in knowing what to do while carrying his inebriated master about the country, or to and from his professional obligations. As Booth rode the odd-looking animal along the highway, goading it into a speedy gallop, dogs barked, Negroes rushed to the side of the road, and farmers' teams ran away, but he always reached his destination. Inhabitants of the region knew him as Farmer Booth rather than as Booth the Great Tragedian. They were often astonished, when they met him at the Baltimore markets, to hear him ask exorbitant prices for his produce. Those familiar with his antics waited, knowing that if he did not get what he demanded, the entire cartload might ultimately be purchased for a few coins. On occasion, however, he sold his produce to great advantage by refusing to enter the theatre where he had been announced to perform until it had all been disposed of, and so forcing the manager to pay an outrageous sum for it. At

A MAD TRAGEDIAN

market he always wore "hayseed" clothes and a broad-brimmed hat slouched over his eyes. If his wagon were overloaded, he rode astride the horse.

He was the first Marylander to advertise for bones and use them as fertilizer. It was not long before carts, wagons, baskets, and even the aprons of old women, were dumping skeletons at his door in exchange for cash. These were deposited in a heap until a sufficient supply accumulated, then they were pounded, burned and pulverized.

Booth's greatest delight was to hitch Peacock and a large horse named Captain in tandem to his carryall, fill it with vegetables, butter, eggs and live chickens, and drive to Washington. There he would peddle the assortment to hotelkeepers and then go to some favorite tavern to look up his friends. Although he thought an actor had no business meddling in national affairs, and said that he would never vote for any office-seeker, he still took an interest in political matters. Like his father, he occasionally burst forth in fervent harangue on some principle of republicanism, drawing a crowd of enthralled listeners with the earnestness of his vigorous declamation. In these Washington haunts he matched his eloquence with that of a congressman, or competed with Sam Houston, defender of Indians, for the title of **Big Drunk**.

Houston was a great admirer of Booth and frequently mailed him a request to play in some city Houston intended to visit, assuring him that he wished to attend the theatre but would not do so unless Booth performed. Booth's compliance generally resulted in Houston accompanying him for a few days on an adventurous tour, thereby increasing the anxiety of the theatrical manager. Booth was an intimate friend of Andrew Jackson, also, and visited him at the Hermitage.

Junius, Jr. (often referred to in the family as "June"), and Rosalie were still young children, learning to walk and talk. Booth always asked after them with affectionate concern in his letters to Mary Ann and his father, but he rarely mentioned his performances on tour. Indeed, he seldom discussed the theatre with anyone at the farm, and as his children grew older he purposely avoided any reference which might dispose them toward his profession. In 1825, another son, of whom no birth record exists, was born to Mary Ann Holmes and named Henry Byron. This third child was unhappily not destined to live very long, but through his short span of years seems to have been a favorite with his father.

The play Booth had been writing for Mr. and Mrs. Wallack was completed under the title of *Ugolino*, and on April 20, 1825, it was first produced at the Chestnut Street Theatre in Philadelphia with these two stars in the principal rôles. This was Booth's sole claim to authorship, but it was praised as a work possessing great poetry of diction. During his lifetime, productions of the play were given in several eastern cities, and after his death it was revived by his son, John Wilkes.

Within twelve years Booth had scaled the heights of fame, established himself in a lucrative and unparalleled career, become the father of two families and the idol of his audiences. But adulation had not turned his head. At twenty-nine he was at heart a simple country gentleman, kindhearted and charitable, full of an innate nobility of spirit. There was much of his own character in his interpretation of Lear. He had a princely dignity, a tenderness for those he loved, but the time was at hand when his self-control was to crack like a broken dam. The force of genius would break loose into unrestrained excess.

CHAPTER III

With characteristically quixotic impulse, Booth suddenly decided to take his American family to England. After spending the summer of 1825 at the farm, the dauntless tragedian, Mary Ann, their children, and a black girl servant boarded a ship for Liverpool, leaving old Richard to look after the premises near Belair. In Liverpool, Booth met his tempestuous rival, Edmund Kean, who was again departing for America. The early feud between them and the riots it had caused were the main topics of their conversation. Booth wrote his father in Maryland that he had passed an hour with Kean and "reconciled our ancient misunderstanding." But Kean's actions at a later date proved that he was not so reconciled as Booth assumed.

Booth was the kind of man who felt no situation too difficult to handle. He still had a lingering sense of responsibility to Adelaide and their son, and he thought this trip would be an opportunity to re-establish her confidence in his fidelity, if he could manage to appear in London without his American brood. In order to make the illusion complete, he packed off the Maryland family, as soon as they landed, to stay with Mary Ann's mother at Reading, while he went up to London alone, so he might create the proper atmosphere for a respectable domestic reunion.

There he found his wife and six-year-old heir boarding not far from his former home, and embraced them as if he had been away only a few hours. Time had not dealt kindly with Adelaide. She had lost her youthful appearance, and now that her husband was back at last she made matters worse by smothering whatever regard he had left with a possessiveness that was in no way congenial to his great independence of spirit. Even old Richard's removal to the United States had not made her suspicious. She assumed that her husband had come home to stay and that she would again shine in London society in the reflection of his glory. Booth was quick to detect the insincerity of her affection: it was different from Mary Ann's simple, generous devotion. Adelaide meant nothing to him now, but for the sake of appearances and his fondness for little Richard, he permitted a family portrait to be painted and continued to act the part of faithful husband during his stay in England.

London was prepared to give Booth a hearty welcome, but an engagement of three nights at Drury Lane proved unsuccessful. The press censured him caustically for refusing to answer his curtain calls during the play, and he replied that the custom was obsolete and should be abolished. His attitude was probably not a matter of arrogance as was supposed at the time, but was due to the fact that in his dressing room, Booth remained saturated with the emotions and idiosyncrasies of his part; he appeared in a trance and like one bewitched. To come before the curtain undoubtedly disturbed his train of thought and made it difficult to resume the part immediately.

He played one other performance in London at the Royalty Theatre, but luck was not with him, for the building burned to the ground and practically all his wardrobe was destroyed.

Booth, undismayed by these unfortunate appearances, went on a tour of the provinces while Adelaide wrote encouraging letters and awaited his return in vain. Then he took Mary Ann and her children and their Negro servant to Brussels, and in some miraculous way, managed to keep them in Adelaide's native city while he acted, without attracting the attention of her relatives. With his ménage he went on to engagements in Holland. At Rotterdam they boarded a ship for their voyage back to the United States, and all the time Adelaide never knew of the Maryland family. Booth's confidence in his strategy had proved well-founded!

On his arrival in New York in the autumn of 1826, he played an extensive series of profitable performances at the Chatham Theatre, ending in January. The warm reception that he received here was all the more gratifying after the disappointments in England, and Booth must have realized once and for all that, though he had originally come to the United States as a brief visitor, the country had become his own by mutual adoption and appreciation. His children would be Americans, raised in the traditions that his father had so admired as a young man. England might be revisited, but his family would be known as the Booths of Maryland, taking pride and interest in the welfare of his new land burgeoning with the promise of greatness.

By spring, he and his family were again at the farm, where, so he said, Peacock greeted him affectionately. The next six years marked the birth dates of three more children born to Mary Ann Holmes and christened Mary Ann, Frederick, and Elizabeth. These three infants seem to have been frail and delicate. Their remittent suffering from severe colds caused Booth's incessant inquiry about them in his family correspondence.

A MAD TRAGEDIAN

He was stage manager at the Camp Street Theatre in New Orleans the following winter and drew capacity audiences on the nights he was announced to act. He gave a single performance of Racine's *Andromaque* at the Théâtre d'Orléans, February 19, 1828, playing the part of Oreste in French.[17] His passionate delivery and the vibrant resonance of his magnificent voice, even in the expression of a foreign language, profoundly moved his audience.

Such linguistic efforts once led him to attempt a London presentation of Shylock "in the Jewish dialect" to ridicule a foreign actor who had played it in Hebrew, but there is no authority for the statement that he spoke in that language throughout the performance. In one city where he was billed in *The Merchant of Venice*, a boy arrived at the theatre early in the morning to inform the manager that his star was getting drunk. A carriage was hastily summoned and Booth driven into the country far from temptation. He was brought back just in time for the performance, complaining that he had not been given anything to eat and was starving. The manager sent out for some sandwiches which he took to Booth's dressing room. One glance at them was enough for the hungry tragedian to exclaim: "What! I am to play Shylock and you give me pork to eat!" Booth plucked the meat violently from each slice of bread, flung it to the floor, and contented himself with the crusts.

His character now showed a marked splitting of personality. At home in Maryland he still had the benign and friendly disposition for which he had always been known. There he was tolerant and temperate, interested in plans for the farm and in the education of his children. Despite the fact that visitors were rare, he never felt lonely, for he enjoyed the opportunity to relax in his library and refresh himself by reading the works of Milton, Ben Jonson, Byron, Shakespeare, and other great men. But once away from this wholesome atmosphere, his mind began to wander, not altogether from the influence of liquor but also from the very lack of balance from which his genius sprang. It was a form of madness akin to greatness. The stimulus of drink was all that was needed to release it.

Booth's friend, Tom Flynn, had arrived in the United States and was now the manager of a new theatre in Annapolis. They met in Baltimore and Flynn suggested that Booth play an engagement for him. He consented and promised to open on the following Monday night. Flynn returned to Annapolis to make the announcement, but on Monday Booth did not appear, nor had Flynn heard from him. Flynn wrote to Mary Ann for his whereabouts, and was told that Booth had left Baltimore some days before. As he walked the streets in perplexity, a small boy ran up and asked Flynn if he were the manager of the theatre.

"Yes," said Flynn, "but why do you ask?"

"Because," answered the urchin, "we've got one of your playing chaps on board our sloop raising the devil with the captain, who wishes you to come and take him away."

He followed the boy, who lost no time in returning to the vessel. When they arrived, Flynn found the captain on his knees, holding a huge bowl in his hands, while Booth was standing a few yards distant pointing a loaded musket at him and crying, "Drink, Sir, drink! You're bilious and require physic; I know it by your eyes; I know it by your skin. Drink, Sir, or I'll send you to another and better world!"

"Pray, let me off," the captain was pleading. "Think of my wife and children. I've drunk six bowls of this damn stuff already, and a seventh will physic me to death!"

It turned out that Booth had taken the sloop to Annapolis instead of going by land from Baltimore, and at the time of its arrival was inspecting the captain's medicine chest. What he found there resulted in the captain's being made the unwilling object of his prank. Flynn succeeded in getting the loaded musket from Booth, explained his occasional mental aberrations to the quivering target, apologized, presented him with a sum of money, and rushed from the sloop with the mad tragedian in tow. Booth was taken to a hotel and locked in a room, but soon escaped and spent the remainder of the day in an adjoining bar, singing Lincolnshire ditties to a drowsy Negro attendant.

Letters written by Booth to his managers are evidence of what they had to contend with, if they were to have their theatres crowded and still preserve their reputations with the public. One of these reads:

My dear Sir:

Please write to me in Boston on receipt of this, for I'm told you've announced me, and I was so damn drunk when we parted that I cannot recollect what was said or done by

JUNIUS B. BOOTH

Another received a letter headed, "Vapor Boat, Saturday," requesting him, "under the exhausting state of existing events and the acerbity of stomach and disposition," not to bill Booth for a farce part on Tuesday. "I should prefer," continued the wavering lines, "Hamlet for the furst piece to Richard & shall cum pervided accordingly. Richard has bin so hack'd & Hamlet is nooer. When u c Amanda giv my 'specks. Ever ate set hurrah J. B. B."

A Boston newspaper of 1829 labeled him "a lunatic of the first water." There, at the Tremont Theatre, beginning November sixteenth, he played for one or two nights with fine effect, but was suddenly taken ill and kept to his room until the first week in December, when he reappeared in *Richard III*. The bill for the seventh had been announced as *Evadne* with Booth as Ludovico, and an afterpiece entitled *Amateurs and Actors*, in which he was to play the part of a comical character. When the curtain went up the house was crowded, and people had been turned away from the doors.

> Mr. Booth's first appearance on the stage denoted something unusual. He was careless and hesitating in his delivery, and his countenance had none of its customary expression. He would falter in his discourse, jumble scraps of other plays into his dialogue, run to the prompter's side of the stage and lean against a side scene, while the prompter endeavored to help him forward in the play, by speaking out his part of the dialogue loud enough to be heard in the galleries. In this manner he made a shift to get through the first two acts of the tragedy. Those familiar with the theatre saw very plainly that something was rotten in the State of Denmark, but a great proportion of the very crowded audience present, not knowing much of his manner of acting, did not comprehend the business, but only looked on, stared, gaped, and wondered, and protested that for an actor of so much celebrity, Mr. Booth played in a very spiritless and bungling fashion.
>
> This *bizarrerie* soon came to a close. In the early part of the third act, while engaged in parlance with the King of Naples, the audience were surprised by his suddenly breaking off from the measured, heroical dignity of his stage tone, and with a comical simper, falling at once into a colloquial gossiping sort of chatter with His Majesty, thus—"Upon my word, sir, I don't know, sir," etc. The audience were thrown into as much astonishment as the King of the two Sicilies at Signor Ludovico's sudden and anti-poetical downcome from his buskined height of declamation. For a moment all was silence; when Mr. Booth, turning round and facing the spectators, began to address them in this manner: "Ladies and gentlemen; I really don't know this part. I studied it only once before, much against my inclination. I will read the part, and the play shall go on. By your leave the play shall go on, and Mr. Wilson shall read the part for me."

Here an overpowering burst of hissing and exclamation arose from all parts of the house, while Mr. Booth continued to face the audience with a grinning look, which at length broke out into an open laugh. Mr. Smith [the stage manager] then rushed from behind the scenes upon the stage, and led him off, Mr. Booth exclaiming, "I can't read,—I am a charity boy;—I can't read. Take me to the Lunatic Hospital!" Here the curtain fell amid the murmurs and hisses of the house.

Smith came before the audience and announced that it would be impossible for Booth to continue the performance and that a substitute play was being considered. He said that, although Booth had for some time been subject to partial insanity, he would not have been permitted to appear had his physician reported him unfit. Smith's exit was the signal for more hissing by the audience and loud calls for "Booth! Booth! *Bride of the Master!*" This brought Smith again to the front. He then stated that Booth's indisposition should not be ascribed to liquor, as persons attending him that day had declared no intoxicants had been given him.

Mr. Booth was immediately carried to his lodgings, and his disorder having increased, it was on Wednesday deemed advisable to obtain a consultation as to the propriety of placing him in the Lunatic Asylum, but on repairing to his room, the patient was *non est*. Search was made for him, and the only information that could be obtained was his application for a seat in the Providence stage, at the Marlboro Hotel; but the stage having previously departed, he went off, and whither no one knew; and it was not till the arrival of a stage from Providence, that intelligence was conveyed by the driver, that on Wednesday he met Mr. Booth between Dedham and Walpole on foot, bearing towards Providence, without his outside garments, and without any extra clothing whatever. He reached Providence on Thursday and, it was supposed, slept in the woods on Wednesday night.[18]

Fortunately, Booth's friends came to his aid and took care of him until he could resume his engagements. They knew that Mary Ann could not leave her family and rush to him so she was not informed of his first serious derangement.[19] But she, too, was shortly to realize the extent of Booth's madness.

Members of the company were always on guard lest Booth fail to distinguish himself from the character he was acting and bring on a real tragedy. Many times in the duel scene of *Richard III*, he chased the Richmond of the evening through the stage door and out into the street; and once in the rôle of Othello he bore down so heavily with a pillow on poor Desdemona that she would have suffocated had not several of the cast rushed onto the stage and rescued her.

Three of the Booth children, Frederick, Elizabeth and Mary Ann, whose health had so concerned their parents, died at close intervals during the year 1833 and were buried in a small graveyard on the farm. Booth was playing in Richmond, Virginia, under Hamblin, when he received news of Frederick's illness. He rushed off without giving Hamblin any explanation, only to find the child dying when he reached home. After burying the infant, Booth started back to Richmond, but in Baltimore he was informed that Hamblin had closed the theatre and departed. While there he received a letter telling of the serious illness of Elizabeth and got back in time to witness her death. During another theatrical engagement he heard of the death of little Mary Ann.

"When he returned a week or more thereafter, he had the body of little Mary disinterred and taken into the house in the delusive hope of bringing her back to life," wrote his neighbor, Mrs. Elijah Rogers. "On one other occasion his old horse [Peacock] had died and he had so much confidence in the prayers of Mrs. Booth he thought she could bring him back to life again; and he insisted upon her lying down upon the dead body. It was easy to see that his mind was disordered; so one of the neighbors went for Dr. Nunnikhuysen. The neighbors, by main force, put him to bed. He had not slept for several days and nights. Finally, sleep overcame him, and he continued to sleep all day, and all night; and when he awoke his mind was all right; though he continued to lament the loss of the child and the horse; and persisted in the belief that if he had been home they would not have died." [20]

The loss of his three children in succession, all this intense and accumulated sorrow, did much to advance the mania with which he was afflicted. Hamblin, still unaware of what had led to Booth's hasty departure from Richmond, brought suit for breach of contract, but old Richard took his son's case in hand and the matter was amicably settled.

On the spectacular night of November 13, 1833, as the stars were falling from the heavens in an outburst of unprecedented brilliance, Edwin Booth, a son destined to fame, made his advent in the world at the log house on his father's farm in Harford County, Maryland. Born under such an exceptional meteoric display, and with a caul, this child, to superstitious natives, was destined for a charmed life. Booth, being chained to Hamblin by another contract, was far away from the natal scene.

A notice in the *Morning Courier and New York Inquirer* is evidence of his absence: "American Theatre—Bowery—The Manager [Hamblin] has great pleasure in announcing, that Mr. Booth, having recovered from his severe indisposition, has arrived in New York, and will make his first appearance this evening" in Shakespeare's tragedy of *Richard III.*

The Bowery had now proved itself a serious rival to the Park Theatre where Booth had been introduced so successfully twelve years before. It was the first place of amusement to install the innovation of gas lights.[21] This marvelous invention revealed an attractive interior, tastefully decorated, in marked contrast to the increasing dreariness of its aging competitor. The exterior of the Bowery presented an imposing façade of simulated marble, which gave the whole building a festive and prosperous air, unusual then in American theatrical architecture.

The bill for November fifteenth was *Othello*, with Hamblin playing the title rôle and Booth Iago. Preceding the performance, Hamblin gave a dinner party for members of the company during which, in the mock interest of temperance, they cried, "Down with all spiritous liquors!" and followed Hamlet's advice in suiting "the action to the word and the word to the action." In the midst of the hilarity, Flynn, who was stage manager, tapped Booth on the shoulder and announced to all that it was time to start to their dressing rooms. Booth went along grudgingly but at the stage door stopped and said, "Now, my good friend, you will have to get another Iago; I'm off!" And leaving Flynn dumb with amazement, he dashed down the street and disappeared in the darkness.

Flynn found a substitute for the part, went before the audience and apologized for the unpreventable desertion of the great tragedian, and offered to refund the price of admission to those dissatisfied with the unexpected change in the cast. This made a considerable dent in the receipts for the evening. About midnight he located Booth in a barroom, haranguing a crowd on the distress and privations of the inhabitants of Texas and calling for volunteers to go and help them. The impromptu oration was probably a compliment to his friend Sam Houston. When people heard of this escapade, they became more curious than ever to see him. At his next performance, he was greeted by a thunderous applause.

Booth played alternately in New York and Philadelphia. On one occasion he was so drunk that the manager whispered from the wings, "Bring your act to a speedy close!" Booth staggered to the footlights.

"Ladies and Gentlemen: I have been requested to end this as soon as possible; so I'll end it now! Here, Wilford, catch me!" Throwing himself into "Wilford's" arms, he enacted a death scene of terrific agony. The curtain was rung down while the audience roared with laughter.

His final New York appearance that year was at the Bowery Theatre, on the night the city celebrated the anniversary of its evacuation by the British. Soon after, he was back at the farm gazing on the latest addition to his family and naming the handsome boy for his two best friends, *Edwin* Forrest and *Thomas* Flynn. Booth was only thirty-seven years of age and he had been on the stage almost half that time.

The theatrical season, now in full bloom, kept him from remaining long at home. In December he started off on another tour. From a letter he wrote to the theatrical manager, Francis Wemyss, postmarked Baltimore, he seems to have been dodging Hamblin again—perhaps for breaking the contract that Richard had fixed up for him. Other things are evident:

> Tuesday Night—Stage office—Once more I am, as the French say, *en route*, and hope to reach Pittsburg in time to begin Monday night—bar sickness, My Lord Judge, and the delays. Messrs. Managers of the West, you are partically the cause of—Had you not announced Mr. Booth as being engaged in Pittsburg and Cincinnati, Hamblin would never have cotched me here as he did. It is best in my humble opinion not to announce me until the beast arrives. Yours in duty bound.
>
> BOOTH
>
> P. S. Good!—Commence with, I am—conclude with J. B. Booth—He conjugates—the villain!

What became of Booth after he wrote this letter was a mystery to Wemyss. Finally, in February, Mrs. Wemyss received a letter from him written at Wheeling, in which he said "Dear Madam—I hope you are in full enjoyment of health, and that your lamp fed with vegetable oil burns well and clear. I take the freedom of making you a present of two handsome turkeys, pets of mine, which I transfer to you on condition that you will not have them killed but let the children give them bread to eat and water to drink, or *pulse*, as Daniel calls it, and let them live until the great Jehovah of the Christians causes them to die of a good old age. . . ."

Two days later, Wemyss was handed a note. "Please pony up and pay my attendant and companion, John, enough to settle with the captain for his passage as I have only by me some silver and fourteen hundred dollars in two large lumps; one for a thousand and other for four hundred dollars." At the bottom of the page was scrawled "Booth" and the words, "I hope your wife received the turkeys."

Soon the mad tragedian came into Wemyss' theatre, accompanied by Sam Houston. Wemyss was to remember them as a strange pair. He said that Booth, when they took the mail coach together from Pittsburgh, was painted and garbed like an Indian chief—fit comrade for the Raven. He did not know what became of them, nor did he see Booth or hear from him for more than a year.[22]

It was at this Pittsburgh Theatre that Junius, Jr., made his début as Tressel in his father's performance of *Richard III*.[23]

On a Sunday night in Cincinnati, Booth strutted up the aisle of a Methodist church wearing his Richelieu robes, and sat down in a front pew. The preacher and his congregation thought they were being honored by the presence of some celebrated prelate from abroad, until Booth solemnly arose after the benediction and announced that he would open his engagement on the following evening. This practice of going about in costume often made him a one-man parade. He would walk the streets in the full regalia of Richard, Shylock or some other character, with a mob following at his heels and scrambling for the coins he tossed into the air. After managing, on this tour, to avoid the keepers of a lunatic asylum, he went back to the farm.

Booth had promised to play Richard at the Bowery Theatre in New York as a benefit for Thomas Flynn. When the time approached and he had not arrived in New York, Flynn took matters in hand and went to the farm to remind him. As Flynn drew near the house he saw what he took to be a young farm-hand digging in the potato patch and called out, "Halloa, boy! Where's Mr. Booth?"

"Here at your service," said the actor, raising his head. "What the deuce brought *you* here?"

"Why, Booth, don't you recollect you promised to play for my benefit?"

"Did I? Very well; come into the house."

The two friends went to New York together, and on the opening night, Booth was greeted by an audience that overflowed to the front sides of the stage. His Richard was never better. Life on the farm had built up a reserve of firm vigor. His tanned skin, his sparkling eyes, and the glowing tones of his voice gave the impression of dynamic virility. Richard is a trying part, requiring sheer bodily stamina. The character is before the audience through almost every scene of the five acts without rest or relaxation. Booth surpassed himself in this performance. Small of stature, he seemed to fill the stage with his personality, to dominate all around him. Soaring to flights of ruthless ambition, melting with tenderness for Lady Anne, and then driving on with inflexible will to gain a crown through murderous villainy, he played the tyrant to perfection.

At the drop of the curtain, he shook hands with Flynn, refused to accept even the expenses of his trip to New York, and next day went back to the farm where he resumed his labor in the potato patch.[24] Cincinnatus himself could not have better performed the agrarian role.

Asia Booth Clarke, the family historian, was born November 19, 1835. In accounts of her father, she referred to the year of her birth as a period in which his aberrations increased in strength and frequency and assumed many singular phases. He was either on the heights of jubilance or in the depths of depression, and so wavered between madness and genius that no one could be certain which would predominate. One performance would be exceptionally fine, another ordinary and disappointing. In rational moments, however, he was most considerate of his family.

The day Asia was born, Booth was again on tour. When he came home, there was discussion between the parents over what to name the baby. They could not decide whether to call her Sydney after the wife of their friend H. L. Bateman, or Ayesha after the favorite wife of Mohammed. Booth, off on tour again, wrote Mary Ann: "Call the little one Asia in remembrance of that country where God first walked with man, and Frigga, because she came to us on Friday, which day is consecrated to the Mother Venus." The matter was not settled for two years, and then there seems to have been a compromise for the girl's early letters are signed Asia Sydney.

Junius, who was now nearly fourteen, was studying Latin and Greek under a Mr. Sandborn in Baltimore. Booth believed that his namesake would make a "scholar of no mean capacity", and planned a liberal education for him. The eldest son resembled both his father and his mother in a heavy, thickset way. Early instruction in boxing and fencing changed him from a flabby, awkward boy into a muscular youth of great agility. He lacked the sensitive features and poetic expression that his brothers later developed, but, on the other hand, he showed signs of possessing a more even-tempered, stable disposition than they ever were able to command. Mary Ann may well have welcomed the boy's traits of patient practicality with the realization that they would soon be put to the test in caring for his father. It was her anxiety over Booth's unpredictable behavior when away from home and her reliance on young Junius' peculiar sense of responsibility that made her feel he should accompany the impetuous tragedian on his tours. Although Booth, like so many actors of the past and present, was strongly averse to having his children embark on a dramatic career, he was persuaded to interrupt the boy's studies, and from time to time, take Junius with him as his dresser. Neither parent had any idea that the glamour of the theatre would appeal to his phlegmatic imagination and gradually overshadow his interest in schooling. Indeed, if Booth had ever suspected this would be the result, it is extremely doubtful if he would have yielded to Mary Ann's insistence. Had it not been for Booth's capricious antics, his imperious thirst for liquor, and Mary Ann's concern for his health and position in the profession, the second generation might never have been allowed the chance to set foot on the stage.

In Washington, Junius and his father were both examined by a phrenologist whose report, so Junius jokingly told his grandfather, revealed that they had "pretty bad characters." Richard hardly needed to be informed about his son's character. At a house in Baltimore which the family occupied in the winter months, Booth had gone to the old man's room in the middle of the night, draped in a sheet for a toga. Richard heard him declaiming lines from *Julius Caesar* as he strode down the passage and prepared for his entrance. The moment Booth opened the door, Richard dashed a bowl and pitcher on the floor to bring him to his senses. "Ah, my son, my son," cried Richard, "will you never have done with these mad freaks!"

Booth gambled on another trip to England in October of 1836 and set forth again with his Maryland family, and Hagar, a Negro servant. Whether he knew it or not before he left America, Adelaide and their young son Richard were conveniently visiting her relatives in Brussels. At any rate, he kept them there by repeatedly promising to come and see them—which he had no intention of doing.

Misfortunes other than matrimonial complications attended this reckless venture. From Pentonville, a few months later, he informed his father in Belair:

> We have at last cause and severe enough it is, to regret coming to England. I have delayed writing till time had somewhat softened the horror of the event. Our dear little Henry is dead! He caught the small pox and it proved fatal —he has been buried about three weeks since in the chapel ground, close by. Guess what his loss has been to us,—so proud as I was of him above all others. The infernal disease

has placed Hagar in the hospital, but she is recovering and the two youngest [Edwin and Asia] who were inoculated are also getting well. Junius and Rosalie had been vaccinated—so had Henry—but on him the vaccine had not taken effect and his general health being so excellent caused us to forget the danger he was liable to.

I shall return (God willing) by packet of April 8th, to Philadelphia, as theatricals on proving them turn out to be not so prosperous as they seemed on my arrival. I played at Drury Lane . . . but was forced to sue Mr. Bunn, the manager, and he is now paying me the hundred pounds he owes me by weekly instalments. . . . I afterwards acted at the Surry with tolerably good success and was honorably paid. Since then I've been to Birmingham where I was when the melancholy news alluded to reached me. I expect to play a few nights more in London at one of the minor theatres and at Edinburgh before I return. Forrest won't play any more, at least he says so now—Hamblin is here—so is Barrett of Boston, Terman of Philadelphia and Rice—the only one it appears who really has bettered his fortune by London is *he*. . . .

Rosalie goes to school and is improving very fast. Junius is gone a few miles in the country with some friends for a week or two. . . . Hoping you are in good health and may long continue so is the prayer of your affectionate son

J. B. BOOTH

M. Ann and Rose join in best love to you.[25]

From that time to the birth of the tempestuous John Wilkes, Booth grieved incessantly.

The loss of his favorite son, together with unsuccessful engagements and unforeseen difficulties brought on by his shiftless brother-in-law, made this last visit to England something of a nightmare.

Jimmy Mitchell was a reprobate of the lowest order. He and Jane, Booth's sister, now had a family of eight children for whom the scapegrace had as little regard and paternal responsibility as a stray tomcat. Jimmy did not intend to bother himself with earning a living when he could bully his brother-in-law by threatening to expose the family scandal. Here was an easy source of income, and he lost no time in taking full advantage of his auspicious position. The idea of staying any longer in England became intolerable to Booth and Mary Ann, and with hearts full of disappointment and anxiety, they looked forward eagerly to a quick return to the United States. More unwilling than ever to have Adelaide back in England, Booth did not inform her of his intended departure until it was too late for her to reach him. In his farewell letter he promised to return in two years and attend to the education of their son. When she read his slight apology, with furious resentment, the Maryland Booths were already on the high seas, sailing homeward.

After they had safely reached Baltimore, Booth sent Jane enough money to bring her and her children to America, with the strict stipulation that her indolent husband was to remain in England. But when the Mitchells arrived at the farm, Jimmy was with them.

Poor old Richard was at his wits' end. Here was this scoundrel, this knave from whom he had fled, not only under the same roof again but forcing him out of his own room and lolling about the place with consummate impudence. The only defense Richard could summon against the caravan of intruders was to refuse to speak to any of the Mitchell tribe. For the rest of his days, the indignant old man managed to ignore the entire swarm of them, underfoot and loud-mouthed as they were.

The peaceful country retreat near Belair now became a gypsy camp. Vocal battles between Jimmy and Jane kept the place in a constant uproar. He refused to lift a finger in any kind of work and treated her as an ill-used servant. The slatternly Mitchell children ran about the farm like so many mischievous animals while Mary Ann and the Booth children looked on in bewilderment. Jimmy put his older boys and girls to work in the neighborhood and promptly and invariably seized their earnings to buy liquor for himself. Booth was left to support a third family. If the little Mitchells did not get enough to eat, they ran clamoring to Mrs. Rogers and imposed on her.

This bedlam in the spot that had once been Booth's only source of relaxation and renewed energy was enough to unhinge the soundest mind. Irritated by the results of his generous impulse and perplexed by the problem of feeding and clothing twenty people, he rushed back into the theatre for funds. His reappearance again drove managers to distraction. His madness knew few intermissions. Often they could bring him to his senses only by threatening him, or keep him sober and fit for engagements only by locking him in jail.

At one performance, he faltered, walked upstage, knocked loudly on a door in the set, and, coming down to the footlights, said, "Ladies and gentlemen, there does not appear to be anyone at home." The stage manager had him pulled into the wings and told him he would be soundly whipped if he did not play the part as written. In a few minutes he continued, and so averted a riot.

At another theatre, quite intoxicated, he fell on the stage and was booed by the audience. As the curtains closed in, a fellow actor lifted him to his feet; Booth staggered, shook his fist at the growling assemblage, and exclaimed, "Wait! Wait! I'll be back in five minutes and give you the goddamnedest performance of *King Lear* you've ever seen!"

Cast as Hamlet, with Mrs. John Drew, he failed to appear at curtain time for the fifth act. Attendants were sent in search of him and had almost given up in despair, when he was spotted on a rafter above the scenery crowing like a rooster. The manager had him hauled down from his perch, and the play went on.

Following these eastern engagements, he boarded the steamer *Neptune* in New York for Charleston, intending to continue his tour southward from that city. Flynn was with him. During the trip, Booth indulged freely in liquor and perpetrated various extravagances, to the terror of the captain and the dismay of the passengers. After being at sea a few days, he came to Flynn to request that he be informed when they passed the spot where Conway, the well-known tragedian, had committed suicide by throwing himself overboard, as he had a message for his departed friend. He went to sleep and Flynn said nothing, but, at a point off Charleston harbor, Booth rushed on deck, announced he was starting on his journey to Conway, and jumped from the stern into the water. A lifeboat was immediately lowered, and Booth was hauled into it. As they tossed over the waves in the small craft, he cautioned Flynn, who had helped in rescuing him, to be steady or he would turn over the boat and all would be drowned.

No city captivated Booth more than Charleston. His vegetarian appetite was thoroughly appeased by what he found in its cool markets. "The Carolinians," he once remarked, "would have few blemishes were it not for the unnecessary and wicked treatment of the colored people." But in this southern city he had the greatest misfortune of his career.

After the opening performance, Booth insisted that Flynn go with him to Truesdale's saloon. There he drank his usual tankards, and Flynn had some difficulty in getting him back to their lodgings at the Planters' Hotel. A little past midnight, Flynn was awakened and saw Booth crawling through the window into his room on the ground floor. Before he could do anything, Booth went to the fireplace, picked up an andiron and struck Flynn with it. As Flynn sprang from his bed, Booth hit him again, wounding him over his right eye. Realizing that Booth was for the moment insane, Flynn, to defend himself, dealt him a full blow in the face, breaking his nose and permanently disfiguring him.

The accident not only ruined Booth's handsome Roman profile but changed the quality of his once magical voice. From this time to his death, his full eloquence was marred by a nasal rasp. Neither passion nor tenderness could he ever utter again with such unerring beauty. The instrument that was the essence of his talent had been permanently injured.

The result of Booth's Charleston debauch did not lessen his drinking or check his vagaries. In April, 1838, the Baltimore *Sun* reported, "Mr. Booth, the mad tragedian, has arrived in our city."

Out at the farm Mary Ann was expecting Booth and the birth of another child. Since the Mitchells had entrenched themselves all her plans to raise her children in a quiet environment had been defeated. The shrieking voices, Jimmy's drunken brawls, and old Richard's murderous oaths, made her feel as though she were living in a madhouse. And then back into this chaos came Booth, the maddest of all.

On May 10, 1838, a son was born to Mary Ann Holmes and Junius Brutus Booth, who was destined to carry the honored name of John Wilkes, which his grandfather gave him, to an ignoble grave. From the moment of his birth he was the darling of his father's heart. Indeed, both his parents so idolized and spoiled him that by comparison they seemed indifferent to the older children.

Grandfather Richard, unable to cope with Jimmy Mitchell's abuse, took refuge with a friend and neighbor of the Booths named Woolsey. From there he moved to a tavern in Baltimore, kept by a Dr. Braretta, where he died on December 28, 1839, at the age of seventy-six. The stone slab marking his grave in Baltimore Cemetery bore a Hebrew inscription.[26] Although the old man had enjoyed a spurt of adventurous spirit in his youth, in his later years he had maintained a calm unruffled attitude toward life, unhampered by ambition for wealth or distinction. The placid pattern of his existence had been colored and jolted by his more impetuous children, but, fortunately for him, he did not live to know the painful pressure of concealed scandal that followed his son and the dishonor brought to the family name by his grandson in a calamity that saddened the American continent he loved so well.

CHAPTER IV

The Booths, as was now their custom, spent most of the winter months in Baltimore, but according to their intimate friend, Mrs. Rogers, they were at the farm when Joseph Adrian was born on February 8, 1840.[27] However, as late as July, letters of devotion from Booth to Mary Ann Holmes, addressed Mrs. M. A. Booth, were sent to North High Street, in Baltimore. Away from home, he still never failed to be concerned about her and their "dear children," six of whom were then living.

Junius, now nineteen, and Rosalie, seventeen, showed a marked physical resemblance to each other. Rosalie, however, had little of Junius' calm common sense, being inclined to a neurotic moodiness that kept her from enjoying the normal social pleasures of a young girl. Apparently she was never able to throw off this morose disposition, even as a grown woman, for we seldom hear of her participating actively in the lives of her brothers and sister. Whether this was due to a blighted romance when she was a young girl or solely to mental traits inherited from her father, it is hard to say. We know only that her girlhood had none of the zest for life that characterized her younger sister Asia.

Edwin, a boy of seven, Asia, a girl of five, and John Wilkes, hardly more than a baby of two, all had their father's penetrating dark eyes, his glossy black hair and slender build. Joseph also grew to show this family likeness. Even at this early age it was easy to see that Edwin had the most sensitive nature of all the children. He was observant and keenly appreciative of beautiful details, but innately shy, and his grave reticence made him seem thoughtful beyond his years. John, however, became a problem the moment he stepped out of the cradle. He was what irritated uncles call a "brat." The affection which his mother and father lavished on him undoubtedly spoiled him from the start. Asia, growing up with two brothers, was more outspoken than Rosalie had ever been, and enjoyed rollicking through the woods, joining in the simple amusements.

Each summer the family returned to the farm where Booth continued his practice of growing and selling produce. There the children relished various diversions. They had a small lake in which to dabble on hot afternoons; they rode horseback, went on picnics to **Deer**

Creek Rocks, and joined with the Mitchell offspring in giving Shakespearean plays, altered to suit themselves. Sometimes a stray pickaninny from the Old Field settlement half a mile away got mixed up in the throng and joined in the frolics. One of these, an old woman who had lived in the neighborhood all her life, recalled "bein' ovah at the Booth place once when ol' man Booth was at home. He was settin' in the yard with his feet propped up 'gainst a tree. Ann Hall come out where I's playin' with the Booth chillun an' told me, 'Don't you go ovah theah an' bother ol' man Booth 'less you want to git hit with his stick.' Mrs. Booth was a handsome woman. She didn't mind the cullud chillun playin' on the place at all. She used to give us food jes' the same as she done her own chillun. We all run ovah the farm together. Sometimes they had a kind o' show ovah theah; thunder an' lightnin' I called it. Many a day they put up a tent in the yard."

Booth finally refused to support the Mitchells, and Jimmy was forced to move his family near a ring factory where he put his children to work. He made his wife take in boarders, while he strutted about and bossed his household. Eventually they all moved to Baltimore, and Jane continued the drudgery which caused her death, long before that of her scallywag husband. A demented son was a newsboy, and a daughter, Eliza, sold cakes and fruit in a Baltimore theatre. Eliza would save enough money to buy her father a new suit of clothes, dress him in it, and proudly exhibit him to the neighbors; but when the old man took the notion, he would sell it and go on a spree. Her marriage to the actor, William Ward, took her from this impoverished background, and she advanced to star rôles on the stage. "No wonder she could play *The Little Barefoot* so well," wrote Mrs. Rogers. "She found out all about bare feet in her childhood." [28]

Junius attended St. Mary's College in Baltimore and for a short time studied surgery. But early trouping days with his father had left an imprint on him, and he finally gave up academic pursuits to become an actor. He had to get his training and experience without parental assistance. During his first years in the theatre he met Clementine De Bar, a popular Irish actress, eleven years his senior. She gave him the advice and encouragement he needed, and undoubtedly her interest in him and the value of association with a favorite star led him to marry her. Certainly, events in later years show it to have been a marriage of convenience rather than romance. They had a daughter, Blanche De Bar, who was Booth's first grandchild.

In March, 1843, Junius and Clementine arrived in New York.

Theatricals were then at a low ebb and many actors out of employment, but the name Booth gave entrée into any playhouse, and they were able to get an engagement with Hamblin at the Bowery Theatre. On the twenty-fifth of that month they made their first appearance there in *Mazeppa* as Zemila and Abder Khan. Junius played but few performances at this time and did not get beyond small parts.

The most notable event of the season was the appearance of the elder Booth, as he was now beginning to be known, in a varied repertoire with his daughter-in-law, who was a great favorite at the Bowery. The next September, Junius, Jr., became a member of the brilliant Chatham Theatre Company under Deverna's management, but early in the new year transferred his activities to the Bowery, where he played successfully until August.

While shifting from one stage to another, Junius had not failed to note the essentials of good management. He saw failures and successes in turn and drew his own conclusions. Large theatres, such as the Olympic, and heavy old dramas resulted in financial losses. Small playhouses and a diversity of entertainment produced profits. The day of burlesque and minstrelsy had arrived. This change was to take Junius from the footlights at a later date and place him in the front rank of theatrical managers.

The elder Booth, knowing that Junius and Clementine were not finding the stage a prosperous source of income, had, in a burst of generosity, given his son some of his priceless costumes. While Junius was at the Bowery in April, 1845, it was destroyed by fire and he suffered the loss of this valuable wardrobe. Next October he joined the Howard Athenaeum Company in Boston, which included Harriet Mace, a beautiful actress still in her 'teens, and sister of the famous prize fighter. Their friendship soon ripened into romance and flourished with their mutual interest in the theatre.

Junius' first appearance of any importance was at the rebuilt New York Bowery on his benefit night, as Sir Giles Overreach, March 31, 1847. That season he alternated between stock engagements in New York and Boston and was in great demand as a leading man. By the end of the summer he had established a fair reputation in the profession. In August he became a member of the Boston Museum company among whom was the elder Booth's drinking companion, George Spear.

Junius had been swept into the current of his father's dynamic style of acting, but had not enhanced his performances with any original interpretations or imaginative flourishes. Such deficiencies became evident when, about this time, he played Iago to his father's Othello.

The elder Booth must have recognized his son's lack of creative ability and realized that it would eventually hinder his efforts to reach distinction as an actor.

The continued friendship between Junius and Harriet led inevitably to domestic trouble with Clementine and a situation like that of Adelaide and the elder Booth. Early in 1848, Junius deserted his wife and child in New York to center his attentions on Harriet in Boston. Left destitute, Clementine followed her father-in-law to Baltimore and told him a story of neglect similar to the story Adelaide could have told old Richard. The fear of having to provide for another family prompted Booth to arrange a benefit for her at the New York Chatham Theatre. He appeared as *The Stranger*, and she sang a ballad entitled, "I've a Silent Sorrow Here." The press was discreet in its comments; but Junius did not return to the New York stage for many years.

Some time after this separation, Clementine secured an engagement in Boston so that she might investigate his philandering. When she saw Harriet Mace flitting about on Junius' arm, she knew there could be no reconciliation and decided to ignore them.

By 1841 Adelaide and Booth's oldest son, Richard, now a young man of twenty-two years, had returned from Brussels to England. Richard, like his father, had shown a decided talent for languages and, although Booth continued to send them money, the young man was anxious to start earning a living for himself. Unable to get a position in London, Richard began tutoring in Greek and Latin while his mother frantically corresponded with people she knew, asking for letters of introduction to prominent persons who might help him along. In May of 1839 she had written her aunt in Brussels that while her husband had sent her funds from time to time, she had received no letter from him during the previous year nor read anything concerning him in foreign newspapers. She added that he had not kept the promise he had made by letter at the time he left England, to return in two years and attend to his son's education, and that she was endeavoring to get in touch with him through friends in Philadelphia. Adelaide, of course, was still ignorant of Booth's other family in the United States, knew nothing of its increasing demands on him and of the deplorable mental condition into which he was sinking. She and Richard went about London and were received everywhere as the wife and son of Booth, the great tragedian.

Richard's attempts to make money were pitifully unsuccessful and in despair he finally wrote to his father for permission to visit him in the United States. Booth sent him money for the trip, but illness and a delay in payment of the draft postponed his sailing and Richard did not arrive in America until 1842. Junius was then pursuing his own theatrical career and the elder Booth was in need of a dresser. Since it was well to keep a watchful eye on Richard's movements lest he learn too much of the Maryland family, Booth decided to take him along on his tours.

Adelaide's son bore such a striking resemblance to his father that strangers seeing them together accepted their relationship at once. Difficulties soon began to arise. Booth had not counted on Richard's devotion to his mother and his unflinching loyalty to her, nor had he taken into consideration the treacherous effect of backstage gossip. Behind the scenes one night, someone accused Richard of putting on airs and informed him that he was an illegitimate son of the great actor, who had a wife and a large family of children living in Baltimore. Richard made inquiries and found out more than he had been told. He then sent word to his mother, begging her to come to the United States and establish his legitimacy. Meantime, not wishing to arouse his father's suspicion, he took advantage of some trivial excuse and separated from him.

Edmund Kean now settled his grudge with Booth by contributing a sum sufficient for Adelaide's voyage, and she sailed for America. But the steamer was stranded on a reef off the Irish coast, and all the passengers, after being removed, returned to Liverpool for a second departure on another vessel. From Baltimore, on December 17, 1846, she wrote to her sister:

My Dear Thérèse:

Thank God, I have at length arrived. I left Liverpool on the 31st of October by the *Great Western*. In spite of the advanced season and the bad weather we accomplished the voyage in seventeen days.

Directly after my arrival in New York I left for Baltimore. I was in a great hurry to see Richard. It was in the morning. I took the idea to go and find him in the establishment where I knew he was giving lessons in Latin and Greek. He was there. I leave you to judge of the joy his presence gave me. He was very much moved. I had great difficulty to keep from exhibiting my happiness too much. We got into the carriage which waited for me, and Richard took me to a furnished house where he had secured a lodging for me.

It was so delightful to be together. Booth was playing in New York when I arrived. He is just about to commence his winter tour. I don't want to do anything to prevent him from making money, so I shall wait until he comes to Baltimore, and as soon as he arrives my lawyer will fall on his back like a bomb. Nobody here has any notion that I am the wife of the famous tragedian. My lawyer tells me that, considering the fortune which remains to him, I may demand 5,000 francs.

Whilst he was traveling with his father Booth used to sing to him the song of the "Tobacco Pipe," and also the romances that poor sister Agatha used to sing, to the guitar. Richard has told me during the last week all about the follies and extravagances of B. He has barely escaped several times being run over by carriages whilst he was drunk. I passed through the street where the Holmes live and I saw the house. It has not a very grand appearance. I have not seen anyone of that set. . . .[29]

The drama that took place in Baltimore soon after this far outrivaled any current production on the stage. When Booth arrived, Adelaide and Richard took him completely by surprise. He lost no time in roaring down Adelaide's fiery accusations and told her to return to Europe immediately. She demanded recognition for herself and her son in the United States, but he refused it. The battle was on.

In order to file a bill for divorce, it was necessary for her to establish a residence in Maryland. As this necessitated living within the state for a period of years, she and Richard moved to a cheaper section of the city, and he continued to teach languages. Booth stopped providing for them, and they were totally dependent upon Richard's earnings, which were scarcely adequate for comfort. By December, 1849, however, their financial condition appears to have been much better, for on the last day of that month Richard married Sarah Ware.

The Baltimore home of the Booths at the time of Adelaide's residence was not far from the Belair market where the elder Booth rented a stall and sold vegetables. His customers often heard the great tragedian cursed to shame by the woman he had abandoned. When Adelaide spied him, a row always followed. Reports of these encounters state that they did not speak in whispers but scattered their invectives to the winds. Mary Ann, who occasionally assisted Booth or was left in charge of the stall if he were off on some errand, would retreat discreetly when she saw Adelaide approaching and try to avoid a public scene in the hope that the scandal might be kept within bounds.

An old resident near Belair remembered having heard Ann Hall, the colored woman who worked for the Booths, tell of "the Belgium wife" coming out to the farm one time and "upbraiding the second Mrs.

Booth." It was doubtless after one of these explosions with Adelaide, that Booth smashed the gravestone above his infants' burial ground, and tore up the family Bible, to destroy the birth records of his American children. Some of these dates were later salvaged by members of the family, though that of John Wilkes' advent was seldom mentioned after Lincoln's assassination.

Mary Ann, of course, knew the truth of Adelaide's rancorous indictments on the day she visited the farm, and since denials were useless, managed to control herself and achieve a certain cool dignity that served only to infuriate Adelaide still further. In spite of the fact that the younger children never heard Mary Ann speak of this storm cloud which had settled over her family, they began to be aware of a strain on outside friendships that had not existed before. Whispered inferences and sly questions from friends and neighbors made them defend her, even though Asia, John, and Joe were still too young to know the meaning of this insidious gossip. The older children, on the other hand, must have been quick to realize that Mary Ann was trying to shield them and loyally joined in her prudent silence. So began a family tradition that remained unbroken as long as they lived; not a few people were to express dislike of the Booths because they were so secretive.

Adelaide waited over five years to establish her divorce. She seems to have been overcome by the futility of pressing a public scandal on Booth and his family, and even the actual bill of divorce was tinged with a forlorn kind of self-effacement. Personal denunciation had proved useless in her attack, and from now until her death she seems to have followed a course of crushed resignation. It was on March 26, 1851, that Adelaide filed her suit, alleging adultery.[30] Booth did not contest the charges, and the decree was granted, April 18, 1851. Since there was no family discussion of these distressing matters even the older children were still uninformed of the full details behind the disgrace, and, however much or little the younger ones had come to understand of it, they accepted their mother's attitude of mute devotion and did their best to lock the skeleton in the proverbial cupboard.

On the tenth of May, John Wilkes' thirteenth birthday, Junius Brutus Booth and Mary Ann Holmes were married in the city of Baltimore, and their union recorded in the city courthouse.

CHAPTER V

Years before the climax of Booth's ill-starred first marriage, the younger Booth children were beginning to assert themselves on the farm. Little Johnnie, as he was called at home, had captured the center of the family scene. To Edwin and his sisters he was a trouble-maker and a vexation, but to his father and mother he was an exceptional child whom they petted for his bright appearance and fiery temperament. They could not keep up with his pranks, and he was allowed to run about like a wild young colt. Edwin in his shy thoughtful manner quietly pursued his less spectacular interests. No member of the family had much influence over the impetuous Johnnie. His father was away on tour during most of his formative years, and when he returned it was to shower "his well-beloved, his bright boy Absalom," with tender-hearted adulation.

Johnnie was extremely fond of his mother, and she frequently forgave his ungovernable antics because of his gentleness toward her. His unwarranted emotional displays reacted on Edwin to increase his own introspective nature.

On summer afternoons Johnnie loitered about the stable, begging Madagascan Joe to let him lead the nags to water. When his first pair of boots were given him, he mounted a horse and rode off down the lane, much to the amazement of the family. From that time on he never let a day pass without spending part of it in the saddle. He would gallop through the woods waving a lance in the air and challenging imaginary foes.[31] Before he reached the age when most country boys learn to ride, young Johnnie could take care of himself on any horse in the vicinity.

In plain defiance he went on hunting jaunts prohibited by his father, driving game from hiding places and banging away with his rifle. He had the reputation of being a good shot, and the scampering targets seldom escaped. If anyone doubted his supremacy, he silenced him by placing an empty bottle at some distance, shooting through its open neck, and blasting out the bottom without nicking it elsewhere.

Johnnie was above average in things he liked to do, particularly outdoor sports. He made friends easily, was popular, and was always willing to share what he had with his companions. When boys came to play on the farm, he was agreeable to the wishes of the majority, but generally was the leader in whatever he desired to do.

Elijah Whistler, who lived half a mile from the Booth farm, went with Johnnie to the first public school in that neighborhood. Recalling those days after many years, he said: "Johnnie was a handsome boy; kind and gentle. Sometimes he did things which seemed a little crazy, but so did his father. There were people around here who thought all the Booths were cracked. At the end of one of the school terms, the pupils gave a play and Johnnie was selected to take the leading rôle. When he stood on the stage speaking his lines his black eyes sparkled with intensity. Every one could see that he would some day be a great actor like his father."

Elijah admitted that the instructors in this first public school were not very commendable. "One was a dope fiend but he left at the close of his first year; another was a drunkard. When we went to school in the morning we looked along the road leading to the village. If we saw our teacher in a ditch we knew there would be no session that day. He ended by falling dead while trying to drag a piano out of a burning house at Belair."

In Baltimore the Booth children made some enduring friendships. One of these was between Edwin and a boy named Sleeper who became the well-known actor, John Sleeper Clarke. Their acquaintance began when Edwin was a slender, delicate lad about twelve years old. His sensitive nature had been offended by the ridicule of a neighborhood bully who had commented unfavorably on Edwin's long black hair and the Italian cloak he was wearing. As Clarke approached them, the bully was trying to drag Edwin into a fight and had struck him. Clarke immediately took Edwin's part. Edwin, encouraged, started punching the bully in the ribs so hard that he made him stagger and fall almost winded. Thereafter Edwin and Clarke were constant companions. This led to Clarke's meeting Asia Booth, whose dark beauty so enthralled him that he would stand for hours at some street corner waiting for a glimpse of her.

Despite the success of his eldest son in the theatre, Booth still hoped that his other children would select careers in more solid professions. He hesitated to take them to see the current plays, not wishing to over-stimulate their active imaginations and arouse a lasting interest in the evanescent world of make-believe. At home he continued to refer but seldom to his professional life, and he told few anecdotes of his theatrical experiences, both because he did not wish deliberately to call the family's attention to his erratic behavior and also because of his stern belief in discouraging the children's interest in his work.

In 1845 the Booths were living on North Front Street, but a year later moved to a home on Exeter Street, where a spacious arbor in the back yard served as a theatre in which many ambitious youths who grew to be prominent actors played their first parts.[32] There they performed, before select juvenile audiences, classic and romantic dramas with the female rôles left out. Edwin organized the company and was its manager. Booth's disapproval soon forced them to move to a cellar in Triplet Alley.

The cellar was under a hotel kept by John Lutz (afterward associated with Laura Keene), who knew nothing of the rental arrangement they had made with his Negro janitor by promising him all the pennies he collected at the door. The admission fee was three cents for reserved seats, one cent for standing room, and there was no free list. Edwin was the star, George L. Stout was prompter and leading man, and Sleepy Clarke, as he was called, was stage manager. Other company members included Theodore Hamilton, Summerfield Barry, Samuel Knapp Chester, and Henry Stuart, who was to be known professionally as Stuart Robson.

Stage properties and funds to promote the venture were obtained by borrowing surreptitiously from their elders. Robson's mother had an old iron stove which was not in use, and the others pointed out to him that he might add something to the treasury by turning it into cash. The fact that his mother never spared the rod on a certain part of his anatomy made him hesitate, but the sale was finally accomplished and the money used to buy an abandoned set piece from a resort at Fell's Point. By some such means, they financed also the purchase of an old nag at the horse market and hired an organ-grinder to fill in as orchestra.

Edwin, whose great desire was to be a clown in a circus, was advertised to perform a daring equestrian act on the opening night, but when they got the old nag into the ring and Edwin was lifted onto his back the horse refused to budge. Efforts to force him into action had no effect, until a rasping tune from the hand organ sent him gallivanting around the circle. One boy's father owned a livery stable, and unknowingly, furnished feed for the animal, who grew so fat that they had to remove a partition to get him out. An account of these Triplet Alley days was given by George L. Stout in his *Recollections:*

> It was in this cellar that Edwin Booth made his first appearance as *Richard III*, and a tragedy indeed it turned out to be. He was anxious to get armour and finally solved the puzzle by getting pieces of oilcloth and covering them with

large spangles cut from the gaberdine worn by his father as *Shylock*. He cut up the garment and transferred the spangles without detection, and had made beautiful armour. Unfortunately, just about this time the old man had a sudden call to play *Shylock*, and in looking over his wardrobe discovered the loss. He went at once to Wilkes and began thrashing him without more ado, promising to keep up until told who did the mischief. On this hint, Wilkes spoke, and confessed that Edwin was responsible, moreover, that he was at the moment wearing the stolen ornaments. The old man lost no time in hastening to the cellar, but was held up at the door by the janitor, who refused to let him pass without the tribute of three cents. Whereupon Booth pitched into the negro and fought his way to the cellar, his anger now at boiling point. Edwin was just saying, "A horse! A horse! My kingdom for a horse!" before an entranced audience, when he heard the well known voice. With a lightning appreciation of his father's form blocking the door, he made a wild dash for the window. He got half way through when the armor stuck, and the old man began to "lay on" with a vigor that produced realistic shrieks from *Richard* who was on the other side of the window being tugged vigorously by a policeman, who thought he was climbing out of the window with burglarious spoils! Between his father and the policeman, poor Edwin was literally torn with contending emotions.[33]

The plays were so well patronized by the boys and girls of the neighborhood that they were kept up for several weeks, and the Negro often took in more than a dollar at each performance. But rivalry among members of the company divided them and led to much trouble. Robson and Hamilton organized another group, claimed all the stage properties they had scraped together, and stole the set. Edwin and his associates fought them and got it back. They foiled further attempts with clubs and sticks, and moved it, when not in use, to a secret hiding place.

Johnnie was then eight years old. He often interrupted rehearsals by suddenly appearing at a window and mimicking an aspiring actor. On one of these occasions, Theodore Micheau threw an oystershell at him, which cut his forehead so deeply that the wound left a small scar. Thereafter he parted his hair so as to cover this slight disfigurement. The older boys later found a more subtle way of stopping Johnnie's interruptions by giving him a triangle to beat on and letting him sing a specialty number called "The Heart Bowed Down."

Johnnie and his younger brother Joseph attended the Belair Academy for about five years. It was directed by Dr. Edwin Arnold, who described the older boy as very handsome "in face and figure although slightly bowlegged." He thought him not deficient in intelligence, but disinclined to take advantage of the educational opportunities offered him. Each day he rode back and forth from farm to school, taking more interest in what happened along the way than in reaching his classes on time. Joseph, who boarded at the Academy, was much more studious.

The two Booth boys belonged to a debating club which the members finally decided to discontinue. As it had been in existence for some time, quite a sum of money had accumulated from dues, and there was a question of its disposition. After discussing the matter, they agreed "to blow it all in on a party" some Friday night before the end of the term. The day scholars were to sneak cakes and confections from their homes, and Hughey Rogers, barkeeper at the Harford House, was enticed into making up pitchers of "hot stuff" sufficiently potent to enliven the members. To insure secrecy, Dr. Arnold's son was invited, as they were afraid he might otherwise hear of it and tell his father. Johnnie was the chief promoter, and this invitation was an indication of his craftiness in handling the situation.

The members arrived and drank freely of Rogers' concoction. Soon pandemonium broke loose. Card-playing gave way to shouts, blood-curdling cries and whoops of hilarity. Dr. Arnold heard the racket and hastened to the meeting place to see what was going on. When he arrived and discovered his son among the revelers, he slipped away again without being noticed, but on Monday morning he told the boys he had visited the party at its height and the only thing that saved them all from expulsion was that "so many were present, to punish the guilty would break up the school."

On another occasion, after the town had fittingly observed the Fourth of July, Johnnie discovered some left-over fireworks in a hotel room and carried them out onto the porch where some old-timers, oblivious of his intentions, were discussing politics. Suddenly there was a terrific explosion and everyone rushed into the street. When they looked around, they saw Johnnie escaping in the opposite direction toward the woods.

The older Booth children, with the exception of Edwin whose academic training was spasmodic, received such education as their father could afford, and the two younger boys benefited by the earnings of their grown brothers after his death.

Asia, about eleven, was attending classes at the Carmelite Convent as a day student. The usual restrictions of a Catholic school had been somewhat modified because of financial difficulties, and she had been admitted despite the fact that her father was an actor. The influence of this religious schooling did much to affect her character. She developed a conscientious integrity in which she never faltered. Through all the tempestuous life of the Booths, Asia sought to vindicate the family honor with an almost puritanical zeal.

Edwin began at a school for boys and girls directed by spinster Susan Hyde in a section of Baltimore known as Old Town. There he was grounded in rudiments and then placed under the care of Louis Dugas, a French West Indian officer. An old Negro taught him to play the banjo and a Signor Picioli gave him instruction on the violin. At intervals he studied with a pedagogue named Kearney, who not only wrote textbooks but coached his students in dramatics. Edwin and Sleepy Clarke frequently gave readings from Shakespeare. At one of these, the quarrel scene between Brutus and Cassius, with Edwin dressed in white pants and a black jacket, the elder Booth suddenly made his appearance in the classroom. He had come to get Edwin and Sleepy to wash the mud from some potatoes he had brought from the farm to his market stall. Often the two boys were employed for this sort of work and got a few pennies for pay.

An incident occurred at this time which Edwin never forgot. His deportment had not been up to Miss Hyde's standard, and she kept him after school. As he gazed from the window he saw Sleepy looking up at him from the street below with a brickbat in his hand. As soon as he was released, Edwin rushed out to join him and asked what he meant to do with the brickbat. "I was watching to catch Miss Hyde come into the room and punish you," said Sleepy, "and the moment I saw her strike, I was going to throw the brickbat through the window at her."

When fourteen, Edwin took matters into his own hands and determined to seek his fortune on the stage, regardless of paternal disfavor. He presented himself to the manager of the Holliday Street Theatre, who cast him in the part of Captain in *The Spectre Bridegroom*. But Edwin's professional début was unhappily not a success. "It was a most painful sight," said Henry C. Wagner, whose uncle owned the theatre. "Young Booth was possessed by a genuine case of stage fright. He stammered and halted and was most uneasy. At a later period I saw him in a tragedy and at that time his performance was marred by the same characteristics. One could not have seen in the nervous young man of those occasions, the brilliant artist of a later day." [34]

Junius Senior was again in need of a dresser and companion who could urge some kind of restraint on his fantastic escapades, so, in 1847, Edwin was packed off as his father's new attendant. In speaking of this period of his life, Edwin later recalled that though his father might often be irrational and overcome with drink, he still maintained a mother-like solicitude for his sensitive young son. He always insisted that Edwin bring his textbooks with him so that he might continue his studies along the way, not suspecting that the boy was learning his most cherished lessons from Booth's own playbooks and a diligent observation of his technical expression.

It is hard to believe that the great tragedian, lapsing from his fixed intention, would have deliberately thrust his child into the environment of the theatre and yet expect him to be completely indifferent to its fascination. At this time he certainly thought little of Edwin's potentialities as an actor, for when a manager suggested that Edwin's name might appear on the bill, he replied with utmost seriousness that his son was a good banjo player and could be announced for a solo between the acts.

Booth's disregard of dates continued to increase his managers' losses. At the Odeon Theatre in Albany, the callboy tapped on his dressing-room door but got no response. A report was made to the stage manager, who searched the theatre from top to bottom and then went before the audience to make the usual announcement, under such conditions, of a substitute play or player and a refund at the box office. This left few people in the house. After the performance an attendant was sent to look further for Booth, and it was not long before he found the mad tragedian in a Trotter's Alley groggery, *The Hole in the Wall*, laid out on a bench, stupidly drunk.

To guard against a repetition, he was taken in a carriage to the old Howard Street jail and locked in the debtors' cell. When his manager arrived the following morning, he found Booth drunker than ever and was forced to remain with him all day to assure his appearance that evening. No one could account for his condition, as he had been confined behind a grating too small for a bottle to be passed through to him. The chore-boy eventually confessed to having obtained brandy and a Shaker pipe for Booth, through which he had sipped the liquor from a cup outside the grating. Again, when he should have been in Buffalo, he was with some drunken companions in a beer garden overlooking the Hudson River, singing ribald songs, while Edwin waited to guide him on.

Travel between cities was a matter of tedious hours in rickety, springless coaches, of jouncing along muddy roads and of being

The elder Booth before his nose was broken by actor Thomas Flynn. A rare photograph from the collection of Gail Merrifield, great-great-granddaughter of John Wilkes Booth and Izola Mills D'Arcy.

Front view of Tudor Hall, the home built by the elder Booth. *(Original photograph by the author)*

The elder Booth at fifty-three and Edwin at sixteen, about the time of their appearance at the Boston Museum, September 10, 1849. After a daguerreotype. *(New York Public Library photo)*

chilled by inclement weather. Whenever he could, Booth would take a river boat or coastwise vessel to escape these discomforts, seldom a train. After a tiresome journey the coach would turn into the cobbled courtyard of some tavern or hostelry, and Booth, with Edwin at his heels, would stride in, arrange for accommodations, and repair promptly to the barroom. There he would revive his good humor, and announce that his engagement would begin on a certain evening. No wonder Edwin's boyhood was filled with tears. What had he to remember from such grim experiences? Rank barrooms, dismal hotels, dirty conveyances, the dim interiors of many theatres. However, he found compensation in an intimacy with celebrated rôles as interpreted by his father.

There is a popular tradition, supported by some writers, that Edwin's first appearance occurred September 10, 1849, in the elder Booth's production of *Richard III*, at the Boston Museum, but it is apparent from the records that he had experienced professional activity before. Such accounts state also that this appearance was unexpected—the result of an actor wishing to be excused from the part; but the fact that his name appears on the program of that performance proves that his billing was premeditated and regularly announced. Years later he wrote of the event: "After my début in the very small part of *Tressel*, my father 'cuddled' me; and gave me gruel (his usual meal at night, when acting) and made me don his worsted night-cap, which when his work was ended he always wore as a protection for his heated head, to prevent me from taking cold after my labors, which were doubtless very exhausting on that occasion, being confined to one brief scene at the beginning of the play! At that time there seemed to be a touch of irony in this overcare of me, but *now*, recalling the many acts of his large sympathy, it appears in its true character of genuine solicitude for the heedless boy who had drifted into that troublous sea, where without talent he would either sink or, buoyed perhaps by vanity alone, merely flounder in its uncertain waves." [35]

Following a Boston performance the elder Booth returned with Edwin to their lodgings so exhausted he could not rest, and insisted on going out again into the street. To keep him from the inevitable barroom, Edwin begged him to retire, offering to play his banjo and sing Negro songs or read from one of his favorite books. The old man, however, was determined and started for the door. Immediately, he found his way blocked by his young son, who cried, "You shall not leave this room!" The words so surprised his father that for a moment he stood transfixed. Then he vanished into a closet and locked the door from the inside. Edwin, alarmed, called to him but got no response. As he was about to run for help, the closet door opened and the elder Booth emerged. Without a word or a glance in the boy's direction, he walked sternly across the room, undressed, and went to bed.

In Providence, Edwin played Cassio to his father's Iago. "Fancy a sixteen-year-old boy calling wine a demon and lamenting his drunkenness," was one comment on that performance. Here he also made a favorable impression as Wilford, in *The Iron Chest*. Barton Hill played with them in Pittsburgh on this tour and described Edwin as having a fine forehead, intellectual features, brilliant eyes and, even then, the somber expression of his later portraits.

The boy went home to study, and his father journeyed southward alone. At Richmond the "evil spirit" came on him again, and manager John Sefton, who kept tab of performances on the backs of playbills, noted: "Clear night. Mr. Booth was drunk and did not appear." The next day he announced through the press that, having disappointed the audience on the previous evening, Booth would not be permitted to play again that season at his theatre.

After this dismissal Booth disappeared, and Edwin, at the request of his mother, wrote to Sefton for information. As he could not help, Edwin was dispatched to Richmond with instructions to locate his father and bring him home. Accompanied by the manager he frantically raced from one barroom to another, inquiring for the great actor, who was finally discovered having a royal time on a friend's plantation. Booth borrowed fifty dollars from Sefton to pay passage for himself and his son back to the farm in Maryland, promising to repay it on a certain day within two weeks. When it was due, Sefton received his money by express in the exact coinage he had loaned to Booth.

Edwin again appeared as Wilford with his father, in Philadelphia, at the end of the season. He then attended a private school in Baltimore, along with two more Booths, Asia and John Wilkes. According to J. R. Codet, their instructor:

> They learned society dancing, taking their lessons in the classes made up from the children of representative citizens, being in no sense 'set apart' because their father was an actor. I have frequently known Junius Brutus Booth, sr., to come to the dressing rooms there to wait for his children and take them home. He seemed to be a plain farmer, and generally had an ample supply of mud on his boots, and resembled closely the ordinary hayseed of to-day. Anyone looked more like an

actor than he. There was nothing theatrical in his appearance. His fame resulting from his unequalled rendition of the *Lord's Prayer* was the cause of many an invitation being extended to him to dine or sup socially, on which occasions he would invariably be called upon to repeat in his reverential, pathetically suppliant manner that most beautiful of prayers.[36]

A friend of Booth's who stayed at the farm overnight heard it in different circumstances. He had retired early and was about to fall asleep when he was disturbed by someone at the door. On opening his eyes, he saw Booth enter the room with a lighted candle in his hand. As he approached his guest, Booth asked in a low, deep voice, "Have you prayed tonight?" The guest admitted he had not done so before crawling into bed. Thereupon Booth demanded that he "rise, kneel, and repeat the Lord's Prayer." Acquainted with the peculiar temperament of his host, the man at once complied. When he had finished, Booth exclaimed, "Is that all you can make out of the grandest utterance in literature!" As the astonished guest gazed up at him, not knowing what to say or do, the mad actor dropped on his knees and demonstrated how it should be interpreted.

Booth was acquainted with numerous creeds. He read the Talmud and strictly adhered to many of its laws, admired the Koran and observed days sacred to its teachings, attended Catholic and Protestant services alike, and often worshiped at a sailors' bethel. An old sea derelict once knocked at the door of his Baltimore home, asking for food. When he heard his story, he invited him in, fed him, then washed and bandaged a bad wound on his leg. Mary Ann, on the other hand, was more reserved in her religious sentiments and frequently took the children to the Episcopal Church, both in Baltimore and in the country.

The residents of Belair had heard of Edwin's stage appearances and asked him to give some readings from Shakespeare while at home. They offered him the use of a room in the courthouse and assured him of a large audience. With John Sleeper Clarke, who was visiting at the farm, Edwin set the date for August second (1850). The youths made selections from their varied schoolday repertoire and galloped off on horseback one hot afternoon to have programs printed in Baltimore. When they returned the next day, they were surprised to find the elder Booth interested in the event and offering suggestions for its success.

Taking a sheet to use as a curtain and a dinner bell to announce the time for it to go up, they rode back to town to arrange the courthouse room. Some country boys, believing that a circus had arrived, gathered at the windows to see what was going on. Edwin rolled in a barrel and, while standing on it to hang the curtain, lost his balance and fell off. This disgusted one of the rustics who turned away from the window, saying, "Aw hell, they hain't circus people; that one cain't even stand on a barrel!"

Madagascan Joe, entrusted with a stack of programs, felt very important as he went about tacking them on trees and fences, crying, "Oyez! Oyez! Tonight great tragedy!" When Edwin and Sleeper rode back to the courthouse that evening they were dismayed to find that he had posted all the programs upside down. Nevertheless, a large and enthusiastic audience greeted them, and their efforts grossed thirty dollars.

Now in his fifty-fourth year, the elder Booth began the construction of a new house at the farm. It was to be built of brick in the Elizabethan style, contain about eight rooms and a spacious hallway on both the lower and upper floors. For this work he employed James Gifford, an architect, and a young carpenter, Edward Spangler, who, at a future date, was to be involved in a certain tragedy at Ford's Washington Theatre. This more substantial residence, which Booth named Tudor Hall, was not completed until after his death, and since his sons continued their theatrical careers and lived elsewhere, it never became the center of family life he had intended it to be.[37]

That autumn, Booth relinquished all hope of restraining Edwin's desire to be a professional actor, and took his son with him trouping through the major eastern cities. Edwin had profited well by studying the characters in his father's prompt books and now assumed a variety of parts. He made his initial New York appearance at the National Theatre playing the rôle of Wilford, in *The Iron Chest* and of Hemaya, in *The Apostate*. In November father and son went to Baltimore for an engagement at the Holliday Street Theatre. Edwin's name was first advertised in that city in connection with his father's benefit performance of John Howard Payne's *Brutus, or, The Fall of Tarquin*. It was announced that Booth would introduce his son in the rôle of Titus. The playwright saw Edwin in this bill not long afterward when it was produced in Washington and was favorably impressed with his ability.

The following April found Edwin and his father in New York. Booth had played a moderately successful engagement at the National Theatre climaxed by a benefit for himself as Iago in the popular bill of Othello. The next night had been set aside as a benefit for Master Murry, an infant prodigy who had taken the fancy of the public. The piece selected was Booth's old favorite, *Richard III*, and he was expected to appear with the child marvel. But when the time came he was obdurate—second-fiddle to a freak, not he! Edwin began entreating his father to start off with him for the theatre, but was silenced by the old man's exclamation, "Go play it yourself!" Confused and distracted, Edwin reached the theatre and repeated his father's words to the manager, John R. Scott, who added to his perplexity by saying, "All right; you can do it."

Edwin rushed to the dressing room and apprehensively put on his father's costume.

The curtain went up, the performance began, and when Edwin made his entrance he was met with bewildering applause. But this wild acclaim was not for him; the audience suddenly saw that they had been deceived. He was not the Booth they had paid to see. Yet his acting mystified them—it was so similar to the great tragedian's style and pattern. Who was this understudy? Scott, anxiously watching in the wings, was pleased Edwin was proving a worthy substitute. At the end of the act he led him before the curtain and introduced him. This brought a renewed round of clapping punctuated by shouts of "Bravo!" and with this personal welcome ringing in his ears, Edwin finished the performance in great style. When he returned to the hotel Booth coolly questioned him about the evening in a preoccupied manner, dismissing the whole affair as a capricious incident. Yet in later life Edwin insisted that his father had quietly slipped into the audience to watch and was moderately pleased with the result.

Edwin now applied to Thaddeus Barton, manager of the Baltimore Holliday Street Theatre, for a place in his company. Barton took it up with the elder Booth, who thought it over and replied, "It has always been my desire that Ted should be a lawyer, as my father was, but I suppose that if I don't let him follow his bent he will run off and join some other company, and if he plays here I will have him under my observation. Let him try it." So Edwin was employed at six dollars a week to do utility parts.

He had had little training beyond what his powers of observation had taught him, and his lack of fundamental technique soon became apparent. Those who saw him in minor rôles and inferior plays at this time found him shy, awkward, confused and completely at a loss to know how to remedy his faults. Asia tells of his attempting a part in a pantomime with the exciting French actress, Madame Ciocca. He was supposed to act with the fastidious mannerisms of an eighteenth-century dandy but instead clumsily bungled about the stage, lacking all sense of dexterity and skill. His *gaucherie* so horrified the clever Frenchwoman that she added to his mortification by bringing sharp abuse down on his head when the fiasco was over.

The rigors of his dynamic style, the hardships of trouping, and the pressure of his personal worries had done much to age the elder Booth beyond his fifty-six years. The next winter he again took Edwin with him to play a series of engagements in the East and the South. These appearances were to be his last visits to all but one of the cities which had acclaimed him for so many seasons. His farewell New York performance was given in *Bertram*, at the National Theatre, on May 19, 1852. There he became aware of a new trend in theatrical patronage. The good old days of the tragic dramas were drifting away. Variety entertainment with minstrel shows, dance tunes, and comic skits sprinkled with popular airs were becoming fashionable. The music hall was no place for him—the afterpiece was as far as he had gone in comedy. Sensing these changing conditions and aware of his advancing years, Booth began to limit his engagements and stay more at home.

Johnnie and Joseph, after attending schools in Baltimore, were sent about this time to St. Timothy's Hall in Catonsville, Maryland. Johnnie's acquaintance there with Samuel B. Arnold, another Baltimore boy, was to result in an association that had a far-reaching effect on their lives.

CHAPTER VI

Back in 1850 Augustus Fenno,[38] a well-known tragedian who had returned to Boston from the California gold rush, gave young Junius glowing accounts of the wealth in the West and advised his going to San Francisco. Other members of the profession, including the Chapmans in New York, heard about his reports and dreamed of trekking westward. Soon the "breaking out of the mines," as it was called, began to look like a real epidemic. Theatrical managers, fearing a sudden exodus of companies and stars, signed many of them to long-term engagements, but this only delayed their departure.

Before Junius had definitely decided what to do, an agent approached him with a contract to manage a new theatre in San Francisco being built by a former New York politician named Thomas Maguire.[39] This seemed to solve his difficulties, and, in the summer of 1851, he and Harriet Mace sailed for the Golden Gate.

With them were Kate Gray and several others well-known in the theatre. They took the fastest route, by way of Panama, going first to Chagres, a port at the mouth of the river of that name.

They were conveyed ashore in a small boat, and remained overnight at a rowdy tavern. Early the following morning they started the journey across the Isthmus in canoes paddled by dark-skinned boys, through territory where bandits, fevers, and insects waited to pounce on weary travelers.

Junius had been warned to buy provisions and quinine for the trip and to keep an eye on the baggage. They had not gone far before he realized the necessity for such advice: only *ranchos* and huts were seen along the river, with occasional groups of jabbering natives who seemed to be discussing the value of their possessions! They spent another night at Gorgona and next morning continued on muleback over the old road to Panama City. Again they climbed into a small boat and were carried out to the steamship *Tennessee*. Their long journey ended in San Francisco on Sunday morning, July 20, 1851.

What they saw there was most disheartening. The month before, fire had again swept over a large portion of the city, leaving misery and desolation for its inhabitants. A few blackened walls and a mass of cinders were all that remained in a number of streets once crowded with shops and dwellings. Many had predicted that San Francisco would never be rebuilt, but new structures were already beginning to appear here and there, and in the lower section of the city, brick buildings were being erected that would bid defiance to the Fire King.

Thomas Maguire, whose first shelter had been a tent on Portsmouth Square, had turned his New York experiences into cash and lost more than he had ever dreamed of possessing. Being in control of the underworld, Tom accumulated dollars between conflagrations. This supplied the gold for his theatrical ventures, which had been profitless. The arrival of his new manager, however, caught him without a playhouse in San Francisco, as the new Jenny Lind Theatre, which was being built of stone on the site of two others successively destroyed by fire, had not been completed. When they met that Sunday, Maguire informed Junius that he and Harriet, accompanied by several members of his troupe, would be sent to Sacramento for an engagement with C. R. Thorne's company.[40]

In the afternoon Junius and Harriet strolled about San Francisco, mingling with strange crowds. They saw few gray-haired veterans but many well-educated youths from the East and the South, as well as a motley collection of adventurers from every nation on the globe. Turbaned Ottomans and Hindus, pigtailed Chinese, diminutive Malayans, tall and vigorous Maoris bargained with Hebrews, Africans, Indians, and illiterates from the border states for fake gold indicators and worthless trinkets. Silver half-dollars passed from hand to hand—the smallest coins exchanged for any service or article. Bearded miners, garbed in woolen shirts and baggy pantaloons, bristled with knives and pistols not worn for ornamental purposes. Those who had "seen the elephant," a term for hardships endured without reward, and others more successful in the quest for gold, looked askance at newcomers.

Efforts to tame these infidels accounted for the gospel shouting of a Reverend Taylor each Sunday in Portsmouth Square, where loud bidding on mules and prospectors' outfits often drowned out his voice and left him doing a pantomime against the devil, much to the delight of his audience.

Women of refinement were noticeably absent in all public places; consequently, when one appeared she was worshiped almost as a divinity and any physical imperfection was overlooked. This scarcity sent miners rushing up gangways of steamers from foreign ports to snatch women for wives before proprietors of resorts could hoodwink them into contracts and start them off in an ancient business. Peruvian and Polynesian girls were in demand for dancing halls, and the French demimonde for the gambling tables. Those who knew how to manage their own affairs often grew rich. A missionary journal reported a prostitute's earning fifty thousand dollars within a few years after her arrival.

The city was overrun with rats of every size, shape and color. By night they pursued their gambols on the planks of the streets and often tripped up pedestrians who sought to find their way by lantern to and from their lodgings. The Oakland *Times* noted that other California cities also were celebrated for the pests in their midst: Stockton for its mosquitoes, Sacramento for its bedbugs, and Oakland for assorted fleas that swarmed everywhere, the church flea being the most ravenous variety as it was starved all week and so had an extraordinary appetite for Sunday.

Pioneers in this new Eldorado never knew what to expect from day to day. Life was hazardous for all. Depressions and booms engulfed them in such quick succession that they hardly had time to recover from the one before they were in the midst of the other. California was no place for weaklings or a tottering generation in 1851; it belonged only to young and blasphemous huskies who could defy all the elements leagued against them in the mountains and valleys of that rugged era.

Supported by as talented a company as any eastern theatre could boast, Junius made his Sacramento début at the Pacific Theatre in *The Stranger*, with Harriet cast as Charlotte, on the night of August twenty-first. The press reported an enthusiastic response to Junius' interpretations and compared his rendition to his father's style. Junius was still an imitator, without a creative flair. In September they moved to the American Theatre, where they played for two weeks before terminating their first engagement on the Pacific Coast.

Having been materially purified by fire, San Francisco arose from its ashes and went on another boom. Shops and dwellings sprang up; bankers and gold-dust buyers moved into new and more spacious buildings; nefarious establishments vied with one another in adding splendor; and new theatres staged productions outrivaling previous efforts.

When Junius returned there with the woman who had acquired his name, he selected a house on Telegraph Hill which overlooked the city. At the highest point on the hill the tilting of a black wooden arm announced the arrival of each vessel. Junius gained an immediate respect in the community by joining the Vigilantes who had recently bound themselves together to curb lawlessness and rid the city of undesirables. Eventually, this brought him into touch with one

La Fayette C. Baker, whose experiences with this organization were to fit him for an important post at the beginning of the Civil War. Their friendship was to prove an advantage to Junius at a much later date.

Harriet was a pleasing actress and very popular. Junius was athletic, exceedingly fond of boxing and fencing, and had the grace of all the Booths. They were spoken of as the handsomest couple in San Francisco. Their generous hospitality soon attracted many friends and their home became a meeting place for all theatrical people. Here, two children were born, the one surviving infancy being named Marion.

Maguire's new Jenny Lind Theatre, with Junius as manager, opened its doors to the public October 4, 1851, and was heralded as "the most beautiful temple devoted to the legitimate drama in The United States." Its scenery had been painted by the celebrated Boston artist, John Fairchild, and its furnishings were the most lavish money could buy. Admission prices made Junius feel as though he had at last reached the promised land. In the New York Bowery Theatre he had played for ten, twelve and a half, and eighteen cents. The Jenny Lind prices soared to three dollars in the parquet and dress circle! Here was something which might attract his father.

The company was composed of many famous actors from Boston and New York, and when the curtain went up on *Faint Heart Never Won Fair Lady* and *All That Glitters Is Not Gold* the house was crowded. Wesley Venua, a popular English actor, spoke the first words; Harriet made her San Francisco début in the initial bill, and Junius, as Stephen Plum, appeared in the afterpiece. This engagement gave Junius his first opportunity in San Francisco to venture in celebrated rôles, and he followed with *Richelieu* and other well-known plays, collecting a string of press clippings along the way. Undoubtedly, now, he was most ambitious as an actor. Edwin had not yet been heard from; the crown of the elder Booth might pass to Junius when his father could no longer wear it.

A benefit performance of *The School for Scandal* was tendered the night of December eleventh to the ex-cabdriver who had become the Napoleon of the Drama on the coast. Tom Maguire arrived immaculately dressed and sat with his shrewd wife in a box, acknowledging the applause of the crowd. Mr. and Mrs. James Stark played the leading rôles, and Junius stayed behind the scenes. The next day some of Tom's associates told him it was the "best show" he had ever put on, but he failed to get their meaning.

Stars were now fast arriving. In February, 1852, Lewis Baker and his famous wife Alexina made their appearance at the Jenny Lind, in *The Hunchback*. Dissatisfied with this connection, they soon took over the new little Adelphi Theatre, engaged a celebrated cast, among whom were the Starks and Frank Chanfrau, and announced an opening for the following month. Another theatre, the American, after having settled into a bog beneath the weight of its large first-night audience, continued to prosper, and rivalry between the three houses was growing.

With expenses cut to a minimum, the little Adelphi looked like a serious competitor to the over-sized and debt-burdened Jenny Lind, and Junius began putting on novelties of the day to avoid losing the patronage which the house required to function. The Bakers then advertised that a succession of novelties would be brought forward, and every care and attention paid to their complete and unapproachable production.

Reminded of the struggle between small playhouses and large theatres in New York, Junius proposed to Maguire, who was already tiring of the elephantine Jenny Lind Theatre, that he sell it and build a smaller house in the neighborhood of Portsmouth Square. He advised Maguire to employ the best talent, to present entertaining farce and burlesque, and to add to the structure as it paid its way for such expansion. This suggestion brought about the building of the San Francisco Hall.

Junius had been planning for some time to return east for his father, and he bound the recently arrived Chapmans under contract, to keep them at the Jenny Lind while he was away. Here, March fifteenth, William B. Chapman made his San Francisco début. The Jenny Lind company had been moved to the American, and resumed carnival attractions. The Adelphi, being a cold, uncomfortable theatre, located on the side of a steep hill, apparently chilled the actors toward one another. Their quarrels and departures forced the Bakers to give it up and join with Junius at the American.

A benefit performance for the Booths on the eighteenth of the month brought Junius before the curtain to announce that he and Harriet would sail in a few days for a short visit with his parents in Maryland.

They reached the farm early in May. Father could hardly call son to account for a *mésalliance* so like his own. The cases were disconcerting in their similarity; consequently, Harriet was accepted without embarrassment as a member of the family.

The elder Booth was certainly in a dilemma. He had tried vainly to keep Junius out of the theatre, and here he was following the pattern of his life in a still more ominous way. What was to become of Mary Ann's loyal efforts to hush family scandal if it became known that Junius had placed himself in this situation?

Junius told of the fortune in California awaiting so celebrated an actor as his father, but the latter was not interested. Though his son reminded him that William Chapman of his Brussels days and many of his other friends were there, it failed to stir him. Descriptions of night life in the gambling halls and barrooms, however, finally aroused the old man and he said he would go—"more for the novelty of the trip than a desire to perform there."

Edwin was not well, and Mary Ann was reluctant to agree to so long a journey for her husband without his guidance. He had learned many of his father's tricks and usually could control him. Junius, with Harriet's interests to consider, was not so dependable. But after further urging she consented to let her husband go without Edwin, and immediately after his last performance of *Richard III*, on June fifth, at the Holliday Street Theatre in Baltimore, he started off, carpetbag in hand, with Junius and Harriet. The new dwelling, Tudor Hall, was still uncompleted. The old man was destined never to occupy the house in which he hoped his Maryland family would gather about him in his declining years.

In New York Junius made reservations on a steamer to Panama, while his father wandered off to look up some cronies. It did not take him long to locate George Spear and coax him into joining the party for California. Arm in arm they went the rounds of the Bowery bidding their friends good-by. At sailing time both of them were drunk and missed the boat. The moment Booth was sober he cried for Edwin and went back to Belair after him. While he was away his amiable companion disappeared and Junius made another reservation, on the steamer *Illinois*. Edwin was now recovered sufficiently to accompany his erratic father and keep him in tow, but when he led the old man up the gangplank George Spear staggered aboard after them.

No passage to California was one of comfort in those days. The Booths crossed the Isthmus of Panama over the original disjointed route although twenty-three miles of railroad between Aspinwall (the new Atlantic port) and Barbacoas were now nearing completion. Harriet slept in a hammock, while other members of the party dozed on blanket-covered wine casks, with loaded pistols in hand ready for use in case the inhabitants of the region went on a rampage with their machetes. The elder Booth predicted that some day a canal would stretch across the Isthmus.

At Panama they boarded the steamer *California*, and on July twenty-eighth arrived in San Francisco. "Booth will arouse and revive the drooping theatricals in this State," proclaimed the press.

Every member of the profession was at the dock to see them ashore. Tom Maguire had a band to greet them and a handsome carriage to convey them to one of his elaborate establishments in Portsmouth Square. All at the dock recognized the old man carrying the carpetbag as Booth, and were not surprised to see George Spear, but the shy and youthful appearance of Edwin caused them to wonder who he might be. When he came closer and they noted his large black eyes and dark hair, they knew him for one of the Maryland Booths.

As the new arrivals passed through the streets, they were amazed to see oriental bazaars scattered among the wooden and canvas structures with shop windows displaying expensive curiosities from all parts of the world; elegantly painted cabs drawn by spirited horses decked in silver-studded harness; shaggy miners garish with clusters of diamonds, gold rings and watch chains, who lounged in the doorways of dives; auctioneers endeavoring to attract bidders with the din of their bells; and tradespeople rushing about as if great international affairs depended on their immediate attention. They caught glimpses of lavishly furnished hotel lobbies and restaurants paneled with mirrors and overhung by glistening chandeliers, and observed the exorbitant prices listed on their advertisements. It was unlike anything they had ever seen before.

After the reception given by Maguire, Edwin was whisked away by Junius and Harriet to their home on Telegraph Hill, and the elder Booth, with his boon companion, George Spear, began a tour of establishments where old-timers propped them up to drink toasts to their reunion. His sons, knowing he was among friends, did not go back for him. By midnight Spear had passed out, and old man Booth wandered off to a blacksmith shop on Montgomery Street where he slept till the following day. Harriet prepared a place for him, but he refused to leave his new haunts and obtained lodgings in the lower section of the city. Thereafter, when they wanted to find him, they looked in at Barry and Patten's or any one of the numerous barrooms in the neighborhood of Portsmouth Square.

His Pythagorean ideas received a shock in the Bay City. Large supplies of fruits and melons were on sale everywhere. But melons cost as much as a dollar apiece; pears and figs, the first raised in San Jose Valley, sold singly for twelve and a half cents; and other edibles brought similar prices. Booth was beginning to wonder if California were really the place for him.

Junius discovered that during his absence Maguire had unloaded the Jenny Lind Theatre upon the people of San Francisco for use as a city hall. However, by agreeing to devote one night to any charitable purpose the Board might wish to nominate, he was able to arrange for his father's appearance there. The announcement was then made that Messrs. W. B. Chapman and H. F. Daly had, at great expense, secured the services of the celebrated tragedian, Mr. Junius Brutus Booth, Sr., his son, Edwin Booth, and the well-known comedian, Mr. George Spear, who, with the popular J. B. Booth, Jr., and other members of their company, would begin an engagement July thirtieth in *The Iron Chest*.

The morning of the first rehearsal, crowds gathered in the plaza opposite the theatre to watch a bulletin board on which were posted woodcuts of Franklin Pierce and Winfield Scott, presidential nominees of the Democrats and Whigs, in comical postures. As Edwin came along a local organization was parading and the holiday appearance of these surroundings made him forget the hour set for his presence backstage. When he finally arrived he took no interest in what was going on, walked about listlessly and mumbled his part. This caused Booth, Sr., to storm the wings with vocal explosions. "That won't do! Come, come, come!" he shouted, snapping his fingers in the air. Edwin began again and drawled out the line, "The weary sun has made a golden set . . ." This threw the old man into another outburst of reproof, and he exclaimed, "For God's sake! Where does the sun set? Well, show it then! Point to it! Nod your head! Damn it, do something!" Then he went over to where his son was standing and made him do it.

"That was the way Edwin learned to act," said J. J. McCloskey, in relating the incident. "We saw nothing in his acting to show that he had any talent. In fact, during the engagement, which lasted about two weeks, he gave no evidence of further greatness." [41] Yet Ferdinand C. Ewer, a pioneer journalist and editor, in reviewing the performance in the *Daily Alta California*, spoke of Edwin as a judicious actor who was applauded throughout. Ewer became one of Edwin's closest friends and staunchest supporters. His astute criticism of the elder Booth's appearance was prophetic in its accuracy. He described him as a splendid ruin, magnificent in decay, a man whose days were numbered and whose absence from the stage would be an irreparable loss.

The *Alta* later reported the Jenny Lind as being nightly one dense pack of mortality from gallery to pit, with great numbers of people being turned away at the doors, and stated it was useless to enter on any criticism of the great Booth's acting, as it had been seen and admired by thousands. Evidently the old man was behaving himself. In accordance with the agreement, the Board appropriated the proceeds of *The Stranger* for the orphan asylum. Many of its inmates had been left destitute by the death of their parents aboard steamers bound for California.

On the fifteenth of August, the Jenny Lind closed with the elder Booth's final appearance in *Macbeth*, after which it was converted into the city hall. Crowded houses had given the impression that the engagement was a financial success, but when salaries and expenses for the journey from New York had been paid, nothing was left for Messrs. Chapman and Daly.

Junius then took a company, including all the Booths, Caroline and William Chapman, H. F. Daly and George Spear, to Sacramento. He guaranteed his father a certain sum of money, and all expected to reap a few bags of gold dust. They packed their luggage and set out for the Long Wharf, from which magnificent steamboats started on the voyage up the river. These vessels were the pride of their owners, having been brought from the East around Cape Horn, and were capable of speed as great as any craft afloat. The usual fare for the ten-hour trip from San Francisco to Sacramento was between five and eight dollars, but competition being keen, opposition steamboat owners trapped approaching passengers by having their "tooters" cry, "One dollar to-night for Sacramento, by the . . . fastest boat that ever turned a wheel from Long Wharf—with feather pillows and curled-hair mattresses, mahogany doors and silver hinges. She has got eight young-lady passengers to-night, that speak all the dead languages, and not a colored man from stem to stern of her." [42]

The company was billed for the American Theatre. The press lauded the arrival of the elder Booth by announcing that "the people of the community would have an opportunity to witness dramatic representations which would repay them for the miserable manglings that had so often grated on their ears." They opened, August nineteenth, with *The Iron Chest*, before a crowded house which was described as fashionable and discriminating. But one of those quick changes in conditions which swept over California during this period came to make men cautious in all their dealings, and those who had been lavish spenders now began to hoard their gold. As audiences became smaller the Booths took benefits, the first being for the elder Booth on August twenty-sixth when Payne's *Brutus* was presented. Edwin was next in line, billed for September second as Jaffer, in *Venice Preserved*. In the black dress of that character, he approached his father, seated on a step at the door of his dressing room. The old man gazed at him a moment and said: "You look like Hamlet; why did you not do it for your benefit?" to which Edwin replied, "If ever I have another benefit, I will." [43]

Once in these California days the elder Booth was standing close to Edwin in the wings when he was asked which son he thought would keep the name at its high level in the theatre. Junius was not far off and the old man, not wishing to discuss the matter or say anything which might lead to jealousy between his sons, simply placed his arm around Edwin for a moment and then walked away. At no time in his life did the modest Edwin ever refer to the incident, but the memory of it must have sunk deeply into his heart and made him determined always to uphold the trust his father had placed in him.

The combat scene of *Richard III* on Junius' benefit night was reported as most exciting and exhibiting a skill in the use of foils rarely seen on the stage. The elder Booth's appearance as Jerry Sneak, in the afterpiece, kept the house in a continual roar of laughter. At the close of the performance, he and Junius responded to many curtain calls, and an old-timer in the audience exclaimed, "Splendid! Splendid! As good as we saw it in '27!", which set the house into another burst of merriment and applause.

The Sacramento venture was financially disastrous to its sponsor. When Junius had made the offer to his father, there had been no indication that business was on the verge of a sudden slump. The effort to bolster receipts by benefits had been negligible. Booth reminded his oldest son of the fortune he had said awaited him in California, and, after the final appearance, he ruthlessly demanded the full sum promised. To pay the obligation, Junius almost emptied his own pockets to fill his father's.

The company straggled back to the Bay City. The elder Booth announced a farewell engagement of four nights only at the Adelphi Theatre before his departure East. His intent to go back probably explains his penurious conduct with Junius. He told his sons that he was anxious to be at home again and meant to retire from the stage. As a slight recompense to Junius he presented him with the diadem he had worn so many years in *Richard III*, saying, "I shall no longer need it; I hope you will wear it with honor." Booth had seen no startling indication that this eldest son and namesake would carry on his traditions, but he passed his crown to Junius as the only one then prepared to wear it.

Edwin offered to return with his father, fearing some catastrophe would happen on the way, but the old man counseled him to remain longer in the West and fight his own battles for recognition. He warned him that he could never achieve independence in acting or in life so long as he leaned on another. Then he went off to ask his friend, kindly D. C. (Dave) Anderson, a widower, to co-operate with Junius in watching over the boy and helping him along. Anderson was a popular actor in San Francisco, known for his characterizations of old-men rôles. He was more considerate and sympathetic than Junius and became one of Edwin's close confidants. There was always a twinkle of mirth in the eyes that were shadowed by heavy brows, and in his face was a benign understanding.

On Monday evening, September twenty-seventh, the elder Booth opened at the Adelphi as Bertram, followed with *Richard III* and *A New Way To Pay Old Debts*, and closed on the thirtieth in *The Merchant of Venice*, before a house crowded in every nook and corner. Again and again he was called before the curtain, and with a wave of his hand he bade California farewell. It was the last performance of the great tragedian witnessed by his sons.

The next day they accompanied him to the docks where the *Independence* was making ready to sail. "My last experience of his vagaries, was at our final parting on the ship that bore him forever from me," related Edwin. "He asked a sailor on deck to take his luggage to his cabin. The fellow replied—'I'm no flunky.' 'What are you, sir?' demanded my father. 'I'm a thief,' responded the brute. Instantly the actor assumed his favorite part of *Bertram* at this 'cue,' and said—'Your hand, comrade, I'm a pirate.' The sailor laughed and rejoined, 'All right, my covey; where's your traps?' and carried the trunk to the stateroom." [44] Soon the steamer was passing through the Golden Gate with old Booth on board bound for San Juan, Nicaragua.

This route took him by native coach and boat over an inland road, lake, and river to the Atlantic Coast. Somewhere along the way he was robbed of a wallet containing most of his California savings. What was left brought him to New Orleans on the steamer *Daniel Webster*, which arrived November twelfth. Noah M. Ludlow, then manager of the St. Charles Theatre, helped him replenish his purse by an engagement of six performances, beginning November fourteenth, before he continued his voyage homeward. His benefit night and final appearance was November 19, 1852, on that stage.

> *The Iron Chest* . . . was played on this occasion, Mr. Booth appearing in his favorite character of Sir Edward Mortimer. To say that he enacted it in a style that delighted every one would be speaking without exaggeration. Indeed, every successful performance during his too brief engagement, ap-

peared to show Mr. Booth's powers to better advantage, and the regret is general that he should stay so short a time with us. Talent like that he possesses is so rare now-a-days, when respectable mediocrity is the chief qualification of the American stage, that we cannot make up our minds to part with Mr. Booth until, at least, we have seen all the faces of the jewel of dramatic genius whose brilliancy has illumined his name not only for the present generation, but for posterity.

Mr. Booth was called out after the play and again after the farce—the famous one of the *Review*. Public curiosity was much excited to see him in a part so opposite to the tragic characters he had represented in the early part of the evening, and it was difficult to recognize in the stupid, awkward Yorkshire clown, John Lump, the form and face and voice that moved the audience in Shylock, Bertram, and such powerful characters.[45]

That evening he caught a severe cold, and upon leaving New Orleans by the river boat *J. S. Chenoweth*, was stricken with fever. The first day of the voyage he drank freely from the Mississippi, which increased his illness. Edwin was not there to care for him, and he was too independent to ask others for aid.

A passenger, James H. Simpson, noticed him in the salon walking back and forth with his hands behind him and his head bowed. He tried to recollect where he had seen him before. When told that his name was Booth, Simpson recognized the great tragedian whose last performance he had witnessed at the St. Charles Theatre. The next morning Booth did not appear. As no one else seemed to be concerned over his absence, Simpson went to the old man's stateroom. He found him in his bunk breathing heavily. Booth stared at him, but nodded assent when Simpson asked if he should have the room cleaned, his linen and bedding changed, and some gruel brought in; and in answer to "Have you a wife?" Booth grunted, "Certainly I have."

Two days later he was so ill he could not move without help. His jaws were becoming rigid and affecting his power of speech. Unable to find any medical supplies on board, Simpson tried to give him some brandy by placing a saturated rag to his lips, but he made an effort to remove it and mumbled, "No more in this world." Though he attempted to tell of his journey from California, all that could be understood was that he had suffered a great deal and been exposed very much. Realizing the old man's condition was hopeless, Simpson inquired if he wished to send a message to his wife and received the feeble reply, "Oh, that I could talk!"

On the fifth day Simpson was with him all morning until the bell rang for dinner at noon. When he was leaving, the helpless old man sighed, "Pray—pray—pray!" and looked after him beseechingly. It was November 30, 1852. The boat was nearing Louisville. Before it docked, the elder Booth was dead.[46]

Mary Ann, informed of her husband's illness by telegraph, had left Baltimore to meet the steamer in Cincinnati and so failed to receive the second message telling of his death. Since no funds had been found on his person and she was unable to meet immediate expenses, she was forced to delay her return until a collection could be taken up for her by the Masons, who had Booth's body placed in a metallic coffin awaiting her departure. People have speculated over what became of the ten hundred and eighty-four dollars paid him by Ludlow for his New Orleans engagement, some contending he lost it while gambling, and others, that he was again the victim of thieves.

His remains reached the Exeter Street house in Baltimore on December ninth. The coffin was placed beside a large marble figure of Shakespeare in a room on the ground floor, from which all furniture had been removed. The walls were draped entirely in white. He looked so natural the family was afraid to bury him until assured by physicians that he was not just in a trance. Two days later his body was carried to the old Baltimore Cemetery, followed by private citizens, members of the theatrical profession, and many colored persons. A request had been made by Mrs. Booth to the leader of Volandt's Band that no music be played until the procession entered the grounds. Within the gates a death march, composed for the occasion, resounded dolefully from a distance. As the assemblage stood bareheaded in the bleak evening air and snow began falling, the coffin was deposited in a mausoleum to await another burial in the spring.

Rufus Choate, hearing of Booth's death, exclaimed, "There are no more actors!" Years later, old Walt Whitman, recalling the days of his youth, wrote in *November Boughs*:

> I can, from my good seat in the pit, pretty well front, see again Booth's quiet entrance from the side, as, with head bent, he slowly and in silence, (amid the tempest of boisterous hand-clapping,) walks down the stage to the footlights with that peculiar and abstracted gesture, musingly kicking his sword, which he holds off from him by its sash. Though fifty years have pass'd since then, I can hear the clank, and feel the perfect following hush of perhaps three thousand people waiting. (I never saw an actor who could make more of the said hush

or wait, and hold the audience in an indescribable, half-delicious, half-irritating suspense.). . .

Without question Booth was royal heir and legitimate representative of the Garrick-Kemble-Siddons dramatic traditions; but he vitalized and gave an unnamable *race* to those traditions with his own electric personal idiosyncrasy. . . .

The words fire, energy, *abandon*, found in him unprecedented meanings. I never heard a speaker or actor who could give such a sting to hauteur or the taunt. . . .

For though those brilliant years had many fine and even magnificent actors, undoubtedly at Booth's death (in 1852) went the last and by far the noblest Roman of them all.[47]

BOOK TWO

THE BROTHERS

Junius Brutus Booth, Jr. *(National Archives photo)*

CHAPTER I

The great economic depression that set in after the elder Booth's departure from California threatened to darken the theatres. Edwin wandered about the streets of San Francisco with no means of support. He was only nineteen, but the vicissitudes that he had to face at this time would have tried the stamina of any veteran. Junius, twelve years older, had assumed the responsibilities of a family man with an established career to maintain. His stolid, unimaginative disposition and conservative business sense inhibited any idea of exploiting Edwin as a possible discovery. Rather than commend his younger brother and give him stimulating advice, his attitude was one of tolerant patronage. Edwin wanted to be an actor—well, let him try it! The elder Booth had asked Junius to help the boy: that he would do whenever possible—so long as Edwin behaved himself. But, as money seemed to have disappeared from circulation, Junius was unable to offer him more than the shelter of his own home.

Balked by inactivity in the theatres, and believing that Junius was uninterested in his career, Edwin had his first real taste of bitterness and frustration. Stronger young men than hothouse actors drowned their troubles in drink and he could not resist the temptation. If he inherited his father's craze for liquor, as Asia asserted, then he needed no more than this environment to cultivate it. Periodic moods of despondency, which were part of Edwin's melancholy nature, led to his drinking, and that, in turn, was responsible for his poor acting. His early career was greatly influenced by this uncontrollable weakness. Junius, however, was one member of the Booth family who had no use for any intoxicating beverage. He had seen his fill of dramshops and their habitués as a boy on occasional trips with his father and thereafter had little patience with intemperance.

Theatrical conditions in San Francisco continued to decline, and late that fall an actor, Willmarth Waller, who, with his wife, had arrived from the East some six months before, began selecting a company of players to take into the northern mining region of the state. In his quest for a good leading man he approached J. J. McCloskey.

"Don't know of anyone in particular," drawled that pioneer. "There are several you might take."

"What do you think of young Booth?" asked Waller.

"Well, he comes from good stock and might fill the bill," replied McCloskey.

"I saw him do some pretty fair acting at the Jenny Lind," said Waller, "and he had a lot of experience in parts with his father before coming out here. Several years ago I saw him in the East as Cassio and in other parts with the old man and was favorably impressed. He's been on the stage most of his life and I believe he'll turn out all right. The name will help me anyway; I'm going to make him an offer."[1]

Waller consulted Junius and found him anxious to have Edwin join the company, because this would not only give him an opportunity to try out some star rôles, but would also keep him away from barrooms where he was becoming too well-known. Junius feared, however, that Edwin would not be interested and suggested that he be the one to win him over. This was not so difficult as he had anticipated. In fact, Edwin's eagerness to go made Junius realize he knew nothing of the hardships to be encountered in the northern mining camps. He therefore advised him to put his last slug (an octagonal gold piece worth fifty dollars) in the bottom of his wardrobe trunk where he could find it if Waller's enterprise failed. Arrangements were completed and a date set for the company's departure. Everyone was delighted with the prospects of the mountain tour.

These strolling players included some of the most talented performers from California theatres. Waller was gifted with a resonant voice and natural ability to act. Mrs. Waller had studied music and languages in various European capitals and prepared herself for a career in grand opera. William Barry, a highly rated comedian, was noted for his performance of the First Gravedigger, in *Hamlet*. Others were D. V. Gates, a well-known mimic, Dave Anderson, George Spear (who had been nicknamed "Old Spudge"), Sam Dennis, and (according to McCloskey) a talented young actor listed as Folland. It was not, as so many writers have maintained, merely a barnstorming troupe.

The infant gold mines of those early days, known as the Mother Lode, covered a territory of several hundred miles in the mountains some distance northeast of San Francisco. The Sacramento, San Joaquin, and Feather rivers bordered the towns and camps, the last-named having its northern terminal of navigation at Marysville. Coming from San Francisco, Waller's troupe changed steamers at Sacramento for this river port. Here they climbed into the rigs of a coach company for the overland journey to Nevada City, where they were to give their first performance. The route passed through Grass Valley and Rough and Ready, two of the towns they intended to play.

Torrential rains had made the roads practically impassable. The horses tugged and pulled. Sometimes passengers were forced to get out and walk a short distance up a hill, and, occasionally, to help push the coach out of the mud. This was not the holiday the troupe had expected. They found food so costly in the interior that a large number of people were almost destitute. As they passed along, only a few miners were digging in the gulches and ravines. Many of the clapboard shanties and cabins nestling under the trees were empty; for miles around the deserted country yawned with man-made cavities.

The mountain theatres of the Mother Lode were similar to the old inn-yards of Shakespeare's time. Large tin horns announced the arrival of a troupe; miners gathered from the surrounding camps and stood at the entrance, awaiting the treasurer of the company who would stipulate the fee and adjust the scales for the required amount of gold dust to admit them. As they poured it out from well-filled leather "pokes," a tap on the arm by someone in the crowd often enlarged the receipts, which were hastily dumped into the company's coffers, while the victim was chided by the laughter and remarks of those responsible for his generosity. Performances were often given under crude shelters covered with cloth and paper, on improvised stages of boards and billiard tables.

Scenery and costumes might be inferior, but it was never wise to count on a spectator's ignorance of the play. A miner's outfit might hide a scholar of classical literature who would not tolerate mistakes or omissions. Many had seen theatrical productions in the East and were able to pass sentence upon any actor. Sometimes a shaggy gold-digger would stop one of the actors and offer twenty-five dollars or more for the privilege of finishing the part for him, and would be letter-perfect in his lines. When exceptional talent appeared, the generosity of the applause and "diggin's" fully repaid performers for all the inconveniences of travel. Even in the toughest camps, they would take in a few hundred dollars each night, and with a woman in the cast they were sure to draw capacity houses.

The troupe arrived at Nevada City and opened in the Dramatic Hall with a Shakespearean repertoire, Edwin playing Iago for the first time. Never before had the classics been presented here on so grand a scale. Miners flocked to the performances, thankful to Waller for having brought into their midst a company which could have appeared with credit in any large city. Their next appearance was at Grass Valley, where Edwin repeated Iago in the tawdry Alta Theatre, above a gambling saloon.

Although Rough and Ready was only a short distance, its inhabitants would not patronize the theatre at Grass Valley, having one of their own which they thought superior. It was located in a large hall on the second floor of Downie's Hotel, with adjoining rooms rented to guests. Here Waller's troupe played and lived during their next engagement. In this hall, a large audience had once applauded a performance by the Chapmans so vigorously that the seats gave way and they landed on the floor.

From Rough and Ready the company traveled some thirty-three miles along the old trail to Downieville, which was far up in the mountainous region of Sierra County. The town itself, however, was in a canyon too steep for any vehicle to reach it. Travelers had to leave the stagecoaches and go down to it on foot or horseback.

> We went down the hill
> Into Downieville
> To pick our pile;
> We came up the hill
> Out of Downieville
> Without shirt or tile,

sang the miners who had been there. It was a lively little town, and the surrounding settlements such as Goodyear's Bar, one of the most celebrated camps on the upper Yuba, contained free-spending crowds who wildly applauded the arrival of the actors. Following a custom then in vogue, Waller auctioned off the first ticket for the opening performance and it brought one thousand and seventy-five dollars.

Snow had been falling for several days, and winds began to whip it into a blizzard. Fearing they might be marooned, Waller cut short the engagement and started the troupe back to Nevada City, where he had promised to play again on the return trip. By the time they reached Grass Valley, the country was snowed under to such a depth that they could not proceed. Hemmed in on all sides, they sought to amuse themselves by collecting a few musical instruments and forming an orchestra. But the storm continued to show no signs of abating.

Unaccustomed to such weather, the inhabitants had not provided against possible misfortune. Food and funds soon disappeared, pack trains could not get through, and people faced starvation. They cursed and damned the merchants of San Francisco, believing the paralyzing scarcity of supplies in the interior to be the result of a monopoly. The price of flour advanced, potatoes became rare, and bacon almost unobtainable. "What are we to do?" was the cry.

At a meeting of the miners and citizens, a preamble and resolution was adopted which ended with, "Resolved, that appealing to High Heaven for the Justice of our cause—we will go to San Francisco and obtain the necessary supplies peacefully if we can, but forcibly if we must." All this was to be accomplished by one hundred and ten able-bodied men when they reached the Bay City, which had a population of about fifty thousand. However, the snow was now from six to twelve feet deep, and it was dangerous to take a trip of even one day's journey until a cold night had frozen the surface sufficiently to hold up a man's weight. Then he would have to start off in early morning darkness and reach shelter before it began to thaw at noon. So the Grass Valley delegation stayed at home.[2] Waller and his troupe wished they had never undertaken a winter tour of the mountains. Edwin's slug had paid for their last dinner.

Aware of trouble brewing in the town, the penniless players, the moment they could safely do so, moved on to Nevada City, where they hoped to play an engagement and collect enough to take them back to San Francisco. But they found the theatre closed and starvation threatening everyone as in Grass Valley. Marysville was nearly fifty miles away and any attempt to reach it was almost certain to end in disaster. Hungry and tired, they all moved into a small hotel and Edwin went off to wander about the town.

The same day a mail carrier, managing to get through, brought a letter to Waller from Junius which gave an account of the elder Booth's death and asked that his mother's enclosed message for Edwin be delivered as adroitly as possible. Junius was much concerned about the effect it would have upon his younger brother.

With tears in his eyes, Waller called Spear to his side and related the sad tidings. "I can't tell the boy," he said. "You'll have to do it."

Spear did not think he was equal to the task. Nevertheless, he took his lantern and started off to find Edwin. On a deserted road, he saw a dark form coming toward him splashing through the snow and mud. Lifting his lantern, he called out, "Hello, Ted, is that you?"

"Yes," answered Edwin, "What's up?"

Spear braced himself and replied, "There is a mail in, and a letter for you."

"What news is there?" was the casual query.

"Not very good news for you, my boy," said Spear.

Edwin was silent; he surmised what he was about to be told. "Spear, is my father dead?" he asked.

"Yes," answered Spear, "your father is dead." Sympathetically, he placed his arm around the boy's shoulder and led him back to the hotel.

Crazed and torn by grief, Edwin sobbed for hours and reproached himself for not having returned East with his father. All that night Dave Anderson watched over him; it was the beginning of a lifelong friendship.

The next morning Edwin realized the urgent necessity of leaving such a wretched place and getting back to the shelter and solace of his brother's home. He wished to know more of what his mother had written and to consult Junius about returning to the farm in Maryland. So, pulling himself together, he went out into the town to discover by what means he could break away from this miserable situation. He soon encountered a hopeless little group of friends shivering on a street corner. Barry, the comedian, and a fiddler named Burridge, whose solitary efforts supplied music for the theatre, were among them. He overheard their plan to start immediately for Marysville and asked to join the party. Other members of the troupe tried to dissuade him, but within an hour he was on his way with those determined to reach some point of safety.

Mile after mile they struggled on foot through great banks of heavy snow, passing Grass Valley, Rough and Ready, and the frozen mining camps of the district. At nightfall they stopped at the home of a lonely old woman who welcomed them with food and dried their clothing. In return for her kindness, Edwin sang some southern songs, accompanying himself on a banjo he had taken from the wall. Before daylight they continued their hazardous journey and reached the river town of Marysville that evening.

Edwin left the party, borrowed some money, and took the boat to Sacramento, where he found the city in ruins from fire and flood. A day later he arrived at Junius' home in San Francisco and read about his father's funeral in a second letter sent by their mother. She suggested, if the future seemed promising, that they remain in the West. Next summer (1853) she would rent the Baltimore house and, with the children, move into Tudor Hall, their new home at the farm. She would then arrange to complete the two-story dwelling, thus making it habitable at all times. There was no need for anxiety—life would go on as it had when their father was on tour. No hint was given of the straitened circumstances in which his death had left the Booths in Maryland, but, for years to come, Junius and Edwin were to share the financial burdens of the family. That they often were harassed by misfortune did not prevent them from sending money to their mother whenever possible.

Soon after Edwin's departure from Nevada City, rain washed away the great barriers and Waller's troupe was able to straggle back from the mountains. A downpour in San Francisco caused the press to complain of "the abominable condition of the streets, almost impassable in many places, and the crazy sidewalks." Boxes, barrels, and rubbish were piled in confusion everywhere, leaving no dry space for those forced to travel. Nevertheless, places of amusement were being patronized, and the San Francisco Hall, ideally located on Washington Street, attracted large crowds. In building it, Tom Maguire had followed the suggestions of Junius to the last detail. Its stage and auditorium were small, but so constructed that they could easily be enlarged without much expense. The gambling hall and saloon, which always connected with his theatres, were planned solely by Maguire. Junius had nothing to do with that side of the business.

The season opened in December with a company composed of Junius, George Chapman, and other favorites, who were so successful that the Hall was declared the most popular playhouse in the city. Maguire's theatrical ventures became profitable, and within a short time an addition was made to the stage, performances being suspended until most of the work was completed.

Edwin's return again placed Junius in the position of having to help his younger brother. Waller had given him a good report of Edwin's performances and of his conduct, so Junius offered him a place in the new company. But he was still skeptical of Edwin's habits and warned him that his future depended upon his deportment in the theatre. Junius was pompous and aloof toward those who indulged too freely in the cup and then came to him for favors. He had no intention of searching barrooms to find Edwin as he had done with their father. Nor had he the time to do so. This younger brother must learn his own lessons! While waiting for the remodeling of the San Francisco Hall, Edwin, with no money in his pockets, met a friend of better days who repaid him a loan of a twenty-dollar gold piece. Elated, he sauntered along thinking of the many needs he could supply with it. At Portsmouth Square another companion proposed that he augment his wealth at a near-by gambling hall. They entered, and Edwin was amazed at the fortune being made by a man who placed small sums on the table and swept back hundreds of dollars. It appeared so simple that he tossed his twenty-dollar gold piece into a game of *vingt-et-un*. Luck, or the house, was against him and he lost. This experience cured him. He always said it was the only time he ever really gambled.

By February second the Hall was again in operation as the San Francisco Theatre. On that date Edwin first appeared there as Fred Jerome, in the three-act drama of *The American Fireman*, which the *Alta* tagged "a very flat thing." Every morning he could be seen galloping to and from rehearsals on Junius' white horse, with his top boots halfway up to his knees, and smoking a small bulldog pipe. Of the many bills in which he was cast with the Chapmans, he made a great hit as Dandy Cox in a Negro farce. His caricature of a local celebrity named Plume so pleased the gentleman that he gave Edwin his hat, coat, and gaiters to add pictorially to the presentation.

But the attitude of Junius toward Edwin during these early California days continued to be more of tolerance than of sympathy. After all, it was up to his brother to work and study if he wished to achieve a place on the stage, and it seemed to Junius that Edwin was not doing all he could to merit his interest. Junius, looking back at himself when twenty years old, thought he was much more established in life than Edwin at the same age. Certainly, he was not so frivolous about his future in the theatre. Stage life was a serious matter with Junius. He counted every hour, every penny, and now at thirty-two he was considered one of the most efficient managers in his profession. San Francisco at the time was a great dramatic center. All the celebrated stars of the day played engagements there and to win approval had to be competent. Junius did not intend to see the Booth name flutter in the wings and fall to earth under his management, and he informed Edwin of this fact in no uncertain terms. Edwin looked upon his brother as a little inflated by his importance in the community, but he was fully conscious of the value of his advice and accepted it. This brought results. Under Junius' direction, Edwin improved.

CHAPTER II

Edwin did not long remain at Junius' home. There were too many unwelcome interruptions. Groups of fluttering, over-attentive women were always bobbing up at his brother's social gatherings, and he was annoyed by all the young flirts, breathless matrons, and indulgent, kind old ladies who clamored to look after him. He was perfectly normal in his attitude toward women, but his innate shyness made him feel uncomfortable in the presence of those who fussed over him. He wanted to go his own way and do as he pleased without either censure or approbation from anyone, so he went to live in a North Beach shack with another Baltimore actor known as Nat Hayward.

When Nat married one of the Chapman girls, Edwin camped with his friend Dave Anderson in a tent on the sandhills off the far end of the Mission Road until they built a suitable house. This new dwelling contained but two rooms and was on a small lot, but they called their place the "ranch," and each had himself listed in the city directory as "comedian and ranchero." Here they attended to household chores and entertained their friends. David Belasco's mother often saw their wash hanging in the yard. Several other actors, including the troubadour, Stephen C. Massett, lived in this neighborhood, and the "four white cottages on the other side of the creek" became known as Pipesville, the actors' colony.

Relieved from the anxiety of being penniless, Edwin was lively, jovial, and always ready to join in some mischief. A shirt would disappear from a neighbor's washline, to turn up a week or so later with a note in a strange hand thanking the owner for the use of it. Another neighbor would return home to find a large poster on his house offering it for sale. Edwin "got all the humor out of every situation if there was any in it," wrote J. J. McCloskey. "He had a very lovable disposition and was always courteous and considerate, except when he was on a lark, for he did love a practical joke better than anyone in the crowd . . . though his manner was quiet . . . when anything would strike him particularly he would smile and wink. There was one subject that he wouldn't talk about, and that was the theatre." [3]

On marketing days, "Uncle Dave" and Edwin drove to the city in an old buckboard, stopping at a butcher shop while one or the other cried, "Any kidneys today?" Frequently they were blinded by the sand drifting along the Mission Road. Nevertheless, it was *the* boulevard and public promenade on which even an omnibus ran at intervals. Sundays saw the road thronged with gamblers, women of pleasure, merchants, clerks, miners, and a motley crowd of idlers, walking or riding in various types of vehicles. Bordering the highway were a variety of gardens, a few elegant homes, and several churches. Congestion of the populace in this region led to many affairs of honor, and the names of some prominent men were listed in the duelling annals of that period. The previous year had been especially "prolific in pistoling," wrote one historian.

Junius had formed a partnership with several well-known men for the purpose of taking over the theatre. One of their members was John Fairchild, the celebrated scenic designer who, according to the custom of the time, was to be given a benefit night for which he had the honor of choosing the play. Fairchild selected *Richard III* and extracted a promise from Edwin to appear in the title rôle. Junius, reluctant to permit his younger brother to undertake such a difficult part, tried to persuade him to wait until he was more qualified for it and better acquainted with the public. But Edwin insisted and was given the opportunity to try his father's favorite character as a reward for his hard work. While he acted out front, Ferdinand Ewer stood in the wings watching every move he made. In the *Alta*, he credited Edwin with a just conception of the character and prophesied that his ability would, in the coming years, place his name foremost among the actors of the day.

Edwin's ability to play tragic rôles also won him the support of Joseph E. Lawrence, another early California journalist and editor, who told Junius that it would be a great idea for his younger brother to try *Hamlet*. Again Junius was reluctant and members of the company who were present laughed at the suggestion. But Lawrence contended that no matter what happened to Edwin's Hamlet, the theatre would be packed—which was the important thing so far as the management was concerned.

When Edwin heard that he might be given the part, he informed Junius of what their father had said to him in Sacramento. His brother then agreed, and the announcement went to the press that on Monday evening, April 25, 1853, Mr. Edwin Booth would take a benefit and appear for the first time as Hamlet. Old George Spear was with him that night too, as Polonius. Ewer, the *Alta* critic, had the honor of being the first to review Edwin Booth's Hamlet:

THE BROTHERS

San Francisco Theatre—For the benefit of Mr. Booth the favorite play of *Hamlet* was produced at this establishment last night, Mr. B. supporting the principal part and making his first appearance in that difficult character. As a first appearance it may be considered highly creditable, and we can even predict a high degree of success for the promising young artist when he shall have overcome a few disagreeable faults in intonation and delivery, and reached a profound conception of the part. Mr. Wilder's *ghost* was tolerably well read, but very poorly made up and but indifferently acted. Miss [Caroline] Chapman's Ophelia, of course, was excellent, as everything is which this most talented woman undertakes. Mr. Chapman as 1st Gravedigger was inimitable. The remainder of the parts were very well sustained.

A number of Edwin's young friends sat down in front and gave him a great round of applause each time he entered. Edwin didn't like it and thought they were guying him. "You fellows overdid it," he told them afterward.

His brother's failure to recognize Edwin's potentialities until attention had been called to them by the critics was due to that lack of vision in Junius which he had shown in promoting his own career as an actor. Junius was not a pioneer in discovering talent. He was too cautious either to take the initiative or to be influenced by others until convinced by tangible proof. This trait steadied his balance in business matters, but it also limited his possibilities. Not until others had pointed out the flecks of gold dust on the surface was Junius sure that under the dross was a vein of precious ore.

On May ninth, Edwin appeared with Mrs. Catherine Sinclair at her San Francisco début in *Love's Sacrifice*, and that month he gave his first performances of *Much Ado About Nothing* and *Katherine and Petruchio*. Mrs. Sinclair's arrival in California had followed matrimonial troubles with her husband, the great American tragedian, Edwin Forrest. He had found, among her effects, a letter and poem sent by an admirer and had at once accused her of indiscretions and hurried off to the divorce courts. This led to scandal and common gossip. In an effort to win over the public, Forrest appeared before his audiences in eastern cities and in Othello's language branded her with "that foul name!" While he was raving and ranting on the stage, she began studying under the tutelage of a well-known New York actor for a professional career in the theatre. This, of course, doubled the wrath of the "roaring bull" as he was often called. When the jury granted the divorce but awarded her three thousand dollars per year during life for maintenance, he exploded and refused to pay it. His bill of exception on appeal had been entered for the October, 1854, term of court, and, while awaiting that decision, she continued to tantalize him by appearing in such plays as *The School for Scandal* and *Love's Sacrifice*.

People were complaining that the San Francisco Theatre had acquired a bad odor from the tobacco juice distributed by miners over the floor, seats, and footlights. It was, in fact, so filthy that patronage diminished and Junius was forced to close it for a thorough purifying. By early June, it had been painted and refitted, commodious boxes made suitable for families, and three ventilators added to the dress circle to insure a free current of air even when the house was crowded.

Many members of the old company remained. Their opening bill was *The Honeymoon*, with Edwin, Junius, and Caroline Chapman in the important rôles. A burlesque on the notorious Lola Montez (a recent arrival) entitled *Who's Got the Countess*, written by Dr. David G. (Yankee) Robinson, became the talk of the town, owing to Miss Chapman's fine impersonation of that eccentric actress. Toward the end of the month, Edwin's first performance of Romeo, with Miss Chapman as Juliet, was highly praised by the critics.

In September, Edwin made his début as Shylock at his own benefit performance, supported by Junius and Catherine Sinclair. Reviews indicate that her influence over Edwin in his early training was not equal to that of Caroline Chapman. Successive efforts to give his brother the advantage of appearing in stellar parts with this fine combination of talent kept Junius in the background, and on several occasions the press asked why he was not seen on the stage more frequently.

Edwin, conscious that he was being hailed as a rising young star upon whom the mantle of his father had fallen, grew cocky. His older brother realized that such praise endangered Edwin's future, slapped him back into comedy and burlesque, and told him he still had much to learn. Edwin did not complain but adjusted himself to the rôles assigned him. In later years he conceded the wisdom of Junius' action. "It was a lesson for crushed tragedians," he said.

As the little playhouse had again taken on the odor of a cuspidor, it was closed a few nights for another purification. Apparently Junius' efforts to keep his crowded theatre habitable after each few weeks of patronage by the miners were not very effective. The fact that it had to be gone over periodically became the joke of the day.

During these intervals Junius went off to box and fence at the Pioneer

Gymnasium on Battery Street, which he had helped his friend, Frank Wheeler, to finance; but the moment Edwin was out of his older brother's sight, he wandered back into his old barroom haunts with his former disregard for the future, so that he again became a problem to Junius.

The theatre reopened under the direction of Mrs. Sinclair with Junius as stage manager. Dave Anderson, William Barry, and others were added to the company, and on October third, Anderson appeared in *The Belle's Stratagem* as Hardy, with Edwin as Dorrecourt. Light bills followed, Junius acting now and then in the leading rôle of *The Barbarian*. *The Queen's Husband* was presented on the fourteenth (which would have brought a blast of curses from old Forrest, had he seen the announcement) with Edwin in the part of Don Manuel.

Ewer, in the *Alta*, qualified his appreciation of the young actor's talent by openly advising him to study his work more carefully and to correct his apparent faults. Other critics shared this opinion, but lacking the personal concern in Edwin's marked promise of fame, reported that "Mr. Booth . . . was habitually spirited." Edwin was back in his cups! But before long Junius once more had him under control.

General William Tecumseh Sherman, recalling the nights he had spent in the pioneer metropolis, too poor to do other than sit on the veranda of his hotel, mentioned the thunders of applause which greeted the young tragedian, Edwin Booth, in the San Francisco Theatre across the way.

After a short and successful engagement with Mrs. Sinclair in Sacramento, Edwin returned to the San Francisco Theatre. In December, she reappeared with him there in *Damon and Pythias*, his initial portrayal of the latter character. Within the month, this versatile actress had leased the new San Francisco Theatre which was nearing completion. A short time afterward, she changed its name to the Metropolitan to avoid confusion with the older theatre. Decoration of the interior was still incomplete when the playhouse was opened on Christmas Eve, 1853. Even in this unfinished condition, the new surroundings with their promise of elegance proved a fitting background for the opening bill—*The School for Scandal*—in which James E. Murdock, the eminent American actor, starred opposite Mrs. Sinclair.

Edwin had the good fortune to support Murdock in all his bills, but several of his efforts received the rebuke that he had not properly studied his part. However, since he was being tossed into new plays so fast, there was some excuse for the imperfections in his lines. Owing to the popularity of the classics, every stock actor of the day was sufficiently versed in parts from Shakespeare and other playwrights to step into a character at once. Each rôle had a well-defined pattern taken from English acting traditions which he was supposed to know. Edwin, on the other hand, found "quick study" as it was called, very difficult and even in his later years limited his repertoire to the classical plays with which he was most familiar. Thus had he not attained stardom, his inability to learn readily would have kept him from ever becoming a good stock actor.

Mrs. Sinclair added the Montplaisir Ballet Troupe to the opera and dramatic companies playing at the Metropolitan and spent a fortune importing stars in her desire to bedevil old Forrest. These expenditures soon paved her way to insolvency.

April sixth the press announced the first night in California of the vivacious comedienne, Miss Laura Keene, at the Metropolitan Theatre, in *The Love Chase*. She was given a hearty welcome, and the critics waited expectantly. They greeted her as the most talented and natural actress that had yet appeared upon the California stage. At the conclusion of the play, she was loudly called for, and appeared with Edwin before the curtain. As she bowed her acknowledgments, a shower of bouquets fell before her.

Successive performances with Edwin, however, failed to display the brilliant acting that San Francisco had expected of Miss Keene. Disappointed by adverse criticism, she turned on Edwin, reproaching him for her cool reception. The sparks flew, and after three or four performances, she closed her engagement in an outburst of temperament. Throughout her life, Laura contended that Edwin was responsible for the failure of her California début, but since he had successfully supported such great stars as Caroline Chapman, Catherine Sinclair, and Matilda Heron, he cannot be blamed for this fiasco.

Laura had once been an English barmaid, a lovely auburn-haired girl with a propensity to spout Shakespeare. She had a graceful figure, a charming voice, and personal magnetism, which were great assets to her employer. Men came to the tavern for their liquor just to look at her. They called her Red Laura. Her career began when she was betrayed into marriage with an officer in the British army or navy, named John Taylor, who set up his own drinking establishment. After the birth of two daughters, she spent very little time in his tavern, and the business failed. Taylor then committed some crime and was banished as a convict to unannounced regions, whereupon his wife drifted to the stage. After a short training under the English actress-manager, Madame Vestris, and a checkered provincial experience, she

Young Edwin Booth. (Original photograph from the collection of the author)

Laura Keene. Oil painting by William H. Powell, 1858. (From 'Dictionary of American Portraits,' Dover; courtesy of The New-York Historical Society, New York City)

Edwin Booth at the age of twenty-four, at the time of his Boston Theatre engagement, April 20, 1857. (*New York Public Library photo*)

Edwin Forrest. Daguerreotype by Mathew Brady. (*From 'Dictionary of American Portraits,' Dover; courtesy Library of Congress*)

was brought to the United States by the elder Wallack for a leading part in legitimate comedies. Her mother and two daughters accompanied her, but on this side of the Atlantic her daughters became nieces.

In order to come to an understanding with Taylor as to their status, should he be released, Laura kept looking for him in out-of-the-way places. Her belief that he might be among the "ticket of leave men" shipped to California from Australia had caused her to rush westward with John Lutz of Baltimore, now reputed to be a first-rate gambler, who furnished funds for the trip. Undaunted by the lukewarm reception in San Francisco, she went to Stockton for a short engagement, then returned to the former city and was more successful.

In the meantime, Mr. and Mrs. James Stark had come back from an Australian tour which netted them sixty thousand dollars. As Fenno had started many actors westward by his tales of California gold, so the Starks now influenced a number of them to depart for the British colonies in the South Pacific.

The possibility of making a fortune in Australia excited Edwin, Dave Anderson, and a number of other players. Visions of a new Eldorado where an actor had the luck of Midas were before them constantly, and they began planning to go there. The cautious Junius was unimpressed by these reports, but he was not averse to Edwin's taking the trip so long as Dave Anderson was with him. Even if they made no money from the venture, the voyage would add to Edwin's experience and broaden his viewpoint of life, thought Junius.

Laura Keene leased the Union Theatre in San Francisco and began an engagement in June. While she directed the arrangement of a scene on the stage, a chandelier fell and struck her on the head, some fragments of glass cutting her severely across the nose. Unable to appear for several nights, she had an opportunity to talk with Mrs. Stark, who told her that her husband, John Taylor, was in an Australian convict camp. When Laura learned of Anderson's contemplated voyage, she went to him and asked to join in the venture, but requested that no one be informed of her intentions. Anderson decided not to let the coolness between Edwin and this redheaded firebrand interfere with their professional obligations, and he told her to come along. His unwarranted optimism that such an arrangement might renew their friendship eventually suffered disillusionment.

On the evening of July 30, 1854, all but Laura boarded the sailing vessel, *Mary Ann Jones*, scheduled to get under way at 4:00 A.M. She waited until that hour to dash up the gangplank and into her cabin unobserved. The captain, however, missed the tide and was obliged to wait until afternoon to navigate his ship out of port. This delay and a large number of unpaid bills kept Laura in seclusion until she was safely at sea.

When she came on deck she found several actresses already aspiring to be Edwin's leading lady. Her unexpected appearance caused considerable fluttering, but it did not end the rivalry, and throughout the voyage of about two and a half months to Sydney (during which the ship often was becalmed), the ladies' frantic efforts to win Edwin's favor afforded much amusement for the other passengers.

Letters arrived at the Booth farm telling of Edwin's sailing. One from him was filled with exclamations over the money he expected to make in that far-off land. Another from Junius to their mother quieted her fears with assurances that Dave Anderson would take care of Edwin and suggested that his expectations of sudden wealth be greatly discounted. Edwin's sisters, brothers, and friends in Maryland now envied him more than ever, and regarded him as an adventurous knight roaming the world.

That September Junius was given a benefit at the Metropolitan Theatre in San Francisco. The press published complimentary notices lauding his ability as manager and actor and the high esteem in which he was held. Suddenly, without a word to anyone, he vanished eastward taking Harriet and their infant, Marion, with him. This hasty exit was prompted by a slip of paper informing him that his wife, Clementine De Bar Booth, was suing him for divorce on the grounds of non-support and abandonment. Junius made every effort to keep this fact from developing into a scandal since Harriet had long been accepted as his legitimate wife.

There had been no time to write to any of the Booths in Maryland, so when Junius with his unlegalized family arrived at the farm, his mother, Asia, Rosalie, and Johnnie were quite surprised to see them. Johnnie had remained to assist in operating the farm while Joe had gone off to school at Elkton. Before they could question Junius, he told them that he had returned East to look after some theatrical matters. This was his first visit since his father's death, and he thought the new house, Tudor Hall, which was being built when he was there last, most attractive.

Again Mary Ann welcomed her guests, and remembering the little Junius in her arms, was kind to Harriet. Joe Hall (Madagascan Joe) and several other Negroes working on the place joyously greeted Junius with "Massa" as they carried in the baggage, while half a dozen colored children stood open-mouthed with curiosity under the tall cherry tree which had been planted by the elder Booth. Asia, in her usual way, tried to monopolize Junius and began to pester him immediately for news of Edwin, but gentle Rosalie took care of little Marion to relieve Harriet. In the buzz of greetings, Johnnie, embarrassed by his rural attire, slipped from sight to put on his "town clothes."

The wise Mary Ann sensed some dubious reason for this unexpected visit and soon had Junius in a corner away from his chattering sister. He at once told his mother of his impending divorce from Clementine. She was then a member of her brother's, Ben De Bar's, company at New Orleans, and reviews indicated she had passed the meridian of attractiveness as a leading lady. The Booths were seldom under one roof, but it seemed they were ever on the verge of some calamity. That the shadow of another scandal might fall over them alarmed Mary Ann. Actors were always before the public—anything they did might cause comment from the press. For more than thirty years she had lived with his father under constant dread that an unforeseen event would lead to the discovery of the family's illegitimacy. Was this affair to bring it about? Junius explained to her that his trip East was solely for the purpose of making a settlement with Clementine and keeping news of it from the public.

Mary Ann was silent. Intuitively, she felt that some day she would be helpless to prevent a revelation of their past. Nevertheless, things must go on as before; the neighbors, no one, must be given any opportunity for suspicion. She accompanied Junius to Baltimore, where he met old friends; there were no questions about Clementine, and the Booths were careful not to mention her. Junius talked of California and told of his name having been among those recently mentioned by the Whigs as a possible candidate for the legislature of that state. He related his father's experiences in the Far West and also those of Edwin. When an excuse seemed necessary for a journey to another city, he said he was looking after theatrical matters. Cleverness in managing his divorce proceedings kept the scandal from the press.

Not wishing to give her oldest son further anxiety, Mary Ann refrained from telling him of the difficulties she was encountering in operating the farm. Nor did she mention attempts made by various people, including James Gifford, who had helped to build Tudor Hall, to collect debts after the elder Booth's death which she was sure he did not owe. Gifford had refused to finish the work until he had been paid the sum he contended was due him. They could not agree on a settlement and she had been forced to employ others to add a roof to the house so that she and the children could live there in the winter. Junius did learn, however, that the money received from the sale of a few Baltimore investments made by his father, and the rental from their home in that city, had been necessary to complete the house and to support the Booths in Maryland. Also that the small sums which he and Edwin had been able to send to their mother from time to time only paid for their younger brothers' education.

The year before, in 1853, Johnnie had been a student at Milton's, a boys' boarding school on the York turnpike about seventeen miles from Baltimore. It was a Quaker institution managed by an elderly Friend named Lamb. "Jack [as Johnnie was known at Milton's] was a bad boy and used to fag the smaller boys cruelly," wrote one of his classmates.[4] "He was a bully until a short, stout boy from the Eastern Shore matriculated and Jack tried to fag him, but that boy turned on Jack and thrashed him terribly and he never crowed again. His scepter was broken, his throne destroyed, his dynasty was ended, he was thoroughly conquered, cowed and humiliated, and all the boys were glad of it." But the girls in the neighborhood of Milton's said "Jack" was the handsomest boy and the best dancer at the school.

Later, Widow Booth had sent Johnnie to Bland's Boarding Academy in York, Pennsylvania, where he remained but a few weeks. From all accounts, this school must have been a rowdy place. Bland, an English ex-soldier who had served in the War of 1812, had deserted in Canada and fled to the United States. He was unqualified to educate or to instruct, and so employed younger and more competent men to take care of his classes, while he attended to the corporal punishment of his students. One of them later credited the old man's health, vigor, and activity to his efficiency as a whipping master, remarking that he "whaled the daylights out of the boys just for fun!" There was no system, no regular course of study nor recitation. After a time the school failed, leaving its owner bankrupt and compelling him to spend his last years as a steward in a Virginia seminary.

During the summer of 1854, Johnnie had tried his hand at tilling the soil while Joe attended to less strenuous chores. Sunshine and wild flowers filled the countryside with warmth and color. Asia was nineteen years old and her Harford County suitors had become so ardent that Sleeper Clarke decided he had better spend more time with her and put an end to their advances. But no matter what the season, life was the same for Rosalie. Neighbors said she was "a little queer."

It had been previous to Junius' and his family's surprise arrival in the fall that Joe had gone to school at Elkton. This youngest son's return to the farm for the Christmas holidays now brought together all but one of the Maryland Booths then living. Edwin was the exception, and Mary Ann keenly felt his absence. It was only at intervals that the different members of this actor-family saw one another. They were always at different points of the compass, and a complete reunion was impossible. The Booths, however, were never divided in their interests, but clung together as one in defense of their clan.

As the eldest of the children, Junius took a more critical attitude toward these younger brothers and sisters than he had before their father's death. Joe and the two girls received less of his attention, as they were orderly and well-behaved. Johnnie was more of a problem. He did not like to study, refused to go to school, and wanted only to remain at the farm, though his efforts to assist in its operation were negligible. Away from home, he had gone on several sprees, and the knowledge of this probably influenced his mother in permitting him to stay with her. Junius' attempts at discipline and fatherly advice were balked by Mary Ann, who requested that he say nothing, as Johnnie would be sure to resent it. She wished everything to be pleasant while they were all at home. This laxity with Johnnie resulted in his having less schooling than either Junius or Joe, though he managed to get more than Edwin who began his trouping days when a mere boy.

On their hurried journey to Maryland, Junius and Harriet had found the railroad at Panama operating only as far as Culebra. With a young child to care for, they had decided against returning to California until the completion of the line so that the crossing of the Isthmus would be less of an ordeal. By February, 1855, when a train was carrying the passengers over the entire distance between the Atlantic and Pacific ports of the Isthmus, Junius made arrangements to leave the farm for the long trip westward.

In New Orleans, he and his family were joined by Jean Davenport, a favorite actress of the time, and they all sailed to Aspinwall. Here, the steamer added its quota to the fortnightly crowd of travelers whose former attire was changed only by the absence of bowie knives and deadly pistols. These adventurers found no other shelter than moldy hotels that lured them in with wide-open doors and sent them out ravaged by tropical fever. At the depot, ghastly natives suffering from this malady sold small boxes of quinine tablets advising everyone to partake liberally of them.

Although few in the crowd were making the trip for the first time, practically all of them were experiencing new sensations in crossing the Isthmus over the forty-nine miles of railroad. Scrambling into the train which moved from its shed along a street scantily lined with leaning structures, they glided smoothly from the view of the harbor, over marshland that led to a jungle luxuriant with color and vegetation. They crossed rippling streams and entered groves where palm trees spread abundant shade over isolated huts. Many miles of trestles and wooden props carried them above deep gorges and over parts of the road where the soil was still soft and yielding. Every shriek of the engine whistle sent monkeys, parrots, and other creatures of this wilderness to the shelter of their haunts as the train jogged on to Gatun, the first stop. From there the journey continued along the Chagres River, left it for the short distance to Tiger Hill, and followed it again to Bujio Solado, where John L. Stephens, explorer, and one of the projectors of the railroad, had lived.

As they entered Panama, dark señoritas in loose-fitting dresses eyed them from balconies above narrow streets; padres shuffled under arched entrances of ancient churches; and vendors of assorted wares scurried along beside the slow-moving coaches, offering their displays at prices twice the amount they were willing to take. Within a few hours, passengers and baggage were aboard the steamer *Sonora*, sailing for California. Edwin had not yet returned from Australia when Junius and his family arrived in San Francisco on March 2, 1855.

CHAPTER III

At Sydney, Edwin and the company were amazed to find a thickly settled city of inhabitants so typically English that it might have been a London suburb. There was nothing colonial about it; household furnishings, dress, everything had been imported—even the cooking was English. Many streets were well paved and lighted by gas. Shops supplied the demands of all Britishers for home products. Handsome residences, with gardens displaying a variety of flowers and fruits, bordered the city. A cathedral and churches, a large botanical garden, the select Australian Club, and a promenade over which splendidly equipped carriages drove in leisurely manner and where a military band frequently gave concerts, offered many *divertissements*.

Edwin opened at the Royal Victoria Theatre, October 23, 1854, with *The Lady of Lyons*. On the following evening *The Merchant of Venice* was given, with Laura Keene as Portia and Edwin as Shylock.[5] The engagement ran almost two weeks, and having been fairly successful, the troupe traveled on to the Queen's Theatre in Melbourne.

There was little similarity between these two cities about six hundred and fifty miles apart. Melbourne, much smaller than Sydney, was a thriving colonial port where young people predominated, and business went on at a brisk pace. The center of this teeming life was in Collins Street and the surrounding neighborhood, with a convivial tavern called *The Shakespeare* at one corner of the market place. A customhouse of dark brown sandstone stood near the lower end of the market slope and the spire of a church near-by pointed upward like the bayonet of a soldier guarding the town. Great stumps of gum trees, left by early settlers in their mad scramble for timber to build dwellings, were to be seen everywhere. In fact, one stump was so large that a wooden building "deviated to go around it."

In Melbourne Edwin observed his twenty-first birthday. He had his photograph taken and then got drunk. Another day he and Anderson went on an inland excursion, and Edwin barely escaped having his skull cracked by a large coconut that fell from a tree under which he was resting. He later wrote to his mother telling her of this and credited his caul for the move he had made in time to avoid it. He enclosed a copy of the photograph, which was greatly admired in far-off Maryland, and said he expected to visit the farm after his return to San Francisco.

But Edwin's anticipation of acquiring wealth and fame so that he could come back a successful star with gold lining his pockets was due for a rude shock. In this outpost of civilization conditions were similar to those in California. Periods of intense activity were frequently interrupted by sudden business depressions, one of which unfortunately had just hit Melbourne. Hence, dramatic productions suffered from a lack of patronage.

The company started off, November twentieth, with *Much Ado About Nothing*, before a sparsely filled house. As expectations of wealth dwindled, the troupers became alarmed lest they find themselves stranded. Good notices did not increase their audiences, and after four performances they closed.

Laura's theatrical activities had limited her quest for John Taylor, so she took advantage of paltry box-office receipts to blame Edwin for another failure. This enabled her to break their agreement and secure the freedom necessary to continue the search for her husband. She jumped about the country playing engagements under her own name, which she lavishly reported to the San Francisco press at a later date in order to conceal her real objective in going to Australia.

After discovering that the father of her two daughters was in prison for life, Laura feared her secret might be found out, and was anxious to be on her way again. She rejoined the company, once more taking advantage of arrangements made for their departure, and sailed with them on the steamer *City of Norfolk*, bound for San Francisco.[6]

The failure of this tour was a great disappointment to Edwin. For such brilliant prospects to end so dismally was almost impossible to believe! Instead of returning to California rich and successful as he had hoped—he must go back unacclaimed and empty-handed!

The ship reached the Hawaiian island of Oahu in February, 1855, and anchored two miles off that port, as the passageway in a coral reef was too narrow for it to enter the bay. Since the steamer was to remain there several days, most of the passengers went ashore in small boats. On approaching the landing they saw the towering cone of an extinct volcano, known as Diamond Head, on one side, and opposite it a steep wall of bluffs reaching out into the sea. Beyond the bay was another extinct volcano with deep ravines at its base. Within this enclosure vine-covered huts of the natives, churches and missionary schools, a number of unpretentious frame buildings—among them the Royal Hawaiian Theatre and a hotel—spread over the part of the plain that was Honolulu.

The knowledge that they would need money when they reached San Francisco to keep them from being thrown on the resources of friends, induced the company to pool their funds, rent the Royal Hawaiian Theatre, and rehearse *Charles II, or, The Days of the Merry Monarch* for their opening performance. Matters relating to the direction of the play, however, caused another dispute between Edwin and Laura, and she resumed her voyage on the same vessel without them.

Since the assets of the company, about fifty dollars, had been used in financing the venture, the actors could not afford the luxury of a hotel and slept in hammocks hung in their dressing rooms. It has been related that Edwin was forced to post his own bills in Honolulu, to keep native boys from eating the paste (poi), but this has been refuted by a contemporary resident of the tropical island.[7]

The theatre in which they appeared resembled an English playhouse, the ground floor being the pit where the mob sat with their hats on, eating peanuts, and frequently scoffing at the performers. Exclusive and fashionable patrons, mostly foreigners, occupied an upper section reserved for them, and reached by a flight of stairs on the outside of the building.

"I always wondered," said Edwin, "at the popularity of my *Hamlet* with the native chiefs; but they used to come night after night, squat on their haunches directly in front of the stage, and listen to the play from beginning to end. Between the acts they would apparently talk it over, of course in their native tongue, in the most animated manner, and then when the curtain rose again they would resume their attitudes and expressions of deep interest and remain until the end of the performance. . . ."[8]

Kamehameha IV, King of the Sandwich Islands, was an educated Hawaiian who spoke English fluently. In his youth he had attended a performance of *Richard III* by the elder Booth at the New York Chatham Theatre and now wished to see Edwin play the same character. As he was in mourning for his father, the King could not appear in public, so a place was fitted up for him backstage. There he sat in state on a throne-chair, attended by two escorts, one a Frenchman and the other "a huge Kanaka wearing a military jacket, white trousers and a long sword." As the Coronation Scene required the use of a throne, the King cheerfully relinquished the chair and remained standing until it could be replaced for him.

By the end of March, Edwin and members of the troupe were anxious to return home and sailed for California on the American schooner *Lady Jane*. After their passage had been purchased, the net profit from the Honolulu engagement amounted to about fifty dollars. Financially and spiritually they left Hawaii in the same condition in which they had arrived.

In San Francisco, Mrs. Sinclair had already heard from Laura Keene that Edwin and Anderson were playing a short engagement in Honolulu and would soon return. From reports Mrs. Sinclair surmised they would be in need, so she sent a letter to the "rancho" offering them jobs in her company at the Metropolitan Theatre as soon as they arrived. Their disappointments were forgotten when they reached home and found her message.

Junius was not so surprised to see them, as to learn that they were without debts and had found employment awaiting them. That in itself was an achievement. It was also a relief, for, although he had been back two months, he had no contract which would permit him to assist his younger brother. Each carefully avoided certain subjects. Edwin said nothing about having been drunk in Melbourne on his twenty-first birthday nor did Junius disclose the real purpose of his trip East. In the discussion of family affairs at the farm, Junius told Edwin that their mother's leniency toward Johnnie, who refused to follow directions, was making him more of a problem from day to day.

Edwin reappeared at the Metropolitan Theatre on May second, as Benedick, in *Much Ado About Nothing*. That he had to delay his visit to the farm did not discourage him and he plunged wholeheartedly into his work. He had no intimation that almost one and a half years would pass before he could go home. But within that time he was to prepare himself for more ambitious undertakings. Reviews praised his acting, and toward the end of the month he was cast as Armand Duval with Jean Davenport, in *Camille*. She dreaded the performance, for she believed Edwin was inexperienced, yet afterward she wrote that he had played his part with the self-forgetfulness, abandon, and intuitive knowledge of an old actor.

The deficit at the Metropolitan finally reached a sum which made necessary an announcement that, on June ninth, Mrs. Sinclair would give up the management of the theatre. She had not prospered, but the press observed that her efforts to please the public had been most satisfactory.

Edwin played a short engagement at the American and in August returned to the Sacramento Theatre, where he gave first performances of *A Midsummer Night's Dream*, *Twelfth Night*, and *A Comedy of Errors*. The feeling that he was working hard and getting nowhere now combined to magnify the failure of his ventures across the Pacific, and again he sought a release from disappointing reality. His inability to impress the critics was accounted for by reports of his intemperance.

At Sacramento this indulgence almost proved fatal. Joseph Murphy, an unemployed actor, had wandered down a street fringing the river where barrooms and gambling houses catered to notorious spenders. On the levee he saw what apparently was a bundle half-submerged, but discovered it to be the limp form of a well-dressed man. Unable to drag him up the bank, he rushed to a near-by saloon for aid. "Restoratives were applied, brandy poured into not unwilling lips, the body roughly shaken and it came to life, opened its eyes, looked around with maudlin indignation and demanded who had dared to interrupt his slumbers?" Friends recognized him as Edwin Booth. Familiar with his drunken habits, they took him to a hotel and watched over him until he could get on his feet. He never learned the name of his rescuer nor knew how narrowly he had escaped being drowned.[9]

Edwin made another appearance at the American Theatre in San Francisco, but his acting still showed lack of study. His indifference resulted in small audiences, so to recapture public attention he was billed as Hamlet. Although he was much better in this rôle, he failed to draw the expected crowds. Earlier in the season Junius, in *Uncle Tom's Cabin*, had been more successful at the San Francisco Theatre.

A magnificent new playhouse was completed in Sacramento that fall and named for Edwin Forrest. Its interior was in gold and white and the drop curtain beautifully painted. There was a greenroom exquisitely furnished and, on the second floor, a Grand Salon. Over the entablature perched the figure of a large American Eagle, and an empty niche in the front of the building awaited the arrival of Forrest—in bronze. Charles A. King and George Ryer were the lessees when the theatre opened in October, 1855.

The Sacramento press threw the gauntlet to San Francisco by stating that the Forrest Theatre had the most talented company of players in California. Its members included Edwin Booth, Caroline Chapman, Sophie Edwin, Mrs. Judah, George Spear, and W. M. Leman—an array of stars and well-known actors plucked from the theatres of the Bay City.

They began November sixth with *Much Ado About Nothing*, but after a few performances the press began a direct attack on Edwin. The critics did not mince matters in referring to the effects of overindulgence in alcohol on his work, and contrary to the claim that jealousy among the company was responsible for his dismissal, these open denunciations of his drunkenness were the actual cause of his failure. He finally interrupted his engagement by staggering too close to a sign marked EXIT.

This prodigal excess was overlooked when Catherine Sinclair arrived and took over the Sacramento Theatre that month. Having just emerged from her San Francisco deficit, she was more cautious in this venture and engaged a smaller company at the beginning, with Edwin as leading man. James Dowling was stage manager, and Wesley Venua was put on the staff as treasurer with power to curb any possible whims of extravagance.

For a few nights Edwin was sober and his performances were noted as being exceedingly fine. But when December rolled around he was again haunting the barrooms and reeling across the stage.

> The opening scene [of *Richard III*] was a grievous farce. When Booth as the Duke of Gloucester came out, the audience felt a short respite from pain. He opened fairly and with promise, but it soon became evident that he was not equal to the task. His elocution was defective. Many passages, by the proper delivery of which the interest and power of the author are illumed, were either spun out at random or in such a novel style that they came out as he came into the world; others, however, were rendered pleasingly and often with effect.
>
> It was palpable that the part had not been studied with the deep concern which an actor of so much promise as Mr. Booth owes not only to an audience but also to himself. Indeed, his memory sometimes failed. He had more than once to halt for language. This, of itself, even if he had only to wait for a second or for a single word, is enough to destroy irreparably the effect of an entire scene. No man, uncertain of his language, can feel confident in himself and can, consequently, feel what he seems. He knows that he is not Gloucester, that he is not a king commanding the text. He fears failure and, while trying to marshal his words, forgets his looks and actions. His auditors soon fathom his shortcomings and, while they overlook much, cannot but regret that a great character must be mangled because of the negligence, not inability, of him who bears it. . . .
>
> The stuff to make a good Richard is in Booth, but it wants much care and cultivation for years to come. Industry and perseverance will in time produce it.[10]

This criticism had some influence on Edwin's behavior and for a while his performances improved.

One evening Jim Dowling, who, with several members of the

company, boarded at a Mrs. Carswell's, announced to the group that he had read a play which he thought would be a great hit. At breakfast the next morning they held a meeting, and Dowling tossed upon the table the script of Charles Selby's English adaptation of *Les Filles de Marbre*, called *The Marble Heart*. Edwin took it to his room, read it, and in an hour returned saying he liked the play and would take the part of Volage, even though it was one of light comedy. When he was informed that this was to be given to Henry Sedley and he was to be cast as Raphael, an argument ensued. The matter was finally settled by flipping a coin which gave Edwin the rôle originally offered to him. Mrs. Sinclair was billed as Marco—whose heart was of marble.

Edwin's attitude at rehearsals was anything but encouraging to the rest of the company. He not only failed to memorize his part, but mumbled as he read it, while others were letter-perfect in their lines. The day before the first performance he had not improved, and the management considered withdrawing it from the bill, although it had been announced as the great event of the season.

When the curtain went up on the night of December 10, 1855, the company was almost certain the play would be a failure, owing to Edwin's indifference. By the end of the first act they had not changed their minds, but in a later scene with Raphael's mother, his expressive voice and emotional acting held both the audience and the company spellbound. The house went wild. That night a play was launched which was to become one of the most popular of the time.

An extended run of *The Marble Heart* made the Sacramento Theatre a veritable gold mine. Long before the doors opened, crowds gathered, clamoring for tickets. Miners came all the way from the Sierra counties to sympathize with the woes of false Marco's victim.

Wesley Venua lived backstage and also cooked his meals there. This often brought complaints from the audience about odors they were forced to endure. On one occasion he left some tripe to boil and Edwin replaced it with a turkish towel. Between acts Venua rushed to stir the contents of the pot but did not discover the change until he was ready to eat. He catered to his appetite for chicken suppers by keeping some live specimens in a crate just outside a rear door. Sooner or later they followed each other onto Venua's plate. One hen, however, before her demise, made a theatrical début with Edwin Booth at his first appearance in *The Corsican Brothers* on New Year's Eve.

In celebrating the end of 1855, George Spear who had just joined the company, and J. J. McCloskey consumed so much liquor before the performance that McCloskey's wobbling enactment of his part was frequently hissed. The next day the press rebuked both of them: "The nonsensical extras introduced into the play marred its beauty. By what authority did Messrs. Spear and McCloskey outrage the feelings of the audience by beating each other with a live chicken? . . . Had it not been for these ridiculous matters, and the mishap which, it was said, befell McCloskey, the play would have gone off creditably. Messrs. Booth and Venua sustained their characters with much credit. . . ."

The bill was repeated, and Edwin took his turn with John Barleycorn. "*The Corsican Brothers* was offered as the attraction last night, but it turned out to be anything else. Mr. Booth, who was cast to sustain the principal character, could hardly sustain himself, but he struggled through it, dragging everything down to the depths of disgust. Speaking mildly, he was intoxicated. He who is to sustain a prominent position in an honorable and polished profession and has so little respect for himself, or regard for his audience, as to voluntarily become incapacitated by drink, is undeserving the countenance of any community—The audience was indeed small, but a few more such nights will cause it to be even smaller."

From further reports it appears Edwin was more or less incapacitated during the remainder of the engagement which closed January 5, 1856, with his benefit performance in *Richard III*. Four days later, Mrs. Sinclair and Edwin, with several members of the troupe, left for Marysville and a tour of a few mountain towns. By the middle of February, they were back in Sacramento at the Forrest Theatre, for a short time under the management of Bennie Baker, affectionately known in the theatrical world as "Uncle Ben." In March this theatre was taken over by John S. Potter, who engaged Baker as stage manager.

Potter had the reputation for building, opening, and closing more theatres in the United States than any other man. It was said that he was a most remarkable character, gifted with an optimistic outlook to such an extent that he could see a silver lining to the darkest cloud. However, he was not often able to infuse his unpaid actors with the same visions and once complained that their insistence on being paid had ruined him; had they not made such demands he could have kept them together and avoided closing the theatre. To an actor who begged for a small part of the money due him, Potter remarked, "Why ask for salary when blackberries are ripe?" He was a versatile gentleman, this Potter. He could play any rôle in any drama on short notice, raise and lower the curtain, look after properties, shift scenery, and at the end of the performance, get to the box office, dump the evening's receipts into his pocket and be out of sight before members of his company missed him.[11]

A succession of new bills forced Edwin to study and keep sober. One of these bore the unfamiliar but significant title of *The Great Moral Drama, A Warning to Youth, or, The Six Degrees of Crime: Wine, Women, Gambling, Theft, Murder, The Scaffold*. He did not appear in *Richard III* with the "extraordinary tragedians", Dumphries and Woodward, when, as Richard and Richmond, they executed the fight mounted on two live jackasses imported expressly for the trying occasion.

Potter soon gave up the management of the Forrest Theatre, and Baker again took it over. One of his attractions was a Mormon girl who had fled from Salt Lake City and for a time drew large crowds as a featured player with Edwin. Another was a retired dancing master, C. C. Clapp, who, fired with an ambition to act, began his antics on the California stage in a début performance of *Hamlet* before a crowd eager to witness what they knew would be a farce.

Clapp seems to have been the only one who believed himself equal to the part. The first and second acts passed without any annoying disturbances, but near the end of the third act (when Edwin reappeared as the Ghost) the fun started. Everyone in the audience joined in the play and, in an effort to make the dancing master feel at home, called out "hands across," "ladies' chain," "down the middle," etc. Clapp stuttered, got entangled in the props, rushed back and forth to the prompter's box for cues, but would not give up until he finished the performance.

Following these innovations, the Forrest Theatre returned to normal. On April nineteenth, under Baker's management, Edwin presented a varied program: *The Iron Chest*, the third act of *Hamlet*, and the farce, *Little Toddlekins*, to which members of the state legislature were invited. Several of them and many of the Sacramento residents, who had been unable to witness this performance, requested him to repeat it. Three nights later it was given as his closing bill. The same month he opened in *Richard III* at the Sacramento Theatre, which had been taken over by Baker and Dunlap. Here he made his début as Brutus in Payne's tragedy. He next secured a place in the company appearing at the Union Theatre in San Francisco where Junius was stage manager and leading man. Before Edwin was announced to play, Junius permitted Clapp to repeat his Hamlet. This could not have been intended for more than a prank on Junius' part, as everyone knew of the dancing master's previous failure. Edwin's next appearance in the title rôle put an end to Clapp's ambitions in San Francisco.

Several years had passed since Edwin had been under his older brother's steady influence. Although he had achieved a certain independence in his career, he was still greatly in need of Junius' kindly admonishments. Instead of turning from his brother's advice with youthful bravado, he seems to have accepted his well-earned discipline with grace and appreciation. Junius must have impressed him with a sense of responsibility, since Edwin, during his last few months in California, became more temperate and tractable.

CHAPTER IV

After the Union Theatre engagement, Edwin played benefit performances for friends in both San Francisco and Sacramento. Criticism now showed that he had improved in his approach to his work which was confirming early opinions of his potential talent.

Ben Baker had been watching Edwin with considerable interest and had collected a number of favorable notices. On one of Edwin's trips to Sacramento, Baker said to him, "Ned, I'm going East; what about arranging for you to appear in Boston, New York, and other cities? Now that your father is dead you will be the coming tragedian." He suggested that Edwin familiarize himself with a repertoire required for these engagements by touring the Mother Lode, where extraordinary activity had been reported among the miners. Why not join a troupe of strolling players under big Ben Moulton and improve his health, acting, and financial condition? Edwin agreed and signed up for the trip.

Moulton was a professional coach-driver and thoroughly acquainted with this mountainous region. He was a rugged, well-proportioned man, proud of his swearing and the fact that he could chew a plug of tobacco before breakfast. Passengers, innkeepers, and lackies respected him. His actress wife, Harriet Carpenter, after their marriage, had faded as a star and taken to the hinterlands. She dragged the handsome Moulton away from flirtatious metropolitan damsels by putting him in charge of her theatrical expeditions. It was in this manner that he became versed in the management of troupes playing the mountain circuits. But he considered all occupations other than coach-driving inferior and had, on more than one occasion, escaped the clutches of his wife by suddenly disappearing from a mining camp without leaving word of his whereabouts.

Sometime before departing for the mountains Edwin purchased a riding horse. It was a pinto pony, fleet of foot, and as odd-looking as his father's imported Peacock had been. Every day he rode it for an hour or so, breaking it in for the journey. Meanwhile, Moulton rented an outfit consisting of a large covered wagon and four splendid horses. He decorated this equipage with signs featuring *The Iron Chest*, or, *The Mysterious Murder* which, with *Katherine and Petruchio,* was the principal bill. On the rear platform of the wagon, he displayed what appeared to be a sinister-looking box by covering a large champagne basket, which Edwin was using as a wardrobe trunk, with a canvas that had a huge skull and crossbones painted on it. As he wished to add prestige to this array, he employed an assistant driver to whom he boomed his orders in the voice of a general commanding an army.

Early on the morning of July second, Moulton's company of about ten players, including his wife, clambered aboard the wagon and, amid the shouts of their friends, rolled away toward the hills, Edwin on his pinto pony in the lead. Beyond the limits of the city, roads extended in all directions over a broad plain almost devoid of trees or houses. Every blade of vegetation had withered, and dust rolled in great clouds above the highway. Lack of rainfall and the sun's burning heat had turned the luxuriant valley into a barren and desolate waste. Along the way they passed caravans of wagons drawn by mules, dragging supplies to the mines. Occasionally a large-wheeled cart, pulled by oxen with closed eyes and pulsing nostrils, swayed lazily in their path and forced them to drive around it.

At roadside inns, they dug the dust out of their eyes and ears, while the horses rested, and Moulton pompously inspected the rigging. Before long they reached the foothills and began the ascent of country spotted with oak and pine trees, affording some shade, but requiring them to walk where grades were so steep that the horses dripped with sweat. Narrow strips of the road filled with rocks and stumps made progress slow and occasionally they came across men digging for gold. By nightfall Moulton and his troupe arrived at Placerville, directly under the snow-capped peaks of the Sierra Nevada, where they had arranged to play on the third and fourth of July. This thriving village had once been known as Hangtown "to commemorate a notable execution under the code of Judge Lynch in 1850." [12]

Camps had grown considerably in the three and a half years since Edwin's first appearance in the northern portion of the Mother Lode. Crowded communities and the proximity of dwellings built with combustible materials often led to disastrous fires. Standards and morals were higher, but a rough element and the continued possibility of crime, over which corrupt officials exercised little control, forced law-abiding men together for the protection of their own interests. Vigilance committees flourished here as well as in other cities.

The day after the troupe's arrival, Placerville began preparing for its Fourth of July celebration by decorating streets and buildings with flags and banners. To these Moulton added a few large signs advertising the company's offering. In the hall at which they were to appear, the actors found they had to play around an unremovable post sticking up through the middle of the stage, and so they called the place Hide and Seek Theatre. About noon the covered wagon with its mysterious chest paraded the streets heralded by a band of several pieces. Crowds of curious spectators followed it back to the theatre entrance where Moulton made a speech which would have elected him to Congress had he not been in the show business.

After the engagement Edwin wrote to a Sacramento friend that he had appeared before the largest audiences ever assembled in Placerville, and looked forward to a successful tour of the mountain towns.

The troupe trekked southward over a country filled with historic interest. They passed Diamond Springs, a rich locality where the Digger Indians had consecrated ground on which they held funeral rites for deceased warriors and members of their tribe. On the outskirts of this town, Moulton's company stopped to give their wardrobe an airing, and, while they were hanging costumes, armor, and wigs on a line stretched between trees, a band of these Indians came that way. Seeing the strange sight of what they believed were scalps, warrior regalia, and a box containing dead enemies, the Indians let out a loud yell and disappeared down the road at breakneck speed.

After repacking their possessions, the strolling players continued on through Amador City, Sutter Creek, and Jackson (which the Mexicans called *Bottileas*—Bottletown—because of the large number of such objects littering its streets), and reached Mokelumne River. Here Edwin experienced the first of several misfortunes he was to share with other members of the troupe. While fording the river on his pinto pony, he barely escaped drowning. Again he credited his caul with having saved his life.

Moulton's caravan then entered a region later made famous by Bret Harte, Mark Twain, and Joaquin Miller. The mountain road they were traveling took them to Angel's Camp, where the annual Jumping Frog Jubilee is still held. After playing there, they journeyed to Columbia and performed before a large crowd of applauding miners, who, the following day, gave them a rousing cheer as they started back for an appearance at Coloma. It was at this latter camp, on the south fork of the American River, that gold was first discovered by James Marshall in January, 1848. Along the way they learned that Placerville and near-by Georgetown, once known as Growlersburg to indicate the nature of its inhabitants, had burned to the ground since their departure.

Before they left Coloma for their next engagement at Auburn, fire broke out a short distance away at Diamond Springs. With a property loss in that area of more than a million dollars, the people became panic stricken and maintained that these holocausts were the work of incendiaries. While the citizens threatened imaginary miscreants, Moulton's players moved from Auburn and opened at Nevada City.

Since Edwin's venture there with Waller it had become one of the most prosperous settlements in the mining section. The boast that it had been built on a gold mine was true. Each shovelful of soil, even loose dirt in the streets, held enough of the yellow ore to make removing it worth while.

On the date *Richelieu* was announced for the bill at Frisbie's Theatre, Frank Mayo, who had been playing the circuit with E. F. Conner's company before going with Moulton, was to take the part of De Mauprat. What happened was later told in these words: "The troupe that was advertised to play on the night of that memorable day had given notice that they would devote the receipts to the relief of the people of Placerville, which had just been destroyed by fire, but the fire demon also laid his hand on Nevada City, and the performance had to be indefinitely postponed."

This blotted the place from existence. The blaze started accidently in a blacksmith shop, and soon took Frisbie's Theatre with it. A few hours before, Moulton's company had unloaded all their costumes and stage properties into the building and these possessions went up in smoke. Water was not available, and the flames spread so quickly it was impossible to control them. Records and documents belonging to the town and county were destroyed. Only a few provisions were left in one or two remaining stores. A number of people were ensnared and burned alive. Edwin was penniless again in the little city where he had first received news of his father's death. Fallen structures were still smoldering here when the near-by town of Grass Valley became a roaring inferno.

Newspapers of San Francisco discussed the origin of such calamities and the *Bulletin* asked: "What mean these piled up accounts that reach our ears of monstrous fires? Scarcely can we realize that one flourishing inland town is laid in ashes, before the telegraph announces another ruined." So the story of Edwin as the Fiery Star grew into the tale repeated by historians, that "there was no obvious link between the strollers and the fires; but the logic of the mountaineers deducted the one from the other, and travel became unsafe for Moulton's caravan." [13]

They managed to save their wagon and horses by a timely exit but the inhabitants of neighboring towns were not interested in theatricals while mysterious fires raged about them, so the troupe struggled on, with a makeshift wardrobe, and debts in their wake. Finally they arrived at Downieville, and Moulton made another of his disappearances leaving the outfit he had rented to be seized by the sheriff who was hot on their heels. The officer also took Edwin's pinto pony and turned it over to Moulton's assistant driver who had not been paid for his last week's services. This was not so disastrous, however, as Edwin knew it would be useless to ride the animal over grassless plains, with no money for feed. But it left him stranded in the tough little village which enjoyed the reputation that it was a dull day indeed when the townsfolk did not "have a man for breakfast"—meaning, of course, that one had usually been killed the night before.

With a blanket, which he had carried on the saddle during the trip, as his only possession, Edwin started out a second time on foot for Marysville. Dejectedly he trudged along wondering how he was to follow Baker East without funds. Other members of the troupe, including Moulton's wife, managed, by various means, to reach Sacramento before Edwin arrived there.

But fortune always seemed to balance misfortune in his life, and in this city he met an older friend, M. P. Butler, who offered to help him on his way. He told Edwin that Boothroyd Fairclough, an actor on the Atlantic Coast, was attempting to usurp the place which should fall to him as the elder Booth's son. Butler volunteered to arrange a benefit performance for Edwin before his departure for San Francisco, but young Booth insisted that benefits for other members precede his and offered to appear in them.

He supported Mrs. Moulton in the first of these, which was given for her. Then he began a brief engagement at the Forrest Theatre, with Junius, Harriet Mace, and Dave Anderson in the company, and opened as Hamlet. On the following evening, they played Payne's tragedy of *Brutus*, and Junius gave his first Sacramento performance as a female impersonator in the title rôle of the afterpiece, *Black-Eyed Susan*.

The deferred benefit for Edwin occurred on August twenty-third when he appeared as Richelieu and outdid any previous effort. At the close, he was called before the curtain to receive a valuable diamond ring, presented by the women of Sacramento. In reporting his plans, the newspapers stated he intended to go to Europe. Many years of hard work were to pass before that ambition was realized.

Receipts from these performances paid his debts but left nothing in his pockets, and on September first he was given a final benefit which turned out to be a great triumph. On this occasion, he took the rôle of Iago and, in appreciation of his marked ability, was given an elegantly bound copy of Shakespeare.

At the dock where he boarded the river steamer *New World* for San Francisco, crowds gathered to see him depart. Several members of the company, including Junius and Harriet, were also going. The band from the theatre played as Edwin waved to friends who were shouting farewells. All this acclaim was very gratifying to him, but he had not yet received the money from his last night's performance which was to finance his trip eastward.

Whistles blew and deck hands made ready to draw in the gangplank. Suddenly, Butler, who had just remembered his part in the ceremony, cried out for them to halt. While they stood by, he dashed aboard, handed Edwin the bag of gold due him, and returned to the wharf. A volley of applause and good wishes followed as the steamer sailed down the river.

In San Francisco, twenty-five prominent men signed their names to a letter stating that they wished to tender Edwin another benefit in the Bay City before he bade California farewell. It was announced for the Metropolitan Theatre on the date his answer appeared in the *Alta:*

> Gentlemen:
> Your kind communication on behalf of the citizens of San Francisco, tendering to me a Complimentary Benefit, prior to my departure for the Atlantic States, has just been placed in my hands.
> The limited time allowed me compels me to name this (Wednesday) evening, September 3 [1856], as the time for the proposed favor, on which occasion, at the solicitation of many friends, I will make my first appearance in the character of "King Lear."

Once more a brilliant and crowded audience showed its appreciation and after the performance gave Edwin one of the greatest ovations ever recorded in a California theatre.

This engagement ended the preparation for his eastern appearance as a star, which Baker had gone on to arrange. Having been called upon to take the scepter of his father's kingdom, Edwin Booth now realized that he was saying good-by to the happiest days of his life and facing responsibilities which meant hard work and long hours of serious study.

On September fifth, he sailed away on the steamer *Golden Age* to Panama. For the first time he crossed the Isthmus by rail and, as chance would have it, voyaged northward on the steamer *Illinois* which had carried him off with Junius and his father on the old man's fateful journey to California.

Junius remained in San Francisco and was connected with various theatres until December, 1856. While stage manager at the Metropolitan he had the sensational Lola Montez as a guest star. Lola was somewhat flamboyant and boasted of horsewhipping men who got in her way. When she appeared at the stage door of the Metropolitan for the first time she was smoking her usual black cigar. Lola's personal representative, an immaculately dressed Frenchman who could speak very little English, accompanied her. Junius warned Lola that no smoking was permitted backstage in that theatre, and Lola retorted that she was Madame Montez and would do as she pleased. Her representative, becoming excited, started jabbering in a language Junius did not understand and so he threw him out. This silenced Lola. When Junius returned to take care of her, the cigar was missing. They had no trouble after that.

The public demand for minstrelsy on a lavish scale made further enlargement of the San Francisco Theatre necessary. Maguire had watched its expansion from a small bandbox to its present proportions and realized the time had come to fulfill the dream of his early days. His ambitions resulted in the famous Maguire Opera House, which became known the world over for its beauty and splendor. He was proud of this imposing edifice and had his name placed higher than it had ever been in the civic life of the city, by locating it above the entrance of the building.

Since he still found his underworld sympathies a lucrative source of interest, he disapproved of Junius' Vigilante affiliations, and did not re-engage him when the new opera house opened in November, 1856. But Junius was well-aware of his share in its success. With the exception of the gambling club hidden under its roof and the adjoining saloon, Maguire had again incorporated all of Junius' suggestions. Maguire soon realized that he could not forfeit the chance to exploit Junius' capable advice and popular appeal, and later enlisted his services as leading man through a long run of engagements.

Competition in the theatre was keen, with many new playhouses going up and old ones being leased under changed names. Aspiring actors poured into the city. Among these ambitious newcomers from Australia were the Land sisters, Belle and Agnes, accompanied by their mother, Mrs. Land Rookes. Agnes, a girl of sixteen years, had made her début as a dancer in Sydney but after her arrival in California she took up dramatics and married a talented actor, Harry Perry. His promising career was shortened by death soon after, and her long association with the theatre ultimately led to a romance with Junius.

Harriet was kept in a whirl of activity. Between playing small parts and being a hostess at popular social functions she drove herself to the point of exhaustion, and during the next three years her health began to fail under the strain. She died on August 28, 1859. Although she had been ill for some time, her death was an unexpected shock to all who knew her. It has been reported that she committed suicide, and it is quite possible that, despondent over her frail condition and fading attractions, she wished to escape the inevitable consequences of watching Junius drift away from her and look upon her as a burden. Whatever the cause of her death, it was timely for her sake.

True to the tradition of the profession, Junius did not permit his personal sorrow to interfere with his work and continued at the opera house without interruption. He remained in California with his motherless daughter, Marion, until 1864, when they returned East. Prior to her mother's death this child had made her stage début in San Francisco.

California had proved an appreciative testing ground for the talents of these two Booth brothers. Junius had established himself as a successful, level-headed manager and Edwin had finally left in a burst of glory. This younger son of the great tragedian was to reach more coveted heights of fame than any other member of the family.

Agnes Booth, wife of Junius Brutus Booth, Jr. *(Original photograph from the collection of the author)*

John Sleeper Clarke, actor, husband of Asia Booth.
(Courtesy National Park Service)

CHAPTER V

Everyone at the Booth farm in Maryland was excited. A carriage was coming up the lane heralded by several neighborhood boys crying, "Ned has come home!" Edwin's mother and sisters rushed out and threw their arms around him. Ann Hall, the buxom and smiling mammy, ran from the kitchen, wiping her hands on her apron, her brood trailing her. Johnnie came galloping across the field on his pony, stopped short and jumped to the ground. In a bound he was at his brother's side.

Edwin had not expected such a welcome. Blushing and confused by all the embraces his mother and sisters showered on him, he was quite embarrassed. Didn't they know he wasn't a baby any more? What would these grown-up country fellows think of him? He was a man now—they must understand that!

Before the Negroes could be called from their work in the fields Johnnie had just left, Edwin's boyhood friends began to unload his baggage. Their whispered exclamations of wonder at the weight of his trunk, which they supposed might contain some gold since he had just "come from the diggin's," amused him.

Asia, standing apart from the others, quietly studied this older brother. She thought he looked very boyish and fragile, that his long dark hair and piercing black eyes made him appear melancholy. However, she noted the poise and suavity that experience had given him. Mary Ann invited the neighboring boys to remain a while, but they were so in awe of their former playmate, that they sheepishly excused themselves by promising to return the next day. When they had passed out of hearing of the Booths, one boy remarked that perhaps it was skulls Edwin had in his trunk.

"What would Ned be doin' with skulls?" asked his companion.

"Actors always carry skulls with 'em," was the reply. "Ain't you never heard of Hamlet?"

Left alone in his room Edwin realized how everything at the farm would remind him of his father who, though he had not lived in this house, had planned it and walked about in it while it was being built. From his window Edwin could see the cabin where he was born. He remembered the many times he and his father had started out on tour from that doorway and returned there after a season on the road. He could see him out in the potato patch, and hear him at the barn giving the help "the devil" for neglecting some task. Others had lived in the cabin since then—some of the Negroes and hired hands—but it was the cabin in which he had grown up and he felt a tinge of regret that they had made the change. Soon he would be on tour, playing the theatres and using the dressing rooms that would again remind him of his father. He hoped that the critics would not compare them—he wished to be *Edwin* Booth on the stage, not the son of a renowned tragedian.

That evening his mother told him of the difficulties she was having with the farm. Since Junius had been there, she had tried several plans, but none had worked out successfully. She had made a deal with a tenant who turned into such a tyrant that they were relieved when his time was up. The winters were so severe she and the girls did not want to remain there much longer. Anyway, Asia would soon marry Sleeper Clarke who had kept coming to the house for years. Rosalie, she knew, would always be with her, but the younger sons would undoubtedly go their own way as Edwin and Junius had done.

She realized now that Johnnie would never be a farmer. It was too lonely a life for him—he could never settle down to it. A year before, he had made an appearance at the Charles St. Theatre in Baltimore as Richmond in *Richard III*. She thought it was hasty, and blamed Sleeper Clarke for inveigling him into it on his benefit night. Clarke, she said, just wanted to have the name of a Booth on his bill. She did not criticize Johnnie for his rashness; perhaps he was to be an actor, too. He seemed to have the theatre in his blood—had been reading and studying many plays. There were times around the house when his declamations reminded her of his father! Yes, Johnnie would make a good actor if he studied.

Edwin cautiously hinted that Junius had said Johnnie needed some correction, but his mother quickly warned him, as she had Junius when he had stayed at the farm, not to do or say anything that Johnnie could interpret as reproof, lest it cause some unpleasantness. Johnnie had time enough to decide what he wanted to do, and she knew when he had made that decision he would take up some definite work.

These were not the only problems she had been forced to meet, she continued. There had been that carpenter, James Gifford, who was employed by John T. Ford, the Baltimore theatrical manager. Gifford had been dunning her for money he said was due for work on the house, but she was sure the elder Booth had paid him in full before he left for California. Edwin promised to attend to Gifford's claim when he saw him in Baltimore. Evidently Gifford never got his money, for he later told Ford that the Booths' failure to pay him had made it impossible for him to settle his debts, and in consequence, he had lost his own dwelling.

The prestige that Edwin had brought East with him affected Asia in a curious way. She could not understand the popularity of this older brother whom she had regarded as a solemn and thoughtful young man, lacking the impetuousness of the younger Johnnie. But when she became reconciled to his unexpected fame, she made the most of it and thoroughly enjoyed standing in the reflected light of Edwin's glory. She even grew jealous of any serious interest he might show in the women who admired him and guarded him with a peculiar possessiveness all her own. This trait in her character was to cause the only friction between them.

Young Johnnie was eighteen now and still the apple of his mother's eye. Junius and Edwin had drifted away from her into a more independent life and it is possible that she still blamed Edwin in her heart for not returning with Booth from the ill-fated trip to California, and possibly averting his untimely death. Whatever Mary Ann felt toward Edwin, she never expressed it openly. We only know of the irony of an incident which took place shortly after his home-coming. He had anxiously examined his father's wardrobe, selecting costumes he had told Ben Baker he could obtain, but was informed by his mother that she was saving them for Johnnie. She seems to have been totally oblivious of the fact that her decision endangered the career of her son at a time when he most needed such material encouragement and assistance.

Unable to arrange for Edwin's appearances in Boston, New York, or Philadelphia, Baker came on to Baltimore. Here he attempted to secure the Holliday Street Theatre, but, finding it occupied by a musical troupe, he was forced to take the old Front Street house which Edwin had requested him not to do. Although again disappointed, Edwin opened there on the night of October fifteenth (1856) in *Hamlet*, supported by the stock company of the Holliday Street Theatre.

This bill, and successive performances of *Richelieu, Richard III*, and others were lauded by the Baltimore critics in their predictions of an eminent career for the son who had inherited so much of his father's genius. This was only the beginning of references to the elder Booth which Edwin had hoped to avoid. The engagement closed with Edwin's benefit on the twenty-fifth of that month.

In November he and Baker arrived in Richmond, Virginia, where Mary Devlin, a young girl of rare musical and dramatic ability, was the leading lady at John T. Ford's theatre. She was the sixteen-year-old daughter of an impoverished Troy, New York, merchant and was then living with the Joseph Jeffersons. Under Ford's tutelage she had advanced professionally and when Jefferson became stage manager of Ford's Richmond Theatre, she accompanied him there.

Mary had large dark eyes and a full sensitive mouth which gave her an expression of pensive serenity. The oval contours of her face were set off by dark brown hair arranged in smooth Victorian fashion. A sunny disposition, responsive manner, and gentle grace charmed and delighted her many friends. Mary's likeness to Edwin's mother as a young girl is arresting. She had the same poised loveliness that had appealed to Junius Brutus Booth so many years before in the Bow Street flower market.

On November twenty-fourth, Edwin began his Richmond engagement as Richard III. Notified that she was to play opposite him, Mary was so awed by the famous name of Booth that she feared she would be unable to act in his presence. But at the next day's rehearsal of *Romeo and Juliet*, something happened which could be explained neither by Jefferson, Edwin, nor Mary. After their performance she exclaimed: "He is the greatest actor I have ever known. I was inspired, and could act forever with him," and Edwin, upon returning to his living quarters, wrote to his mother: "I have seen and acted with a young woman who has so impressed me that I could almost forget my vow never to marry an actress." By the end of the week, their friendship had progressed to Edwin's presenting Mary with an exquisite turquoise bracelet.

Jefferson, knowing the proclivities of the Booths toward first-loves, did not want a brokenhearted protégée to console after the young star's departure and instructed her to return the gift. When Mary repeated the words of her foster father to Edwin, he told her not to worry, that he had a plan whereby their romance would be accepted. Excusing himself for a short while, he hurried away to return with a duplicate of her turquoise bracelet. Then, with Mary, he took it to Mrs. Jefferson who beamed with pleasure. When next they saw Jefferson, and fell upon their knees in mock-heroic manner pleading, "Father your blessing," he was much moved and gave them his benediction.[14] But the close of that engagement left Baker with a gloomy Romeo and Jefferson with a sad Juliet.

Edwin toured through the South, playing in Washington, Charleston, Mobile, and New Orleans where the *Daily Crescent* proclaimed him the best tragedian on the American stage, already rivaling his father in his most famous characters, and excelling him in some of them. Prompted by such notices, Baker began billing him as "The World's Greatest Actor." At each stop along the way, Edwin read in glowing terms of his ability and claims to international distinction.

Averse to these exaggerations, he asked Baker to desist, or at least to modify his announcements, but Baker had ideas of his own regarding publicity, and the compliments increased instead of diminishing. As they continued northward to St. Louis, with Boston and New York still their objectives, nothing was left to chance by Edwin's promoter. From each new engagement Baker collected a fresh batch of press clippings.

During his first Chicago appearance, Edwin was invited to the home of an acquaintance and there met a girl who took a great fancy to him. Her mother, formerly a widow named Runnion, had married J. H. McVicker, one of the leading theatrical managers of the Midwest. The precocious youngster sang in concerts with Signor Brignoli and played juvenile parts. After adopting her step-father's name she became known as Mary McVicker. In so short a time Edwin had met both his future wives.

Performances were given in Pittsburgh and Wheeling with Edwin's shabby wardrobe in constant need of repair or some ingenious alteration in order to make it adaptable to a repertoire. He threaded the needle and Baker did the sewing.

Wheeling's theatre was over a carriage-maker's shop and not unlike several of the halls in the Mother Lode. The night was cold and the audience huddled around two potbellied stoves. Edwin strode onto the stage repeating his lines, but, glancing over the house, could locate no spectators. Without a pause in his performance he sauntered to the prompter's side occupied by Baker and whispered, "Where's the audience?"

At Rochester, they were in so impecunious a condition that Baker was forced to attach some imitation fur to the collar and skirt of his frock coat in order that Edwin might have a costume for the announced bill. Edwin also wore Baker's boots, and the latter had to squeeze his own feet into Edwin's shoes rather than go barefoot.

Baker had discovered that their audience would be composed mainly of Germans, and so advertised his young star as Herr Edwin Booth, who would present Schiller's *Robbers* in the original language. When the curtain went up and Edwin began to speak in English, a riot broke out. Fortunately, he was able to pacify them by his fine acting, and the performance continued without further interruption.

In Buffalo, he renewed his acquaintance with Barton Hill, and they spent afternoons smoking clay pipes in Edwin's room at the old Clarendon Hotel and watching Baker sew concaves on a shirt of mail to complete armor for *Richard III* and *Macbeth*.

Edwin next appeared in Detroit. Again an argument arose with his manager over the superlatives in his billing. A proof of the first broadside bearing the old familiar phrases, "The World-renowned Young American Tragedian," "The Inheritor of his Father's Genius," etc., was sent over to Baker for correction and fell into Edwin's hands. Snatching a pencil from the printer's devil who had delivered the proof, he drew heavy lines through the words and told the boy to go at once with the corrected bill to Mr. Garry Hough, manager of the theatre in which he was to play. "Tell Mr. Hough," demanded Edwin, "that I will not have all this; that it must be cut out; that I insist on being announced as simple Edwin Booth, nothing more; tell him just what I have said!"

Hough's sense of humor prompted him to comply explicitly with the directions, and the announcement was published:

Engagement for One Week Only

of Simple

Edwin Booth

Upon seeing it, Baker went into a tantrum, rushed to the printer's foreman, and began to rave about the ridiculous mistake. The foreman pointed to the corrected proof and apprised Baker of the fact that "it was a printer's business to follow copy even if it took him out of the window."

The efforts of Edwin's manager were finally rewarded with the coveted engagement at the Boston Theatre, then under the direction of Thomas Barry. On the night of April 20, 1857, he opened as Sir Giles Overreach, in *A New Way to Pay Old Debts*. Critics were lavish in their praise of him. "We seriously think that Mr. Booth last night showed the possession of more talent for the tragic drama than any actor that we have seen upon the stage of the Boston Theatre," declared the *Courier*. Other journals hailed his appearances as a succession of the most brilliant and complete triumphs, and stated they had found in him a finished actor and tragedian of the best school, and that he had attracted larger audiences than any other actor playing there.

Edwin had decided, while traveling eastward from California, to let his future be governed by the reception of his efforts in Boston. If critics hailed him, he would continue his star billing; if not, he would become a stock actor. One thing was certain, he would never again appear with Laura Keene! She had made Baker an offer to take on Edwin as her leading man, but Baker had rejected it. Far from western audiences her alibi of failure there loomed as an asset. It was fortunate for Edwin that he was not associated with her in several other unsuccessful ventures.

Having won, after some trepidation, the approval of a city whose judgment was known for its severity, he was not only inspired, but confident in the fulfillment of his plans. The effect of this success was noticeable in all he undertook.

Such acclaim put him in line for New York. Baker rushed there to secure a contract with William E. Burton, who was now determined to make the most of an opportunity he had once passed by. Edwin had asked Baker to bill him as Sir Giles Overreach for his first night in New York, hoping to duplicate the ovation he had received in Boston. But Burton, in a published fanfare expressing his pleasure in introducing the eminent young tragedian, Edwin Booth, whose undeniable success in California, Australia, and elsewhere had stamped him THE HOPE OF THE LIVING DRAMA, announced that Edwin would begin his engagement May fourth at his Broadway Metropolitan Theatre in *Richard III.*

Edwin celebrated his Boston success with a spree, then climbed on the train for New York. He took one look at Burton's announcements and exclaimed, "I am ruined!" He felt he had been placed in a position too exalted to attain and was more than sober when he arrived at the theatre on Monday morning for rehearsal. In the company supporting him was a young actor named Lawrence Barrett, who became one of his most intimate associates. Barrett's ill nature, however, often kept him at odds with others, and Edwin had his share of such misunderstandings.

Reviews compared Edwin to some of the great dramatic actors and credited him with fine personal endowments, but his Richard was censured for too much malice and not enough of the sardonic, humorous mockery of the older tragedians. The very comparison which he had hoped to avoid was freely reiterated by his critics. Memories of the elder Booth clogged the minds of many and prevented their isolating the father's achievements in appraising his son. Whenever they did get away from the old man, it was only to remark that Edwin was "promising." But on *The Albion,* a weekly periodical, was a young, and more tolerant, writer also embarking upon a career. He began under the pseudonyms of Hamilton and Mercutio and eventually disclosed his real name by signing himself William Winter.

As Ewer had written of Edwin in the West, so Winter continued his helpful criticism in the East. In two of his articles that month he called attention to the hard fate of the son of an illustrious father. He sympathized with Edwin's problem of being the butt of critical comparisons and the impossibility of his talent being measured with a fresh perspective. "A famous son makes his father famous by reflection, takes him up, as it were, on his filial shoulders and bears him out of the chill obscure . . ." noted Winter. "But the service is rarely reciprocated, and I can comprehend, at least, if I may not commend, the state of mind of that hapless gentleman, who blew out his brains to escape being presented as the son of his renowned sire."

Winter's attitude enabled him to see Edwin as an individual with his own faults and merits. He commended him on the control of his outward appearance but advised him to approach his work with a better intellectual perception. Winter saw Edwin as a man scintillating with genius and predicted that when he came to a deeper understanding of his work he would "eclipse any name which has adorned the English stage within the memory of living man."

From a summer tour, Edwin returned to New York for a week's engagement at the Metropolitan Theatre, which later became known as the Winter Garden. Having terminated his association with Baker, he played under the management of E. L. Davenport at the Howard Athenaeum, Boston. It was in 1858, at the Richmond Theatre, that Edwin staged the first production in the United States of Shakespeare's *Henry V*. March of that year he appeared at the Baltimore Holliday Street Theatre where Mary Devlin was playing and their romance was renewed. Between performances Edwin continued his courtship at Mary's boarding house, in the rear of Guy's Hotel. Since the family were then in Baltimore, this undoubtedly gave him the opportunity of introducing his mother and sisters to the charming young actress of whom he had already written in such glowing terms.

On the ninth of March, local newspapers described a heavy snowfall in the city and announced Edwin's bill for the evening as *A New Way To Pay Old Debts*. That same day, Adelaide Delannoy, first wife of Junius Brutus Booth, Sr., died. After her divorce, she and her son Richard Junius, had continued to live in Baltimore where Richard obtained a position as an instructor of languages at a seminary for young women.[15] Mrs. Elijah Rogers noted that the elder Booth's "first wife was not pretty," and the writer George Alfred Townsend disclosed that Adelaide "went down to a drunken and brokenhearted grave."

THE BROTHERS

Immediately after his mother's death, Richard placed a stone above her burial ground which read:

> Jesus—Mary—Joseph
> Pray for the soul of
> Mary Christine Adelaide
> Delannoy
> wife of
> Junius Brutus Booth, tragedian
> She Died in Baltimore
> March the 9th 1858
> Aged 66 yrs.

So Edwin, to refute this claim of the "wife of Junius Brutus Booth," and to establish his mother's right to the title, now commissioned a Boston sculptor to design something appropriate for the Booth lot in Baltimore Cemetery where his father was buried. Within a month a steamboat brought a marble obelisk nine feet high ornamented by a medallion representing the elder Booth and Edwin had it set in place on May first, his father's birthday. It was inscribed:

> Behold the spot where genius lies,
> O drop a tear when talent dies!
> Of tragedy the mighty chief,
> His power to please surpassed belief.
> Hic jacet matchless Booth.[16]

Thus the two families of the great tragedian, who carefully avoided each other, sought to confirm their right to his name.

The romance of Edwin and Mary Devlin was now in full bloom though professional engagements kept them apart most of the time. Edwin made several appearances in New York that summer, but did not equal his former success. In June Mary appeared there at Niblo's Garden as Juliet to the versatile Charlotte Cushman's Romeo, and later went on with the company to Boston.

Those who knew Mary Devlin described her as having more personal magnetism than beauty. She was an intelligent woman, refined and accomplished; otherwise a man of Edwin's qualities would never have been attracted to her. Asia, for no other reason than jealousy, violently disliked her and, the moment she realized they were seriously considering marriage, began scheming to upset their plans. There was no indication that Mrs. Booth was not fond of Mary or that she disapproved of the wedding.

Evidently Asia did not have the same attitude toward actors as she had toward actresses, for she would not promise to marry Sleeper Clarke until he had definitely decided to adopt the dramatic profession. By 1859 he had gained some fame, and on April twenty-eighth of that year they were married at St. Paul's Church in Baltimore. Shortly after, they went to Philadelphia where Clarke was then living. Junius' first child, Blanche, and her aunt, Mrs. Ben De Bar, visited them and were none too cordially received. Asia made it clear that she disliked this tall and graceful young girl, with the brilliant, black eyes characteristic of the Booth beauty, almost as intensely as she did Mary Devlin, and referred to the child as being merely her brother's stepdaughter.[17]

In Boston a well-known lawyer was ardently pursuing Mary, and Charlotte Cushman advised her to accept him. Undecided, she wrote to Edwin in New York telling him of this. Her letter so unbalanced him that he ignored theatrical engagements, got drunk, raved, and alarmed his friends, who feared he might commit suicide. They hastily sent word of his condition to Mary, who left everything and rushed to him. That settled the matter. Edwin asked her to give up the stage and continue her studies in music and languages until they could arrange for a wedding. But Asia, determined not to accept Mary as a member of the Booth family, accused her of having inveigled Edwin, during one of his sprees, into a promise to marry her so that she might get his money and provide for her parents.

Edwin went on to Philadelphia and rented a home for his mother and sister Rosalie with the intention that he and Mary Devlin would live there after their marriage. While Mary studied in New York, he rounded out his tour, came back to Philadelphia for an engagement, and telegraphed her the date she could expect him, adding that he would leave immediately after his final curtain. Asia cried and stormed about, though other members of the family remained silent, but Edwin was firm, said nothing, and went on with his plans. His return to Mary ended his visits to Asia's home for many years.

He found Mary hysterically happy. As they embraced and she wept and smothered him with kisses, he fervently vowed never to be separated from her again. Each had prepared for an impressive appearance at this reunion, but now they looked as though they were shipwrecked. They laughed and clung together. A tornado could not have swept them apart.[18]

On July 7, 1860, Edwin's friend, Adam Badeau, and his brother, John Wilkes, witnessed the marriage ceremony at the home of Reverend Samuel Osgood in New York City. Here they signed their names to a certificate attesting that Edwin Booth of Philadelphia and

Mary Devlin of Hudson City had been married in their presence. Asia had lost. Edwin took Mary, his mother, and youngest brother, Joseph, to Niagara Falls.

Asia, paddling around in bloomers at a seaside resort near Philadelphia with her husband, hoped "Miss Devlin," as she called her new sister-in-law, would topple into the water, or try to swim in the whirlpool and get drowned. In the autumn the Clarkes went to Baltimore for a visit with relatives and childhood friends, taking along little Asia, their six-months-old firstborn. Some time after their return to Philadelphia, Edwin brought Mary to his mother's home. Asia still refused to accept her and was determined not to visit any public or private place where she might possibly encounter her. Since Edwin was financing the Philadelphia home, his mother advised him to give it up under the circumstances and plan to live in a more pleasant environment. This promised to be the only solution to the problem of restoring peace in the family.

Edwin's marriage to Mary Devlin seemed fortunate. She was a delightful companion, and her cheerfulness checked his tendency toward melancholia. Encouraged by her helpful suggestions and advice, he took a new interest in his work and controlled his appetite for liquor, which was a great relief not only to his mother but also to his friends. On more than one occasion, Adam Badeau and others had been called upon to guide his staggering form to the shelter of their dwellings or to some temporary address he called home. At times he had seemed to rival his father in the barroom rather than on the stage. Mary's influence directed his energies to the theatre and undoubtedly saved him from sinking into mediocrity.

By November, 1860, they were living at the Fifth Avenue Hotel in New York, and on the twenty-sixth of the month after an absence of almost two years from the footlights of that city, Edwin began his first theatrical engagement since his marriage, as Hamlet at the Winter Garden. Forrest had emerged from retirement in Philadelphia, and had reappeared at Niblo's Garden where he remained until late spring.

It was now that young Edwin Booth crossed swords with him in a royal battle for the supremacy of the American theatre. Forrest was like an aged bull who had earned his leadership with ferocious might. Sweeping aside all the intricacies of studied interpretation, Forrest had stormed through one part after another until by his very roar he had gained the respect of the American public. His career had been marked by the blood and thunder he expounded. In 1849, the Astor Place Opera House had been the scene of a serious riot, instigated by a dispute over the sovereignty of the English actor Macready or Forrest upon the stage. A number of people were killed or injured and the crowd had threatened to destroy the building. Forrest was triumphant in the eyes of the American public and had retained his leadership in spite of his years. Now his position was to be challenged by Edwin Booth. The situation was similar to that of the elder Booth and Kean forty-three years before in London. It was to be the turning point in theatrical history in the United States. The critics were to choose between Forrest's lusty bombast and Edwin's calmer naturalism, and the choice was to have decisive effects.

The press, viewing first one and then the other rendition of Hamlet, began to hum. The *Tribune* said: "Since we saw him last, Mr. Booth has been at work, and his work has borne such noble fruit as can only be fully appreciated by those who knew him when he was the crude, unpolished, but still startling and original actor of three years ago, and who see him now, and note what gigantic strides he has taken toward the highest excellence. Mr. Booth's performance of Hamlet . . . last evening was a triumph for himself, and . . . all things considered, by far the best for many years." Edwin played it for three nights, and the *Times* added, "Of all those who have essayed the character of Hamlet, for a night or fifty consecutive nights in this country, Mr. Booth is unquestionably the best." Such tributes jarred Forrest, who had presented the Dane for a total of nine performances.

After the first three weeks of the New Year, when Edwin played at the Philadelphia Academy of Music with Charlotte Cushman, he returned to New York to continue his rivalry with Forrest. Efforts were made to draw the two tragedians together in the same play, but Forrest politely refused. They did, in fact, perform *Richelieu* on the same evening, but in separate houses.

Forrest's acting stimulated interest in Edwin, and the marked preference for certain of the young man's productions prolonged his engagement. Each attracted more than the usual attention. The advisability of restoring the episode in the King's closet in *Hamlet*, as Edwin had done, and his arrangements of text and stage-business in other plays, were widely discussed. Defects in Forrest's acting "which even dull-witted persons recognized" were the subject of sharp attacks by the critics, though they conceded he was still a man of might and genius in the theatre.

Forrest followed traditions; Edwin's conceptions were more novel and his execution more modulated. Attendance at performances had shifted during their engagements. Edwin began with small audiences which increased until multitudes acclaimed him; Forrest suffered a reverse. A majority of the older patrons championed him, but many

THE BROTHERS

of them and all the younger groups were won over by Edwin, who was setting a fast pace for pre-eminence in the profession.

The popularity Edwin achieved drew his attention to the public's trend for less ranting on the stage. Blood and thunder melodrama was passing with actors such as Forrest. "The conversational, colloquial school you desire to adopt is the only true one, Edwin, for the present day; but, as you reasonably add, 'Too much is dangerous,'" advised his talented and discerning young wife in one of her letters.[19] After knocking Forrest against the ropes, Edwin was cautious in his movements. He knew he stood midway between the old and the new in the theatre. Many critics did not see that he was blazing a new trail back of the footlights, and took his digressions from established rules as mistakes. But the approval of a majority gave him the decision over the tottering tragedian.

At this point in his career, Edwin's attitude toward publicity methods was slightly altered. He even permitted excerpts from good reviews to be inserted in his advertisements. Now that he had defeated Forrest, made more money, and gained applause beyond his expectations, Edwin turned his thoughts to England. He was not only eager to increase his prestige in the theatrical world but he was also anxious to find respite from the harassed conditions in his own country. Talk of secession was heated and ominous. Lincoln's election had cast the threat of civil war over the United States. Hostility was growing on all sides, and although Edwin's delivery of the lines:

> Beneath the rule of men entirely great,
> The pen is mightier than the sword. . . .
>
> Take away the sword;
> States can be saved without it . . .

had been seized upon as pertinent to the very hour, fate was to intervene and make a mockery of these hopes.

Mary Devlin, Edwin Booth's first wife. *(Courtesy Museum of the City of New York)*

BOOK THREE
CONFLICT

A rare photograph of John Wilkes Booth, from the collection of Gail Merrifield, great-great-granddaughter of Wilkes and Izola Mills D'Arcy.

CHAPTER I

On the evening of August 14, 1855, a seventeen-year-old stripling by the name of John Wilkes Booth made his début as Richmond, in *Richard III*, with a Mr. Ellis in the title rôle, at the Charles Street Theatre in Baltimore. In one notice he was incorrectly announced as J. M. Booth. It was a benefit for his sister Asia's beau, John Sleeper Clarke, who was winning laurels as a talented young comedian, and on this night appeared in an afterpiece entitled *Toodles*. Wilkes, as he was now beginning to be known, was billed as the son of the lamented Junius Brutus Booth. For this leap into the family profession he was as unprepared as for an aerial act in a circus. All he had to recommend him were the costumes of the elder Booth that had been given to him by his mother. The critics, remembering his father, were kind, and reported that, for a beginner, he had given a fair performance. But the old man was not there to tell him the truth, and young Wilkes took their condescensions as applause. The next day, in imitation of his great sire, he galloped back to the farm on his pony and told of his imaginary success.

Although Wilkes had followed his older brothers in and out of stage doors, he had reaped no harvest of cues from the prompt books of the elder Booth. Junius and Edwin had prepared themselves for theatrical careers by study and rehearsal, but Wilkes thought he could attain by some royal road the perfection of the greatest tragedians. He skipped lightly over his apprenticeship and, two years after the Baltimore début, plunged disastrously into his ill-starred vocation. It happened in Philadelphia, and the City of Brotherly Love never forgave him for it.

Determined to be an actor, he went to his future brother-in-law, John Sleeper Clarke, for help. Through Clarke's efforts Wilkes secured a contract to appear in minor parts, at eight dollars per week, in the stock company of the Philadelphia Arch Street Theatre. He had decided not to use the name of Booth until he was more capable, and had himself billed as J. Wilkes. According to the agreement he was compelled to attend daily rehearsals, but his acting improved very little. He was careless, and his blundering spoiled many productions. On several occasions he was hissed off the stage. Once he took the part of a Venetian comrade in Hugo's *Lucretia Borgia*, and was to have said in his turn, "Madam, I am Petruchio Pandolfe," but instead he got confused and blurted out, "Madam, I am Pondolfio Pet—Pedolfio Pat—Pantuchio Ped—damn it! What am I?"[1] The audience did not hiss this time, but shrieked with laughter.

The following evening they booed en masse the moment he appeared on the stage as Dawson, in *The Gamester*, by Edward Moore. He completely forgot his lines, his legs went out from under him, and "Dawson" was dragged back of the wings. To make matters worse, Wilkes had invited a young woman to the theatre to see him act, and his failure ended their acquaintance. The stage manager bellowed that there was no hope for anyone like him. Wilkes said he had studied his parts faithfully but had no confidence in himself.

In later years he never forgot the ordeal of those Philadelphia performances and always dreaded playing there. Those who knew him blamed his failure on his lack of enterprise and his neglect to study other and better parts than the minor rôles assigned him. They said his indifference was responsible for all his mistakes, and that he was unable to apply himself or to progress as Edwin was doing.

Among the many ambitious students, artists, and actors, living in a boarding house on Arch Street near the theatre, Wilkes was noticeably idle. His companions there admired his "superb masculine beauty," said he was "a young Apollo in face and figure," but when he paced the floor exclaiming, "I must have fame! fame!" they were at a loss to know how he expected to achieve it without effort. He attained some local notice by challenging one of them to a duel, and received a great deal of chiding from those who saw the paper on which he had scrawled his defiance, as it was poorly spelled and looked as though it had been written by a boy of seven. Wilkes bewailed his wounded honor, but nothing happened, and it became evident that the challenge was merely a bid for attention.

His early escapades in Philadelphia included several amorous adventures similar to those of his father at about the same age in London. The handsome Wilkes also had the sort of appeal that no woman could resist. His fascinating dark eyes and melodious voice made them susceptible to his advances. At this same boarding house was a beautiful girl who fell desperately in love with him. Each night she entertained Wilkes with charms that finally got him into trouble and caused him considerable expense. That he managed the entire affair with but few intimate friends' knowing of it flattered his ego and gave him a false assurance. He considered himself especially adept at intrigue.

The Booths were a strange assortment of contradictions. Junius the elder started out in life as a flighty Romeo and became the devoted companion and husband of one woman. His only moral defect was his weakness for liquor. Junius, Jr., never touched intoxicants, yet repeated his father's infidelity by leaving a wife and child to go away with a young mistress. Edwin took to drink at nineteen but was shy and ignored the fair sex until he fell in love with Mary Devlin. Throughout his life Wilkes was a libertine and certainly no teetotaler. Joseph's only stimulant was an occasional glass of wine, and his marriage vows were strictly observed. Asia and Rosalie, too, were opposites. Asia was gay, though snobbish; she married, and became the mother of seven children, including twins. Rosalie was morbid, uncommunicative, and remained a spinster all her life.

The applause that Edwin had won as a star since his return from California made Wilkes envious of his early training. Wilkes had been too young to troupe with their father, and he fully realized the advantage Edwin had over him in that respect. Nor had he had Junius' guiding hand to direct him. However, his mother never would have permitted him to go so far from her had he wished to work under Junius in San Francisco. Nor would Junius have welcomed him as an added responsibility. But of the three younger boys, Wilkes was the one who most needed the rigid discipline which this older brother could have given him.

By the autumn of 1858 Wilkes had accepted an offer of twenty dollars a week, with a promise of better parts, from George Kunkel, manager of the Richmond Theatre, and was at home preparing to go South. Edwin was playing at the Holliday Street Theatre in Baltimore and on August twenty-seventh took a benefit as Richard III. To encourage Wilkes and please their mother, Edwin had him cast as Richmond under his real name, John Wilkes Booth, and not according to his Philadelphia billing as J. Wilkes. The impression that Wilkes had made at the time of his Baltimore début three years previously was so ineffectual that one newspaper now announced Edwin would be supported by a younger brother who had never before performed in Baltimore, but had played last season in Philadelphia. His failure to attract even a little notice in comparison to the attention given Edwin made Wilkes feel inferior. Edwin was conscious of this and tried to banish such an idea from Wilkes' mind by complimenting him at every opportunity.

At rehearsal he saw that Wilkes would be extremely difficult to direct for he did not easily follow instructions, but centered his efforts on imitating the old bombastic actors. As Edwin stood aside and watched this younger brother, he recognized the heritage of their father's endowments. Wilkes had the same classic features, restless energy and mental alertness. Physically he was equal to any demands the profession would make of him. There was a certain originality in his gestures and a lightning agility of his movements that were not unlike those of the elder Booth. To Edwin this resemblance brought back the image of his father upon the stage and reminded him of their trouping days. It was the sentimental link which bound him to his brother.

But with all his natural attributes, Wilkes' acting was crude. At twenty his stage experience was as nothing compared to Edwin's at the same age. Wilkes seemed at this time to lack the artistic sense which might eventually help him reach perfection. He plunged into his part as if determined to succeed at all costs. He had no control of his voice, mispronounced many words, and often ranted his lines. These were not trivial faults. They would endanger the career of any budding actor if not remedied before they became habits. An actor's voice is the instrument upon which he plays—without it, talent, ability, experience, popularity, fame, could not assure him of lasting success.

Edwin knew that Wilkes was temperamentally unfit to accept corrections or advice and could only overcome his defects by hard work and study. Would he be equal to the task? To keep matters pleasant between them, Edwin refrained from any suggestion in stage business which might put his younger brother out of range of the footlights. Even on the night of their performance he let him have his own way and covered up his mistakes whenever possible.

With the exception of Edwin's ovations which he shared, Wilkes made no sudden stride toward his dreamed-of triumph until he reached Richmond. There he received the applause of a friendly and hospitable people who proclaimed him the handsomest man on the American stage. His graceful manner was enhanced by a gift for sparkling conversation and an air of gay romance that bewitched hearts. As J. Wilkes, the name he had resumed, he immediately became a great favorite in theatrical circles and a brilliant addition to Richmond society.

Such approval was music to ears that had heard Philadelphia hissing. The encouragement he received in this southern city gave him confidence in himself and stimulated his efforts. In a letter to Junius, his mother boasted, "John is doing well in Richmond. He is very anxious to go on faster. When he has a run of bad parts he writes home in despair."

In this city, Edwin and Wilkes made another appearance together on October first, Wilkes playing Horatio to Edwin's Hamlet. Again Edwin arranged to have his brother's name prominently placed on the bill and, for the first time in Richmond, it was given as Wilkes Booth. When the curtain fell Edwin, a little shorter than Wilkes, not quite so dashing in appearance but with a heart full of generosity, led his younger brother down the stage and pointing to him, said to the audience, "I think he has done well. Don't you?" The applause increased and cries of "Yes! Yes!" responded throughout the theatre. Once more Wilkes' success was due to Edwin. His departure forced the younger brother to carry on alone and he continued to appear under his former billing of J. Wilkes.

What Edwin really thought of Wilkes following that engagement was written in a letter to Junius, who apparently had requested a candid opinion regarding the status of the family name after Wilkes' mishaps in Philadelphia. "I don't think he will startle the world . . ." wrote Edwin, "but he is improving fast, and looks beautiful on the *platform*." [2]

Years later, however, Edwin remarked, "John Wilkes had the genius of my father, and was far more gifted than I," and Walt Whitman's commentary on Edwin partly substantiates this opinion. "Edwin had everything but guts;" said old Walt, "if he had had a little more that was absolutely gross in his composition he would have been altogether first-class instead of just a little short of it. His father had more power and less finish." [3]

Edwin endeavored to cast aside the influence of his father's acting and to acquire a technique of his own. He replaced the swagger and bombast of older actors with milder gestures which had less power and more finish. Had Wilkes learned to control his voice and modulate his gymnastics, he might have combined certain elements of power and finish and achieved a distinction unequaled by his contemporaries.

Wilkes occasionally played in other provincial cities and, in the latter part of 1858, appeared in Petersburg, Virginia, at the theatre where the popular Maggie Mitchell was a star. Leonard Grover, who later became manager of the National Theatre in Washington, saw him there in the character of Uncas, an Indian, and thought him the most talented actor in the company. As he was cast under the name of John Wilkes, Grover did not then know he was a member of the celebrated Booth family. Wilkes told an acquaintance that when he had made a reputation as an actor, he would take back his family name.

Despite his handsome features, many of his close friends often chided him about his bowlegs, resembling his father's, which he attempted to conceal by wearing a long cloak. According to John M. Barron, a member of the Richmond company, many of Wilkes' antics were also imitations of the old man's vagaries. One afternoon while arranging their costumes for a performance of *Much Ado About Nothing*, in which Wilkes was to take the part of Don Pedro and Barron that of Don Claudio, Wilkes suddenly informed Barron that he must play Don Pedro that evening. Barron looked at him in amazement and replied, "I do not. I play Don Claudio, as I rehearsed it. What do you mean?"

"No matter what I mean," exclaimed Wilkes. "You go and tell old Phil [stage manager Phillips] that you play Don Pedro and he plays Claudio. I am going to Petersburg."

Barron was dumbfounded, but, knowing that "to argue with him would have been as effective as trying to widen the Royal Gorge of the Colorado by whistling in it," he said nothing. Phillips was forced to do Wilkes' bidding and the performance naturally suffered. After several days' absence Wilkes walked through the stage door as if he had never infringed upon the management and requested another assignment, which was given him.[4] Had he not been one of the Booths, it is probable he would have been tossed back into the street.

In this southern city many women fell violently in love with him, but if he eloped with one of them and married her in Connecticut on January 9, 1859,[5] as has been reported, no record of such a wedding is in evidence. The statement by a descendant of this reputed union, that the Booth family knew of Wilkes' secret marriage, is disproved by numerous letters, particularly those to Wilkes from his mother, Mary Ann, in which she refers to his fiancée, lovely Bessie Hale, daughter of a New Hampshire senator.[6] Certainly she would not have discussed his betrothal to a young woman so well-known socially as Miss Hale, had she known of a previous marriage. Wilkes played in Richmond throughout the season of 1858-1859 and could hardly have had time to make the long journey to Connecticut between his engagements without someone being aware of his absence. It was noted that he did go to Baltimore about three months later for a few days to attend the wedding of his sister Asia and John Sleeper Clarke.*

He then returned to Richmond and became more intimate with several young men of prominent families whom he had recently met. They belonged to various organizations composing the militia and were considered the coming leaders in society and politics. Parades, balls, civic gatherings, brought them forward in colorful uniforms which won the admiration of all Virginians. Under these peaceful conditions, Wilkes concluded there would be no danger if he donned a uniform. Thus he could gain a prestige equal to that of any of his friends.

At the Maryland farm where he spent the summer, he expressed his desire to join one of these military groups. He had no premonition at

* See Supplement I, page 387.

the time, that a sample of soldiering he was soon to get would disillusion him. His mother was definitely opposed to it and requested him to leave sword-rattling to others and to continue his career on the stage. He promised to do as she wished and went back to the Richmond Theatre in the fall of 1859 to play stock. Since he was again cast under the pseudonym of J. B. Wilkes, it may be presumed that the name Booth was still in need of protection.

Richmond papers soon began to report events more dramatic than any listed on theatrical boards. In October, John Brown, the fiery Abolitionist, armed some Negroes, seized the arsenal at Harper's Ferry, near Charlestown, and staged a black revolt against slavery. Virginians, aflame with excitement and indignation, expressed their views in no uncertain terms. Talk of war was in the air. Wilkes was swept along in the current. His sympathies were naturally bound to the people who had befriended him so warmly, and he became an ardent champion of the southern cause. He began to regard the northern states with increasing bitterness and suspicion. Even his ambitions in the theatre were colored by his opinions. He went about voicing his allegiance, threatening to shoot every Abolitionist he encountered. What was no more than a pose grew to be fanatical sectionalism.

Yet he did not join the militia when it was ordered to entrain for Harper's Ferry to quell Brown's rebellion. With actual danger confronting him, Wilkes explained his decision not to go by professing regard for his mother's request that he continue in the theatre. However, the troops went no farther than Washington, for the insurrection had been suppressed, and Brown captured. Back in their barracks at Richmond they held themselves in readiness to hasten to the scene should a new outbreak occur.

Brown's trial in Charlestown, where he was confined, lasted one week and ended November second. He was found guilty and sentenced to be hanged a month later on charges of treason to the State of Virginia, murder in the first degree, and inspiring slaves and others to commit the same. November nineteenth, the militia at Richmond was ordered to Charlestown to guard against any attempts by Brown's adherents to rescue him before he could be executed.

As the bell in the old tower of Capitol Square in Richmond tolled its signal for the troops to muster and proceed to Charlestown, Wilkes was sauntering to a minor comedy rôle at the theatre. He passed groups of men in uniform on their way to the depot, accompanied by applauding citizens. Swayed by this display of southern fervor and the knowledge that now there would be no danger, he determined to join them. Suddenly he stopped, turned about, and started off in another direction. A few minutes before the train puffed out of the station, Wilkes arrived wearing a borrowed uniform, armed with pistols and knife. Soldiers repeatedly pushed him off the coaches, but he "secreted himself in the baggage car until the train had got far upon its journey, when he showed himself and was made either an Assistant Commissary or Quartermaster." [7] Asked how George Kunkel, the manager of the Richmond Theatre, was going to get along without him, he replied that he didn't know and didn't care.

Ten crowded cars carried the contingent, high in spirits at the prospect of meeting the aiders and abettors of the uprising, to Charlestown in the Virginia hills. There they occupied close quarters in an abandoned tin factory and slept on pallets of straw. On evenings when he was not assigned to sentinel duty, Wilkes entertained his companions with dramatic readings while John Brown, in his prison cell not far away, read the Bible and prepared for death. The day preceding the hanging, the Richmond *Dispatch* published the following under a heading of *General Content:* "Old Brown says he is ready to die; the Abolitionists say they want a martyr; the Conservatives think he ought to be hung, and the Virginians will swing him off with great gratification. We never heard of a public execution which promised so much satisfaction to everybody concerned."

The Richmond Grays formed a part of the guard under Colonel Robert E. Lee, which surrounded the scaffold and saw the Sage of Ossawatomie die.[8] Wilkes enjoyed his military rôle until the trap fell and John Brown's body dangled in the air. Then he became pale and asked for a good stiff drink of whisky. Later in life he took credit for assisting in the capture, but since he did not arrive upon the scene until Brown was safely in jail, this vaunted heroism was only a figment of Wilkes' imagination. The moment he returned to Richmond, he got out of his uniform and was never seen in one again. This time Kunkel discharged him for taking so sudden a leave of absence, but a large group from the regiment in which he had served marched to the theatre and forced the management to reinstate him.

At the close of the Richmond season, Wilkes played short engagements elsewhere before returning north for the summer and attending Edwin's marriage. The reopening of stage doors took him back south where he tried stardom, under the name of J. Wilkes, at Matthew Canning's Columbus (Georgia) Theatre. The night he was to play Hamlet another actor was with him in his dressing room when Canning entered and jokingly threatened to shoot both of them. The gun unexpectedly exploded and Wilkes "was shot in the rear." This accident kept him off the stage for several weeks.

Reading in the Montgomery *Daily Post* that Edwin had just received five thousand dollars as his share of the profits for a month's engagement in Boston, Wilkes "resolved to transform himself from a stock actor to a Star. As many will read this who do not understand such distinctions," wrote George Alfred Townsend after Wilkes' death, "let me preface it by explaining that a Star is an actor who belongs to no one theatre, but travels from each to all, playing a few weeks at a time, and is sustained in his chief character by the regular or stock actors. A stock actor is a good actor and a poor fool. A Star is an advertisement in tights, who grows rich and corrupts the public taste. [Wilkes] Booth was a Star, and being so, had an agent. The agent is a trumpeter who goes on before, writing the impartial notices which you see in the Editorial Columns of county papers and counting noses at the theatre doors.

"Booth's agent was one Matthew Canning, an exploded Philadelphia lawyer, who took to managing after passing the bar, and J. Wilkes no longer, but our country's rising tragedian, J. Wilkes Booth, opened in Montgomery, Alabama, in his father's consecrated part of Richard III." [9] The date was Monday, October 29, 1860, and the play was not *Richard III* but *The Apostate*.

Success in such well-known title rôles made him feel he was on his way to fame and fortune. A magnetic personality had given him an entrée into the social life around him, and his physical perfections had reaped a harvest of hearts. His slender form, youthful but manly face, and the grace of his movements occasioned the remark that no photograph ever did him justice. His skill in certain sports, especially fencing, also made him extremely popular.

Wilkes' income increased and his independence began to assert itself in elegant attire. He wore a silk hat, kid gloves of the finest material, expensive and well-selected linen, and boots of superior quality. Fluttering females showered him with compliments and presents. They wrote passionate letters to him imploring his attention. One of his Virginia sweethearts gave him her beautiful light brown locks which had been cut from her head during an illness of typhoid fever. After her death Wilkes had the hair converted into a wig, which he carried about the country in a trunk containing a *Hamlet* skull and other theatrical paraphernalia.

The South became so defiant during the winter of 1860-1861 that no opinions other than those favoring her cause were permitted to be expressed within her borders. Following Lincoln's election to the presidency, advertisements appeared in southern publications offering property for sale "before the country goes to the dogs." With war looming before them, theatricals began to wane, and Wilkes went north. It was about this time that he joined the Baltimore order of a rebel secret society known as The Knights of the Golden Circle. In December he visited his mother and sister Rosalie in Philadelphia, where they were boarding with a family on Marshall Street. Canning's bullet was still in him and the wound had not entirely healed.

From his mother Wilkes heard more of Edwin's earnings and by February, 1861, he had invaded his brother's territory in the north. According to the New York *Clipper*, Richard III was a Booth again:

> During Mr. Wilkes Booth's engagement in Rochester, he appeared as Richard III, and, during the combat between Richard and Richmond (Mr. Miles), the latter was severely injured by the breaking of Richard's sword, the point of which struck Mr. Miles just above the eye, inflicting quite a wound.

Traveling under the star system, Wilkes appeared only in the cities large enough to support a stock company. He began his northern tour and indulged his desire for notoriety by quoting slave-state slogans among his companions. But the words he used were not his own; they were repetitions of sentiments he had heard in a land of potential rebellion. It was the effect on his listeners that fascinated Wilkes. George Wren, an actor, had known him in Richmond, and while stage manager for Laura Keene in New York, met Wilkes, who was then going about blindly working himself into a fever-heat against the "damn Yankees." Thus Wilkes continued his part in a great national drama, a part that he understood as little as he had his early rôles on the stage.

However, there were newspapers in the North proclaiming views similar to Wilkes' parrot talk, and prominent persons who insisted that the Federal Government had no right to compel the South to do its bidding. At the beginning of the year it had been proposed that Manhattan Island, Long Island, and Staten Island secede from the Union and form a combination to be called Tri-Insula. This attitude of northern renegades encouraged Wilkes in the belief that men coming into power were unscrupulous tyrants if they used armed force against the South to impose their convictions upon them.

Wilkes' first performance in Albany, New York, was at the Green Street Gayety Theatre, where he starred as Romeo to Annie Waite's Juliet. Here he also was proclaimed the handsomest actor on the American stage. The next evening he appeared as Pescara, in *The Apostate*, and had the misfortune to fall on his dagger, inflicting a serious wound in his right axilla which forced him to suspend engagements for several evenings. With nothing to do, he went about declaring himself a staunch Secessionist and at Stanwix Hall, where he was stopping, tactlessly expressed opinions antagonistic to public feeling. This compelled the management of the theatre to send its treasurer, Mr. Cuyler, to caution the new star against further denouncements and to warn him that, unless he desisted, he would not only endanger his engagement but also his person.

"Is not this a democratic city?" exclaimed Wilkes.

"Democratic, yes; but disunion, no!" replied Cuyler.

The rebuke silenced Wilkes for a time but his sentiments only grew stronger with each suppression.[10]

On the date of Wilkes' Albany début, Abraham Lincoln left Springfield, bound for Washington to assume his duties as President of the United States. His journey eastward was to have been without ballyhoo as a matter of precaution against threats he had received. However, when he reached Albany on February eighteenth a roar of artillery greeted him, troops lined the streets, and crowds of excited citizens fought for a glimpse of the tall, gaunt figure from the midwestern prairies. That day Wilkes first gazed upon the man who was to become the object of his smoldering hatred.

The same evening Wilkes resumed his engagement at the Gayety Theatre and romped through another performance of *The Apostate* with his right arm bandged and tied to his side. A witness of the performance reported that he fenced like a demon with his left arm, as if enraged by something other than a wound, and it is permissible to presume that the reception accorded Lincoln was responsible for his exasperation. Those who knew Wilkes said he was growing more morose and sullen each time they met him and that from a genial gentleman he had changed into a sour cynic.

At eight o'clock that evening, Lincoln and his suite left Albany. In reference to him the *Atlas and Argus* had this to say: "The President-Elect—While Mr. Lincoln carefully preserved silence during the electoral campaign, and long afterwards, the public accorded him the credit of withholding something too precious to be wasted! . . . but lo! the wine is out, the cord severed and the cork released, and instead of sparkling champagne that bubbled over, there is a frothy rush of root beer—yeasty foam, inspired flatulence, slops and dregs."

As Lincoln's train moved on toward the Capital, Wilkes continued his Albany engagement and played his benefit performance in *Richard III* on Washington's birthday. The comment on his appearances in the above newspaper was much more complimentary than that which had been given to Lincoln: "Booth, the tragedian—Gayety—The young gentleman has succeeded admirably in gaining many warm admirers in this city, all of whom he never fails to delight with his masterly impersonations. Mr. Booth is full of genius, and this with his fine face and figure, and his artistic conceptions of the characters he performs, will always render him a favorite." He closed his engagement in *The Robbers* on the following night. Many thought Wilkes the best actor they had seen in Albany and ranked him above his father in several parts. As Wilkes had no agent with him in that city, press opinions were unbiased.[11]

The opening bill on his return to Albany in April, 1861, was a double attraction: "Mr. Wilkes Booth, and Signor Canito, the Man-Monkey," which proved to be his last appearance there. On the day of his arrival Union flags draped doorways and windows in protest to the firing on Fort Sumter. This display brought on a tirade of invectives from Wilkes, and he boldly proclaimed his admiration for the rebels, designating their deed the most heroic of modern times. His denunciations so enraged some of the residents that they threatened him with violence.

There were members of the theatrical profession in the East who said Wilkes should not be allowed to go at large so long as he continued treasonable utterances, but many of his friends defended him as a tragedian of superior ability, originality, and promise, and denied ever hearing him denounce the North when he was not in his cups. The admiration he boasted for Brutus and Charlotte Corday seemed to them no more than a pretended infatuation for these assassins, and they paid little or no attention to it. In fact, those who knew Wilkes intimately never regarded his remarks as sincere, nor indicative of any deep feeling, in matters concerning the war which was now inevitable.

The excuse that a promise to his mother prevented him from enlisting in the Confederate service may have been partially true, but usually Wilkes did as he wished, regardless of others. Edwin once remarked that his younger brother's theatrical career suffered because Wilkes did not like to be corrected, and probably this aversion to discipline kept him from entering the ranks as a private. Wilkes was looking for a short cut to fame, and his restless ambition had little time to pause along the way. When war broke out Wilkes' stock days were over; he was a star, and he was determined to remain a star until the end.

That end might have come at several different periods in his life but Wilkes was destined to play a part in the drama of the Civil War, and at the final curtain hold the stage alone. At that moment, in his mad estimation, he had reached his pinnacle as a star. Canning's bullet was not the only missile which could have disposed of him and kept the name of Booth from the pages of history. Back of the footlights Wilkes was often so rash with his sword that he severely injured himself, or missed his cues and frequently suffered at the point of his opponent's blade. Of all these, the one that nearly proved fatal occurred offstage at the close of his last engagement in Albany.

On April twenty-sixth, the date that eventually marked his death, an attempt was made on his life by a beautiful young actress, Henrietta Irving. She was madly in love with Wilkes, and it is not improbable that he had promised to marry her. During a drinking orgy in his room at Stanwix Hall she accused him of having won her favors under false pretentions, and in a jealous rage slashed him across the face as he threw up his arm to ward off the blow that would have pierced his heart. He barely missed an injury which might have marred his classic features and been equal in disfigurement to his father's broken nose. Henrietta believed she had killed Wilkes and rushed to her own room where she stabbed herself, but the wound was not serious and she survived. That night Wilkes packed his bags and hurriedly left the city. Not long after, he arrived in Baltimore.

During the month there had been a riot in that city when hundreds of southern sympathizers endeavored to prevent a Massachusetts regiment from passing through its streets on the way to join Union forces at Washington. The people of Maryland were so divided in their attitudes toward slavery, secession, and the Civil War, that no one knew what moment the state might suddenly declare itself for the Confederacy and devote all its energies to her cause. To prevent the possibility of its being won over by the rebels, General Benjamin F. Butler moved loyal Union troops to Federal Hill and built forts which would protect Baltimore from invasion by the southern army. But within the city itself, many rebels were still active. One of these, named Hazlett, enlisted men for Confederate service, paying each ten dollars in gold at Baltimore, and guaranteeing ninety dollars more of the same specie upon arrival at Charleston, South Carolina. All this excited the imagination of young Wilkes, who was now sharing a room with an actor friend, William A. Howell, at Brown's boarding house on High Street.

Wilkes proposed that they round up a company of volunteers and march them on to Richmond. Howell, as his lieutenant, was to remain in Baltimore and look after matters; Wilkes to ride out to Harford County and canvass the vicinity for recruits. Word of their intentions was forwarded to Confederate headquarters, but, while they awaited instructions, Union troops seized seditious agents and cut off all communications with the South. The action by the Federal Government halted Wilkes' efforts to attain military glory and sent him back to the theatre.

Joseph's appearances on the professional stage were few. One who had seen him play Orson, in *The Iron Chest*, with Edwin at the Baltimore Front Street Theatre, said, "Joe will never make an actor." Joe agreed with this and decided to be a doctor.

At the beginning of hostilities between the North and South, he was attending a medical college in Charleston. There he joined one of the Confederate staffs as a physician and served with the rebels attacking Fort Sumter. Immediately after the combat, he returned to Baltimore and occupied a room at Barnum's Hotel. This was just previous to Wilkes' visit in the city. On the street one day, Joe met Howell, whom he had known for some time. He showed an unwillingness to converse with Howell there for fear of being recognized by others and suggested that they go to his room at the hotel. Howell knew him to be a quiet, dreamy, indolent fellow full of romantic ideas, who was always hoping that something extraordinary would occur for his special benefit. But he could not account for his strange actions except that recent events had made everyone in Baltimore a bit nervous as to what might happen from hour to hour.

When they arrived at Barnum's, Joe locked the door, looked about the room to make certain they were alone, and confessed his recent service in the Confederate army. He opened a trunk, and, taking out a collection of skulls, bones, and exploded shells, gave a wild account of how he had obtained them.

Howell realized Joe was unnecessarily upset and tried to allay his fears of being discovered and arrested for the services he had rendered the Secessionists. Joe became more composed after Howell pointed out that many Baltimoreans, more actively helpful to the rebel cause, had not fallen into the clutches of General Butler.

Family references to this youngest son over the long period of the Civil War are extremely scarce. Reports that he made a voyage to Australia fail to disclose any purpose for the trip. It is known that for some time he was employed by Wells Fargo Company in San Francisco. One thing is certain: Joe did not long remain in Baltimore, but went to visit his mother and sister Rosalie in Philadelphia, where Federal authorities were not so diligent.

Like so many households, the Booths were divided in their sympathies between the North and South. Junius and Edwin were unswerving in their devotion to the Union, Wilkes to the Confederacy. Their brother and sisters wavered from one side to the other, but the mother remained neutral in her effort to keep peace among them. The ambitions of both Junius and Edwin were in the theatre. They hated war and had no intentions of delaying their own interests by joining in this civil strife. Throughout the greater portion of it, Junius remained in the West.[12] Shortly after guns began to boom in the East, Edwin and Mary sailed away to England.

On September 30, 1861, Edwin began his first London engagement at the Haymarket Theatre Royal, under the management of J. B. Buckstone. There he played on alternate nights which were filled in by the inimitable comedian, Charles Mathews. The Haymarket was an old theatre, having opened in July, 1821. It was a handsome building of stone and brick with a portico in the Corinthian style and a spacious interior decorated with gold ornaments and crimson curtains. Edmund Kean, the Kembles, and other great stars had appeared there in its prime.

A popular actor, C. A. Fechter, was storming the boards at the Princess Theatre Royal in *Hamlet,* and so Edwin wished to make his début in *Richelieu.* Buckstone, however, insisted that he open in the character of Shylock, which was not one of his best parts and placed him at a disadvantage in a theatre that had lost its prestige with audiences preferring the classics. Added to this was the growing hostility of the King's subjects toward Yankees, which the press supported by its encouragement and justification of the secession movement.

Critics were caustic and patronage was meager. "Mr. Edwin Booth is the son of Mr. Junius Brutus Booth, who some forty years ago measured his strength with Kean and lacked not admirers to pronounce him, in many parts, a successful rival," reported the London *Era.* "With a remembrance of the characteristics of the father, it was natural to expect that the fiery and impulsive school of acting was again to be represented on the stage, and most probably it was from a nervous feeling of anxiety on these grounds that Mr. Edwin Booth repressed rather than revealed his energies on the opening night, for fear of being considered a mere imitator of his father and a servile follower of old traditions."

Reviews of his second appearance were more favorable; yet there was no rush to the box office. For his fourth night, Edwin played Sir Giles Overreach, but again the public would not concede that a potential genius had arrived in their midst. The third week, he repeated these bills and from other notices it seems spectators were not so prejudiced as critics, probably because of the number of Americans among them. Their interest was sufficient to carry Edwin on to *Richard III* after a week's intermission, during which time he and Mary had strolled about London wishing they were back in the United States.

Another sharp and rather misinformed attack from the *Era* failed to discourage Edwin. In comparing him once more to the elder Booth the dramatic critic pointed out that since the American actor had been too young at the time of his father's death to remember the great tragedian's mode of rendition, Edwin was handicapped from the start! His ability was spoken of with considerable reservation, but his attempt to veer away from bombast and to create a style of his own was still unrecognized and unappreciated. After such reviews Buckstone relented and *Richelieu* went on.

When the curtain rose, men had gathered to mock the performance, but Edwin's fine acting of the crafty old cardinal aroused the audience to the wildest cheers and made any adverse demonstration impossible. The "decided advance on his previous personations . . ." acknowledged one critic, "was not merely distinguished by the judgment and intelligence that we have had to recognize in other parts, but by a vigor in delivery that won for him frequent and well merited plaudits. There might have been a little more dignity in some portions, and a little more keenness of sarcasm in others; but, on the whole, it was an excellent conception of the part, well wrought out.

"The energetic manner in which he threatened the King's emissaries with the vengeance of the church, should they invade the circle of its protection, and his reply to the taunt of his enemy, Baradas, produced an impressive effect, and obtained for him a warm recall at the end of the Fourth Act . . . and the summons before the curtain at the end of the Play was a fair tribute to his merits."

With money coming in a little faster, Buckstone realized his mistake in not permitting his star to open in Bulwer-Lytton's papal play, but it was too late, as Edwin was booked elsewhere. He took a benefit and journeyed to Manchester and Liverpool, leaving Mary in London expecting the birth of their first child. During his engagement in Manchester he played various title rôles and among the cast was Henry Irving whose fame was not yet in the ascendancy.

Edwin found these industrial towns as belligerent toward Americans as London and made no effort to extend his performances beyond that month. This was fortunate, as the Trent Affair strained the tension between England and the United States almost to the breaking point.

That his first child was to be born in a foreign land displeased Edwin. "I worried over it to myself," he said in later years, "and all at once I had it! I saw my way to outwit that imp called Fate. I had Old Glory draped over my wife's bed. Under her country's flag she lay, and our child was, literally, born under the Stars and Stripes." [13] They named this daughter, born at Fulham, December 9, 1861, Edwina.

While in England, Edwin attended the funeral of his grandmother Holmes. The following spring he took his family to France, and in Paris he was presented with the sword worn by Frédéric Lemaître, in *Ruy Blas*. Here Edwin secured the services of a Mlle. Forrnier to attend the young mother and child during the return voyage on the steamer *Great Eastern* which docked in New York, August 28, 1862.

In boldface type newspapers blazoned the accounts of terrific fighting between the Confederate and Union forces at Manassas, Virginia. Edwin rubbed his eyes and read of daring exploits by men under Lee, Longstreet, Stonewall Jackson, Pope, Porter, and their subordinates. But as time went on and the war continued he kept his activities within the theatre. Guns and bayonets were not for him.

CHAPTER II

Ever since Edwin had set sail for England, the drums of war had been beating throughout the North and South. State after state had seceded from the Union. Maryland, standing on the brink of the battle, wavered and vacillated but did not join the Confederacy. The battles of Rich Mountain, Bull Run, and Wilson Creek, had inflamed and intensified emotions already kindled. Civilians on every hand were leaving plantations or factories to join in the bloody struggle.

Yet Wilkes, with all his southern sympathies, remained in the North. He had a new purpose in view, and temporarily restrained his political ideas so that he might win a more personal victory for himself on the stage. He was out to capture the Booth laurels in Edwin's absence, and for the first time he made every effort to fit himself more carefully for his career. His efforts were rewarded, since it was generally granted that he had only to control the fierceness of the inherited fire in his blood to achieve greatness as an actor.

He opened in St. Louis at the beginning of the New Year 1862, with *Richard III*, and was acclaimed an artist of the highest order. After two weeks of appearances, the Missouri *Republican* gave him credit for his admirable performances and the large audiences he attracted.

The manager of this St. Louis Theatre was Ben De Bar, the brother of Junius' former wife, Clementine. Ben was a British subject who had lived in St. Louis since 1839 and had no intention of becoming a citizen of the United States. He was a sympathizer with the rebellion, and "at the outbreak of the war was several times admonished by provost marshals for pandering to rebel tastes on the stage of his theatre," but later, "to protect his pecuniary interests, modified his demonstrations." [14] When the shadow of the provost marshal fell over him again in 1865, he also minimized his relations with the Booths of Maryland in giving an account of his association with them.

From St. Louis, Wilkes went on to his Chicago début at McVicker's Theatre, where his performances were reported as the most brilliant ever played in the city. His first Baltimore appearance in a title rôle was as Richard III at the Holliday Street Theatre, February seventeenth (1862), under the spectacular billing I AM MYSELF ALONE. He was acknowledged the youthful and gifted tragedian whose brief career within the past few months had been one of matchless success. In this city of his boyhood days, he was applauded as the rival of Edwin, and there were persons who thought him somewhat superior. A Grand Boothenian Festival tendered by the young men of Baltimore was given him as a complimentary benefit on the evening preceding his final appearance.

Mary Provost, who had been unable to interest New York managers in starring her, took over the Wallack Theatre there and put on her own productions until forced to retire because of illness. As older houses were commanding the support of established reputations, it was necessary after her departure for the management to offer engagements to actors of rising fame who had not yet been given a metropolitan hearing. Wilkes was one of these, and believing he might be good box office, they made him an offer. He accepted and lost no time in moving into an empty dressing room of the theatre. This engagement of three weeks, and a single performance of *Julius Caesar* in November, 1864, marked his only appearances in New York.

Wilkes captivated the entire company when he appeared at rehearsal for *Richard III* on March seventeenth. After being introduced, he began directing them in a sharp, jerky manner, suggesting new business which stimulated the interest of all concerned. He told members of the company not to be surprised or frightened if he threw a little more fire into his evening's performance and warned E. L. Tilton, a powerful man over six feet in height, to be fully prepared to defend himself in the rôle of Richmond. Tilton, who was an excellent swordsman, thought himself capable of taking care of Wilkes. Whether he fell into the orchestra pit or was knocked off the stage has been a controversial subject, but Tilton said he believed his shoulder was dislocated by the blow from "Richard's" sword. Reviews spoke well of Wilkes' efforts and called attention to the striking resemblance between him and his brother Edwin.

The position Maryland had taken in the war led to a dispute backstage at a rehearsal of *The Robbers*. Some of the cast contended that the Federal Government had forced the state to remain in the Union, others argued that Maryland had expressed the wishes of the majority by not seceding. Wilkes paid little attention until a newspaper account was read of the arrest of a Baltimore police marshal, George P. Kane, and of Stanton's order for his confinement in Fort McHenry. An uproar followed in which the War Secretary's act was approved by certain members of the company and denounced by others. One declared Baltimore to be a hotbed of rebels and said it should be wiped from the earth; another contended Stanton ought to be put out of the way with a pistol.

After this last remark Wilkes flew into a rage and cried, "Yes, sir, you are right! I know George Kane well; he is my friend, and the man who could drag him from the bosom of his family for no crime whatever, but a mere suspicion that he may commit one some time, deserves a dog's death!" For a moment after hurling his words into the air, Wilkes stood transfixed, then, in a sharp, ringing voice, ordered them to go on with the rehearsal. The name of Lincoln was not mentioned nor was the discussion continued. They all felt as though the stage had been struck by lightning.

From New York, Wilkes went on to Boston, where one of the most constructive criticisms he received during his theatrical career was published by the *Daily Advertiser*, a week after his début on May twelfth. The portion which should have warned Wilkes that he was striding toward an abyss read:

> With a view to observing if Mr. Wilkes Booth were winning for himself his father's triumphs, or if he were likely so to do, we have taken pains to see him in each of the characters which he assumed during the last week, Richard III, Romeo, Charles De Moor, and Hamlet. We have been greatly pleased, and greatly disappointed. . . .
>
> In what does he fail? Principally, in knowledge of himself—of his resources, how to husband and how to use them. He is, apparently, entirely ignorant of the main principles of elocution. We do not mean by this word merely enunciation, but the nature and proper treatment of the voice, as well. *He ignores the fundamental principle of all vocal study and exercise*—that the chest, and not the throat or mouth, should supply the sound necessary for singing or speaking. . . . When Mr. Booth wishes to be forcible or impressive, he produces a mongrel sound in the back of the mouth or top of the throat, which by itself would be unintelligible and without effect; by a proper use of his vocal organs he might draw from that fine trunk of his a resonant, deep tone whose mere sound in the ear of one who knew not the language should give a hint of the emotion to be thereby conveyed. In this connection we need simply say that his proclivity to a nasal quality is most apparent, and bodes great harm to his delivery if not checked at once. . . .

Had Wilkes heeded this advice, the story of the Mad Booths of Maryland might have been less tragic.

In the Midwest Wilkes rivaled such firmly established actors as James Murdock and added to his popularity by appearing in some light comedies which revealed the variety of his talent. That he also shared the financial burdens of the family during this successful period is shown by this extract from one of his letters:

> I wrote Joyce the other day, telling him I would either send him the money now, or pay him when in Boston. I prefer the latter, as I do not fancy sending money by express. I have now been waiting (with all the patience in the world) for over two weeks to hear of $800 I sent to my mother. My goose does indeed hang high (long may she wave). I have picked up on an average this season over $650 per week....[15]

These achievements during the year that Edwin was in England were now in danger of being diminished by his return, and Wilkes redoubled his efforts to retain them. Though unsuccessful, Edwin's London début had given him a certain prestige in New York. There he made his reappearance as Hamlet at the Winter Garden, September 29, 1862, under the management of T. B. Jackson. In the cast on his opening night were some of his old California friends: Alexina Fisher Baker, Lewis Baker, and George Ryer. Critics praised him conditionally, yet this engagement marked the beginning of his gradual rise to unrivaled fame in America. Thereafter, he appeared only in productions of established merit.

Forrest was playing at Niblo's Garden and again challenged Edwin by treading on his heels in similar parts. When they reached the romantic characters, their emulations were comical. Forrest was too old and Edwin not adept in such rôles. E. A. Sothern once remarked to Edwin: "The worst performance ever seen was my Claude Melnotte," to which Edwin replied, "The worst? Did you ever see my Romeo?"

During the early winter months, Edwin and Mary attended many gatherings at the homes of intimate friends. The social cup was much in evidence and Edwin slipped back into his weakness for liquor. Mary had not entirely regained her health and began to worry. At the end of his engagement in November, Edwin, upon the advice of their physician, took her to the quieter surroundings of Dorchester, Massachusetts, where they occupied a comfortable home.

His engagement of four weeks at the Boston Theatre, beginning November twenty-fourth, was enviously watched by Forrest who followed him there. Reviews had flattered Edwin more than they did Forrest, who at the end of two weeks went on, disgruntled, to Philadelphia. In the Midwest, Wilkes scanned criticisms of them while eagerly awaiting his invasion of their territory. His greed for fame made him feel that by a swift decisive blow, he could capture all the laurels they had won. Soon he was on his way for appearances at the Boston Museum.

Had misfortune not overtaken Edwin at this time, it is probable that the efforts of these three actors for supremacy on the stage would have resulted in a battle royal. The direction he was taking, however, would have been disastrous under any circumstances. An attempt to relieve the strain of these engagements led him to a point where his craze for drink again became uncontrollable.

Wilkes arrived and opened at the Boston Museum, January 17, 1863. Edwin remained in Dorchester and Wilkes' visits to his home were not marred by unpleasant controversies about the war. Wilkes was still intent on his career in the theatre. On the twenty-first he appeared as Pescara, in *The Apostate*, and for the first time Edwin, as one of a large audience, saw his fiery young brother give a performance that was wildly cheered. It was obvious that he was following in the trend of Forrest and, like him, still had no conception of Edwin's determination to moderate the old bombastic style of acting, yet Edwin thought Wilkes full of promise. Edwin had won by presenting a classical repertoire, Forrest and Wilkes successively vied with melodramatic rôles. Each had followed the other and received his share of applause. Edwin had drawn from a select group, Wilkes more from the daily rabble, and Forrest from both. Encouraged by notices, and attendance at his performances, Wilkes decided to pursue Forrest to Philadelphia. The opportunity to compete with this great American tragedian submerged his painful memories of his earlier disagreeable reception there and he made arrangements for an engagement at the Arch Street Theatre, the scene of his former failures.

Edwin returned to New York, leaving Mary at their Dorchester home, and began another series of performances at the Winter Garden, once more opening in *Hamlet* on February ninth. Mary saw reviews of his acting and needed no one to tell her that he was staggering on and off the stage at every performance. She wrote to their New York friends to look after him, as she was too ill to get there. Richard Henry Stoddard, the poet, and others tried to rescue him from the cup, but were unsuccessful. Sculptor Launt Thompson, who could imbibe more liquor at a sitting than Edwin could drink in a week, was one of these.

At the close of his Boston engagement that month, Wilkes left for his rivalry with Forrest in Philadelphia. On his way there he stopped over in New York and told Edwin that Mary had a severe cold from which she seemed to be recovering. He was unaware that it had now developed into pneumonia.

On February twentieth, Edwin was playing *Richard III*, and the empty bottles in his dressing room outnumbered those which had not yet been drained. Several unopened telegrams lay on his table. As each one was delivered, he tossed it aside, took another drink and returned to the stage, too drunk to hear the loud comments in the audience. When a telegram came to the manager of the theatre asking why Edwin had not answered the previous messages, the drunken actor was shaken out of his stupor and made to listen while the last one was read to him. It requested that he return home at once—Mary was dying.

He drank quantities of black coffee, but by the time he was sober, the midnight train to Boston had gone, and he was informed there would be no other until eight o'clock the next morning. He arrived at Mary's bedside too late. She had died at the hour he was leaving New York.[16]

Wilkes had not yet begun his Philadelphia engagement, and with John Sleeper Clarke returned to Boston where they found Mary Ann Booth. Asia's unrelenting nature kept her from rushing to her grief-stricken brother or attending the funeral. She ignored her last chance to show some respect for the woman who had been so helpful and devoted to him. Mary's death did not end the estrangement between Edwin and Asia until autumn, when he visited her in Philadelphia and extended the forgiving hand. Only recently was their feud revealed by the discovery of unpublished family letters.[17]

From this time on he was less intimate with many of his former friends (Stoddard and his wife among them), probably because he had reason to believe they were responsible for reports that he had neglected Mary. After his wife's burial in Mount Auburn Cemetery, Cambridge, Edwin's mother stayed with him until he gave up the Dorchester house and bought a home at 28 East Nineteenth Street in New York, where she and Rosalie watched over him during his temporary retirement from the stage. "Do you think it is possible for me to recite some passages in a play without a something in my heart and throat?" he wrote to Adam Badeau. "God help me! Madness would be a relief to me, and I have often thought I stood very near the brink of it. . . ."

Edwin was right. Melancholia pursued him throughout his life. But never, after Mary's death, did liquor gain so great a grip on him.

Wilkes' return to Boston for Mary's funeral delayed his appearance at the Philadelphia Arch Street Theatre for a week. His opening on March second forced Forrest, at the Chestnut Street Theatre, to cope directly with a Booth whom he considered of less promise than the one he had encountered before in New York. The hearty applause now showered upon Wilkes atoned for the former hissing in this city and gave him courage, on his last benefit night, to defy Forrest's popularity by announcing the same bill of *Macbeth*. Forrest ignored him, but knew where part of his audience had gone. He had no desire to see any of the younger Booths approaching the throne upon which he sat, and Wilkes was his pet aversion.

The aspiring young actor fought the roaring bull on his own ground and left him staggering in the arena. Audiences preferred the handsome and fiery Wilkes to the aging and rigid Forrest. Thereafter any mention of the Booths sent him into one of his swearing tantrums which gave him an illusion of victory.

Heralded by announcements such as the following in the Washington *Evening Star*, Wilkes continued his theatrical triumphs, opening in the Capital city with *Richard III*:

> Grover's Theatre
> Saturday Evening, April 11, 1863
> J. Wilkes Booth
> The Pride of the American People
> The Youngest Tragedian in the World
> who is entitled to be denominated
> **A STAR OF THE FIRST MAGNITUDE**
> Son of the great
> Junius Brutus Booth
> and brother and artistic rival of
> Edwin Booth
> Who is engaged to commence this evening
> and who will remain
> **ONLY SEVEN NIGHTS**

The same issue told of Lincoln's return to the White House the previous midnight from a visit to the Army of the Potomac. So, for the second time the two names had been linked together in the news of the day. Such coincidences were now to be mere repetitions.

Washington, encircled by forts, continued to seethe with activity. Day and night one heard the rattle of army wagons, the clatter of horses' hoofs, the tramp of marching feet over deeply rutted streets often filled with mud or obscured by dust. Temporary structures served as hospitals which overflowed with wounded. After a great

Ford's Theatre, site of Lincoln's assassination. *(Courtesy National Park Service)*

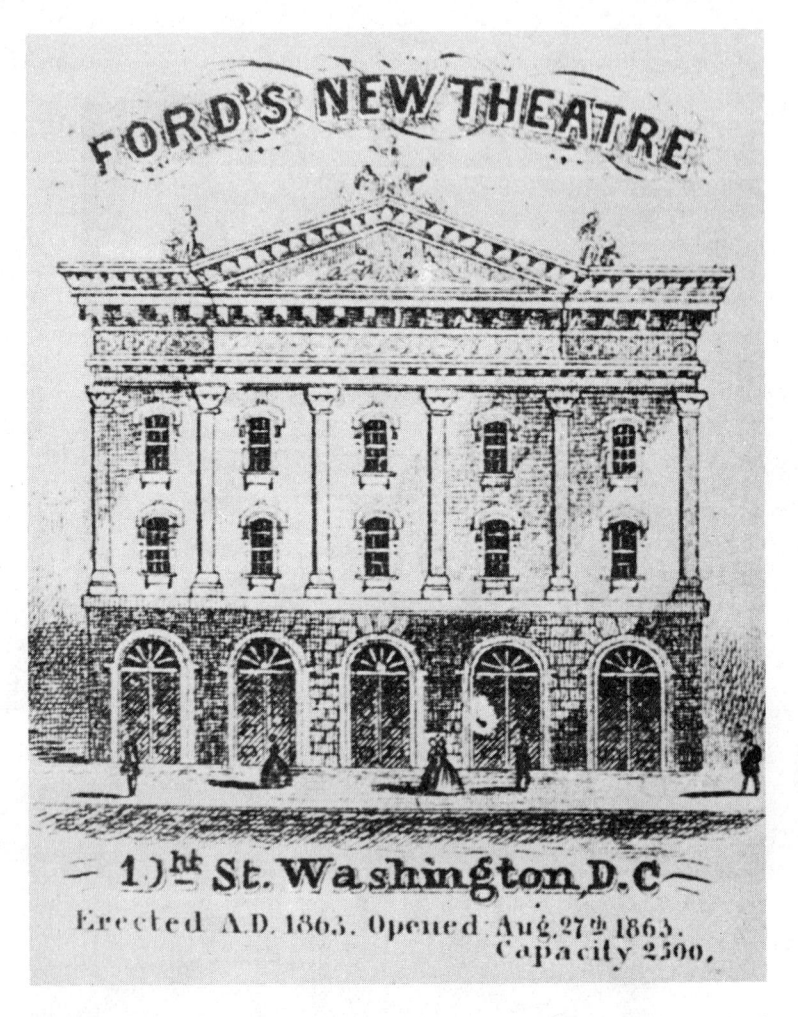

Ford's poster advertising his new theatre. *(Courtesy National Park Service)*

Original painting of John Wilkes Booth in the possession of the author.

John Thompson Ford, owner of Ford's Theatre. (From 'Dictionary of American Portraits,' Dover)

David E. Herold, Wilkes' accomplice. (Courtesy Library of Congress)

battle, the city suddenly became crowded with civilians in search of friends or relatives. They peered into ambulances and hunted in sheds lined with dead, seeking information of them.

The injured and maimed straggled along, stopping to rest in doorways, on the steps of government buildings or against hitching posts. Prisoners were brought in and transferred to near-by camps and the outlying districts.

Federal officers in their blue and gold, sentries, privates, government employees, war profiteers, women in mourning, and old men, made up the curious and moving pageant. Occasionally a paroled Confederate officer in his gray uniform enraged a group of Northerners by his insolent stride and became the target of mud or pebbles thrown by urchins. Everyone discussed the latest reports—news of the naval battle in Charleston harbor, rumors that Lee had routed Hooker's army, the attitude of foreign nations toward the belligerents. Any slight remark favoring the rebel cause was sure to provoke someone on the street into accusing the speaker of being a Copperhead. These were the days when Walt Whitman, in his big hat and open collar, sauntered about handing out gifts to cheer disabled soldiers.

In so crowded a city the stage supplied the most popular form of relaxation and, on Tenth Street, John T. Ford was rushing the completion of his new theatre on the site of the one destroyed by fire the previous December. It was to be the most elegant in the Capital, a massive and enduring structure of red brick with an ornamental interior that would seat about twenty-five hundred. The best acoustic properties were to be combined with a stage mechanically outfitted to present the finest and most spectacular productions. There John Wilkes Booth was to give his last performance—there, less than a month later, he was to assassinate the President, Abraham Lincoln.

A review of Wilkes' *Richard III* at Grover's Theatre in April of 1863, said that he had been flatteringly received and predicted he would be a reigning favorite in Washington. Lincoln was attracted by Wilkes' popularity and at Ford's Theatre, November 9, 1863, he saw him in a performance of *The Marble Heart*.[18]

It was twice presented during Wilkes' engagement, and on one of these nights he happened to meet a David E. Herold. This slender youth with small, weak eyes and a stolid face bearing an immature growth of hair, was foolhardy and undependable, with a mentality half his age. His access to lethal compounds, as an apothecary's clerk in Thompson's drugstore, that supplied the White House, was said to have been responsible for his name being linked with a scheme to poison Lincoln, but it is probable he put nothing other than an overdose of cathartic in prescriptions sent to the executive mansion.[19] He was seldom employed steadily, for he forgot jobs in his pursuit of partridge shooting and in his childish interest in brass bands. One of these he once followed down into lower Maryland where he joined in a serenade to a Mrs. Mary Surratt of rebel alliance. To be associated with the popular J. Wilkes Booth, flattered Herold, and he trailed him whenever possible.

He went along with him to Dr. Frederick May for the diagnosis of a distressing irritation on the back of Wilkes' neck. The doctor found a large fibroid tumor somewhat to the left side. Wilkes asked if the removal of it would prevent him from fulfilling his engagement. "I told him, if he would be careful not to make any violent efforts, it would not," related Dr. May. "He then agreed to have the operation performed. I took the tumor out and united the wound very closely. . . . Booth played his engagement and came regularly to my office for some two weeks afterwards to have the wound dressed. He came some four or five days after the wound had united, with it all torn open, stating that in some part of the play, in which he said Miss Cushman (who he remarked was a strong, powerful woman) bore a part, she had either to throw her arms around his neck or to strike him—perhaps to strike him a blow—and that she struck him on the tender cicatrix, tearing it completely open, and made a gaping wound which had to fill up by the process of granulation." [20]

Years later, Dr. May read his article *The Mark of the Scalpel*, before the Columbia Historical Society in which he disclosed that Wilkes had asked him to answer all inquiries regarding the operation by replying that it had been for the removal of a bullet, but he would not promise to do so, as he had found nothing to verify such a contention. Why Wilkes made this request, or what became of the bullet left in his body after Canning accidentally shot him, was never known.

Apparently Wilkes thought himself capable of running the whole show, for he took over the Washington Theatre, announced himself as lessee, manager, and star, and began another engagement. The company included many favorites of the Capital. Newspapers gave their efforts favorable notices, but box-office receipts fell off the second week, as a result of the Union defeat at Chancellorsville which cast a spell of gloom over the entire city and lessened the patronage at all public places. Wilkes had not taken into consideration the experience necessary for an undertaking of this kind, and realizing at its close that he had been more fortunate than wise, he made no other attempts to act under so pretentious a billing.

Evidence that he was again assailing the Federal Government reappears about this time and it may be that seeing Lincoln occasionally, during his Washington sojourn, had something to do with his attitude. Edwin's return to the United States might also have irritated him and aggravated his peevishness. At Ben De Bar's theatre in St. Louis, where Wilkes went after his Washington stand, he and T. L. Conner, a member of that stock company, were arrested for utterances against Lincoln's administration. Conner was committed to a military prison, while Wilkes was hailed before Colonel H. L. McConnell and accused of having said he "wished the whole damned government would go to hell." Upon taking the oath of allegiance to the Union, and paying a fine, Wilkes was released. This seems to have had no effect upon his engagement, for reviews invariably stated that he had given a fine performance and been well received by the audience. Ben De Bar, the British subject and violent Secessionist, escaped the attention of Federal officers until after the war, despite the fact that his theatre was a hotbed of rebels.

Wilkes continued to spout invectives against the North, and in Chicago he was said to have remarked: "What a glorious opportunity there is for a man to immortalize himself by killing Lincoln." Frequently he quoted the lines:

> The ambitious youth who fired the Ephesian Dome,
> Outlived in fame the pious fool who reared it—

though when asked to name the youth he could never do so.

He created a furore at the Cleveland Academy of Music, managed by John Ellsler, and justified the expectations of those who were led to expect something more than ordinary from a Booth. On his last night, Clevelanders shouted for more appearances of the rising young star, and before Wilkes departed Ellsler made arrangements with him for a return in the fall.

Concluding this tour, Wilkes visited Edwin in New York and was there in July, when riots broke out in protest to the alternative of answering the military draft, or paying three hundred dollars, which the poor strenuously opposed. Mobs stormed about in the streets, burned buildings, hanged Negroes, and were responsible for many deaths. The police thought they knew how to handle such outbreaks until they tried to suppress this one. Reinforcements were unavailable as most of the loyal citizens had joined the Union army and were in service elsewhere.

Edwin's friend, Adam Badeau, now a Union officer, had been wounded near New Orleans and was convalescing in New York at a relative's home which was in danger of becoming a target for the rioters. Badeau was removed to the house that Edwin was occupying, and Wilkes helped carry him from a carriage to a room on one of the upper floors, where he looked after him until the riots were quelled and he could be taken to the country. Badeau always spoke of Wilkes' kindness and described him as a more handsome man than Edwin, yet not so intellectual or distinguished in appearance.

During this visit to Edwin's home Wilkes refrained from saying anything against the North. His conduct in this respect was not influenced by any consideration for his brother or Badeau but for himself. Edwin regarded Wilkes "as a good-hearted, harmless, though wild-brained boy," and laughed at his "patriotic froth whenever secession was discussed." He thought that no one who knew Wilkes well could doubt that he "was insane on that one point."[21] This attitude on Edwin's part humiliated Wilkes. He was afraid Edwin's efforts to give the impression that he was not serious would make him appear ridiculous, and he withheld such verbal outbursts before others than the family when Edwin was present. Despite Edwin's fondness for Wilkes, the two brothers frequently were at odds, Edwin treating Wilkes as one for whom an apology was due and Wilkes boiling under the impression that he was inferior in Edwin's esteem. Hence, the chasm between them grew wider, and Wilkes rarely visited in Edwin's home when their mother was not living with him.

There was also a sort of impish glee in Edwin's suggestion to Wilkes that each of the three Booth brothers take over a section of the United States as his theatrical territory—Wilkes the South, Edwin the North, and Junius the West. This is a good example of the manner Edwin used to humor Wilkes into doing something he thought best for him. He knew that it would be much to Wilkes' own interests, and safety too, for him to be among people whose political views were in accord with his own and hoped that his younger brother's desire to be the idol of the South would take him in that direction.

Wilkes devoted more time this summer to securing engagements for the coming season. Letters to John Ford, Ben De Bar, and others brought contracts for appearances, which filled his purse with greenbacks and his mind with visions of outrivaling Edwin in theatrical fame.

Edwin's first appearance following the death of his wife was as Hamlet, at the New York Winter Garden, on September twenty-first. The theatre was still under the management of T. B. Jackson, and Lawrence Barrett was a member of the company. Opinion was divided; some of the critics thought Edwin's Hamlet the best they had ever seen, others that he overacted. If he were to become the greatest tragedian in the country, the latter maintained, he must cater to the intellectual and not the gallery portion of his audience. The ability to benefit from such criticism led him to achievements only dreamed of by Wilkes. Bills for this engagement included the first production in the United States of *Ruy Blas*, with Edwin in the title rôle and Barrett as Don Caesar de Bazan.

On his previous visit of reconciliation with Asia in Philadelphia Edwin had discussed with Clarke a joint purchase of the Walnut Street playhouse, which was now effected. This theatre was so successfully managed that within three years it had paid for itself. One evening while playing there, Edwin sat calmly smoking a cigar and remarked: "What a difference between my father and myself there is. My father, waiting for his cue here in this dressing room, could no more smoke this cigar than I could fly. He used to make up at the mirror there, and as he settled the hump on his shoulders, he seemed to put on the character with it. From that moment on he was Richard. He wished to be spoken to by nobody. If I told him anything about the house or ventured to remark about the news of the day he would glare at me like a fiend.

"There are many things that my father did as Richard that I cannot do. I cannot say, 'Off with his head' as he said it. By striking one hand into the other, thus, he would picture to the audience the headsman, the block, and the victim so vividly that everybody shuddered. And yet when I use exactly the same gesture to illustrate the same speech it seems to mean nothing." [22]

From Edwin's home, Wilkes went to Boston and opened at the Howard Athenaeum. So many women flocked to see him that on one occasion he complained because their attendance outnumbered that of the men. His liaisons with actresses, however, kept him from straying into many private homes. In fact Wilkes' amorous affairs with leading ladies were often more successful than his efforts on the stage. Reviews at this time and during a short tour he made with the beautiful Fanny Brown, stated that his performances were marred by hoarseness, but these warnings failed to impress him with their significance.

Wilkes' engagement at Ford's New Washington Theatre in November reached its zenith when he appeared as Romeo, and more than one Juliet thrilled to the passion he professed. The *Daily National Intelligencer* proclaimed it "the most satisfactory of all renderings of that fine character," and H. L. Bateman, who later managed the London

Lyceum, so admired it that he once considered presenting Wilkes to English audiences in the rôle.

A stage balcony and artificial moonlight were unnecessary for this Pied Piper of romantic lines. As his contribution to the parlor entertainment of society women in the Capital and elsewhere he often recited a poem entitled *The Beautiful Snow,* which he compared to "the lost purity of some young girl." No one could equal Wilkes' delivery of it. As he repeated the words, he gazed heavenward, and tears filled his eyes. Before he had finished, all his listeners were weeping. *The Beautiful Snow* was an entrée to every woman's heart and could be relied upon to open any boudoir door. Requested encores brought from his pockets clippings of verse which he read to his audience in the same impassioned manner.

Wilkes returned to fulfill his agreement with Ellsler, and the Cleveland *Leader* predicted he would repeat his sensational performance of a previous visit as Richard III. This was a weak prophecy compared with what really happened:

UNFORTUNATE ACCIDENT
AT THE
ACADEMY OF MUSIC

In the combat scene in the closing act of Richard the Third, which was presented at the Academy of Music last night, Mr. Booth, who was playing Richard, met with a very unfortunate accident. In the course of the combat—a most terrific one—in which Mr. Booth as Richard and Mr. McCollom as Richmond are the combatants, Mr. Booth's sword was broken. He caught it by the blade, intending to fight the scene out, holding it in that manner. But his grasp was necessarily a loose one, and on the next blow from his opponent the sword flew back cutting his forehead severely above the eye. He nevertheless fought the scene out, its effect being greatly heightened by the accident. A doctor was immediately sent for and measures taken for the relief of the wounded man. Mr. Booth's wound is not so severe as to interfere with his engagement, which continues this week.

Ellsler, who had known the elder Booth and was an admirer of Edwin, said Wilkes had "more of the old man's power in one performance than Edwin can show in a year. He has the fire, the dash, the touch of strangeness. . . . Full of impulses just now, like a colt, his heels are in the air nearly as often as his head; but wait a year or two till he gets used to the harness and quiets down a bit, and you will see as great an actor as America can produce." [23]

Wilkes was now trouping over a circuit of theatres that guaranteed him three hundred dollars a week. These engagements enabled him at times to assist in sending medical supplies into the South.[24] He attended to this matter so shrewdly that little is known of such activity. A Nashville critic compared him unfavorably with both the elder Booth and Edwin, saying Wilkes was too violent by half, but his tirade had no ill effect on the box office nor on other critics. One of the latter remarked that although Wilkes insisted Edwin was the Hamlet of the family, Nashvillians thought Shakespeare could scarcely have wished for a better Hamlet than himself.

Wilkes' appearances were again threatened by a return of the bronchial trouble which had been hovering over him for months, and from Wood's Theatre, Cincinnati, he wrote to a friend telling of his recovery and of his departure for New Orleans to play a five weeks' engagement at the St. Charles Theatre under the management of Ben De Bar.[25] The anticipation of a new conquest in the country he hoped to make his own thrilled him. There was no doubt in his mind that the Confederacy eventually would win the war, and he fully intended to live within its boundaries when peace brought back the prosperous days of the theatre. New Orleans would be but the first of many future triumphs in the South. Though the city was in the hands of Federal troops, Wilkes felt that he was on the way to the promised land. At Vicksburg he received a military pass from General Grant which took him through the Union lines.

His idea changed the moment he arrived and saw the number of decorations which had marked the inauguration on March fourth of Michael Hahn, the first governor to be elected on a straight Free State ticket. Lafayette Square and the surrounding streets were still embellished with Union flags and with large replicas of state seals. Inscriptions, too, told Wilkes of the change that had come to New Orleans since David Farragut's Union fleet had captured the city in April, 1862. One read, "The Star of Louisiana as she was in 1860 so stands she now in the bright galaxy of 1864." Others proclaimed her loyalty to the Federal Government and her belief in the Union cause. No, this was not the defiant New Orleans Wilkes had expected to find. The memory of General Ben Butler's iron rule over the city for a year after its surrender held rebels in check more than the presence of General N. P. Banks and the force now under his command in that region. Yet, everywhere Wilkes heard mutterings of Secessionists.

"It is true," wrote one northern correspondent, "that you can walk through the city without being spat upon, scowled at, or hissed; the people are civil, but only from a conviction that, however the war may result elsewhere, their condition is temporarily irremediable, and they must needs make the best of it."

Wilkes' New Orleans début, March 14, 1864, as Richard III, took place in the theatre where his father had given his last performance. Ovations which he received from capacity audiences outrivaled those of other cities. This engagement became one of supreme achievement, fulfilling his ambition as an actor and his desire to be the idol of the southern people.

At the moment of this triumph the dreaded bronchial trouble recurred, causing the *Times*, on the day following his fifth performance to take note of his condition: "It is a matter of regret that he is at present laboring under a severe hoarseness, in consequence of which his efforts have been much less satisfactory to himself than to his friends, but we trust his speedy recovery may enable him to consent to the merit of his endeavors. He has certainly created a furore here, which will continue through his engagement."

Reports of Wilkes' hoarseness now followed at alarmingly close intervals. On March twenty-first the same newspaper stated he had given a vivid impersonation of Gloster, but that his raucous voice kept him from being up to his usual standard. Regarding his Othello the succeeding night, the critic was much pleased, yet regretted that a severe hoarseness marred his articulation. Two days later a review of his Macbeth also expressed concern over the hoarseness which was impeding his obvious talent.

Wilkes played a second benefit performance in *The Merchant of Venice*, Friday, March twenty-fifth, and on the following evening the blow fell. Local newspapers and several national publications chronicled his misfortune. The Sunday edition of the *Times* contained this:

> *Notice*—The management of the St. Charles Theatre regret to inform the public that in consequence of the severe and continued cold under which Mr. Booth has been laboring for several days, and at the suggestion of his medical adviser, he is compelled to take a short respite from his engagement. Due notice will be given of his next appearance.

It was a humorous coincidence that here among rabid Secessionists Wilkes' adversity forced him to discontinue his utterances against Federal control of their city. Monday night, however, he was warmly greeted on his return, but the condition of his voice still affected his performances. On the following Sunday his engagement closed.

The day of reckoning had arrived. Wilkes' "hoarseness" was not due to a bronchial infection resulting from a severe cold but was the reprisal from the lack of early study and training in voice control. He knew his future as a star was doomed. He might continue his engagements at intervals, perhaps play a few benefit bills, but soon the curtain would fall before him for the last time and in the dim light of some empty theatre he would make his final exit. The name of Booth would still dominate the boards, but it would be filled in by Edwin—not John Wilkes.

As he journeyed overland through rebel country, memories of brilliant audiences applauding him confirmed his belief that he was still destined for fame, and he sought some objective to attain it; but his mind could not get away from the theatre; he had been a part of it too long.

CHAPTER III

While Wilkes had been on his way to New Orleans, his brother Edwin had presented some notable plays at Grover's Theatre in Washington. On March second, by special appointment with the President and Mrs. Lincoln, he had appeared there as Hamlet.

It was not only his appreciation of Edwin's acting that accounted for Lincoln's applause. Once near the beginning of the war, young Robert Lincoln was standing on the platform of the Pennsylvania Railroad Station in Jersey City, watching passengers purchase sleeping-car reservations from the conductor. There was some crowding at the entrance when the train began to move, and young Lincoln was pushed against the car so that his legs went down into the narrow space between the train and platform. Someone grabbed him, pulled him up, and set him on his feet again. He turned to thank the man who had rescued him and recognized Edwin Booth. Later, Robert Lincoln told Adam Badeau, who was on Lieutenant General Grant's staff, of the almost fatal accident, saying he was very grateful to Edwin.[26] As soon as Grant heard of it, he wrote a letter to Edwin saying that if ever he could serve him he would be glad to do so, and Edwin cannily replied that when Grant was in Richmond he would like to play for him there.

Edwin's first New York appearance as Bertucchio, the deformed jester in *The Fool's Revenge*, at Niblo's Garden on March twenty-eighth, caused much excitement and was hailed by all the critics for its dramatic power. The play had been adapted by Tom Taylor from Victor Hugo's *Le Roi S'Amuse* and given its initial performance at a London theatre several years before. It was *Rigoletto*—without music.

Edwin had presented it in other cities and now kept it on until the middle of April, then appeared in *The Iron Chest* and *Katherine and Petruchio* on the benefit night for the Sanitary Commission. His sole New York production of *The Marble Heart* followed.

In far-off San Francisco, Junius was tendered a farewell benefit in *Camilla's Husband*, after which he appeared before the audience in a bout with a Professor Clark and fenced with a Colonel Monstery.

Some of the spectators enjoyed it, but others thought Junius showed too much of himself as he jumped about the stage, stripped to the waist. This was the last view they had of him for some time. Shortly before the war, he had met with reverses and Edwin, in appreciation of his early assistance, had aided him with money. A return of prosperity had tempted Junius to invest heavily in California real estate, and now he was facing another slump. Edwin did not think much of his acting, but respected his ability as a manager and offered him employment.

On April twenty-third, accompanied by Marion, he sailed East to help with the management of the New York Winter Garden and Walnut Street Theatre, Philadelphia, in which his younger brother was financially interested. Eleven years after Edwin had secured an engagement with Junius in San Francisco, Junius was under contract to him. The agreement did not restrict Junius in his stage appearances, and occasionally he performed elsewhere. During this time Marion stayed at her Aunt Asia's home in Philadelphia and later attended Notre Dame school there.

At the Winter Garden, Edwin presented *Romeo and Juliet* with Avonia Jones, for the benefit of the Central Park Shakespeare Statue fund, and continued playing there into May. While Junius was journeying eastward, Edwin and Sleeper Clarke took over the lease which had not been renewed by Jackson, and made William Stuart their nominal manager.

Stuart, whose real name was O'Flaherty, had been associated with various New York theatrical ventures for a number of years. Articles which had appeared in the press flaying the aging Forrest and praising the youthful Edwin were said to have been written by him. His extremes in advertising Edwin put Baker in the amateur class for trumping up stars' merits. Posters of the size used by circuses proclaimed the name of Edwin Booth and his attainments in large letters; busts, pictures, pamphlets, with his name on them were seen in all public places; there were long reviews of his productions; and critics acknowledged his Hamlet in glowing terms. Women raved about his handsome dark features and made overtures to him, men of influence in the financial and artistic world sought his friendship.

Edwin's personal triumph was greater than that known by the elder Booth at any time during his career, and his fame was casting a shadow over other members of the family. Junius applauded him, but Wilkes began wondering what he could do to prevent his own total eclipse by this ambitious brother.

Wilkes' appearance at the Boston Museum in May was his last in that city. He was in constant fear that his voice would fail him, and he modified his articulation to avoid a catastrophe such as had occurred in New Orleans. He knew now that he could not continue—much less succeed—under such a handicap. Kate Reignolds, who was a member of the company supporting him, applied the term madman to Wilkes in the account of her life behind the footlights. "It is my earnest belief that if ever there was an irresponsible person, it was this sad-faced, handsome, passionate boy," she declared. "He was as undisciplined on the stage as off. . . . How he threw me about! once even knocked me down, picking me up again with a regret as quick as his dramatic impulse had been vehement. In *Othello*, when with fiery remorse, he rushed to the bed of Desdemona after the murder, I used to gather myself together and hold my breath, lest the bang his scimitar gave when he threw himself at me should force me back to life with a shriek." [27]

It was at his farewell benefit on the twenty-seventh of May (the month in which he and his father had been born) that he took the part of Count Ugolino in the play written by the elder Booth. Perhaps Wilkes gave it in honor of his famous parent, although the program made no mention that it was a memorial performance.

While in Boston, Wilkes went about bitterly denouncing Lincoln. Other actors avoided him, and he was frequently cautioned to be careful in his remarks. He was fortunate that two of the afterpieces played during this engagement, *Turn Him Out* and *Hit Him, He Has No Friends*, were enacted only on the stage.

The Confederates had suffered their greatest defeat at Gettysburg, and Vicksburg had fallen into Federal hands. After bloody Chickamauga, the battles of Chattanooga, Lookout Mountain, and Missionary Ridge had further darkened the hopes of southern generals for a Confederate victory. In March, 1864, Grant had taken chief command of the Union forces and, in May, Sherman had started his triumphant march to the sea while the Battle of the Wilderness raged. Political mud-slinging had indicated another national election. Anti-Lincoln cartoonists were hard at work, and men as prominent as Wendell Phillips were hurling epithets of "imbecile" and "honest incompetent" at the President.

In early June, the Republicans met for a short session of shouting at Baltimore's Front Street Theatre, and on the eighth, renominated Lincoln with an ex-tailor from Tennessee named Andrew Johnson as his running-mate. Under the roof of this building, Edwin had been wildly cheered after speaking the lines:

> You have among you many a purchas'd slave,
> Which, like your asses, and your dogs, and mules,
> You use in abject and in slavish parts,
> Because you bought them.—Shall I say to you,
> Let them be free, marry them to your heirs?
> Why sweat they under burdens? Let their beds
> Be made as soft as yours, and let their palates
> Be season'd with such viands? You will answer,
> The slaves are ours:—So do I answer you.
> The pound of flesh, which I demand of him,
> Is dearly bought; 'tis mine, and I will have it:
> If you deny me, fie upon your law!

At the termination of his Boston engagement Wilkes made use of Edwin's New York home as a convenient stopover while he considered what to do. The hoarseness that had troubled him all through the winter now prohibited professional appearances. In private he rehearsed his lines, but they stuck in his throat. All the will power he summoned could not bring them forth. Again and again he repeated *To be or not to be*—that was as far as he could go. Good God! if he could not speak the part, how could he act it! He saw an audience waiting—he tried again—he heard mumbling beyond the footlights—it grew louder—people were hissing—booing— No! No! he would not give up—*To be or not to be*—the words were lost even to himself—a roar of voices pounded on his brain—the curtain was being lowered—footlights becoming dim—a last effort—a cry in the darkness!

Wilkes' reason returned to torment him. He, one of a family of actors, son of a great tragedian, brother of another, to be forced off the stage by so intangible an enemy as his voice! He could not believe it! What was he to do now? He had always been an actor, he knew no other craft. Where was he to win fame, fortune, immortality if not in the theatre?

He said nothing to anyone of the calamity which had befallen him nor did he discuss his future plans. Although their political views differed widely, Edwin was kind and hospitable toward Wilkes. He hoped that by giving Wilkes a home in which he could come and go freely, he might in some way mitigate the violence of his brother's denunciations against the government. With the realization that his theatrical career was practically over, Wilkes made several trips to the oil regions of Venango County, Pennsylvania, where he had invested a small sum on an earlier visit at the first of the year. Desperately he increased his speculations, splurged in a grand manner and entertained so lavishly that his friends began to think he intended retiring from the stage. But the dreams of gaining power with profits in this new field of endeavor never materialized. After the illusion of the fortune in them had passed, these investments led to many strange events and were the source of fanciful reports regarding his income and the money he was said to have squandered in sensual indulgences.

Ella Turner Starr became a favorite companion after accompanying him on one of his jaunts to Pennsylvania. She was about twenty-one years old and a native of Baltimore. Wilkes and Ella returned to Washington where she lived with her sister, Nellie, whose home on Ohio Avenue was a rendezvous for gentlemen of means seeking pleasure. Another diversion often took Wilkes to the shooting gallery of Benjamin Barker, who said Booth attracted much attention by his skill with a pistol. He practised to shoot with accuracy in any position, and outclassed all others in ringing the bell on the target. Such amusement was common in that era and indicated no motive on his part except the desire to be a superior marksman.

He spent idle hours loitering about the streets of the Capital, where marching soldiers, cheered by the crowds, recalled the plaudits he had received in the theatre. This and Edwin's success irked Wilkes and set him planning some heroic deed which would lift him to immediate fame and compensate for the loss of his voice. Grant's order the previous April, prohibiting the exchange of soldiers between the North and South, crystallized the project in his mind.[28]

The first intimation of Wilkes' plot to abduct Lincoln dates from a trip he made to Baltimore in September. Samuel Arnold, recently discharged from Confederate service, had come to the city from his brother's farm in Hookstown for a visit with his father. A few years older than Wilkes and of medium height, Arnold's nature was reflected in his sullen lips and distrustful eyes. While staying at Barnum's Hotel, Wilkes learned that Arnold was in town and sent word that he wished to see him. They had not met since their student days at St. Timothy's Hall, and Arnold, flattered that Wilkes should remember him, immediately responded to the invitation.

When he arrived at Wilkes' room, he was greeted heartily by his former chum. This delighted him, as he had expected to find Wilkes aloof because of the public attention lavished on him. They smoked and talked of the war, and Wilkes said he had heard that Arnold had served with the South. In the midst of their conversation there was a knock on the door. Wilkes opened it and admitted a younger man whose features somewhat resembled his own, with the exception of a pointed tuft of hair on his chin known as an imperial. He was introduced to Arnold as Michael O'Laughlin. This Marylander had

Samuel Arnold, one of the conspirators.
(Courtesy Library of Congress)

Michael O'Laughlin, one of the conspirators.
(Courtesy Library of Congress)

George A. Atzerodt, one of the conspirators.
(*Courtesy Library of Congress*)

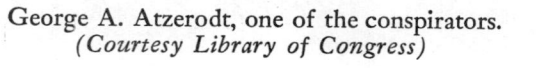

Edward Spangler, one of the conspirators.
(*Courtesy Library of Congress*)

also enlisted in the Confederate army, but later had given up fighting and taken the oath of allegiance to the Union. Although this facilitated his entrance into the produce business with his father and brother, who had offices in Baltimore and Washington, it did not change his attitude toward the Federal Government.

Wilkes ordered wine, and the talk of war continued. When the refusal of Federal officials to exchange prisoners with the Confederacy was mentioned, Wilkes told them he had a plan which would compel the release of southern soldiers then in northern prisons. He made no secret of the matter, but boldly outlined his plot to kidnap the President of the United States and hold him as hostage in Richmond. The plan amazed the two men, but they eagerly listened as Wilkes outlined the details concernings its accomplishment.

Lincoln, Wilkes told them, often went out to the Soldiers' Home alone and his capture at such a time would be a simple matter. He would then be rushed by carriage to the Potomac River, where a boat would be waiting to convey the party across to the Virginia shore. There, another carriage would take them on to Richmond where "Old Abe" would be presented to the Confederate Cabinet with their compliments. Neither Arnold nor O'Laughlin were to be financially obligated in any way; all Wilkes asked of them was their assistance in carrying out the project. At the proper time, they would meet again, and each one be assigned a certain duty to perform.

After drinking more wine and debating the possible success of such a venture, Arnold and O'Laughlin agreed to be ready when called on. Wilkes informed them he would take the early morning train to New York City, wind up personal affairs by making over property to different members of his family—but reserve funds sufficient for the kidnaping project—and return to Baltimore. This brought to a close the first discussion of Wilkes' preposterous scheme, and Arnold returned to Hookstown.

In New York Wilkes suffered another attack of bronchitis. Again he tried to convince himself that it was not severe, but as it continued he became despondent. His voice needed constant attention; at times he could not talk above a whisper. This condition placed him at the mercy of his overactive mind. Past frustrations and the fear of being denied coveted fame increased his neurotic sense of inferiority. He pictured himself always as an actor before an enthralled audience— all the fame he ever dreamed of had its setting on the stage. Even the scheme he had unfolded to Arnold and O'Laughlin grew to be a great drama in which he would play the leading rôle with but few words to speak.

Frantically he plunged ahead with his mad project. He wrote Arnold to select a good horse that he would purchase later, and enclosed money for his expenses. Then he returned to Pennsylvania and closed out all his unprofitable investments in oil speculation.[29]

Determination to proceed with his plans to abduct Lincoln sent Wilkes scurrying about to strange places. In October he told his friends that he was going to Buffalo to play an engagement, but instead started off for Montreal, Canada. There he lived in a back room of a once-fashionable residence on Cote Street. Nearby were the Theatre Royal, a famous riding school, and the home of the Christian Brothers, a religious sect originally from France. Cote Street was an interesting little thoroughfare and always humming with activity. Within easy walking distance was the St. Lawrence Hall, a leading hotel operated by Henry Hogan, who could not read or write, yet grew rich from the profits of rebel agents who made his place their headquarters.

Upon his arrival, Wilkes immediately got in contact with these Secessionists. Among them were Jacob Thompson, controller of the Confederate bank account in Canada, Beverly Tucker, George N. Saunders, Dr. M. A. Pallen, a Dr. Blackburn of Kentucky, a Mr. Lee from Virginia (related to General Robert E. Lee), J. D. Wescott of Florida (whose sitting room in suite number four was their meeting place), and several others.[30] Wilkes was not secretive about his connections. He thought it flattering to be seen openly with such men, drinking wine at their tables, and appearing on familiar terms with them. As they seldom had anything to do with persons outside their own clique and were known to be plotting against the Union, this intimacy aroused the suspicions of other guests and Wilkes was questioned by a few of his former acquaintances.

Those who encountered him observed that his conversation had a wandering character, and that the wild ideas he expressed showed excitement and mental derangement. During a game of billiards he compared his play to a plan he had "to bag the biggest game this side of hell," and added, "You'll hear of a double carom one of these days." When someone spoke of the presidential campaign then going on in the States, he exclaimed, "It makes damned little difference, head or tail! Abe's contract is nearly up, and whether he is re-elected or not, he'll get his goose cooked!" Later he slapped his opponent on the back and cried, "By God, I like your Canadian style; I must post myself on Canuck airs, for some of us devils may have to settle here shortly."

Wilkes borrowed many volumes of classical literature from friends and carried them about with him. He wished to impress these Confederates, who were important men in his estimation, that he was well-versed in the works of great writers. His knowledge of titles had been gained from the library of his father, which included the books brought to America by Richard Booth. On cold days in Montreal, Wilkes wore a yellow foxskin cap with a sheltering beak and was so proud of this headgear that he had his photograph taken in it. Some time later, the photographer's gallery was burned and the negative of Wilkes' picture destroyed. One afternoon following a snowstorm, he drove in a sleigh to Lachive, eight miles from Montreal, but a gale at twenty below zero was more than he expected, and he never repeated the experience.

On the twenty-seventh of October, Wilkes went to the Ontario Bank in Montreal, where he opened a small account by depositing a check from a broker named Davis and two hundred dollars in currency. He bought a bill of exchange for a little over sixty-one pounds and told the bank employee, "I am going to run the blockade." Then he asked, "In case I should be captured, can anyone make use of the exchange?" The employee informed him that no one could unless he indorsed the bill, for it was made payable to his order. Wilkes handed over the amount in United States gold coin.

Early in the war a group of Confederates, including one named Martin, seized a steamer in lower Maryland. As it was about to be retaken, Martin escaped to Canada and established himself in the blockade-running business. Confident of success in abducting Lincoln, Wilkes now entrusted Martin with the shipment of his theatrical wardrobe trunk into rebel states. Among its contents were a splendid collection of fine costumes made of silk, velvet, satin, and ermine; hats, caps, plumes, boots, buskin shoes, and a case containing a large variety of handsomely mounted swords and pistols, all valued at about fifteen thousand dollars. Some of these had belonged to the elder Booth and had been given to Wilkes by his mother. His purpose in sending this wardrobe south was to have such possessions where he could get to them again after his flight from Washington to Richmond, with the President of the United States as hostage.

Martin put Wilkes' trunk on board the schooner *Marie Victoria*, but neither reached its destination. The vessel was wrecked, and although the trunk was salvaged, its contents were sold at public auction in July, 1865, by decree of the vice-admiralty court. Much damaged by salt water, the collection only brought about five hundred dollars. George Rankin, brother of the actor McKee Rankin, bought most of the articles. Eventually they came into the possession of Edwin Booth.

Wilkes returned to New York about the first of November, bought two carbines, three pairs of revolvers, three dirks, and two pairs of handcuffs. These he packed away in his trunk and started for Baltimore, where he met Arnold. Fearing that the weight of his trunk might arouse suspicion, he had Arnold take charge of some of the weapons and ship them to him at the National Hotel in Washington, where he arrived a few days later.

His actions at this time seemed peculiar to George Wren, who was then engaged as prompter at Grover's Theatre in the Capital. Wilkes' laxity in securing engagements puzzled him. He noticed that Wilkes had become absent-minded—different from what he used to be. Instead of going about with many comrades, he was always alone except for the occasional company of Clay Ford, brother of the theatrical manager, and Billy Barron, an out and out Secessionist from Boston, who was a member of Grover's stock company.

On Friday, November eleventh, Wilkes journeyed down into lower Maryland to visit a Dr. Queen who lived near Bryantown, with a letter of credentials to him from the notorious Martin in Canada. The following Sunday he accompanied the doctor and his family to St. Mary's Catholic Church in the vicinity and occupied a pew with them. As they stood in front of the church before the services, Dr. Samuel A. Mudd arrived and was introduced to Wilkes by Dr. Queen's son-in-law, John C. Thompson.

Dr. Mudd, a moderately tall, slender man, had a long, narrow face with small piercing eyes and a high forehead. His thin sandy hair, drooping mustache and chin whiskers made him seem older than his thirty-one years. He had obtained an early education at Georgetown College, then studied medicine and surgery at the University of Maryland, after which he returned to the estate of his father, a wealthy planter and slaveowner living a few miles from Bryantown. There Dr. Mudd began the practice of medicine and soon after married a young woman who had just graduated from a convent. They built a home on a portion of his father's land and were occupying it at this time.

Wilkes let it be known that he wished to purchase a carriage-horse suitable for travel over the roads of lower Maryland, and Dr. Mudd mentioned that George Gardiner, his neighbor, had several for sale. Booth spent the night at the doctor's home and early the next morning went with him to the neighbor's farm. Gardiner said he could not recommend the three horses he had for sale as buggy-horses and showed Wilkes a young mare, which he rejected. When Gardiner brought out an old dark bay saddle-horse, blind in one eye, Wilkes said it would do as he intended to use it only one year. He paid Gardiner eighty dollars in cash and returned to Dr. Mudd's house alone.

After telling Mrs. Mudd good-by, he took his overcoat from a parlor chair where he had tossed it the night before, and departed. Later Mrs. Mudd found a letter from New York which he had dropped, and read enough of it to be convinced that "some poor man's home had been wrecked by the handsome face and wily ways of Booth." That day Wilkes rode the horse he had purchased from Gardiner back to Washington. On November sixteenth he went to Baltimore, where he met Junius and returned with him to New York.

Edwin Booth and John Sleeper Clarke were now in the second season of their management at the Winter Garden. Since August, Edwin had been preparing new sets and costumes for a production of *Hamlet* in the fall which he hoped would be a crowning event. The return of Junius from California and Wilkes' presence in New York the previous summer had given Edwin the idea of presenting *Julius Caesar* with the three important rôles to be played by himself and his brothers.

Never before had Junius, Edwin, and Wilkes been seen behind the footlights at the same time. On November 25, 1864, they appeared together in *Julius Caesar* for the purpose of increasing the fund to erect a statue to Shakespeare in Central Park, and the program announced that the three Booths came forward "to do honor to the immortal bard from whose works the genius of their father caught its inspiration, and of many of whose greatest creations he was the best and noblest illustrator the stage has ever seen."

Edwin had made an apt and fortunate selection for the three "sons worthy of a worthy father." They were indeed a triumvirate. Junius had the patrician dignity for Cassius, a part often played by the elder Booth, Edwin the decisive eloquence of Brutus, and Wilkes, Marc Antony's brilliant flair for demagoguery. It was to be a strange coincidence that this younger brother, an embryo assassin, should cry for vengeance against the murders of Brutus in a performance never to be forgotten by those who saw it. The rest which Wilkes had given his voice helped him to sustain his rôle that evening, but he knew that he could not continue to be absent from the stage over such long intervals and achieve lasting renown in the family profession.

More than two thousand people crowded into the Winter Garden, the largest audience ever assembled there. The proud old mother, with other members of the Booth family, sat in a private box and silently looked on. It was a performance which had no precedent and which was unlikely ever to be duplicated. When the brothers entered side by side in the first act the ovation they received was deafening.

What must have been the thoughts of Mary Ann as she watched her three eldest sons that memorable evening! Ordeals of the past must have seemed negligible to her then. She had played her part well; the end would come some day, quietly, peacefully, and she could say that life had been worth while. The final words of the first act were followed by an outburst of applause and cries of "Bravo! Bravo!" When her three sons stood before the private box she occupied and paid her homage, it was the proudest moment of an old woman's life. The audience, not to be silenced, clamored for the performance to continue.

Just as the curtain rose on the second act, firemen came rushing into the vestibule of the theatre crying "Fire! Fire!" One of the front rooms of the Lafarge Hotel in the same building was in flames. A panic was averted only by Edwin's appealing speech to the audience that they remain quietly seated until the end of the play. Later a rebel plot was uncovered that had aimed to burn the city by setting inflammable material on fire in every hotel and in Barnum's Museum.

In reviewing the performance of the Booth brothers, the New York *Herald* commented: "Brutus was individualized with great force and distinctness—Cassius was brought out equally well—and if there was less of real personality given to Marc Antony, the fault was rather in the part than in the actor." The scene of Brutus and the conspirators, that of the death of Caesar, and the famous quarrel scene, were reported to have been perfect pieces of dramatic art. The general opinion was that Edwin's great superiority was brilliantly manifested. The next evening he gave the first of one hundred successive performances of *Hamlet*. This was the production which had been in preparation for some time, but he had no intention of playing so long an engagement when it opened.

All New York was wildly excited over the attempt to burn the city, and it was the subject of conversation in Edwin's home after the family had gathered at the breakfast table. Here a "quarrel scene" of a different nature from that in *Julius Caesar* was enacted. Junius firmly maintained that a vigilance committee could do a great deal of good in New York, that the whole pack of incendiaries would have been caught and hanged from the window of the Vigilante headquarters on Sacramento Street had it happened in San Francisco. Wilkes argued that the exploit was in retaliation for atrocities by Union forces in the Shenandoah Valley and therefore equitable as an act of war. Junius was sure that Federal officers would round up the culprits within a short time. They did, and a Robert C. Kennedy confessed that he was the leader of the rebel band and had set fire to Barnum's Museum and several hotels while his accomplices did likewise in other places. For his part in this undertaking Kennedy was hanged.

The discussion between the Booth brothers became heated, Edwin declaring he had voted for Lincoln and hoped only for the victory of the Union forces. Wilkes, infuriated by his brothers' loyal remarks, exclaimed that if the North won the war Lincoln would proclaim himself king. Unfortunately neither Junius nor Edwin then realized how swiftly such thoughts were carrying Wilkes on to madness.

Mary Ann began to question the security that had seemed to envelop her the evening before while watching these three sons on the stage. For the first time she felt that some danger was hovering over Wilkes. She tried to calm her fears by the thought that he had promised her not to enlist in the Confederate army. He was the dearest of all her boys and would keep that promise, she told herself. But why was he not seeking theatrical engagements? What was he doing in Washington? Had he some motive back of all this talk? She did not wish to involve herself in their dispute, fearing perhaps that would prolong it, so she did not reproach them nor show any partiality toward either side, but remained pitifully silent, waiting for the quarrel between her sons to end.

CHAPTER IV

Samuel Knapp Chester, who had known Wilkes in his early days in Richmond, was a member of the Winter Garden company. They met again at the *Julius Caesar* rehearsals and Chester, wondering why Wilkes had not been on the stage over a long period, asked what he had been doing. Wilkes explained that he had sent his wardrobe south and told him he did not wish to play again in the North after this performance. He said nothing about the plot he was hatching until the night of the production, and then only mentioned a big speculation he had on hand. He suggested that Chester should join it, but did not tell him what it was. A few days later Wilkes was with some friends on lower Broadway, who joked about his oil investments. Chester came along and paused to hear their banter. Immediately Wilkes took him by the arm and walked with him up the street, saying they would not laugh when they heard of his speculation. Later in the week, Wilkes again suggested that Chester join him in it, but Chester replied it would be impossible as he had no funds. Wilkes told him it was not necessary to have money in order to come into the deal, that he had always liked him and would finance him. Even at this time, he did not reveal the nature of his scheme.

On his way to Washington, Wilkes stopped off in Philadelphia to leave a large envelope with Asia for safekeeping. As he had frequently done this, the Clarkes presumed it contained private papers that were difficult to carry about while traveling. While here, he met his former manager, Matthew Canning, and unsuccessfully tried to inveigle him into the plot without disclosing its real purpose. From Washington, Wilkes wrote to Chester saying he was sure to make money from his land investments and that Chester should join him in the enterprise. A few days later Wilkes made a second journey to Dr. Queen's home.

From rebel associates he learned of a widow Surratt and her children, who owned a farm in lower Maryland at a place called Surrattsville. It was here that Herold had made her acquaintance. Wilkes was told that she often sheltered blockade-runners and he was anxious to get in touch with her. But he found that she had moved to Washington that fall and leased her rural home to a tavernkeeper named John M. Lloyd.

This Mrs. Surratt, a domineering woman about forty-five years of

Mrs. Mary Surratt. (Courtesy National Park Service)

Dr. Samuel Mudd. (Courtesy National Park Service)

Anna Surratt, daughter of Mary Surratt. *(National Archives photo)*

John Surratt, son of Mary Surratt. *(National Archives photo)*

age, had little regard for others. Shortly after her marriage, her home at Conden Mill was set on fire by mutinous slaves lashed to vengeful fury by her ruthless treatment of them. The Surratts almost perished in the flames but survived to raise a family of three children. At the time Wilkes became interested in their household, Mrs. Surratt had been a widow for two years. Her oldest son Isaac had enlisted in the Confederate army, while her two other children, Anna and John, remained with her. She had opened a boarding house in Washington on H Street where "some of the most stupendous deviltry of the world's history" was concocted.[31]

Young John Surratt had left St. Charles College at the outbreak of the war to take active part in sending information regarding movements of Federal troops from Washington and carrying dispatches to Confederate boats on the Potomac. Being unmarried, he was given most of the hard riding to do, and soon established himself in the esteem of Richmond officials as a capable rebel errand boy. He was not yet twenty-one and was described as being about six feet tall, and having a prominent forehead, large nose, sunken eyes, a goatee, and long light-colored hair. The information Wilkes obtained concerning him proved that he knew the roads of lower Maryland leading to the Potomac River intimately, and therefore would be indispensable in the plot to kidnap the President of the United States.

On Sunday morning, Wilkes attended services at St. Mary's Church and again met Dr. Samuel Mudd. After roaming about in the vicinity of Bryantown for almost a week, he returned to Washington; a day later (December twenty-third), Dr. Mudd arrived in the Capital.

Louis J. Wiechmann, a fair-complexioned, stockily built son of German parents, was several years older than Surratt. They had been classmates at St. Charles College, and, when the Surratts came to live in Washington, Wiechmann boarded at their home. As the two young men strolled down Seventh Street that December evening, they heard someone call, "Surratt, Surratt," and, on looking around, Surratt recognized Dr. Mudd, whom he introduced to Wiechmann. Dr. Mudd, in turn, introduced Wilkes to both of them.[32] Wilkes invited the three men to his room at the National Hotel, where he ordered wine and cigars. Presently Dr. Mudd got up, went into an outer passage, and called to Wilkes, who followed him. After a moment they returned to the room, only to make a second exit with Surratt, leaving Wiechmann to sit alone on a lounge near the window. From their actions and secret conversations, Wiechmann concluded that something mysterious was going on of which he knew nothing.

No matter what may be said concerning Wiechmann's unreliability as a witness at the trial of the conspirators, events proved that he was not wrong in his general deductions.[33] There can be no doubt that Wiechmann, employed in the office of the commissary general of prisoners in Washington, had given Surratt important information which he had passed along to rebel authorities in Richmond. It was probably because of this concession that Wiechmann could not understand why he was not a party to any intrigue involving Surratt.

From the National Hotel, they all went to the Pennsylvania House, where Dr. Mudd was stopping, and the mysterious interview continued between Wilkes and Surratt, while Dr. Mudd talked to Wiechmann. At about ten-thirty, Wilkes, Surratt, and Wiechmann departed. The next morning, Dr. Mudd returned home, and Wilkes went to New York to spend the holidays with his mother.

Christmas day, McVicker wrote to Wilkes from Chicago, asking: "What do you say to filling time weekly with me, May twenty-ninth? I have not yet filled your time in January and see no chance of doing so with an attraction equal to yourself. There are plenty of little fish but I don't want them if I can help it. So, if you can come then, come at the above date." Wilkes must have been good box office in Chicago to have received such a letter from one of the best midwestern managers, but he was too busy playing his new rôle offstage to accept McVicker's offer.

A few days after Christmas, Wilkes called on Chester and asked him to walk over to the House of Lords for some food and drinks. Chester accompanied him there, and they remained about an hour, then went to another saloon under the Revere House, and later strolled up Broadway. Although Wilkes had a great deal to say about his speculation, he managed to keep from divulging its true character. Each time Chester asked about it, Wilkes put him off, saying he would tell him by and by. As they approached Bleecker Street, Chester bade him good night. Wilkes suggested they continue their walk, for he wished to tell him his secret, and turned in the direction of Fourth Street where, he said, there were fewer people.

When they reached an unfrequented portion of the street, Wilkes stopped and disclosed his conspiracy to capture the heads of the Federal Government, including the President, and to take them to Richmond. The abduction was to take place at Ford's Theatre in Washington, explained Wilkes, and he wished Chester to help in carrying out the plan. The task he was to perform seems to have wavered in Wilkes' mind between two possible actions. Chester was either to turn off the gas at a given signal so that the audience would be in confusion during the abduction, or to guard the rear door of the theatre and have it open for the hasty exit of the kidnapers.

Later Wilkes asked Ford to get in touch with Edwin and to suggest exchanging Chester for an actor in Ford's Washington company. Ford could not understand why he should attend to the matter, and told Wilkes to make the arrangements himself. As this would have connected Edwin directly with the plot, Wilkes did nothing more about it.

Wilkes' vitriolic denouncements of Lincoln and the Union were responsible for the growing unfriendliness between him and Edwin. In an effort to repress these outbursts, Edwin finally prohibited any discussion of the war while Wilkes was at his home. George L. Stout, an actor friend of the Booths, contended that "Edwin then was making all the success of the family and he was unwilling for Wilkes to come to New York." It was not Edwin, however, who kept Wilkes from playing there; nor did the condition of his voice influence managers in that city. They considered Wilkes too unreliable and refused to make him offers. All knew of his tendency to applaud the rebels and did not want to risk their reputations by billing him. Reproof generally sent Wilkes off on a drinking bout and made him more vindictive than before, and they wanted nothing to do with such an actor.

Following one of his rows with Edwin, and in the midst of preparations to kidnap Lincoln, Wilkes wrote to Junius:

Dear Brother:

I have just received yours from Philadelphia in which you complain of my not writing. I wrote you some days ago to Philadelphia and I know my letter must have been waiting for you, yet by yours, you have not received it directed to Chestnut Street Theatre. I therein stated why I had not written before. You ask me what I am doing. Well, a thousand things, yet *no more*, hardly than what I could attend to if I was home. But dear brother, you must not think me childish when I say that the *old feeling* roused by our loving brother has not yet died out. I am sure *he thinks I live upon him*. And its only for dear mother that I have gone there at all when in New York, and as I cannot live in that city without him at home, and as this season I would be home all the time, I thought it best not to be in the city at all, and as I like *this place next* [Washington], and my business calls me here I thought I would here make my stand. I hope you received my last, it was a little better than this as this is in haste. Give my love to all. When does John [Sleeper Clarke] come here, if I was him I would put it off till March as all's dull now. I don't know how the Philadelphia papers will use you but if they are as kind to you as to me, *why God help you say I*.

Your loving brother,

I received Joe's letter.[34]   JOHN

On his return trip to Washington, after spending Christmas at Edwin's home, Wilkes stopped over in Baltimore and purchased a horse Arnold had selected for him. The last day in December, he arrived in the Capital and began haunting the Surratt house on H Street. John Surratt was then working for the Adams Express Company in that city, but Wilkes' plan for kidnaping Lincoln appealed to him, and soon he was devoting all his time to it. By so doing, he unknowingly placed a noose around his mother's neck. The two young men became conspicuous as well-dressed loafers and, when asked why he was not working, Wilkes replied he could make more money in oil. Mrs. Surratt helped substantiate their story by referring to them as gamblers. After the closing out of Wilkes' legitimate holdings in the Pennsylvania speculations, the word *oil* in communications between the conspirators meant *abduction*.

Wilkes now approached another actor, John Matthews, and offered him the rôle intended for Chester, which Matthews refused. Although he later denied that Wilkes had mentioned the matter to him, Matthew's flight to Canada after Lincoln's assassination indicated more than a desire to travel.

Wilkes' next departure from Washington occurred on January 10, 1865. It is presumed that he went to Baltimore. In his absence, Arnold and O'Laughlin drove a horse and buggy from that city to Washington, left the outfit at Nailor's livery stable and took a room for themselves at Rullman's Hotel. Two days after Wilkes' mysterious disappearance, he returned to the capital.

James Maddox, property man at Ford's Theatre, had rented a stable in the rear of the alley leading from that building into F Street, and Wilkes paid him to keep his saddle-horse there. With the arrival of the horse and buggy, the stable was altered to accommodate the outfit by Edward Spangler and James Gifford, employees of John T. Ford, who used materials belonging to him without his knowledge. Spangler had helped Gifford in partly building the elder Booth's new home at the farm. He was a middle-aged widower now, over-fond of his liquor and of crab-fishing in season. His mild-looking face was marked by a scanty growth of brown hair and eyes that often were bloodshot. After Wilkes' horse and buggy had been placed in the stable, Spangler and a chore-boy known as Peanut John took care of them. The latter also attended the rear door of Ford's Theatre during performances and sold various refreshments between the acts.

Later in the month, John Surratt went to Port Tobacco to scout for men skilled in secret service for the rebel government. There a Confederate introduced him to a blacksmith and coachmaker named George

Atzerodt, who had been born in Prussia some thirty years before. He came to the United States while still a boy and had spent practically all of his life in southern Maryland. He was a stubby, round-shouldered individual whose ill-kept brown hair, goatee, and sickly-looking skin were made more objectionable by a dull-witted countenance with no semblance of intelligence. About 1857 he had moved to Port Tobacco, where he lived with a woman not his wife, by whom he had one child. The traffic in blockade-running had demoralized most of the mechanics and loungers in that village by its easy gain of money, and Atzerodt had turned from his petty trade to this more profitable occupation. He was exactly the man Surratt wanted to meet, and willingly joined the little group of conspirators.

After the first of the New Year, Wilkes continued his occasional trips to New York, and each time endeavored to drag Chester into his nefarious scheme. Inadequate assistance, bad roads, and a lack of money, probably had more to do with temporarily checking the abduction plans than the failure of Lincoln to appear at Ford's Washington theatre on the night Wilkes expected him to attend, during Forrest's January engagement. As his funds dwindled, he began to borrow money from Edwin, for he had no intention of drawing on his Canadian resources until he needed them in his flight from Washington.

On a journey to New York at the end of January he concluded another matter preparatory to this flight. He stopped off in Philadelphia, reclaimed the sealed envelope he had left with Asia for safekeeping, and took it along. It is supposed that while in New York, he added his signature in a different ink from that used in the body of an enclosed letter addressed *To Whom It May Concern*. Before returning to Washington, he again visited the Clarkes in Philadelphia and left the envelope, sealed, and labeled with the name J. Wilkes Booth. He never divulged its contents to anyone, nor was the mystery of it solved until he was hiding in the swamps of lower Maryland.

Early in February, Arnold and O'Laughlin called on Wilkes at his room in the National Hotel and were introduced to a "Mr. Cole." When he left, Wilkes informed them the man's real name was Surratt, and that he was one of those engaged in the abduction plot. He mentioned having received a letter from his mother describing fearful dreams she had about him, and saying his continued idleness worried her. She could see no purpose in his remaining in Washington unless he intended to play there, and had sent Junius to beg him to come back to New York. Between him and his mother, Wilkes added, there existed a bond, and frequently she had written to ask him if he were ill or had suffered some misfortune when such was actually the case. In order to prevent Junius from insisting on his return to New York, Wilkes had told him he held a commission in the Confederate army, but asked that he keep this information from the family. As he was afraid Junius would hear of the three horses he had at Cleaver's stable and demand an explanation, he asked Arnold to go there and say he had purchased them from Wilkes and thereafter would be responsible for their keep. Arnold did so and later Wilkes repaid him.

Delays and discouragements which impeded the progress of his plot began to irritate Wilkes. His mental condition grew more unstable, his drinking increased, and he became the victim of morbid impulses, delusions, and manias.

That month he again went to New York and threatened to ruin Chester in his profession, if he did not join him, declaring he was sorry he had not sacrificed Matthews for refusing to do so. When Wilkes realized his remarks were having no effect upon Chester, he became calm and, with the apology that he was short of funds, accepted the return of a fifty-dollar bill he had sent Chester from Washington.[35]

On the Sunday following his arrival in the Capital, Wilkes persuaded John McCullough, an actor who had appeared with him on several occasions, to go for a horseback ride, though McCullough was reluctant, as he did not care for the sport. They rode some distance from the city and into lonely lanes along the river known as the Eastern Branch, while Wilkes pointed out spots where a man might hide if he were in a tight fix. McCullough thought his remarks rather queer and said, "When I leave Washington I shall leave on the cars; I am all raw now with riding this old horse. For God's sake take me back to the hotel!"

While awaiting orders from Wilkes, Arnold and O'Laughlin had moved several times and were now living at the home of a Mrs. Mary J. Van Tine. Nearly every Saturday the two men went to Baltimore and spent the week end with Arnold's father, who understood from what he was told that they were in the oil business with John Wilkes Booth.

Toward the end of February, Arnold felt his idleness had made government detectives suspicious of him and that they were following his movements in an effort to obtain some clue as to his activities. (It was the constant association of Arnold and O'Laughlin that later led detectives to search for them at the same time on the day after the assassination). "Prisoners were now being exchanged," wrote Arnold in his *Narrative*,[36] "yet he [Wilkes] insisted still upon carrying out the abduction. Patriotism had converged into heartless ambition on his part, and I looked upon him as a madman, and resolved, if the project were not speedily executed to sever my connections with him."

Lewis Paine Powell was a tall husky young rebel whose heavy-set jaws, scowling eyes, and shock of black hair dangling over a low forehead, gave his beardless face a vicious appearance. He had been wounded and captured at Gettysburg by Federal troops and dispatched to a Baltimore prison hospital in which he served as an attendant. Although he hoped to be released from such duties by an exchange of prisoners between the North and South, the chance to escape came first and he started out to rejoin his Confederate regiment. As Union lines prevented his success, he managed to reach a unit of southern cavalry in Virginia and secure himself within its ranks. In January of 1865, he became convinced he was fighting for a lost cause and deserted the rebels.

At Alexandria, Powell sold his horse and took the oath of allegiance to the Union, signing his name Lewis Paine, a refugee from Fauquier. Returning to Baltimore, Paine, as he was now known, rented a room from a Mrs. Branson and got into trouble there by beating a female colored servant unmercifully. He was arrested and brought before the provost marshal, who ordered him north of Philadelphia. Had Paine gone, he might have escaped the gallows, but, while loitering about the steps of Barnum's Hotel on the morning of February twenty-eighth, he was recognized by Wilkes, who was delighted to see him again.

The date of their first meeting is not known. W. E. Doster, in his defense of Paine at the trial of the conspirators, gave it as having been on the night of a performance by Wilkes in Richmond at the beginning of the war, but Wilkes was not then playing in the South. Since Paine was reported to have taken part in the St. Albans, Vermont, raid and escaped to Canada about the time of Wilkes' visit in Montreal, it is probable they became acquainted there.

In all the world Wilkes could not have found one more suitable for his purpose than this finely proportioned but poorly dressed ex-soldier on the verge of starvation. Paine joined his mad scheme without hesitating and accepted the money placed in his hand as if it were manna from heaven. The day after their Baltimore meeting, Wilkes was back in Washington with Paine in tow. In the evening Paine turned up at the Surratt house. From then on he became a frequent boarder under several aliases. Herold, the shiftless drug clerk, and Atzerodt, were also occasional visitors.

Wilkes ran in and out of the house as if he lived there. His secret conversations with John Surratt and Atzerodt kept Wiechmann in a state of constant curiosity. Wiechmann asked Atzerodt what it was all about and was told that Wilkes intended to rent the Washington

Theatre and employ him as a ticket agent. At another time, Wiechmann questioned Surratt and was informed that Wilkes was preparing him for a theatrical career in Richmond.

"Would you become an actor?" asked Wiechmann.

"Of course I would; it's no disgrace," answered Surratt.

On the night of March third these two young men accompanied Wilkes to the closing session of Congress. The following day (Saturday), a few hours before the second inauguration of Lincoln, John McCullough walked into Wilkes' room at the National Hotel without knocking and found Wilkes sitting behind a table studying a map which was spread out before him. He was wearing a slouch military hat, gauntlets were on his hands and spurs on his boots. On the table were a pistol and a large knife. As McCullough entered, Wilkes looked up, seized the knife and rushed at him. McCullough cried out, "What's the matter with you, John; are you crazy?" Wilkes, recognizing McCullough, placed his hands over his eyes as if trying to regain his senses and said, "Why, Johnnie, how are you?" Others saw him dressed in this regalia at the inauguration ceremonies and thought his actions erratic.

He was now becoming desperate in his determination to accomplish the abduction and realized he might have to take some drastic action or bear the humiliation of defeat. On the afternoon of March seventeenth, when Lincoln arrived at the National Hotel to attend a ceremony for receiving flags captured in the Shenandoah Valley, Wilkes was reported to have been in the crowd swarming about his carriage and to have watched him with such a demoniacal expression that he was noticed by those standing near him. A woman described as having a dignified appearance spoke to Wilkes but he waved her off with a motion of his hand saying, "No, no, not now. Be quiet. I will let you know."

What Wilkes was up to on these occasions no one knows. In the last instance Lincoln was probably in no more danger than when a girl named Lizzy Murty had "tried to spit upon his head" while he was making a speech in front of the hotel.[37]

That evening, Paine, Surratt, and two young women boarders from the latter's home attended a performance by Edwin Forrest at Ford's Theatre, and occupied the box usually reserved for the President. Between acts, Wilkes joined them. The three men thoroughly examined the box, noting that the lock was in such condition as to make the door impossible to fasten.

Wilkes arranged to meet them at Gotier's Eating Saloon after the play, and went to find Herold whom he sent to round up other mem-

Lewis Paine (Powell), assailant of Seward.
(Courtesy Library of Congress)

Telegram from Wilkes to O'Laughlin, March 13, 1865 (the printed form says 1864). (*War Department, Office of the Judge Advocate General, 1940*)

Lincoln's second inaugural. Photograph by Alexander Gardner. One of the men in stovepipe hats in the top row at right of the stand above Lincoln has been identified as John Wilkes Booth, while Paine, Herold, Atzerodt, Surratt, and Spangler have been identified in the group standing just beneath the President. (*Courtesy National Park Service*)

The National Hotel in Henry Clay's time. Wilkes was a guest there at the time of the assassination. (*Courtesy National Park Service*)

bers of the group. It was the first time Wilkes had brought them all together, and he took this opportunity to assign a part to each. Paine was to seize the President in the box, O'Laughlin and Herold were to turn off the gas, Arnold was to jump upon the stage and assist in lowering the President from the box, while Surratt and Atzerodt were to wait on the other side of the Eastern Branch Bridge to act as pilots and assist in conveying their prize to the boat which would be waiting to take them across the Potomac.

Arnold did not think Wilkes' plan was practicable and said so. Infuriated, Wilkes threatened to shoot him. Arnold retorted that two could play at that game and a general row followed.[38] Surratt feared the government had information of their plot, for a stockade being built at the Navy Yard Bridge had gates opening toward the south as if danger were expected from within. He therefore suggested that the whole project of abducting the President be dropped. Everyone agreed except Wilkes, who got up, banged his fist on the table, and exclaimed, "Well, gentlemen, if the worst comes to the worst, I shall know what to do!"

A spirited controversy began, during which one declared, "If I understand you to intimate anything more than the capture of Mr. Lincoln, I, for one, will bid you good-by." All expressed the same opinion, arose, and commenced putting on their hats. Wilkes perceived he had gone too far, asked their pardon and admitted he had drunk too much champagne. Thereupon the difficulty was straightened out. They all became friendly again and separated at five o'clock in the morning.[39] There can be little doubt that Wilkes at this time had insinuated assassination if the plot to kidnap the President were to fail, regardless of subsequent denials from other members of the group that such an action was ever thought of or mentioned by any of them.

When Wiechmann saw Surratt early that morning, he asked where he had been, and was answered, "Al, mind your own business." Surratt was unaware that Wiechmann had already told a Captain Gleason, employed in the same office, of the mysterious activities that had aroused his curiosity and that these tales had reached the ears of government detectives. Why such information did not lead to a quick round-up of the plotters before the assassination instead of after it is amazing. Probably government officials also learned from the same source how the Surratts had often sheltered the blockade-runners, Mrs. Slater and A. S. Howell, in their H Street home.

In compliance with a request from John McCullough to appear on his benefit night, Wilkes played his last performance as Pescara, in *The Apostate*, at Ford's Theatre in Washington, March 18, 1865. He did this more for the purpose of providing himself with an excuse to offer his family for remaining there, than through any desire to accommodate McCullough, though he greatly admired him. Bronchial trouble still threatened Wilkes, as this announcement shows: "If he shall be well, *and in good voice*, we venture to predict that he will create a sensation to-night." Reviews gave no criticism of Wilkes but stated that the audience was unusually demonstrative and manifested its appreciation of his efforts by stamping on the floor and loudly cheering when he appeared. As Surratt, Wiechmann, Herold, Atzerodt, and others were there on passes received from Wilkes, they may have had something to do with the ovation.

Wilkes and Surratt had heard of another plot to kidnap Lincoln and were anxious to get hold of him before some other group made such an attempt. O'Laughlin had gone to Baltimore, so Wilkes sent him a telegram (March thirteenth) reading: "Don't you fear to neglect your business. You had better come at once. J. Booth."

A week later, Paine reappeared at the Surratt home in Washington, dressed in a new suit, and announced himself as a Baptist minister and Union man. Wiechmann was puzzled, as he and the Surratts were Catholics and the garb Paine wore did not have the appearance of belonging to a priest of any faith. This time he asked Mrs. Surratt why her son brought such men to her house and associated with them. Her answer was, "Oh, John wishes to make use of them for his dirty work." Wiechmann asked what that was and she said, "John wanted them to clean his horses."

If events taking place in the Surratt home aroused the curiosity of Wiechmann to such an extent, they should also have acted similarly on Mrs. Surratt. Known as an efficient landlady, she could not but be aware of what was going on in so small a house. John Surratt claimed that Wiechmann "was constantly begging to be allowed to become an active member of the group," though he told him he could not join in the plot "for the simple reason that he could neither ride a horse nor shoot a pistol." His refusal nettled Wiechmann. Wilkes, suspicious of him, once asked Surratt if he thought he could be trusted, and Surratt replied he thought so, as Wiechmann was a Southerner.

Rumors of Lincoln's intention to be present at Campbell Hospital for a performance of *Still Waters Run Deep* prompted Wilkes to call the conspirators together again hurriedly and tell them that the time had arrived to bag their prize at some lonely spot along the way.[40] The plan he gave for capturing the President was somewhat spectacular. His coachman was to be overpowered, Surratt was to seize the reins and drive him over the Eastern Branch Bridge, to a point where the carriage would be abandoned, and continue with fast horses obtained along the Rebel underground route.

If they found sentinels at the bridge, salutes and hurrahs were to be given to impress them with the idea that the band of horsemen were the protectors of the President as he dashed southward on some important mission. Herold was sent to T. B.,[41] a village in lower Maryland, with guns, a coil of rope, and a monkey wrench to await them and guide them from there to Port Tobacco. They intended to travel the distance of about forty miles south of Washington to a point on the Potomac River during the night, be ferried over to the Virginia shore early in the morning, and by afternoon, arrive safely behind Confederate lines.

In the company performing at Campbell Hospital was the actor-manager E. L. Davenport who was well acquainted with Wilkes. During an intermission in the play, Davenport went to the rear of the theatre where there was a garden. Wilkes suddenly appeared attired in boots and spurs, which seemed odd to Davenport, for he was otherwise elegantly dressed. He was somewhat excited, but, on seeing Davenport, said, "Hello, Ned; who is in the house?" Davenport mentioned several well-known names, and Wilkes inquired, "Did the old man come?"—meaning Lincoln. Told that the President was not there, he turned on his heel to go.

"It seems to me you are in a great hurry," said Davenport.

"Yes, I'm trying a new horse and he is rather restive," replied Wilkes, and disappeared.

For some time Wilkes and his group of conspirators watched the road, waiting for Lincoln, but, when one of the White House coaches galloped by and disclosed an unfamiliar face at the moment the attempt at abduction was to have been made, they became alarmed. Believing that Federal authorities had discovered their plot and sent a decoy to trap them, they quickly scattered in opposite directions.

Soon after, Surratt returned home very much disgruntled and entered the room where Wiechmann was reading. In about ten minutes Paine arrived brandishing a pistol, and was followed by Wilkes who paced back and forth as he slapped his boot with the whip in his hand. Wiechmann spoke to him and Wilkes said curtly, "I did not see you." The three men went upstairs, remained there half an hour, then came down and left the house together.

Surratt and Atzerodt rode out toward T. B. to get Herold and met him early in the morning as he was starting back. They stopped in at Lloyd's tavern, got a drink at the bar and went to the parlor. Lloyd joined them and they asked him to keep the wrench, rope and guns that Herold had brought, all of which were on the sofa. Lloyd objected, as he did not know where to store them, but Surratt took him into a rear room and pointed out where they could be concealed between the joist and ceiling. He told Lloyd that they intended to call for the articles within a few days.

Following the frustration of their attempt to kidnap the President on his way to Campbell Hospital, the conspirators disbanded, and Atzerodt was delegated to sell the horses. Arnold and O'Laughlin returned to Baltimore, and told their families they had ceased to be in the oil business with John Wilkes Booth and had severed all connections with him. The next day (March twenty-first) Wilkes started for New York City, but stopped in Baltimore. He went to Barnum's Hotel and wrote two notes, one to O'Laughlin, and the other to Arnold.

From New York Wilkes wired Wiechmann, asking him to have Surratt "telegraph number and street at once." Surratt said the conspirators seldom used their own names in communications, and that Wilkes often sent messages under the name of Lewis J. Wiechmann "because Wiechmann knew of the abduction plot." On this occasion, however, when Wiechmann inquired what particular street and number Wilkes wished to know, Surratt told him not to be "so damn' inquisitive."

That night, the wily dispatch-carrier, Mrs. Slater, made one of several sojourns under the Surratt roof in Washington on her way from Canada with dispatches for rebel chiefs in Richmond. As A. S. Howell, who had been ferrying Confederates across the Potomac River, had been captured and sent to a Federal jail, John Surratt accompanied her on the journey southward which they began under the guise of a drive into the country with his mother.

Wilkes was in New York when Edwin played his one hundredth consecutive night of *Hamlet* on March twenty-second at the Winter Garden. Until then no actor had ever achieved such a record in that play. "Stuart [manager of the theatre] during rehearsals, was confident that *Hamlet* would run six months. Afterwards he gave it eight weeks; and at length he agreed with me that if we got four weeks out of it we should be satisfied. . . ." admitted Edwin. "I was heartily sick and wearied of the monotonous work, and several times during it suggested a change of bill, for I felt that the incessant repetition was seriously affecting my acting, as at that time I was unused to such a thing. But Stuart, with his (!) wonderful success, would exclaim, 'No, not at all, my dear boy! Keep it up, keep it up! If it goes a year, keep it up!' And so we kept it up." [42]

Edwin once remarked that he preferred *Richelieu* to *Hamlet*. However, he was so aptly endowed with the characteristics of the Dane that his performance took the public's fancy and it became his most popular rôle. The acclaim given him at this time must have forced Wilkes to another realization of his own shortcomings. He knew he could never have equaled, much less surpassed, the superiority of this older brother on the stage. All the Booths were now fully conscious that Edwin was to wear his father's crown. "There is but one Hamlet to my mind—that's my brother Edwin," Wilkes acknowledged. "You see, between ourselves, he is Hamlet—melancholy and all."

The death of Edwin's wife, Mary Devlin, had deepened this trait in him which his intimate friends believed to be the result of constant brooding over the family's early illegitimacy. Yet Wilkes, knowing that he would undoubtedly call public attention to this stigma, went on with his plans. Three days after Edwin closed in *Hamlet*, Wilkes again stopped over in Baltimore on his way to Washington and went to see Arnold. As he was not at his father's home, Wilkes left a message asking him to call at Barnum's Hotel. In a sealed letter he also stated that he desired to give the abduction scheme another trial during the next week, but if unsuccessful, to abandon it forever. Later that day, Wilkes arrived in Washington.

In spite of the fact that Edwin was being toasted and fêted as were only the great war heroes of the day, Mary Ann continued to be troubled and anxious. Edwin could take care of himself—but John Wilkes? Still her favorite, this hot-headed young man was full of some dangerous objective. What it was, she was only left to guess and, in grief-stricken dismay, she wrote to him immediately after his departure, begging him to be cautious for her sake as well as his own.[43]

Paine was now living at the Herndon House in Washington, where John Surratt had procured a room for him before going to Richmond. Mrs. Surratt, according to several of her boarders and her niece, visited Paine there. O'Laughlin, still in Baltimore, received a telegram from Wilkes, reading: "Get word to Sam. Come on without him Wednesday evening. We sell that day sure. Don't fail. J. Wilkes Booth." This message is ambiguous, for Lincoln was then at City Point, having gone there from Washington via steamer with Mrs. Lincoln and Tad, and there was no possibility of his returning to the Capital by the time mentioned in the telegram. But Arnold and O'Laughlin did not fail to get there—for the purpose, so Arnold stated, of obtaining five hundred dollars Wilkes had borrowed from O'Laughlin.

They called on Wilkes, and, instead of continuing with the details of the abduction plan, he repeated his intention of giving it up. Arnold asked about a letter he had sent him in which he suggested they wait until a more propitious time to carry out the scheme, but Wilkes said he had not received it. Arnold requested him to destroy it when it arrived and he promised to do so. Federal officers found it in Wilkes' trunk at the National Hotel after his flight from Washington.[44]

On All Fools' Day the three cavaliers went to Baltimore. O'Laughlin remained there, Wilkes returned to New York, and Arnold accepted a position as clerk in a store owned by a Mr. Wharton at Old Point Comfort, Virginia.

Within the next twenty-four hours Jefferson Davis and the Confederacy were somewhat upset. While His Excellency was attending St. Paul's Church in Richmond on Sunday, April second, a messenger tiptoed down the aisle and handed him a telegram from General Lee, stating that it would be impossible to hold the Confederate line much longer and advising that preparations be made for leaving Richmond that night. At this news, Davis hurried back to his Capital home, packed his traveling bags, and left on the next train, his wife and children having departed earlier that week.

When word reached northern cities that Richmond had been captured and was occupied by Union troops, people rejoiced in the streets, national colors fluttered from all public buildings, and church bells rang triumphantly. But the certainty of Lee's formal surrender did not change the attitude of many whose sympathies were with the South. By various acts some of them got their names into the records. James P. Ferguson, who owned a café on the upper side of Ford's Theatre, asked Gifford, the chief carpenter of that playhouse, if he didn't have some Union flags stored in the building.

"Yes, I have; I guess there is a flag about," drawled Gifford.

"Why don't you run one out on the roof?" asked Ferguson.

"There's a rope, isn't that enough?" scowled Gifford.

"You are the hell of a man; you ought to be in the Old Capitol Prison," shouted the café owner.

In less than a month Gifford was confined there. Mrs. Surratt drew down the shades and closed the blinds, like one in mourning. "Her house was gloomy and cheerless," said Wiechmann. "To use her own expression, it was 'indicative of her feelings!'" National events had no effect on Atzerodt, however. He was still leading the useless horses of the abduction fiasco from stable to stable trying to sell them.

John Surratt arrived in Washington that Sunday and told Wiechmann he did not believe the news, as he had talked with Davis and Benjamin, and they had each assured him that the Confederate Capital would never be evacuated. If Surratt were in the company of these rebel authorities as much as he professed, he must surely have informed them, at one time or another, of Wilkes and his abduction project. To escape being intercepted by detectives who had heard of his trip South and inquired for him at his mother's home that day, Surratt went to a hotel.

Early the next morning Surratt continued his journey to Canada, stopping over for a few hours in New York. There he called at Edwin's home, which he said was the most elegant he had ever seen. When he asked for Wilkes, he was told that he had gone to Boston where Edwin was playing an engagement. But a fair companion was with Wilkes, and they loitered along the way.[45] His reputed betrothal to Bessie Hale, daughter of a New Hampshire senator, did not seem to affect his relation with other women.

In Boston, Wilkes spent an afternoon at the shooting gallery of Floyd and Edwards, which was then in a basement near the Parker House. When he entered he saw Edwards, who had the reputation for being a fine marksman, and immediately challenged him. Edwards accepted, the two men selected revolvers, and the contest began. Wilkes shot up and down the line of targets, making a perfect score; Edwards did the same. Wilkes turned his back, firing first over one shoulder and then the other, and scored as before. Edwards followed but scored badly. Wilkes fired under each arm, looking back of him to take aim and the score was still in his favor.

Then Wilkes began some fancy shooting, using each hand alternately. A crowd gathered about him and marveled at the accuracy of the distinguished-looking man with the thick black hair. After he had gone Edwards told them who it was and they were all amazed, for they thought they had been watching a professional marksman. At the end of this visit, Edwin and Wilkes got into another unpleasant argument about the war, and Wilkes' last words to him were: "Good-by, Ned; you and I could never agree upon that question."

One week previous to the assassination Wilkes sat in the House of Lords in New York City sipping brandy and talking to the actor, Chester. "What an excellent chance I had to kill the President if I had wished on Inauguration Day," exclaimed Wilkes, and added that he was then as close to Lincoln as he was to Chester at the moment. This privileged position near the President had been granted Wilkes by a card obtained through Senator Hale's daughter. He also told Chester that he had given up the idea of the abduction and was selling the horses bought for that purpose, as keeping them too long in one place looked suspicious.

On Saturday, Wilkes arrived in Washington and heard reports that

Lincoln had lolled in Jeff Davis' chair while at the Confederate Capital, "crossing his long legs and rocking back and forth as if he were at home." This so enraged Wilkes that he damned his having gone to Boston and shooting at a target instead of to Richmond and killing the President.

Journalists, lawyers, army officers, and the better class of actors patronized the Grand Saloon owned by Chris Mades at Tenth and E Streets, but Wilkes preferred a less pretentious place run by a German widow named Volkner, half a block from there. Her patrons were a beer-drinking crew of truckmen, mechanics, and stagehands, who seemed to fit Wilkes' inferior moodiness much better than his fellow players. Here, he could boast and strut without being ridiculed by those of his own profession. In such an atmosphere, he was the star and could nourish his vanity with the envious glances and paltry praise of shabby nondescripts.

Having received no word concerning Lee's surrender, Lincoln decided to return to Washington on the steamer *River Queen*, and arrived there about nine o'clock Sunday evening. A carriage was waiting for the presidential party, and they all climbed in. As they passed along the streets on their way to the White House, they saw groups of excited people gathered about bonfires. Curious, Tad Lincoln wanted to know what was going on, and the President had the driver stop the carriage while one of the party asked a bystander what had happened. Not recognizing the occupants of the carriage, the man replied, "Why where have you been? Lee has surrendered." Lee had met Grant at Appomattox that afternoon.

The city of Washington was just beginning a celebration which was to continue for days. Secretary of War Stanton ordered a royal salute of two hundred guns fired at all army posts; Vice-President Andrew Johnson got drunk and made a speech to a howling mob from the steps of the Willard Hotel, saying that he would hang every rebel south of the Potomac if he ever became president.

On the morning of April eleventh, Mrs. Surratt sent Wiechmann over to the National Hotel to ask Wilkes for the use of his horse and buggy as she wanted to drive to the country. Wilkes told Wiechmann he had sold the outfit but gave him ten dollars to hire another one. About nine o'clock Wiechmann and Mrs. Surratt started for Lloyd's tavern, her former home, ten miles from the Washington Navy Yard Bridge.[46]

That evening Wilkes and Herold were in the crowd at the White House, listening to Lincoln's plans regarding the floundering rebel states and their defeated pilots. When he had finished his speech and the band was playing *Dixie,* Wilkes told Herold that the President's remarks indicated "nigger citizenship," and added, "Now, by God, I'll put him through!" [47]

The day before the assassination, the prompter at Grover's Theatre was reading a manuscript to Manager C. D. Hess in the rear office of the building when Wilkes walked in, seated himself in a chair, and started a conversation. He asked if Grover's would be fully lighted and was told it would be on the following night, which had been set as the time for great illuminations throughout the Capital. Wilkes said if that were so he would have a good chance to dispose of some coal oil and asked if the President were to be invited to Grover's Theatre. "Yes," answered Hess, "that reminds me, I must send the invitation at once."

He then sent a note to Mrs. Lincoln, as she was the one who usually made decisions regarding such affairs. The two men were rather surprised by Wilkes' manner, since he had not been in the habit of entering the office unless invited. As he seemed in no hurry to go, the manuscript was tossed aside for a moment and the prompter said to him: "John, when are you going to Richmond again?" Abstractedly, he replied, "I never shall go to Richmond again—I never shall go to Richmond again—" At the time they concluded that Wilkes' intense sympathy for the South made him feel he did not wish to witness the result of its subjugation.

During the evening Wilkes and Herold went to John Deery's billiard room, and Wilkes introduced Herold to the former champion, who described Herold as "scarcely more than a big beardless boy . . . backward and slow of speech," his manner toward Wilkes having "the air of a sort of body-servant." Herold had attached himself to Wilkes like a stray dog from the streets. Unkempt, dull-witted and easily led, he idolized the handsome young actor who had lifted him out of his shabby obscurity. What Wilkes saw in him or why he confided in this indolent craven no one will ever know. Herold's dogged devotion to Wilkes was the result of cowering gratitude. It is doubtful that he even had the intellect to realize the risks that were ahead of him.

Wilkes asked Deery if he would send down to the Grover's ticket office and secure a private box in his (Wilkes') name for the following evening's performance of *Aladdin,* an oriental spectacle with the subtitle of *The Wonderful Lamp.* He pulled out some bills and counted a number of them, suggesting as he did so that Deery let one of the boys employed at the tables attend to the matter. Deery was surprised at his request, as he knew Wilkes had the freedom of any theatre in Washington and could obtain a box from Grover simply by asking for it.

He mentioned this to Wilkes who answered that he didn't care to accept favors from Grover at the time.

Deery called one of the boys and Wilkes handed the money to him, including a tip, saying he must not accept any other box than the one he had specified. The boy returned with the reservation and Wilkes was much pleased. The box he had reserved was the one next to that retained for the President. Wilkes and Herold did not appear to be in a hurry but left later and were not seen again at Deery's. Herold went home. Wilkes did not return to his room at the National Hotel. It is presumed he spent his last night in Washington with Ella Starr.

BOOK FOUR
CATASTROPHE

Title page of a song dedicated to John Wilkes Booth. Copies of it are extremely scarce. *(Theatre Collection, Harvard College Library)*

CHAPTER I

Dark clouds hung over the Capital on Good Friday of 1865, threatening to drench the gaily decorated city with rain. Cheering crowds surged along Pennsylvania Avenue; delegations paraded waving Union flags, and bands played.

It was past noon when Wilkes came sauntering up Tenth Street toward Ford's Theatre to get his mail. He was elegantly dressed, and his thorough grooming showed that he had been to a barber shop that morning. As he appeared, Harry Ford said to others at the entrance, "There comes the handsomest man in Washington." Familiar with Wilkes' aversion to jokes about the war, Harry decided to have some fun, and, handing him a letter remarked, "The President will be here tonight with General Grant. They've got General Lee a prisoner, and he's coming too. We're going to put him in the opposite box."

"Oh, no, they haven't got Lee a prisoner; they certainly wouldn't bring him to Washington," replied Wilkes as he sat down on the steps to read his letter. Upon finishing it he suddenly turned to Harry Ford and asked if he were positive Lincoln and Grant would attend the evening performance, a benefit and last appearance of Laura Keene in *Our American Cousin*. "Yes," said Harry, "they are surely coming." [1]

This did not alter the plan Wilkes was concocting when he secured a box at Grover's Theatre in the belief that Lincoln would be there to see the oriental spectacle of *Aladdin*; it merely changed the location of his act. He had been wavering between abducting the President and murdering him. The decision he made that day was not sudden, but it was final. Apparently he made it because he lacked aid for the kidnaping project. Arnold was at Old Point Comfort clerking for Wharton. O'Laughlin had come to Washington from Baltimore for the celebration, but missed seeing Wilkes at the National Hotel, and had no connection with the assassination plot. Herold, Paine, and Atzerodt were not enough men to abduct Lincoln. Even with John Surratt in the Capital, the number would have been insufficient for that purpose.[2]

After conversing with Harry Ford, Wilkes walked rapidly down the street in the direction of the Kirkwood House, where Atzerodt had registered earlier in the day. He had told Atzerodt that it would be easy to obtain a military pass from Vice-President Johnson who lived there.[3] Wilkes knew Johnson and his secretary, W. A. Browning, also a guest at the hotel, having met them in Nashville. If such a pass could be secured through the courtesy of the Vice-President, it would take the conspirators into southern Maryland that night. Atzerodt waited while Wilkes wrote on a card, "Don't wish to disturb you; are you at home? J. Wilkes Booth," and presented it at the desk. The clerk informed him that neither Johnson nor Browning was in and placed the card in the latter's box.

Failure to procure the pass made it important for Wilkes to get information concerning the sentinels guarding the road to Surrattsville, at a point three miles out of Washington, over which the conspirators would have to travel; so he called on Mrs. Surratt and asked her to make the trip over this route that afternoon. She consented, and Wilkes started for his hotel to get a field glass he wished her to take to Lloyd at Surrattsville. He stopped in at Pumphrey's Livery Stable directly across the street from his rear room and asked that the sorrel horse he had been accustomed to ride be ready for him at four o'clock. As the horse was in use, he engaged a small bay mare without inquiring into her habits. Then he went to his room for the field glass and took it to Mrs. Surratt.

A holiday, granted to government employees who wished to attend religious services, enabled Wiechmann to drive Mrs. Surratt to Lloyd's tavern a second time. She gave Wiechmann ten dollars to hire a conveyance and told him to return for her. As he left, he met Wilkes at the door with the package containing the field glass under one arm and his hand on the bell. They greeted each other and Wilkes walked into the parlor. Wilkes gave Mrs. Surratt the package she was to deliver and requested her to notify Lloyd that the articles and "shooting irons" left with him by the conspirators would be needed that night and to have them ready. Wiechmann returned in a carriage for Mrs. Surratt and saw Wilkes leaving the house.

While his emissary was traveling to and from Lloyd's tavern Wilkes attended to other matters. He went to the stable back of Ford's Theatre to arrange for sheltering the bay mare he had engaged from Pumphrey so that she would be close at hand and ready for use that evening. Between two and three o'clock he stood in a rear doorway of the theatre talking to several members of the cast after the rehearsal of *Our American Cousin*. Old George Spear, who had witnessed so much in the lives of the Booths, was there. At this historic performance he took the part of Binney. Some of the company were inside practising the patriotic song which was to be an added feature on the program. As soon as they had finished Wilkes and the others went into the theatre.

He saw Edward Spangler and the chore-boy, Peanut John, removing the partition between two upper boxes looking down upon the stage from the right side and arranging them for the accommodation of the presidential party. Wilkes then went back to the Kirkwood House to see if Johnson had returned. He was taking no chances that Mrs. Surratt's report regarding the pickets on the road leading out of Washington might be unfavorable to his plans. But Atzerodt informed him that the Vice-President had not yet come in. Soon after Wilkes had gone, Herold sauntered into the hotel and went up to Atzerodt's room. They were there only a short time and left for Naylor's Livery Stable, where John Fletcher was foreman. Atzerodt rode a horse that he had hired from another stable and Herold walked. At Naylor's, Herold rented a roan horse which he was to call for later in the day, and Atzerodt turned his horse over to Fletcher with instructions to have it ready for him at 10 P.M. Herold returned alone at four o'clock and asked for the roan horse he had selected. It was brought to him, and he agreed to have it back at the stable by nine o'clock that evening.

About four o'clock Wilkes arrived at Pumphrey's stable to get the small bay mare he had engaged. Near the entrance he met Colonel C. F. Cobb, a friend and schoolmate, who had served in the Union army, and asked if he had heard "that dirty tailor [Vice-President Johnson] from Tennessee speak in front of Willard's Hotel." Cobb replied that he had not heard him but had read his speech in the *Chronicle*. Wilkes then began a harangue against the Vice-President, and Cobb concluded he was drunk. "If I had been there, I would have shot the sonofabitch," boasted Wilkes. An old man standing near by heard Wilkes and told him he should have joined the southern army and "gotten his fill of shooting."

Wilkes went into the stable and asked for a tie-rein to hitch the mare, saying he wanted to stop at a restaurant and get a drink. Pumphrey advised him not to try hitching her as she was in the habit of breaking her bridle. "Get a boy to hold her for you," suggested Pumphrey. Wilkes answered that was not always possible, and Pumphrey said, "There are plenty of bootblacks about the streets who will hold your horse." Wilkes told him he was going to Grover's Theatre to write a letter and there would be no necessity to tie her, for he could put her in a stable close by. He questioned Pumphrey as to the best ride he could take out of Washington. "You have been around here for some time now and ought to know," said Pumphrey. "How about Crystal Springs?" asked Wilkes. "A very good place, but it is rather early for it," answered Pumphrey. "Well," said Wilkes, "I will go there after writing a letter at Grover's Theatre." That was the last Pumphrey saw of him or the bay mare.

Wilkes rode up the avenue, hailed John Matthews, who was appearing with Laura Keene's company, and handed him a sealed envelope, asking that it be delivered to John Coyle, publisher of the *National Intelligencer*, if he did not reclaim it by one o'clock next day. Matthews promised to follow Wilkes' instructions and put the letter in his pocket, but completely forgot about it until that night, when, rushing from the stage to his dressing room to discard his costume immediately after the assassination, it dropped from his coat which he had thrown to the floor in his excitement. He left the theatre, went to his room, read the letter, and was so alarmed that he burned it. He was the only one who ever saw what Wilkes had written therein and later quoted the closing paragraph as: "The moment has at length arrived when my plans must be changed. The world may censure me for what I am about to do, but I am sure that posterity will justify me." To this Wilkes had signed his own name and those of Paine, Atzerodt, and Herold.

Wilkes did not ride out to Crystal Springs but stopped on the upper side of Ford's Theatre near James P. Ferguson's café. Here he sat astride his horse, talking to Maddox until Ferguson came out. "See what a nice horse I have," said Wilkes. "Now watch; she can run like a cat." He then spurred the animal, and went racing down the street. Shortly after, he rode to the stable back of the theatre and called to Spangler for a halter. Spangler was busy on the stage, so Jacob Ritterspaugh, another employee, brought it out.

Spangler went to the stable with Wilkes, put the halter on the horse, and commenced to take off the saddle. "Never mind, I do not want it off. Let it and the bridle remain," said Wilkes. "She is a bad little bitch." He afterward took the saddle off himself, locked the stable, and passed into the theatre. Maddox, Peanut John, and Spangler then accompanied him to Peter Taltavul's bar adjoining Ford's Theatre on the lower side, and Wilkes bought the drinks. When they parted, Ford's employees went to supper. It is possible that Wilkes, taking advantage of their absence, went into the theatre, bored a gimlet hole through one of the inner doors leading to the President's box so he could view the occupants, loosened screws on the keepers of locks to both inner doors, and placed a wooden rod behind the door of the outer passage which, when properly arranged, prevented entrance from the balcony.[4]

Atzerodt returned to the Kirkwood House about six o'clock and was told a young man had called. He took a seat in the lobby, and soon Herold came in and said Wilkes and Paine wanted to see him at the Herndon House. They all met there and Wilkes assigned each one the part he was to take. Wilkes was to assassinate Lincoln and Grant; Atzerodt, Vice-President Johnson; and Paine, Secretary of State Seward. Paine eagerly accepted his rôle but Atzerodt balked, saying he had only agreed to assist in the kidnaping and would not kill. Wilkes informed him that it was foolish for him to back out now, as he was too involved in the plot to escape hanging. Herold's only duty was to act as guide and carry the smaller firearms they took with them out of Washington. They separated, and Wilkes went to the bar adjoining Ford's Theatre.

Before going backstage that evening, the orchestra leader, William Withers, Jr., entered the bar and saw Wilkes standing at one end of the room. His coat was off and thrown over one arm, and his hat was in his hand. Several men were with him, and all seemed to be in a jovial mood. Wilkes invited Withers to join them and ordered another round of drinks. While discussing the preceding generation of the theatrical profession, someone tauntingly remarked that Wilkes would never be as great an actor as his father. A sardonic smile curled Wilkes' lips as he replied, "When I leave the stage for good I will be the most famous man in America." Withers left the group at the bar and went to his place in the orchestra pit.

President Lincoln had been delayed at the White House,[5] and the second act was well along when he entered the theatre. With him were Mrs. Lincoln, Major Rathbone, and Miss Clara Harris. Wilkes afterward said, in lower Maryland, that waiting so long for Lincoln to arrive had almost driven him crazy.

The President, with his usual consideration for others, endeavored to remain unnoticed as he passed to the balcony rear aisle leading to the box reserved for him and his guests. *Hail to the Chief* was played, but only a ripple of hand-clapping greeted him, for the audience was too disappointed in not seeing Grant to respond with much enthusiasm. The General and Mrs. Grant had left the city late that afternoon to visit their children at a school in Burlington, New Jersey.[6]

The moment Lincoln was in the theatre, Wilkes rushed to Mrs. Surratt's home. She had been to Lloyd's,[7] attended to Wilkes' requests, and returned only a few minutes before he came in. He learned from her that the pickets on the Surrattsville road had been withdrawn at eight o'clock.[8]

Wilkes now hurried to the stable and saddled the bay mare. He led her up the alley to the rear door of Ford's Theatre and called several times for Spangler, but the actor J. L. Debonay appeared. "Tell Spangler to come to the door and hold my horse," demanded Wilkes. Debonay repeated his words to Spangler, who went outside to do as he was requested.⁹ Wilkes then entered the theatre and asked Debonay if he could get across the stage. Upon being told he could not cross at that time, as the dairy scene was on, he went down under the stage and came up on the other side.

Spangler called to Debonay, "Tell Peanut John to come here and hold this horse; I have not time. Mr. Gifford is out in front of the theatre, and all the responsibility of the scene lies on me." Peanut John was attending the stage door, keeping out those who had no business behind the scenes, and gave the excuse that he could not leave his post. Spangler said he would be responsible for what happened at the stage door, but that Peanut John should come out and take charge of Mr. Booth's horse. If anything happened, he was to blame Spangler for it. Peanut John then went out, took the reins from Spangler, and sat down on a carpenter's bench near the back door.

When the second act of *Our American Cousin* was ended and people began strolling into the vestibule and bar, Wilkes had completed his preparations and was talking to two men in front of the theatre. The President's carriage was at the curbstone and a Sergeant Joseph Dye thought that they were expecting the President to come out. Had Lincoln appeared, Wilkes might have shot him, but this is improbable as he had not done so on similar occasions when such opportunities occurred. His anxiety at that moment was caused by the possibility that Lincoln would depart and defeat his plan to put on the act before an audience *inside* the theatre. The crowd returned to their seats, and Wilkes went into the bar loudly calling for brandy. Many who saw him thought he was getting drunk.

Impatiently Wilkes glanced at the clock and came back to the entrance. He asked doorkeeper J. E. Buckingham for a chew of tobacco and got it. Buckingham saw him go into the bar again, gulp down a large glass of brandy, return to the theatre, pass into the house, and pause to look at the audience before going out. Soon he reappeared and went upstairs to the balcony, humming a tune.¹⁰ When John Miles, a colored employee in the fly-gallery above the stage, gazed out of an upper window, he could faintly see Peanut John lying on a bench in the alley holding Wilkes' horse.

Wilkes could not have asked the Washington Metropolitan Police for a man better suited to his purpose than Lincoln's indolent guard, John Parker. He had never seen a performance of *Our American Cousin* and was watching it from a seat in the balcony below his post at the doorway of the passage leading to the President's box.¹¹ With no one to stop him, Wilkes was soon inside adjusting the wooden rod against the door to prevent anyone following him.

Handbills for the performance at which Lincoln was shot. The version with the patriotic song was printed after it was learned that the President was to attend. *(Courtesy National Park Service)*

The Treasury Guard flag, torn by Wilkes' spur in his leap from the President's box. *(Courtesy National Park Service)*

CATASTROPHE

The play had progressed to the second scene of the third act, and the occupants of the box were also intently observing the action on the stage. Mrs. Muzzy, in the role of Mrs. Mountchessington, was repeating the lines to Harry Hawk, playing the part of Asa Trenchard: "I am sure, Mr. Trenchard, you are not used to the manner of good society, and that, alone, will excuse the impertinence of which you have been guilty." Wilkes was now standing behind the door of the box in the outer passage; the hands of the clock were nearing ten-thirty.[12] As Mrs. Muzzy made her exit, Hawk, left alone on the stage, began his comical reply: "Don't know the manners of good society, eh? Well, I guess I know enough to turn you inside out, old gal—you sockdologizing old man-trap." These were the last words Lincoln heard. The audience roared with laughter. It was Wilkes' cue to act. He went into the box quickly. With his pistol pointed at the back of Lincoln's head, he fired.[13] In a flash he dropped the pistol,[14] raised a dagger and cried *"Sic Semper Tyrannis!"* [15]

No one in the box saw what had occurred.[16] Rathbone's back was toward the door when he heard the discharge of the pistol. He turned and could see, through the smoke, a man whom he did not recognize, between the door and the President. Instantly he sprang toward the man and seized him. Wilkes wrested himself from Rathbone's grasp and made a violent thrust at his breast with the dagger. Rathbone, who was skilled in swordsmanship, parried the blow by striking it up, and received a wound several inches deep in his left arm.

Wilkes then rushed to the front of the box, and Rathbone tried to seize him again, but Wilkes leaped over the railing onto the stage fourteen feet below and his coat was jerked from Rathbone's hold. This undoubtedly caused Wilkes to catch his spur in the folds of the Treasury Guard flag [17] which hung down over the railing of the box, and he was thrown heavily to the stage floor, alighting on his left side and breaking the tibia just above the ankle of his left leg. As Wilkes jumped to the stage, Rathbone cried out, "Stop that man!" Before anyone knew what had happened, Wilkes was on his feet again and headed for a rear door, crossing the stage with a motion like "the hopping of a bullfrog," and leaving behind him a hat and spur. That he paused to utter another dramatic phrase is doubtful. If he said anything at all, he probably cursed his misfortune in falling.

Meanwhile, Mrs. Lincoln had leaned forward to look down on the stage. She thought the President had fallen out of the box, but found him still sitting at her left, his head drooping on his breast. Rising and gesticulating toward the audience, she cried, "The President has been shot! Is there a surgeon here?" She then caught the President by the arm and around the neck and began screaming for water.

Harry Hawk had his back toward the President's box, when he heard the report of a pistol, then heard something tear and somebody fall upon the stage. He whirled around and saw Wilkes coming in his direction with a dagger in his hand. Hawk, terrified, ran up a flight of stairs. John Deveny was in the audience and cried out, as Wilkes crossed the stage, "He is John Wilkes Booth and he has shot the President!" [18]

Laura Keene was standing near the prompter's desk on the side of the stage opposite the President's box when Wilkes pushed by her, striking her on the hand. She stared at him, unable to comprehend what was happening, until she heard the cry that the President had been shot. A second later the audience was in a panic. Women and children were screaming, men crying, "Stop the murderer!" Miss Keene went to the front of the stage and addressed them, "For God's sake, have presence of mind and keep your peace, and all will be well." [19] Miss Harris called to her from the box to bring some water, and she immediately responded.

Withers was backstage trying to find out why he had not yet been given the signal to begin the patriotic song delayed by Lincoln's tardy arrival. Suddenly Wilkes, whom he recognized, rushed by, striking him twice with the dagger, which rent his clothing but failed to injure him. Wilkes next bumped into Jacob Ritterspaugh and struck at him with his knife. Then he ran out a rear door and slammed it shut. [20]

The door through which Wilkes made his escape was not the stage door of the theatre. It was a small opening in a larger door used for moving scenery in and out, unknown to several members of the company at the time. The regular stage door was at the end of a long passage from the front of the building on Tenth Street. Peanut John was still sitting on the carpenter's bench holding the horse when Wilkes ran out of this back door, shouting, "Give me the horse," snatched the reins, knocked him down, mounted, and galloped off through the alley. Peanut John saw no one follow Wilkes out of the door to intercept him. Wilkes was well on his way before J. B. Stewart reached the alley, where he has so often been credited with having made the attempt to capture Lincoln's assassin. [21]

Grant's presence would not have prevented the assassination, nor would a hundred guards at the entrance of the presidential box have saved Abraham Lincoln that night. "I would have made no failure with either," said Wilkes during his flight, "as I had laid my plans for success only." John T. Ford had given Wilkes "the privilege of entering any part of the theatre, a courtesy always extended to actors in good standing." Had Wilkes seen guards at the entrance to the box, there is no doubt that he would have gone backstage and, at a chosen moment, from some position in the wings, shot the President and escaped as he had planned. His marksmanship would not have failed him. In fact, such a procedure would have been much easier than the one he took, but Wilkes could not omit the dramatic leap from the box before an astonished audience. He was an actor determined to steal the show.[22]

CHAPTER II

When Atzerodt came back to Naylor's Livery Stable for his horse at nine o'clock (an hour earlier than expected), Herold had not yet returned with the roan horse as he had promised. Atzerodt's mention of his own plans so aroused Fletcher's suspicion that when he left, Fletcher lighted a lantern and followed him. He saw Atzerodt stop at the Kirkwood House, dismount, and enter. Before long Atzerodt reappeared, mounted his horse, and started off along D Street, turning up at Tenth. He made no attempt to assassinate Johnson, who had gone to bed in a drunken stupor. Atzerodt had the reputation of being a coward. He was so afraid of firearms that in barroom brawls between other men, he would vanish at the sight of a drawn pistol.[23]

Fletcher lost track of Atzerodt and began looking about the streets for Herold; but that rascally apothecary's assistant was off with Paine to carry out his part of the plot.

Early in April Secretary of State William H. Seward had been injured when he and his son jumped from a carriage during a runaway and left two women to the mercy of the horses. He had been confined to his bed since that time, and Wilkes had concocted a ruse designed to give Paine easy access to Seward's bedroom for the purpose of murdering him. While Wilkes carried out his part of the plot at Ford's Theatre, Paine and Herold were to ride to Seward's house, and Paine was to present a package of medicine, saying he had been sent by Seward's physician, Dr. Verdi, with orders to deliver it plus a message, personally, to the Secretary.

When Paine and Herold arrived at the Secretary's house, William Bell, a colored boy, came to the door. He told Paine he would take the package and message to Sergeant Robinson, the Secretary's nurse, as no visitors were permitted to go upstairs. Paine, however, forced his way into the hall and convinced the colored boy of his sincerity. As he ascended the stairs the boy called after him to go quietly. On the landing above, Paine met Seward's son, Frederick, and repeated his reason for being there. Frederick looked into his father's room, found him sleeping, and told Paine he could not be disturbed. Paine then started down the stairway but suddenly turned and attacked young

Seward, beating him over the head with his revolver. As young Seward staggered to his sister's room, Sergeant Robinson opened the door of the Secretary's room to see what was happening, and Paine hit him on the forehead with a heavy knife. The cries of Miss Seward aroused another brother, Augustus, who came running in his "shirt and drawers," but there was so much confusion that he could not tell what was happening. He had been resting until time for him to sit up with his father.

Paine entered the bedroom of the Secretary and attempted to stab him in the head and neck, having found his revolver jammed from the blow he had given Frederick Seward. When Augustus rushed into the bedroom, he saw two men scuffling on the bed and at first thought his father had become delirious, then concluded the nurse had gone insane. Joining in the tussle, he tried to separate them, and was injured. Meanwhile, Secretary of State Seward had managed to free himself and roll under the bed. The steel bandages that were placed around his neck to support his fractured jawbone, the result of his accident, had prevented Paine's knife thrusts from penetrating a fatal spot. The colored boy, realizing that a murder was in progress, ran from the house and down the street crying for help. In fear of capture, Herold galloped off without waiting for Paine, who believed that he had accomplished his purpose and, rushing from the house, stabbed another attendant, thus leaving five wounded men behind him. He leaped for his horse with such force that he went on over his saddle but mounted again and galloped away.[24]

As Herold came down Pennsylvania Avenue, he spied Fletcher in front of the Willard Hotel. Fletcher called to him, but, instead of stopping, Herold spurred his horse and galloped up Fourteenth Street, then turned east on F Street. He believed Paine had been captured in his effort to murder Seward and was hastening to inform Wilkes, who had planned to meet them at a point along the escape route. Positive that something mysterious was happening, Fletcher rushed back to the stable, secured a horse, and went in pursuit of Herold. Wilkes was then in Ford's Theatre, so Herold waited near by on F Street to warn him about Paine.

Lincoln's assassin lost no time in making his escape and dashed out the alley to F Street, where he was joined by Herold. They hurriedly rode by the Herndon House and Patent Office to the corner of Fifth and F Streets. From there Wilkes raced ahead, speeding over a cinder pathway under the trees of Judiciary Square to Indiana Avenue, thence past the rear of the Capitol on First Street N. W., and the south side of it on B Street, to Pennsylvania Avenue S. E., and down

Eleventh Street S. E., to the Navy Yard Bridge. Not once on their route out of Washington were Wilkes and Herold intercepted by anyone nor did they encounter the suspicious Fletcher.[25]

The shiny skin of the small bay mare that Wilkes was riding made her look as though she had just come out of a race. At the bridge, which he reached before Herold, the sentry challenged him, and Sergeant Silas T. Cobb, who was on guard duty, advanced to see if he were a proper person to pass.

"Who are you?" asked the sergeant.

"My name is Booth," answered the rider.

"Where are you from?"

"The city," drawled Wilkes.

"Where are you going?"

"I am going down home in the Charleses."

"What town?"

"I don't live in any town; I live close to Beantown."

Cobb said he had not heard of that place, and Wilkes exclaimed, "Good God, then you never was down there!"

"Well, don't you know, my friend, that it is against the law to cross here after nine o'clock?"

"No, I haven't been in town for some time, and it is new to me."

"What is your object to be in town after nine o'clock when you have so long a road to travel?" continued Cobb.

"It is a dark road, and I thought if I waited a spell I would have the moon."

"I will pass you, but I don't know as I ought to."

"Hell! I guess there'll be no trouble about that," retorted Wilkes.

He walked his horse across the bridge, then raced on toward Lloyd's tavern.

Not more than ten minutes later, Herold came riding up, less rapidly, was challenged and similarly questioned. He answered that he was "a friend" and on the way home to White Plains. When asked why he was out so late, he said he had "stopped to see a woman on Capitol Hill, and couldn't get off before." The sergeant had him brought close to the guardhouse door, so that the light could shine full on him and his horse. He was then allowed to proceed.[26]

Some distance beyond the bridge, Polk Gardiner, who lived near Bryantown and was on his way to Washington, passed two horsemen, one half a mile behind the other, and both riding very fast. They were Wilkes and Herold, bound for Surrattsville, their first stop. When they arrived about midnight Wilkes was on the roan horse, Herold on the small bay mare. This exchange of horses between them probably took place at Hill Top before the fugitives reached Lloyd's tavern and was due to the gait of the bay, known as a *rocker*, which irritated Wilkes' injured leg. The roan was a lady's horse and easier to ride.

Herold rushed into the tavern and called to Lloyd, "For God's sake, make haste and get those things." Since Mrs. Surratt had given him Wilkes' message that afternoon Lloyd knew exactly what to do. He immediately got out all the articles, except the rope and monkey wrench, and handed them over to Herold. Wilkes did not come in but remained on his horse. Herold took out a bottle of whisky, and Wilkes drank most of it. After returning the bottle, Herold drank from a glass inside the tavern, handed Lloyd a bill and said, "I owe you a couple of dollars; here." Later Lloyd discovered he had given him but one dollar and remarked it "just about paid for the liquor out of the bottle."

They took only one of the carbines, Wilkes explaining to Lloyd that he could not manage the other because of his broken leg. As they were ready to leave, he added, "I will tell you some news if you want to hear it." Lloyd said he didn't care whether he heard it or not. "Well," said Wilkes, "I am pretty certain that we have assassinated the President and Secretary Seward." Wilkes' boast of this fact to so many along the way makes it doubtful that anyone sheltering him was ignorant of his crime.

He and Herold were at Surrattsville about five minutes and then galloped off on the road to the village of T. B. There they stopped long enough to mend a broken saddle girth before going on to seek Dr. Samuel Mudd's aid. He was not the only physician in that vicinity.

Dr. Mudd and his wife were asleep in their bedroom, the only one on the ground floor of the house, when Wilkes and Herold arrived at daybreak on the morning of April fifteenth. Herold's loud rapping awakened the doctor and his wife, and there was a hasty conference between them as to who would go to the door. Fearful that it might be someone with evil intent the doctor first inquired who was there. He was told that they were two strangers from St. Mary's County on their way to Washington, but that the horse of one of them had fallen and broken the rider's leg. The doctor looked out the window, and convinced that he was being told the truth, opened the door. He was greeted by a well-grown boy of about eighteen who had never yet shaved (Herold), and a man of medium size, with black hair, thick whiskers, and a mustache (Wilkes).

Herold asked Dr. Mudd if their horses could be placed in the stable for the one he was holding would break away if tied. Wilkes, who had been Dr. Mudd's guest only a few months before, was carried by him into the parlor and laid on a sofa. The doctor lighted a candle and called his colored boy to go out and put the horses in the stable. Then Herold came in and helped take Wilkes upstairs to the room Wilkes had previously occupied.

The disguise of whiskers which Wilkes wore and intended to use all along the escape route, was not to hide his identity from rebels in whom he confided and whom he expected to shelter him, but to keep members of their households from noting his real features. The Mudds were the only ones who saw him in these thick whiskers, for Wilkes found them impracticable and discarded them as soon as he left their home. Since both men were heavily armed, Wilkes with pistols and knives under his coat, and Herold carrying a carbine impossible to conceal, Wilkes must have informed Dr. Mudd immediately of what had occurred in Washington and that they were on their way South.[27] He probably told him also that the reason Herold said they were going to Washington was to allay undue curiosity so that no one in the house would know that the doctor had been involved in their affairs. Wilkes believed himself a hero and at this time looked forward to the blessing of all Confederates for his assassination of Lincoln.

Herold asked Dr. Mudd to do something to ease Wilkes as soon as possible for they had to be on their way. The doctor was unable to examine the injury to Wilkes' left leg without first cutting and removing the boot.[28] He found Wilkes had fractured the tibia about two inches above the ankle, and, having no adequate surgical supplies, bound it with splints made from an old bandbox. Wilkes also complained of the pain in his back but the doctor could do nothing more for him. He suggested that if his condition did not improve, they stop on their way south and see Dr. Richard H. Stewart, a Confederate who lived on the other side of the Potomac.[29] He then left Wilkes with Herold and went to his room downstairs.

About seven o'clock a servant was sent to notify the visitors that breakfast was ready. Herold came down and told the Mudds that Wilkes would remain in bed, so food was sent up to him. But he did not eat it. Back in Washington at twenty-two minutes past seven, Abraham Lincoln died.[30]

Herold was most talkative. He said that he had often been in Bryantown and knew several families in the vicinity. He was sure that he had seen Dr. Mudd before and it is possible that the doctor also recognized him. After breakfast Dr. Mudd took him into the back yard and pointed out the shortest way to the Potomac River. It was across Zachiah Swamp. Before the doctor left to direct some farm work, Herold asked for a razor to take to Wilkes who thought he would feel better if he shaved.

The fugitives stayed close to their room until noon, when Herold came down for dinner. Food was again sent up to Wilkes, but the servant returned with it and the breakfast, reporting that neither had been touched. Herold inquired if he could obtain a carriage so that Wilkes might travel more comfortably. The doctor had none, but said if Herold would accompany him to Bryantown where he had to visit a patient, one might be hired there.

When they had finished eating the two men went up to see Wilkes. He seemed to be suffering a great deal, yet insisted on paying the doctor twenty-five dollars for his services. As he took the money from him, Dr. Mudd noticed that his patient had shaved off his moustache but still wore the thick whiskers. Herold asked if some crutches could be made for Wilkes so Dr. Mudd, with the help of his gardener, built a pair for him and sent them up with an old shoe, which had been slit open, for the swollen foot.

After the doctor and Herold left that noon, Mrs. Mudd took a few oranges, some cake and wine, on a tray to Wilkes and inquired how he was feeling. He kept his face turned toward the wall as he replied, "My back hurts me dreadfully. I must have hurt it when the horse fell and broke my leg." He still refused to eat, but wanted to know if the doctor had any brandy. Mrs. Mudd told him all he had was good whisky and offered to get some for him but Wilkes declined it. She excused herself for not having been to see him all day and asked if she could help him. He did not answer or turn from the wall, so she left the room.

On the way to Bryantown, Herold and Dr. Mudd stopped in at his father's place to see if a carriage were available. Dr. Mudd's father was not at home, and the son who talked with them would not take the responsibility of lending their father's carriage, as it would be needed to carry the family to Easter service at St. Mary's Church the next day. Herold galloped off toward the village with Mudd following. A short distance ahead he wheeled around and rode back to the doctor whose horse was much slower. He told him that he had decided not to bother about a carriage—he and Wilkes would continue their journey on the horses.

He returned to the house, notified Mrs. Mudd that they were leaving, and went upstairs for Wilkes. Soon they came down, Herold carrying the carbine, Wilkes painfully supporting himself on the improvised crutches. Mrs. Mudd was startled to see Wilkes' whiskers become partially detached, but the agony in his face so aroused her sympathy that her suspicions faded. She suggested that the cripple remain until he felt better. Herold said that if Wilkes suffered much they would not go far, as they could stop at the home of a woman he knew. Once outside Wilkes tried to adjust the false whiskers but they would not stay in place and disgustedly he removed them. While he hobbled off down a rear lane, Herold went to get the horses. Just as he came from the stable, Dr. Mudd returned home frightened and visibly upset by the sudden appearance in Bryantown of some Federal soldiers searching for Lincoln's assassin. When Herold heard of this he mounted the small bay mare and hastily caught up with Wilkes. Excitedly he repeated the alarming news. After some difficulty he managed to get him on the roan horse and they headed into Zachiah Swamp.

Wilkes' escape route. (1) The old Navy Yard Bridge (Anacostia Bridge) over which Booth and Herold left Washington. (*Courtesy Library of Congress*)

Wilkes' escape route. (2) Lloyd's tavern (the Surratt house) in Surrattsville. *(This photograph and the 21 which follow were taken by the author in 1934.)*

Wilkes' escape route. (3) The village of T. B.

Wilkes' escape route. (4) Junction of the main road with the side road leading to the Mudd house.

Wilkes' escape route. (5) The home of Dr. Samuel Mudd, where Booth and Herold arrived about daybreak on April 15, 1865.

Wilkes' escape route. (6) The pathway leading from the Mudd house.

Wilkes' escape route. (7) The approach to Zachiah Swamp.

CHAPTER III

The day after Lincoln's assassination, Secretary of War Stanton sent a telegram to the chief of the United States Secret Service, Colonel La Fayette C. Baker (then in New York making plans for the capture of bounty jumpers) to come to Washington immediately to track down the murderer of the President. He arrived in the Capital accompanied by his cousin, Lieutenant Luther B. Baker, and found that no detectives from his force had been out on the trail of the fugitives, nor had any reward been posted for information leading to their capture. His first move, therefore, was to have handbills printed offering twenty thousand dollars from the city of Washington, and ten thousand dollars from the War Department, for the capture of Lincoln's assassin and the unknown person who had attempted to kill Seward. This sent men of every rank in search of them. Later rewards, amounting to approximately two hundred thousand dollars, resulted in many more joining the hunt.[31]

After entering Zachiah Swamp, Wilkes and Herold soon lost all sense of direction and wandered about until nine o'clock, when they encountered a colored man, Oswald Swan. Wilkes was not wearing the false whiskers then and since they were never seen or heard of again, it has always been presumed that he disposed of them in the swamp. After the Negro brought the fugitives some whisky and bread, he was ordered by Wilkes to take them to the home of Samuel Cox. Before they reached there, Wilkes warned Swan, "Don't you say anything; if you tell anybody that you saw anything you will not live long." [32]

At the beginning of the war, Samuel Cox, a wealthy slaveowner, had served the rebel states as captain of a volunteer company with headquarters in Bryantown. He occupied a large frame house surrounded by outbuildings and Negro quarters, about fifteen miles from that village and an equal distance across Zachiah Swamp from the home of Dr. Mudd. His acreage, far removed from any public road, contained much woodland, and was known as *Rich Hill*. He had a foster-brother named Thomas Jones, also of that vicinity. Jones was a short, slender man with a thin and melancholy face. He gave the impression of being dull-witted, but back of his gray-blue eyes was a cunning brain which had served the Confederacy since the outbreak of hostilities.

It had been his duty to get spies and messengers carrying contraband mail across the Potomac River on their trips to and from Richmond.

In the fall of 1861 he was arrested by Federal officers and lodged in a Washington jail for six months. There he met more Confederate prisoners who related their experiences and taught him how to improve his service. When he was released by a general jail delivery ordered by Congress in March of the following year, he had completed a course in blockade-running second to none, and eventually became the chief signal agent of the Confederacy in lower Maryland. At the time that Wilkes and Herold came that way, he lived in an old cabin on a farm known as *Huckleberry*, about a mile from the Potomac River.

On the afternoon following the assassination, two Federal cavalrymen met Jones and one called out, "Is that your boat down at the creek?"

"Yes, it is," replied Jones.

"Well you had better keep an eye to it," said the cavalryman. "There are suspicious characters somewhere in the neighborhood who will be wanting to cross the river, and if you do not look sharp you will lose your boat."

"Indeed, I will look after it," Jones answered. "I would not like to lose it, as it is my fishing boat and the shad are beginning to run." The boat was lead colored, had a flat bottom, and was about twelve feet long. Jones had purchased it in Baltimore the year before for eighteen dollars.

The two horsemen conferred for a moment, then one asked, "Have you heard the news from Washington?"

Jones said he had not, and the soldier continued, "Then I will tell you. Our President has been murdered."

This brought a mournful look over Jones' face, and he exclaimed, as if the news touched him deeply, "Is it possible!"

"Yes," said the soldier, "President Lincoln was killed last night, and the men who did it came this way."

Early the next morning Jones had a visitor. He was an adopted son of Samuel Cox and said his father wished to see him about getting some seed-corn. But Jones knew Cox had reasons other than seed-corn for wanting to get in touch with him. When he arrived, Cox met him at the gate and casually spoke to him of several matters before he mentioned that he had had visitors.

"Who were they and what did they want?" asked Jones.

"They want to get across the river," Cox replied, and then whispered, "Have you heard that Lincoln was killed Friday night?"

Jones said that two soldiers had told him of it on the previous evening. Cox then related how he had been disturbed about four o'clock that morning by a knocking at his door. On opening it, he had found a strange man standing there, while another on horseback, accompanied by Oswald Swan, waited at the gate. He went out to the man who, when convinced that he was Samuel Cox, took him beyond hearing of the Negro and told him what he had done, showing the initials J. W. B. in India ink upon his left hand to prove his identity. He explained how he had broken his leg and thereby been prevented from reaching the river that fateful Friday night. As a ruse to make the Negro believe they had been ordered from the place, Wilkes had gone off cursing Cox. After paying Swan twelve dollars and dismissing him, the fugitives had returned to the house where they had remained until Cox's overseer, Franklin A. Robey, took charge of them.[33]

"Tom, we must get these men who were here this morning across the river," continued Cox.

As southern Maryland was then "swarming with soldiers and detectives . . . eager to avenge the murder of their beloved President and reap the reward," Jones felt that the odds were against him, but said he would see what he could do and asked where the men were hiding. Cox told him that Robey had guided them to a place in the thick pines about one mile to the west of the house. He had advised them to remain quiet and had said someone would be sent to look after them. They had agreed upon a signal, a low and peculiar whistle, by which they were to know who approached. Sufficient food and a pair of blankets had been left with them. "Take care how you approach them, Tom," warned Cox. "They are fully armed and might shoot you through mistake."

Near the hiding place to which Jones had been directed, he saw a bay mare grazing in an open space made for a tobacco bed. The saddle and bridle were still on, and Jones, supposing the mare belonged to some neighbor, tied her to a tree. At the agreed spot, he stopped and gave the whistle. Herold slowly emerged from the thicket, carrying the carbine, and instantly demanded what he wanted. Jones answered that he had been sent by Cox. Satisfied, Herold said, "Follow me." They entered a dense underbrush and came to Wilkes, about thirty yards farther, lying on the ground wrapped in a blanket and wearing a slouch hat. His pistols, knife, and crutches were beside him.

"This friend comes from Captain Cox," said Herold. Wilkes was courteous and polite, despite the intense pain from his broken leg. Jones promised the fugitives that he would get them across the river as soon as possible but said they must wait until an opportunity presented itself, for to attempt it then would be suicide. In the meantime, he would arrange to bring food to them each day. Wilkes held out his hand and thanked him. He told Jones of his crime and said he knew the Federal Government would do everything possible to capture him. "But," he added, "they will never take me alive."

The flash of determination in Wilkes' dark eyes convinced Jones that he meant what he said. He was anxious to know what was being published about him and asked for newspapers. Jones pointed out a near-by spring where they could obtain drinking water and informed them they must get rid of their horses, or the animals would betray them.

The horses disappeared, but Jones never knew definitely what became of them, notwithstanding the fact that Cox told him he had seen the horses at a distance being led away and heard shots which he supposed killed them.[34]

On Tuesday Jones rode over to Port Tobacco to see what was going on among the officers and soldiers combing the country for the fugitives. In the barroom of the Brawner House, he met William Wells, a detective, who suspected he knew more than his face indicated, and offered to guarantee one hundred thousand dollars to the man who would tell where Lincoln's assassin was hiding. Jones looked blankly at him and drawled, "That's a right good sum to give for one man."[35]

Each day, Jones sent Henry Woodland, his Negro, on a fishing trip in the lead-colored skiff he kept down by the Potomac River, so that Federal officers, seeing it in constant use, would not destroy it. When Woodland returned in the evening, he left the boat near a creek flowing into the river just below Dent's Meadow. This land separated Jones' farm from the shore of the Potomac River.

From Sunday morning until Friday night, the fugitives were forced to remain in the pine thicket.[36] The weather was not suitable to outdoor life. Fog and mist kept the ground wet, and the dampness chilled them. In all that time their hiding place was never suspected by their pursuers, although the fugitives "once heard the clanking of sabers and tramping of horses, as a body of cavalry passed down the road within two hundred yards" of them. Even Jones did not see much of Wilkes and Herold, as he rode through the woods pretending to look for his stray hogs, and never lingered with the two men after delivering provisions and newspapers.[37] It was while he was in the thicket that Wilkes read the first accounts of his crime and wrote in his diary:[38]

>April 13, 14, Friday, The Ides
>Until today nothing was ever thought of sacrificing to our country's wrongs. For six months we have worked to cap-

ture. But our cause being almost lost, something decisive and great must be done. But its failure was owing to others who did not strike for their country with a heart. I struck boldly, and not as the papers say. I walked with a firm step through a thousand of his friends; was stopped but pushed on. A colonel was at his side. I shouted Sic semper before I fired. In jumping I broke my leg. I passed all his pickets. Rode sixty miles that night, with the bone of my leg tearing the flesh at every jump.

I can never repent it, though we hated to kill. Our country owed all our troubles to him, and God simply made me the instrument of his punishment.

The country is not what it was. This forced union is not what I have loved. I care not what becomes of me. I have no desire to outlive my country. This night (before the deed) I wrote a long article and left it for one of the editors of the *National Intelligencer*, in which I fully set forth our reasons for our proceedings. He or the Gov't . . .

The abrupt ending of the diary at this point probably was due to Jones' arrival.

Thursday, April twentieth, Jones had another boat in his possession brought up from Allen's Fresh, a village three miles east of his house, and instructed his Negro to leave it at a certain point along the Potomac near Dent's Meadow. Jones was away from home most of the afternoon and spent that night waiting for a favorable opportunity to send the fugitives across the river. But too many soldiers were still in the neighborhood and he gave up hope of doing anything immediately. Before daylight on Friday morning he went down to the river's edge and concealed the boat his Negro had left there by drawing it into the marsh. This was a precautionary measure should something happen to the fishing boat in daily use. About sunrise Jones returned to his home.[39]

During the late afternoon he rode to Allen's Fresh and sauntered into Colton's store. He had not been there long when Federal cavalry, guided by John Walton, arrived and dismounted. While some of the soldiers were in the store ordering drinks, Walton entered and exclaimed, "Boys, I have news that they [the fugitives] have been seen in St. Mary's." Immediately the men rushed to their horses and galloped off in that direction.

Jones waited a few minutes, then leisurely rode away in a manner not to excite suspicion. A light mist had been falling throughout the day, and darkness was now beginning to blot everything from sight.

Well out of the village, he raced his horse to where Wilkes and Herold were concealed. It was the first time he had visited them at night, and he approached their hiding place with a great deal of caution. "The coast seems to be clear," said Jones, "and the darkness favors us. Let us make the attempt."

Wilkes was lifted into the saddle on Jones' horse and their possessions strapped around him. Herold led the horse, and Jones walked ahead to make sure the way was clear. Every fifty or sixty yards he stopped, gave a low whistle, waited until they appeared, then repeated the performance. In this way, they traveled about one and a half miles over a cart track to a public road, then down that road another mile to Jones' farm, and through the farm to the Potomac River, one mile farther on. The public road was the most dangerous part of the way over which they had to pass, chiefly because of two houses close to it. One of these was occupied by a Negro whose children were always curious to see who passed, and Jones dreaded the dogs at the other place, as they might bark and give them away. Nothing happened, however, and about ten o'clock they reached his farm.

Jones told them to wait near the stable and he would bring out food, but the glow of a lamp and the thought of a warm room tempted Wilkes to ask if he could not go into the cabin and drink some hot coffee. It distressed Jones to refuse him but he said that it would not be safe for those in the house to see him and jeopardize their last chance to get away.

In the kitchen Jones found his colored man, Henry Woodland, eating supper, and casually spoke to him of the fishing he had done that day. Finally, he said, "Henry, did you bring the boat back to Dent's Meadow?" The Negro replied that he had left it there, and Jones continued his random conversation while getting food for the fugitives. After taking it out to them, he returned, ate his supper, and again disappeared. His children and other members of his household, knowing his rebel connections, never inquired about his movements or asked what such nightly prowlings meant.

The three men now continued their journey as before. A few hundred yards from the river a fence crossed their path and made further use of the horse impossible. Jones and Herold carried Wilkes down a steep and narrow footway to the shore of the Potomac, where they found the flat-bottomed fishing boat left by the Negro. Wilkes was placed in the stern of it with his crutches, firearms, and an oar to steer, and Herold got in amidships to row. "Here," said Jones, "is a bottle of whisky I brought along for you; it will keep you warm." A candle was lighted (and shaded by a coat) so that Jones could point

Wilkes' escape route. (8) The Samuel Cox house.

Wilkes' escape route. (9) Mary Swan (Old Aunt Mary Kelly), ex-slave of Cox who observed the conspirators at Cox's house.

Wilkes' escape route. (10) The cabin of Thomas Jones, who cared for Booth and Herold when they were in hiding near Cox's house.

Wilkes' escape route. (11) The stream below Dent's Meadow.

Wilkes' escape route. (12) The shore of the Potomac where Jones guided Booth and Herold.

Wilkes' escape route. (13) Nanjemoy Stores, where the tide carried the fugitives.

out to them on a compass the course to Machadoc Creek across the river.

"Mrs. Elizabeth Quesenberry lives near the mouth of this creek. If you tell her you come from me, I think she will take care of you," Jones informed them, as he was about to shove the little skiff from shore. Just then Wilkes exclaimed, "Wait, old fellow; here, take this," and offered Jones some money, which he refused. Wilkes insisted, however, that he pay him something, and Jones accepted the price of his boat, certain that he would never see it again. "God bless you, my dear friend, for all you have done for me. Good-by, old fellow," said Wilkes, and the boat glided out into the darkness of the river. Not until the sound of the oars had died away did Jones return to his little cabin at Huckleberry farm.[40]

CHAPTER IV

Land conditions were favorable to the escape of the fugitives from Maryland that night, but conditions on the Potomac River were not. Wilkes and Herold, having no experience in navigation, could not manage the boat when left to the mercy of the flood tide. In seeking to evade a Federal gunboat they were thrown entirely off their course. At daybreak, Herold saw familiar landmarks near by and, recognizing the home of a Colonel John J. Hughes, knew they were not yet on Virginia soil. Instead of crossing the river from Pope's Creek, as Jones had directed and as they supposed they were doing, they had drifted eight miles west to a point on the Maryland shore known as Nanjemoy Stores.

Herold pulled the boat up into the marsh, where Wilkes remained, while he took the risk of asking for food at Colonel Hughes' house. Hopeless and alone, Wilkes scrawled his misery over the pages of his diary:

Friday 21 [41]

After being hunted like a dog through swamps, woods, and last night being chased by gunboats till I was forced to return wet, cold, and starving, with every man's hand against me, I am here in despair. And why? For doing what Brutus was honored for—what made Tell a hero. And yet I, for striking down a greater tyrant than they ever knew, am looked upon as a common cut-throat. My action was purer than either of theirs. One hoped to be great. The other had not only his country's, but his own, wrongs to avenge. I hoped for no gain. I knew no private wrong. I struck for my country and that alone. A country that groaned beneath this tyranny, and prayed for this end, and yet now behold the cold hand they extend me. God cannot pardon me if I have done wrong. Yet I cannot see my wrong, except in serving a degenerate people. The little, the very little, I left behind to clear my name, the government will not allow to be printed. So ends all. For my country I have given up all that makes life sweet and holy, brought misery upon my family, and am sure there is no pardon in the Heaven for me, since man condemns me so. I have only heard of what has been done (except what I did myself), and it fills me with horror. God, try and forgive me, and bless my mother. Tonight I will once more try the river with the intent to cross. Though I have a greater desire and almost a mind to return to Washington, and in a measure clear my name—which I feel I can do.[42] I do not repent the blow I struck. I may before my God, but not to man. I think I have done well. Though I am abandoned, with the curse of Cain upon me, when, if the world knew my heart, that one blow would have made me great, though I did desire no greatness.

Tonight I try to escape these blood-hounds once more. Who, who can read his fate? God's will be done. I have too great a soul to die like a criminal. O, may He, may He spare me that, and let me die bravely.

I bless the entire world. Have never hated or wronged anyone. This last was not a wrong, unless God deems it so, and it's with Him to damn or bless me. And for this brave boy with me, who often prays (yes, before and since) with a true and sincere heart—was it crime in him? If so, why can he pray the same?

I do not wish to shed a drop of blood, but "I must fight the course." 'Tis all that's left me.

Fortunately for them Hughes, though frightened, was in sympathy with the fugitives. He gave them food and milk in place of whisky and that night they got across a three-mile stretch of the river. Daylight, however, forced them to seek the shelter of Gambo Creek, some distance from Mrs. Quesenberry's home which would have been more accessible had they gone up Machadoc Creek. Herold pulled the boat ashore and about noon started off to seek her aid, Wilkes waiting under a walnut tree.

Herold was informed by Mrs. Quesenberry's daughter that her mother was not in and he asked that someone be sent for her. When she returned Herold inquired if she would furnish a conveyance which could take him into the country. She refused and wanted to know why he did not walk. Herold explained, "I can but my brother, who is sitting down by the river, cannot, for his horse fell and broke his leg." He then divulged that they were escaped prisoners and entreated her to sell them a horse. Mrs. Quesenberry was still unwilling to assist them and Herold decided to come to the point at once. Jones had said that she might take care of them so he blurted out, "The man who killed Abe Lincoln is within a mile of this house." The danger of being held as an accessory prompted her to demand his immediate departure, but as he turned to go she asked if they had eaten anything.

He told her they had been without food all day and she promised to send some to them.

Thomas Harbin, a stepbrother of Jones, delivered the supplies in a satchel belonging to Mrs. Quesenberry.[43] Harbin found Wilkes stretched on the ground, suffering from his injured leg. He talked very little, but expressed the belief that the worst part of the journey was over. Thus far it had been attended with some danger but now he anticipated no difficulty in escaping southward. He confided to Harbin that he was Lincoln's assassin. Wilkes asked where he could get some sort of vehicle to carry him to Dr. Stewart's home (eight miles distant) and was told old man Bryant would accommodate him. The fugitives were being passed from one rebel to another!

William L. Bryant, the man Harbin referred to, was a neighbor of Mrs. Quesenberry. Herold arrived at his house about an hour before sundown and repeated his plea for a means of travel. Bryant looked him over and said he could not help him. "Well," said Herold, "I was recommended to Dr. Stewart to have something done to my brother's leg. I'll give you ten dollars to carry us there."

One of Bryant's horses was in the yard and another not far off. He saddled them and was directed by Herold to where Wilkes was sitting in a field about a quarter of a mile from the house. Wilkes said less to Bryant than he had to Harbin but Herold talked incessantly. On the way to Stewart's house, Bryant tried to find out why they wished to go there when other doctors were more convenient, and Herold repeated that "he was recommended to Dr. Stewart." In answer to Bryant's question as to what caused the injury to Wilkes' leg, Herold explained, "He got it broke in Richmond in a fight; a horse threw him and broke his leg, and he was paroled to go home."[44]

Dr. Richard H. Stewart was considered one of the wealthiest men in that community and the most prominent Confederate. He had two homes, one in a wooded section, which he called *Cleydale*, where he spent the summer months with his family, and another, used as a winter residence, on the bank of the Potomac River. During most of the war, the Stewarts lived at the former retreat, as it not only avoided the malaria and heat of Mathias Point in the summer, but was distant from Federal gunboats patrolling the river throughout the year. Two of General Lee's daughters lived with them part of the time their father was at the front, and many rebels, traveling on Confederate missions, stopped over here or at Mrs. Quesenberry's. For such services to his countrymen, Dr. Stewart had been twice arrested and confined, once in Washington and once in a prison ship near his waterfront home.

Late that Sunday afternoon, Bryant, Wilkes, and Herold arrived

Wilkes' escape route. (14) The point at which the fugitives crossed the Potomac.

Wilkes' escape route. (15) Gambo Creek.

Wilkes' escape route. (16) The Quesenberry house (remodeled since 1865).

Wilkes' escape route. (17) Slave quarters on the Quesenberry property.

at his summer residence, slightly drunk. Dr. Stewart had just finished tea with his family when they came. He went to the door and found them all on horseback except Herold. As it was dark, he could not very well distinguish them and asked, "Who are you?" Herold answered, "Two of us are Marylanders in want of accommodations for the night." Dr. Stewart replied it was impossible to keep them, as he had no room. Herold then mentioned Wilkes' broken leg and acquainted him with the fact that Dr. Mudd had set it and recommended him to aid them on their journey.

Dr. Stewart answered that he was a physician not a surgeon, that he had heard of the Mudds in Maryland but did not know them, and that no one was authorized to recommend anyone to him. Again Herold appealed for assistance, saying that they were very weary and hungry. The doctor insisted that he had no room but would give them something to eat. Wilkes then urged, "If you will listen to the circumstances of the case you will be able to do it." Dr. Stewart was firm. Their appearance and actions made him suspicious of them and he had no desire to hear anything that they had to say. Herold was still carrying the carbine and Wilkes' face was partly obscured by a large shawl. The doctor thought the leg injury and crutches merely a sham to get his sympathy and aid. He was beginning to fear that they might be connected with Lincoln's assassination of which he had heard the previous Tuesday. Since he had returned only recently from his second imprisonment, he did not want to take chances on harboring fugitives.

Herold would not cease chattering and disclosed that they wished to get to Mosby. Dr. Stewart bluntly informed him that this leader of a rebel band engaged in guerrilla warfare had surrendered. Herold next asked if he knew of anyone who could take them to Fredericksburg, and Stewart suggested a colored man named William Lucas who lived near by and sometimes hired out his wagons. Lucas had often conveyed the doctor's "guests" to Port Conway on the Rappahannock River.

After Wilkes and Herold had gone into the house for supper, the doctor questioned Bryant about them. Bryant alleged all he knew was that they had come to him from the marsh and asked if he could get them to Dr. Stewart's place. The doctor retorted, "It is very strange; I know nothing about the men; I cannot accommodate them; you will have to take them somewhere else," and went into the house.

Bryant started for home, but the doctor, hearing him depart, ran out and chased him two or three hundred yards up the road. "I can't accommodate these men," he shouted. "You must take them away!"

Bryant came back, and the doctor once more went into his house. He announced to his uninvited visitors, "The old man's waiting for you; he is anxious to be off; it is cold; he is not well and wants to get home." When they finished their meal, Wilkes and Herold returned to Bryant outside. They had been in the house about a quarter of an hour. The doctor lost no time in having Bryant mount them on his horses. As they were leaving Wilkes asked Bryant if he would take them over to the Negro, William Lucas, which was about a quarter of a mile down the road. Bryant said it was his nearest way home and he would do so.

When they approached the cabin, dogs began to bark. Herold called to Lucas but the Negro would not open the door until he knew who was there. Only after he heard Bryant's voice would he come out. Herold again did most of the talking. "We want to stay here tonight," he declared.

"I's a cullud man and got no right to take care o' white people," replied Lucas. "I's only one room in my house and my wife am sick."

"We are Confederate soldiers," said Herold. "We have been in the service three years; we have been knocking about all night and don't intend to any longer; so we are going to stay."

In the meantime Wilkes had hobbled into the house. Old Lucas began to remonstrate with them. "Gen'lemen, you has treated me very badly," he complained. Wilkes, who was now sitting down, took out a dagger and brandished it at him with, "Old man, how do you like that! We were sent here—we understand you have a good team." In a quivering voice Lucas replied, "I's don't like dat at all. I's afraid o' a knife," but told them they could not have the team for he had hired hands coming in the morning to plant corn.

Wilkes then turned to Herold, "Well, Dave, we will not go any further, but stay here and make this old man get us his horses in the morning." They forced Lucas to give them some whisky and began another drinking bout.

Poor Lucas was afraid to go to sleep, and took his wife out on the steps where they stayed for the rest of the night. About seven o'clock on Monday morning Wilkes ordered the horses hitched to a wagon. After Lucas had done so Herold helped Wilkes get in. The Negro asked if they were going to take his horses without pay. Wilkes' reply was to inquire what he got for driving to Port Conway. He answered ten dollars in gold or twenty dollars in greenbacks, and asked that his son go with them. Wilkes refused, saying they might want to go further but Herold interrupted, "Yes, he can go; you have a large family, and a crop on hand, and you can have the team back again." Then old Lucas bravely ventured, "I's thought you would be done pressin' teams in de Northern Neck since de fall o' Richmond." Wilkes menacingly exclaimed, "Repeat that again!" Lucas said no more.

Wilkes had torn a page from his diary and written a querulous note, in which he had rolled up some money, for Lucas to deliver to Dr. Stewart.[45] Wilkes paid Lucas' wife for the use of the team and young Lucas drove the fugitives off on their ten-mile journey to Port Conway. Simultaneously Major General W. S. Hancock appealed, in the Washington *Star*, to the colored people to "go forth . . . watch and listen and inquire and search and pray, by day and by night, until you shall have succeeded in dragging this monstrous and bloody criminal from his hiding place." Several days before some of Mosby's guerrilla bands had come within the Union line at Fairfax Station and surrendered themselves, but a few were still along the lower Potomac and on the banks of the Rappahannock near Fredericksburg. It is most probable that the fugitives, being in the vicinity, heard of them and hoped to join these outlaws still at large in that section of the country.

When Wilkes and Herold reached Port Conway during the early afternoon in the rickety wagon driven by young Lucas, he refused to take them farther and returned home. The owner of the Rappahannock River ferry, William Rollins, was preparing to go fishing and did not notice them, until Herold, at his yard gate, asked him if he could have a drink of water for his brother with a broken leg in the wagon at the wharf. He took it to Wilkes, then returned and tried to persuade Rollins to convey them from Port Royal, on the other side of the river, to Orange Court House. Rollins answered it would be impossible but Herold induced him to promise that he would drive them to Bowling Green, fifteen miles away.

Just then a man waiting for Rollins to go fishing, hailed him and he started off. Herold called to him to ferry them across the narrow river, and Rollins answered he would do so when he returned if the ferryboat had not arrived there before that time. It could not be brought over just then as the tide was very low and so the fugitives were forced to wait. Though anxious to forge ahead they did not wish to travel after dark because they needed rest. Rollins, they thought, was disinclined to start before sundown and they decided to try someone else.

While they were discussing other means of procedure, eighteen-year-old Willie S. Jett, of the 9th Virginia Cavalry, and two of his companions, A. R. Bainbridge and Mortimer B. Ruggles, who had been with Mosby's command, arrived on horseback at Port Conway. They reached a hill about fifty yards from the river and saw the wagon at the wharf, but, since it was a common occurrence for such conveyances to be waiting for the Port Royal ferry, they paid no attention to it. As they approached the wagon, Herold jumped out, put his hand in the inside breast pocket of his coat as if reaching for a weapon, but did not speak. They rode on down to the landing and signaled the ferryman. No sooner had they done so than Herold approached them and said, "Gentlemen, what command do you belong to?" Ruggles answered, "To Mosby's command." Jett and Bainbridge were silent. Herold continued, "If I am not inquisitive, can I ask where you are going?" "That is a secret," parried Jett, "nobody knows where we are going because I never tell anybody." He then turned toward the ferry landing across the narrow river and said nothing more. One of Jett's companions inquired of Herold under what command he had served, to which he replied, "We belong to A. P. Hill's corps; I have my brother with me, a Marylander, who was wounded in a fight below Petersburg." Jett asked their names, and Herold gave his as David E. Boyd and Wilkes' as James William Boyd.

At this moment Wilkes got out of the wagon and began to hobble toward the wharf on his crutches. Jett and his companions had turned in the direction of the opposite shore and were ignoring Herold. Somewhat exasperated, he said, "Come, gentlemen, I suppose you are all going to the Southern Army?" They did not respond, and Herold added, "We are also anxious to get there ourselves and wish you to take us along." The three men continued to disregard him and he proposed, "Come, gentlemen, get down; we have something to drink here. We will go and take a drink." They thanked him but rejected the offer.

Jett rode off about twenty yards and tied his horse to a tree. Herold continued to beg Ruggles and Bainbridge to take him and Wilkes across the river to a place of safety, and to quiet him, they promised to do so. Wilkes, haggard and pinched with a beard of some ten days' growth, and eyes sunken but strangely bright, came up to them. He must have suspected Herold of disclosing his identity for he said, "I suppose you have been told who I am?" Ruggles, concluding he referred to Herold's account, answered in the affirmative. Wilkes quickly drew his revolver and leaned back on his crutch. In a calm, steady voice he announced, "Yes, I am John Wilkes Booth, the slayer of Abraham Lincoln, and I am worth just one hundred and seventy-five thousand dollars to the man who captures me."

Ruggles retorted that they did not sanction his act as an assassin, but were not men to take blood money. Since they had promised Herold to assist them, they would do so. Wilkes then replaced his weapon.

Jett returned and saw them all sitting on the steps of a near-by house. He went over to them, and Herold rose, saying he would like to speak with him. They walked toward the wharf and Herold began, "I take it for granted you are raising a command to go south to Mexico, and I want you to let us go with you." Astonished, Jett asked, "Who are you?" Herold unhesitatingly boasted, "We are the assassinators of the President!" He added that, if Jett would carefully notice the lame man's left hand, he would see the letters, *J. W. B.*, which were not the initials of the names he had given him, but of John Wilkes Booth. Ruggles interrupted them, and Jett exclaimed, "Here is a strange thing!" then repeated what Herold had just told him. Wilkes now joined them, and Herold, after inquiring their names, introduced him as Mr. Booth. To prove it Wilkes threw back the shawl he had just put on and showed them the initials on his left hand.[46]

Rollins, back from his fishing, was at the wharf when he heard rapping at the door of his house. He turned and saw Jett and Herold beckoning to him. After counting his shad, he went to them, and Jett asked if he had any ink. He took them into the house where they copied paroles, on notepaper procured by Herold from Wilkes, forging the name of a provost marshal. They took this precaution in case they were met and questioned by Federal officers. Herold's possession of this notepaper probably accounts for several of the missing pages in Wilkes' diary.

As the ferryboat started across the river from the Port Royal side, Wilkes hobbled to the edge of the wharf where Ruggles and Bainbridge were waiting on their horses. Herold and Jett came from the house followed by Rollins, and Jett went to get his horse while the other two men sauntered toward the landing. Herold informed Rollins that he and Wilkes would not need to hire his wagon, as they would go on with their friends. Wilkes was lifted onto Ruggles' horse, and when the scow arrived, all but Rollins boarded it.

The Negro poling the ferry glowered at Wilkes whose refusal to dismount violated the law regarding passengers. Wilkes gazed ahead as if he could hardly wait to reach the opposite shore. The moment they were off the scow he cheerfully exclaimed, "Thank God! Now I am safe!"

Jett was well acquainted in Caroline County, and told Wilkes he would find someone to look after him until Herold could hire a conveyance to carry them on. Wilkes asked that he be spoken of and introduced as a Confederate soldier by the name of Boyd, and Jett galloped off toward the home of Sarah Peyton, a spinster living in Port Royal. The other members of the party followed at a slower pace. By the time Miss Peyton had consented to care for him a few days, Wilkes and his companions were at her gate. He was lifted from Ruggles' horse, but when he hobbled into the house, Miss Peyton saw the variety of pistols and knives under his coat and changed her mind. She called Jett aside and informed him that, since her brother was not at home, she would be unable to shelter his wounded friend. "Get him in somewhere up the road—Mr. Garrett's or some other place," she said.

Jett did not argue with her, but, before going on, crossed the street to the home of another friend named Catlitt, while Wilkes went back to the gate. Finding no one in, Jett returned to his companions and said, "Now, boys, I propose to take our friend, Booth, up to Garrett's house. I think they will give him shelter there and treat him kindly."

"Whatever you do with me, I'll agree to be satisfied," replied Wilkes.

"Jett knows what is best, and I think it will be well to act as he directs," said Ruggles.

"I am in your hands," answered Wilkes, "and will go wherever you suggest."

"Well, let's take Mr. Booth to Garrett's," said Jett, "tell the family who he is, and trust to their hospitality to make him comfortable until he sees fit to seek other quarters."

Wilkes was again placed on Ruggles' horse and the journey continued, Ruggles riding with Bainbridge, and Herold with Jett. It was then about one o'clock in the afternoon. During the two or three miles travel to the farm very little was said. Herold pushed up his sleeves and showed Jett an image of a heart tattooed on his right arm, also an anchor on his left, with the initials, *D. E. H.* The *H* had been partly rubbed out, and Herold explained that he had tried to remove the initials. Wilkes grimly remarked that, if he found himself in danger of being captured, he did not intend to be taken alive. "If they don't kill me, I'll kill myself," he declared.

At the outer gate, leading directly from the public road into the farm of Richard H. Garrett, Herold got off Jett's horse to go on to Bowling Green with Bainbridge. He exchanged places with Ruggles, who then rode with Jett, and the two accompanied Wilkes up a lane to the large, old-fashioned Garrett home, at one side of which was a tobacco barn. Slightly to the rear of it were two smaller structures used as corn-cribs, and behind them a cow-shed and stable. All of these frame buildings stood on a knoll surrounded by broad patches of open fields and dense forests.

Jett introduced himself to Mr. Garrett, saying he had not met him

Wilkes' escape route. (18) The back road at the left of the picture is the one leading from the Quesenberry house to the Stewart house.

Wilkes' escape route. (19) Rear of the Stewart house, where the office door was and where Booth and Herold arrived. (The lean-to is a later addition.)

Wilkes' escape route. (20) Front view of the Stewart house.

Wilkes' escape route. (21) Cabin similar to the Lucas cabin, near the Stewart house, where Booth and Herold spent one night.

Wilkes' escape route. (22) The road from the Lucas cabin where it meets the ferry landing at Port Conway.

Wilkes' escape route. (23) The Garrett house, where Booth died and Herold was captured. (No longer standing.)

before but had seen him at the courthouse. As Jett knew Garrett to be a staunch Southerner, he continued, "Here is a wounded Confederate soldier that we want you to take care of for a day or two; will you do it?"

"Yes, certainly I will," replied Garrett.

They helped Wilkes off Ruggles' horse and assured him that for the present this was the best place to stay. Jett, who had a sweetheart at Bowling Green and wanted no more delay in getting there, rode off at a gallop with Ruggles trailing him.

Many of Garrett's neighbors believed that Jett, after leaving Wilkes at the farm, first stopped at a place called Ashland, and notified Washington by telegraph of where they could find Lincoln's assassin;[47] but this was not possible.

In the Capital that afternoon, Lieutenant Edward P. Doherty received an order from the War Department to report with a detachment of twenty-five men to Colonel L. C. Baker. Doherty, Baker's cousin Lieutenant L. B. Baker, and former Lieutenant Colonel E. J. Conger, were to have control over the movements of the detachment in the pursuit of Lincoln's assassin. Colonel Baker pointed out to them on coast survey maps, the escape route taken by Wilkes and Herold through Maryland toward Virginia. He stressed the importance of capturing them unharmed and bringing them back to Washington for trial.

The activity in Baker's department which resulted in these men's dashing southward, began before noon; hence Jett could not have been responsible for it. Nor has such a telegram or any record of it been found. Apparently, no one in the community ever questioned the telegrapher then at Ashland, yet all were convinced that Jett betrayed the fugitives. To this day the source of Colonel Baker's information is unknown, yet at the time he gave as his informant a mythical Negro in order to throw out other claimants to the reward.[48]

When Colonel Baker's men boarded the steamer *John S. Ide* and left Washington at two o'clock in the afternoon of April twenty-fourth, they took the most direct route to Port Conway, which was down the Potomac River to Belle Plain, where they arrived about ten o'clock that night. The experienced Conger, knowing the roads in that vicinity, went ahead of the party with Lieutenant Baker, while Lieutenant Doherty remained with the detachment which followed about half a mile behind. Conger and Baker stopped at the homes of prominent Confederates and said, "We are being pursued by Yankees, and in crossing the river we have become separated from two of our party; one of them is lame; have you seen them?" But the answers and the scowls they received frightened Conger and Baker, and they soon decided they had better not use such pretense.

After traveling all night, the detachment halted early in the morning for rest at the home of a Dr. Ashton who lived near the Rappahannock River. The party then separated. Conger and Baker, accompanied by a few soldiers, combed the country along the Rappahannock, and Doherty, with the remaining men, followed the shore line of the Potomac. A short distance from Port Conway, they met again, had dinner at the home of a planter, and fed their horses. At this point, most of the men were so weary they fell asleep, and Conger, distressed by a wound received in the war, was exhausted. Baker went on to Port Conway, hoping to get some information of the fugitives. There he spied the Negro ferryman who acted dumb and told him nothing. While engaged with him, however, Baker saw Rollins and his wife sitting in the doorway of their house.

He went to them and inquired if they had seen two citizens, one lame, pass that way. They told him of the men who had been there the previous day. He showed them several photographs, and Rollins selected those of Wilkes and Herold, saying, "There are the men, only this one had no mustache." He also mentioned the three Confederate soldiers who had crossed the river with the fugitives and gave their names. Baker asked if he knew the direction they had taken, and Rollins drawled, "Wal, this fellow Jett has a lady-love over at Bowling Green, and I reckon he went over there." Unaware of the stop made at Garrett's farm, Rollins suggested to Baker that Goldman's Hotel, kept by the parents of Jett's sweetheart, "was big and would make a good hiding place for a wounded man." This convinced Baker he was not far from his objective, and he informed Rollins he would have to accompany him to Bowling Green. Rollins replied he did not wish to incur the hatred of his neighbors by going willingly, and added, "But you might make me your prisoner and I'll have to go."

Meanwhile, Doherty had arrived with the detachment, but Conger was still missing, so Baker sent his orderly back for him. He then hailed the ferry and told Doherty to get the men over as quickly as possible. But the boat was not large and it required three trips to get them across. By that time it was almost sundown. Apprehensive lest Wilkes and Herold be warned if it became known Federal troops were close on their heels, Baker circulated the information that the detachment was on its way to join the command at Fredericksburg. With Rollins as their guide, they set out from Port Royal for Bowling Green.

CHAPTER V

Bidding Jett and Ruggles good-by, Wilkes remained on the porch, talking to two of Garrett's sons, John, who had just returned from Appomattox, and his younger brother William, until they were all called in to supper.[49] When Wilkes had finished eating, he asked if he might retire, for his wound pained him. He was taken to one of the upper rooms in which the Garrett boys slept. Wilkes removed his coat, and little Robert Garrett saw that he had two revolvers and a pearl-handled knife. Wilkes slept peacefully through the night and was the last to get up in the morning. After breakfast with the family he went into the yard, where the younger children were playing, and lay down upon the grass. He spoke very little, but the Garretts supposed it was because he was suffering.

Early in the morning, the eldest son, John, went to have his boots repaired at a shoemaker's shop about a mile from the house. Another resident of the community was there and showed him a newspaper which a friend had brought from Richmond telling of Lincoln's assassination, and containing an advertisement offering one hundred and fifty thousand dollars reward for the capture of J. Wilkes Booth. During dinner that noon, John told of having seen the paper and mentioned the large reward offered for the assassin. "I wish he would come this way, so that I might catch him and get the reward," exclaimed Robert. Wilkes turned to him and asked, "If he were to come this way, would you inform against him?" The boy laughed and replied that he would like to have the money. Wilkes showed no emotion at all and said it would not have surprised him had the offer been half a million, adding that he had heard Lincoln's assassin had been captured between Baltimore and Philadelphia and taken to Washington. Garrett's daughter, Joanna, expressed the view that the man who killed the President had been well paid for it, whereupon Wilkes replied, "It is my opinion he wasn't paid a cent, but did it for notoriety's sake."

As Wilkes had told them he was a Marylander, someone asked if he had ever seen the Booth who shot Lincoln. "I saw him once in Richmond," said Wilkes, "about the time of the John Brown raid."

"Is he an old or a young man?" asked another of the family.

"Well," answered Wilkes, "he was rather a young fellow."

Old man Garrett informed them he had never heard of any Booth except the great actor, Edwin Booth. Wilkes smiled at that remark, remembering the reply he had given to the barroom banter: "When I leave the stage for good, I will be the most famous man in America."

At the end of the meal he accompanied the older Garrett boys into the yard where they practised shooting with their pistols at a post in front of the house. Wilkes hit the target each time and amazed them with his marksmanship. They had no idea that their amiable guest was a murderer, nor that a cloud of tragedy was hovering over them.

In Bowling Green the next morning, Herold and Bainbridge met Jett and Ruggles. Jett told them that Garrett did not want to shelter Wilkes, but with some coaxing he had finally permitted him to stay even though he feared he was taking a great chance. Garrett must have known his visitor's name and kept other members of his family ignorant of it. Ruggles decided to accompany Herold and Bainbridge to Garrett's, and Jett returned to the home of his sweetheart intending to visit her several days.

Herold supposedly had gone to Bowling Green for a pair of shoes, but his real purpose was to obtain information of rebel troops who, Wilkes hoped, might aid and protect them in their escape. He brought back the news that only some straggling Confederate cavalry was to be found at Milford, a short distance away. General Joseph E. Johnston and the last of the guerrillas had surrendered.

Mrs. Garrett had spread some quilts under the trees in front of the house for Wilkes to lie upon, and he was there talking with John when Herold got down from Bainbridge's horse and came toward the house. Wilkes went to meet him, and they walked slowly back to the porch, speaking rather low until they reached young Garrett, to whom Herold was introduced as "Davy." They told him they had decided to go to Milford the next day, and asked if they could hire horses from him and his brother to take them there, but John refused and suggested they get Ned Freeman, a colored man living close by who had a wagon.

Wilkes returned alone to the lawn where Ruggles joined him and they talked of what Wilkes had done. Wilkes told him that he was sure he could end the war by putting Lincoln out of the way and thus serve the country; he had not believed the conflict was over. He was chagrined that the people in Virginia were so inhospitable to him, and although he was resigned to anything that might happen, he would never be taken alive. Ruggles wanted to know why he did not attempt to reach Europe and Wilkes replied that there was no refuge for him in countries ruled by kings, for they were constantly in fear of assassins. Since he had learned that the war was definitely at an end and that the South could not protect him, he was resolved to go to the silver mines in Mexico. Had he not hurt his leg so badly, he would now be much farther along. Ruggles examined Wilkes' injury and, from his previous experience with wounds, thought that even amputation could not save him from death by gangrene.

He and Bainbridge left, and Wilkes went into the house with Robert Garrett. The latter took a United States map off the wall for Wilkes, who spread it on the floor and began marking routes leading from different southern cities to Mexico. Herold entered and closely followed his tracings. Soon they returned to the yard and Wilkes again lounged on the grass.

Federal cavalrymen under Conger and Baker were now coming along the public road leading to the Garrett farm on their way from Port Royal to Bowling Green. Ruggles and Bainbridge had gone only a short distance when they met another soldier of Mosby's command who informed them of the approaching Yankees, and advised galloping in an opposite direction unless they had their paroles or did not fear capture. This soldier lost no time in making his escape, but Ruggles and Bainbridge raced back to warn Wilkes of the danger. As they rode up to the gate, he hobbled out to them.

"Well, boys, what is in the wind now?" he asked.

"Yankees are coming! Get over there at once and hide yourself!" cried Bainbridge, pointing to a densely wooded section. "In those ravines you will never be found!"

"Yes! and get there as quickly as you can!" urged Ruggles.

Wilkes turned to look for Herold, but he had gone into the house. "I'll do as you say, boys, right off! Ride on! Good-by! It will never do for you to be found in my company. Rest assured of one thing, good friends, Wilkes will never be taken alive!" He called to Herold who brought out the pistols and carbine, and they hurried to the woods as Ruggles and Bainbridge rode away to find another hiding place. But curiosity got the better of these ex-soldiers, and they stopped on a hill to have a look at the Yankees. They saw two men (Conger and Baker) leave the detachment and start toward them, so they charged into a forest which the fading light of early evening failed to penetrate. The two Federal officers, believing the fugitives to be with Jett at Bowling Green, decided not to enter such a forbidding spot to chase horsemen for whom no reward had been offered and, rejoining their detachment, passed the Garrett farm.

As Garrett returned from some work near his house, he was surprised to see Wilkes and Herold head for the woods. When Herold reappeared later, Garrett was in the yard and told him supper would soon be ready. Herold called to Wilkes, who came out of the woods, and brought the firearms with him. It was then dark. After supper, Garrett murmured he did not feel well, and went to his room. A Yankee detachment passing his house, two criminals under his roof, and a tobacco barn filled with valuable furniture entrusted to his care by rebel neighbors who supposed it safely hidden under a covering of fodder and hay,[50] were enough to give him more than a headache. Apparently that last supper was a hurried one for all of them. No sooner had Garrett gone than Wilkes and Herold, realizing the danger of remaining longer in that vicinity, cornered his sons, John and William, took them to the porch, and asked that they help them make a hasty departure.

"We have heard there are Marylanders at Orange Courthouse who are endeavoring to get west of the Mississippi River and we wish to go with them," said Wilkes. "Can you get us a conveyance which will take us a part of the way tonight?" John repeated the suggestion he had made earlier: that they hire the Negro to take them in his wagon. "Why can't you let us have the horses we saw you riding this evening?" asked Herold. Wilkes' and Herold's excitement led the two Garrett boys to conclude that their insistence on leaving had something to do with the arrival of Federal troops in the neighborhood. Equally anxious to get them off the place as the men were to go, one of the boys went for the Negro in the hope that he would be willing to accommodate them, but he was not at home. Young Garrett returned and Wilkes offered him ten dollars to take them twenty miles farther before sunup. He refused to assist them that night but promised to do so the next morning. When Wilkes said they would wait, they were denied shelter in the house. Herold proposed sleeping under the front porch but was told the dogs on the place would annoy them. Wilkes suggested one of the outbuildings, and they were directed to the tobacco barn. This structure was boarded with slats having narrow spaces between them for drying the leaves stored inside. It was possible for anyone standing close to the tobacco barn to see inside and similarly one from the interior could see out through the openings.

The collection of firearms in the possession of Wilkes and Herold alarmed the older of the two Garrett boys, and both feared their uninvited guests might be planning to steal the horses for a quick getaway during the night. Their father was not informed of what had occurred, but the sons, who had taken charge of the situation, were determined to thwart such an attempt. They decided to take their blankets and remain in one of the corn-cribs between the tobacco barn and stable. The danger of being shot, should they openly defy the men, then dawned upon them, so John got a padlock and key, sneaked to the door, and locked Wilkes and Herold in the tobacco barn.[51]

At Bowling Green, Doherty left several of his men to guard the road leading into the town, and the rest of the detachment proceeded to Goldman's Hotel, where their arrival was announced by the loud barking of dogs. A light flickered from within the building as the Yankees surrounded it and demanded entrance. Conger went to the rear and Baker waited at the front door. It opened a crack and a woman's voice asked what was wanted. Baker quickly thrust his foot inside and pushed back the door but found only a frightened woman who said her name was Mrs. Goldman.

Meanwhile, Conger had entered the hotel through a rear door, and was being led to the main hallway by a Negro whose stammering answers to questions were more comical than enlightening.[52] The officers questioned Mrs. Goldman regarding the number of men in the house, and she answered that there was only her wounded son. On being warned of the consequences of giving false information, she admitted there was also an ex-Confederate cavalryman sleeping in the room with him. She was then ordered to direct the officers to the room and told that everyone found in the hotel would be taken to Washington as prisoners and the place burned, if any Federal was fired upon. It is possible that Jett had boasted to the Goldmans of having met and assisted Lincoln's assassin, and that Mrs. Goldman knew why the officers wanted him.

Candles were lighted, and the party ascended to the room on the second floor occupied by Jett and Mrs. Goldman's wounded son. When the officers threw open the door, Jett sprang from his bed clad only in his shirt. "Who do you want?" he cried, as he glared at pistols pointed in his direction. The officers announced they had full knowledge of what he had done, and one of them read Stanton's proclamation regarding the death penalty to be given persons assisting the fugitives in their flight. They threatened Jett with hanging if he did not tell what he knew, and promised him protection if his statements proved truthful. Not until he had disclosed all the facts did they permit him to dress and have his horse taken from the stable. He was then placed under guard, and the detachment started back over the dusty road they had just traveled.

It was now midnight, and the countryside was blotted out by darkness. At the edge of the town, Doherty found the men he had left there, fast asleep. The entire detachment, having been so long without rest, was exhausted and could hardly be kept moving. To prevent losing any of his men, Doherty ordered a sergeant named Boston Corbett[53] to the rear to see that no one fell out of line.

About two o'clock in the morning, the detachment drew up at the side of Garrett's orchard, and the officers, with Rollins in their midst, made their plans for the capture. A part of the fence was removed, and Doherty assigned men to surround the buildings on the premises and allow no one to pass, without giving the countersign, "Boston." All were instructed not to fire upon the fugitives unless in self-defense or to prevent their escape. From the orchard, the detachment cautiously moved toward the house, quietly opened the gates, and encircled the dwelling. Their movements, however, brought the dogs into the yard, and they began an uproar which awakened Garrett, who opened a window and discovered that the number of his uninvited guests had increased.

"What's going on here?" he shouted at the men.

"Never mind; light a candle and open the door," commanded Baker.

By this time someone was loudly knocking at his side-porch door, so Garrett hastily lighted a candle, slipped into his pantaloons, and rushed downstairs. When he opened the door, Baker grabbed him, and he felt the cold barrel of a pistol against his head, as a voice asked if there were two men staying at his house. Garrett had a slight impediment in his speech and at first was unable to reply, but finally stammered that two men had been there before he went to bed; he did not know what became of them afterward. Conger, now at the door, ignored Garrett's explanations and ordered him taken into the yard and hanged to a tree. This frightened the old man out of his wits, and he began sputtering nonsense as he was led to a spot where several soldiers greeted him with the cry, "Hang the rebel. Hang him! Here is a rope!"

The danger in which their father was placed brought John and William Garrett running from the corn-cribs, and they too were grabbed by the officers, who demanded where the fugitives were hiding. "They are in the tobacco barn," answered John. Old Garrett was denied permission to get extra clothing and was left shivering in the yard under guard. When he saw Jett he turned to him angrily and demanded why he had left such men at his farm and brought this calamity upon him. Jett explained that he had wished to get rid of them and had taken the first opportunity to do so. He said he had told the officers at Bowling Green that Garrett did not know the two men were fugitives.[54]

Conger now ordered Doherty to have the horses taken to the rear of the house and left there. He posted the soldiers about thirty feet from the tobacco barn on all sides but the front. Meanwhile Baker questioned John Garrett and, learning that he had locked the door of the barn, took a lighted candle and hustled him off in that direction. Conger joined them and Baker told John that since the men were on his father's place, he (John) must go into the barn, get their firearms, and demand their surrender. Baker then unlocked the door and shoved him inside.

In the darkness Wilkes had suddenly awakened. He had heard the low voices of several men near the door and stealthy footsteps on all sides. He aroused Herold and told him that they were surrounded by Yankee soldiers. Herold asked him to give himself up, but Wilkes said he would die first. He told him to lie still so that the cavalrymen would think no one was there and go on. It was then that young Garrett nervously announced that the soldiers had come for them, that their identity was known, and that they must give up their firearms and yield to arrest. Wilkes made no reply, but started to draw his pistol. "You have betrayed us; get out of here," he said menacingly. John rushed to the door and pleaded for Baker to open it. Baker threw it back and, when John emerged like a frightened animal, quickly closed it again, locked it, and kept the key himself. John warned him that Wilkes was a walking arsenal so Conger quickly extinguished the candle which had made them a target for the men inside. Neither Baker nor Conger had any desire to go in and get the fugitives. Baker then commanded Wilkes and Herold to surrender and told them if they did not do so within fifteen minutes the tobacco barn would be burned and they would have a shooting match. Wilkes' request, that he be given a few minutes to consider what he should do, was granted.

Soon he called, "Captain, this is hard; we are guilty of no crime." He proposed that Baker draw his men up twenty yards from the door and permit him to come out and fight the whole command. He was answered by a second order to surrender and this time given ten minutes in which to do so. Wilkes asked what authority Baker had to take him and received no reply. Herold pleaded with him to give himself up or permit him to, but Wilkes threatened to shoot him and also blow out his own brains. Baker now notified them that there were only five minutes left before they would fire the barn. Herold, frantic at the prospect of being burned alive, told Wilkes that he would not stay any longer and went to the door. Before he knocked on it,

Wilkes asked him to say nothing when questioned of his two revolvers, cartridges, bowie knife, and carbine. Then as Herold rapped, Wilkes called for Baker to let Herold out as he was innocent.

Baker, having been informed by Rollins that Herold carried the carbine, ordered him to bring it along, but Herold denied having it. Baker then commanded, "Whoever you are, come out with your hands up." When Herold appeared Baker searched him, took his gloves and a piece of map, and turned him over to Lieutenant Doherty, who had him tied to a tree where he could see all that was going on. He became so excited and jabbered at such a rapid pace that one officer shouted, "If you don't shut up we will cut off your damn' head!"

Conger directed one of the Garrett boys to pile some brush against the corner of the tobacco barn to give the impression that it was to be set on fire. Wilkes spied young Garrett from inside and warned him to go away from there if he valued his life or he would shoot him. Conger now went to Baker and said they had better start the fire. Wilkes was advised that he had only two minutes more to surrender, but he repeated the crazy proposition he had made to come out and fight the whole command. There was no answer and summoning all that was left of a voice once known for its dramatic power, he cried in hollow tones, "Well, my brave boys, you can prepare a stretcher for me. One more stain on the old banner!" Again Wilkes was the actor. His last performance was given in a tobacco barn more brilliantly lighted than any theatre in which he had previously appeared.

All along the escape route, he had boasted he would not be taken alive, and his mouthings at the end were the cries of a madman speaking the lines of others. His request to Baker was that of John Brown to another officer, when soldiers surrounded the engine house where he was captured.

Conger had gone to the rear of the building and made a torch of straw which he now lit. He thrust it inside and ignited some straw that was gathered in a corner. The flare brightened the interior of the barn so that Wilkes could be seen through the openings between the slats. He stood almost in the center of the barn, supporting himself with one crutch and holding his carbine under his right arm ready for action. He walked across toward the burning corner, and at that instant so resembled Edwin that Conger half-believed the whole pursuit to have been a mistake. Baker, having seen the fire spring up, had gone to open the door, and was standing there holding the lock in the hasp. Wilkes peered through the cracks of the wall trying to see who had started the fire, then stooped and picked up a piece of furniture by its leg to throw on it. But he decided not to, for the flames had

CATASTROPHE

now risen to within two-thirds of the top of the barn and he knew he could not smother the blaze. In bewilderment he glanced around and caught sight of a gun pointed at him through one of the crevices. His expression changed, he dropped his crutch and carbine and turned in the direction of the door. He had advanced about ten or fifteen feet, when suddenly he drew his pistol, placed it back of his right ear and fired.[55] Sardonically, he had selected a spot opposite to the one he had chosen for Lincoln.[56] This mad gesture left unmarred the face that so often had been spoken of as eminently handsome. Still clutching the revolver in his hand, Wilkes fell to the floor.

Baker heard the shot and rushed inside to where Wilkes lay apparently dead. To make sure, Baker took hold of his arms and found him limp and helpless. He removed the pistol from Wilkes' clenched hand and noticed the carbine lying near by. He then threw back Wilkes' coat and discovered the bowie knife and other pistol which he had in his belt. From outside Conger had seen Wilkes start for the door, and was rushing there himself when he also heard the shot. He hastened in and found Baker examining Wilkes. Conger crouched and stared at the unconscious form, observing to Baker that Wilkes must have shot himself.

"No, he did not!" exclaimed Baker curtly.

Conger asked, "Where is he shot?"

Baker thought it was in the neck. Conger raised Wilkes' head and saw the bleeding wound below the right ear. It made him positive that Wilkes had shot himself but aimed low. A second time he said, "He shot himself."

Again Baker snapped, "No, he did not!" and looked at him suspiciously. "Did you shoot him?" he asked.

"No, I did not!" was Conger's emphatic reply.

Baker concluded that if Conger had done it, they had better keep it quiet, as it was in disobedience to the orders they had received before leaving Washington.

Carefully they lifted Wilkes and carried him from the burning building to the cool grass. Young Garrett had followed Baker into the tobacco barn and then run out calling to the soldiers to extinguish the fire. Conger went back to direct the men but saw that it was impossible to save the barn and withdrew them.[57] Now was his chance to discover if anyone in the detachment had fired the shot. In answer to his question, Sergeant Boston Corbett, grasping this opportunity for fame, boastfully announced that he had done it. Corbett was the one who had aimed the gun which Wilkes saw pointed at him through the crack. However, it was not his bullet that killed Lincoln's assassin.[58] Conger demanded why Corbett had disobeyed orders. Corbett clicked his heels together, saluted, pointed heavenward and replied, "God Almighty directed me."

"Well," remarked Conger, "I guess He did, or you couldn't have hit Booth through that crack in the barn." He added that under such circumstances he would leave him to the mercy of Providence and the Secretary of War.[59]

Baker dashed water in Wilkes' face and gave him some to drink in the hope of reviving him and getting information. Wilkes opened his eyes and weakly blew out the water, in an effort to speak. Baker leaned over him and was able to distinguish faint whisperings of "Tell mother—tell mother—" as Wilkes again swooned away. The fire from the barn was now so hot that Wilkes was removed to the Garrett house. They had started to take him inside but were stopped in the doorway by men bringing out a mattress. It was dropped there and Wilkes placed on it so that his head and shoulders were inside the living room and his body and legs on the porch.

Ice water was brought and his face and wound bathed, while a messenger was sent for Dr. Urquhart of Port Royal. Revived somewhat by the ice water, Wilkes opened his eyes and pleaded with the officers to kill him.

"No, Booth," said Baker, "we do not wish to kill you, and we hope you will recover; you were shot against orders." While Baker and Conger searched his pockets, Baker inquired as to Jett's whereabouts, and Wilkes, turning his eyes toward them, feebly asked, "Did Jett betray me?"[60] to which Baker replied, "Never mind about Jett."

Wilkes continued to plead, "Kill me, kill me," and gasped, "Tell mother—I died for my country—I have done—what I have thought—was for the best." After Wilkes tried several times to cough, Conger told him he could see no blood, and Wilkes murmured, "My hands—" Baker washed one of his hands with the ice water and held it up, but Wilkes had no control over it. As Baker let it drop, Wilkes sighed, "Useless—useless—"[61]

Dr. Urquhart arrived and started to probe the wound, but Baker informed him that the ball had gone through. He asked the physician if there were any chance to get Wilkes back to Washington alive and was told it would be impossible as he was slowly breathing his last. Conger realized the end had come and immediately set out for the Capital with news of the capture and some of the articles taken from Wilkes as evidence that they had the right man.[62] At a quarter past seven on the morning of April 26, 1865, within a fortnight of his twenty-seventh birthday, John Wilkes Booth died.

The picture of Bessie Hale, Booth's fiancée, found among his effects. (*War Department, Office of the Judge Advocate General, 1940*)

Col. (later Brig. Gen.) La Fayette Curry Baker, Chief of the Secret Service, who organized the manhunt for Booth. Engraving by Robert Whitechurch. (*From 'Dictionary of American Portraits,' Dover*)

A contemporary rendering of the return to Washington of Herold and the body of Booth.

CHAPTER VI

As the body of Lincoln's assassin was being sewn into an army blanket the Negro, Ned Freeman, whom young Garrett had tried to engage the night before to take the fugitives southward, arrived for that purpose. He and his one-horse wagon were immediately commandeered by officers of the detachment. Herold was set on a horse, his feet made fast by a rope stretched under the animal's belly, and Corporal John Winter, with two privates, assigned to guard him on the journey back to Washington.

While other members of the detachment were having breakfast at Garrett's, Baker and an orderly started off for Port Royal with Freeman, in whose wagon the corpse of Wilkes had been placed. Baker expected the cavalrymen to overtake them before reaching the Rappahannock River but they failed to do so.

After crossing the river, Baker took a road which the Negro said would lead them to Belle Plain thirty miles away, where the steamer *John S. Ide* waited to convey the party to the Capital. Some distance from the Rappahannock, Baker became alarmed, as they seemed to be on a desolate road in rebel territory without sufficient protection. He sent his orderly back to Doherty with instructions to have him rush the cavalry along; but they did not appear, and Baker was left alone with the Negro and the body of Wilkes. His anxiety increased when he perceived a few Confederate soldiers approaching and feared they intended to attack them.

"What have you got there, a dead Yank?" asked one.

"Yes," replied Baker and grinned nervously as they passed by.

He was now beginning to wonder if the detachment had been forced to escape from some band of rebels who might at any time pounce upon him and snatch the corpse. He had been three days in the saddle, and his horse was dragging along so wearily that he would be useless in any encounter. The sand in the road was deep, the Negro's rickety wagon creaked, and his old horse could hardly pull the load up the hills. On one of them a king-bolt snapped and the tilting of the wagon threw the dead body into an upright position. Blood trickled from the blanket, and ran down on the Negro's hands as he crept under the wagon to fix it. Half-paralyzed by fear, Freeman looked at his hands and moaned, "It am de blood ob a murderer and will neber, neber, wash off," then started for the woods as if intending to abandon the whole outfit. Baker grabbed him and commanded that he continue the journey. Late in the afternoon they reached the Potomac, but saw that the steamer was docked a mile up the river. Baker discovered the Negro had taken him to the old landing, which had been changed during the war.

Apprehensive that shouts to the crew for assistance might attract possible enemies, he and the Negro hid the body in some near-by willows. Baker ordered Freeman to wait while he rode two miles farther over a wandering road to the landing for aid. At the steamer, he found his orderly with Doherty and the entire detachment. Baker demanded of his orderly why he had not returned with the detachment, and was told Doherty had prohibited him from doing so. Baker secured a rowboat and went back with two members of the crew for Wilkes' body, which was hoisted onto the deck of the *John S. Ide* and placed under guard as the steamer started on its trip up the river.

Conger, having gone on ahead, reached Washington about five o'clock, April twenty-sixth, and reported the capture to Colonel Baker who rushed him posthaste to Stanton, thinking he would rejoice in the news. When Stanton was told and some of the articles taken from Wilkes' person were placed before him, he covered his eyes a moment with his hands and said nothing. Then he got up, put on his coat, and gave Colonel Baker his instructions.

At ten-thirty that night as the steamer *John S. Ide* neared Alexandria, a tugboat with Colonel Baker on board met it, and both Herold and Wilkes' body were removed. Three hours later, they were transferred to the monitor *Montauk* anchored off the Anacostia Navy Yard. Herold was manacled, and a canvas hood padded with cotton, having slits in it for breathing and eating, was drawn over his head. This was the garb worn by the other conspirators, with the exception of Mrs. Surratt. The corpse in its blanket sack was carried to a carpenter's bench on the forward deck of the *Montauk* and a guard placed around it.

Commodore J. B. Montgomery, Commandant of the Navy Yard, sent notice of their arrival to Gideon Wells, Secretary of the Navy, with the information that Wilkes' body was changing rapidly, and asked what disposition should be made of it. The next morning at eleven o'clock Surgeon General Barnes, with other Federal officers and a number of men who had known Wilkes, went aboard and Barnes sliced open the covering in which the body had been wrapped. After viewing it, those who were called upon to make the identification went

CATASTROPHE

to the cabin of the commanding officer, where a coroner's inquest was held and affidavits taken by Judge Holt. Among these was Dr. May, who had operated on Wilkes' neck and recognized the scar left by the accident with Charlotte Cushman.[63]

Stanton was determined to have no Confederate flag waving over the tomb of Lincoln's assassin. To prevent any possibility of Wilkes' rebel friends obtaining his body, he instructed Colonel Baker to dispose of it secretly and make no report to the War Department. As soon as Barnes had completed an autopsy,[64] Colonel Baker and Lieutenant Baker went to the old penitentiary prison, known as the Arsenal, on the mysterious mission of finding a burial place. From there they continued to the Navy Yard, secured a small boat, and pulled up beside the *Montauk* at sundown.

Word of Wilkes' body and several prisoners being on board had attracted many persons along the shore. When the corpse was taken from the carpenter's bench and lowered into the boat, Colonel Baker feigned to be working with a ball and chain for the purpose of giving his spectators the impression that the body was to be sunk in the river. To further this idea, he and his cousin paddled down the Potomac, with the crowd following them along the shore, until the boat reached a point where the curious could no longer see it. But they continued their macabre voyage to a burial ground used by the government for dumping condemned mules and horses and there went through the motions of burying Wilkes' body in a watery grave. Then they returned through the darkness to the side of the old penitentiary wall in which a hole had been cut, large enough to admit the corpse. Inside, a sentry had been posted with orders to allow no one to enter without giving the countersign. Into this convict's cell, the body of John Wilkes Booth was lifted and buried under a stone slab.[65]

CHAPTER VII

The talent Wilkes inherited from his father was of little value, as he did not know how to develop it, and there was no one to direct him toward the renown he wished to achieve. The appeal of his handsome features and natural ability often was submerged by boisterous interpretations, yet he was highly regarded by many in the profession who lamented the fate which abruptly ended the possibility of a brilliant theatrical career. His friends considered his damnable deed the result of a vain nature and of a lifetime longing for acclaim, and spoke of him as having had nerve without stamina, impulse without direction, enthusiasm without judgment. Had he been in the West under the guidance of Junius during his early years, the great tragedy in the lives of the Booths of Maryland might have been averted. Wilkes had discovered, too late, that hard work was the only road to fame; he had squandered his youth in seeking short cuts instead of applying himself to study.

No matter what kept Wilkes from joining the Confederate ranks at the beginning of the war, he believed toward its end that he had missed another opportunity to achieve distinction. Flattered by the applause given him in the South, he became more violent in his verbal defense of her cause than most rebels. He had gone about the country jabbering belligerent phrases against those opposed to slavery and secession. This had gained him nothing more than the taunts of many who knew him, and he began to brood over the fact that they were making him the butt of their conversations. While he had talked, other men had risen from nonentity to recognition in the martial affairs of the Confederacy and of the Union. Wilkes soon perceived that to become a hero he must act quickly or sink forever into insignificance.

"When I leave the stage for good, I will be the most famous man in America," he had declared over the brandy glasses on the evening of the assassination. And at Garrett's he had said that he believed the man who shot the President did it "for notoriety's sake."

The realization that he could never became prominent in the theatre because of the condition of his voice turned his mind to other means of reaching the pinnacle he wished to attain. A voice which had been applauded night after night by appreciative audiences, a voice which had been unable to withstand the ordeal of constant performances, a voice which had mocked his desire for fame, drove him to that act of madness. There can be no doubt that this was the underlying cause of his determination to kill Lincoln.[66]

Many theatrical organizations throughout the country published resolutions in the press deploring the fact that one of their number should have committed such a crime.[67] In Columbus, Ohio, the Ellslers and other members of their company refused at first to believe the report. When Mrs. Ellsler found it was true, she shed tears "for the mad boy." Everyone crept about quietly and "winced at the sound of the overture. It was as if one dead lay within the walls . . . one who had belonged to us." [68]

After Wilkes' friend, Billy Baron, brought the news of Lincoln's assassination and Wilkes' flight to Ella Turner Starr at her sister's Washington home early on the morning of April fifteenth, she tried unsuccessfully to end her life by taking chloroform. Ella's act caused all the occupants of the house to be arrested and led to her sister's confession that the place was one of prostitution.[69]

John T. Ford was in the shattered town of Richmond that fateful Friday, having gone there on a government pass for the purpose of attending to the needs of his wife and relatives. He did not hear of the assassination until it was reported there Sunday evening that Edwin Booth had killed the President. "I said it was impossible, as I knew he was not in Washington," stated Ford. "That moment I recollected Wilkes Booth was in Washington; that he was boyish and foolish enough for it. He had pluck. He was always training, riding, shooting, at the gymnasium." [70] Early Monday morning as Ford boarded the boat for Baltimore, he read the first details of the tragic occurrence at his theatre. From Baltimore he hastened to Washington, where he was immediately committed to Old Capitol Prison.

Laura Keene, John Doytt, and Harry Hawk of the *American Cousin* troupe, were arrested on a Northern Central train near Harrisburg. John Lutz, Laura's transcontinental lover, came to their aid and telegraphed the War Office for an official permit so they could proceed on their tour. This was granted by Colonel Baker who said that he knew of no reason for detaining them. Other actors of this company who remained in Washington were required to make daily reports to the police. They were unable to gain access to their trunks because of orders given soldiers on guard at Ford's Theatre that nothing inside the building was to be removed. Several of them, including George Spear, sent requests to the War Office asking permission to obtain such possessions. This kindly old actor pointed out that it was impossible for him to pursue his professional work without his wardrobe. The release he received directed Colonel H. H. Wells to accompany him "to see that he takes only his own property, and to take proper receipts." [71]

On July third, a "Card" appeared in Washington newspapers signed by Ford stating that his theatre had not been sold and would reopen at the earliest possible moment, but the "private box occupied by our late lamented President will remain closed." Stanton, however, decided against any more theatrical performances in that building, and the War Department took it over for use as a surgeon general's office.

Wilkes' fellow conspirators fared almost as badly as he. Among those accused only John Surratt evaded punishment. He fled the country, and when brought back for trial, managed to get acquitted because he was charged with murder and not with conspiracy. Paine, after his unsuccessful attack on Seward, found himself deserted by Herold and did not know which road to take. He met with a number of misadventures and wandered back to Mrs. Surratt's house on April seventeenth just as she was being arrested. Atzerodt was not found until the twentieth and, though at the last he had refused to do Wilkes' bidding, enough evidence was discovered to connect him with the conspirators. Herold, while the plot was brewing, had talked so much that those who knew him never understood why Wilkes confided in him nor how he ever kept the plans of the conspiracy a secret; but after his capture he surprised everyone by his silence. This change was due to the pressure brought to bear on him by his counsel, Frederick Stone, who later remarked that if he had not been able to shut Herold's mouth every rebel in lower Maryland would have been hanged.

Among those who figured less prominently in the murder, Dr. Mudd was undoubtedly the most unfortunate, for if Wilkes had not injured his leg he probably would never have become involved. Spangler was charged with having aided Wilkes by various means, and O'Laughlin and Arnold, who had been under suspicion for some time, were found and arrested three days after the assassination.

Mrs. Surratt, Paine, Atzerodt, Herold, Dr. Mudd, Arnold, O'Laughlin, and Spangler were removed to the Arsenal for trial and legal aid was obtained for them.[72] But the latter proved of little avail. On the afternoon of July 7, 1865, in the enclosed yard of the Arsenal the traps of a scaffold were sprung and under a scorching sun Mrs. Surratt, Paine, Atzerodt, and Herold writhed in mid-air until dead. All were buried in the Arsenal yard not far from the wall of the building separating them from Wilkes' body. Before the end of the month Dr. Mudd, Arnold, O'Laughlin, and Spangler were serving their sentences behind the shark infested moat of Fort Jefferson prison on Dry Tortugas Island off the coast of Florida.

BOOK FIVE

A CHILD OF TRAGEDY

Edwin Booth. *(National Archives photo)*

CHAPTER I

The night that Wilkes was playing his murderous rôle in Washington, Edwin, on the stage of the Boston Theatre, as Sir Edward Mortimer, in *The Iron Chest*, was repeating the prophetic lines, "Where is my honor now! Mountains of shame are piled upon me!" Edwina, not yet four years old, was visiting her little cousins, the Clarkes, in Philadelphia, where Asia, expecting the birth of another child, was remaining close at home.[1] Marion, Junius' daughter, also was there. Rosalie and Mary Ann were living quietly at Edwin's East Nineteenth Street house in New York.

The morning following the crime, Mary Ann, harassed by worry over her favorite son, heard newsboys in the streets crying, "President Lincoln murdered!" She could hardly believe the lines she read that John Wilkes Booth was suspected as the assassin. A cold fear gripped her—those premonitions, the awful dreams, had they been sent to her as a warning? Tears blinded her as she sobbed, "O God, if this be true, let him shoot himself, let him not live to be hung! Spare him, spare us, spare the name that dreadful disgrace!" [2]

Scarcely had she uttered the words when the postman delivered an affectionate letter to her from Wilkes written on the previous afternoon. In anguish she clung miserably to the stunned Rosalie. But this mother of the Maryland Booths did not permit herself the solace of long sorrowing. Asia must be thought of—in her condition this sudden shock would be difficult to bear. So Mary Ann left immediately for Philadelphia where she found the Clarkes barricaded against representatives of the press and an outraged public. Sunday afternoon as Asia opened the packet which Wilkes had left with her at the first of the year, Mary Ann anxiously awaited the revelation of its contents, while Clarke looked on surly and resentful of being involved in this Booth disgrace.

The packet contained bonds worth about four thousand dollars, an assignment of some Pennsylvania oil stock to Junius, and several letters. One of these, to his mother, exonerated all the Booths from any connection with Wilkes' plots. It was never seen again, nor were the contents reported after it had been turned over to Federal authorities by the Clarkes. Another addressed *To Whom It May Concern* was the one signed by Wilkes with a different colored ink from that used in the body of the letter. In it Wilkes sought to vindicate himself for plotting to abduct Lincoln, who he contended had plunged the South into such disaster. There was no hint in the letter that Wilkes intended to murder Lincoln. The Philadelphia *Enquirer* published it on April nineteenth.[*]

In Boston, the morning following the assassination, Edwin's colored servant rushed into his bedroom exclaiming that it was being rumored "Massa John" had killed President Lincoln. Edwin was horrified. He felt as though he had been struck down by a hammer. Could the report be true? Yes, his headstrong young brother must have done it! He was reckless enough to commit such an irrational deed. Edwin's mind became a jumbled mass of worry. Where was Wilkes? Would others in the family be held accountable for his crime? What could any Booth do now? Still dazed for a solution as to how to proceed, he received this discreet note from the manager of the Boston Theatre:

> My Dear Sir:
>
> A fearful calamity is upon us. The President of the United States has fallen by the hand of an assassin, and I am shocked to say suspicion points to one nearly related to you as the perpetrator of this horrid deed. God grant it may not prove so! With this knowledge, and out of respect to the anguish which will fill the public mind as soon as the appalling fact shall be fully revealed, I have concluded to close the Boston Theatre until further notice. Please signify to me your co-operation in this matter.
>
> In great sorrow, and in haste,
>
> I remain, yours very truly,
> HENRY C. JARRETT.

Edwin appreciated his consideration, and on that dismal Saturday penned the first of few letters in which he ever referred to Lincoln's assassination:

> With deepest sorrow and great agitation, I thank you for relieving me from my engagement with yourself and the public. The news of the morning has made me wretched indeed, not only because I have received the unhappy tidings of the suspicion of a brother's crime, but because a good man, and a most justly honored and patriotic ruler, has fallen, in an hour of national joy, by the hand of an assassin. The memory of the thousands who have fallen in the field, in our country's

---

[*] See Supplement V, p. 396.

defense, during this struggle, cannot be forgotten by me, even in this, the most distressing day of my life. And I most sincerely pray that the victories we have already won may stay the brand of war and the tide of loyal blood. While mourning, in common with all other loyal hearts, the death of the President, I am oppressed by a private woe not to be expressed in words. But whatever calamity may befall me or mine, my country, one and indivisible, has my warmest devotion.[3]

Friends rallied to Edwin, but the ill-feeling of the public against the Booth family forced him to remain in his room. Unaware of his mother's departure for Philadelphia, he telegraphed her that he would take the midnight train and be home early Sunday morning, but Federal officers detained him for a severe questioning and a thorough search of his baggage. Had it not been for the influence of several prominent men, he would not have been released. Dressed in a long dark cloak and a soft hat pulled down over his forehead, he managed to make the journey to New York without being recognized, his ghostlike appearance frightening those who met him. William Bispham and others watched over him during the weeks that followed. All were alarmed lest he should suddenly become insane.[4]

Edwin resolved never to act in public again, but on April seventeenth, the New York *Tribune* published one of many appeals for his reappearance upon the stage. These were later to bear results. "No community," the *Tribune* prophesied, "could be so cruelly unjust as to allow the stigma of Wilkes Booth's crime to tarnish the fame of so true and loyal a citizen as Edwin Booth. The intended engagement at the Winter Garden, which was to have commenced in a few weeks, will doubtless be relinquished; but Edwin Booth's friends will not consent to his sharing the odium of disgrace which must be visited upon his wretched and unworthy brother."

When the news reached Junius at Cincinnati, he paced back and forth in his room like a madman. The hotelkeeper was compelled to guard the hallway leading to Junius' quarters while he fled through a rear door and escaped a mob waiting to lynch him. He managed to keep his whereabouts a secret until he arrived at the Clarkes' in Philadelphia late Wednesday night and reported to a United States marshal. In San Francisco, Dave Anderson, Junius' business agent, took special care that his property should not be destroyed by hoodlums who disliked Junius' Vigilante affiliations and might take this opportunity for revenge.

La Fayette C. Baker, once associated with Junius in this organization, was in the East at the outbreak of the war. He had intended to return to California but remained and became the organizer and first chief of the United States Secret Service. The tactics Baker had employed to terrorize lawless citizens in the West, convinced Junius that his brother could not escape a man who had received his early training in such a school. Innocent of any connection with Wilkes' plot, Junius had no thought of being implicated, but a letter he had written to his younger brother in care of Ford's Theatre was turned over to the Washington police, and aroused their suspicions. In it Junius had advised Wilkes to give up the "oil business" as his friends believed it would not be profitable since Richmond had fallen and Lee had surrendered. Federal authorities, concluding that this related to the conspiracy, sent a telegram to Philadelphia ordering Junius' immediate arrest. The press secured the letter and on the morning of April twenty-fifth, Junius saw a copy of it in a newspaper. About three o'clock that afternoon, he was taken into custody by United States Special Agent Isaac M. Krupp who called at Clarke's home and informed Junius that he had a warrant for his arrest in irons.

Junius was dumbfounded and asked, "Do you know if it is in regard to that letter?" The officer would not answer but said that, although he had authority to take him in irons, he would dispense with the use of them. Considerably agitated, Junius thanked him and they left the house at once. At the police station, where he had to remain for several hours, he became quite dejected and employed his time in copying extracts from the Bible or reading the Forty-ninth Psalm. That same evening, he was taken by carriage to the railroad station and put on the eleven o'clock train for Washington, with Officer Krupp. Junius had little to say during the trip other than that he "wished John had been killed before the assassination, for the sake of the family." [5]

Upon his arrival in Washington, Junius was questioned at the War Department and confined in Old Capitol Prison. At four o'clock on the afternoon of April twenty-sixth, as Wilkes' body passed along the lonely road in Virginia and Lincoln's funeral train moved slowly across the state of New York, Junius, not yet aware of his brother's fate, heard the creaking door of a gloomy cell close behind him.[6] But he was not hooded and chained as were the men known to have taken part in the conspiracy, owing to the fact that Colonel Baker remembered Junius' attitude toward Maguire's crooked politics in San Francisco and believed this Booth irreproachable.

John T. Ford, still in Old Capitol Prison, was questioned by Colonel Olcott regarding him, and replied that Junius always had been loyal to the Union and had hoped for its ultimate triumph. John Sleeper Clarke was also arrested and placed in the same prison but in a different cell.[7] The dishonor of the Booths in which he had become embroiled so infuriated him that he was ready to divorce himself from the entire family. Edwin's freedom added coals to the fire.[8] He had gone to Washington voluntarily and appeared before the authorities. Two days after Wilkes' burial, a newspaper there noted his arrival "at the instance of his mother, to obtain the body of his brother," and added, "if such is the case, he has been unsuccessful up to the present time."

Ford remarked that Wilkes' "mad act was a terrible blow to Edwin Booth, and, though time softened the anguish and humiliation it brought upon him, he shrank ever after from the scene of the tragedy, and never played in Washington again."[9] Repeated efforts were made at intervals to have him renew his engagements there. Letters by Supreme Court Justices, Cabinet members, and Congressmen, implored him to return. Even President Arthur added his request, but no one was ever able to induce Edwin to break the vow made after his brother's crime. He knew, if he returned to any theatre in the Capital, there would always be the memory of the tragedy to haunt him.

When he played in Baltimore, railroads ran special trains from Washington in order to accommodate the throngs wishing to see him. Ford contended that such a calamity would have ruined any other actor, but it swelled box-office receipts for Edwin. However, Edwin detested the notoriety he received from his brother's crime, and refused to discuss it except with very intimate friends.

Messages came to Edwin's New York home threatening members of the Booth family, yet within the household no unkind word was uttered by anyone against the bearer of the name that had brought such disgrace upon them, nor was his picture removed from the prominent place Edwin had given it.

The money Wilkes had deposited in the Ontario Bank at Montreal never fell into Booth hands. Advertisements appeared in Canadian newspapers requesting Wilkes' heirs to present their claims, and Mrs. Rogers, the Harford County neighbor of the Booths, offered to accompany some member of the family to Montreal, but Edwin would not permit any of them to go. Later a final notice gave warning that unless claimed by a certain date the deposit would be converted into the British treasury. Edwin still refused to let anyone attend to the matter, and the money was lost to the family.

Joseph seemed to have been forgotten by the authorities until one J. H. Brown of the Treasury Department in Washington sent Stanton a note saying:

May 17, 1865

I have just received information from California that Joseph A. Booth left San Francisco for New York on one of the last steamers, and that he was aware of the plot and conspiracy against the Executive officers of the Government.[10]

Joseph knew no more about the conspiracy than the man who informed against him. Nevertheless, he was arrested upon his arrival in New York and held until officials were thoroughly satisfied of his innocence.[11]

When Edwin Forrest was asked if he believed Wilkes had assassinated Lincoln, he exclaimed vehemently, "Certainly I do! All those goddam Booths are crazy!" [12]

The scandal of their father's matrimonial affairs had made the Maryland Booths a supersensitive family. His marriage to Mary Ann Holmes, after ten children had been born to them, haunted their daily lives. They were ever on the alert for disclosures of it and hence shunned social obligations. There is some evidence of an intention to blackmail Edwin when these facts regarding the family history were brought to light.[13] Wilkes' crime centered public attention on all the Booths, and they became more recluse than ever before, dreading the notoriety with which they were faced.

In some quarters the name became a part of blasphemous epithets, threats, and denunciations, that resounded like a death knell to those who had made every effort to place it on the highest pinnacle of untarnished fame. Asia, torn by grief and anxiety for the future, inscribed in the first book about her father: "We, of all families, secure in domestic love and retirement, are stricken desolate! The name we would have enwreathed with laurels is dishonored by a son—'his well-beloved —his bright boy Absalom!' "

Three weeks after the assassination, Edwin was still in seclusion in New York, avoiding any public appearance because he feared possible demonstrations against him. Had it not been for the letters of friends and the personal attention of those closely attached to him, he might have given up the stage, though he was less than thirty-two years of age at the time. His mother and little daughter, Edwina, remained in Philadelphia with Asia, who, at the advice of a physician, had not yet been told of her husband's imprisonment. The once proud Mary Ann steeled herself because of the duty she owed her children. She held to the conviction that the hatred of common minds would pass, and that the future would bestow upon her family the compassion and understanding their misfortune so justly deserved.

A CHILD OF TRAGEDY

Junius and Sleeper Clarke were released from Old Capitol Prison in Washington as abruptly as they had been arrested. Still somewhat dazed by their entanglement in the tragic web, they returned to Clarke's home in Philadelphia. Asia was now fully aware of what had happened and, bitter in her denunciations against the Federal Government, she spared no words in expressing regrets for the assistance given by members of the family to various relief organizations in the North during the war. Most of all she was incensed that her home continued to be the focal point for vicious curiosity-seekers who forced the family to conduct its movements in secrecy.

Before the end of May, the moment he could safely do so, Edwin had come to take Edwina back to New York. Mary Ann also returned there to greet Joseph, the least agitated of the Booths. In the mother's absence, the tension under which they were all straining broke loose with Clarke's suggestion for a separation from Asia. Edwin recognized this as a gesture to be free from them and indignantly offered to release Clarke from their joint ownership of theatrical property; but no immediate action was taken, and after these impulsive outbursts had been reconsidered, the domestic life of the Clarkes remained unchanged. In time the two men dissolved their partnership solely for business reasons.

As soon as Edwin left Philadelphia with Edwina, Asia caustically spoke of his betrothal and possible marriage to a Blanch Hanel. This romance, of which there are no details, never culminated. Presumably Edwin found his fiancée also prejudiced against the Booths and willing to relinquish him from further obligations. In all the family correspondence there are but a few casual references to her.

Clarke finally sold his interest in the Winter Garden to Edwin shortly before it burned and went to England, taking one of his sons with him. His London theatrical ventures were successful, so Asia followed with their family and a nurse in March, 1868. Joseph had planned to accompany them but decided to remain in the United States. They lived in a comfortably furnished cottage in St. John's Wood, a short drive from the city through a countryside blooming with flowers. Asia was glad to be in a land removed from the stigma of her brother's crime, and hoped that the rest of her family would soon join them. At first she looked upon England as something of a paradise, but the difficulties of managing a household in a foreign country soon disillusioned her. She was cheated by tradesmen; the cook could not prepare dishes to which they were accustomed; and servants, entitled to three pints of beer a day, added to this supply and became drunk by nightfall. Soon Asia was submerged in the loneliness of a strange environment.

Edwin had not altered his decision in regard to the theatre, for he was still timorous of appearing before the public. However, by December, 1865, necessity compelled him to forget his qualms and take to the boards again. While preparing for his return to the stage he confided to a friend, Mrs. Richard F. Cary:

> Sincerely, were it not for *means*, I would not do so, public sympathy notwithstanding; but I have huge debts to pay, a family to care for, a love for the grand and beautiful in art, to boot, to gratify, and hence my sudden resolve to abandon the heavy, aching gloom of my little red room, where I have sat so long chewing my heart in solitude, for the excitement of the only trade for which God has fitted me. . . .[14]

On the night of January 3, 1866, he came back to the stage as Hamlet at the New York Winter Garden. The *Herald* published a tirade against him and asked concerning his manager Stuart: "Can the sinking fortunes of this foreign manager be sustained in no other way than by such an indecent violation of propriety? The blood of our martyred President is not yet dry in the memory of the people, and the very name of the assassin is appalling to the public mind; still a Booth is advertised to appear before a New York audience!" Obviously, people did not agree with these sentiments. Tickets for the performance were soon sold out with speculators getting more than their share of them so that admission prices boomed.

Great crowds gathered in the street. Some cheered, some booed, but policemen were on hand to curb any demonstration. When the curtain went up, the house was filled with noted men and women, who greeted Edwin with rounds of applause, tossed flowers on the stage, and shouted words expressive of their sympathy, leaving no doubt in his mind as to his future. He was back upon the boards to stay. But the interest of a morbid public, because of his brother's crime, was to be his most trying experience. *Hamlet* was followed by a lavish production of *Richelieu*, after which Edwin triumphantly appeared in Boston and Philadelphia. Success in these and other cities gave him confidence that, through constant effort, he could redeem the Booth name.

In the spring of 1866 he and Clarke were operating three first-class theatres in as many cities, and engaged Junius as stage manager for their Boston Theatre. Again Junius proved his solid managerial ability by bringing together one of the finest stock companies in the country and featuring the most celebrated stars. The next season Agnes Land Perry joined the company. This revived their former attraction for each other and, in February, 1867, she and Junius were married. Agnes was twenty-five years his junior and three years younger than his oldest daughter, Blanche De Bar Booth. They spent part of the summer with their friend, Benjamin W. Thayer, at his seaside home in Manchester, a short distance from Boston. That September Junius purchased from him the first tract of land later to be a part of the large estate known as the Masconomo property. It was named for the Indian chieftain of this territory who had greeted the first white settlers. The village of Manchester soon became a popular resort for theatrical people, Joseph Proctor, John Gilbert, and others having homes above a beach called "Singing Sands."

Edwin continued his tours and within less than a year had re-established the name of Booth with the public. In December, 1866, he played an important engagement as Iago to the Othello of Bogumil Dawison, the renowned German actor, in a polyglot performance at the Winter Garden. Maria Methua-Scheller, a talented and beautiful actress who had abandoned the German stage in hope of reward in America, appeared as Desdemona. She addressed Dawison in German and other members of the company in English. Apparently, the audience liked it. Among other noted foreign stars who appeared with Edwin in later years were Mmes. Ristori and Janauschek.

When the last lines of *Hamlet* had been spoken at the Winter Garden on the night of January 22, 1867, the stage was reset with a drawing-room scene. It formed a background for a noted assemblage of guests before whom Edwin was presented with an inscribed gold medal. Oval in shape, it was surrounded by a golden serpent, in the center of which was a head of Edwin as Hamlet, topped by a Danish crown with two wreaths of laurel and myrtle. The pin to which it was attached bore the head of Shakespeare between two other heads symbolizing tragedy and comedy. It commemorated Edwin's achievement of one hundred nights in the rôle of the melancholy Dane. The engagement had ended shortly before Lincoln's assassination, but the medal had not been finished on the closing night and Edwin's temporary retirement had caused further delay of the ceremony. Though thoroughly satisfied with the success of this unprecedented long run, Edwin never repeated the ordeal.

After a sumptuous production of *The Merchant of Venice* had been on for some time and single performances had been given of several other plays, Payne's *Brutus* (in which the burning of Rome was realistically displayed) was performed. Fire used in this final scene led to the destruction of the theatre on the morning of March twenty-third, when flames burst from under the stage and furiously spread throughout the building, destroying a valuable collection of costumes and mementoes belonging to Edwin. The conflagration supposedly had been caused by sparks from the scenic fire which were fanned into a blaze by the opening of a door early that day.

In Edwin's last year at the Winter Garden he appeared in the full maturity of his powers. He was master of all his characters and displayed an ease and fluency unsurpassed by any of his contemporaries. At thirty-four he had achieved success, not only as an actor, but also as a speculator in theatrical property. This encouraged him to embark upon an ambitious venture which had been in his mind for some time. He began planning for the construction of a theatre to perpetuate the Booth name in stone where he could fulfill his most cherished desires in the production of Shakespeare's plays.

The replacement of the Winter Garden, "the house of great actors," offered the opportunity for which he had been waiting. But the full amount needed was not in his pocket, and he started off on a professional tour in search of the balance. His itinerary took him to Chicago where he played Romeo to the Juliet of Mary McVicker, whom he had met before. This small, energetic actress, about half his age, with dark hair and gray eyes, was unsuited physically for the tragic rôles she insisted on playing. Nevertheless, behind the scenes she took her part so well that she roused the usually diffident tragedian to another romance, and before the closing performance they were engaged. From that time on she seldom let him get far away from her. Edwin believed that he had found a companion for himself and his young daughter. When the tour continued his new Juliet went with him.

The political excitement which was caused by his reappearance at the Holliday Street Theatre in Baltimore on September 9, 1867, after an absence of six years, brought out an extra police force with strict regulations for the traffic swarming before the entrance. He opened as Sir Giles Overreach, and two nights later his *Richard III* netted the largest receipts ever known in that city for a single Shakespearean production.

At the performance of *The Apostate* he was accidentally stabbed in his right arm and hand with a dagger wielded by Charles Vandenhoff in the stage duel near the end of the tragedy. Since Edwin's benefit had been announced for the next bill, he had to go on with his arm in a sling, but it was covered by his costume and unnoticed by most of the audience. When *Richard III* was repeated, however, the bandages attracted much attention, as he was forced to fight the final battle scene with his left hand. Inflammation set in the wound and he was ordered by Dr. Christopher Johnson to stop playing for a few nights, during

Edwin Booth; Mary McVicker, his second wife; and his daughter Edwina, whose mother was Mary Devlin. *(Courtesy Museum of the City of New York)*

Booth's Theatre at Twenty-third Street and Sixth Avenue in New York. Woodcut from *Harper's Weekly*, January 9, 1869.

which interval, Mary McVicker made herself indispensable to his welfare. Yet she was not what Mary Devlin had been. Never did this second romance compare with the first.

In New York City, on April 8, 1868, the cornerstone of Booth's Theatre was laid, and the building shot upward on the southeast corner of Twenty-third Street and Sixth Avenue. R. A. Robertson, a Boston businessman with a flair for the arts, was taken in as a partner; J. H. Magonigle, a brother-in-law of Edwin's first wife, became their representative, and Joseph Booth treasurer. Edwin, on tour, sent in checks to meet expenses, but as thousands of dollars rolled in an equal amount rolled out. In fact, money flew past Joe at such a terrific pace that he was soon lost in a maze of accounts. Even marriage did not seem to have a stabilizing effect on him, and he did not shoulder responsibilities seriously until he was over thirty. "I'm in a very big puddle," acknowledged Edwin to a friend. "If I can wade it, well; if not, why, as Bunsby would say, 'Well, too.' . . . Certain it is, I have had enough vexation regarding this same theatre to drive me mad. . . ." [15]

He was quite debilitated that summer and tried every medical water on the market for a cure, but in September, after placing seven-year-old Edwina in a school near New York, he started off on another quest for funds to meet the demands of creditors. When finished, the theatre was a massive and imposing structure of granite. It had a spacious and elegantly decorated auditorium with three galleries (in all accommodating about eighteen hundred) and perfect acoustic properties. Beside the stairway above a marble foyer was sculptor Thomas R. Gould's bust of the elder Booth. The stage was supplied with elaborate and ingeniously devised machinery, and with a curtain painted by Russell Smith, one of the best scenic artists of his time. Edward Mollenhauer was engaged as leader of the orchestra and Mark Smith as stage manager. The opening was to be a great event.

Edwin sent Barton Hill to Forrest with the suggestion that he play Othello to Edwin's Iago on this occasion. Hill had permission to arrange matters on the spot. He was to accept Forrest's terms unconditionally, wire Edwin, and then forward the agreement. Whatever the old lion demanded for his services, he was to have without question. Forrest listened, smiled, complimented Edwin—and declined the honor. His business agent, Joseph McArdle, later disclosed Forrest's reason for the refusal: Edwin had supported Catherine Sinclair in California, and Forrest wanted nothing to do with anyone who had touched the fringes of her gown. When Hill told Edwin, he remarked, "Well, then, Barton, my early good luck was a great misfortune." [16]

Edwin's million-dollar theatre, on the way for two years, opened its doors to the public on the wintry evening of February 3, 1869, with an extravagant production of *Romeo and Juliet*, in which Edwin and Mary McVicker played the title rôles, the part of Mercutio being taken by Edwin Adams and that of the nurse by Fanny Morant. A. W. Fenno was also a member of the company. Before the play began, loud calls for Edwin brought him to the footlights, and he was obliged to make one of the speeches he so detested. In part he said:

> . . . Let me bid you a welcome, warm as heart can make it, to my new theatre. It has long been my desire to build a theatre that might be regarded as worthy of our metropolis; and at last my ambition is realized. . . . When the Winter Garden was burnt down I had been announced to play Romeo; and it has seemed to me fitting that I should resume my professional labours before you, precisely at the point where they were so abruptly ended.[17]

As the audience gazed upon the scenes, they were amazed at settings which included a solidly constructed house sixty feet high, with balconies one above the other, wherein dwelt the lovely Juliet. They were delighted too by the presentation of new business, such as the street fight between the Montagues and the Capulets. The critics did not think much of Edwin's Romeo. They felt that he could not mold his glacial countenance to the character. His performance had not enough of passion in it, they said; he never soared to a lover's paradise; he was out of tune with this part and could not act it. He should stick to tragedy, they hinted between the lines. Nor did Mary McVicker score better. The new theatre itself was the real drawing card. More space was given to it in reviews than to the stars. This interest enabled Edwin to keep the bill on for ten weeks and to reap a profit of sixty thousand dollars.

A magnificently produced *Othello* followed in April with Edwin as the Moor, Mary as Desdemona, and Edwin Adams as Iago. The two actors later exchanged rôles, and on the twenty-ninth of the next month, Mary gave her farewell performance as Desdemona. Her romance with Edwin had been more successful than her acting, and it was at his request that she left the stage. Mary Devlin had done the same. Edwin did not want his wife in the theatre, but to Mary McVicker this did not mean that she was to be excluded from his dressing room. Her continued insistence on being there was to drive him almost to distraction.

They were married on June seventh, at the summer home of the bride's parents in Long Branch. The ceremony was performed by her grandfather, Reverend B. F. Meyers of California, with Edwin Adams and his wife present. Since Mary Devlin's death six years before, Asia had not meddled in Edwin's affairs. Now her former critical attitude toward him flared up again, and in letters from England to relatives and friends she condemned his selection of another actress for a wife. As usual, their mother was silent and hoped that this son would regain some of the happiness he had lost.

Mary Ann had become more concerned than ever over the welfare of the Booths after the tragedy in Washington had enveloped them. She had been brave in her sorrow over her favorite's shameful death, and had borne her humiliation without complaint. Unable to keep her family together in life, she now was grimly determined to unite them after death. She grieved constantly over the incarceration of Wilkes' body in the dirt floor of the Arsenal cell. Her intense desire to have him buried beside other Booths actuated two years of effort by Edwin to obtain his body so that it could be placed in a family burial ground.

His first request was made to Grant, who was then Secretary of War. Their mutual friend, Adam Badeau, had reminded Edwin of Grant's offer to serve him at any time in return for his rescue of young Robert Lincoln in the Jersey City railroad station. The letter sent from Barnum's Hotel during Edwin's Baltimore engagement of September, 1867, carried this plea:

> Sir:
> Having once received a promise from Mr. Stanton that the family of John Wilkes Booth should be permitted to obtain the body when sufficient time had elapsed, I yielded to the entreaties of my Mother and applied for it to the Secretary of War—I fear too soon, for the letter was unheeded—if, indeed, it ever reached him.
> I now appeal to you—on behalf of my heart-broken mother—that she may receive the remains of her son. You, Sir, can understand what a consolation it would be to an aged parent to have the privilege of visiting the grave of her child, and I feel assured that you will, even in the midst of your most pressing duties, feel a touch of sympathy for her—one of the greatest sufferers living.
> May I not hope too that you will listen to our entreaties and send me some encouragement—some information how and when the remains may be obtained? By so doing you will receive the gratitude of a most unhappy family, and will—I am

sure—be justified by all right-thinking minds should the matter ever become known to others than ourselves.

I shall remain in Baltimore two weeks from the date of this letter—during which time I could send a trust-worthy person to bring hither and privately bury the remains in the family grounds, thus relieving my poor Mother of much misery.

Apologizing for my intrusion, and anxiously awaiting a reply to this—I am, Sir, with great respect

Yr. obt. servt.,
EDWIN BOOTH [18]

He received no answer. When the main part of the old penitentiary building was torn down within the year, Wilkes' body was removed to a large warehouse on the eastern side of the Arsenal grounds and reburied with the four who had been hanged. About the time of Edwin's letter to Grant, the Washington *Express* made known a communication from the popular comedian C. B. Bishop to the proprietors of the National Hotel on behalf of Edwin. Bishop had asked that Wilkes' trunk, which had been left there, be shipped to Baltimore as the family were anxious to obtain his effects. He had added that Edwin was willing to pay the amount of his brother's indebtedness on presentation of the bill. The letter was forwarded to the War Department, but permission to release the trunk was refused.

While crowds jammed Edwin's New York theatre in February, 1869, he again endeavored to obtain Wilkes' body from the government by engaging John H. Weaver, a Baltimore undertaker, to go to Washington as his representative. This time he took no chance on his request not reaching the right official and wrote a letter to President Johnson, which was to be personally delivered by Weaver. Upon arriving in the Capital, Weaver arranged for the undertaking firm of Harvey and Marr to assist him. Accompanied by Harvey, he called at the White House and presented the following:

Dear Sir:

May I not now ask your kind consideration of my poor mother's request in relation to her son's remains?

The bearer of this (Mr. John Weaver) is sexton of Christ's Church, Baltimore, who will observe the strictest secrecy in this matter—and you may rest assured that none of my family desire its publicity.

Unable to visit Washington, I have deputed Mr. Weaver, in whom I have the fullest confidence, and I beg that you will not delay in ordering the body to be given to his care. He will retain it (placing it in his vault) until such time as we can remove other members of our family to the Baltimore Cemetery, and thus prevent any special notice of it.

There is also (I am told) a trunk of his at the National Hotel—which I once applied for but was refused—it being under seal of the War Dept., it may contain relics of the poor misguided boy—which would be dear to his sorrowing mother, and of no use to anyone. Your Excellency would greatly lessen the crushing weight of grief that is hurrying my Mother to the grave, by giving immediate orders for the safe delivery of the remains of John Wilkes Booth to Mr. Weaver, and gain the lasting gratitude of

Yr. obt. servt.,
EDWIN BOOTH.[19]

President Johnson instructed them to return on the fifteenth, at which time he stipulated that no monument or mound would be permitted to mark the actual location of Wilkes' grave; then he signed a release for his body. About three o'clock that afternoon, Weaver received the final order permitting its delivery. Since all trace of Wilkes' birth date disappeared from the family records it is probable that there was an understanding between President Johnson and Edwin about it. Officials seem to have had some fear that the day might be celebrated in the South.

Harvey and Marr went with Weaver to the Arsenal and all were escorted to the warehouse where Wilkes' body had been reburied. There they saw a pile of flagstones and dirt beside a large open trench exposing boxes in which were the remains of Atzerodt, Paine, and Captain Henry Wirz.[20] These had been left when the boxes containing the bodies of Mrs. Surratt and Herold were claimed and given interment in Washington cemeteries.[21] The one holding Wilkes' remains had been placed underground beside Herold, but, after the latter's exhumation, it had been re-covered with dirt. Within forty-five minutes, a number of soldiers dug it up, and the lettering identifying it was seen by those present. At five o'clock it was placed in a furniture wagon and driven from the Arsenal grounds by W. R. Speare, a boy employed by the undertakers.

To safeguard Harvey's and Marr's establishment near Ford's Theatre from a possible siege by the morbidly curious, Weaver had the corpse temporarily deposited in the stable where Wilkes had kept his horse, back of the theatre and fronting the alley through which he had escaped.[22] "When the box was opened," stated one account, "and the body taken from the army blanket which enshrouded it, it was seen that four years had brought decay. The skull was detached, and, when lifted out, a dentist identified his work, thus proving the identity of the body beyond a doubt." [23]

As the box was not in good condition, it was encased in a larger one made of pine and shipped to Baltimore. Two days later, on the seventeenth, Joseph, Rosalie, and their mother arrived in that city and went to Weaver's establishment where the body had been placed in a rear room awaiting further identification. It was confirmed as being that of John Wilkes Booth by Joseph's recognition of a peculiarly plugged tooth,[24] and the added corroboration of Dr. Theodore Micheau, George L. Stout, and other former intimates of his brother. While the examination was in progress, Rosalie tried to console Mary Ann, who sat to one side weeping.

The Booths had purchased a family lot in Greenmount Cemetery, to which they intended removing the bodies of the elder Booth and Richard from Baltimore Cemetery, and those of the children, Frederick, Elizabeth, and Mary Ann, who had been buried in 1833 at the farm.[25] The part their old Harford County neighbor, Mrs. Rogers, took in these proceedings was related by her in an unpublished letter:

> Mrs. Booth wrote to me to go to Mr. Weaver's and give him the directions as to how he should proceed to the "farm" to procure the remains of her children who had been buried there, and to bring them to Baltimore. I complied with her request, and the bodies were brought on and placed in a casket together; and were deposited in Mr. Weaver's vault for a few days. John's body was, at the same time, placed in an elegant casket by itself and was kept a short time until arrangements could be made for burying all together.[26]

This was the "mysterious burial of John Wilkes Booth" so often described as having occurred at midnight. It was no more than a temporary depositing of his body in the vault by Weaver without ceremony of any kind.

On the afternoon of Saturday, June 26, 1869, Mary Ann, Junius, Rosalie, Edwin, Joseph—all the Maryland Booths but Asia—gathered at Greenmount Cemetery in Baltimore for the ceremony. Surrounded by a large group of relatives and friends, the undaunted family waited before an open grave, as the handsome casket containing the body of Wilkes was lifted from Weaver's hearse. The pallbearers, selected from members of the theatrical profession acquainted with Wilkes, included a Mr. Gallagher, the only survivor of those who had carried the elder Booth to his resting place seventeen years before. A small casket holding the remains of the children that had been brought from

A CHILD OF TRAGEDY

the farm was then set down beside the larger one in the shadow of the elder Booth's monument which, with his body and Richard's, had been previously removed from Baltimore Cemetery. The only marker to signify that these children were buried there is the added inscription on one side of the memorial shaft, which reads—"To the Memory of the Children of Junius Brutus Booth and Mary Ann Booth: John Wilkes, Frederick, Elizabeth, Mary Ann, Henry Byron."

During most of the solemn ritual Mary Ann was calm, but when the Reverend Fleming James,[27] a Protestant Episcopal minister of New York City, began the benediction over the caskets being lowered into the grave, she gave way to uncontrolled grief. Edwin comforted her with the reminder that she now had all her departed ones, except Henry Byron, in a family burial ground. Her other children looked silently on, hoping that her life would be prolonged by the contentment which would follow this fulfillment of her wish.[28]

CHAPTER II

Booth's Theatre had no shops on the street level, but the building contained a number of artist's studios, rented to bring some revenue to the owner. Edwin had furnished one of these for himself and Mary who, when her mania for accompanying him and being present in his dressing room at each performance occasionally abated, remained in New York while he was on tour. The amount he received from the rentals was so small, however, that it caused no more than a splash in the puddle he was wading. At the end of 1869 the books showed a profit of over one hundred thousand dollars on the theatre, but the construction debts took all of that, and it was evident, from the costs of productions, to which side of the ledger the figures were moving.

By January 5, 1870, Edwin was back in his theatre playing *Hamlet*. Time and money had been spent in an effort to make it the most perfect production ever staged in America. The costume of Hamlet contained purple, the mourning color of the early Danes, which had not been used before in the dress portraying the character. Edwin's acting companions and soldiers were all blonde Norsemen who wore finely wrought steel armor, and the castle of the Danish kings had the massive fortress-like appearance of tenth- or eleventh-century architecture, in which period the action of the play was placed. The cast included David Anderson, Willmarth Waller, Theodore Hamilton, and Edwin's niece, Blanche De Bar.

This outstanding production of the season placed Edwin's Hamlet beyond the reach of all his contemporaries. His performance was "now mellowed to the point of richness which from this time forward for years stamped the impression indelibly on the public consciousness. Thereafter . . . Booth was Hamlet and Hamlet was Booth, one and inseparable." [29]

Charles Fechter, of London, staged his version of the Dane at another theatre and gave burlesque comedians an opportunity to make the most of such rivalry, but Edwin played to packed houses. The financial spurt encouraged him—until he saw another expense account. After several changes in the plays, John Sleeper Clarke, who was back in the United States, began an engagement in Booth's Theatre in the spring. At this time, Edwin sold his half-interest in the Philadelphia Walnut Street Theatre to him.

On July 4, 1870, a son was born to Edwin and Mary in the apartment they occupied in the theatre. He was christened Edgar, but lived only a few hours. "In the birth of the child it was necessary to crush its head," Edwin confided to a friend.[30] A small stone marks his grave near that of Edwin's first wife in Mount Auburn Cemetery at Cambridge, Massachusetts.

The birth of Edgar was a crucial moment for Mary. What would have been the outcome had Edgar survived cannot be guessed, but the ordeal left Mary in a grave mental condition, the precursor of a more serious mental instability to come. Again the shadow of insanity was to touch a child of Junius Brutus Booth.

But this misfortune was still in the future. That summer was a quiet one for Edwin and his family. They lived in a house at Long Branch, which Edwin had purchased, and Edwina came from school to stay with them. It was a comfortable dwelling, surrounded by pine woods, affording a cool and pleasant retreat from the city. After another vacation there Edwina took up her studies at Notre Dame in Philadelphia, where Marion was a student.

Although Edwin kept in touch with his theatre, debts continued to pile up. No effort was made to curtail expenses. Scenery, dress, and appointments were heralded as beyond comparison to all others in the world. Productions continued which left no balance to pay off the cost of the building, and in the autumn Edwin started off on another tour for more money. After this debt was paid he intended to make few appearances and spend most of his time in retirement. By the middle of November, he was back in New York, and, in a letter to Edwina saying he was going to call on his mother, he wrote, "Uncle Joe went on to Baltimore the other day to see about selling Grandma's farm (the place where your old pap was born)."[31]

January of the following year found Edwin again at his theatre as the central figure in a magnificent revival of *Richelieu*, with Lawrence Barrett in the rôle of Adrien de Mauprat. Having similar artistic inclinations, the two men were drawn to each other by a common objective in perfecting theatrical productions of the classics. Their friendship began shortly after Edwin's return to the stage in 1866 and, except for the intervals caused by some petty squabbles, continued until Barrett's death. The press complained of the poor support given Edwin by the company, but *Richelieu* had a fair run. After Edwin's departure, Barrett went on starring in other bills until July, when the house was closed for the first time during the summer.

Doors were thrown open again next season, the most important engagement being that of Charlotte Cushman, who made her reappearance after a long retirement. About this time Edwin and Robertson got into a wrangle concerning their agreement, which resulted in Edwin's ending the partnership by an outlay of cash and property amounting to nearly two hundred and fifty thousand dollars. Toward the end of the year he presented *Julius Caesar* in sumptuous settings, playing on different nights the parts of Cassius, Brutus, and Marc Antony, supported by Frank Bangs, Lawrence Barrett and, later in the season, his brother Junius. This bill carried them into the spring of 1872 and somewhat reduced Edwin's debts.

But the cares of management soon began to weigh heavily upon him and he discussed with Junius means of being relieved from such responsibilities. Junius believed he could put the theatre on a paying basis if he had it entirely under his control and offered to take it over as a lessee. Edwin had confidence in his older brother and thought himself fortunate in the arrangement. He could not possibly have found a man more qualified to uphold the reputation of Booth's Theatre. The two brothers had never had any difficulty in their business relations and Edwin felt certain of success. In January, 1873, Junius signed a contract to guide the theatre through the next five years of its existence, but he did not assume his managerial duties until June.

In the basement of the building was one of Wilkes' old trunks, filled with his theatrical effects, some of which had belonged to the elder Booth. It was the one he had left in Montreal for Martin to run through the blockade. Edwin had obtained the trunk from McKee Rankin whose brother had bought it at auction from the Canadian government. Now that the management of his theatre was being transferred, Edwin attended to a matter that had been on his mind for some time, and early one wintry morning, burned the entire collection in the furnace. Thereafter, all that remained of John Wilkes Booth in his possession, was the one small photograph, now on a wall of his room at The Players.[32]

The great Panic of 1873 played havoc with any plans Junius may have had for his new venture and forced him to borrow money. Joseph Jefferson opened at Booth's on September first in the popular *Rip Van Winkle* which drew a large and brilliant audience, although his support was "too cold and hard to make his delightful picture of Irving's hero as sound and perfect in its surroundings as in itself." Maggie Mitchell next appeared there. She was followed by Edwin who began a four weeks' engagement on November third in *Hamlet*. That month, the press repeated complaints by managers of a general depression and the possibility of darkened houses.

In an attempt to revive business Junius continued to bring in star after star. Among others, he featured his wife, Agnes Booth, but this did not help matters, though in Shakespearean rôles she received some complimentary notices. The climax came at the beginning of the New Year. Edwin found it necessary to file a petition of voluntary bankruptcy in the United States District Court. For several months, however, Junius kept the doors of the theatre from closing, and in May John McCullough achieved a short triumph in *The Gladiator*. The last bill was *King John* in which "Mrs. Booth as Constance gave new evidence of her great dramatic power," but the title rôle, played by Junius, was criticized as having been "disfigured by staginess and mannerisms." This concluded Junius' management of the Booth Theatre. "His career was checkered like that of his predecessors . . ." read one review. "Mr. McCullough's performances wound up the season in a way that prevents the comment that it feebly flickered out. . . ." [33]

Maurice Grau took over the theatre for a short time, then it fell into the hands of Jarrett and Palmer, who secured the lease at an annual rental of forty thousand dollars. When Edwin protested against the use of his name in connection with the theatre, a downtown printer, also named Booth, was taken into the organization for the purpose, and it was called Booth's Theatre as long as it remained a place of amusement. The property was sold at foreclosure in December and bought by the Oakes Ames Estate, the plaintiff in the action.

The exact cost of Booth's Theatre was never known, as expert accountants were unable to separate the sums Joe had listed for the construction work from those of several plays first presented. Edwin's mind had always been on the artistic success of his theatre. He trusted others in financing the project, and when the panic came he was trapped. Soon after bankruptcy had snatched his million-dollar theatre from him, he confided to his friend, William Bispham:

> This is by no means the heaviest blow my life has felt, and I shall recover from it very shortly if my creditors have any feeling whatever.
>
> My disappointment is great, to be sure, but I have the consciousness of having tried to do what I deemed my duty. Since the talent God has given me can be made available for no other purpose, I believe the object I devote it to to be worthy of self-sacrifice.
>
> I gave up all that most men hold dearest, wealth and luxurious ease; nor do I complain because that unlucky "slip 'twixt the cup and the lip" has spilled all my tea.
>
> With a continuance of the health and popularity the good Lord has thus far blessed me with, I will pay every "sou" and exclaim with "Don Caesar," tho' in a different spirit, "I have done great things—if you doubt me ask my creditors."

Of course I see some years of hard work before me, all for a "dead horse" too, not a very cheering prospect. But I'll "worry" it thro', and thank God with all my heart when I can cry "quits" with my neighbor.[34]

After the failure of Edwin's theatre the three brothers went their separate ways. Joseph made no attempt to succeed behind the footlights, but lived with his wife at Long Branch, New Jersey, where he acquired considerable real estate. The experience kept Edwin from ever again participating in such ventures, and during the next twenty years he traveled as a star. Junius' connection with his brother's theatre was also his last undertaking of any importance in that respect. A large portion of the once ample fortune that he had accumulated in his long career as a theatrical manager was lost in this speculation. The standards of the Booths were back in the dust. But Edwin was determined that every cent of his obligations should be paid, that the Booth name might again be the proudest in the American theatre.

Junius' connection with Booth's Theatre had lasted less than a year. When the management passed from his control in the summer of 1874, he paid a hurried visit to the Clarkes at Boulogne Sur Mer, France, with whom his daughter, Marion, had been staying. To him and the many former companions who stopped over at their home while on European tours, Asia expressed her desire to be in America again. She explained, however, that she not only dreaded recrossing the ocean, but feared that a reunion with her mother might cause her aging parent more unhappiness when she would again have to return to London, where her husband was firmly entrenched in theatrical investments. But these interests did not deter Clarke from making some stage appearances in the United States.

Several years before Junius met with reverses, he had purchased, at various times, more shore property in Manchester near Boston. He now owned a total of fifteen acres and began planning to retire from the stage so that he could live there permanently with his family. The need for money to pay his debts and release him from professional activities, sent him and his wife to California in October. Here they hoped to replenish their finances by the sale of valuable real estate Junius owned in San Francisco, and by a theatrical engagement starring Agnes. But it is evident from his will made four years later that he did not dispose of all these investments.

While her husband was attending to such matters, Agnes played a two weeks' engagement at the California Theatre under the management of John McCullough, opening late that month in *Romeo and*

Juliet, supported by Joseph Wheelock. Junius made his only appearance during this visit in the title rôle of *King John* on her benefit night. Her final bill was *Elene*, one of Adolph Belot's plays, which the press condemned as having a plot entirely without purpose, founded on absurdities, and giving no opportunity for good acting. Agnes was enthusiastically received, but the engagement, financially, was disappointing.

Junius did not care for the growing metropolis and deplored the widening of Kearney Street, which prevented friends "from shaking hands across it." San Francisco was not the city he had known as a younger man. Before departing, he divulged to a former associate that those involved with Wilkes in the Lincoln plot went to trial on Wilkes' birthday.[35]

The return trip to Manchester was interrupted by a stop-over in Nevada, where Junius fought a contest with the champion swordsman of France which lasted one hour, the newspapers lauding Junius' great ability as a duelist.

At first the New England villagers were a bit skeptical of the actors in their midst, but the charitable willingness of the Booths to participate in any local entertainment dispelled such doubts. The townsfolk were forced to admit that the theatrical celebrities who had come there and transformed what had been an unprofitable tract of stony property into valuable estates had done more for the community than its regular inhabitants could have accomplished in a century. They had entertained almost every well-known member of their profession, many of whom returned to build summer homes, which gave the place a great deal of publicity, and resulted in every foot of land's being purchased. Manchester became a mecca for actors, artists, writers, and many wealthy people who appreciated its scenic qualities and its easy access to supplies.

But there were no hotels to accommodate these visitors, and Junius saw an opportunity to invest money advantageously by building one. This would necessitate his disposal of more San Francisco real estate, and after their house had been converted into winter quarters, Junius and Agnes made a hurried trip to California at the beginning of 1876 for added funds.[36] Agnes' mother, Mrs. Sarah Smeatham (formerly Mrs. Land Rookes) and her daughter Belle, who lived with the Booths in Manchester, took care of the four sons, Junius Brutus, III., Algernon C., Sydney Barton, and Barton J., in their parents' absence.

When Junius and Agnes returned, they arranged for the construction of the hotel on their seaside property to be known as the Masconomo House. In the fall of 1877 the building was underway.

Agnes had continued her professional engagements in eastern cities, and much of the money that she earned plus all that Junius could raise went into it.

The house they had first occupied remained as their private quarters when the gigantic hotel, extending from it on one side, was completed. As Edwin had built his theatre, so Junius built his hotel. The Booths did nothing halfway. Junius wanted a show-place and he got it. The grounds surrounding the hotel were transformed into beautiful gardens with broad lawns sloping down to the *Singing Sands* beach. A bowling alley and dance hall occupied a separate building near the hotel; and back of it, at the foot of the hill, was a fully equipped stable, with horse stalls and carriage space for rent. Other buildings sheltered about fifty Negroes employed by Junius.

Operating expenses for such a place were enormous, but the Masconomo House drew great crowds of wealthy patrons and made money while Junius had it under his control. Gay parties were held there, and special trains ran from Boston to accommodate summer guests. Theatrical productions were given for their entertainment on the spacious lawns, and saddle horses were always at hand to take them on popular jaunts through the Essex woods to Agassiz Rock. Junius was reminded of his family picnics on the boulders of Deer Creek during his boyhood days in Maryland. Only the deaths of their two small sons, Algernon C., in January, 1877, and Barton J., in July, 1879, marred the happiness of Junius and Agnes. Both children were buried in Rosedale Cemetery, Manchester, and their graves marked by stones representing broken columns.

"We called Mr. Booth *J. B.*," said an old Manchester citizen. "He was a handsome man, very dignified, but always pleasant. I was just a young fellow then and never talked with him very much, but I played a lot with his two boys, Sid and Wid (Junius III). They had a raft anchored off shore from the hotel beach where we went in swimming. The boys called that big island rock down there Monte Cristo. Wid told us about the play, so we used to swim over to the rock and stage a little drama. We were all going to be great actors. When theatrical performances were given on the lawn, we used to hide in the bushes and watch the grown-ups. The Booths were well-liked by everybody in the town. I never knew of Edwin Booth being at J. B.'s place, but I suppose he came sometime or other. Boston papers were always printing things about him. I never heard J. B. speak of John Wilkes."

Junius' daughter, Marion, was thrust into her theatrical career by John T. Ford in October of 1877, at Richmond, when he asked her to substitute for an actress who was taken ill and could not go on in the play, *Pink Dominoes,* at Mozart Hall. Marion told him that she had never attempted an important rôle on the stage and could not prepare herself for such an ordeal before curtain time that evening. But Ford insisted, and she performed so well that he declared his indebtedness to her for having saved him from disappointment. That December John Sleeper Clarke, again appearing in the United States, was at the Broad Street Theatre in Philadelphia and engaged her as his leading lady. She also supported him for two weeks at the Fifth Avenue Theatre in New York City. With Blanche making her own way as an actress (after a successful début in 1865), Junius now had two daughters doing very well upon the stage.

While Junius promoted his seaside resort, Edwin worked to pay his debts. As if this were not enough burden in itself, in 1875 he suffered an accident that put an additional load upon him. While he and his family were at Cos Cob during the summer, he and Dr. A. O. Kellogg crawled into a carriage behind a rather frisky team. One of the animals, newly purchased, set a pace which Edwin tried to check. Its mate joined in the spree, and all went flying down the road at cyclone speed with the dust shooting up behind them. Suddenly, the carriage tipped, and Edwin was dumped out. The doctor went on a short way, then felt the earth jar him and found himself in a ditch. The team was finally corralled, and Edwin was picked up severely bruised, one of his arms and several ribs broken. He had experienced other runaways, but this one had been a close call. The rest of the summer was spent in bandages.

In October he had recovered enough to play a delayed Hamlet at Daly's Fifth Avenue Theatre, New York, where he received a demonstrative welcome after an absence of two years. The following month he gave one of his finest impersonations as Richard II, and while there wrote to Edwina: "My forty-second birthday (yesterday) was passed (day and evening) in the theatre, with *Richelieu* and *Shylock,* two weary old boys."[37] He was still feeling the effects of the accident. His arm had not yet healed, and he never wholly regained the use of it.

The southern tour Edwin made under the management of John T. Ford at the beginning of 1876 was a great success artistically and financially. For fifty performances Ford paid him thirty thousand dollars, and everywhere Edwin received ovations that far outrivaled those given to any other actor. But the curiosity in regard to him because of Wilkes' crime made Edwin so dislike attention outside the theatre that Ford was compelled to have a member of the company impersonate him when their car stopped at railway stations along the route where crowds shouted for his appearance. As the substitute was not only delighted but also fully equal to the task, and the throngs were not well-acquainted with Edwin's likeness, everyone, including the great tragedian himself, was satisfied.

Upon reaching Richmond, Edwin wrote to his daughter, "'Twas in this city, darling, just twenty years ago, that I first met your angel mother. . . . My last visit here was seventeen years ago (before *you* knew me). . . . Your grandfather Booth was much beloved here, and made his first appearance (in 1821) before an American audience in this city." [38]

Frederick Warde, a member of Ford's company, was often surprised by the humorous remarks made by Edwin in the midst of some tragic scene, which, because of Edwin's tendency to melancholia, were very unexpected. When the company arrived at Mobile, Alabama, mosquitoes pounced upon their tender bodies and during performances took advantage of the inactivity against them to remain longer than usual upon an unprotected spot. One evening, in the rôle of Lear, Edwin, wearing the garb of the demented old king, was sitting on a log. "I, as the assumed madman Edgar, was lying at his feet," recalled Warde. "Lear, taking Edgar to be a learned philosopher, asks him: 'What is your occupation?' to which Edgar, humoring the old king, answers: 'How to prevent the fiend and to kill vermin.' To my intense astonishment, Mr. Booth, without a change in the vacant eye, or a muscle of the pain-drawn, reverend face, asked 'Skeeters and sich?'"

At another time and place, they were playing *Richelieu*. Between acts, Warde, in his costume of the Chevalier, went to Edwin's dressing room and found him sitting before the mirror, made up as the great Cardinal, in the full crimson robes, with the biretta on his head and the jeweled cross on his breast, smoking a corncob pipe. The incongruity of the situation struck them forcibly, and they both laughed.[39]

Edwin's incessant smoking was to be the direct cause of an illness later in life. He was not well then and during the tour did not play every night. While still in Alabama, he experienced one of several incidents in the aftermath of his brother's crime. His morning's mail contained a note which read:

Dear Sir:

My wife and self have always been great admirers of you. We want to see you play very much, but cannot afford to buy our tickets. Will you please send us a couple of seats? I am sure you will not refuse this request when I tell you that I am the United States soldier that shot and killed your brother who assassinated President Lincoln.

A CHILD OF TRAGEDY

Edwin investigated and found it was from Boston Corbett. Tickets were sent to him and that evening he and his wife attended the performance. Edwin always regarded Corbett's act, if authentic, as having averted a more terrible fate for his brother than would have been his had he reached Washington alive and fallen into the hands of the mob or been strung up on the gallows.[40]

Toward the end of February, the company was in Nashville, Tennessee, where great crowds followed Edwin about the city from the moment he arrived until his departure. "Swarms of females (they can't be called 'ladies')," he scribbled to his daughter, "gathered in all public places. It is unpleasant for me, who hate notoriety and publicity. They point at and touch me, exclaiming to one another, 'That's him! that's Booth!' Today they tried to get on the carriage that brought me to the hotel." [41]

Edwin ended the tour under Ford's management in March, 1876, but continued playing as a visiting star with various stock companies throughout the Midwest, and in April was billed at his father-in-law's Chicago theatre.

Barton Hill had gone to San Francisco and associated himself with John McCullough in the management of the California Theatre. McCullough, knowing the extent of Edwin's bankruptcy from the account given him by Junius, urged his return to the Golden State. Edwin accepted the offer of an eight weeks' engagement, and Hill was sent to Chicago for him, while McCullough remained in San Francisco to arrange for his appearances.

Hill secured one of the best hotel-cars from the railway company, which included a Pullman conductor, cook, and porter, and Edwin, with Mary and Edwina started westward. Prevented from reading or studying because of an eye trouble, Edwina was now being educated orally by her stepmother. Eleven days had been allowed for the usual five-day trip by rail "on account of the extreme nervousness of that charming lady, Mrs. Booth, whom I had great difficulty in persuading to consent to travel at night," said Hill. "But the mosquitoes of the first night of side-track rest on the way to Omaha, and the quiet motion of the Union Pacific trains assisted in eventually overcoming her scruples, and, with one day's rest at Omaha, three at Salt Lake, and one at Virginia City, we reached San Francisco after a most delightful trip." [42] At Virginia City, Hill suggested they inspect a mine, but Mrs. Booth would not go nor allow Edwin to make the descent.

They arrived in San Francisco twenty years to the day after Edwin had departed. Everything had changed—but Edwin's financial condition.

He told McCullough he had about the same amount in cash that he left with in 1856—five hundred dollars. Dave Anderson (who had returned in 1873 and married Mrs. Marie Everard, once a favorite California actress) and many other old friends were there to welcome him.

Additional scenery and costumes had been procured by McCullough, and the company engaged to support Edwin was one of recognized merit. Most of them had played with him before and were familiar with all the plays in his repertoire except *The Fool's Revenge*. Public enthusiasm was at its height, and enormous premiums were paid for tickets. The California Theatre was packed from top to bottom each night, and hundreds were turned away at the door. The house echoed with affectionate calls to Edwin and boomed with applause. McCullough and T. W. Keene, his leading man, played opposite him during this engagement. Each day, at the end of rehearsal, Anderson, Edwin, and a few intimates would go to the California Market for a glass of buttermilk, after which they sat smoking and talking. Invitations were showered upon him, but no one could get him to a friendly home unless it belonged to some old crony. It was a pleasant holiday for Edwin and beneficial in more ways than one. His health improved, and when the engagement ended he had fifty thousand dollars—for his creditors.

In November he returned to New York under his father-in-law's management and played to profitable houses, although the loss of more than three hundred lives in the panic and fire of the Brooklyn Theatre on December fifth later ruined the business of other companies throughout the city. At the beginning of the year 1877, he started off on another eastern tour, ending with an engagement in May at the Globe Theatre, Boston.

Edwin's earnings for this period had been close to seventy-two thousand five hundred dollars, which he also passed into the hands of waiting creditors.[43] He had now paid the last of his obligations. The struggle to do so had occupied years which might have been spent in securing personal luxuries and future ease. His feverish efforts to re-establish his financial standing had once again placed the name of Booth above reproach.

CHAPTER III

Tongues had been wagging about Edwin and Mary. Occasionally, little tales slipped out, similar to one told by Margaret Townsend:

> That part of the community who only knew . . . Edwin Booth as our country's most celebrated actor would probably have experienced surprise had they obtained a glimpse of his domestic life with the second Mrs. Booth—to have witnessed the meekness of manner, you might say, with which he complied with her suggestions. That last, however, is scarcely the word for the place, as she was usually in the imperative mood.
>
> The Mrs. Booth I refer to was one of the most extraordinarily small and precise of women, and it was difficult for the observer to discover wherein lay her attraction for the great actor, likewise her claim to such absolute control as she practised over her family.
>
> As an instance of the latter I may cite the following, which occurred nightly, and with absolute regularity, at a summer resort where a number of people, including the Booths, were passing a part of the season.
>
> Miss Booth would possibly be engaged conversing with some of her acquaintances; Mr. Booth immersed in a book. On the stroke of ten, Mrs. Booth, with index finger pointing dramatically at the clock, would enunciate warningly the single word—
>
> "Edwina!"
>
> Without an instant's hesitation, Miss Booth would bid her friends good-night and retire.
>
> In possibly half an hour's time, Mrs. Booth, in the same warning voice would remark:
>
> "Mr. Booth."
>
> Booth, glancing dreamily up from his book, would regard the small lady for an instant as if gradually collecting himself from some other sphere, and then, as obediently as Edwina, he would gravely bid good-night to those present, and likewise retire.[44]

The second Mary had given Edwin little peace of mind. She nagged him day and night, was extremely jealous, watched every move he made, allowed no reference by him or Edwina to the latter's mother, and often flew into temperamental outbursts. The situation was difficult for all, but especially for Edwin. Once, in a dejected mood, he called at the home of Reverend Samuel Osgood in New York and asked to see the clergyman's study where he had, years before, "secured his greatest happiness."

The gossips did not know that Mary's dictatorial manner was but a phase of the mental illness which was gradually taking hold of her—increasingly since the birth and death of Edgar. Edwin and his daughter indulged her whims only to keep her from becoming too excited. Although Dr. A. O. Kellogg supposedly visited them at Cos Cob in 1875 for no other purpose than friendly chats with Edwin, the condition into which Mary was slipping probably had something to do with his sojourn there. While they talked of Hamlet's insanity, this specialist was not apt to overlook a matter closer at hand. Two summers later, while Edwin rested at Benedict's home in Greenwich, Mary was in a private sanitarium for neurotic patients. The situation in which Edwin was placed compelled Edwina to stay with other members of the Booth family during her vacation.

The apparent improvement of the imperious little wife enabled her to continue traveling with Edwin. No one could swerve her from this fixed decision until she became so nervously exhausted that Edwin insisted upon her remaining for a time with the McVickers in Chicago. The next two seasons he toured the Midwest and East, appeared under his own management at Booth's Theatre in New York and published fifteen volumes of his prompt books, edited by William Winter.

In April of 1879 Edwin and his family were in Chicago, where he played an engagement at his father-in-law's theatre. As he delivered the last-act soliloquy in *Richard II* on the twenty-third of the month (the anniversary of Shakespeare's birthday) he deviated from his usual stage business and did something he had never done before. He leaned over to steady himself as he got up. As he did so, a bullet whizzed over his head. Another shot was fired, and looking up, he saw a man standing in the gallery, pistol in hand, ready to pull the trigger once more, had he not been prevented by several persons from behind who seized his arms.

Edwin calmly walked to the front of the stage, pointed him out, and cried, "Arrest that man!" For a few moments, the audience was panic-stricken, but was quieted after the would-be murderer had been taken from the house. Edwin addressed them, saying he wished to speak with his wife who was backstage and would then finish the performance. Mary, much more frightened than he, was in a state of collapse. For several nights after that she awakened screaming that she had recurrent visions of guns aimed at him. Fortunately, Edwina was not in the theatre. Mary Ann and other Booths were shaken by the news and believed the attempt to shoot Edwin was in revenge for Wilkes' assassination of Lincoln.

When questioned, the man gave his name as Mark Gray, twenty-three years of age, a clerk and resident of St. Louis. His reasons for wishing to kill Edwin were somewhat confused. He first stated he was avenging the honor of a female relative, then said Edwin had defeated his ambitions for histrionic glory, and boasted that for three years he had been preparing to kill him and was disappointed in not having accomplished his purpose. The critics, however, facetiously declared Gray had tried to murder Edwin for "restoring" Shakespeare's intolerable *Richard II* to the stage, but Edwin dubbed Gray's performance "The Fool's Revenge."

After the final curtain, he dug out the bullet which had gone into a stage prop instead of his head and later had it mounted in a gold cartridge bearing the date and an inscription, "From Mark Gray to Edwin Booth." It dangled from his watch chain the rest of his life. Once more he attributed escape to his caul. But the attack of a madman and the constant companionship of a neurotic wife were too strong a combination for Edwin, and his temporary self-control threatened to give way. The day following the incident he became nervously excited but continued his engagement. From Chicago he went to more quiet surroundings and another summer of relaxation.

While Gray was in a Chicago prison, Edwin wrote to an attorney of that city: "I trust that our friend Gray may become gray indeed—yea, positively hoary-headed—in kind but careful confinement, or if earlier released, that his exit may be from this earthly stage of his dramatic exploits to that celestial scene where idiots cease from shooting and actors are at rest. If he be ever again at liberty my own life I shall not value worth a rush. But I hope the Elgin guardians will not be deceived by his seeming harmlessness." [45]

In October Edwin returned to the stage and played in Baltimore, Philadelphia, and New York, but the first two months of the New Year he was inactive professionally and often attended performances of light opera and comedies as a spectator. The press kept track of him and made reports such as, "Mr. Edwin Booth enjoyed *Traviata* Tuesday night but was not looking very well." Edwin protested and the *Dramatic Mirror*, in February, declared he was in better health than he had been for years. He wrote to Anderson: "Because I choose to 'loaf and invite my soul' this season for needed rest in preference to working for wealth, which I don't want, the papers occasionally fling at me that illness and failing power, etc., prevent my filling engagements." [46]

Other Booths were also in New York. Mary Ann and Rosalie were living at the Grand Central Hotel which had been built on the site of the old Winter Garden Theatre. Junius' daughter, Marion, was with Frank Mayo's company at the Grand Opera House, playing the hardhearted Alida Bloodgood, in *The Streets of New York*, and "creating a very favorable impression." His wife, Agnes, "the best leading lady on the American stage," was at the Park Theatre. The Booth name was always on the boards somewhere—and in the papers.

Edwin's spring engagements were under the management of Henry E. Abbey and began at the Academy of Music, where he appeared "in aid of the Sufferers of Ireland," as Hamlet, Iago, and Petruchio. His niece, Marion Booth, took the rôle of Katherine in the latter bill, which was given in its entirety. From there the company went to the Park Theatre in Boston for three weeks. Before half the time had passed, Edwin regretted that they had not arranged to stay longer—all tickets had been sold for remaining performances and the box office closed.

Mary continued her vexing trips to his dressing room, but he saw little of Edwina, who was much in demand and having a gay time socially. She was an attractive girl in her nineteenth year, with features and a wholesome nature like those of her mother. Edwin's adoration of his daughter aroused much of Mary's jealousy and antipathy toward her.

In April they were back in New York, where Edwin appeared at Booth's Theatre—"My old shop," he called it. An engagement in Brooklyn concluded this short season which critics summed up by pointing to his undiminished popularity and sovereignty over the American stage. They complained, however, that the company supporting him was very inferior. Some accused him of having procured the support of secondary actors so that he could appear to advantage. It was a stock phrase which also had been aimed at Forrest and others.

His anxiety over Mary increased owing to a distressing cough she had difficulty in repressing at certain times. Her mental state had not improved, and her hallucinations were becoming more frequent. Between the acts at one of Edwin's New York performances, she had bluntly told him that Dave Anderson had just died. It was remarkable that the shock did not prevent him from going on with his next scene. "By Jove! it staggered me!" he wrote to his old California friend. "But knowing that if any such calamity had occurred, I would be one of the first to know it, I held myself together. . . ." [47]

This was only one of the inconsiderations he endured from Mary's wandering mind. She had started an autograph collection and forced him to induce such celebrities as Ole Bull, the great Norwegian violinist, to inscribe some bars of music and a poem above his signature for her. Edwin's apologies to persons of note for these intrusions revealed how necessary it was to humor and keep Mary occupied. He was constantly harassed by her wild demands and unbalanced accusations at home and in the theatre, but he patiently resigned himself to the fate that made him the melancholy Dane both off and on the stage.

Edwin wanted to return to England and had been negotiating for an opportune appearance at the London Lyceum during the time of Henry Irving's proposed tour in America. Irving, then playing a Shakespearean repertoire at this theatre, had reached fame by his performance in *The Bells*. A letter to Irving remained unanswered, and the matter dragged along for about a year until an agent in London was able to secure the services of Walter Gooch, a manager who was constructing a new playhouse on the site of the old Princess Theatre. To protect himself, should his efforts be unsuccessful, Edwin feigned indifference to his secret ambition for European approval. At the same time, he hoped that Mary's health and mental condition would be improved by a change of scenery and planned various excursions for her benefit, which would also be interesting and instructive to Edwina. But in England, tuberculosis of the throat and lungs was to place Mary beyond all hope of recovery.

"It is still uncertain when I'll act in London," Edwin wrote to William Winter. "I shall be slow and very cautious in all my movements. Acting will not be my chief aim this time, but recreation, health, and a protracted loaf. . . . My sister [Asia] sends all sorts of fearful messages regarding my advent and Irving's influence in London! There's a man named Clement Scott who publishes ugly things about the Booth family constantly, and is very anxious to know if, and when, I am going." [48]

A public breakfast, attended by many prominent men, was given for Edwin at Delmonico's in June, and on the last day of the month he sailed away for a second engagement in England, taking Edwina and his wife with him. After a disappointing view of Ireland, Scotland, and Wales, they settled down in London.

Some English critics wondered why Edwin deserted the throne he had won in America and again journeyed overseas in an effort to gain the approbation of a people who had given him and other American actors nothing more than rebuffs and poor box office. Yet this scramble for English acclaim continued, each actor thinking he could, by a successful leap to London, surpass contemporaries in his own country. Upon Edwin's arrival he found John McCullough, Lawrence Barrett, and others there arranging for appearances.

When Edwin called upon the Clarkes in their suburban home, he learned that Asia was trying to combat the family scandal by rewriting and issuing another volume about their father. She asked him to give her some new material, but Edwin said he could not while he felt so wretched in mind and body. He gave her some advice, however, which he thought more important, and in the next edition of her book the word *mésalliance* was omitted.

Edwin soon discovered that the Princess Theatre in London had a reputation equal to the Bowery in New York for melodramatic productions catering to a cheap clientele. Irving still ignored him, and Edwin found it difficult to gain attention from the London populace without some recognition from this eminent tragedian. He did not want to be managed or heralded by his brother-in-law, Clarke, who operated two theatres in London, but preferred a responsible and well-established English manager. However, it was Clarke who finally looked after his interests and secured his contract. Since there was no other, Edwin agreed to open the new Princess Theatre which Gooch expected to have ready by November.

While awaiting its completion, the Booths visited Stratford-on-Avon, then traveled on to the continent, hurriedly skirting the Rhine by rail in order to reach Oberammergau for the Passion Play. There they did not fare so well. They could get no accommodations other than a bed in a hayloft and their anticipations of an unusual performance suffered great disappointment. Edwin thought it theatrical, greatly exaggerated, and saw no religious fervor in either actors or spectators. He declared it unsuitable for the professional stage and later helped prevent an attempt to present it at Booth's Theatre in New York. The family went on to Paris, but Edwin's appreciation of the fine acting of Coquelin, a celebrated French comedian, failed to dull his unpleasant impression of repulsive odors and squalor in the city.

When they returned to London and Edwin beheld the gaudy interior of the Princess Theatre, met the company, and looked over the sets, he knew it was not the right address for Shakespeare. But on November 6, 1880, he opened there in *Hamlet*. As usual, Mary insisted on accompanying him to the theatre and remaining in his dressing room. He permitted her to do so in order not to aggravate her nervous condition, although her presence there always upset him. He had been warned that some critics were waiting to snipe him and the prospect of such a reception made him unresponsive to the demands of his rôle.

Clement Scott of the London *Telegraph*, who Asia said had circulated base reports about the Booth family, was the first to deride him. After contrasting his well-cut, animated, intellectual features, and elastic walk, with the "poor and unattractive dress . . . tangled black hair, well off the face but hanging in feminine disorder down the back," he scoffed, "This was Edwin Booth, who looked as if he had stepped out of some old theatrical print in the days of elocution and before the era of natural and real acting." Then asking, "Is this Hamlet?" he continued: "The play proceeds, scene after scene and act after act, and the naturally ideal Hamlet seems omitted from the programme. He never makes the blood course through the veins, warms the emotions, or touches the sympathies . . . his Hamlet . . . is cold and classical to a fault. . . ."

Others, however, did not agree with these opinions. In a long review the *Times* commended Edwin's Hamlet as eminently interesting and successful. The reviewer mentioned Booth's early struggles and many vicissitudes such as the loss of a million dollars in an attempt to present the finest productions of the classics, and concluded that any man who, surviving so much, could walk to the front of the stage and calmly point out an assailant as a pistol was being unloaded in his direction, had nothing to fear from the critics.

Supported by a company far below par, Edwin was forced to play night after night to houses that barely paid his expenses. But letters of encouragement from private sources made him confident that if he continued through the spring season he would gain the hearty approval of the English public, after which he planned to test the German temper. *Richelieu* followed *Hamlet*, and for two weeks the box office boomed, then fell back to its first average, and *Richelieu* was withdrawn.

Edwin and Asia spent their first Christmas together since their childhood. She was still occupied with her writing, and he now helped her by cheerfully recalling many of his early experiences which she included in *The Elder and the Younger Booth*. Their discussions poignantly reminded them of how seldom the family had been together, and the improbability of a future reunion, as Asia was determined never to return to the land of their brother's crime.

Edwin continued his engagement with *The Fool's Revenge* which also suffered from several scathing reviews and increased his gratitude for the praise given him in the United States.

In January, Irving came down out of his ivory tower and called on him, after which they met several times and became friendly. The season at the Princess dragged on, and Edwin began to regard his period of exile as little better than wasted.

Although his wife had been under the care of an eminent physician, her condition had not improved, and Edwin limited rather than increased his social obligations. She still insisted on accompanying him to the theatre, and her presence kept him constantly on edge during performances, fearing she might suddenly be taken by violent convulsions. Shortly after the first of the New Year his engagement with Gooch was extended, much to the latter's financial benefit, regardless of his first agreement that any renewal was to be on the same terms. *Othello* did not improve Edwin's notices, but a production of *Lear* in February brought Charles Reade, the well-known English novelist and critic, whom the tragedian later met, into the theatre.

On the night Reade attended, Mary became ill in Edwin's dressing room. Her physician was summoned and it was thought she would die before the performance ended. Tuberculosis was now taking its toll of Mary. Edwin rushed from the stage to his wife, and from her to the stage, his self-control deceiving the audience who supposed his emotions a part of his acting. Reade, unaware of the facts, commented to E. H. House, an American author, on Edwin's fine impersonation, "Poor old man; they have broken his mind, but see how he holds his dignity." [49] At the close of the play Edwin found Mary's physician still unable to relieve her. Physical complications and suffering were further affecting her mind. Madness was beckoning to her as it had to his father, to Wilkes, to himself. Edwin seemed destined always to live within its reach. Since nothing could be done for Mary in the theatre, she was rushed home in a carriage through streets where galloping horses would attract the least attention. Physicians now refused to care for her unless she was kept away from the theatre. Fees for constant medical attention and nurses so increased Edwin's expenses that he was compelled to move from his comfortable rooms to less cheerful quarters.

His early efforts to win approval in England had been interrupted by the war, and now domestic tragedy threatened the furtherance of his ambition. While he doggedly continued in the theatre, Edwina took charge of social and household obligations. The pressure of his adversities bore down on him to such an extent that he wrote to Winter: "The strain of *Lear* every night is in itself enough to drain the life of a stronger man that I; but add to this the anxiety on Mary's account, and loss of sleep, and you may guess how *sane* I am. I sometimes feel as though my brain were tottering on the verge. Perhaps acting mad every night has something to do with it. I once read of a French actress who went mad after a continued run of an insane character she personated." [50]

Tennyson was present at the performance on March seventh and invited Edwin to dine with him on the following day. Not knowing of the tension under which he was acting, the poet expressed the opinion that Edwin's Lear was effectively given but was not a true interpretation of the character.

Edwin's spirit was at its lowest ebb, yet he did not want to leave England until he had been presented with a first-class company. He therefore began planning, before the final curtain at the Princess, for another engagement. In his conversation with Irving one day, he suggested appearing at the Lyceum in a series of varied parts during the morning or afternoon. Irving at first agreed, then decided it would be better for them to appear in alternate parts of Othello and Iago at the usual evening performances. Edwin was surprised and delighted. He had not expected such generosity.

Irving said the prices would have to be doubled and Edwin was considerate enough to remark that Irving was taking all the risk by the combination. But when the public learned they could see them act together for this increase in admission Edwin's own patronage dwindled to almost nothing. His engagement at the Princess closed near the end of March with *The Merchant of Venice* and *Katherine and Petruchio*.

"I would not have missed *Shylock* on any account," Reade told House. "The scene with Tubal is the biggest thing I have seen on the London stage this many a year." After commenting at length on Edwin's exceptional ability and the faint praise he had received from English critics, Reade exclaimed, "The London press is an ass!" His approval overshadowed the opinions of the unfavorable critics, but it came too late. "I wish Mr. Reade would say as much for poor old *Shylock* publicly as he does privately," remarked Edwin when told of his approbation. "No matter—I thank him most heartily for his good opinion of my efforts. His judgment is to me beyond all price." [51] When the curtain went down on the final scene, Edwin wrote to his poet-friend E. C. Stedman, "At last my great London engagement is ended. Thank God, a thousand times, again and again repeated!" [52]

The productions he had wished to stage at the Princess could not be adequately mounted owing to poor properties. Everyone in the company had wanted to star in the bills and had taken no interest in the part assigned. From the beginning, it appeared that the management had assumed the engagement would be a failure and did nothing to save it. Only a few of the critics and a small part of the theatre-going public had recognized Edwin's genius, yet he had never acted better. "He had not the spirit which can combat such treatment as he received at the Princess'," said Ellen Terry in her account of his London experiences.[53]

Irving and Edwin began their private rehearsals while friends and enemies fought for or against the combination. Although the two actors were thoroughly in accord, their detractors made every effort to separate them by malicious reports of distrust, selfishness, and trickery. Irving's friends, and those opposed to Americans who supported him, felt that he was undertaking a venture which would add nothing to his popularity and might embroil him in unpleasant circumstances. Others, jealous of his rapid rise to fame, joined Edwin's champions. Fortunately, neither actor was influenced by such intrigue. Irving asked to play Iago first, for the part was new to him and the public would be curious to see him in that rôle.

Ellen Terry, who was to play Desdemona, met Edwin in Irving's dressing room. Edwin did not see her as she entered and when he heard Irving say, "Here's Miss Terry," Edwin turned and quickly looked up at her. "I have never, in any face, in any country, seen such wonderful eyes," she related. "There was a mystery about his appearance and his manner—a sort of pride which seemed to say: 'Don't try to know me, for I am not what I have been.' He seemed broken and devoid of ambition.

"At rehearsals he was very gentle and apathetic. Accustomed to playing Othello with stock companies, he had few suggestions to make about the stage-management. The part was to him more or less of a monologue.

" 'I shall never make you black,' he said one morning. 'When I take your hand I shall have a corner of my drapery in my hand. That will protect you.'

"I am bound to say I thought of that 'protection' with some yearning the next week, when I played Desdemona to Henry's Othello," continued Ellen Terry. "Before he had done with me I was nearly as black as he."[54]

A week before the opening night several thousand pounds had poured into the Lyceum till and all good seats had been reserved. With preparations for this important event going forward, Edwina was taken ill, Mary became a raving maniac and was not expected to live more than a few weeks, and the McVickers arrived in London to blame Edwin for her condition. Stunned by the force of circum-

Henry Irving, who acted with Edwin Booth. *(From 'Dictionary of American Portraits,' Dover)*

Asia Booth Clarke in 1884. (*Original photograph from the collection of the author*)

Mary Ann Booth, mother of the Maryland Booths, in her old age. (*New York Public Library photo*)

stances that loomed against him, he retreated into a shell of silence but resolutely went on with his theatrical plans.

The engagement began May 2, 1881, with Edwin in the rôle of Othello and Irving as Iago. The first performance was so noteworthy that it left this indelible impression with E. H. House:

> To describe the reception accorded to Booth is no more possible than to analyze the effect of a great victory upon the imagination. It carried everything before it, like the rush of a stately river. Noisier welcomes I have heard, but never one more eloquent. It must have gone far to compensate the troubled stranger for the petty miseries he had endured. I think it shook him a little; for, though his acting was all his friends could have wished, a few deviations from his accustomed manner were perceptible in the early scenes, unaccountable except by the supposition of some overmastering strain upon his composure. And the plaudits were not confined to the first greeting. As often as he appeared, a wave of sympathy thrilled through the assemblage, and the house resounded with exhilarant acclamation. Not till then had Booth received his just tribute from England.[55]

The critics, however, did not rush in with bravos. The *Times* wrote "the Moor of Mr. Booth is by no means one of his best performances," and reported Mr. Irving's Iago "extremely spirited and original," but that it was exactly "at all points the Iago of Shakespeare one hardly likes to say." After seeing them in their alternate rôles the *Times* placed "the American's Iago above the Englishman's."[56] It was agreed that both Othellos were inferior to the Iagos.

In the midst of what promised to be the success for which Edwin had labored so persistently, the imp of fate stalked him again. From his Portland Place address he wrote to William Bispham:

> The McVickers are here, and we have concluded it to be best to take Mary home (if she lives so long) on June 18 (my engagement with Irving terminating June 10), and have the parting in New York rather than here. She is a surprise to her doctors—being quite strong, though a mere shadow, and at times is as sane as ever. . . . The doctors say, however, that she may die at any moment. . . .
> The Lyceum business is still great, and creates as much excitement as at first. I've not done myself justice yet, being so depressed by my domestic troubles. Irving is very kind, and is a splendid fellow, as well as the best director of stage-art I have ever met. . . .[57]

The engagement at the Lyceum was most important in that it brought together two of the noted tragedians of the day, but Edwin's departure did not end the wrangle over their merits and demerits. In fact, it is still a matter of discussion. Their contemporaries thought Irving behaved very generously toward Edwin and said, had it not been for the friendly hand he held out to him, Edwin would have returned to the United States once more without acknowledgment in England. The formal coolness which was to affect their friendship was apparently the aftermath of some private grievance between them.

The Booths, McVickers, and an English physician attending Mary, sailed from Liverpool on the steamer *Bothnia* and arrived in New York June twenty-ninth. Edwin engaged quarters for his family and the McVickers at the Windsor Hotel, where he was besieged by reporters. His comments on Irving were most flattering and there was no outward indication of a rift between them. The London public had received Edwin cordially, he said, and he had no complaints. "I had already partially engaged a company for the Provinces, and was in negotiations with some German managers when compelled to abandon my European plans by my wife's sickness," he added. Later, however, he admitted it had been necessary to forfeit a large sum of money in order to secure his release from these cherished ambitions.

Such misfortunes were not the only mental torments Edwin suffered at this time. He had no more than unpacked his trunks when newspapers flared with accounts from Washington of the attempt on President Garfield's life by Charles Guiteau, "another crazy assassin." For eleven weeks preceding the President's death there were daily references in the press to Wilkes Booth's crime.[58]

Both Edwin and his daughter had to be constantly on guard in Mary's presence lest something they said or did would bring on one of her raving spasms which made her difficult to control. If they tried to pacify her, she often became violent and ordered them from her sight, or screamed so loudly she could be heard throughout the neighborhood. Edwin's visits to her room threw her into such convulsions that he was finally forced to remain away from her. Each time she came out of these periods of mental derangement, she had no recollection of what had happened; but her mother and stepfather accused Edwin of having provoked them. The situation between the Booths and the McVickers was at the breaking point when the latter moved Mary to lodgings they had engaged elsewhere. Their disregard of Edwin's feelings did not keep him from paying all the bills. Nevertheless, the separation lifted the strain for both him and Edwina.

That summer, after he took Edwina to his mother, who was living with Rosalie at Joseph's home in Long Branch, he went on to visit E. C. Benedict and J. H. Magonigle. Mary's condition did not improve, and the McVickers insisted she remain with them. Hence, Edwin began his plans for the winter season. Supported by a large and expensive company, he opened in New York during the first week in October at the theatre still bearing his name. Dave Anderson who had come East with his wife at Edwin's bidding was now a member of the troupe. The prestige gained in England renewed interest in Edwin at home, and receipts were enormous.

A hotel-car was fitted up with a piano, bookcases, and other luxuries for him and Edwina, and a pullman attached to accommodate the company. Their second engagement was in Philadelphia, and while there, on his forty-eighth birthday, he was notified by telegram of his wife's death.

He returned to New York for the funeral service, at which he and Edwina sat apart from the McVickers while a Reverend Robert Collyer mixed his eulogies of the departed Mary with hints that Edwin was responsible for what had happened. His friends, however, knew otherwise, and later Reverend Ferdinand C. Ewer, who had given up journalism in California to become a clergyman, expressed himself concerning Collyer's disregard for "taste, sound judgment, and . . . the first principles of Christianity," declaring "the whole harangue a bare-faced insult . . ." to Edwin and his daughter.[59] Laurence Hutton and William Winter went with Edwin when he and the McVickers accompanied Mary's body to Chicago. Immediately after her burial in Rose Hill Cemetery, he returned to Philadelphia. Later, he considered placing the body of their infant son Edgar beside her, but it was never removed from Mount Auburn Cemetery in Cambridge.

The following month the company played in Boston, and Edwin wrote to Bispham of his intentions to provide for "Uncle Dave" Anderson and his wife, who was traveling with them although she did not appear in any of the bills. He asked him to find a comfortable place for a "dear old couple of antique babies" to live in New York, adding that he wished to have them near him during their few remaining years.

He and Edwina were then staying at the Hotel Vendôme, and on Christmas Eve invited a party of intimate friends to join them in a late supper in their private sitting room after the performance. Although weary, Edwin seemed happy and entertained royally. At midnight Edwina retired, but the others remained, listening to the anecdotes he told of his father, his home, and his recent experiences in England. Before he realized it, he had mentioned the name of John

Wilkes. "Yes, my brother, John," he repeated, and stopped. His guests looked at one another and were silent. Slowly moving his hand across his eyes as if to brush something from them, he murmured, "Yes, my *unfortunate* brother, John." Suddenly he pulled himself together, got up, and said, smiling, "Come, come, I have displaced the mirth. Let us drink to a Merry Christmas." It was one of the few times since that Good Friday of 1865 that the name of this brother had passed his lips. When their glasses were emptied, the guests knew it was time to depart and leave him alone with Dave Anderson. As the door closed behind them they realized that Edwin was struggling to withhold his grief.

The tour continued, and members of the company spoke of Edwin's thoughtfulness concerning their welfare and the courtesy he extended to everyone connected with the theatres in which they played. "It made no difference whether it was the leading man or woman, or the humble utility people; all were treated alike," said Louisa Eldridge, a favorite member of the troupe and "Aunt" to all the profession. "Edwin Booth never passed the stage door-keeper, or the stage-carpenter, or the property-man, without a kind *good-morning* or a cheerful *good-night*." [60] At the close of his engagement he always gave them each a present. Every few days en route he invited as many of the troupe as could conveniently be seated, into his hotel-car where delightful luncheons were served, after which Louisa Eldridge sang, Dave Anderson told stories, and Edwina played piano solos or duets with the daughter of another actor.

When the winter season had passed, he turned his thoughts to the fulfillment of the tour he had planned in the English provinces and on the Continent which had been interrupted by his domestic difficulties. But in May Edwina was stricken with an attack of pleurisy and pneumonia which Edwin thought would delay their departure. However, she rallied and was well enough to go on with her father the next month.

So on June 14, 1882, they sailed for England on the steamship *Gallia* accompanied by their physician, Dr. St. Clair Smith, Edwina's friend, Miss Julia Vaux, and a colored maid. In London Edwin found he had made another mistake in having leased the Adelphi Theatre, which was not highly rated owing to the sensational type of plays staged there. This time, however, he did not open in *Hamlet* but in *Richelieu*, and the reputation he had established during his previous engagement at the Lyceum brought money rolling into the Adelphi's box office. He played from the latter part of June into August and closed with a benefit for his manager, Wynn Miller, at which he gave his first performance in England as Don Caesar de Bazan. This short London season was successful and, after a pleasure trip to Switzerland with his daughter, he began a tour of the English provinces, ending in December at the Theatre Royal in Birmingham. He and Edwina spent the Christmas holidays at Morley's Hotel in London, alluded to by William Winter as "that cosy hermitage in the very center of the world." Edwin saw Irving's production of *Much Ado About Nothing* at the theatre which had once echoed with applause for him and spoke of it as having been superbly presented. His praise of Irving was always generous, but Irving waited until Edwin was dead to return the compliment.

Edwin and his daughter celebrated New Year's Eve in Paris, and then they went on to Berlin. He had hoped to play at the Victoria Theatre there but found the manager unwilling to replace a successful bill by a gamble on a Booth. The contract he offered Edwin included a clause which stipulated that the American tragedian agree to wait until a theatre could be procured for him. Fortunately, before Edwin fell into that snare, he set a German agent to work who came to him with the information that the small and fashionable Berlin Residenz Theatre was available, as the actress who had been starring there was ill. Edwin called this a miracle, though there is no record of the ailing star's thoughts on the matter. He opened there January eleventh in *Hamlet*, playing the part so intelligently in English to the German of the supporting cast that Oscar Welten in the *Tägliche Berliner Rundschau* commented: "Booth is the best Hamlet I have ever seen. Neither Rossi, Devrient nor Barnay—not to mention the minor celebrities—can be put on the same level with him. . . . You can understand Booth perfectly, although you may not know a single word of what he utters. . . ." The *Unterhaltungs-Blatt der Berliner Presse* proclaimed, "Edwin Booth is Hamlet by the Grace of God and of Shakespeare." His somber acting of the part had infinite charm, was simple, noble, "and free from all attempts at mere effect." Night after night Edwin was greeted at the Residenz with cries of *Meister! Meister!* He was heralded as a phenomenal artist, and before the end of the month, his engagement was renewed for twelve additional performances.

The Crown Prince and Princess had attended the theatre several times and taken so much interest in the engagement that it was thought Edwin would receive a command performance from the Emperor, but the death of Prince Charles put an end to the public appearances of Royalty and prevented that honor being conferred upon him.

Edwin's tour of the German cities was a succession of triumphs.

From Berlin to his final bill at Leipzig, on March twenty-first, he was acclaimed and presented with trophies and mementoes. When he left theatres, his supporting companies formed a line from his dressing room to the stage door, pressed his hand, kissed him, and reverently touched portions of his clothing as he passed. In the streets and at his hotels, crowds hailed him and repeated the approval they had shouted at his performances. It was "the realization of a twenty-years' dream." Far from the associations of family scandal and a brother's crime, Edwin yielded to the vanity of a normal man.

He went on to Vienna where he played a short, but extremely successful, engagement at the Stadt Theatre. Declining invitations to act in Russia, Italy, France, and Spain, he revisited Paris with his daughter and then sailed for home, somewhat fatigued from the ordeal of performances in a mixture of tongues before foreign audiences. Yet his health was excellent, and he had received the recognition he valued most at the time. His earnings were another matter, but he had not expected them to measure up with his ovations. When he arrived with Edwina in New York, he had crossed the Atlantic Ocean for the last time.

On the thirtieth of April, a final performance of *Romeo and Juliet* by Madame Modjeska closed Booth's Theatre in New York with the same bill which had opened it fourteen years before. Shortly after this workmen demolished the building to make way for shops and commercial establishments.

CHAPTER IV

In September, 1883, Agnes Booth was appearing in Augustin Daly's drama, *Pique*, at the Philadelphia Chestnut Street Theatre when she received word from Manchester that Junius, who had been suffering with Bright's disease for some time, was in a critical condition. She left immediately and arrived on the thirteenth of the month at the cottage the family was then occupying back of the Masconomo House. Joseph and Edwin followed her on succeeding days, but the mother of the Maryland Booths was too old and feeble to make the journey, so Rosalie remained with her at Joseph's home in Long Branch, New Jersey. As Junius was in a coma and it was not certain how many days he might linger on, Edwin went back to Newport where he and Edwina were spending the summer in a house they called *Boothden*, which he had bought upon his return from Europe. On the sixteenth Junius was sinking rapidly and Agnes did not leave his bedside. Although later bulletins stated he died at ten minutes past eleven o'clock that night, he did not breathe his last until the following day.[61]

Edwin returned for the funeral, and a special train from Boston took many notables to Manchester. Services were held in the parlor of the cottage, which was filled with elaborate floral tributes. The burial of Junius at Rosedale Cemetery had been preceded by interments of his two sons and his wife's sister, Belle Land Hosmer.[62] Four of his seven children were still living: Blanche De Bar,[63] Marion, and by his last marriage, Junius III and Sydney Booth.[64]

Junius had inherited little of the elder Booth's genius for the stage. Of the three sons who followed theatrical careers, he showed the least ability as an actor, the only important character he played well being King John. His success had been behind the scenes. Years of activity as a manager had made him one of the most prominent men in the profession. He had been connected with several of the largest theatres and had known every stage celebrity of his time. His modesty, good nature, and keen sense of humor had made him popular among his many friends.

Retirement from the theatre during the last ten years of his life had again separated him from Edwin. Within that time this younger brother had helped to mitigate the infamy of Wilkes' crime by lifting the Booth name to world renown. Junius was never given the recognition due him for his share in these accomplishments, yet his early training and discipline in California directed Edwin to the fame he achieved.

Junius' will left all his property, both real and personal, to his wife Agnes. He had taken this means of protecting her from any loss of the hard-earned money she had put into the estate, which was valued at about sixty-six thousand dollars, with almost half of it subject to mortgage. During her husband's illness, John B. Schoeffel, a well-known producer and intimate friend of the family, assisted Agnes in operating the Masconomo House, but his help, after Junius' death, caused considerable gossip. Within a few months their marriage was predicted. Schoeffel denied it as a vicious attempt to ruin Agnes' business. But on February 4, 1885, they were married.[65]

From Newport, the first week in October, following Junius' death, Edwin and his daughter went to Boston and inspected a winter home at 29 Chestnut Street, which he purchased. A few days later they arrived in New York, and Edwin began rehearsals with a company which had been selected for him there. Agnes, too, went back to the theatre, and that season they both were on the road, Edwin opening in November at Boston.[66]

He played until summer and, following a short stay at their Boston home, returned with Edwina to *Boothden* at Newport. Late in the season he bought a small yacht, and they made daily cruises in near-by waters. November found them again at their Boston address, interested in plans for the memorial window Edwina wished to place in the Bishop Berkeley Memorial Church, Newport, as a tribute to her mother. Edwin's engagement in Boston that month ended in competition with Henry Irving who was at another theatre in the same city. The report that they were still friendly was the cue for an old actor to remark: "Yes; like two icicles hanging together from the same roof."

Reviews of Edwin's performances covering this period indicate no waning of his ability. His New York engagement early in 1885 brought in sums totaling fifty thousand dollars to the Fifth Avenue Theatre from audiences that packed the house to standing room practically every night for a period of four weeks. After engagements in other cities, he returned to Boston in May, and from there wrote to Bispham:

... Since I left New York I have felt and acted better than at any time during the entire past season, and here a perfect ovation was given me every night. In Philadelphia the size of the house chilled the audience and actors, and although the business was excellent, it was not so great as here or in New York.

The Philadelphia critics (justly, I think) rather condemned the polyglot business. By the by, I had a worse fall there than in New York—a very dangerous one, too. In the last scene, when I was brought on with hands tied behind me, my foot caught on the door-sill and I pitched headlong to the stage—it might have broken my neck. ... The first night here, as I ran into *Iago's* dark house,—after stabbing *Cassio*,— I tripped and fell again, but 't was behind the scenes: about the same time young Salvini flopped flat on his back on the stage. It must be the Italian School of acting, I suspect! The elder Salvini remarked after my second fall, "The public seem to like to see you fall!"

I gave him a breakfast, and invited an Italian whom I thought his friend; afterward I heard that they were foes—but all went well at table.[67]

For the past month Edwina had been preparing for her wedding to Ignatius R. Grossman, a Hungarian who had once taught languages but was now a broker of financial and social standing. In frequent letters to his daughter, who was almost twenty-four years old, Edwin had discussed his theory of marriage. He explained it had not only to do with the heart but also included mental affinity, which together would bring real happiness, and that he looked forward to their union as a merging of these two essentials.

He approved of young Grossman, yet he could hardly realize that his daughter had reached the age when he must share her affections with another. Her motherless years and absence from him while at school, the terrible experiences with mad Mary McVicker, had bound them together more securely than the joyous trips and periods of quiet companionship.

A few days after their marriage on May 16, 1885, at the Chestnut Street house in Boston, Edwina and her husband sailed for Europe. They had scarcely passed Sandy Hook when Edwin wrote to her: "Darling, I can't tell you just how I feel—the separation has been a wrench to my nerves; but when in the midst of my selfishness the thought comes of your happiness and the good that will come to you, I cease to grieve, and somehow enjoy your pleasures as if I were with you. ..."[68] He added that in two weeks he would return to New

York and help his mother move there from Joseph's home in Long Branch, New Jersey.

A year before Joseph's wife had died. As he now planned to attend New York University to resume his study of medicine, he took a house on West Twenty-third Street. It was to this address that Mary Ann and Rosalie were moving. Until late in life Joseph frequently went back and forth between his two homes and continued to deal in Long Branch real estate.

While she lived in New Jersey, the mother of the Maryland Booths had fallen and broken her leg. She had never experienced any serious illness, and it was difficult for her to become accustomed to this incapacity. Doctors said that she would not be able to walk again, but Edwin allowed no one to tell her the extent of her injuries. In frequent visits he endeavored to keep her cheerful by pretending that it would not be long until she could leave the wheel-chair and go about as usual.

Everything was arranged for her convenience in Joseph's New York home. Each day she was wheeled to her place beside a window, that she might interest herself in what went on outside and forget her disability. Neighbors always looked for the kindly face and spoke of her as Edwin Booth's mother without thought of the fact that she was living in Joseph's house. She was happy to know that most of her hopes had come true. War wounds had healed, much of the hatred toward the Booths had passed, and the name had been restored to a prestige above that attained for it by the elder Booth.

The patient old woman's misfortunes were now nearing an end and her days drawing to a close. In October of 1885 she was stricken with pneumonia. At first her condition was not alarming, but on the twenty-second of the month she suddenly became worse and Edwin was quickly summoned.

"Poor grandma passed away at three this morning," he wrote to Edwina. "I did not arrive till seven. How strange that it should be my lot always in such cases to arrive too late! . . . The doctor, yesterday, did not think it necessary to send for me then. She fell into a stupor about 7:30 last night, and died so at three. . . . 'Tis for poor Rose I feel most anxious. She has just sighed, barely loud enough for me to hear, 'I wish I was gone too.' Poor, poor soul! I must now arrange something for her." [69] Weary Mary Ann had lived beyond her eighty-third birthday. A cable was sent to Asia, and in far-off England she mourned the mother she had not seen for seventeen years.

Funeral services were held and Mary Ann's remains taken to Baltimore by her sons, daughter, and grandchild, Marion Booth. They arrived about noon and were driven directly to Greenmount Cemetery in two carriages following the hearse. There was no floral display, and only a Reverend P. Wroth accompanied them. Newspapers had announced that her burial in the family lot, beside her husband, would take place at two-thirty in the afternoon. However, the burial service was so hastily completed, before the stated hour, that one noted: "The accompanying members of the family did not even wait to witness the sad part of the program of filling in the grave, but drove immediately to the Hotel Rennert, where they partook of dinner and left on the five o'clock train for New York."

This seemingly inconsiderate conduct was for the purpose of avoiding morbidly curious spectators, who they knew would be attracted by the news of another burial in the lot containing the body of John Wilkes Booth. Their action was not unwarranted, as people began gathering at the cemetery before they departed, and a large number of later arrivals would not leave until convinced that the interment had taken place.

Edwin discontinued his engagements for a while, then returned to the road, and in New York visited Edwina and her husband, whose happiness and varied accounts of their European journey cheered him. The vigor of his acting at the beginning of the New Year excited great interest and favorable comment. Later he appeared with Tomasso Salvini in Boston, and then at the Academy of Music in New York. Here, while playing Iago to the Italian's Othello, he tossed another morsel of unmerited gossip to the scandal-mongers. On the afternoon of April twenty-eighth, he rehearsed with the company until three o'clock and went home ill from lack of food and too much smoking. As he was subject to attacks of vertigo, his physician advised him not to perform that evening; nevertheless, when the curtain went up he was on hand.

During the third act, "in the most exciting part of the play, Iago fell among the footlights, and was pulled out by Othello," reported the New York *Post* after accusing Edwin of having been intoxicated. A number of persons in the audience hissed, some applauded, some departed, and others called for Edwin, who appeared twice in answer to their shouts. "I was dizzy from the effects of dyspepsia, and being *jerked* up from the stage by Salvini [which was part of the action in the play], who let me go before I had regained my footing, I stumbled on my heels, and a rent in the carpet laid me flat on my back. That was all of it," he explained. "It's an infamous thing that one's reputation should be at the mercy of a set of scoundrels." [70]

Years after Edwin's death, Salvini alleged that Edwin had taken too much liquor as a stimulant that evening and could not stand on his feet.

In defense of Edwin, one of his friends pointed out that he had finished the performance and sarcastically asked upon what he had stood during all the long time before and after his fall.

Edwin, after several spats with Barrett, had become friendly again, and spent the summer with him at Cohasset. Barrett suggested an extended tour supported by a company which he would get together, although a previous contract prohibited him from traveling with it as an active member. He offered to assume all responsibilities of the venture and Edwin finally consented, notwithstanding the fact that he had planned to lessen the number of appearances during the next few years in order to retire eventually from the stage. Rehearsals were held at the New York Academy of Music and the company went to Buffalo for its opening engagement in September.

They traveled up and down the old circuits, playing the Midwest and reaping another financial harvest before returning to New York in November. A month later they started out again on the road and headed southward over a route to California. The tour was an unbroken triumph. Theatres were crowded and engagements of several nights or a week were not sufficient to accommodate those clamoring for tickets, many of whom came long distances only to be disappointed. The car in which the company traveled, christened "The David Garrick," was commodious and comfortable, but incessant jerks and vibration during long jumps made the western journey tedious. After a three-day passage through the desert, Edwin was exhausted.

The changes he perceived in the San Francisco of March, 1887, from "a mere sand-hill thirty years ago," amazed him. It was there that old friends shook their heads when they saw his Hamlet; the Prince of Denmark looked a little antique with gray hair. "I told them," he said afterward, "that I didn't mind wearing a wig."

He had not intended playing in the Bay City more than two weeks, but crowds greeted him at each appearance, and he was urged to continue. At the end of the fourth week, he gave an afternoon and evening performance of *Hamlet* and said farewell. The press proclaimed him without a peer in his profession. This engagement netted Edwin ninety-six thousand dollars. California had given him another bag of gold.

The return trip was made through a territory that yielded still more profits. From Denver the company made an excursion to Colorado Springs to see the Garden of the Gods. Edwin took an intense delight in such diversions, and wished he might roam about the country as a sightseer, not as an actor. On several occasions he expressed a desire to visit Florida and Dry Tortugas Island where the Lincoln conspirators had been confined. He had journeyed thousands of miles, but seen very little outside of theatres, hotels, and city streets.

"Once in *David Garrick* days," related Katherine Goodale, who, as Kitty Molony, was a member of Edwin's company, "Mr. Booth, in telling of the Booth children, was so carried away that his eyes filled with tears—merry ones, too. I, alas, forgot, and asked: 'How many brothers and sisters did you have, Mr. Booth?' I hated myself for my thoughtlessness. Any word of mine now could not but make the situation worse. I left it to him—and Mr. Booth took care of it. It made my throat ache that many another forgetful one may have schooled him for such handling. He smoked on a bit, then said unemotionally: 'I forget the lot of us. I'll name them—you count them for me! Junius Brutus—after my father, of course—Rosalie, Henry, Mary, Frederick, Elizabeth—I come in here—Asia, Joe—how many is that?'

" 'Nine, Mr. Booth.'

" 'What big families they used to raise!'—he smoked on.

"There were ten Booth children, and the name of Wilkes was not spoken. Indeed, I well knew it would not be." [71]

Upon his arrival East, he was asked to deliver an address at the dedication of the Actors' Monument in Evergreens Cemetery, Long Island. He seldom took part in any public ceremony not connected with the theatre and even on those occasions would never consent to make a speech if he could help it. As usual he pleaded having other matters to attend to on that date, but finally consented to say a few words. After one glance at the immense throng that surrounded the platform on which he was seated, he whispered to a companion: "This is a fearful moment for me. I would rather wing a leading part in a five-act tragedy than to face that audience today." Once before he had told a friend that every time he was called upon to talk in public he became so shy that he wished he had taken his father's advice and learned a trade. Some thought that it was Edwin's consciousness of his lack of education that made him timid in such instances.

That summer E. C. Benedict invited Edwin, William Bispham, Lawrence Barrett, T. B. Aldrich, and Laurence Hutton to join him in a cruise to northern waters on his yacht *Oneida*. This voyage of about a month was spent principally in discussing the establishment of a home for the profession. Edwin had first mentioned it to several members of his company, including Katherine Goodale, while crossing the Rocky Mountains on their return from California. He had thought of it as a memorial to his father. Eventually it became known as **The Players**, a name suggested by Aldrich.

Edwin was only fifty-four, yet his thoughts were turning to the time when he would be but a memory in the minds of men. By the endowment of a club and by generous donations to individuals, he hoped to perpetuate the good he could do in his lifetime. His ample funds were more than sufficient to take care of such bequests, and of all the Booths, if ever they were in need. He felt that he could not be at ease until these matters were settled.

Soon after their sailing trip, Edwin and Barrett began their professional partnership (which was to last until the latter's death) by a joint appearance at Buffalo in September, 1887. As they traveled from city to city Edwin's plans for The Players developed. Membership was now extended to include others than those of the theatrical profession, as he believed actors became stilted by mingling only with one another. At the close of the New York engagement in January, the club was incorporated by the "crew" of the *Oneida* (with the exception of its owner and Aldrich), the two Dalys (Augustin and Joseph), Samuel Clemens, John Drew, Joseph Jefferson, Brander Matthews, John A. Lane, James Lewis, Henry Edwards, Stephen H. Olin, Albert M. Palmer, and General William T. Sherman.

The Booth-Barrett combination toured the country until summer, following the route Edwin had taken to California and back the year previous. In his correspondence with Bispham, whom he had entrusted with selecting a shelter for The Players, he mentioned the possibility of another establishment, an "Actors' Home for charitable purposes"—which never materialized. He assured Bispham that he would not be associated with Barrett in his scheme for a new theatre, but would limit his activities to the professional side of such a venture, and thus quieted Bispham's fears in regard to his disbursements. He was not to be inveigled into a second undertaking of this sort!

Details sent by Bispham for the purchase of a four-story stone house at 16 Gramercy Park (costing the modest sum of one hundred and fifty thousand dollars), suitable for The Players, reached him at St. Joseph, Missouri, in April. Although this put an end to his more benevolent designs for the Actors' Home, Edwin telegraphed Bispham to accept the terms. The sale was completed upon his arrival in New York the following month and Stanford White was given the contract for remodeling the building. This was retarded, however, by the difficulty of ejecting the tenants whose lease, it was discovered, would not expire for another year.

From the outset of their tour, Barrett insisted on doubling admission prices, which, in the end, broke all records in the United States for box-office receipts during a like period. What it did to certain individuals along the way was related by Milton Nobles, a less-brilliant star in the theatrical firmament:

> This is an era of "trusts" and "combines," and the Booth-Barrett tour was a mammoth "trust," and the local managers and more humble attractions have been the victims. . . . The Booth-Barrett tour swooped down upon the profession at large after the manner of a cyclone or a stroke of paralysis. Throughout the country—particularly, the one and two-night stands—they simply killed the business for six or eight weeks in the midst of the season.
>
> The coming of the great "combine" was known months in advance. It was an event that no theatre-goer could think of missing. The theatre . . . is supported by the industrial classes. The clerk, book-keeper, artist, artisan and small tradesman, with incomes ranging from nine hundred to two or three thousand a year, are the main support of the drama. They allow themselves a certain amount of money during the season for amusement. To see the Booth-Barrett "combine" cost them just five times what it would cost to see Louis James, Annie Pixley, Fred Warde, Maggie Mitchell, or Milton Nobles. . . . So great an event demands unusual preparation in the matter of toilets, gloves, carriages, etc., for wife or sweetheart. All of these extra expenses must be met by rigid economy before the coming, and total abstinence after the departure of the great "combine."
>
> In point of fact, the one attraction has absorbed the amusement fund for the season.
>
> Booth and Barrett played to a three thousand dollar house and the local managers got three hundred dollars. Three or four attractions preceding this engagement had, on former visits, played to houses ranging from four hundred dollars to eight hundred dollars. Owing to the great expectations aroused by the coming of the "combine," their business this season was less than half. . . . This rule applies with still greater force to the month following the great event. . . . The Booth-Barrett tour cost me five thousand dollars in the Southern States alone, local managers, of course suffering proportionately. Several managers in the South told me that their season had been ruined by the Booth-Barrett tour, and that the organization could never play these cities again excepting upon the same terms and at the same prices as other first class attractions.
>
> Mr. Barrett in his *Tribune* talk also referred to "their brilliant San Francisco engagement." He did not, however, refer to the disaster that followed in their wake. . . .[72]

Many years had passed since Edwin had seen Asia in England. Within that time her letters to him had told of her suffering from a rheumatic affliction and heart trouble. Her eldest son, Edwin Booth Clarke, who had attended Annapolis Naval Academy, had perished in a wreck of an English merchant vessel off the Australian coast while he was employed in the Indian trade. She was never able to reconcile herself to his loss, for she believed he would return. This catastrophe and the death of her mother were shocks from which she could not recover. Clarke's trips to the United States and her separation from the Booths for so many years engulfed her in loneliness, but did not alter her determination to remain abroad. She was always eager for information of the family and urged that they visit her.

Another son, Creston, had made his début in his Uncle Edwin's production of *Richelieu*. He was appearing in the United States with his father when Asia's failing health became so serious that they were called back to England. A month after their departure, Edwin received a cablegram from his brother-in-law telling of her death at Bournemouth on May 16, 1888. Twenty of her fifty-three years had been spent in self-imposed exile.[73]

Clarke and his son returned immediately with the body and, accompanied by Edwin and Joseph, went on to Baltimore for Asia's interment in Greenmount Cemetery on the last day of that month. There was no haste this time. Many friends attended the service which was read by a Catholic priest above her white oak casket surrounded by floral offerings.

Asia was said to have been a beautiful woman, but the gentle nature often attributed to her is not discernible in some of her unpublished letters. The books she wrote about the Booths are misleading in many incidents because of her efforts to suppress the family scandals. Although she spent her entire life in the atmosphere of the theatre, her only contribution to the stage was a play entitled *Social Events*, which her husband produced in Philadelphia the winter preceding her death. Of four children surviving her (one of whom, a daughter, married Rhys Morgan, an English barrister, and lived in London), only Creston achieved distinction.

Prior to the message of his sister's death, Edwin had promised to appear as Hamlet at the Metropolitan Opera House in a benefit for Lester Wallack on the twenty-first of May. While awaiting the return of Asia's remains to the United States, he played that performance, supported by the greatest array of stars ever assembled in one company. Lawrence Barrett was cast as Ghost; Joseph Jefferson with William Florence enacted the parts of First and Second Grave-diggers;

Frank Mayo was Claudius; John Gilbert, Polonius; Helena Modjeska, Ophelia; Gertrude Kellogg, Queen; and Rose Coghlan, Player Queen. Other rôles were taken by well-known actors, and even the names of those appearing as soldiers, couriers, and ladies-in-waiting were familiar to the stage. A volunteer orchestra was conducted by Walter Damrosch.

Such a constellation, however, was not favorable to a good production of *Hamlet*. The press stated that the performance suffered from the inevitable lack of rehearsals, but acclaimed Edwin for the force and eloquence of his acting. So far as Wallack was concerned, the best part of the program was an "afterpiece" a few days later, in which theatrical manager A. M. Palmer presented Mrs. Wallack with a check for twenty thousand dollars. The personal advantages he received from this source were of short duration, for in September the celebrated old actor died.

Upon Edwin's return to New York from Asia's funeral, he collected his theatrical library, paintings, and mementoes which were to be installed in the clubhouse. Early in July he and Clarke were at Newport, and later in the month he visited his daughter.

> A fair correspondent writes that there is no more interesting spectacle at Narragansett Pier than that of Edwin Booth, seated on the Casino verandah, teaching his grandbabies to say *moo, bow wow*, etc., to the great delight of the guests who see the great actor in this unstudied role. His daughter and son-in-law, Mr. Grossman, are a very devoted couple. Grossman is a Hungarian and speaks with a marked accent. Their oldest child—a girl two-and-a-half years old—has eyes like Mr. Booth. The little boy is blind.[74]

Several months later Edwin denounced this rumor in a letter to a friend: "The absurd report anent my grandson's eyes has no foundation whatever; both children are perfect in every particular—full of health, beauty, and baby charm." [75]

Edwin and Barrett planned more elaborate and costly productions to startle the natives of the hinterlands—and ruin helpless managers. The next September, when the "combine" again took to the road, they opened in Kansas City. There Barrett got into one of his squabbles with a member of the profession which made him unpopular among them.[76] But he was an efficient executive and continued to be a pleasant companion for Edwin, so there was no trouble in their camp. They played engagements in six midwestern cities and when November rolled around, were back in New York gazing with admiration at the nearly completed clubhouse in which the third floor had been reserved by Edwin for their living quarters. His room was in front, facing Gramercy Park, Barrett's in the rear above a garden. Stanford White was supervising decoration of the interior, and Edwin took the time carefully to select mottoes for the walls. On appointed days he sat for several artists who made portraits of him in painting and sculpture.

The moment workmen were out of the building, Edwin's valuable theatrical costumes, armor, paintings, photographs, books, and knick-knacks, including those donated by others, were moved in. Stragglers from the surrounding neighborhood thought the building was to be used as a museum when they saw what was being deposited there. "Mr. Booth's club is a very generous gift," remarked the New York *Dramatic Mirror*. "Let's wait and see of what moral sort of use it's going to be to the profession. The actors have been seeing as much of each other in the past as is good for 'em. They don't need any gilded halls and hammered brass grill rooms to make 'em acquainted or better their condition. And as for tiger skin rugs and tiled fireplaces making a man's soul bigger or making a bum actor more of a gentleman, go to! Thou talkest rot!"

As the number of eligibles was limited, and select, a subsequent issue of the same weekly noted: "The Players' Club does not appear to have excited much interest among the profession whose members look upon it as an exclusive, proprietary affair, which offers few inducements and many obstacles to membership. The directors have found that the only class anxious to become enrolled is the class of outsiders. These they have accepted in large numbers."

Some maintained that the gift of so lavish a club to men of considerable means was the expression of Edwin's secret desire to equalize himself with those who he believed had acquired wealth, knowledge, and social prominence superior to his own. "If it were not the fulfillment of such an aspiration," argued an old thespian, "why did it completely obliterate the Actors' Home for charitable purposes?"

But Edwin was sincere in his efforts and hoped that at least ten per cent of the club members would always be composed of actors. "He sought to establish an institution in which influences of learning and taste should be brought to bear upon the members of the stage," explained William Winter, "a place where they might find books and pictures, precious relics of the great players of the past, intellectual communion with minds of their own order, and with men of education in other walks of life, refinement of thought and of manners, innocent pleasure, and sweet, gracious, ennobling associations. He wished the

Players' Club to represent all that is best in the dramatic profession, to foster the dramatic art, and to exalt the standard of personal worth among the actors of America." [77]

Shortly before midnight on December 31, 1888, The Players, then numbering about one hundred members, gathered at the clubhouse for the dedication ceremony. Standing before a large fireplace in a spacious room, Edwin, as president, made a brief speech and handed to Augustin Daly, vice-president, the title-deed conveying the property, with all its furnishings, to the organization. Daly accepted the lavish gift, not only for those present, as he said, but also for members who would follow them.

Lawrence Barrett then read a letter from Edwin's daughter, and a poem she had enclosed, written by Thomas W. Parsons, sent with a laurel wreath to be presented to her father. As the words, "Tragedian, take the crown," were spoken and the wreath handed to him, a clock tolled the hour of midnight. Edwin, emotionally stirred, responded briefly—and the Yule log was lighted. The log had come all the way from Boston, he told them, as his daughter's "offering of love, peace and good will to the Players." Only the din of a boisterous city greeting the New Year broke the silence of that room. Edwin watched the log, and so did Stanford White; each wondered if it would burn in the new fireplace without smoking.

When the flames leaped toward the chimney, Edwin said: "Let us drink from this loving cup, bequeathed by William Warren to our no less valued Jefferson and by him presented to us—from this cup and this souvenir of long ago, my father's flagon, let us now, beneath his portrait and on the anniversary of this occupation, drink to the Players, perpetual prosperity." [78] The cup was passed from hand to hand, inaugurating a custom which is followed at this hour each year on Founder's Night. A supper served in the large dining room ended the formalities, but many members remained until dawn.

Edwin was happier than he had been for a long time. Now he could rest more peacefully. When he went to his room, however, he could not sleep, for the scenes he had just left kept revolving in his overstimulated mind. Gradually the characters in the setting changed. One by one they were replaced by faces strange to him, yet friendly. The procession was endless. Generations circled about him gratefully acknowledging this gift. They crowded out all remembrance of failures and disappointments. The purpose that had been uppermost in his mind for almost two years had been accomplished. His affairs were in order. The future could hold no regrets for him.

CHAPTER V

Edwin and Lawrence Barrett started off on another tour in January of 1889 and opened at Pittsburgh. There, an announcement that they were next to play in Baltimore stated, "Manager Albaugh has arranged to give the theatre-goers of Washington, where Mr. Booth never appears, an opportunity to witness the performance. Two nights will be set apart for Washington, in which city tickets at the regular price will entitle the holder to a free trip to and from Baltimore on a special train."

This Baltimore engagement began at the Holliday Street Theatre on the fourteenth of the month. The following night, Edwin received the sad news that his sister, Rosalie, had died in New York. She had been ill for several years with bulbar paralysis. Burial was in Greenmount Cemetery, Baltimore. The services were conducted by a rector of the Protestant Episcopal church.[79]

Rosalie was sixty-six years old and had never married. Few people knew of her existence. She was seldom mentioned in accounts of the Booths for she took no active part in their public life. Family efforts to shield her were probably meant to conceal her deep melancholy which led to reports questioning her sanity. Of all the Maryland Booths only Edwin and Joseph remained.

In February this younger brother passed his forty-ninth birthday and that spring received his medical degree at New York University. Soon after, he became attending physician at the Northern Dispensary in Christopher Street, intermittently lecturing on surgery at various institutions in the city. About 1894 he married Cora Elizabeth Mitchell, one of his North Carolina cousins half his age. A son was born to them but died when fifteen months old.

The latter part of Joseph's life was spent at his residence in East Twenty-first Street. He took little interest in social affairs and gave up professional activity shortly before his death from pneumonia on February 26, 1902. He survived Edwin nine years and was the last of the Maryland Booths to be buried in Greenmount Cemetery.[80]

After Rosalie's funeral, Edwin continued his engagements with the company and played numerous one-night stands before returning to New York. On March 30, 1889, a midnight supper was given in his honor at Delmonico's by Augustin Daly and Albert M. Palmer, in recognition by The Players for his gift of a clubhouse. It was attended by many prominent men who spoke eloquently of him as a loyal citizen, most eminent tragedian, and greatest benefactor of the profession. This homage thrilled Edwin and added to the satisfaction in having fulfilled one of his greatest desires.

He resumed his tour with Barrett, although he was not feeling well and had been subject to attacks of vertigo. In Rochester, the next month, he suffered a slight stroke of paralysis. On his way to the performance in a carriage with Barrett, he realized that he could hardly speak. He did nothing about it immediately thinking the condition would not last, but grew alarmed and embarrassed when he found himself unable to return the greeting of the doorman at the theatre. As he changed to his Othello costume, he earnestly hoped that he would have no difficulty in delivering his lines out front but, after reaching the stage, knew he could not make himself understood. The curtain was lowered, and Barrett, quite overcome, told the audience Edwin was very ill and might not ever act again.

A messenger was sent across the street for Dr. C. R. Sumner, who hurried to Edwin's dressing room. Many lingered about the theatre anxiously awaiting word of his condition. He was finally removed to his hotel where he showed improvement, and a bulletin was issued stating that a week or ten days of absolute rest would be required to restore him.

Before this stroke he had played with an artistic freshness and no small amount of his usual vigor, but now his health steadily declined. It vacillated between spells of weakness and spurts of energy. Press and friends noted this condition and accused Barrett of overworking him. Edwina wrote urging her father to give up his engagements and to rest, but he gently rebuked her, saying that Barrett was not to blame, and promised to be more careful in preserving his strength. Nothing could down him, and soon he was on the road again with Barrett, filling engagements that took them westward. San Francisco failed to interest him on this trip. When an earthquake rocked his bed and jarred him from sleep, he denounced the place in a letter to his daughter. "I wouldn't live here if the city were presented to me free of taxes," he declared.

The company toured until late June, the last engagement being in Portland, Oregon. Barrett had become ill from a glandular disease, and was brought back by Edwin to their rooms at The Players in New York. That summer Edwin went again to Narragansett Pier for a visit with the Grossmans, and from there sent five hundred dollars to the women of Belair who were collecting funds for a library in the village. In compliment to this native son, a memorial tablet, inscribed with his name, is prominently displayed above a fountain in front of the Harford County courthouse. It attests to the fact that the inhabitants of the community are not adverse to linking its past with a Booth. They have not permitted their rancor toward John Wilkes to overshadow the high esteem in which they hold his older brother, Edwin. They point with pride to the achievements of the man who spent a part of his early youth in that vicinity.

No one will ever know the extent of Edwin's generosity during his lifetime. Sensitive to the publicity given his contributions, he seldom mentioned them. He was ever ready to assist financially those in need, and never forgot friends who had helped him along the way. On their birthdays he sent Ben Baker and others sums from one hundred to a thousand dollars. Each Christmas he played the part of Santa Claus as well as any character he acted upon the stage, but the public rarely saw him in that rôle. Once he even became the unconscious benefactor to a lad in Jacksonville who made over a thousand dollars at a fair, ballyhooing imitations of phonograph cylinders recording Edwin's voice. The fraud was discovered by Edwin while on tour with Madame Modjeska, but he did nothing about it other than to denounce the boy.

His engagements with this distinguished Polish actress had begun at Pittsburgh in September, under the management of Lawrence Barrett whose ill health prevented his accompanying them.[81] The tour was not very successful and the strain of constant travel and performances began to tell on Edwin before it ended in May at Buffalo.

Meanwhile Barrett had attempted a few rehearsals in a play he intended producing, but had finally been forced to give it up and go to a spa in Europe for treatment. By autumn he had returned somewhat improved. Edwin was then combating a severe attack of sciatica, and during the next six weeks Barrett starred alone. In November they began another season together, opening at Albaugh's Lyceum Theatre, Baltimore.

There Edwin celebrated his fifty-seventh birthday and received congratulations from all parts of the country at his rooms in the Mt. Vernon Hotel. Many people called on him, among them a Mrs. Charlotte Hyde, whom he immediately recognized as one of his Mitchell cousins. Upon learning that she was in need, he gave her enough money to cover expenses to her brother's home in North Carolina and promised to settle a yearly allowance on her.

The community of Belair observed his birthday by placing Louis Dietrich's painting of him in the courthouse on the site where he and Clarke had given their reading from Shakespeare. Edwin had sent the portrait in answer to their request "as a token of my fond recollection of and affection for my native country."

At his evening's performance of *Julius Caesar* in Baltimore, he was repeatedly called before the curtain and finally responded to the shouting audience by making this brief and characteristic reply: "I thank you all from the bottom of my heart—fifty-seven times!" Many perceived he was not the Edwin Booth of other days. It was his last engagement in that city. The short tour ended on December fifteenth in Providence, Rhode Island.

Barrett now continued ten weeks without Edwin, who remained inactive until their appearance at the Broadway Theatre, New York, in March, 1891. Critics (*"crickets,"* Edwin dubbed them) were unreserved in their estimate of his acting at this time, using such words as comparatively ineffective, feeble, and inadequate, in describing it. His voice was husky, his speech halting, he could not always be heard, he walked with difficulty, he had been ill and lacked the strength to continue—why didn't he retire? they asked. But Edwin persisted and somehow his work improved.

On the eighteenth the bill was announced as *Richelieu*, with Edwin as the Cardinal, and Barrett as De Mauprat. Edwin was informed, early in the evening, that Barrett, who had arrived and gone to his dressing room, seemed very ill. He found him sitting in a chair beside the wall quietly weeping and still wearing his overcoat and hat. "I urged him to go home," said Edwin, "but he insisted on playing, and he managed to get as far as the end of the third act; but when he bent over me, after I was on the Cardinal's bed, he whispered, 'I can't go on.' " [82] He was taken to his apartment at the Windsor Hotel where he lived with his wife when she was in the city. Mrs. Barrett, then in Boston, returned immediately upon receiving a telegram announcing his illness. Two days later he died, unable to struggle through pneumonia because of his weakened condition, and was buried at Cohasset, Massachusetts. Barrett's death greatly agitated and distressed Edwin. Their long association together had made him totally dependent upon Barrett's management, and now that he was gone, Edwin had no further ambition to act. But, for the sake of the company, he continued playing another week in New York, and then fulfilled a short engagement at the Brooklyn Academy of Music. Here, on April 4, 1891, he made his final appearance in a matinee performance of *Hamlet*.

Early in the morning crowds gathered in the street before the theatre, young and old, waiting for admission. Word had been circulated that Edwin Booth might never play again, and they had come to bid farewell to the actor and the man for whom they had a great affection. The house was packed to the doors and in the audience were many well-known people in the commercial and professional world.

Those who went "hoping to see the *Hamlet* of Edwin Booth at its best—the greatest *Hamlet* of history—must have been grievously disappointed. The framework of the great creation was there . . . and the mysterious melancholy . . . but the whole performance seemed to be palsied. . . . In truth, that *Hamlet* of yesterday could never have run one hundred nights . . ." observed the Brooklyn *Eagle*. "Mr. Booth spoke so faintly that much of his speech was inaudible even in the front of the house, and several times he heightened the difficulty by delivering long speeches in a low tone with his back to the audience. . . .

"In the first act the players went shivering around complaining of the cold when leaves were green all over the trees, while in the graveyard the property man had neglected to give the digger any earth to throw out of the pit and the dummy that was supposed to represent Ophelia's body and was not a bit like it was deposited in a pit about a foot and a half deep. . . ." The shabbiness of the sets and costumes, the listless company supporting him, and disregard for consistency in the scenes and dialogue were all "chargeable to the leading actor's indifference," continued the *Eagle*, and then acknowledged, "We shall look in vain for the successors of Edwin Booth."

At the close of the performance, prolonged applause brought him before the curtain, and, as the audience stood in reverence, he spoke for the last time from the stage:

> I scarcely know what to say, and, indeed, I can only make my usual speech—of thanks and gratitude. I thank you for your great kindness. It will never be forgotten. I hope that this is not the last time I shall have the honor of appearing before you. When I come again I hope that I shall be able to give greater attention than I have ever given to whatever part I may play. I hope that my health and strength may be improved, so that I can serve you better; and I shall always try to deserve the favor you have shown.[83]

The crowd renewed its salvos of praise. Exhausted, Edwin bowed and departed. The dynasty of the Booths had ended. Outside the theatre a great throng gave him another ovation as he stepped into his carriage. A few moments later the cheers were only an echo. He was jogging through the evening light, a tired man ready for sleep.

A CHILD OF TRAGEDY

Most of the summer he spent at Edwina's home in Narragansett Pier, where he smoked, dozed, and indulged in revery. His letters to correspondents boasted that his health had improved and that he had been able to walk about without the need of a cane. But on several occasions, when he was dressing himself, his hands failed for a moment to do his bidding. He knew that he was not equal to the demands of his profession and canceled all future engagements.

Soon he was back in his room at The Players, reminiscing with intimates, or with an out of town visitor—telling some of them good-by.[84] He was shown drawings by Walter Hale of a schoolhouse in Belair and of the *Booth Mansion* near there, but said he remembered very little of his boyhood days in Maryland. To his recollection their place in Harford County had always been called *The Farm*, and in reality was as near the villages of Churchville and Hickory, as it was to Belair. He pointed to the drawing of the *Booth Mansion* and indicated where the trees stood that had shaded the original log cabin in which he was born. The gable and bay window in the *Mansion*, he said, were "modern improvements." He gazed at the drawing of the schoolroom and remarked that in his time all such places looked alike, then added, "This must have been where I learned my early lessons, but my life has been so busy and varied since, that those days are dim now."[85]

He took a great delight in the Founder's Night festivities and thought this year's superior to all previous gatherings. It was probably the most remarkable of the period, as every distinguished member of the organization was present. Each one endeavored to cheer him and to make him forget his infirmities. All seemed moved by presentiment; and Edwin himself appeared apprehensive that it might be his last New Year's Eve. At midnight the loving cup was passed around, and the Yule log burned, while outside bells and whistles announced the arrival of 1892. Happily, he was to be with them again on such an occasion.

During the winter he stayed close to his rooms, taking only short walks or jaunts to his daughter's New York home for tea or dinner. It was evident to those associated with him that he was, to use his own term, "mentally and physically about played out." But he always had the welfare of The Players in mind and never missed a meeting of its directors if able to attend. He said he wanted as many young men as possible in the organization to "keep it going." No one ever received more homage or respect than the benefactor of The Players in the home he had so generously provided for them.

Toward the latter part of the season he felt stronger and attended the theatre where his favorite nephew, Sydney Booth, was appearing in *Amy Robsart*. Barton Hill was stage manager and after the performance asked Edwin what he thought of the young man, still in his 'teens. "I suppose he was one of the merry-makers outside of the castle," replied Edwin. "To tell the truth, I didn't notice him." When Hill told Edwin that Sydney had taken the part of Mike Lambourne, Edwin did not at first believe him. "It took some time to convince the tragedian that the bearded ruffian who had strutted before him was his smooth-faced young nephew. When he was convinced, he expressed pride in the boy's achievement." [86]

Edwin took a great interest in Junius' sons and always was delighted to hear of their activities. What would they do with the name, he wondered. Although it was not then perceptible, Junius III was another problem to the Booths. If he did not inherit much of the family's talent for the stage, he inherited enough of their madness to end tragically.[87] Sydney came out a little better and attained some prominence in the theatrical world.

Edwin's last Founder's Night was another gala New Year's Eve. President-elect Grover Cleveland attended and made a speech in which he referred in terms of affection to Edwin, who modestly responded before passing the loving cup at the usual midnight ceremony. Time passed slowly now. Edwin lounged about the club, talked with friends, smoked more than was good for him, strolled over to the park and back.

On April eleventh he attended a performance of a humorous play entitled *The Guardsman*, at the Lyceum Theatre, then under the management of Daniel Frohman. He occupied a box with his daughter and her husband. Edwina noted "with a pained heart how great an effort it cost him to sit through a performance, however enjoyable, yet he never complained of fatigue, and seemed all unconscious that he was the central figure upon whom the audience admiringly gazed between the acts." [88] It was his final view of the stage.

The same night, at the Union Square Theatre, a boy prodigy was playing *Hamlet*. His name was Walker Whiteside.

One evening Edwin was called upon, as president of The Players, to preside at a directors' meeting. He took his accustomed seat but, at intervals, while matters relating to the club were discussed, seemed to be far away. Several times, as motions were in order and he failed to proceed with his duties, members had to nudge him or call his attention to what had been said. And then, alone in his room, on the night of April eighteenth, he had another attack which was not discovered until morning when he was found in his bed, unconscious. The right

Rare photo of Edwin Booth taken in Baltimore, March 1890. *(New York Public Library photo)*

Statue of Edwin Booth as Hamlet in Gramercy Park, New York, opposite The Players. Edmond T. Quinn, sculptor. Erected by The Players, and dedicated November 13, 1918. *(Courtesy of the Walter Hampden Memorial Library at The Players, New York City)*

side of his face was drawn and his eyes half-closed. Dr. St. Clair Smith, his physician, diagnosed it as a paralytic stroke.

Edwina rushed to his bedside and intimate friends waited anxiously at the door. They believed that he was dying; but Edwin's great vitality kept him alive. Twice within the next seven weeks he emerged from stupor or delirium to recognize those around him and, between strange mumblings and inarticulate sounds, was able to speak distinctly. "His last coherent words were addressed to our little children, whom we had taken to his bedside two days before he died," wrote his daughter. "My boy called gently, 'How are you, dear grandpa?' and the answer came loud and clear, in the familiar, boyish way, 'How are you yourself, old fellow?'" [89]

Gradually, he sank into another state of coma. Before midnight of June sixth (with Dr. Smith and two nurses in attendance) Edwina, her husband, William Bispham, J. H. Magonigle, and Charles P. Carryl gathered round him knowing the end was near. Outside, a summer storm had pelted the city with rain as lightning flashed and thunder rumbled, but now there was silence again in Gramercy Park. Suddenly the lights of the neighborhood went out, and in Edwin's room a woman's voice exclaimed, "Don't let father die in the dark!" Almost instantly the lights came on again. A moment later Edwin Booth died. It was seventeen minutes past one o'clock on the morning of June 7, 1893.

Announcements of his death headlined front pages of newspapers; telegraphs sent it around the world; men and women throughout the United States, England, and Germany paused to remember the voice and figure that had entranced them before the curtain fell. But the scandal of the Mad Booths of Maryland would not die, and on the date that was to mark Edwin's tombstone the press began rattling the bones of the family skeleton. "Thousands of Booth's admirers have vainly asked to know the secret of his morbid melancholy," asserted the New York *Sun*. "Now that he is gone they may be answered, in part at least. It is undeniable that he inherited his father's tendency to madness, and his life was a constant fight against dangerous excesses, but the blight that most affected him was undoubtedly the stain caused by his father's early matrimonial affairs. . . ."

To this the *Times* added: "Edwin's mother was always recognized as his father's wife, yet another woman claimed that place, and Edwin's friends have thought that he was always very sensitive about his birth and exaggerated the family dishonor. He realized with bitterness that the infamy of his younger brother served to advertise him, and he hated the advertisement."

There had been no escape; reminders of Wilkes' crime had haunted him at every turn. On the cruise with E. C. Benedict and his friends on the yacht *Oneida*, they put in at Boothbay to get medicine for Edwin, who was ill from too much indulgence in tobacco. He asked the druggist how the bay was named and received the answer: "There is a tradition that a ship captain by the name of Booth was shipwrecked here and began a settlement. But I can assure you, sir, he was no relation of that damned scoundrel who shot Lincoln." Edwin glared at the druggist, paid his bill and strode from the premises with his lips tightly set.[90]

During a visit with Laurence Hutton he had noticed a death mask in his library and questioned him about it. When Hutton was forced to reply that it was of Lincoln, Edwin picked it up, gazed at it, then replaced it without comment. A similar incident occurred at Lorrimer Graham's home where a cast of Lincoln's hand attracted his attention. His private life was also clouded by the early death of his first wife and his unfortunate marriage to Mary McVicker. These afflictions kept him in a half-world and the melancholy madness of Hamlet was always hanging over him. Members of The Players were silent when Edwin, after Barrett's death, hearing some sound in the room he had occupied, would say, "There comes poor Lawrence now." It would have been impossible for Edwin's morbidly sensitive nature to have survived the mental torture of all these memories much longer.

The normal pursuits of childhood passed him by, and in many of his early letters to his daughter he insisted that she play and study, as he had not been able to. This fact did not escape the *Herald*, who told its readers: "When the lad had only grown into roundabouts he was taken away from the birch and the Fourth Reader to follow in the footsteps of his father . . . at a time when he ought to have been sleeping all night and playing out of doors in the daytime."

After achieving fame, Edwin deplored his lack of a college education and the fact that he had not endeavored to remedy such a deficiency until he was past the age when most young men had received their degrees. He had a keen appreciation of music, and talent for both writing and sculpture which was never developed. In answer to a compliment, he remarked that his theatrical career had been "tediously successful." Vicissitudes of the road were taken lightly. He enjoyed telling of once giving a "cold performance" in a new playhouse before the roof was finished, and of his appearance as Hamlet in street clothes when the baggage failed to arrive before curtain time.

Extremely superstitious, he permitted no omens of bad luck to enter a theatre where he was playing if he could prevent it. During one of his engagements in San Francisco, Katherine Goodale went shopping in Chinatown and returned with some peacock feathers which she placed in her dressing-room trunk. When she innocently told Edwin what she had done, he exclaimed: "Peacock feathers are bad luck! The worst of luck! I have a horror of them! I let that bird come into my theatre. . . . They sent it as a present to me—'something to adorn my office' . . . *and I lost my theatre!*" Before they left San Francisco, the Interstate Commerce Law went into effect and the cost of transporting the company's baggage soared upward. "I told you something would happen . . ." said Edwin. In her New York dressing room Katherine Goodale broke a mirror: "You'll see! It has come again. . . . It's to the theatre! No—it is to *me!*" he cried. The next day she came to replace it and saw a card on the bulletin board stating that the theatre would be closed until further notice. She inquired and was told that Mr. Booth was ill.

Edwin was convinced it was good luck to be born with a caul if one kept it with him, but he had lent his caul to a friend going into danger, and it was lost. "I knew my luck would turn," he said afterward. "Misfortune came. I think few have had more." [91]

The failure of Booth's Theatre started the rumor that he did not have much ability in business matters, but when his papers were examined after his death everything was found in order. Valuation of his estate fixed it at $602,675, from which a residue of $462,335 was left, after debts, legacies and expenses were deducted. This went to Edwina, with the provision that it be divided among her children at the time of her death.[92] The many bequests made to charitable organizations, relatives, and friends, included one of ten thousand dollars to Marion Booth, who, a newspaper disclosed, had recently appeared before the Overseer of the Poor for Neptune Township in New Jersey, alleging that her husband, Barton Douglas, actor, had gone to England, leaving her and their son destitute.

Edwin had no patience with fluttering society and was bored by the adulation of women and the futile chatter of drawing rooms. For a time, after the death of her husband, it was believed that the lovely actress Ida Vernon, who had often been Edwin's leading lady, would lead him back to the marriage altar, but the failure of two previous performances in the nuptial rites warned him against trying it again. With every dwelling in New York City open to him, he visited in less than a dozen and accepted as confidants only those few people who had weathered the years of friendship. Solely for them had he occasionally unlocked his store of humor and become a jester full of surprising wit.

Condolences from all over the world cluttered a table at The Players and flowers banked the walls.[93] On the morning of June ninth, Edwin's body was taken from his room to the Little Church Around the Corner,[94] previous to its journey to Boston for burial in Mount Auburn Cemetery, Cambridge. A long line of carriages followed the hearse, and behind them walked members of The Players led by Judge J. F. Daly and the comedian, James Lewis. While services were being conducted by Bishop Potter, two events occurred reminiscent of John Wilkes Booth. As the result of excavations made under Ford's Theatre in Washington, which had been remodeled for the use of the War Department, three floors gave way and crashed to earth, killing a number of government employees and injuring many others; and the book by Thomas A. Jones telling of Wilkes' flight after the assassination came off the press.[95]

About noon, a funeral party composed of Edwina and her husband, Dr. Joseph A. Booth, Junius Brutus Booth III, Sydney Booth, and several friends started northward by train with Edwin's body. At sundown, in the presence of many noted men and women, it was placed in a tomb beside his first wife, Mary Devlin.

Today one may visualize the acting of Edwin Booth only through reviews of his performances and portraits of him in character. Some of his critics contended that he was not a creator, as few new plays were ever among his offerings; that rôles such as Raphael and Bertuccio, which he was first to enact in the United States, had previously been seen in Europe. But his letters to Horace Furness, the noted Shakespearean scholar and editor, disclose many original ideas for the staging of productions in which Edwin appeared. Others regarded him only as an interpreter who used his voice as Joseph Joachim used his violin, to preserve the melody of poetical verse. Yet Edwin's interpretations were so essentially his own that he left no successor and was acclaimed the last of the great tragedians.[96]

Of all those who saw him on the stage, an old woman best summarized the opinion of his time. Years after Edwin's death she left a theatre with tears streaming from her eyes, and upon being asked why she wept, replied, "Oh, I remember Edwin Booth's Brutus, his slow, stately movements, his perfect art—I have just seen a raving, ranting, ignorant fool attempt to play the part, and the desecration has made me unhappy."

But it is as Hamlet that Edwin will be remembered—as we now see him in the bronze image facing The Players in Gramercy Park— youthful, courageous, noble—undaunted by the misfortunes which befell the Mad Booths of Maryland.

COMMENTS

WAR DEPARTMENT

OFFICE OF THE JUDGE ADVOCATE GENERAL

WASHINGTON

December 2, 1940.

Mr. Stanley Kimmel,
    Ebbitt Hotel,
        Washington, D. C.

Dear Mr. Kimmel:

      We appreciate your having ascertained, by diligent and patient research, that Exhibit #8, marked "Herold's photograph", in the trial of the so-called Lincoln conspirators (M.M. 2251), is erroneous and is in reality the picture of Dr. Joseph A. Booth, younger brother of John Wilkes Booth.

                 Sincerely yours,

                 Joseph L. Lyons
                 Joseph L. Lyons,
                 Chief Clerk.

Letter relating to the photograph of Dr. Joseph A. Booth reproduced earlier in this volume (facing p. 39). *(War Department, Office of the Judge Advocate General, 1940)*

COMMENTS

BOOK ONE

[1] On one of the few existing pages of his diary (now in the Helen Menken Collection) Booth wrote:

> Louisville, May 1839.
>
> This day, May 1st, 1796, I was born [in the parish of St. Pancras, London] at as nearly as can be judged by parental record, a quarter before 2 P.M.—a day which ushered into existence one who has witnessed some most extraordinary vicissitudes and endured [not] a little in this big world. . . .
>
> 'Tis strange that although certainly old enough to identify and retain knowledge of my mother I have not the slightest shade of remembrance of either her person, features or form. My grandmother, i.e., my father's mother, is the earliest link in Memory's chain which I can trace; next, my father then two or three casual faces—my brother —again a lapse until nine years old when I can form a remembrance of my sister. . . .

[2] In the diary previously referred to Booth gave as the reason for having been "served with a subpoena as a witness to some cause in London," his father's determination to keep him from taking up arms against the country he so admired. Booth did not mention Elizabeth Walters, but dates prove her suit to have been responsible for this summons. Notice of the proceedings appeared in the London *Morning Herald*, September 11, 1813.

A clipping from the Portland, Maine, *Argus* (date unknown) erroneously states that Booth was brought into Portland as a prisoner of war after the fight between the *Boxer* and the American *Enterprise* that same month and year.

[3] William Oxberry, *Dramatic Biography and Histrionic Anecdotes*, G. Virtue, London, 1826.

[4] *Actors and Actresses of Great Britain and the United States*, edited by Brander Matthews and Laurence Hutton, Cassel and Company, New York, 1886, Vol. 3.

[5] Asia Booth Clarke, in *Booth Memorials*, declared: "By a boyish *mésalliance* contracted in Brussels in the year 1814, there was one son, who, if alive, is still a resident of London, and of whom we possess no further knowledge."

Baltimore directories prior to publication of this book in 1866, list members of Booth's two families as living in that city at the same time, so Asia must have been fully aware of the fact.

[6] Thomas R. Gould, *The Tragedian*, Hurd and Houghton, New York, 1868.

[7] Asia Booth Clarke, *Booth Memorials*, George W. Carleton, New York, 1866; *The Elder and the Younger Booth*, James R. Osgood and Company, Boston, 1882.

[8] This is confirmed by Bureau of Immigration records. In her books about the elder Booth, Asia gives this date and number of days for the voyage, but makes an obvious error in stating that her parents left the island of Madeira in April.

[9] Noah M. Ludlow, *Dramatic Life As I Found It*, G. I. Jones and Company St. Louis, 1880.

[10] Ruth Crosby Dimmick, *Our Theatres Today and Yesterday*, H. K. Fly Company, New York, 1913.

[11] There has been a great deal of controversy regarding the birthplace of this child. In a Maryland Historical Society unpublished manuscript of May, 1887, entitled *Junius Brutus Booth, Sr.* (now in possession of the Municipal Museum, Baltimore), Dr. William Stump Forward wrote that Dr. John R. Quinan, a noted historian of that city, after careful examination of the subject, expressed the belief that Junius Brutus, Jr., was born in Baltimore. In the same manuscript, however, a letter from Booth's Harford County neighbor, Mrs. Elijah Rogers, maintains that all the Booth children were born in Harford County, Maryland. Records recently discovered by the present writer in Washington prove each of these contentions to be wrong. The list of Free Inhabitants at the Census Bureau for the Fifth Ward in Baltimore, taken on July 17, 1850, at the time the Booths occupied a house on Exeter Street, gives the birthplace of Junius Brutus Booth, Jr., as South Carolina, and among documents in the War Department Archives is one in which Junius stated, at the time he was brought before Federal authorities after the assassination of Lincoln, that he was a native of Charleston, South Carolina. (Book Five, Comment 6.)

[12] Dr. Joseph Booth, the youngest of the Maryland clan, made known at the time of Edwin's death that a trusteeship had been undertaken shortly after his father acquired the property "because he was an alien." Edwin Forrest, the noted American tragedian, was appointed trustee for Junius and Rosalie. "The office," said Joseph, "was faithfully discharged and nobly relinquished when requested. . . . The friendship that existed between my father and Forrest was enduring till death, cemented by the most cordial business relations."

Assertions of the Booth children are at variance as to the year their father acquired this property, but the present writer found, among the records of the Belair courthouse, one dating the "lease for one thousand years," etc., by Richard Hall and others to Junius Brutus Booth, Sr., as June 4, 1824.

[13] Asia Booth Clarke, *op. cit.*

[14] The possible exception was Joseph Adrian. (See page 59).

[15] Joe Edwin Hall, son of Madagascan Joe, still lives in Belair. He was the first child born after his parents left the Booth place and moved into their own cabin on the thirty-five acres of land which they bought just at the close of the war. During an interview he said many of his brothers and sisters had been named for the Booth children. They were about the same in number. One child died in infancy, and Joe was positive she was buried in the Booth family graveyard on the farm. His father was drafted for service in the Union army, and Booth had to pay for a substitute. He died when Joe was a small boy, but Joe's mother lived until July, 1904, when she was ninety-four years old. Two of the Hall children, belonging to Mrs. Rogers, ran away while they were still slaves. One did not return for forty years.

"I remembah hearin' da oldah folks talk 'bout Asia Booth," said Joe. "She used to cum ovah to da cullud settlement at Old Field. When I's a boy, da roads 'round heah wah terrible. Da white folks rode horseback, but da cullud folks walked. Dey had lots o' time."

COMMENTS 339

[16] On May 9, 1824, Booth wrote to his father:

Dear Sir:

I am sorry you refuse to take any interest in my affairs, even to so small a charge as overlooking the servants and labourers, that I may not be cheated and robbed on every side. However, argument with you is out of the question. I do not at all mean or wish to offend you, but to beg you, for your own sake, to refrain from that destructive and sense-depriving custom of getting intoxicated. Madness will be the result if you persist. I have witness'd often with regret the terrible ravages it has made both on your mind and body. Even the occupation of looking now and then after the garden, or any part relative to agriculture (not laborious) would, I sho'd think, give you greater pleasure than feeling every faculty besotted. I had no idea you'd have left the negroes the option of doing as they pleased in my absence, or Sampson, either. These people are receiving my money and eating, as 'twere, the bread that I *earn*, without deserving it, because no check is offered whenever they deviate. I do not ask you to work, but I ask *you* to see that *they* work. Surely the request is not exorbitant.

Look at the folly of that man Curtis! On my return I shall not continue him in my employ. Drinking made him break the carry-all. Whatever tends to deprive man of his reason, of his money, of his nerves and physical powers, and render him temporarily, in some lamentable instances, *forever*, an idiot or a maniac, ought not to be drunk as mother's milk.

On my arrival here, I was astonished at the negligence shown by everyone I had left on the premises. Mr. Walton has (from some cause or other) been excessively dilatory. I have left a letter with Harriet to give him. Why can you not stay here now! There are several articles that might be stolen both from the stable and kitchen, and it appears to me a wonder such has not been the case, for the negroes, when you are away, will sleep here. I shall endeavor to come down on Tuesday or Wednesday and I shall feel happy to see you.

Yours affectionately,
J. B. B.

Helen Menken collection of Booth letters.

[17] Discussions of this performance have divided theatrical historians for many years, the point at issue being Booth's rendition of the part in French. Noah M. Ludlow (Comment 9), most active in theatrical circles in the South and Midwest at the time, and Asia Booth Clarke (Comment 7) give opposite views on the subject. An appreciative *critique* in a New Orleans newspaper on the morning following his performance is so worded that, though indefinite, one is led to accept Asia's statement that her father played the part in the French language.

[18] William W. Clapp, *A Record of the Boston Stage*, James Munroe & Co., Boston, 1853.

[19] Mary Ann rarely accompanied Booth on tour. She was not a professional actress, as often reported, and her performances were few. In the anonymous account of *The Actor* (Comment 24), written and published before Booth's death, containing many incidents in his career none of which he ever denied, there is a passage crediting her with a first appearance on any stage in the comedy, *Town and Country*, at the Holliday Street Theatre, Baltimore, as Rosalie Somers, with Booth in the rôle of Reuben Glenroy. However, Francis C. Wemyss (*Chronology of the American Stage*, W. Taylor and Co., New York,

1852), friendly with the Booths, records her first stage appearance in America at the Chestnut Street Theatre, Philadelphia, in 1831, as Susan Ashfield in *Speed the Plough*. A "Mrs. Booth" listed on numerous playbills of the time was not Mary Ann Holmes.

[20] William Stump Forward, *Junius Brutus Booth, Sr.*, Maryland Historical Society Manuscript, Municipal Museum, Baltimore.

[21] Ruth Crosby Dimmick, *op. cit.*

[22] Francis C. Wemyss, *Twenty-Six Years of the Life of an Actor and Manager*, Burgess, Stringer and Company, New York, 1847.

[23] The year 1839 is recorded by Asia Booth Clarke (Comment 7); William Winter (*Brief Chronicles*, Publications of the Dunlap Society, New York, 1889), and several others, give it as 1834.

[24] Anonymous, *The Actor*, William H. Graham, New York, 1846.

[25] Copied from the original letter in the Helen Menken collection. Asia, in books about her father, gives a different version of it, and notes the name Hagar as being that of a "slave." Booth never owned any slaves but hired them from his neighbors.

[26] When Edwin had the bodies of the Booth family removed from Baltimore Cemetery to Greenmount Cemetery, a Latin translation of this was inscribed on Richard's gravestone.

[27] The births of the Booth children were:

Junius	December 22, 1821
Rosalie	July 5, 1823
Henry	(month and day unknown) 1825
Mary Ann	(month and day unknown) 1827
Frederick	(month and day unknown) 1829
Elizabeth	(month and day unknown) 1831
Edwin	November 13, 1833
Asia	November 19, 1835
John Wilkes	May 10, 1838
Joseph	February 8, 1840

[28] William Stump Forward, *op. cit.* Mrs. Rogers incorrectly gives Eliza's name as Maggie Mitchell, a famous actress of that time.

[29] F. A. Burr, *Junius Brutus Booth's Wife Adelaide*, New York *Press*, August 9, 1891.

[30] The Bill of Divorce to the Judge of the Baltimore County Court sets forth that:

> On the 8th day of May in the year one thousand eight hundred and fifteen (1815) the said Junius Brutus Booth was then a citizen and subject of said Kingdom of Britain but now a citizen of the United States and for many years a resident of the city of Baltimore, Md., and that the oratrix now is and for more than two years past has been a resident of the city of Baltimore, State of Maryland. The said Junius Brutus Booth and your oratrix lived together as husband and wife for several years in the said city of London—during which time she bore to her said husband a son now living named Richard J. Booth and a daughter who died in her infancy; that on or about the month of January in the year 1821 the said Junius Brutus Booth without any intimation whatever to your oratrix of his intentions or any particular cause whatsoever abandoned your oratrix and came to the United States where he has since remained and that said abandonment

has continued uninterrupted from said month of January in the year 1821 to this date more than twenty-nine years and your oratrix alleges that said abandonment is deliberate and final and that the separation of the said Junius Brutus Booth and your oratrix is beyond any reasonable expectation of reconciliation. The said Junius Brutus Booth left the Kingdom of Great Britain and came to the United States as aforesaid in company with a woman with whom he has been in the habit of adulterous intercourse from that time to the present and that he has lived for many years last passed and now does treat and recognize said woman as his wife and that he has by her a large family of children. Your oratrix asks leave to state that in charging this fault she is impelled alone by the necessity for the vindication of her own rights (and not by any desire to add infamy and disgrace either to said husband or to the said woman whom he has professed to himself or to the children, the fruits of said adulterous intercourse).

She alleges adultery as the cause for divorce.

To this is attached a true copy of the

Marriage solemnized in the Parish of Saint George, Bloomsbury, in the County of Middlesex in the year 1815. Junius Brutus Booth, of this Parish, and Adelaide Delannoy, of this Parish, were married in this church by Banns, this eighth Day of May in the year One Thousand Eight Hundred and Fifteen (1815) by me, Nathaniel Forth, B.A., curate. This marriage solemnized between us
Junius Booth
Adelaide Delannoy
In the presence of Tho. Blyth
John Harrison

Note: In the original document, lines are drawn through the words included in the above parentheses.

[31] In the often quoted letter of Edwin Booth to Nahum Capen, dated Windsor Hotel, New York, July 28, 1881, he wrote: "I can give you very little information regarding my brother John. I seldom saw him since his early boyhood in Baltimore. He was a rattlepated fellow, filled with Quixotic notions. While at the farm in Maryland he would charge on horseback through the woods 'spouting' heroic speeches with a lance in his hand, a relic of the Mexican war, given to father by some soldier who had served under Taylor." (Edwina Booth Grossman, *Edwin Booth*, The Century Co., New York, 1894.)

If one follows John Wilkes' boyhood days in Belair and on the farm this will not seem to indicate any freakish conduct on his part. As Edwin acknowledged, he saw very little of his younger brother at this time, and it is possible that, when he wrote to Capen, he did not remember, or had never attended, the Tournaments which were held each year at Deer Creek Rocks. While exploring these rocks, the present writer came upon the names of W. H. Schuck, a boyhood playmate of John Wilkes Booth, and of J. Booth carved on a large boulder. It was a place to which the Booth children often rode on horseback during their vacations, and the Tournaments were surely witnessed by John Wilkes, who was at home much more than Edwin. Old Belair newspapers of the time gave a description of these Tournaments which appear to have been the source of his "Quixotic notions."

On an announced day, horsemen arrived at Deer Creek Rocks dressed in imitation armor of knights and ancient warriors. Bars were put up from which rings dangled, and each horseman, lance in hand, rushed his mount full speed toward the rings in an effort to spear them. Crowds gathered to watch the contest and to applaud the winners. Smaller and smaller rings were placed on the bars until finally the one who had succeeded in spearing the most rings received first prize. Such Tournaments are still held at various points in the South.

Like any other boy, John Wilkes was looking forward to the day when he could join the knights in their contests at Deer Creek Rocks, and his "charge on horseback through the woods" was no more than a desire to imitate his elders and practise feats he had seen at the Tournaments.

[32] Baltimore city directories give the addresses of the Booths as:

1842, J. B. Booth, tragedian, east side High, North of Gay.

1845, 72 North Front Street.

1846-1852, 62 North Exeter Street.

This last address is now 152 Exeter Street. "In the elder Booth's time it was a two-story and attic dwelling, but in recent years an additional story has been put on." Baltimore *Sun*, December 12, 1898.

[33] Baltimore *American*, July 27, 1902.

[34] Henry C. Wagner, "Reminiscences," included in the unpublished manuscript of Alonzo May, Municipal Museum, Baltimore, Md.

[35] Matthews and Hutton, *op. cit.*

[36] Unpublished manuscript of Alonzo May, Municipal Museum, Baltimore, Md.

[37] All books and periodicals containing photographs or drawings of the Booth birthplace in Maryland, including the most recent volume, by Otis Skinner (*The Last Tragedian*, Dodd, Mead and Company, Inc., New York, 1939), give it as Tudor Hall, the house now standing on the property formerly owned by the elder Booth. Writers have accepted this regardless of the fact that he did not begin its construction until about ten years after the birth of the last child. Family letters indicate that it was not occupied until 1853.

In the unpublished manuscript of Dr. W. S. Forward, he mentions visiting the Harford County retreat of the Booths with his daughter one afternoon in May, 1885: "The present dwelling [Tudor Hall] which has the air of newness and freshness about it, which quite surprised us, was built by the senior only a short time before his death, according to his own plans, which are said to represent the English cottage style; but the change in bay-windows, of modern pattern, which had puzzled us, we discovered has been added by the present proprietor.

"The location of the little log house, which had been the home of the family during the greater part of their residence in Harford County, was pointed out to us as having stood beneath some ancient and umbrageous trees, within about fifty yards of the present dwelling."

Questions concerning the disposition of the log house remained unanswered for some time; few inhabitants of the neighborhood remembered it. By various clues, however, it was finally located as a part of a modern dwelling. On its third site, the original home of the Booths began another transformation. Its interior dimensions, fortunately, remain the same (except for the removal of a partition between the two rooms on the lower floor), and the stairway leading to the upper bedrooms bears the imprint of many Booth feet. Logs from the first cabin can plainly be seen in the basement and attic, but added rooms and porches have changed its exterior and hidden the secret of its former history for many years. An account of his discovery of it was related by the present writer in "Home of Assassin Booth Famed for Disappearances," Washington *Sunday Star*, January 19, 1936.

COMMENTS

[38] Whether Fenno or a strolling minstrel who preferred to be called Jeems Pipes of Pipesville rather than Stephen Massett (one of the pioneer group that included the Booths) arrived first in that wilderness of hopeful faces is not known. However, an article in the New York *Herald* of January 30, 1849, entitled "Movements to California," which mentions Augustus W. Fenno as a member of the party sailing on the brig *Sarah McFarland* that morning for San Francisco, makes it appear that Fenno preceded the singing mimic of celebrated characters.

[39] Illiterate Thomas Maguire was a hoodlum ex-cab driver who had taken up politics and become efficient at stuffing ballot boxes for the party then in power. Between elections he had been entrusted with collecting revenue from gambling halls, barrooms, dance dives, and houses of prostitution and had learned the intricate details of their management. When the discovery of gold in California was announced, he and Mrs. Maguire had been among the first to join the stampede westward and in San Francisco Tom found an opportunity to do for himself what he had once done for others. But he had a dual personality: his dreams of political power through nefarious enterprises were often interspersed with visions of great theatrical ventures in which he was the dominating figure. This ambition was to be realized in California.

[40] Immediately after the May fourth fire, Maguire rebuilt the Jenny Lind to have a theatre ready for Junius. The fire of June twenty-second, shortly after it opened, had occurred while Junius was on his way to California. The destruction of this building forced Maguire to erect a third Jenny Lind Theatre. His misfortunes at this time have led some writers to contend that he would not have sent East for a manager, as he had no theatre, and that Junius was not engaged until they met in San Francisco. They do not consider the fact that Junius was engaged before these disasters and that the time required for correspondence made it impossible for Maguire to notify him of events until Junius reached San Francisco.

[41] *Edwin Booth in Old California Days, The Green Book Album,* June, 1911.

[42] J. D. Borthwick, *The Gold Hunters,* Outing Publishing Company, New York, 1917. A reprint of the original published in Edinburgh, 1857.

[43] Asia Booth Clarke, *The Elder and the Younger Booth,* James R. Osgood and Company, Boston, 1882.

[44] Matthews and Hutton, *op. cit.*

[45] New Orleans *Daily Picayune,* Nov. 20, 1852.

[46] Column headed *Driftwood,* New York *Dramatic Mirror,* July 31, 1880.

[47] Walt Whitman, *November Boughs,* David McKay, Philadelphia, 1888.

COMMENTS
BOOK TWO

[1] *Edwin Booth in Old California Days, The Green Book Album,* June, 1911.

[2] Jesse Healy, "My Reminiscences," *History of the California Pioneers Quarterly,* Vol. IX, No. 4, San Francisco, 1932.

"The Hunger Convention at Grass Valley," by Old Block, in Harry L. Wells' *History of Nevada County,* Thompson and West, Oakland, 1880.

[3] *Edwin Booth in Old California Days.*

[4] James W. Shettel, "J. Wilkes Booth at School," New York *Dramatic Mirror,* March 26, 1916.

[5] This was not his first performance in that character, as stated by William Winter (*Life and Art of Edwin Booth,* The Macmillan Co., New York, 1893) and others, a previous appearance having been recorded from the San Francisco press in these pages.

[6] Many of these facts about her are from the column headed, "The Romance of Laura Keene" (an interview with "a well-known and retired member of the New York Bar"), New York *Dramatic Mirror,* January 15, 1887.

[7] John F. Thrum, "Reminiscences of the Stage in Honolulu," *Hawaiian Almanac and Annual;* compiled by Thomas G. Thrum, Honolulu, 1906.

[8] *Pacific Commercial Advertiser,* Honolulu, September 5, 1893.

[9] Frederick Warde, *Fifty Years of Make Believe,* International Press Syndicate, New York, 1920.

[10] Reviews of this engagement are from the Sacramento *Democratic State Journal.*

[11] Walter M. Leman, *Memories of an Old Actor,* A. Roman Co., San Francisco, 1886.

[12] *Ibid.*

[13] Facts, however, discredit this statement by William Winter (*Life and Art of Edwin Booth,* The Macmillan Co., New York, 1893) and similar comments by others. Moulton's troupe, having lost their wardrobe in one fire, would hardly have been accused of incendiarism by these miners, many of whom were not the ignorant class so often depicted. Towns in which Edwin appeared where fires occurred are here given from California historical records and do not substantiate Winter's assertion that "each town took fire as soon as Moulton's cavalcade had left it."

[14] Anne M. Fauntleroy, "The Romance of Mary Devlin," *The Ladies Home Journal,* September, 1904.

[15] Advertisement in the Baltimore *American and Commercial Advertiser,* September 11, 1856:

> Seminary for young ladies,
> W. Fayette St., near Franklin Square,
> Northwest corner of Carlton street.
> Samuel T. Lester, Principal.
> Miss R. W. Saumenig, Assistant.
> R. J. Booth, Languages.
> John Schaefer, Music.
> Emil Kett, Drawing and Painting.

Reports that Richard Junius Booth served with the Confederate army and that he practised law in Boston and Philadelphia have not been substantiated. F. A. Burr, in the New York *Press*, August 9, 1891, wrote of his interview with the sexton of a Baltimore Catholic cemetery who told him that before the Civil War a man who looked like a priest often visited Adelaide's grave and paid him well to keep it in order. The sexton had not seen the man since the war and no other person had taken an interest in the grave. Burr claimed to have received a communication from a distinguished professor of languages in one of the prominent educational institutions in this country saying that a number of letters in his possession might be of interest and if Burr would call he could read them. In this collection was also the painting of Booth, Adelaide, and their son, which had been made in England. Burr, however, did not disclose the name nor the address of the professor in his article, although copies of the letters appeared in it.

On one of his trips to London after Lincoln's assassination, Edwin (with Asia, her youngest son Wilfred, and others) was driving in a carriage when he (so Asia's son reported years later) saw a man resembling John Wilkes Booth and stopped to talk with him. As Edwin had stepped from the carriage to the sidewalk and was some distance away, young Clarke did not hear what was said, but when the stories of Wilkes' escape began to circulate, he was sure it was his "Uncle John" whom Edwin had met that day in London. This is undoubtedly a clue to the whereabouts of Richard Junius after his disappearance in America. That neither Edwin nor Asia ever disclosed the identity of this man to young Clarke was not for the purpose, as he later thought, of keeping John Wilkes' "escape" a secret, but to withhold from him any knowledge of his grandfather's matrimonial affairs which they always feared would besmirch the family honor.

[16] Edwin eventually had these lines removed.

[17] "Junius Booth is father of this girl [Blanche De Bar Booth]. . . . He left Boston some twelve or fifteen years ago with a prostitute named Harriet Mace and went to California. I applied for a divorce for my sister and got it."

Sworn statement of Ben De Bar (who had adopted her), St. Louis, April 22, 1865: War Department Archives.

Confirming this adoption is a letter addressed to J. Wilkes Booth, 28 East 19th St., New York, care of Edwin Booth, dated St. Louis, March 18, 1865:

> Dear John
>
> I enclose you the brilliant success of Blanche. I do this because *you* will be pleased and glad to hear how well she has begun. I have sent June [Junius] a bill to prove to him, I have no wish that the girl should have any other than my name.
>
> Yours Sincerely,
> B. De Bar

Enclosed in the letter were a newspaper account of Miss Blanche De Bar, "the now established favorite of St. Louis," and a playbill announcing her at the St. Louis Theatre on the evening of March 16, 1865, in *The Love Chase*, and *Miss Somnambula*.

[18] Anne M. Fauntleroy, "The Romance of Mary Devlin," *The Ladies Home Journal*, September, 1904.

[19] Edwina Booth Grossman, *Edwin Booth, Recollections by His Daughter*, The Century Co., New York, 1894.

COMMENTS

BOOK THREE

[1] George Alfred Townsend, *Life, Crime and Capture of John Wilkes Booth*, Dick and Fitzgerald, New York, 1865.

[2] Francis Wilson, *John Wilkes Booth*, Houghton Mifflin Company, Boston, 1929.

[3] Horace Traubel, *With Walt Whitman in Camden*, Small, Maynard and Company, Boston, 1906. Vol. 1.

[4] John M. Barron, *With Wilkes Booth in His Days as an Actor*, Baltimore *Sun*, March 17, 1907.

[5] Date given by Izola Forrester, *This One Mad Act*, Hale, Cushman and Flint, Boston, 1937.

[6] One of these letters, now in the War Department Archives, reads:

My dear boy

I received yours on Friday, I had written to you a day or two previous and our letters must have passed each other, you in some measure answered the questions, I asked you—and the secret you have told me, is not exactly a secret, as Edwin was told by someone, you were paying great attention to a young lady in Washington—Now my dear boy, I cannot advise you how to act—you have so often been dead in love and this may prove like the others, not of any lasting impression—you are aware that the woman you make your wife you must love and respect beyond all others, for marriage is an act that can not be recalled without misery if otherwise entered into—which you are well aware of, to be united to a woman that you only think you love is not the thing—You are old enough and have seen so much of the world, to know all this, only a young man in love does not stop to reflect and like a child with a new toy—only craves the possession of it—think and reflect—and if the lady in question is all you desire— I see no cause why you should not try to secure her—her father, I see has his appointment, would he give his consent? You can but ask, just be well assured she is really and truly devoted to you—then obtain his consent, you know in my partial eyes you are a fit match for any woman, no matter who she may be—but some father may have higher notions—God, grant if it is to be so, it will prove a source of happiness to you both—Now I expect you will turn around and laugh at my preaching and may say 'it was all your nonsense' if you really are in earnest and don't meet with a return of your affection—do pray come away from there, at once; it's the height of folly to live on in anxiety and hopes delayed, turn your attention at once to other subjects and try and forget in other pursuits the present trouble—as to politics I have no idea that females should have anything to do with, but leave them to their husbands—but not so the women of these disunited states. Well I think I have written enough on one subject— to make you smile.

I am all alone today—I told you in my last, Rose, June and baby and nurse were gone to Philadelphia—and yesterday after matinee Edwin went—I thought June might have come back after being there a week, he must have felt I was lonely—but I don't think I am much cared for—well to console me, yesterday I had a beautiful letter from Josey, he sends love to all and he was well—It was written on his birthday, the 6th of Feby,—it gave me great pleasure for he seems to be attending to business—and sees the advantage to him to remain there,—he says whoever writes to him to direct his—to the care of Wells & Fargo, he gets them sooner—

Now I am going to dinner by myself why are you not here to chat—and keep me company—no you are looking and saying soft things to one that don't love you half as well as your old mother does. God bless you my dear darling boy, its natural it should be so, I know, so I wont complain, I cannot expect to have you always— Write me soon and relieve my suspense for I am as anxious as you are; once more God guard you forever and ever,

Your loving mother,

M. A. BOOTH.

I don't know if I told you, we have had the little dog Mollie back with us—the woodman begged Edwin to take him as his father intended to give him away or have him drowned—because he said she had consumption—she has a very bad cough—that is very disagreeable—otherwise she looks the same—so Edwin brought her home— but her breath smelt so bad it was horrid—and Edwin was just saying he wished they would take her back, for he couldn't stand it. When lo and behold, in they both came, rushing to Edwin—to beg him to give them back the dog—for they were fretting themselves to death, without her, so he gave her back at once, and I was not sorry, Adieu —write tomorrow.

Note: The young woman to whom Mrs. Booth refers was Miss Bessie Hale, daughter of Senator John P. Hale of New Hampshire, who, with his family sailed from Boston, June 21, 1865, via England, to Spain as United States Ambassador. It is doubtful if Wilkes would have married Miss Hale had he lived to greet her when she returned from Spain.

In this letter Mrs. Booth also refers to "Josey" (Joseph), who was then in San Francisco, and gives February sixth as the date of his birth; other family records give it as February eighth. Edwin, in regard to his own birthdate, once wrote to Edwina: "It seems there is some doubt as to the exact date of my arrival here. Grandma [Booth] says I was born on the night of the great 'star shower' in 1833, and insists that it was November 15; but Uncle June says he remembers well—both my birth and the 'star shower' occurred on November 13, 1833. So you see, I do not know which is the day—for, although I was there, I was too young to pay attention to such weighty matters, and can't remember much about it."

Edwina Booth Grossman, *op. cit.*

[7] Edwin Adams, unpublished letter to "My dear Reakirt," dated Long Branch, N. J., April 17, 1865. War Department Archives.

[8] G. S. P. Holland, "A Visit to the Lincoln Country," *Tyler's Quarterly Historical*, July, 1928, expressed the opinion that "John Brown was a worse assassin than John Wilkes Booth, for while the latter murdered one man, the

former murdered more than a dozen and attempted to involve thousands in massacre. If the purpose of Brown was unselfish, the same could be said of the purpose of Booth. Brown wanted to rid the country of the tyranny of slavery and Booth of the tyranny of Abraham Lincoln, who had caused the slaughter of thousands."

[9] George Alfred Townsend, *op. cit.*

[10] H. P. Phelps, *Players of a Century*, J. McDonough, Albany, N. Y., 1880.

[11] From this Albany engagement Wilkes went to Portland, Maine. After his departure the following appeared in a local newspaper:

> J. Wilkes Booth—A few days ago our citizens were favored with the presence of the gentleman named above; and the reception he met with was no doubt most flattering to his professional pride. We do not propose to discuss his merits as an actor; but our experience with him shows that he lacks the requisites of a gentleman. During his engagement he contracted here, through his agent, a small bill at this office for advertising and printing. He was extremely liberal in his offers, and not sparing of promises. Just before his departure, we called on him for the amount of his indebtedness, but were referred to his agent. The agent referred to his principal; the principal back to the agent; and so, like a shuttlecock, our collector was batted backward and forward between their falsehoods, wearing out more shoe leather than the whole thing was worth. To cut the story short, we have not yet seen the color of the gentleman's money; and we wish merely to say to our brethren of the press that when 'J. Wilkes Booth' may appear on the boards in their vicinity, if they make any contracts with him, the safest way is to adopt the advance principle.

[12] *The Magazine of History*, February, 1906, states that in Richmond, during the first year of the war, Junius appeared in a play entitled *Bombastes Serioso*, in which the names of characters were changed to ridicule Lincoln and several other prominent Unionists. The play was given, but Junius was in San Francisco. The fact that his divorced wife, Clementine De Bar, was a member of the Richmond stock company and had in her possession a prompt book inscribed with his name accounts for this mistaken report.

[13] Katherine Goodale, *Behind the Scenes with Edwin Booth*, Houghton Mifflin Company, Boston, 1931.

[14] Report of Colonel J. H. Baker, Provost Marshal General of the Department of Missouri, to the Honorable C. A. Dana, Assistant Secretary of War, April 24, 1865. War Department Archives.

[15] Gratz Collection, The Historical Society of Pennsylvania, Philadelphia, Pa.

[16] The theatrical event of the past week was the discontinuance of Mr. Edwin Booth's engagement at the Winter Garden, in consequence of the severe illness of his wife, who died on Saturday last, at Dorchester, Mass. We . . . refer to the subject here only to set at rest the prevalent reports prejudicial to Mr. Booth's reputation as an actor. It is very true that Mr. Booth's performances during his recent engagements have been far below his usual standard; but this resulted from his anxiety in regard to his wife's illness, which completely prostrated his nervous system and even affected his mind.

We cannot excuse the Winter Garden management for allowing Mr. Booth to appear under such circumstances. It would have been better to disappoint the public by closing the theatre, or substituting some other performance, than to place Mr. Booth upon the stage when he was really unfit to act, and thus injure his reputation and disgust the audiences, who were, of course, ignorant of the real cause of Mr. Booth's trouble.

Seldom have we seen Shakespeare so murdered as at the Winter Garden during the past two weeks; and now, that the truth is known, we hold the management, and not Mr. Booth, responsible for the nightly repetition of this crime.

New York *Herald*, February 23, 1863.

[17] These letters are in private custody and will not be available to the public until 1970.*

[18] On this date, John Hay, Lincoln's assistant private secretary, noted in his diary: "Spent the evening at the theatre with President and Mrs. L., Mrs. Hunter, Cameron and Nicolay. J. Wilkes Booth was doing the 'Marble Heart.' Rather tame than otherwise."†

[19] After the assassination the War Department received word of a window pane, discovered in room twenty-two of the McHenry House at Meadville, Pa., on which was scratched, "Abe Lincoln departed this life Aug. 13, 1864, by the effects of poison." Wilkes had stayed at this hotel on his trips to the oil regions in the summer and fall of that year, but had not occupied room twenty-two. Herold's connection with drugs and his association with Wilkes led to the belief that both might have been involved in a plot to poison the President. The window pane and Wilkes' signature taken from the McHenry House register are now in the War Department Archives.

[20] Dr. May's statement at the time he identified Wilkes' body. War Department Archives.

[21] Letter to Nahum Capen, an extract from which is also quoted in Book One, Comment 31.

[22] Anonymous, "Edwin Booth, Life and Anecdotes of the Great Tragedian's Life Before and Behind the Footlights," New York *Dramatic Mirror*, June 24, 1893.

[23] Clara Morris-Harriott, *Life on the Stage*, McClure, Phillips and Co., New York, 1901.

[24] In the War Department Archives is an affidavit by Henry C. Higginson, who had been a prisoner at Andersonville, which discloses:

> I had frequent conversations with Ritchie, [a Confederate soldier] and he often referred to the men North who were their friends and aiding them. One day in speaking of actors in general, he particularly mentioned the name of J. Wilkes Booth. This name was mentioned off and on every day for a week or so. He made this remark: "We find in him a firm friend." Shortly after he came into the prison and spoke of the benefits the South were daily receiving from the North. Says he, "Here, Higginson, I have a letter in my pocket from as able a man as the North can produce." He took it out and showed it to me. It was dated Louisville, December, 1863. I think it was about the 12th of that month. The letter was headed "Dear Fellow," and it went on to state that a man of the name of Perkins had started down the Kanawha Valley (he named two or three little towns he had passed through down there) with a wagon load of medicine, saying that they had better send a small cavalry guard to meet him. This letter was signed "J. Wilkes". . . .

[25] Original letter in the collection of the Manuscript Division, Library of Congress, Washington, D. C.

* See Supplement II, p. 391.

† See Supplement III, p. 392.

[26] Robert Lincoln, in "Edwin Booth and Lincoln," *The Century Magazine*, April, 1909, verifies this account. Several versions of the incident, including one attributed to John T. Ford, have been published.

[27] Catherine Mary Reignolds-Winslow, *Yesterdays with Actors*, Cupples and Hurd, Boston, 1887.

[28] Lieutenant General Grant to Major General Butler, April 17, 1864:

> Until there is released to us a sufficient number of officers and men as were captured and paroled at Vicksburg and Port Hudson not another Confederate prisoner will be paroled or exchanged.

Official Records of the Union and Confederate Armies, Series 11, Vol. VII.

[29] Wilkes' business agent, J. H. Simonds, Franklin, Pa., sent the following, dated April 25, 1865, to Captain D. V. Derickson:

> In accordance with your request I am happy to give you correct information with regard to the property of J. Wilkes Booth in this section, more especially as newspaper rumor has assigned to him extensive and valuable interests here. The first time he was ever in Venango County was in January 1864 when he made a small investment in connection with two gentlemen of Cleveland in a lease on the Allegheny River directly opposite Franklin he owning an undivided third interest in the same. During the summer the lease was placed in my hands for management and at that time on the occasion of his second visit here in June last he made an investment of $1000 in a property on Pithole Creek owned by an association of gentlemen in Boston the management of whose affairs here was also placed in my hands. From neither of these interests did he ever derive a single dollar benefit. In September he made his third and last visit here during which time a purchase of the land interest in the Allegheny River property was consummated furnishing his third of the purchase money and by agreement between all the owners the conveyance was made in my name as Trustee and at my suggestion the accounts settled, and operations suspended as in my opinion, work did not promise to prove remunerative. This was no sooner consummated than he requested me to prepare deeds conveying all his title and interest in the Allegheny River property to his brother, Junius Brutus Booth, two thirds and to myself one third, and all his interest in the Pithole property to his sister, he giving as a reason that his oil speculations had proved unprofitable and he wished to dispose of every interest he had in this section as they served to draw away his mind and attention from his profession to which he intended to devote all his faculties in the future. This request I complied with and as soon as they were executed he left for New York since which time I have never seen him. Thus you will see that so far from his having realized a large fortune from Oil Speculations as rumor has averred his were a positive loss, he never having owned but two small interests and neither of these have as yet been any source of profit, although both have now become moderately valuable. This is all that he ever owned in the Venango Oil Region or was interested in, unless he has purchased since I saw him oil stocks in the cities, of which I know nothing, but my impression is that such is not the case. The stories of the newspapers of the large fortune made by him in this section were coined in the brain of some romance-writer. His whole investment in this section would not amount to more than six thousand dollars from which he never

received a dollar return. I have endeavored to make this statement as clear and concise as possible and you are at liberty to use it as you may see fit resting assured that you will be stating the truth in denying the exaggerated rumors which fill the prints with regard to his great fortune, which I have the impression will be found to be nothing more than what he has gained in his profession. . . .

War Department Archives.

[30] Letter to the present writer from Mr. George Iles who was then living in Montreal.

[31] These facts relating to the Surratts appeared in the Baltimore *Sun*, May 13, 1865.

[32] Among War Department affidavits is one by George W. Dutton, Captain of the guard conveying the Lincoln conspiracy prisoners to Fort Jefferson, Dry Tortugas Island, Florida. In it Dutton declared that Dr. Mudd admitted having gone to Washington on this date "to meet Booth by appointment, as the latter wished to be introduced to John Surratt; that when he and Booth were going to Mrs. Surratt's house to see her son, they met . . . Surratt. . . ."

[33] The excuse for his faltering and contradictory testimony is apparent in his communication to Colonel H. L. Burnett, Judge Advocate, War Department, after his arrest as a member of the Surratt household: "You confused and terrified me so . . . that I was almost unable to say anything." Wiechmann believed that he was to be hanged and he became panic-stricken.

[34] Original in the William Seymour Collection. Princeton University.

[35] It was at this time that Wilkes was supposed to have made his trip to Europe. In the *Journal de Edmond Got* (Plon-Nourrit et Cie, Paris 1910)—Got was for many years dean of the Comédie Française—is an account of Wilkes' arrival at his home in the French capital. The date of the entry is April 30, 1865, and the alleged visit is stated to have been "within three months" of that time.

G. W. Bunker, clerk at the National Hotel, Washington, presented evidence at the trial of the conspirators of Wilkes' sojourns there from November 9, 1864, until the night of the assassination, proving that the individual Got so vividly described could not have been Wilkes. No ocean liner of that era could have completed a voyage in any interval occurring in Bimker's memoranda.

[36] Samuel Bland Arnold, "Lincoln Conspiracy and the Conspirators," a series of articles in the Baltimore *American*, December, 1902.

[37] Headquarters Department of Washington, Office Provost Marshal General, Defences North of Potomac, Washington, D. C., Apr. 26th, 1864:

> I have just seen Kate Cannon at the "National." The woman brought here yesterday was probably not the one referred to—it is a girl named Lizzy Murty—Kate says—who roomed in No. 15. . . . Kate Cannon and Lizzy Murty are the genuine Secesh. . . .
> Murty on one occasion while President Lincoln was making a speech (in front of the National I believe) tried to spit upon his head —this Kate tells me and said it is well known to all in the house.
>
> C. COWLAN

War Department Archives.

[38] Samuel Bland Arnold, *op cit*.

[39] "Surratt's Story of the Booth plot," Washington *Sunday Star*, April 12, 1908. (A lecture delivered by him at Rockville, Md., December 6, 1870.)

[40] Mrs. C. C. Sniffen, then of Washington, informed the present writer: "It is not strange that writers have confused Campbell Hospital with the Soldiers' Home (a mile beyond) as both were in the suburbs and anyone would have to go out Seventh Street to reach either one." She added:

> The week of March 13, 1865, the great actors, Davenport and Wallach, played *Still Waters Run Deep* in the Washington Theatre at 11th Street near Pennsylvania Avenue, and *The National Intelligencer* on Saturday, March 18, stated that they took their company to the Campbell Hospital "yesterday afternoon for the second time" —but the paper failed to state whether or not the *first* time was the *16th*—as would seem to be indicated in Wiechmann's testimony of the supposed plans for the abduction of President Lincoln. Booth could not have expected him to be there on the *17th*, for a large gathering assembled at the National Hotel that afternoon, at which Lincoln delivered an address, and which had previously been noted in the papers. On the other hand, the President had denied himself to all visitors, because of not feeling well, for several days prior to and including the 15th, which leaves only the 16th available for his attendance. Booth himself played for the last time at a benefit of John McCullough in Ford's Theatre the night of the 18th, and, *if* Lincoln planned to go to Campbell Hospital on the 16th, Booth could have learned of it from Davenport with whom he is said to have been very intimate. I have never been able to locate any news item of his intention of attending, although it has been written in articles that he could not go and sent Secretary Chase in his stead.

[41] The initials of Thomas Brooke on a stone, which stood at the crossroads, marking a section of the land he owned.

[42] William Winter, *Life and Art of Edwin Booth*, The Macmillan Company, New York, 1893.

[43] From New York, on March 26, 1865, she wrote:

> My dear Boy:
>
> I have just got yours. I was very glad to hear from you. I hope you will write often. I did part with you sadly, and I still feel sad, very much so. June has just left me. He stayed as long as he could. I am now quite alone. Rose has not returned yet. I feel miserable enough. I never yet doubted your love and devotion to me— in fact I always gave you praise for being the fondest of all my boys, but since you leave me to grief I must doubt it. I am no Roman mother. I love my dear ones before country or anything else. Heaven guard you, is my constant prayer.
>
> Your loving mother,
> M. A. Booth

War Department Archives.

[44] Letter headed, Hookstown, Baltimore County, March 27, 1865. *The Trial of the Assassins and Conspirators*, a report of the proceedings published by T. B. Peterson & Brothers, Philadelphia, 1865.

[45] Alfred Smith, Newport, R. I., under date of April 16, 1865, informed Secretary of War Stanton:

> J. W. Booth was in this city on the 5th inst. arriving in the steamboat from New York on that morning, and going with a lady to the Aquidneck House registering his name "J. W. Booth and lady."

COMMENTS

After taking breakfast, they went out walking and were out till 2 P.M. when they returned to the hotel and requested dinner to be sent to the room for the lady, the excuse being indefinite—but before the dinner could be served, they left on the 3 p. m. train for Boston. . . .

War Department Archives.

[46] Mrs. Surratt contended she had gone there to see a Mr. Nothy who owed her some money on a note, and Wiechmann confirmed this by stating that she saw Nothy before returning to Washington. The note and the interest on it had been due for thirteen years. Efforts made by Mrs. Surratt to collect on it at this particular time turned out to be extremely unfortunate for her.

[47] Wilkes' exact words as stated by Herold to his counsel, Frederick Stone. This, and evidence relating to Paine, points to the probability that both men were with Wilkes at the time.

COMMENTS
BOOK FOUR

[1] No sooner had James Ford sent an announcement to the afternoon papers that Lincoln and Grant were to be present, than stage manager J. B. Wright rushed to the printing shop of H. Polkinton, had him stop the press, and insert in the program a verse of a patriotic song to be sung by the company that evening. Not many of the first lot had been printed before the change was made, but they were added to the number distributed at the theatre, and account for the variation in the programs.

[2] Search began for O'Laughlin and Arnold on Saturday (which verified Arnold's fear that detectives had been trailing them), but they were not found and arrested until three days after the assassination. At the trial of the conspirators they were given life terms and sent to the Federal prison at Fort Jefferson on Dry Tortugas Island, Florida, where O'Laughlin died of yellow fever. On March 21, 1869, Arnold was released through a pardon granted by President Johnson.

Although thirteen persons swore they saw Surratt in Washington on April fourteenth, he contended he was in Elmira, New York. Immediately after the assassination he fled from the United States to Canada, was concealed there by Catholic priests for nearly five months, then went on to London and finally to Rome. In that city he enlisted in the Pope's Zouaves under the name of John Watson. A Baltimore acquaintance recognized him and informed the authorities of his whereabouts. He was taken into custody, but managed to escape. After being recaptured in Alexandria, Egypt, he was brought back to the United States for trial as one of Lincoln's assassins. Two months of effort to convict him ended when the jury disagreed, and his case was dropped. His alibi of having been in Elmira at the time of the crime did not convince the jury that he was not in Washington. They entirely agreed that, had he been indicted for conspiracy instead of murder, he would have been convicted upon their retirement.

[3] "He [Wilkes] then told me to go to the Kirkwood [House] and get a pass from Vice-President Johnson. He said he would be there with a man to recommend me. . . ."

Unpublished affidavit of Atzerodt, April 25, 1865, War Department Archives.

[4] Spangler was accused by the government of having done all this, but conclusive evidence was lacking. With the exception of the one damaged lock on the inner door, which a Ford employee had broken previously, the mystery was never solved.

[5] Mr. Matthew Page Andrews, the historian, under the title, "Lincoln's Neglected Friends," (Baltimore *Sun*, February 9, 1930) gives an account of the little-known General James Washington Singleton, closely associated with Lincoln in reference to the President's restoration policy. Through the courtesy of Mr. Andrews who forwarded extracts from his correspondence with Mrs. Lily Singleton Osburn (General Singleton's daughter), the present writer obtained confirmation that her father's unexpected call was responsible for Lincoln's delay in leaving the White House, a fact heretofore overlooked by other historians.

COMMENTS

[6] Lincoln had invited Lieutenant General and Mrs. Grant to be his guests at Ford's Theatre, and Grant had accepted provided they remained in the Capital overnight. He told Lincoln they wished to visit their children, who were in school at Burlington, New Jersey, if he found he could get away during the afternoon. This excuse was merely an evasion. The social feud existing between Mrs. Grant and Mrs. Lincoln was responsible for the regrets sent to the White House and the departure of the Grants from the city at six o'clock that evening. Grant delayed sending the message, hoping Lincoln himself, upon the advice of others, would decide not to attend the theatre on such a rowdy night in the Capital and thereby make it unnecessary for him to decline the invitation. Their places were filled by Major Rathbone and the daughter of a New York senator, Miss Clara Harris, who was Rathbone's stepsister and fiancée.

[7] Lloyd was arrested but eventually released as a witness for the government. In an effort to escape the gallows and to account for the confusion of his statements when questioned, he claimed he was drunk that afternoon. He was sober enough, though, to notice a broken spring on the carriage hired by Mrs. Surratt and to place himself directly back of the horse's heels to fix it. This and other facts have been overlooked by writers seeking to absolve Mrs. Surratt in contending that Lloyd's drunken condition disqualified him as a witness.

[8] Mrs. Surratt told Wiechmann that she had received another letter in regard to the money due her from Nothy and must see him. On the way to Lloyd's tavern the carriage was halted about three miles out of Washington while she obtained the information about the pickets.

Without seeing Nothy, Mrs. Surratt (and Wiechmann) returned to Washington, reaching home shortly before 9 P.M. This gave Mrs. Surratt an opportunity to see that the pickets had been withdrawn and report it to Wilkes. On their return trip from Lloyd's, Mrs. Surratt told Wiechmann she expected a caller. While Wiechmann was eating his supper, the doorbell rang. It was answered by Mrs. Surratt; someone came into the parlor, but went out again almost immediately. Wiechmann contended it was Wilkes making his third and last call. His assertion regarding this final visit was corroborated by what occurred later that night. When detectives arrived to search the Surratt house in quest of Wilkes and John Surratt (confirming the latter's belief that the government was suspicious of them), those living there were gathered together in the parlor and told of Lincoln's assassination. As Wilkes' name was mentioned, Anna Surratt sobbed, "Oh, Ma, all this will bring suspicion on our house; just think of that man [Wilkes] having been here an hour before the murder." There could be no other purpose for Wilkes' appointment with Mrs. Surratt than to obtain information she had gotten for him of the roads leading into southern Maryland.

That Wilkes might have inveigled her into assisting him under the pretext of abducting Lincoln should be considered, but no halo of total guiltlessness can ever crown her name. Although she swore she knew nothing of any plot against the President, less than a minute had passed from the time of the crime until Wilkes was dashing toward the road leading to Lloyd's tavern where she had carried out his instructions that afternoon.

[9] It is amazing that Spangler's defense did not call attention to this fact when he was accused of having been assigned by Wilkes to turn off the gas inside the theatre immediately after the murder.

[10] J. E. Buckingham, *Reminiscences and Souvenirs of the Assassination of Abraham Lincoln*, Rufus H. Darby, Washington, 1894.

[11] That he was certain to have a divided interest in the play seems to have been ignored, or never thought of, by Parker's superiors. Long before that April evening he had been in trouble at headquarters. Complaints against him for conduct unbecoming an officer, sleeping on his beat, willful violation of the rules and regulations, and similar offenses began in October, 1862, and did not end until August, 1868, when he was finally dismissed from the force. Accounts of his whereabouts that Good Friday night differ, and the *Specification* in the charges later brought against him, for which he was never punished, merely states that he "allowed a man to enter the President's private box and shoot the President."

Stanley Kimmel, "Fatal Remissness of Lincoln's Guard Unpunished," Washington *Sunday Star*, Feb. 9, 1936. This was the first account of Parker's record to be published.

[12] In the notebook of army surgeon Charles Sabin Taft, who was present at Lincoln's assassination, death, and autopsy, 10:30 P.M. is given as the time the President was murdered.

"Abraham Lincoln's Last Hours," *The Century Magazine*, February, 1893.

[13] Mr. Otto Eisenschiml (*Why Was Lincoln Murdered?*, Little, Brown and Company, Boston, 1937) quotes the affidavit of Lincoln's attendant, Charles Forbes, made in September, 1892, in which Forbes declared he was in the President's box when Wilkes "fired his fatal shot." This statement twenty-seven years after the event should not be taken seriously, for the affidavit of Lincoln's coachman, Francis Burns, made at the time of the assassination, refutes another assertion by Forbes in the above document that the coachman made two trips from the White House that evening; first with Mrs. Lincoln and their guests, and second with the President alone. In fact all other accounts describe the President as having arrived with his guests.

[14] An affidavit in the War Department Archives discloses that a Will T. Kent picked up the pistol which L. A. Gobright, Washington telegraphic correspondent of the Associated Press, turned over to the police.

[15] This incident is so described in Herold's unpublished affidavit in which he quotes Wilkes. War Department Archives.

[16] Lincoln's position in the box made him visible to only a few persons in the audience, but actor W. J. Ferguson in *I Saw Booth Shoot Lincoln* (Houghton Mifflin Co., Boston, 1930) wrote that the President *could not be seen by anyone in the audience* as the box was in reality on the stage and in front of the orchestra pit giving a view of its occupants only to actors on the stage, or at the wings of the left side. Affidavits of several persons, however, who were seated in the audience far down on the left side make it apparent that the presidential party was not so isolated as Ferguson would have his readers believe. It was to his advantage in telling his story to place the President in view of no one but himself at the moment of the assassination. Since he was standing in the wings on the left side of the stage near Laura Keene, he, of course, was the only person looking directly up at the box when the shot was fired. However, at the trial of the conspirators, restaurant owner James P. Ferguson testified that Harry Ford (who knew the theatre from top to bottom) had helped him "select one of the best seats from which to observe the occupants of the presidential box" and that he (restaurant owner Ferguson) had seen "the flash of the pistol in the box." This was one of several similar statements accepted by Federal authorities without contradiction.

COMMENTS

[17] In Washington two flags are displayed as having tripped Wilkes. One is the Stars and Stripes, the other, the Treasury Guard Flag. When members of the court trying the conspirators visited Ford's Theatre "for the purpose of examining the premises and the localities adjacent figuring in the evidence concerning the assassination," the box occupied by the President was decorated with the picture of Washington and some of the flags which had been used that night, "but not the Treasury Guard Flag, which caught Booth's spur on the occasion." Washington *Evening Star*, May 16, 1865.

[18] Many in the audience were in a quandary as to the identity of the assassin. When L. A. Gobright, of the Associated Press, reached the theatre at five minutes before eleven o'clock, he heard some people assert that the man who jumped from the President's box and crossed the stage was John Wilkes Booth, while others contended the murderer differed in appearance from the actor accused of the crime. So far as Gobright could ascertain there did not seem to be any certainty, and he was not thoroughly satisfied in his own mind that night as to who was the assassin. As late as April twenty-second, the New York *Clipper* published: "Up to the time of going to press, J. Wilkes Booth, the alleged murderer, we are sorry to say, has not yet been arrested. We look upon it as additional and *prima facie* evidence of his guilt that he has not given himself up."

The delay in most reports of the assassination reaching other cities was caused by the grounding of telegraph wires which, fifteen minutes after the murder, severed Washington from all outside communication except a secret government connection with Old Point. It is probable that John Surratt managed this interruption. Among the known conspirators, only he would have been intelligent enough to have given such assistance to the fleeing criminals, and only he would have had rebel accomplices capable of following his directions if he were absent. It was Surratt who commented upon the stupidity of Federal detectives and hinted that he had been responsible for more sabotage than they knew. When wires were again in operation two hours later, it was the first time in history that the telegraph had been called upon to spread the news of such a tragedy throughout the world.

[19] John Creahan, *The Life of Laura Keene*, Rodgers Publishing Company, Philadelphia, 1897.

[20] An official report stated that the passageway behind the scenes through which Wilkes escaped was "remarkably clear." Spangler was also accused of having attended to this matter. Such evidence resulted in a prison sentence of six years. He was sent to Dry Tortugas Island, but did not serve the complete term. On the date (March 21, 1869) that Arnold was released, Spangler also gained his freedom by a pardon from President Johnson. This information is given in the descriptive book of Dry Tortugas Island prisoners. The book is now in the National Archives, Washington, D. C.

[21] A denunciation of him in an unidentified newspaper clipping of 1878 reads: "There is a gigantic pettifogging lawyer in Washington named J. B. Stewart. Every few weeks he turns up somewhere in a row with somebody, and whenever he does the statement is always made in the newspapers that he is the heroic person who chased Wilkes Booth through Ford's theatre on the night of Lincoln's assassination and came near capturing him. Of course, he is a fraud. He was in the theatre on the night of Booth's crime and tore around considerably, but the story about his having caught Booth's horse and having been knocked on the tender sconce by Booth's whip handle is a fraud. . . .

"It is not probable that a man of giant frame, with all his limbs intact, should pursue another much smaller with a broken leg and not catch him, especially when he was so close upon him, and the painfully crippled man had a horse to mount. . . .

"Newspapers partial to the cause of Truth will hereafter refrain from advertising Mr. Stewart as a loyal hero of the Lincoln assassination."

[22] John T. Ford said Wilkes often introduced the most extraordinary and outrageous leaps into his productions, one occurring in the Witch Scene of *Macbeth* when Wilkes jumped from a rock higher than any box in Ford's Theatre, and made the leap to the stage with apparent ease. Ford added the Baltimore *Sun* had condemned this by "styling him a gymnastic actor."

[23] It is doubtful that Wilkes had any confidence in Atzerodt or believed he would carry out the part assigned to him.

The items found in Atzerodt's room at the Kirkwood House were probably planted there for the purpose of connecting Atzerodt's name (in case he failed to act) with those of the conspirators on the document Wilkes had given Matthews to be published in the *Daily National Intelligencer*.

About two o'clock on the morning following the assassination, Atzerodt appeared at the Pennsylvania House and engaged a room. He left before daylight to avoid paying the bill. By Sunday, he had reached Barnesville, Maryland, twenty-two miles from Washington. There he was reported to have been asked if he thought Grant had been assassinated, and to have replied, "No, I do not suppose he was. If he had been killed, it would have been done probably by a man that got on the same train of cars that he did." John Surratt's name has been linked with this intimation, too. At the home of Hartman Richter, a cousin, Atzerodt was arrested at four o'clock on the morning of April twentieth. The prediction Wilkes made turned out to be correct. On the sunny afternoon of July 7, 1865, Atzerodt was one of four to be hanged.

[24] Herold's flight left Paine without a guide. Two bridges crossed the Eastern Branch, the Navy Yard Bridge and Bennings Bridge, about a half a mile apart. Unacquainted with the streets leading to each, Paine, while trying to find the road to southern Maryland, was thrown from his horse and left to wander on foot about the wooded entrenchments of Washington. That night he slept in a tree. At one o'clock on the following morning his horse was captured by a hospital sentinel some distance southeast of the Capitol. It was lame from having tripped and was blind in one eye. Sweat was pouring from it, as if it had been ridden at a fast pace. This was the horse Wilkes had purchased from Dr. Mudd's neighbor, George Gardiner.

Shortly before midnight on April seventeenth, Paine returned to the home of Mrs. Surratt as she and several members of her household were being taken to prison. With the sleeve of an undershirt covering his head and a pick over his shoulder he answered questions of Federal officers as to his identity and reason for calling at that hour by saying he was a poor laborer who had come to dig a ditch for Mrs. Surratt—which proved to be metaphorically true. When she went to the gallows on the afternoon of July 7, 1865, Paine went with her.

[25] In pursuit of Herold, Fletcher had taken a course along Pennsylvania Avenue to Thirteenth Street, up Thirteenth to E, along E to Ninth, and down Ninth to Pennsylvania Avenue. From that point, he had gone in the direction of the Capitol, for he believed Herold might ride out that way to meet Atzerodt, who would take the Navy Yard Bridge road to his home in Port Tobacco.

At the moment Wilkes escaped from Ford's Theatre, Fletcher was riding along

COMMENTS

Pennsylvania Avenue between Ninth Street and the Capitol. Had Wilkes gone from F street directly down Ninth and turned into Pennsylvania Avenue, the route most historians have accepted, he would have passed Fletcher. The fact that Fletcher saw no fleeing horseman on lower Pennsylvania Avenue, nor was told of one by people whom he questioned, is conclusive that neither Wilkes nor Herold galloped out Pennsylvania Avenue toward the Capitol. Nor would they have taken the street fronting the Capitol, as it not only led past an imposing prison but also over a steep hill which would have tired their horses at the outset and slackened their pace.

Fletcher's account authenticates the portion of the accepted route after passing the Capitol on the southeast side and continuing to the Navy Yard Bridge by way of Pennsylvania Avenue and Eleventh Street. When he reached this section of the city, he met an acquaintance and inquired if he had seen a horseman galloping by that way. Informed that two men had just passed on horseback, Fletcher, presuming the two men to be Herold and Atzerodt, rushed on to the Navy Yard Bridge.

Stanley Kimmel, "New Evidence Challenges Story of Booth Flight," Washington *Sunday Star,* April 12, 1936.

[26] When Fletcher rode up, he was told by the sentinel of the two horsemen having passed at intervals a few minutes earlier, and that he would be permitted to follow them but refused a right-of-way over the bridge should he return that night. Fletcher then started back to Naylor's stable. Before he reached there he heard of Lincoln's assassination and went to General Augur's headquarters to report the facts he had learned at the bridge. However, his statements were disregarded, and no effort was made to follow his clues until many hours later. This delay enabled Wilkes and Herold to get far beyond the reach of men sent in pursuit of them Saturday. The failure to question Cobb immediately after the crime is as perplexing as the failure to question Parker. The former can only be explained by Colonel Baker's statement that the name Booth, having been given to Cobb, resulted in the authorities' belief that it was a ruse to put them on the wrong trail in pursuing the assassin of Lincoln.

Stanley Kimmel, "New Evidence Challenges Story of Booth Flight," Washington *Sunday Star,* April 12, 1936.

[27] Fate was against Dr. Mudd. Had Wilkes not injured his leg, Dr. Mudd probably would never have been brought to trial. He was given a life sentence and was taken to the Dry Tortugas Island prison. The affidavit of Captain George W. Dutton, War Department Archives, states that Dr. Mudd, on his voyage there, "confessed that he knew Booth when he came to his house with Herold, on the morning after the assassination of the President; that he had known Booth for some time, but was afraid to tell of his having been at his house on the 15th of April, fearing that his own and the lives of his family would be endangered thereby."

Dr. Mudd's efforts accomplished much in stamping out yellow fever on the island. He, too, was pardoned by President Johnson, and upon his release, March 9, 1869, returned to his Maryland home.

[28] This boot was cast aside and later discovered by a Federal officer.

[29] "His friend urged me to attend to his leg as soon as possible, as they were very anxious to get to Washington," Dr. Mudd stated to a Federal officer, "and then, it is my impression, he inquired if they could reach some point on the Potomac, where they could get a boat to Washington." This was a bad alibi for Dr. Mudd, since Dr. Richard H. Stewart, who lived on the other side of the

Potomac, was questioned regarding the fugitives and, in an unpublished affidavit now in the War Department Archives, swore that "Dr. Mudd had recommended them to me."

[30] That day, the baggage Wilkes had left behind him at the National Hotel was examined, and in a trunk were found a colonel's military dress coat, two pairs of handcuffs, two boxes of cartridges, a gimlet, a secret cipher of the Confederacy, and a package of letters, among which was the one signed *Sam*. This was the letter from Arnold that Wilkes had promised to destroy. The row between them at the Gotier restaurant meeting was probably responsible for Wilkes having left this incriminating evidence.

[31] Although Colonel L. C. Baker has been given credit for originating the idea of placing photographs of criminals beside printed descriptions of them on bills to be posted in public places, he was acting upon the suggestion of two Philadelphians, as disclosed in the War Department Archives. About a week after the distribution of handbills describing and offering rewards for Wilkes and the unknown who had attempted to assassinate Seward, Baker began sending men out to tack up these additional posters. Since a photograph of Wilkes was on them, any deliberate substitution of his likeness by authorities at the conspiracy trial, or elsewhere, would have been inconsistent.

[32] Unpublished affidavit of Oswald Swan, War Department Archives.

[33] Mary Swan, one of Cox's ex-slaves, swore (in an unpublished affidavit, War Department Archives) that three men came to the house on Easter Saturday night, but she did not know who they were; the people had all gone to bed when someone rapped, and Captain Cox got up, put on his pants, and went to the door; she looked out of the window and saw the forms of three men in the yard, one standing with a cane in his left hand; Cox refused to let them come into the house, as they were strangers to him; she did not see any horses; it was almost daylight before they went away; no one got them anything to eat or drink that she knew of; the next night some persons came and stayed until morning.

When the present writer interviewed her she was known as Old Aunt Mary Kelly. Although it was pointed out that the statement she made as a girl was not quite in agreement with the facts later established, she insisted she had told nothing but the truth. "I's sho' saved Massa Cox's life," she said. "Ef I's hadden tol' what I's tol' Massa Cox wud hab been hung; yessah, he sho wud hab been hung."

[34] The most probable of many stories regarding this incident was recently sent to the present writer by Mrs. Margaret C. Powers, of Stafford, Virginia:

"The man who disposed of the horses was Mr. Franklin Robey. He told my father many years after the war, when he was a near neighbor, just how he did it, and the facts as I recall them are as follows:

"There was a spot in the marsh where a limb of a large tree extended out over the water, deep enough to cover the horses after they were shot. He rode one horse and led the other out as far as he could in the water, climbed on the limb, and shot them. They sank out of sight, and I'm sure few ever knew what became of them. Mr. Robey, in my father's opinion, was a man of integrity, and thoroughly reliable, and there was never a doubt in our minds as to his story. Only a short time before my father's death, in 1932, at the age of eighty-five, we were discussing the book by Jones, and he remarked that he regretted so much that Jones had not known at the time he wrote the book what became of the horses."

³⁵ Later in life Jones remarked that he never once thought of taking the money, as his "sympathies were enlisted for the pale-faced young man so ardent to get to Virginia and have the comforts of a doctor." Evidently Wilkes told him that Dr. Mudd had recommended Dr. Stewart.

³⁶ Given by Jones in his account as the period in which he took care of Wilkes and Herold.

³⁷ Some newspapers reported defamations against the martyred President and listed the punishment given offenders. Up in Swampscott, Mass., George Stone said the assassination of Lincoln was the best news he had heard in four years. He was tarred and feathered and dragged through the town with an American flag in his hand.

A Westminster, Maryland, newspaper had a vituperative article about Lincoln in an issue just before the assassination, and when his death was reported a mob stormed its office, smashed the presses, and burned the contents of the building. A Baltimore photographer's gallery was wrecked by a rabid crowd when the rumor spread that it contained negatives of John Wilkes Booth.

In Cleveland, Ohio, J. J. Husband, a prominent architect, got hilarious when he heard of the assassination and yelled at a group of Unionists, "You've had your day of rejoicing, now I'll have mine!" After a terrific beating he was told to get out of the city and never return unless he wished to die suddenly and violently. His name was scraped from the courthouse stone which listed him as the architect, and the Unionists went in search of another son of Ohio who had said it was too bad Lincoln had not been killed when he was first elected president. This man also was severely beaten, but escaped and took refuge in a jail.

At Shelton, Vermont, a preacher delivered a long eulogy on Lincoln to a congregation which included an old Copperhead. After listening for some time, the old Copperhead got up and started for the door of the church. When he was about to open it and step out, the preacher shouted, "Don't you stop, brother, 'till you get to Canada!" and the congregation cried, "Amen!"

In Canada the rebels were celebrating, and the Toronto *Globe* felt called upon to say, "It caused a thrill of horror in this city when it was made known that Southern refugees assembled in our chief hotel, as soon as the deed was known early on Saturday morning, and entered upon a noisy debauch in honor of the event; and a clergyman among them said publicly at the breakfast table at the same hotel that 'Lincoln had only gone to hell a little before his time.'" *

³⁸ References to newspaper reports of his crime, et cetera, refute its having been written on the dates given. The original diary is now in the War Department Archives.

³⁹ Unpublished affidavits of Henry Woodland, War Department Archives.

⁴⁰ Federal officers obtained enough incriminating evidence to involve both Cox and Jones. The two were arrested but after several weeks' imprisonment, during which time they divulged nothing, they were released.

⁴¹ This date is as misleading as those above the first part of Wilkes' diary. (See page 234 and Comment 38). No attempt was made to cross the Potomac River until Friday night, April twenty-first.

⁴² Not knowing that Matthews had destroyed the letter left in his care, Wilkes supposed the government had suppressed its publication, and he had the crazy notion that he could return to Washington and clear his name.

⁴³ Federal officers located the satchel and found Mrs. Quesenberry's initials inside it. She was taken to Washington on the steamer *John S. Ide*, but nothing was

*See Supplement IV, p. 394.

proved against her and she was released. On board were a number of others charged with aiding the fugitives, and the boat in which Wilkes and Herold had crossed the Potomac. A newspaper reporter described it as a small bateau in a very dilapidated condition that looked as though it would not bear up under even a slight gale, the oars appearing to have been made of several distinct pieces of wood. Upon arrival in Washington, relic hunters were so active in chipping off pieces from the seats and other portions of the boat that officials were forced to have it locked in a shed on the wharf to prevent it from being torn to pieces.

[44] Unpublished affidavit of William L. Bryant. War Department Archives.

[45] That evening Lucas gave the note (War Department Archives) and money to Mrs. Stewart, as the doctor was not at home. When the doctor returned he read this message:

> Dear Sir:
>
> Forgive me, but I have some pride. I hate to blame you for your want of hospitality; you know your own affairs. I was sick and tired, with a broken leg, in need of medical advice. I would not have turned a dog from my door in such a condition.
>
> However, you were kind enough to give me something to eat, for which I not only thank you, but, on account of the reluctant manner in which it was bestowed, I feel bound to pay for it.
>
> It is not the substance but the manner in which kindness is extended that makes one happy in the acceptance thereof. The sauce to meat is ceremony; meeting were bare without it.
>
> Be kind enough to accept the enclosed two dollars and a half (though hard to spare) for what we have received.
>
> Yours respectfully,
> STRANGER.

April 24, 1865.

Judge Holt's description (in 1867) of Wilkes' diary indicates Wilkes rewrote this page from the original, and changed the sum from five, to two-and-one-half dollars.

The doctor was about to destroy the note but someone suggested that it might prove useful as evidence of his unfriendly attitude toward the fugitives, should he be questioned. Mrs. Stewart, however, tore his name off one corner. No doubt its contents aided him in obtaining his release after he was arrested and taken to Washington for questioning. Bryant and other rebels from that vicinity were also taken into custody but later discharged. Bryant's affidavit and that of Dr. Stewart were not helpful to Dr. Mudd.

[46] Unpublished affidavit of Willie S. Jett, May 6, 1865, War Department Archives. In a lengthy footnote to Ruggles' *Narrative* ("Pursuit and Death of John Wilkes Booth," *The Century Magazine*, January, 1890) Bainbridge stated that the initials were on Wilkes' right hand.

[47] As stated in the letter of Miss L. K. B. Holloway entitled, "The Capture and Death of John Wilkes Booth," Confederate Museum, Richmond, Virginia.

[48] Among sources which might have led to the capture of the fugitives was the report that Major James O'Beirne gave to Captain S. H. Beckwith at Port Tobacco, who, in turn, telegraphed to Washington that two men had crossed the Potomac River. Although these men proved to be laborers from a nearby farm, and their crossing not identical in time nor place with that of the fugitives, it unwittingly pointed out the direction taken by Wilkes and Herold.

COMMENTS

The admission by the frightened Colonel Hughes who immediately told officials in Port Tobacco that the fugitives had stopped near his house in a boat earlier in the day might also have put Baker on the right trail.

[49] The elder Garrett in a letter dated April 2, 1872, to the editor of the New York *Herald*, refers to these two sons as John M. and William H.

In an interview reported in the New York *Times*, April 29, 1865, Lieutenant Baker stated that both of the older Garrett sons were dressed in Confederate uniforms on the night Wilkes and Herold were captured at the Garrett farm.

[50] So described by Garrett's sister-in-law, Lucinda Holloway, in the letter mentioned in Comment 47.

[51] Had there been another unfastened door in the rear, as some writers have contended, it would have been useless to lock this door. About forty persons (exclusive of Rollins whom Doherty had sent to Port Conway to get his boats ready for the detachment's recrossing of the Rappahannock River) were at Garrett's when Wilkes and Herold were captured, yet no one at the time reported the tobacco barn as having a rear door through which Wilkes could have escaped, leaving a man in his place to pay for his crime. The Garretts always ridiculed this story, calling attention to the fact that they sheltered Wilkes for several days and knew that he was the same man taken from the barn to their porch where he died.

[52] Doherty, in his account of events at Bowling Green, also claimed that he was inside the hotel when the demand was made for Jett, and that he was the officer who took charge of the occupants. The rivalry between these officers from the moment they left Washington until the final payment of the reward offered for the capture of the fugitives make their statements regarding the part each one took in the round-up a confused mass of contradictory testimony.

[53] Thomas P. Corbett was born in England. After coming to the United States, he learned the hatter's trade, married, and lived in New York City. At the birth of their first child, his wife died, and he became despondent. Seeking to drown his sorrow in liquor, he lost his job, wandered aimlessly until he staggered into a Boston Salvation Army meeting, and was inducted into religion. This led to his baptism, after which he "declared that Christ, when he called his disciples, gave them names, and that his name henceforth should be Boston Corbett." (B. B. Johnson, *Abraham Lincoln and Boston Corbett*, Waltham, Mass., 1914.)

His evangelical inclinations prompted him to conduct religious services in the North Shore community. A long prayer one night attracted two sisters of the street who stopped for the sole purpose of enticing him to their quarters. Their solicitations so affected him that, in a deranged manifestation of fervid retribution, he suffered self-castration and was sent to a Massachusetts hospital.

He joined the Union army early in the war, enlisting as a private, and got into considerable trouble through his religious bigotry and assertions.

[54] Following events at Garrett's farm, Ruggles and Bainbridge lost no time in getting to their homes as they had heard they were to be arrested, tried, and hanged for aiding the fugitives. This merely delayed their capture, and about ten days later they were taken into custody by a squad of United States cavalry and hustled off to the Old Capitol Prison at Washington. "We were not alone in our misery, however," wrote Ruggles, "for Dr. Stewart . . . William Lucas . . . and a number of others, were there, among them being Jett, who had escaped from Captain Doherty, and had been recaptured at his home in Westmoreland County."

"Pursuit and Death of John Wilkes Booth," *The Century Magazine*, January, 1890.

[55] The report now on file at the medical museum, contributed by Surgeon General Barnes, states that Wilkes was killed by a conoidal pistol ball which "entered the right side, comminuting the base of the right lamina of the fourth vertebra, fracturing it longitudinally and separating it from the spinous process, at the same time fracturing the fifth through its pedicle and involving that transverse process. The missile passed directly through the canal with a *slight inclination downward* and to the rear, emerging through the left bases of the fourth and fifth laminae, which are comminuted, and from which fragments were embedded in the muscles of the neck. The bullet in its course avoided the large cervical vessels." The word *carbine* in the line "a conoidal carbine ball entered the right side" is crossed out and the word *pistol* written above it, but on the index card following it the words "carbine bullet" have been copied without alteration. Other memoranda in the United States Army Medical Museum at Washington are also indefinite.

[56] The statement that the shot which killed Lincoln was the same in character as that which killed Wilkes is disproved by the copy of assistant surgeon Dr. J. J. Woodward's Autopsy on Lincoln at the Army Medical Museum.

[57] The United States Government refused to pay Garrett for the loss of his tobacco barn but Edwin Booth later sent him money to rebuild it.

[58] Doherty maintained that he had placed Corbett "at a large crack in the side of the barn, and he, seeing by the igniting hay that Booth was leveling his carbine at either Herold or myself, fired to disable him in the arm, but Booth, making a sudden move, the aim erred, and the bullet struck Booth in the back of the head. . . ." Corbett subsequently declared, "When the fire was lighted, which was almost immediately after Herold had been taken out of the barn, he [Wilkes] started at first towards me, and I had a full front dress view of him. I could have shot him much easier then than at the time I did, but as long as he made no demonstration I did not shoot him. I kept my eye on him steadily; he turned towards the other side; he brought his piece up to an aim and I supposed was going to fight his way out; I thought the time had come and I took a steady aim upon him and shot him. . . ."

Years later Robert Garrett told of being awakened that morning by the light of the burning barn flaring at his bedroom window, and rushing downstairs with his pants on backward. But when he reached the yard nobody paid any attention to him because he was so small a child. "I was standing within six feet of Corbett when he fired the shot, and Booth never made a motion to shoot," said Robert. Of all persons there, he turned out to be the only one who made any claim of actually having seen Corbett fire into the tobacco barn. This was an illusion of Robert's youth, for the sight of Corbett's aim made the boy believe Corbett had fired the shot he heard.

Baker admitted that, when he heard the shot and saw Wilkes fall in the burning barn, he thought Conger had shot him, but after Conger's denial "the idea flashed on my mind that, if he did, it had better not be known." At that moment however, Conger was in no position to have fired the fatal shot. Baker's position also eliminates any possibility that he could have fired the shot, and the absurdity of contending he did so after opening the barn door is apparent when one realizes Wilkes would not have permitted any officer or soldier to enter. Had Baker rushed in, Wilkes would have shot him.

The distance between Corbett and Wilkes was reported to have been not over eight or ten yards when Corbett fired. Doherty said Corbett used a

COMMENTS   365

carbine. There was no testimony at any trial as to the condition of the pistol Baker admitted taking from Wilkes' clenched hand when they reached him inside the tobacco barn. J. M. Barron, who had been an intimate friend of Wilkes, did not believe that Corbett killed him. "I can but feel certain that the misguided erratic young man ended his life with his own hands . . ." wrote Barron (May Manuscript, Municipal Museum, Baltimore). "The hole in Booth's head was made by a small pistol shot. Had Corbett shot him with the large slug of an Enfield or Springfield rifle, his head would have been blown off, or nearly so."

Ruggles' conclusion was similar: "Knowing the barn well and judging from all the circumstances connected with the burning of it, I feel convinced that Sergeant Boston Corbett has a reputation undeserved as the slayer of Mr. Lincoln's assassin. From the spot where Sergeant Boston Corbett was, he could not have seen Booth where he stood and certainly could not have been able to shoot him in the back of the head. Having asked Captain Doherty to fall back fifty paces with his men and give him a chance to come out, and very properly and naturally being refused his request by that gallant officer, deserted by Herold, the barn on fire, and seeing that he must perish in the flames or be taken to Washington and hanged, Booth, hopeless, alone, and at bay, placed his pistol to the back of his head and took his own life. No man saw Corbett fire, and one chamber of Booth's revolver held in his hand was empty; and I am by no means alone in the belief that he killed himself." ("Pursuit and Death of John Wilkes Booth," *The Century Magazine*, January, 1890.).

No member of the 16th New York Cavalry believed Corbett shot Wilkes. Upon arrival in Washington, the men drove him out of the company's quarters, crying, "Liar! Liar!" Their refusal to let him remain in the barracks that night forced him to take refuge with the animals and sleep in a horse stall. Others who knew him said "he was crazier than Wilkes Booth and might have killed Lincoln had his mind happened to turn that way."

The direction taken by the bullet indicated the pistol was held higher than the wound; hence, the shot could not have been fired by anyone in direct line with Wilkes, as was Corbett, but the wound could have been made by holding the pistol above the spot and shooting downward.

[59] When Corbett was brought before Stanton on a charge of having disobeyed orders in shooting Wilkes, the Secretary of War quickly disposed of the matter by saying, "The rebel is dead—the patriot lives—he has saved us continued excitement, delay and expense—the patriot is released."

[60] Wilkes' question probably referred only to Jett's return with the detachment, but the accusation that Jett wired authorities in Washington directing soldiers to that community flared up at intervals and resulted in Jett being outlawed by family, friends, and Mrs. Goldman's daughter, to whom he was engaged. He finally left the neighborhood, but the thought that he had been responsible for the arrest of several members of the Garrett family and for pecuniary loss to the old man haunted him, and he spent his last days in an asylum, muttering, "Oh, Mr. Garrett, forgive me for having done you so much wrong." (Charles L. Shipley, "Thirty Years Ago," *Maryland Journal*, Towson, Md., April 20, 1895.).

[61] A wound of the spinal cord, such as Wilkes had, would produce complete paralysis of the arms, legs, and lower portion of the trunk, while respiration and the action of the heart would continue, as the nerves which proceed to those

organs pass off from the cranium and not from the spinal cord. An uninjured brain left his mind active in a dead, helpless body, subjected to the most excruciating and agonizing pain.

[62] Wilkes' weapons, a number of small items, five daguerreotypes, his dairy, money and Canadian bill of exchange, were taken from him by Conger and Baker. They did not know of the field glass which Wilkes had left in the house, but Baker returned later and found it at the home of Garrett's daughter where one of the family had taken it.

Although George Alfred Townsend mentioned the diary in the New York *World* following Wilkes' capture, officials in Washington withheld knowledge of its contents until 1867 when a controversy arose over its mysterious disappearance and supposed spoliation, some eighteen pages having been deleted. The reason for its suppression following Wilkes' death appears to have been his having taken full blame for his act at the time when Federal authorities were endeavoring to incriminate well-known rebels in the assassination plot. The diary was first published by the Washington *Daily Morning Chronicle*, May 22, 1867.

Concealed with the diary were the daguerreotypes, four of which were of actresses easily identified as Fanny Brown, Effie Germon, Alice Grey, and Helen Western. The fifth, however, has always been labeled a "Washington Society Woman" and her identity has never been divulged. On the back of it is written in fastly fading pencil marks, "John F. Coyle's daughter—Rough guess Anna Coyle." Recently the present writer found among the effects of Mr. William Seymour, the well-known actor-manager, long associated with Edwin Booth, a note in Mr. Seymour's handwriting which unquestionably identifies the photograph as that of Bessie Hale, to whom Wilkes was engaged.

In the account mentioned above, Townsend also stated the sum taken from Wilkes was "one hundred and seventy-five dollars in greenbacks!" Herold (affidavit, War Department Archives) and Ruggles (*Century Magazine*, January, 1890) gave smaller amounts. Officials failed to include in any report the cash found on Wilkes and the Garretts believed that, knowing escape was impossible, he threw the money in the fire.

[63] In 1887 Dr. May wrote his article entitled "The Mark of the Scalpel" (Manuscript Division, Library of Congress), in which he stated that Wilkes' right leg was the one fractured. This has been cited as proof that it was not Wilkes' body lying on the *Montauk*. Dr. May's blunder can be excused as he was recounting his observations twenty-two years after the event.

Another who identified Wilkes' remains on board the *Montauk* was Charles Dawson, clerk of the National Hotel, who stated: "I distinctly recognize it as the body of J. Wilkes Booth—first, from the general appearance; next, from the India-ink letters, J. W. B., on his wrist, which I have very frequently noticed; and then by a scar on the neck. I also recognize the vest as that of J. Wilkes Booth." His affidavit ends with:

"Q. On which hand or wrist are the India-ink initials referred to?"
"A. On the left."
War Department Archives.

[64] The Surgeon General cut out a part of Wilkes' head and neck through which the bullet had passed and removed the third, fourth, and fifth cervical vertebrae, and a portion of the spinal cord from the cervical region. These specimens are now in glass bottles marked *J. W. B.* in the Army Medical Museum at Washington. There are no records or specimens which prove that his brain and heart also were removed.

COMMENTS

[65] That was Colonel Baker's story. There are several others. One of these is the account of Dr. George L. Porter, Assistant Army Surgeon, entitled "How Booth's Body Was Hidden," *Columbian Magazine*, April, 1911. Dr. Porter was stationed at the Arsenal as the Medical Officer, and claimed Colonel Baker delivered the corpse to a landing on the Arsenal grounds, placed it under guard, and departed. At midnight, the body was hauled directly to a large storage room having doors wide enough to admit the cart and team which carried it to the grave prepared in the dirt floor.

The antics of Colonel Baker and his cousin on the river, however, were responsible for reports that Wilkes' body had received a watery burial, and a large drawing labeled "an authentic sketch," showing the Bakers about to drop the corpse into the Potomac, appeared in Frank Leslie's *Illustrated Weekly*.

In 1868 a song commemorating the supposed event was published by A. E. Blackmar, New Orleans, with the title *Our Brutus*. Another tribute, a poem, *John Wilkes Booth*, written by Miss Helen Mullins, appeared in the *Commonwealth Magazine*, June 22, 1932. There was once a monument to Wilkes' memory at Troy, Alabama, but it has been removed.

[66] The hanging of John Yates Beall, a Confederate officer, for his piratical activities in the North, often has been given as a motive for Wilkes' assassination of Lincoln, and various reasons offered for his interest in Beall's case: one, that he was a cousin (which was denied by Edwin); another, that he was madly in love with Beall's sister Mary; and a third, that the two men had been fraternity brothers during their college careers. Any one of these is as good as the tale itself, which now has many variations, all more or less circulating around that written into the records of the Daughters of the Confederacy by Mrs. B. G. Clifford, Corresponding Secretary of the South Carolina Division. Authors of these stories ignore the fact that Wilkes, in the letter left with his sister Asia, in the so-called diary written while he was in hiding, and in statements reputed to have been made to others, did not mention the name of Beall or in any way allude to him, which there was no reason for not doing had Beall's hanging prompted such a revenge.

[67] Information was sent to the authorities that the actor, Edwin Adams, who knew the habits and characteristics of Wilkes Booth intimately, believed that he could be found "at or near his own home, closely concealed, well-armed, and ready and desirous to take the life of any one, or more, who might attempt his arrest, and probably that he would commit suicide if escape were impossible."

When a request came to the War Department from Thomas A. Hall, manager of Ford's Theatre in Baltimore, asking that he be given permission to inspect the former home of the Booths at Belair, it was immediately granted. In reporting his visit, he said, "The old residence is vacant at the present time, but an old servant of the family named Jane [Ann] Hall is living near there. She was in the family some twenty years and was much devoted to them; and the boys were in the habit of visiting her when they came to that vicinity."

Hall stated that Wilkes had visited Belair about a year before the assassination and stopped at a hotel kept by a man named Hannah who had gone to the old family servant of the Booths shortly after the assassination and asked her if she would feed Wilkes in case he came there, and she answered that she would. Hall, in speaking of the old residence as being vacant, alluded to the original home of the Booths on that site which was still standing but unoccupied. The story of Federal troops surrounding the property and searching for Wilkes on the night following the assassination has been related by old residents of the neighborhood, and by relatives of Mr. Patrick Henry King, whose family was then living in the new structure called Tudor Hall.

[68] Clara Morris-Harriott, *Life on the Stage*, McClure, Phillips and Co., New York, 1901.

[69] A few days later a letter postmarked New York and addressed to J. Wilkes Booth, Washington, D. C., with the signature *Etta*, fell into the hands of officials and John Kennedy, Chief of Police in New York, investigated the matter. To Col. John A. Foster he wrote: "Every public and private house of prostitution of a class such as Booth would visit has been thoroughly overhauled, from which it appears that, although a frequent visitor to many of them, at but one was he regarded as a lover . . . and in this case he was lover of the landlady. One other person was found, between whom and him a close intimacy had existed, but had been broken off by himself. . . . This woman has undoubtedly had promises for the future from Booth and seems to be attached to him, but has not seen him within three months or more."

The tenor of the *Etta* letter, and the fact that it was dated April thirteenth but not posted until the nineteenth proved it to be a hoax, and was so labeled by Kennedy. Apparently such establishments in other cities were searched, as a note to Stanton assuring him that Wilkes was secreted "in a house of ill fame at 16 Tenth Avenue, Chicago, Illinois," is marked "acted upon. B." These, and many similar communications, are in the War Department Archives.

[70] Affidavit of John T. Ford, War Department Archives.

[71] Spear spent his last days in the Edwin Forrest home for retired actors, near Philadelphia.

[72] Despite the fact that Colonel Baker subpoenaed for the prosecution and defense "more than two hundred witnesses," and had the "task of procuring, compiling, and arranging" testimony given at the conspiracy trial, the Military Commission did not call his cousin, Lieutenant Baker, to testify at this time. And the deposition Lieutenant Baker made before Judge Holt on board the *Montauk* immediately after the arrival of Wilkes' body had, in less than two months, disappeared.

When questioned later concerning this, Lieutenant Baker expressed the opinion that he had been the butt of foul play among some of the officials who wished to see others reap the reward.

An announcement that the sum was to be divided resulted in a battle among the claimants who took their grievances to the House of Representatives the following spring. At that time Doherty declared he had commanded the expedition, Conger and Baker having only the authority of detectives under him. The Chairman of the Committee on Claims answered Doherty, accusing him of cowardice at Garrett's farm and charging him with having concealed himself in one of the outbuildings far from danger, leaving only a half-dozen of his men to assist in seizing the fugitives while the others followed his example by scampering back to the orchard. The Chairman gave Conger full credit for the capture, and the fact that he had previously been "twice shot through the hips" and was then "dragging a withered limb" was cited as evidence of his gallantry as a soldier. In the final adjudication of the rewards, Conger received fifteen thousand dollars; Doherty five thousand two hundred and fifty dollars; Colonel L. C. Baker three thousand seven hundred fifty dollars; Lieutenant L. B. Baker three thousand dollars; and Boston Corbett one thousand six hundred fifty-three dollars and forty-eight cents, his portion as divided among the non-commissioned men of the detachment. Other claimants also shared the rewards.

COMMENTS

BOOK FIVE

[1] Twins, Creston and Lillian, were born to her August 20, 1865.
[2] Mrs. Thomas Bailey Aldrich, *Crowding Memories,* Houghton Mifflin Company, Boston, 1920.
[3] These two letters are quoted by Willian Winter, *Life and Art of Edwin Booth,* The Macmillan Co., New York, 1893.
[4] William Bispham, "Memories and Letters of Edwin Booth," *The Century Magazine,* November, 1893.
[5] Baltimore *American,* April 28, 1865.
[6] Tucked away in the War Department Archives are the affidavits Junius made while imprisoned, three of which are here published for the first time:

War Department, Washington, D. C.
April 26th, 1865.

Statement of *Junius Brutus Booth*

I have seen the letter that has been published in the newspapers purporting to have been written by me to J. Wilkes Booth and signed "Jun," which letter is altogether different in intent and phraseology from the one I wrote to J. Wilkes Booth. When I read the letter as published in the newspaper I was thunderstruck, and quite believed that I should be arrested. The letter I wrote was, substantially, as follows:

It urged him to have nothing to do with the rebellion. Knowing his sympathy for the South I was very much afraid he might go over the lines, and I begged of him not to be so foolish. I told him to follow his profession; to give up oil speculating; and that I was expecting to meet him in New York City on the 22nd, Saturday, to play with his two other brothers. I then said if he wished I would go with him to the oil regions and see how wells were being sunk there. I told him that this rebellion was now all over; Richmond had fallen; Lee had surrendered; Johnston would do the same shortly, and all there would be left would be a few bands of guerrillas to rove over the country, and these would very soon be routed out. In the postscript I said, "Give my love to Alice." That is all the letter contained.

We have always been fearful of J. Wilkes, knowing his sympathy for the South, and have again and again advised him to have nothing to do with it. We have tried to get him away from Washington, knowing that here he would see so much of military life, and besides being so close to Southern soil.

If I had known that I was writing to a conspirator, I should have so worded my letter that my language could not have been misconstrued. I thought I was writing to a brother. If the original letter had been in the hands of the Judge Advocate I think he would not have desired any further explanation.

369

Statement of *Junius Brutus Booth*
Committed April, 1865.

Is a native of Charleston, S. C., age 43 years, and by profession an actor. Has resided in California for the past ten years, prior to 1864, and since his return East in May, 1864, has claimed New York City as his place of residence. Had not seen his brother *John Wilkes Booth* during his stay in California, and until his return as above stated. Found his brother Wilkes strongly in sympathy with the Southern cause and endeavored by frequent and earnest arguments to dissuade him from his views on that subject. Believes that his brother Edwin and brother-in-law J. S. Clark made similar efforts but were equally unsuccessful. Told his brother that his views of a Southern independence would never be realized and begged him for his own and his family's sake not to meddle in the family quarrel, as it might be styled, and only obtained a promise from him that he would not join the rebel army. Says that on the 1st of September last he and his brother Edwin were engaged in their theatrical business, and that his brother Wilkes went to Canada, as he said, to fulfill an engagement there, and that he did not again see him until he met him in Baltimore, at the late presidential election when his brother's conversation was solely about oil stock, in which he appeared to be largely interested.

Says that he and his brother Wilkes played together one night at the Winter Garden Theatre, New York, at the close of which his brother returned to Washington, which he seems to have regarded as his home. Says his brother seldom visited his family and only remained with them a few days. Saw his brother in Washington, in February last and was told by him that he had played there one night, in borrowed clothes, having previously shipped his theatrical wardrobe to the South, while in Canada, and had otherwise disposed of much of his property, intending in the future to reside and play in the South, but the vessel containing his property having been sunk by a gunboat had changed his purpose and induced him to devote his attention to the oil business, in which he expected to be quite successful.

Says he left Washington next day for Philadelphia, and did not see his brother Wilkes until about February 11th, when he stopped for one day, and met his brother in New York on the 14th. Went to Boston and returned to New York and found that his brother Wilkes had gone to Washington; also found that his brother's reputed oil speculations were not as successful as he had represented them to be.

The last time he saw his brother was in the last week in March, in New York City, and was told by him that he was in love with a lady in Washington who was worth more to him than all the wealth of the oil regions. Two days afterwards says his brother returned to Washington. On the 12th of April (late in the afternoon) he received a few lines from his brother Wilkes in New York, saying he had been to Boston, and would return to Washington in a day or two; that he had given him a few shares of oil stock which he thought would soon be valuable, if held on to. Says he replied in a few hurried lines, advising his brother to resume his professional business and hoped to meet him in New York on the 22nd of April to play for the benefit of the Shakespearean Fund, also reminding him of the fall of Richmond, the surrender of Lee, and the probable early termination of the war.

On Saturday, 10 A.M., says he first heard of the President's murder, and remained in Cincinnati until Wednesday night, when he left for

COMMENTS

Philadelphia and arrived there April 19th, 12 M., and immediately reported himself to W. Willisard, U. S. Marshal. Says he found the oil stocks given to him by his brother dated and recorded, he thinks, in September or November last. Was about starting for Washington for the purpose of correcting some newspaper misstatements of his connection with his brother's affairs, but was persuaded by some friends not to do so, and on the Tuesday following was arrested by an officer and conveyed to Washington. Says he has always been a Union man, and associated with loyal men; that his letters also, while in California, to his brother and his letters to and conversation with him and others since his return, have always favored and sustained the Union cause.

J. B. Booth says he has given a full and truthful statement of his knowledge of his brother's recent actions such as came under his notice, or that he could derive from any other source with which he is acquainted, and positively disclaims any knowledge of the plot which resulted in the death of President Lincoln.

May 3d, 1865.

Junius Brutus Booth states:

I do not know what amount of oil stock my brother had. He had some stock in some company in Orange County. He wanted me to go in the oil business with him. I told him no, that I had no faith in it. That was in July or August last. There was a third partner with a man by the name of Ellsler and a man by the name of Meerz. As I said, he wanted me to go into the oil business. I have been so unlucky in mining speculation that I said I had no faith in it. "Well," said he, "I will give you some some day." Said I, "If you do I will take it, but I will never buy a cent's worth."

About three weeks ago, I think it was, he wrote to me, saying, "I have given you some oil stock, and I do not want you to sell it because it will be good some day, although it is not worth much now." When I returned from Cincinnati I found a deed at the house of my brother in Philadelphia. I forget the date—it was since the murder. It was along with a lot of documents that were left there. This was addressed to me. That deed, I think, is dated November. I do not know but think it is November. The deed is for one-third, I think, of the stock in Orange County. It is only acknowledged, and everything seems legal about it. It was recorded— I do not know when. I paid no attention to it at all when I saw the thing but threw it in a drawer. I do not know that there was any deed of trust for my sister. That is all I know about it. I have not seen it since. I left it in a drawer and never gave it another thought.

Do not know what company he has interest in, but Mr. Joe Simons [Simonds] knows all about it. He was for some time his agent. They dissolved connection and Simons went on his own responsibility when they shut the well up. I think that ended their connection.

Q. Who else was connected in the oil business with him?
A. I do not know. The other two were John Ellsler and Reuben Meerz—I think that is his name. They could not agree, and the works were stopped for some time. Ellsler lives in Cleveland, Ohio; is a manager of a theatre. That is all the connection he had with John—they held stock together and had a difficulty. Meerz, I think, lives on the premises.

Q. Did your brother say anything about leaving part of it in trust for your sister?
A. No, sir. I have a sister Rosalie. He told me some time ago that he had given her some shares in oil stock and that it had turned out much more valuable than he had any idea of.
Q. Did he ever give you any idea of what portion of the stock he gave you?
A. No, sir; I had an idea that he gave me more than a few shares. I think it was in February last that he told me about giving our sister this stock.
Q. When did he tell you that it had turned out more valuable than he had supposed it would?
A. At that time. I do not know whether she was aware that she possessed it at that time. She lives at my brother Edwin's house.

[7] Affidavit of *John S. Clarke*, War Department Archives:

May 6th. 1865—I have not seen John Wilkes Booth since February 1865—I have no recollection of receiving but one letter from him in four years, which was *purely upon a theatrical matter*. I have had no conversation with him upon political subjects for at least two years, as our views were entirely different—I am and have always been entirely loyal to the United States Government—and have had no sympathy with man or woman of rebellious principles—Contrary to a fixed rule of my own, I have repeatedly volunteered (gratuitously) my professional services in aid of the United States Sanitary Commission, and have made many private contributions beneficial to the Federal cause—I do and have always believed every member of the Booth family (save Wilkes) to be in sentiment and feeling loyal to the U. S. Government. John Wilkes Booth has repeatedly within, say, two years left at my house in care of his sister (my wife) large envelopes sealed and directed to himself, saying for "safe keeping" as he was obliged to travel through the far west to meet his professional engagements—invariably stating that they contained "stocks etc" —These envelopes have remained sometimes months, and he has called for them—About the latter part of November '64, while I was acting in New York, he left a sealed envelope at my house in Philadelphia in this way. During January he again visited my house and asked for it, took it and shortly after returned it, (or a similar one) and it was again placed as usual in my safe—On the Saturday Afternoon following the assassination of the President Mrs. Booth, the Mother, came to my house from New York—The whole family was of course much depressed and excited—On the Sunday Afternoon we thought of the envelope, and Mrs. Booth, my wife, and I determined to open it. We found the letter which was published—and for his Mother a letter, 5—20 bonds to amount of $3000. Phila. City 6s to amount of $1000— and an assignment of some oil land in Penna. to his brother Junius, and nothing more — I kept these papers in my possession during Monday, thinking that probably the authorities would enquire at the residences of his family for his papers—no one called—On Tuesday I handed them over to the United States Marshall suggesting to him that if consistent I should like him to cause to be published the letter for his mother as in that he exonerated his entire family from any sympathy with his secession propensities, I was surprised the next day to find the other letter published and *not* the one for his mother which I suggested should be made public—Upon the arrival at my house of Junius B. Booth on Wednesday 19th of April from Cincinnati,

I casually remarked, at such a time a *Booth* entering my house might cause a talk, whereupon Junius instantly desired that his arrival should be made known. I called at Marshall Milward's—he was out—On hearing that I had called, the Marshall visited me the next morning and I introduced to him Mr. Junius B. Booth on Thursday April 20th—

JOHN S. CLARKE

Sworn to and subscribed before me this 6th day of May 1865

L. C. TURNER
J. Advocate.

Born in Baltimore Sept. 3rd 1832
Philadelphia has been my residence since August 1852—

J. S. CLARKE

8 "It was only by the powerful influence brought to bear that he escaped arrest after the murder of Lincoln. His brother, Junius Brutus, Jr., and brother-in-law, John Sleeper Clarke, were not so fortunate; both were in prison with me. Clarke was furious over his incarceration, and could not understand it, with Edwin at liberty. They were released, as I was, without reason given for their arrest, or excuse offered."
John T. Ford, "Recollections," Baltimore *American,* June 8, 1893.
9 *Ibid.*
10 War Department Archives.
11 In rounding up the Booths, government authorities swooped down upon the De Bar ménage in St. Louis and found not only evidences of sedition but also an account of the scandal which duplicated the youthful escapade of the elder Booth. A heretofore unpublished report of April, 1865, from Colonel J. H. Baker, Provost Marshal of Missouri, to the Honorable C. A. Dana, Assistant Secretary of War, reads:

Sir—
Your telegram of the 22nd inst., directing me to "make a thorough search of the premises of Miss Blanche Booth and Ben De Bar for any correspondence of J. Wilkes Booth," etc., was received Saturday evening.
In reply I have the honor to state that I immediately directed my Chief of Police to arrest the parties named and bring them to this office, which was done without delay, and their sworn statements were then taken to ascertain what their relations with Booth had been; whether they knew or had reason to believe he meditated the murder of the late lamented President. . . .
In the meantime two of my officers with a sufficient police force seized and held possession of the residences of Ben De Bar, when the house was searched from garrett to cellar and all the papers of whatever nature were brought to this office, where they were examined.
From these papers and effects, and from the statements of the parties, I learn that Miss Blanche Booth, alias De Bar, is the adopted daughter of Ben De Bar, proprietor of the Saint Louis Theatre, Saint Louis, and of the Saint Charles Theatre, New Orleans. She is the daughter of Junius Booth, Jr., from whom, when she was but a child, her mother procured a divorce, he having previously gone to California, in company with a prostitute by the name of Harriet Mace, by whom he has had children. Harriet Mace has since died.
It appears, from the papers, and from information obtained from De Bar, that all intercourse between Blanche Booth and her father

long since ceased. Her mother whose maiden name was Clementina De Bar, and who was a sister of Ben De Bar—has for a long time lived in Richmond, Va., and has been connected with the New Richmond Theatre. Although Ben De Bar was instrumental in procuring a divorce for his sister from her husband, there has been a bad feeling existing between them for some time, and he will not allow Blanche to have any intercourse with her mother, whose character it is alleged is decidedly questionable.

At the breaking out of the rebellion Miss Blanche Booth (De Bar) was in New Orleans, where she had for some time previously resided. She was educated in Memphis, and has been an unmitigated rebel, as indicated by her papers, by poetry addressed by her to rebel officers, by correspondence received by her from the same parties, and by various expressions of sentiment found in her writings. The two first portraits in her album were those of Jeff Davis and Semmes, the pirate: an exact and minute map, sketched in pencil, of Island, No. 10 with explanations of the positions of Federal gunboats and fortifications, was found among her papers. Many of the letters, pictures, mementoes, scraps of poetry and extracts from newspapers found in her possession indicate, unmistakably her rebel sentiments. She is a young lady of 24 years, of fine appearance and bearing the Booth family likeness in a very distinct manner. She is possessed of considerable personal attractions, of a vigorous mind and marked histrionic ability. She recently made her *debut* on her uncle's stage and was quite successful. She is continuing her preparations for a stage career and informs me that it is still the purpose of her life. She avows she has a deep abhorrence for the act of her uncle. She admits it is true that in the outbreak of the war, being in New Orleans, surrounded by young rebel officers, her sympathies were warmly with the South, but that since her return North, her mind has been entirely changed with regard to the contest, and she says, she now thinks the South is wrong and that the old flag of the Union should be sustained.

A large number of family letters were found among the papers of Miss Blanche Booth, but no communications of any character from her uncle John Wilkes, with the exception of a card on which was written in pencil the following:

"Dear Blanche—
"Excuse me this evening for not keeping my word.
"Will see you tomorrow.
"Your *Nunkee*
"JOHN."

The other papers from him were in the possession of Ben De Bar, but they were simply three short notes relative to his engagements at the St. Louis Theatre. The following copy of one is a sample of the rest:

"Sept. 22'/63

"B. De Bar, Esq.
"Dear Ben
"Yours of 20th rec'd.
"All right, Book me for the two weeks
"to begin Jan 4th/64. Share after $140. per
"night, and benefit each week.
"With regards to all,

"I am Truly Yours,
"J. WILKES BOOTH."

Both Ben De Bar and Blanche Booth state that John Wilkes was exceedingly fond of money, that he was niggardly and avaricious and they never knew him to squander money in rioting or excesses of any kind—except possibly with women. They had noticed this as a marked trait in his character.

The letters of Edwin Booth are numerous. They breathe a kind and amiable spirit, and contain no allusion to political matters or public men.

He married a Miss Mary Devlin a woman of extraordinary beauty and amiability, to whom he was devotedly attached. She died about four years ago, since which time Edwin has lived with his mother.

There were some letters from Asia Booth, the Aunt of Blanche and next elder to John Wilkes. She is the wife of Mr. Clark, low comedian and joint-proprietor with Edwin Booth of the Winter Garden Theatre, New York. Asia's letters evince a high order of intellect, combined with an amiable disposition and heart. There are no references in any of them, or in any letters found in Blanche's possession, to John Wilkes, except that Asia once incidentally refers to John as her "brother" and to Edwin as her "darling." . . .

De Bar, also, has separated from his wife. Misfortunes of this kind seem to attend every member of the family, sooner or later.

In a letter of characteristic vigor and elegance from Asia to Blanche entreating her not to make the stage a profession she relates that Eliza Mitchell, a cousin of hers who married well and then made her appearance on the stage giving every indication that she would excel, "had unfortunately gone the wrong way, has parted from her husband (William Ward) and is now a miserable creature."

Blanche Booth lives with her uncle Ben De Bar, in his house adjoining his Theatre. . . .

[12] William Winter, *Vagrant Memories*, George H. Doran Company, New York, 1915.
[13] Dr. W. Stump Forward's letter to Dr. G. W. Archer (the Harford County physician of the Booths) October 7, 1891. Municipal Museum, Baltimore.
[14] Edwina Booth Grossman, *Edwin Booth*, The Century Co., New York, 1894.
[15] *Ibid.*
[16] Barton Hill, "Personal Recollections of Edwin Booth," New York *Dramatic Mirror*, December 25, 1896.
[17] William Winter, *Life and Art of Edwin Booth*, The Macmillan Co., New York, 1893.
[18] H. H. Kohlsaat, "Booth's Letter to Grant," *The Saturday Evening Post*, February 9, 1924. (The original of this first request is owned by Dr. A. S. W. Rosenbach.)
[19] *Ibid.**
[20] Keeper of Andersonville prison, convicted and hanged for atrocities perpetrated there on Union soldiers.
[21] All were later removed and buried elsewhere.
[22] It was reported that Edwin waited in the undertaker's office to view his brother's remains, but this was not possible, as he played through the entire month at Booth's Theatre in New York. Junius did not go to Washington or Baltimore at this time, so it must have been Joseph who was seen at Weaver's establishment.
[23] Dr. George L. Porter, "How Booth's Body Was Hidden," *Columbian Magazine*, April, 1911.

* See Supplement VI, p. 399.

[24] A filled tooth which he did not mention had been done too recently for him to have known of it, and was not unusual enough to be accepted as definite proof for identification. A Dr. Merrill was the Washington dentist who had identified these two teeth which he had filled. Another fallacy is noticeable in the affidavit of "Colonel" William M. Pegram, given to the Maryland Historical Society, in which he says that a "manufactured shoe" made from the original boot was on Wilkes' left leg. It is an undisputed fact that the entire boot, with the slit in it cut by Dr. Mudd at the time he removed it, was later found under the bed Wilkes had occupied in his house. It is now in the War Department collection in Washington.

[25] Records of Greenmount Cemetery state that "six bodies from Baltimore Cemetery, and farm at Belair," were removed to Greenmount in June, 1869. Little Henry Byron was buried in England, hence only five bodies can be accounted for by the Booth records. Negro Joe Edwin Hall's assurance that one of his small sisters was buried in the Booth graveyard at the farm may account for the sixth body. The Booths surely knew the correct number of dead to be brought from the farm, but it must be realized that they could not identify in the bones exhumed after such a long period of years the one they could not account for, and therefore had to accept them all.

[26] William Stump Forward, *Junius Brutus Booth, Sr.*, MS. Municipal Museum, Baltimore.

[27] This Reverend James, then visiting the Reverend Dudley, Rector of Christ's Church, in Baltimore, paid rather dearly for his part in the affair. A gentleman called to ask Reverend Dudley if he would officiate at a burial service in Greenmount Cemetery, but, as he was not at home that day, Reverend James, without inquiring the name of the deceased, consented to officiate, not knowing until he reached the gate that he was to read the sermon over the dead body of Lincoln's assassin. When his flock in New York learned what he had been doing in Baltimore, they told him to stay there. He did—and at different times was associated with several churches in that city.

Henry W. Mears, a young man at the time of Wilkes' burial, who became a Baltimore undertaker and occupied the building formerly used by Weaver, later recalled: "I saw the body of John Wilkes Booth lowered into the grave, and for many years had charge of the lot. While Edwin Booth was alive he evidenced a desire to beautify it, and sent for me to arrange the details. Each grave was discussed, but when that of John Wilkes Booth attracted his attention he turned to me and said: 'Let it remain as it is—unmarked.' "

[28] Thomas B. Florence had been a Philadelphia hatter and a congressman before he established and edited the Washington yellow journal known as the *Constitutional Union*. If news were not sensational enough to suit him, he embellished it; if he had a grievance against any party, he concocted reports to suit his purpose. He had been bitterly opposed to the Lincoln administration and published a story to the effect that the body brought from the Garrett farm by Federal officers to Washington was not that of Lincoln's assassin, implying that Wilkes had escaped. The story took on momentum, and impostors later sprang up in different parts of the country claiming to be John Wilkes Booth. Some looked like him, kept silent, and let gossip clothe them with that identity; a few made the claim verbally. Each one failed to have all the marks of identification on his body; no one had the India ink initials, *J. W. B.*, on either hand. Investigation proved they were all frauds.

The most famous of the impostors was John St. Helen, who professed to a Tennessee lawyer, Finis L. Bates, that he was John Wilkes Booth. He told a long story of startling facts, including a number of blunders in relation to the Booth family, which could never have been attributed to Wilkes, had Bates been aware of the truth. As to the man killed at the Garrett farm, St. Helen "had the impression . . . from having heard his name called by a Mr. Jones . . . that it was Ruddy or Roby . . ." whom he had sent back to retrieve "letters, pictures, et cetera," from the Lucas wagon where he had lost them in coming to Port Conway. At Garrett's farm, St. Helen, as John Wilkes Booth, had been warned of the approaching Federals and made his escape, while "Ruddy or Roby" had arrived and been captured in his stead.

Thirty-eight years later, when a David E. George, contending he was John Wilkes Booth, committed suicide in Enid, Oklahoma, Bates identified him as John St. Helen. That George and St. Helen were the same man is doubtful. Bates' efforts to prove that both names were aliases of John Wilkes Booth, occupied the greater part of his life and were published by him in *The Escape and Suicide of John Wilkes Booth* (Memphis, 1907), but apparently Bates never discovered that Franklin A. Robey died, in December, 1896, at the age of sixty-seven, and was buried at Hill Top, Charles County, Maryland. The tales of Major James R. O'Beirne, Basil Moxley and others asserting that Wilkes escaped, have also been refuted by facts.

The body of David E. George was embalmed and subsequently became the property of Bates. Since then it has belonged to several different persons and has been carted about the country as an exhibition.

[29] George C. D. Odell, *Annals of the New York Stage*, Vol. 8, University of Columbia Press, New York, 1936.

[30] Unpublished diary of Edward V. Valentine, The Valentine Museum, Richmond, Virginia.

[31] Edwina Booth Grossman, *op. cit.*

[32] Otis Skinner, "The Last of John Wilkes Booth," *American Magazine*, November, 1908.

[33] New York *Herald* reviews of May 26 and 31, 1874.

[34] William Bispham, "Memories and Letters of Edwin Booth," *The Century Magazine*, November, 1893.

[35] Unpublished Theatrical Notes of Charles Phipps, San Francisco, California. The trial began May 10, 1865.

[36] Both these journeys westward were at a much later date than the time Junius (and his mother) were supposed to have met Wilkes in California. In fact during the period so designated by certain writers seeking to prove that Wilkes was never captured, all the Booths were about as far away from California as they could be without leaving the United States.

[37] Edwina Booth Grossman, *op. cit.*

[38] *Ibid.*

[39] Frederick Warde, *Fifty Years of Make Believe*, International Press Syndicate, New York, 1920.

[40] Ford Scrapbook, Municipal Museum, Baltimore.

Corbett had many offers to give platform lectures, and relate his version of shooting Lincoln's assassin, but he would not do so. In 1887 he was chosen assistant doorkeeper at the Kansas State Capitol, and a story originated that, believing he had been discriminated against, he drew a revolver during the session of the legislature and chased members of the House of Representatives from the building. The session which was thus adjourned happened to have been held by the clerks who were trying to imitate members of the House by comical antics, and Corbett, feeling such mimicry blasphemous and uncomplimentary, had taken it upon himself to break up the mock session. Someone gave an alarm and the police were called in. While one of them diverted his attention, another came up behind him and grabbed his arms. This escapade landed him in jail for the night. On the following day he was taken before a judge who pronounced him insane and committed him to the State Institution at Topeka. The judge on this occasion was Charles Curtis, who became Vice-President of the United States.

When Corbett was sent to the asylum it was necessary to appoint a guardian for him but, since all were afraid of him, no one would take the job. His interests were then looked after by Judge John J. Huron. The following year Corbett escaped from the insane asylum by jumping on a horse, which the son of the superintendent had left at the entrance to the grounds, and galloping away. A few days later Richard Thatcher, who had been a prisoner with him at Andersonville during the war, saw him riding the horse in Neodesha, Kansas. Corbett told Thatcher the government had treated him so unfairly that he intended spending his remaining days in Mexico. Thereafter, he was marked dead on the asylum records.

At one time Corbett was supposed to have been a medicine peddler. What finally became of him is a mystery. A medicine peddler, assuming his name, once made an effort to collect the pension due him from the government, but when their ages were checked it was found that the impostor was fifty years old while Corbett would have been about seventy at the time, and that the impostor was six feet tall, while Corbett was only five feet and four inches in height. This impostor was sent to the penitentiary at Atlanta, by Judge Huron.

[41] Edwina Booth Grossman, *op. cit.*
[42] Barton Hill, *op. cit.*
[43] Sally MacDougall, "Edwin Booth Counted His Ducats," *The Century Magazine*, December, 1928.
[44] Margaret Townsend, *Theatrical Sketches*, The Merriam Co., New York, 1894.
[45] William Winter, *Life and Art of Edwin Booth*, The Macmillan Co., New York, 1893.
[46] Edwina Booth Grossman, *op. cit.*

According to reports it was during this period of his life that Edwin suffered from what was termed Black Tongue, a strange ailment that puzzled physicians, this case being the third known to them. Dr. G. Durant of New York City diagnosed it as a growth about the size of a silver dollar which made the tongue feel dry and too large for the mouth. He did not believe it was the result of too much smoking, as that would have left a brown coloring instead of the black spot. At first Edwin, fearing it was cancerous and that it would end his career, spent hours before a mirror dejectedly looking at it. Expert surgical scraping by Dr. Durant over a period of months removed the growth so thoroughly that Edwin was never troubled with it again. For this service Dr. Durant received not only a large sum of money but also a loving cup specially designed by Tiffany.

[47] Edwina Booth Grossman, *op. cit.*
[48] Jefferson Winter, "As I Remember," *The Saturday Evening Post*, October 30, 1920.
[49] E. H. House, "Edwin Booth in London," *The Century Magazine*, December, 1897.

COMMENTS 379

[50] William Winter, *op. cit.*
[51] E. H. House, *op. cit.*
[52] Edwina Booth Grossman, *op. cit.*
[53] Ellen Terry, "Memories of Booth and Sarah Bernhardt," *McClure's Magazine*, March, 1908.
[54] *Ibid.*
[55] E. H. House, *op. cit.*
[56] "Chronic grumblers used to complain bitterly of Booth's support, saying he was afraid to gather good actors around him for fear of diminishing his own powers. What do these people say now, since our great tragedian has successfully bearded Irving, the British theatrical lion, in his own den?"
New York *Dramatic Mirror*, May 28, 1881.
[57] William Bispham, "Memories and Letters of Edwin Booth," *The Century Magazine*, December, 1893.
[58] It was from this hotel that Edwin wrote the well-known letter about Wilkes to Nahum Capen (referred to in Book One, Comment 31, and Book Three, p. 176) whose request for information undoubtedly was prompted by a revived interest in Lincoln's assassin.
[59] Richard Lockridge, *Darling of Misfortune*, The Century Co., New York, 1932.
[60] Aunt Louisa Eldridge, "One Christmas Night," New York *Dramatic Mirror*, December 25, 1896.
[61] In legal documents concerning his property, September 17, 1883, is the date given on which he died.
[62] "Miss Belle Land, Mrs. J. B. Booth's less fortunate sister, died in great misery, but it was her own fault. Mrs. Booth adopted Belle Land's daughter on condition that she should never become an actress."
Note of Charles Phipps from an unidentified press clipping, probably the *Beetle and Wedge*, a Manchester publication.
[63] The New York *Dramatic Mirror*, and several other publications reported that Blanche De Bar Booth was not his daughter.
[64] Numerous discrepancies appear not only in the Book and Card Record but also in the inscriptions of the gravestones in the Booth lot at Rosedale Cemetery, the most amazing being that on Junius' gravestone which gives his birth date as December 22, 1822, and the date of his death as September 15, 1884, although the Book and Card Record gives the correct date of his death at the age of sixty-one years, eight months, twenty-three days. Mrs. Agnes Booth, later married to John B. Schoeffel, and her mother, Mrs. Sarah Smeathman, who also survived Junius, are buried there, but not Junius III, who killed his wife and committed suicide in England. Sydney Booth died at the Stamford (Connecticut) Hospital, February 5, 1937, aged sixty-four years, but was not buried in the family lot at Rosedale until the following summer.
Legends of Lincoln's assassin can be heard in Manchester, too. Miss Grace Prest, clerk of the town's Board of Cemetery Commissioners, informed the present writer that "periodically, over a great many years, someone pops up to ask if it is true that John Wilkes Booth was buried secretly at night in the Booth lot at Rosedale Cemetery, but the Superintendent's father who was Superintendent before him told his son he had often been asked the same question and knew positively that John Wilkes Booth was not buried there."
[65] Blanche De Bar and Marion Booth, having been disinherited by their father's will, immediately brought suit, and Agnes, as Mrs. Schoeffel, paid each a thousand

dollars to quitclaim all their rights and interests in the estate. Sydney, through his guardian, R. P. Owen of Boston, also brought an action against his mother, demanding one individual one-half part or moiety of a certain parcel of land with the building thereon situated in Manchester, of which, it was alleged, she had unjustly and without judgment disseized him to the damage of ten thousand dollars. The same action was brought against her by Junius III.

S. H. Halstead and Alfred Clarke, who had been employed by Junius in operating the Masconomo House, gave their testimony at this time. Halstead had been manager of the hotel, had attended to many of Junius' financial matters, and witnessed his will. He stated Junius told him, when making it, he wished "Aggie" to have all of his property so that the boys would be dependent upon her, as she could tell what their dispositions were and whether they ought to have anything; that he had always consulted her and relied implicitly upon her judgment, both in the management of his property and care of his family, and that he had provided for his daughter Marion out of the proceeds from his California investments, and meant to leave nothing more to her.

Alfred Clarke had purchased all the furniture and appliances for the hotel and looked after the buying of provisions. He said Junius once told him that he knew of a man in California who made his will on a cellar door with a piece of chalk, "and it stood so he did not need a lawyer to make a will." He verified all of Halstead's testimony and added that, several years after making his will, Junius called his attention to some mischief the boys had committed. Among other things, they had set fire to the beach bank which he had carefully protected, as the tides would otherwise wash it out. At this time Junius had said he was glad he fixed his will as he had, since the boys were careless and thoughtless, and their mother could control them better if she had the property; that if they behaved themselves and were good, he had no fear of "Aggie's" action in the matter.

The court found for the defendant and presented Sid with a bill of fourteen dollars and seven cents for the cost of the suit, which Wid (Junius III) had to share. That ended the family litigation over the Masconomo property. Under the Schoeffel management, a bandstand was built in the rear yard and performances of light opera were given. Later, the hotel was partially torn down, and several cottages were erected on the grounds, which still are used as a resort for summer visitors.

[66] Daniel Frohman, in *Encore* (Lee Furman, Inc., New York, 1937) states that Edwin Booth appeared in Washington during February, 1884. The present writer was referred to the following in the Chicago *Evening Journal*, Saturday, February 2, 1884, as the authority: "After refusing for nineteen years to play in Washington, Edwin Booth . . . will appear in that city next Monday night."

At the close of his Philadelphia engagement on Saturday, February second, Edwin went immediately to Baltimore and opened there at Albaugh's Holliday Street Theatre, Monday evening, February fourth, in *Richelieu*. His engagement ran through February sixteenth. He then went to Boston and opened at the Globe Theatre two nights later, closing with a matinee performance on Saturday, March first. Hence he did not make a Washington appearance in February, 1884, nor is there any record of his having acted there after Lincoln's assassination.

[67] William Bispham, "Memories and Letters of Edwin Booth," *The Century Magazine*, December, 1893.

[68] Edwina Booth Grossman, *Edwin Booth*, The Century Co., New York, 1894.

[69] *Ibid.*

[70] *Ibid.*

[71] Katherine Goodale, *Behind the Scenes with Edwin Booth*, Houghton Mifflin Co., Boston, 1931.

[72] Milton Nobles, "The Booth-Barrett Tour," New York *Dramatic Mirror*, June 2, 1888.

[73] Baltimore newspaper accounts of her burial state that the brass plate on her casket gave her age as fifty-one years (which is that in the records of Greenmount Cemetery), but in November, 1856, Asia confided to a friend that she would be twenty-one years old on the nineteenth of that month.

[74] New York *Dramatic Mirror*, July 28, 1888.

[75] Edwina Booth Grossman, *op. cit.*

[76] Charles Redfield had been treasurer at McVicker's Chicago theatre and was to have a benefit night given him at the Chicago Opera House on a date during the engagement of the Booth-Barrett combine there. He wrote to Barrett about the matter, then went to Kansas City and got his permission. After tickets had been on sale, Barrett withheld his consent for the benefit, forcing Redfield to put a card in newspapers announcing it could not be given and that money would be refunded. Redfield was generally liked and had many friends in Chicago. The press took up the matter, and the New York *Dramatic Mirror* commented:

> What ever may be the opinion in which Lawrence Barrett is held by his personal friends, it is unquestionably true that no man of similar prominence is more universally unpopular among his brothers and sisters in the profession. In marked contrast is the regard in which his associate Edwin Booth is held. No actor is more widely respected and dearly beloved. Mr. Barrett seems to have positive genius for doing disagreeable and priggish things. The latest specimen is just now agitating professional people in Chicago.

[77] William Winter, *op. cit.* For the sake of harmony among members, dramatic critics later were tabooed and Winter resigned. This did not interfere with the lifelong friendship between him and Edwin.

[78] Richard Lockridge, *op. cit.*

[79] The present writer interviewed several old citizens in Long Branch who had known Dr. Joseph Booth. One, Mr. Leonard Van Dyke, had been a member of the police force during the time Joseph lived there, and was well acquainted with him. When told of the report by Izola Forrester (*This One Mad Act*, Hale, Cushman and Flint, Boston, 1937) that Rosalie's death was the result of a blow from a missile thrown at her as she opened the door of Joseph's home, Mr. Van Dyke was positive such could not have happened without his knowledge of it. The record of her death on file at Greenmount Cemetery states that she died from "paralysis of throat."

The house on Ocean Avenue in which Joseph lived was still standing, but had been altered and enlarged by a Mr. Medzigian, who had purchased it from Joseph's widow.

"Doc Joe," said Mr. Van Dyke, "had a neighbor who operated a retail and wholesale ice-cream business next door. Doc complained of too many horses and carriages standing in the yard, and the flies that swarmed from there to his house, so he built a spite fence twenty feet high. The fence blew down twice but each time he put it up again."

[80] Joseph's widow outlived him thirty-four years and also is buried in this cemetery, but no tombstone marks the grave of his first wife. Izola Forrester (*This One Mad Act*, Hale, Cushman and Flint, Boston, 1937) states that the deed to the Booth family lot specifies that no one not of blood relation shall be buried there. Presuming this to be the cause for no gravestone having been erected to the memory of Joseph's first wife (his second wife having been his own cousin), a letter was sent to Superintendent E. E. Dove, who answered, "I have no information that the Booth family prohibits any burial there of anyone not of blood relation."

[81] Some years before the New York *Dramatic Mirror* had exposed a plan to make public certain foul attacks on Booth and Barrett. Now scandalous reports began to circulate about Booth and Modjeska. But writers who hoped to spread these unwarranted accusations over the front pages of newspapers took to cover when they felt themselves in danger of being sued for libel and slander.

[82] William Winter, *op. cit.*

[83] *Ibid.*

[84] Edward V. Valentine called on him and under date of October 6, 1891, wrote in his unpublished diary:

> I was at the Players, and went up to Edwin's room. . . . In my conversation with Booth he said he had success early. Speaking of fame he told me an anecdote of his father—who was to play but got quite intoxicated so that he could not. (He lifted his eyebrows to express drunkenness when he spoke of his being drunk.) The next morning the papers told of what a fine performance it was but Booth had not played. His father spoke of being descended from Madoc, the Welshman, and his grandfather used when intoxicated to speak of his descent from Modac or an Indian. . . . Edwin Booth said that his brother Wilkes had fine talent, but he did not like correction— Spoke of how strong he was physically. He remembered his grandfather with long white hair and toe nails as he walked the house. Said that Barrett's death mask was brought to the Players Club and the boy was told to take it upstairs. . . . [He should have taken it to the library but he put it in Edwin's room] and Edwin said, "think of my seeing on the table when I came in, the mask of my friend."
>
> Speaking of Mary Devlin I said, "I will describe her to you. She had black hair, greyish eyes, and very white skin. Is that a description of her?" said I.
>
> He said, "No, her hair was brown—and her complexion was not so white." He said that George Boughton painted a picture of his daughter Edwina when she was a baby and said he could paint his wife from recollection—he painted her with light hair. I spoke of her sad expression of eye. He said, "I have seen her sitting with such an expression of eye that I thought she was dead." I walked like his father and he said it was his way—or manner.
>
> He said to me, "We have had some ups and downs" and then repeated something I think Horatio says to Hamlet. Gave me a metal stamp box which he had used. Said he did not like the photographs taken of him in character. He may have been speaking of those which he had there. He gave me some and one for Mrs. Mayo on which he wrote "To my friends' friend Mrs. Kate C. Mayo from Edwin Booth." Eastman Johnson, he said, gave as an excuse for not joining the Players' Club that he "did not sing songs." While Booth was sitting at his desk writing the names on the photographs he sighed and said, "did you hear that?" I told him it was physical and he agreed

to it. Said that he was on the stage with "Roderigo" and found that he could not speak clearly and I think the actor said, "What is the matter with Mr. Booth?" Barrett, who was standing behind the scenes, said, "Go for a doctor." Another attack which he had was after his bath—was making his toilet when his hand moved without his control. Spoke of how finely Wilkes Booth played Mark Anthony. He said he nursed his last wife for 12 years— She had talent but was too small in person to succeed. . . .

The Edward V. Valentine Collection, The Valentine Museum, Richmond, Virginia.

[85] "Our Pictures" (Editorial page), New York *Dramatic Mirror*, December 26, 1891.

[86] Column headed "In the Wings," New York *Dramatic Mirror*, March 5, 1892.

[87] At an early age Junius III deserted the schoolroom for the stage dressing room. After minor experiences playing juvenile rôles, he appeared with several well-known stars, including Dion Boucicault, and under the management of A. M. Palmer during engagements of his mother, Agnes Booth. A year before his father's death he followed the course taken by him in his youth and left the stage to study medicine. He was not successful as a physician, however, and resumed his theatrical career in stock companies of the United States and England, his most important associations being with the Boston Museum and Richard Mansfield's London Lyceum.

Later, he toured the manufacturing centers of Great Britain with his own company, but the venture was not profitable and he purchased a motion-picture theatre at Brightlingsea. There he and his wife occupied rooms in a cheap lodging house, and, on December 7, 1912, were found dead from the wounds of a revolver in Junius' hand. Beside them was a note he had written which read: "I have given my wife a sleeping draught to ease her pain. As I cannot live without her, I will give myself another." He was nearly forty-five years of age. Reports stated his last failures and involvements in a lawsuit were responsible for his actions, but at the inquest certain witnesses testified that he had a highly excitable nature, and that they believed he was addicted to the use of drugs. Official records gave the verdict as "wilful murder and suicide while insane."

[88] Edwina Booth Grossman, *op. cit.*

[89] *Ibid.*

[90] *Valentine's Manual of Old New York*, No. 6, Valentine's Manual, Inc., New York, 1922.

[91] Katherine Goodale, *op. cit.*

[92] She died in New York City, December 25, 1938, as Mrs. Edwina Booth Crossman. Years before her husband's death they had made this change in their name. Previously she had signed the name Grossmann to some of her writings. A son, Edwin Booth Grossman, who retained his father's original name, and a daughter, Mrs. Mildred Booth Tilton, survived their mother.

[93] The New York *Dramatic Mirror* observer wrote: "Speaking of Irving, I was glad to see that he cabled a message to Booth's daughter, and sent a tribute, with other English actors, to place beside the bier at the funeral. The relations of the two foremost actors of our time have been strained for several years—ever since Booth played in London."

The man who represented the English actors at the funeral was Clement Scott, of the London *Telegraph*, who happened to be in New York on his honeymoon.

The *Dramatic Mirror* also commented on the lack of sentiment shown by managers of many theatres in not flying their flags at half-mast, as did Daly and Palmer, on the day of Edwin's funeral.

[94] Five years later The Players presented an Edwin Booth Memorial window to the church, and in 1926 a bust of him was placed in the Hall of Fame at New York University. The Shakespeare Gallery, Stratford, England, also contains a portrait of him.

Richard Lockridge, *op. cit.*

[95] A younger friend of Jones named Mattingly induced him to write this book (*J. Wilkes Booth*, Laird and Lee, Chicago, 1893), predicting it would have a large sale at the Chicago World's Fair. They put up a tent on the grounds, and Mattingly ballyhooed the presence of Jones on the inside selling his book to patrons who wished to read the account of Wilkes' escape into Virginia by one who had aided him. An old Union soldier, claiming to have been a boyhood friend of Lincoln's happened by that way and heard Mattingly's announcement. "Just let me get in there and I'll fix him," exclaimed the Yankee as he started through the entrance. When he got inside, Jones was missing, having crawled under the rear of the tent and disappeared. That ended the sale of the book at the Fair. But in it Jones had written:

> No act ever committed has called forth such universal execration as the murder of that great and good man, Abraham Lincoln. Today I speak of the murdered President as "great and good;" thirty years ago I regarded him only as an enemy of my country. But now that the waves of passion stirred up by the storm of war have all subsided and passed away forever, and I can form my opinions in the light of reason instead of the blindness of prejudice, I believe that Lincoln's name justly belongs among the first upon the deathless roll of fame. I can now realize how truly he was beloved by the North, and what a cruel shock his death, coming when and as it did, must have been to the millions who held his name in reverence. And with that realization comes the wonder that the revenge taken for his murder stopped when it did.

[96] "The Career of Edwin Booth," the New York *Times*, June 7, 1893.

SUPPLEMENTS, 1969

John had one daughter Ogretia and one son Alonzo. Ogretia was beautyfull Alonzo was very much like the old Mr Richard Booth. Johns wife is still living. her name was Izalia. I do not know her Maden name. John told Roslie he would give her two oil wells, and he wished her to take care of those two Children, which she did although they ware with there Mother Rosie calls them her Children. John was not Married to there Mother. after Johns Death Izaliey she went with the Children A way to the Almouise they the Children both Married now. poor Children Oh the trouble bad people do and cause trouble, trouble, to others Mrs Junius Brutus Booth, the trouble she had, was almost insuportable, but

Excerpt from the letter of Mrs. Elijah Rogers discussing John Wilkes Booth's common-law family. *(Courtesy Library of Congress)*

SUPPLEMENT I

JOHN WILKES BOOTH'S COMMON-LAW FAMILY

That John Wilkes Booth followed in the footsteps of his father and older brother Junius Brutus Booth, Jr., and lived with a woman who bore him children out of wedlock, was very definitely established by their Harford County neighbor, Mrs. Elijah Rogers. In a letter, dated August 16, 1886, to Dr. W. Stump Forward, a Maryland friend, she wrote (the spelling is corrected here for clarity):

> John had one daughter, Ogretia, and one son, Alonso. Ogretia was beautiful. Alonso was very much like the old Mr. Richard Booth [Wilkes' grandfather]. John's wife is still living. Her name was Izalia. I do not know her maiden name. John told Rosalie [his sister] he would give her two oil wells, and he wished her to take care of those two children, which she did although they were with their mother. Rosie calls them her children. John was not married to their mother. After John's death she ["Izalia" is written above "she"] went with the children away to Illinois. They ["the children" is added just above] are both married now, poor children. Oh the trouble bad people do, and cause trouble, trouble, to others. Mrs. Junius Brutus Booth [Wilkes' mother], the trouble she had, was almost insupportable. . . .

In this letter, Mrs. Rogers also wrote: "None of the family takes any account of John Wilkes' children but Rosalie. She is very kind to them; does not visit them, but sends them money every spring and fall."

According to Izola Forrester in *This One Mad Act*, the actual name of Wilkes' common-law wife was Izola Martha Mills D'Arcy, and their daughter was named Ogarita Rosalie. She acted under the name of Rita Booth.

(The above is adapted from the author's article "Old Neighbor's Story Reveals More of Booth's Private Life," Washington *Post*, May 9, 1943.)

During the summer of 1953, Mr. Richard Merrifield, the great-grandson of John Wilkes Booth, came to Washington and asked me to take him over the escape route traveled by Booth and Herold on the night of Lincoln's assassination.

He was then the editor of *Yankee*, a monthly magazine published in Dublin, New Hampshire, and said he wished to write a story about the trip.

We discussed his family connection and I showed him my copy of Mrs. Rogers' letter which, I said, confirmed my conclusion in the first edition of *The Mad Booths of Maryland* that there had been no marriage of his ancestors at Cos Cob, Connecticut, at least not on the date January 9, 1859, as recorded by his mother, Izola Forrester, in her book *This One Mad Act*.

In the October 1953 issue of the magazine he published his account of the trip from which the following interesting excerpts are quoted:

> One of his [John Wilkes Booth's] romances seems to have resulted in a marriage. How much it meant to him is not known—he either kept it a secret from his family (except his sister Rosalie), or they kept it a secret themselves. The lady was Izola Martha Mills D'Arcy, a Richmond belle, half Yankee, half Spanish.
> Izola fell in love and, according to her story (still extant in her family papers), eloped to Cos Cob, Conn. and there married John Wilkes Booth.
> She had a daughter, Ogarita, who became a well-known actress in the 1880's, as Rita Booth. . . .
> A mood of tragedy hung over her [Izola's] life and that of her children. Her daughter Ogarita felt it especially. So—though less tragically—did Ogarita's children, one of whom now directs a summer theatre in New Hampshire (Beatrice Booth Colony); another of whom [Izola Forrester Page (1878-1944)] wrote a book about [her grandfather] John Wilkes Booth—*This One Mad Act*.

Izola Forrester was Richard Merrifield's mother. In the account of the trip over the escape route, he wrote:

> Kimmel and this writer had discussed the wisdom of telling our family connection. At first, we had planned to be only an editor from New England, doing a story. We had no desire to become involved, much less trade upon the connection. If this plan were to be deviated from, Mr. Kimmel and we had agreed on a certain signal. . . .
> The Mudd house was not hard to find—a corn and tobacco farm of good size, suffering under the drought. Unchanged, the house stands on a height of land overlooking fields sloping toward Zachiah Swamp. We knocked. No answer. We called through a window and a voice bade us enter. Within—the very room where Dr. Mudd had set Booth's leg—we found a tired man, with tousled brown hair, in farm clothes, taking the morning off while he thought over his drought problem, his poor farming equipment, and lack of dependable help. His attractive wife was visiting an ailing brother. His children were grown up, one in the armed forces. He received us in an uncommunicative mood, more especially so when told that one of us was doing a story. This was, we ventured, the Mudd house?
> "Don't know anything about it," said our unwilling host, and there was a grim edge in his voice. We looked at the mantel, where hung a large and famous portrait of Dr. Samuel Mudd. "Is that Dr. Mudd?" we asked.
> "Ye-es, that's Dr. Sam. But I don't want to talk about it."
> He warmed enough to say that he was Joe Mudd, Dr. Sam's grandson. But, he added, "You fellows ought to know how my family felt about all that. As for me, I don't know anything and don't care." Yet this Joe Mudd, not caring, had seen to it that the old place stayed in the family. He was farming it.
> Joe finally showed us a file of newspaper stories—some headlining Dr. Mudd as a martyred hero. On one page of an album, start[l]ingly, was a picture of John Wilkes Booth. But Joe was growing more displeased with us all the time. Kimmel looked at us and we nodded.
> "Joe," said Kimmel, "what I'm going to tell you may make you

Izola Martha Mills D'Arcy, Wilkes' common-law wife. From the collection of Gail Merrifield, their great-great-granddaughter.

Ogarita Booth, daughter of Izola and John Wilkes Booth. From the collection of Gail Merrifield, her great-granddaughter.

want to run us off your place. But we think you ought to know. You're Dr. Sam Mudd's grandson. This fellow here is Booth's great grandson."

Only men of the soil can swear, as Joe did, with a profanity so slow, deep and rich that it is almost like a noble incantation in a Druidic rite. And Joe swore so, rousing himself from his despair to come across the room and shake hands warmly. It was a curious brotherhood of descendants, and we for one quite frankly relished the historic quality of the moment.

Joe relaxed. We were all good friends. And Joe showed us the lane leading to Zachiah Swamp. "If you ever have time," he said, pointing it out, as his grandfather had to Booth, "I could show you every inch of the route they took down there.". . .

[We had to cover the entire route before dark so we moved along the trail, as pictured in this volume, stopping at other places where Booth and Herold had been in hiding.—S. K.]

Up from Port Conway today runs a wide highway, flanked by a military reservation. Two miles and you come to a marker, the official end of the Booth trail. Garrett's house and tobacco barn are long since gone. There are only the gray marker on the highway, and a dark, Poe-esque thicket. We made our way far into the thicket, seeking the foundation, but without success. . . .

. . . For our story . . . it was the end of our trail; the end of the day's labors and searchings. . . . In the early twilight we reread the marker, and remembered our great grandmother, John Wilkes Booth's wife, who lies in a grave at Canterbury Plains, Conn. For her sake we dropped at the base or [of] the marker, a bit of Queen Anne's Lace, which in a way was a touch of New England, for we had lived in Canterbury, too. [Then we turned the car around] and returned to Washington.

During the preparation of this edition I received the following from Mr. Merrifield's daughter, Gail, who is now the custodian of the John Wilkes Booth family archives:

Izola Martha Mills D'Arcy: Her full name was Martha Lizola Mills. She signed all her letters and most of the poems she wrote, Martha Lizola, or just M. L. I have her diaries, many of her poems, and some of her letters, in her own handwriting and signature. For a while, as a child, she lived with relatives named D'Arcy, and used their name.

I don't know when the photograph I gave you was taken. She died in 1887 at the age of fifty years (she was born September 11, 1837), so probably the photograph was taken during the early 1880s. At that time (1881) she was married to Edwin Bates and lived in Canterbury, Connecticut. She made regular trips to Boston to see her family and old theatrical friends, so it might have been taken then.

Incidentally, I have certified copies for three of her marriages:

(1) 1855: She married Charles Still Bellows in Boston.

(2) 1859: She was supposed to have married John Wilkes Booth. This marriage was not in Cos Cob, Connecticut, as my grandmother [Izola Forrester] supposed. Cos Cob was merely where Rev. Peleg Weaver, the minister who she stated performed the ceremony, spent his last days, and where his descendants remained. Rev. Weaver was somewhere else in 1859, and I am still trying to find out his location at that time.

(3) 1871: She married John H. Stevenson in Boston.

(4) 1881: She married Edwin Sylvanus Bates in Pascoag, Rhode Island.

According to my records, she had at least four children: A boy born out of wedlock in 1852 who died in 1856. Probably his father was George Shepperd. Ogarita Booth, born in 1859, and her brother, Charles Still, born in 1861, both of whom have the last name Bellows on their birth certificates. They probably were John Wilkes Booth's children. In 1871 she had another son, Harry Stevenson, whose father was John Stevenson.

Ogarita Booth: Her full name was Ogarita Elizabeth Booth. Her middle name was not Rosalie (as mentioned in my grandmother's book) either in the record left by her own mother, or on her birth certificate, both of which gave it as Elizabeth. (I have the birth certificate.)

The photograph I gave you of her was taken during her 1888 engagement at the People's Theatre in Minneapolis, Minn. She was about twenty-nine or thirty then (born October 23, 1859) and her stage name was Rita Booth which is on all of the programs I have. That was the first year she openly wore the brooch with her father's [John Wilkes Booth's] photograph, or had her photograph taken wearing it. Reasons? From her letters, the chief reason was economic. Her mother had died the year before and she was in desperate financial circumstances which she sought to alleviate by selling stories of her family relationship to John Wilkes Booth.

SUPPLEMENT II

THE FEUD BETWEEN ASIA AND EDWIN BOOTH

The location of the letters that tell this story has been given little publicity, since staff members of the museum guarding them do not wish to be besieged as the staff of the Library of Congress, before the Robert Todd Lincoln Collection of his father's papers was opened to the public, was besieged by historians, biographers, and others seeking to gain information of their contents previous to the date designated for release.

It can be said, however, that the most important of the forty-five letters making up the collection relate to Edwin Booth and Mary Devlin, his first wife, but all disclose the turmoil of the Booth family covering the years from 1852 to 1874. The story in which Edwin's sister Asia played the leading rôle against his marriage to Mary Devlin was fully revealed for the first time in the first edition of *The Mad Booths of Maryland*.

(The above is adapted from the author's article "New Slant on the Booths," Washington *Sunday Star*, July 27, 1947.)

SUPPLEMENT III

LINCOLN SEES WILKES BOOTH ACT

The Marble Heart was one of the popular sensational dramas of the time. Edwin Booth had played the lead in it in California when it was first seen in the United States about eight years before. But it was Wilkes who had gained a reputation in the dual rôle of the sculptors Phidias and Raphael Duchalet, and made the drama one of his greatest efforts on the stage. It was Wilkes who put life into the romance of that drama—the love of a young sculptor for an unscrupulous woman. It was Wilkes who kept his audiences spellbound during the highly emotional scenes of the play; Wilkes who stood before the curtain at the close of each performance while the crowd applauded and shouted approval. *The Marble Heart* was his play, and performances by other actors were weak and listless compared with his fiery interpretation.

"By his earnestness, his vigorous grasp of genius, and his fervor of style, he invests it with an interest beyond the author's ideal, and claims in the result the most brilliant honors," wrote one critic. "The rôle is peculiarly well fitted to Wilkes Booth, and it is not to be wondered at that he has achieved in its embodiment his richest distinctions."

Nothing more than a desire to see Wilkes at his best could have induced Lincoln to attend a play having so inane a plot as *The Marble Heart*. It was Faust in reverse. And Wilkes, like his father, was neither dependable nor consistent in his performances. In the first scene, a prologue disclosing the dimly lighted studio of the sculptor Phidias at Athens, Wilkes' entrance aroused a deep interest. Dressed in a slate-colored shirt with white Grecian border, his dark hair partly covered by a Phrygian cap, and wearing a small beard and mustache, he achieved an appealing, ethereal quality with his finely molded features.

But in the performance Lincoln saw, Wilkes' blustering refusal to deliver the statues he had created for the wealthy Gorgias, because of his infatuation for them, did not carry conviction. When the statues awakened to momentary life, and by gesture indicated their preference for Gorgias rather than for the artistic Phidias, Wilkes' denunciation of them lacked the sneering bite of contempt. That night the young actor was not up to his usual standard.

A modernized version of this theme which followed, with Wilkes in regal velvet as Raphael Duchalet, the reincarnation of Phidias, gave him an opportunity to redeem himself. However, only in the scene with Mademoiselle Marco, the reincarnation of one statue, did he display the fiery emotion with which he was gifted. For a few fleeting seconds when he upbraided Marco for her mercenary nature and disdain of his love, he soared toward the heights of inspired acting. In despair he threw himself upon a divan and sobbed bitterly as the audience burst into applause. Lincoln, too, joined in the loud acclaim with all that genial heartiness for which he was so distinguished.

It was Wilkes' only spurt of effort that evening. Throughout the remaining scenes he was indifferent and apathetic. He seemed to be waiting for the end of the play. When told of the President's appreciation of his acting, Wilkes curtly replied that he would have preferred the applause of a Negro. Although Lincoln once expressed a desire to meet him, Wilkes evaded making the President's acquaintance; yet he was generally aware of his whereabouts and public appearances.

Was it just a coincidence that on the evening Lincoln attended *The Marble Heart* at Ford's Theatre, Wilkes' interpretation of his rôles lacked the fervor of his other performances? Or did reports of the Union bombardment of Charleston and a Union victory at Rappahannock Station, where Meade had surprised Lee and captured many prisoners, join with the presence of Lincoln to bring on one of the despondent, moody spells Wilkes labored under so often when defeat of the Confederate cause seemed imminent? Probably it was the combination of all these facts that gave the critics, and John Hay, such an uncomplimentary estimate of Wilkes' acting that evening.

(The above is adapted from the author's article "Lincoln Had Deep Appreciation of Acting of John Wilkes Booth," Washington *Sunday Star*, April 15, 1941.)

SUPPLEMENT IV

CRANK LETTERS ON LINCOLN'S ASSASSINATION

The crank-letter writer is the bane of every police chief whose city has ever investigated a major murder. That the breed had forebears as far back as the Civil War is revealed by some faded letters discovered in Government files. Among them are several written to members of President Lincoln's Cabinet shortly after his assassination. Most of them follow a familiar pattern, but some have a ring of authenticity.

One was addressed to Secretary of State William H. Seward after Lewis Paine tried to kill him. It read:

Mr. Wm. H. Seward:
I wish I had cut off your damn head while I was at it instead of only half doing it; if only I had you and Johnson and Stanton out of the way I would feel as if I had done my duty to my country, but knowing that I could not get at Stanton as he did not come out of the house until I saw someone come for him, and knew that my partner had done his part of the work, I thought it best to "light out" of that damn abolition hole as soon as I could, and now I have got here and am not afraid of being caught by your damned hirelings.

I may not be seen in this part of the world again but one thing sure you will never see me alive for I will put a ball through my own head before I will be taken.

The South is avenged and one of the U.S. Presidents gone to Hell or some other port with a ball through his head.

Sic Semper Tyrranis [sic]
JORGEN

On the very day that Wilkes Booth was captured and died at Garrett's farm, the following letter was sent to Secretary of War Stanton:

Dear Sir:
I have the pleasure of addressing you. I am the fellow who put the bullet through Old Abe's head on Good Friday night in Washington and I have got to Canada safe and sound. Of course you will think me a fool to let you know where I am here but you will be mistaken. I have good reason in letting you know that I am in Canada. I might also tell you that I have seen Jake Thompson [a Confederate agent] since I came here, so now you can send your detectives to Canada and search for me and see what the result will be—see will they catch me or not.

I cannot finish this without letting you know how I crossed at Buffalo. I dressed myself in woman's clothes and painted my cheeks and escaped splendidly; got over to Hamilton, from there to Toronto, from there to a place that will be nameless.

I am with pleasure, the assassin of Old Abe.

J. W. BOOTH
per R. S. P.

Booth is sleeping while I am writing. R. S. P., an accomplice—he told me to write this to you.

SUPPLEMENT IV

General Christopher C. Augur, commander of the troops in the Capital, while searching for Wilkes Booth received a letter which read:

> Sir:
> I'm still in your midst. I will remain in this city. God will'd that I should do it. I defy detection.
> J. W. BOOTH
> Actor and Assassin of President Lincoln.
>
> P.S.: The ways of the most high are past finding out.

Another letter, apparently sent to harass authorities, was addressed to John Wilkes Booth in Washington. It had been written five days after Lincoln's assassination. Wilkes Booth and David E. Herold were then hiding in a densely wooded section of Samuel Cox's farm in lower Maryland.

> John:
> I take the present opportunity to write you a few lines. I am well today but there are many rumors that we are all unhappy. I hope you will be able to get to N. Y. as there would be more room for you. I saw Mary off yesterday; the things were sent as you requested through Mr. F. I have been trying to find where H. went but cannot yet. I was at the White House on Tuesday [the day Lincoln's body was on view in the East Room]. The old tyrant looked very natural.
> I shall send this by Ben as he is the only one whom the detectives would not suspect. Send me a reply by him and tell me if you will try to get to N. Y. this week. I think you had better keep still for a few days, as you know your head is not worth much if they once get you. Hoping you may get out of this place soon, I remain
> Your friend,
> T. E.

Not all of these letters were from cranks. Some were sent with good intentions and bore authentic signatures. One, dated West Troy, April 20, 1865, and signed Silas S. Jones, was addressed to Stanton.

> Sir:
> From information in my possession, I believe J. W. Booth to be secreted in the city of Chicago, Ill., in Tenth ave., No. 16, in a house of ill fame. He is disguised as a female, so my informant says.

A similar letter expressed the opinion that, since Wilkes Booth and several of his accomplices were known to have "lived in sin with women," it might be well to ferret out these women. It was marked "acted upon. B."—probably Colonel Baker.

(The above is adapted from the author's article "Cranks Had a Field Day over Booth," Washington *Post*, February 7, 1947.)

SUPPLEMENT V

A LETTER WRITTEN BY JOHN WILKES BOOTH

The following is the text of the letter published by the Philadelphia *Enquirer* on April 19, 1865:

1864

My dear Sir:

You may use this as you think best. But as *some* may wish to know *when*, who and *why* as I know not *how* to direct, I give it (in the words of your master)—"To whom it may concern."

Right or wrong, God judge me, not man. For be my motives good or bad, of one thing I am sure, the lasting condemnation of the North. I love peace more than life. Have loved the Union beyond expression. For four years I have waited, hoped and prayed for the dark clouds to break and for a restoration of our former sunshine. To wait longer would be a crime. All hope for peace is dead. My prayers have proved as idle as my hopes. God's will be done. I go to see and share the bitter end.

I have ever held the South were right. The very nomination of Abraham Lincoln, four years ago, spoke very plainly of war, war, upon Southern rights and institutions. His election proved it. "Await an overt act." Yes, till you are bound and plundered. What folly. The South was wise. Who thinks of argument or pastime when the finger of his enemy presses the trigger? In a *foreign* war, I, too, could say "country right or wrong." But in a struggle *such as ours* (where the brother tries to pierce the brother's heart) for God's sake choose the right. When a country like this spurns *justice* from her side, she forfeits the allegiance of every honest freeman and should leave him, untrammeled by any fealty soever, to act as his conscience may approve. People of the North, to hate tyranny, to love liberty and justice, to strike at wrong and oppression, was the teaching of our fathers. The study of our early history will not let me forget, and may it never.

The country was formed for the white, not for the black man. And looking upon African slavery from the same standpoint held by the noble framers of our Constitution, I, for one, have ever considered it one of the greatest blessings (both for themselves and us) that God ever bestowed upon a favored nation. Witness heretofore our wealth and power: witness their elevation and enlightenment above their race elsewhere. I have lived among it most of my life, and I have seen *less* harsh treatment from master to man than I have beheld in the North from father to son. Yet, heaven knows, *no one* would be willing to do *more* for the Negro race than I, could I but see the way to *still better their condition*.

But Lincoln's policy is only preparing a way for their total annihilation. The south *are not, nor have they* been fighting for the continuation of slavery. The first battle of Bull Run did away with that idea. Their causes for war have been *as noble and greater far than those that urged our fathers on. Even* should we allow they were wrong at the beginning of this contest, *cruelty and injustice* have made the wrong become the right, and they stand now (before the wonder and admiration of the world) as a noble band of patriotic heroes. Hereafter, reading of their deeds, Thermopylæ will be forgotten.

When I aided in the capture and execution of John Brown (who was a murderer on our Western border and who was fairly tried and convicted before an impartial judge and jury, of treason, and who, by the way, has since been made a god) I was proud of my little share in the transaction, for I deemed it my duty that I was helping our common country to perform an act of justice. But what was a crime in poor John Brown is considered (by themselves) as the greatest and only virtue of the whole Republican party. Strange transmigration. *Vice so* becomes a *virtue,* simply because more indulged in. I thought then as *now* that the Abolitionists were the *only traitors* in the land and that the entire party deserved the fate of poor John Brown, not because they wish to abolish slavery, but on account of the means they have ever used to effect that abolition. If Brown were living I doubt whether he *himself* would set slavery against the Union. Most or many in the North do, and openly curse the Union, if the South are to return and retain a *single right* guaranteed to them by every tie which we once revered as sacred.

The South can make no choice. It is either extermination or slavery for *themselves* (worse than death) to draw from. I know my choice.

I have also studied hard to know upon what grounds the right of a state to secede has been denied, when our very name United States, and the Declaration of Independence *both* provide for secession.

But there is no time for words. I write in haste. I know how foolish I shall be deemed for taking such a step as this, where on the one side, I have many friends and many things to make me happy, where my profession *alone* has gained me an income of more than twenty thousand dollars a year, and where my great personal ambition in my profession has such a great field for labor. On the other hand, the South have never bestowed upon me one kind word: a place where I must become a private soldier or a beggar. To give up all the *former* for the *latter, besides* my mother and my sisters, whom I love so dearly (although they so widely differ from me in opinion), seems insane: but God is my judge. I love justice more than a country that disowns it, more than fame and wealth; more (Heaven pardon me if I am wrong), more than a happy home.

I have never been upon a battle field; but, O my countrymen, could you all see the *reality* or effects of this horrid war as I have seen them (in every state save Virginia) I know you would think like me, and would pray the Almighty to create in the Northern mind a *sense of right and justice* (even if it should possess no seasoning of mercy) and that He would dry up the sea of blood between us which is daily growing wider. Alas, poor country. Is she to meet her threatened doom?

Four years ago I would have given a thousand lives to see her remain (as I had always known her) powerful and unbroken. And even now I would hold my life at naught to see her what she was. Oh, my friends, if the fearful scenes of the last four years had never been enacted, or if what has been was a frightful dream from which we could now awake, with what flowing hearts could we bless our God and pray for His continued favor. How I have loved the *old flag* can never be known. A few years since and the entire world could boast of *none* so pure and spotless. But I have of late been seeing and hearing of the *bloody* deeds of which she has been *made the emblem*. O, how I have longed to see her break from the mist of blood that circles round her folds, spoiling her beauty and tarnishing her honor. But no, day by day, has she been dragged deeper and deeper into cruelty and oppression till now (in my eyes) her once bright red stripes look like *bloody gashes* on the face of heaven. I look now upon my early admiration of her glories as a dream. My love (as things stand to-day) is for the South alone. Nor do I deem it a dishonor in attempting to make for her a prisoner of this man to whom she owes so much misery.

If success attends me, I go penniless to her side. They say she has found that "last ditch" which the North has so long derided and has been endeavoring to force her in, forgetting they are our brothers, and that it's impolitic to force on an enemy to madness. Should I reach her in safety and find it true, I will proudly beg permission to triumph or die in that same "ditch" by her side.

A Confederate doing duty on his own responsibility.

J. WILKES BOOTH

SUPPLEMENT VI

GHOSTS OF THE NATIONAL HOTEL

In 1942 the old National Hotel, known as the National Guard Armory, at Sixth Street and Pennsylvania Avenue, Northwest, was demolished. One of Washington's oldest landmarks, the building began its historic career in 1826. During the years that followed, new additions were made and it became one of the largest hotels in the United States. It once boasted a garden and fountain in a courtyard with balconies extending from the rooms above. The Grand Ballroom was the scene of many brilliant political and social events attended by famous men and beautiful women. Its most distinguished guest was Henry Clay, the great statesman and orator of his time.

H. S. Benson was the owner when Wilkes Booth resided there. He came to Washington from Philadelphia, purchased the hotel in April 1863, and operated it until his death in 1869.

All the theatrical celebrities stayed there during their engagements in the city. It was the favorite hotel of Edwin Forrest, Charlotte Cushman, the popular Joseph Jefferson, John Wilkes Booth and his friends, John McCullough. Senator John P. Hale of New Hampshire and his family often were there, and it is possible that Wilkes met his daughter, the lovely Bessie Hale, to whom he was engaged at the time of his death, while they were guests at the hotel.

G. W. Bunker, who was the clerk there during Wilkes' visits, testified at the trial of the conspirators in May 1865:

> From the register, which I have examined, I find that Booth was not at the National Hotel during the month of October 1864. He arrived in the evening of November 9, and occupied room 20; left on an early train on the morning of the 11th; returned November 14, in the early part of the evening, and left on the 16th. His next arrival was December 12; left December 17 on the morning train; he arrived again December 22; left on the 24th; arrived December 31; left January 10; arrived again January 12; left on the 28th; arrived again February 22; occupied room 231, in company with John T. H. Wentworth and John McCullough. Booth left February 28 on 8:15 a.m. train, closing his account to date inclusive. His name does not appear on the register, but another room is assigned to him, and his second account commences March 1, without any entry on the register of that date. On the 2nd, 3rd, and 4th he is called at 8 o'clock a.m.; 21st of March, pays $50 on account; and left that day on 7:30 p.m. train; arrived again March 25—room 231; took tea; and left April 1 on an afternoon train; arrived April 8, room 228, and remained there until the assassination of the President.

It was then that the National Hotel played a part in a drama which has become one of the most interesting chapters in American history. During the early morning hours following Lincoln's assassination, Wilkes' friends stood about in the lobby awaiting his return. They could not believe that he had committed such a crime. They hopefully expected him to stride in at any moment and deny the rumors they had heard in the streets. At daybreak they strolled out into Pennsylvania Avenue to ask questions and listen while others talked.

As the walls of the building were being torn down, Robert E. Welch, the last chief engineer employed there, told the present writer that he had taken up his duties in April 1917:

> The hotel was then much the same as it was in 1865. It had about 300 rooms, one large dining hall, and several smaller quarters which were used for private affairs. It was operated as a hotel until January 1931. The following month all the furnishings were sold. The furniture in all the rooms was much the same, large pieces in dark walnut, the kind you see in the antique shops today. In March the Government troops moved in and it became the National Guard Armory.
>
> I remember rooms 116, which was once number 32, and 228. Henry Clay died in room 116 in June 1852. When the hotel furnishings were sold, a gentleman from the South purchased all the contents of that room. I do not know what he did with them. John Wilkes Booth was occupying room 228 at the time he killed President Lincoln. No, I don't know who bought the furnishings from that room. I don't suppose anyone would want them as relics. They might bring bad luck.

Joseph Keefer was one of the city's oldest inhabitants when the present writer interviewed him:

> I was a boy working in Washington at the close of the Civil War. Every day I passed by the rear of the National Hotel on C Street, Northwest, on my way home. Pumphrey's livery stable was just across the way. Wilkes Booth often hired a certain saddle-horse from Pumphrey. It was a fine animal—not that little bay mare he rode out of Washington after shooting Mr. Lincoln. Many afternoons I saw Wilkes Booth standing at the hallway window in the rear of the National Hotel calling to Pumphrey's man to have the horse ready for him. Soon Wilkes Booth would come out, mount the horse, and gallop off up the street. He was a handsome man, I tell you, and he knew how to manage a horse. Every one in the street always turned and watched him when he passed.
>
> One afternoon I came by the rear of the hotel and saw Wilkes Booth leaning out of a window. He was letting down a long piece of heavy cord to the sidewalk near a cellar doorway. An old Negro who worked in the hotel was fastening a bottle of wine to the end of the cord. Just as Wilkes Booth began pulling it up on the cord the bottle slipped off and hit the old Negro on the head. Wilkes Booth did not laugh; I could see he was afraid the old Negro had been hurt. The old Negro rubbed his head, grinned, and tied the unbroken bottle onto the cord again. That time it went up all right.

(The above is adapted from the author's article "Ghosts of Old National Hotel Must Find Other Halls to Haunt," Washington *Post*, September 22, 1942.)

INDEX

INDEX

Abbey, Henry E., manager for Edwin, 298
Actor's Home, 318, 322
Adams, Edwin, 278, 279
Adelphi Theatre, San Francisco, competes with Jenny Lind Theatre, 83; Junius Brutus Booth at, 88-89; London, 308
Aladdin, 211
Albany, 72, 158
Albaugh's Lyceum Theatre, 326
Aldrich, T. B., on cruise with Edwin, 317
Alien Office, 21
All That Glitters Is Not Gold, 82
Amateurs and Actors, 47
American Fireman, The, 101
American Theatre, in Sacramento, 81, 87
American Theatre, in San Francisco, 83, 119
Amsterdam, Junius Booth in, 19, 27
Amy Robsart, 330
Anderson, Dave, becomes Edwin's confidant, 89; in Waller's troupe, 96; sympathy for Edwin, 100; goes to Australia with Edwin, 109-110; at Forrest Theatre, 129; protects property of Junius, Jr., 269; at Booth's Theatre, 284; in California, 294; Edwin writes to, 297-298; joins Edwin's troupe, 307
Andromaque, 45
Angel's Camp, 127
Annapolis, 45
Antwerp, 19
Apostate, The, 76, 157, 158, 159, 170, 276
Arnold, Dr. Edwin, 70
Arnold, Samuel B., acquaintance with John Wilkes, 78; plots against Lincoln, 186-187, 203-208; meets John Surratt, 199; grows restless, 200; at Old Point Comfort, 215; imprisoned, 264, 354; pardoned, 354
Arthur, Chester A., requests Edwin to play in Washington, 271
Ashton, Dr., 248
Aspinwall, 113

Assassination of President Lincoln and the Trial of the Conspirators, 6
Astor Place Opera House, 143-144
Atlas and Argus, quoted, 159
Atzerodt, George, plots against Lincoln, 199, 203-208, 218-219; visits Surratt home, 201; hires horse, 217; followed by Fletcher, 224; hanging and burial of, 264, 281, 358; quoted, 354; movements of, 358

Badeau, Adam, at Edwin's wedding, 142; letter from Edwin, 171; cared for by John Wilkes, 175-176; learns of Robert Lincoln's accident, 182; remembers Grant's offer, 279
Bainbridge, A. R., at Port Royal Ferry, 243-245; helps John Wilkes escape, 246-247, 250; arrested, 363
Baker, Alexina, at Jenny Lind Theatre, 83; at Winter Garden, 169
Baker, Ben, manages Forrest Theatre, 122, 123; interested in Edwin's acting, 125; as Edwin's manager, 135-140
Baker, Colonel La Fayette C., friendship with Junius, Jr., 82, 269-270; heads search for fugitives, 231, 360; learns of John Wilkes' death, 260; buries John Wilkes, 261, 367; at trial, 368; receives reward, 368
Baker, Lewis, at Jenny Lind Theatre, 82-83; at Winter Garden, 169
Baker, Lieutenant Luther B., pursues fugitives, 231, 247-248, 251; at Garrett farm, 254-258, 364-365; with John Wilkes' body, 259-260; buries John Wilkes, 261, 367; receives reward, 368
Baltimore, 35, 45, 56, 59, 64, 67-71, 91, 135, 140, 142, 149, 151, 154, 161, 162, 166, 186, 191, 276, 297, 324, 326
Baltimore Cemetery, 141
Baltimore *Sun*, 58
Bangs, Frank, 286
Banks, General N. P., 179
Barbarian, The, 107
Barker, Benjamin, 186

403

INDEX

Barnes, Surgeon General, performs autopsy on John Wilkes, 260-261, 366
Barnum's Hotel, 186
Barrett, Lawrence, becomes Edwin's friend, 139; at Winter Garden, 176-177; at Booth's Theatre, 285-286; in England, 300; tours with Edwin, 316, 318-319, 321, 324-327; in *Hamlet*, 320-321; unpopularity of, 321, 381; and The Players, 323; illness and death of, 325-327
Barron, Billy, 190, 263
Barron, John M., scene with John Wilkes, 153-154; believes John Wilkes shot himself, 365
Barry, Summerfield, 68
Barry, Thomas, 138
Barry, William, 96
Barton, Thaddeus, 76
Bateman, H. L., 177
Battle of Bull Run, 166
Battle of Chattanooga, 184
Battle of Chickamauga, 184
Battle of Lookout Mountain, 184
Battle of Missionary Ridge, 184
Battle of Rich Mountain, 166
Battle of Vicksburg, 179, 184
Battle of Waterloo, 19
Battle of Wilderness, 184
Battle of Wilson Creek, 166
Beall, John Yates, hanging of, 367
Beckwith, Captain S., telegraphs Washington, 362
Belair Academy, 70
Bell, William, 224
Bell's Stratagem, The, 107
Bells, The, 299
Benedict, E. C., Edwin visits, 307; Edwin on cruise with, 317
Berlin, 309-310
Berlin Residenz Theatre, 309
Bertram, 78
Bishop, C. B., 280
Bispham, William, worried about Edwin, 269; Edwin writes to, 287-288, 305, 312-313; on cruise with Edwin, 317; at Edwin's bedside, 331
Blackburn, Dr., 188
Black-Eyed Susan, 129
Bond, Dr. Elijah, 38
Booth, Adelaide, courtship and marriage of, 20-21; popularity of, 26; learns of husband's trip to America, 32; in London, 36-37, 62; husband's visits to England, 43-44, 54-56; letter to sister, 63-64; gets divorce, 65, 340-341; comes to United States, 63-64; death of, 140
Booth, Agnes, at Booth's Theatre, 286-287; at Park Theatre, 298; at Philadelphia Chestnut Street Theatre, 311; death of Junius, Jr., 311; marries J. B. Schoeffel, 312; buried at Rosedale Cemetery, 379; *see also* Agnes Land
Booth, Algernon C., in Manchester, 289; death of, 290
Booth, Algernon Sydney, birth of, 17
Booth, Asia, childhood and education of, 59-60, 70-71, 74; and John Sleeper Clarke, 67; tells of Edwin's adventures, 77; requests news of Edwin, 110-111; interest in Edwin, 133, 135; marries Sleeper Clarke, 142; attitude toward Mary Devlin, 141, 142, 143, 171; in Philadelphia, 267, 272; hears of assassination, 267; bitterness of, 272, 273; in England, 273; condemns Edwin, 279; investigated, 375; death of, 381; *see also* Asia Clarke
Booth, Barton J., in Manchester, 289; death of, 290
Booth, Blanche De Bar, birth of, 60; visits Asia, 142; at time of father's second marriage, 275; at Booth's Theatre, 284; at time of father's death, 311; adopted by Ben De Bar, 345; investigated, 373-375; report regarding father, 379; brings suit against estate, 379-380
Booth, Clementine, ignores Junius, 62; *see also* Clementine De Bar
Booth, Edgar, birth and death of, 284, 285; in Mount Auburn Cemetery, 307
Booth, Edwin, research on, 5-7; birth of, 49, 347; youth and education of, 59-60, 66-67, 71, 74-75, 332; first stage experiences, 68-69, 71; becomes father's attendant, 72-74; in Boston, 73, 135, 137, 139, 140, 307, 312, 315; on stage with father, 76-77; illness of, 84, 325, 326, 330-331, 378; sails for California, 84-86; in California, 86-88, 100-109; at Metropolitan Theatre, 107, 118, 130; bids father farewell, 89; discouragements of, 95, 171; in *Hamlet*, 104-105, 117, 135, 144, 170, 191, 274, 286, 300, 309, 316; in Waller's troupe, 96-100; father's death, 99-100; lives with Nat Hayward, 103; camps with Dave Anderson, 103-104; excessive drinking of, 107, 119, 120, 122, 169, 170, 315-316; sails to Australia,

INDEX

109-110; superstitions of, 115, 332-333; in Australia, 115-116; in Honolulu, 116-118; accidents to, 119, 276-277, 291; becomes temperate, 124; joins Moulten's troupe, 125-129; benefits for, 129-130, 135; returns home, 133-135; is refused father's costumes, 135; in Philadelphia, 74, 142, 143, 144, 183, 273, 297, 307; tours under Baker's management, 135-140; plays opposite Mary Devlin, 136; in Washington, 136, 182; in Chicago, 137, 276, 293; success of, 137, 139, 151, 157, 183, 275-276, 284, 291, 309-310, 319; at Winter Garden, 140, 143, 169, 170, 183, 191, 206-207; in New York, 140, 143, 171, 191, 291, 297-298, 312, 315; under Davenport's management, 140; courts Mary Devlin, 140, 141-142; erects family tombstone, 141, 345; marries Mary Devlin, 142-143; rivalry with Forrest, 143-145, 169; helps John Wilkes, 151-153; loyal to Union, 163; in England, 163-165, 299-306, 308-309; at Dorchester home, 169-170; at Niblo's Garden, 182; appears with brothers, 191; effect of assassination on, 268-269; letters of, 268-269, 279-281, 287-288, 291, 292, 293, 297-298, 299, 302, 303, 312-313, 341; leaves stage, 269, 271; refuses Canadian bank money, 271; debts of, 274, 285-286, 291, 294; returns to stage, 176, 274; receives Hamlet Medal, 275; inscription to, 326; and Booth's Theatre, 277-278, 284-288, 296; marries Mary McVicker, 278-279; obtains John Wilkes' body, 279-283; burns John Wilkes' trunk, 286; files bankruptcy, 287; on southern tour, 291-293; illness of Mary McVicker, 295-297, 298, 300, 302, 304, 305-306; publishes prompt books, 296; attempted murder of, 296-297; attends theatre, 297; and Henry Irving, 299-306, 312, 379; visits Asia, 301; death of Mary McVicker, 307; in Europe, 309-310; at *Boothden*, 311, 312; at Edwina's home, 315, 321, 329; tours with Barrett, 316, 318-319, 321, 324, 325-327; on cruise, 317; and The Players, 317-320, 322-323, 329, 330; and grandchildren, 321, 333; in benefit for Wallack, 320-321; dinner in honor of, 324-325; and Helena Modjeska, 326, 382; death of, 331; family skeletons of, 331-332; will of, 333; funeral of, 334; criticisms of, 348-349; replaces Garrett's barn, 364; escapes arrest, 271, 373; investigated, 375; recollections of, 382-383; tributes to, 384

Booth, Edwina, birth of, 165; in Philadelphia, 267, 272; in school, 277; at Notre Dame, 285; illness of Mary McVicker, 295, 298, 306; in Chicago, 297; social life of, 298; in England, 299, 302, 306, 308-310; illness of, 304, 308; in Europe, 309-310; at *Boothden*, 311; marries Grossman, 313; at father's bedside, 331; letter to The Players, 323; *see also* Edwina Grossman

Booth, Elizabeth, 44, 49, 283
Booth, Emilie, birth and death of, 21
Booth, Frederick, 44, 49, 283
Booth, Harriet, makes San Francisco début, 82; visits Maryland, 83-84; returns to California, 84-85; welcomed by Mary Ann, 110; death of, 132; *see also* Harriet Mace
Booth, Henry Byron, birth of, 41; death of, 54
Booth, Jane, birth of, 17; marries Jimmy Mitchell, 37; *see also* Jane Mitchell
Booth, John (father of Richard), 16
Booth, John Wilkes, research on, 5-7; named for John Wilkes, 16; revives father's play 42, 184; birth of, 58; boyhood of, 59-60, 66-67, 69-70, 74, 78, 341-342; appearances in *Richard III*, 134, 149, 151, 157, 158, 159, 166, 167, 168, 172, 173, 178, 180; at Tudor Hall, 110; becomes family problem, 112-113, 118; welcomes Edwin home, 133; at Edwin's wedding, 142; makes début, 149; in Philadelphia, 150-151, 172; failures of, 151-152; in Richmond, 153-156; attends Asia's wedding, 154; uses pseudonym, 155, 156; with militia, 155-156; accidents to, 156, 178; under Canning's management, 157-158; denounces North, 158-160, 168; in Albany, 159-160; attempt on life of, 161; in Baltimore, 161-162, 166-167; in Chicago, 166; in St. Louis, 166, 175; successes of, 166-167; in New York, 167; criticisms of, 168; in Midwest, 169-170; in Boston, 170, 177, 184; rivalry with Forrest, 170, 172; manages Washington Theatre, 174; under Dr. May's care, 174; denounces Lincoln, 175, 184; arrested, 175; visits Edwin, 175-176; in New Orleans, 179-180; sends medical supplies to South, 179,

INDEX

349; bronchial trouble of, 179, 180-181, 184, 185, 187, 204; speculations of, 185, 188, 350; diversions of, 186; and companion, Ella Starr, 186, 212; plots against Lincoln, 186-190, 194, 195-212, 216-221, 349, 352, 355; in Montreal, 188-189; strange actions of, 188, 190; at Dr. Mudd's home, 190-191, 227-230; appears with brothers, 191; letter to Junius, Jr., 197; unfriendly toward Edwin, 197; becomes morbid, 200; attends Lincoln's ceremonies, 202; appears at Ford's Theatre, 203-204; at shooting gallery 209; at White House, 210-211; writes note to Johnson, 215-216; questions Pumphrey, 217; at Taltavul's bar, 218; trips over flag, 221, 357; assassinates Lincoln, 221-223; dramatic leaps of, 222, 358; flight with Herold, 225-258; aided by Jones, 232-237; diary of, 234-235, 238-239, 366; writes to Dr. Stewart, 243, 362; at Garrett farm, 246-247, 249-258; shoots himself, 257, 363-364; death of, 257-258, 365; body returned to Washington, 259-261; body identified, 260-261, 366, 376; buried in convict's cell, 261; motive for assassination, 262-263, 367; burial by family, 279-283; reburial in Arsenal grounds, 280; stories of escape of, 345; letters from mother, 346-347, 352; debts of, 348; supposed trip to Europe, 351; baggage examined, 360; letter from Etta, 368; impostors of, 376-377; common-law family, 387-390

Booth, Joseph A., birth and youth of, 59-60, 70, 78; high morals of, 151; appearances on stage, 162; during Civil War, 162; arrest of, 272; contemplates trip to England with Asia, 273; treasurer of Booth's Theatre, 277; at John Wilkes' burial, 282-283; death of first wife, 314; becomes a doctor, 324; marries Cora Mitchell, 324; death of, 324; at Edwin's funeral, 334; quoted, 338; at undertaker's office, 375; home on Ocean Avenue, 381; death of widow of, 382

Booth, Junius Brutus, trial of, 15, 337; birth of, 17, 337; professional ambitions of, 17-18; begins stage career, 18-19; marries Adelaide Delannoy, 20-21; birth of children, 21, 26, 33, 35, 37, 41, 44, 49, 53, 58, 59, 340; success of, 21-22, 24-26, 42, 53; rivalry with Kean, 21-24, 35; escapade at Manchester, England, 25; in Amsterdam, 27; elopes with Mary Ann Holmes, 27-31; comes to United States, 30-31; writes to Adelaide, 32; début in United States, 32-33; applies for lighthouse post, 35; life on Maryland farm, 35-41, 45, 52, 53, 58; excessive drinking of, 36, 41, 45-46, 50-51, 56-58, 72, 74; leases land from Dr. Hall, 37, 338; eats no meat, 39-40, 45; writes play, 41-42; visits England, 43-44, 54-55; in New Orleans, 45, 89-90, 339; letters of, 46, 51, 54-55, 339; madness of, 47-48, 50, 56-58; death of children, 49, 54-55; under Hamblin's management, 49-50; disfigured by Flynn, 57-58; appears with daughter-in-law, 61; acts with Junius, Jr., 61-62; gives benefit for Clementine, 62; takes Richard on tours, 63; divorce of, 65, 340-341; marries Mary Ann Holmes, 65; and family at Baltimore, 67-71; with Edwin as attendant, 72-74; religious sentiments of, 75; acts with Edwin, 76-77; builds Tudor Hall, 76; farewell performance in New York, 78; in California, 84-89; sails for home, 89-90; illness and death, 90-91; bust in Booth's Theatre, 277; burial at Greenmount Cemetery, 282-283; diary quoted, 337

Booth, Junius, Jr., birth of, 35, 338, 340; in Richard III, 52, 340; education of, 53; with father, 54, 61-62; youth of, 59-60; marries Clementine De Bar, 60; on New York stage, 61; friendship with Harriet Mace, 61-62; in California, 79-82, 84-85, 288; birth of children, 82; manager of Jenny Lind Theatre, 82; visits Maryland, 83-84, 110-114; attitude toward Edwin, 95, 101-102, 104-105; at San Francisco Theatre, 106; worries about John Wilkes, 118; at Union Theatre, 123; as female impersonator, 129; throws manager of Lola Montez out of theatre, 131; after Harriet's death, 132; loyal to Union, 163; returns East, 182-183; appears with brothers, 191; hears of assassination, 269; arrested, 270, 373; release of, 273; stage manager of Boston Theatre, 274; marries Agnes Perry, 275; at John Wilkes' burial, 282-283; manager of Booth's Theatre, 286-287; in France, 288; in sword contest, 289; in Manchester, Mass., 289-291;

INDEX

Booth (cont.)
death and burial of, 311, 379; will of, 312, 379-380; mistaken report of, 348; affidavits of, 369-372
Booth, Junius III, in Manchester, Mass., 289; at time of father's death, 311; a problem, 330; at Edwin's funeral, 334; death of, 379, 383; brings suit against mother, 380; stage career of, 383
Booth, Marion, birth of, 82; stage début of, 132; in Philadelphia, 183, 267; at Notre Dame, 285; first appearances of, 290-291; on New York stage, 298; at time of father's death, 311; receives bequest from Edwin, 333; brings suit against father's estate, 379-380
Booth, Mary Ann, goes to meet husband, 91; troubles of, 111-113, 134-135, 193, 207, 279; in New York, 171, 298, 314; at sons' play, 191-192; in Philadelphia, 267, 272; hears of assassination, 267; at John Wilkes' burial, 282-283; at Long Branch, 307, 311; death and burial of, 314-315; stage appearances of, 339-340; letters to John Wilkes, 346-347, 352; *see also* Mary Ann Holmes
Booth, Mary Devlin, in England, 163-165; ill health and death of, 169-171, 207; *see also* Mary Devlin
Booth, Mary McVicker, birth and death of Edgar, 284-285; in California, 293; mental illness of, 295-297, 298, 300, 302, 304, 305-307; in England, 299-306; death of, 307; *see also* Mary McVicker
Booth, Mildred, *see* Mildred Tilton
Booth, Richard, at son's trial, 15; escapades of, 16; family life of, 17; in America, 37, 39; and son's mad actions, 54; ignores the Mitchells, 56; death of, 58; buried at Greenmount Cemetery, 282-283
Booth, Richard Junius, birth of, 26; comes to United States, 62-63; instructor in seminary, 140, 344; lives in Baltimore, 140-141; disappearance of, 345
Booth, Rosalie, birth of, 37; youth of, 59-60; at Tudor Hall, 110; in Philadelphia, 162; cares for Edwin, 171; at John Wilkes' burial, 282-283; in New York, 298; at Long Branch, 307, 311; death and burial of, 324, 381
Booth, Sally, 21, 26
Booth, Sydney Barton, in Manchester, 289; at time of father's death, 311; in *Amy Robsart*, 330; at Edwin's funeral, 334; death of, 379; brings suit against mother, 380
Boothden, 311, 312
Booths of Maryland, *see* Maryland Booths
Booth's Theatre, building of, 277; opening of, 277-278; difficulties of, 284-287; in bankruptcy, 287-288; Edwin at, 296; torn down, 310
Bothnia, 306
Boston, 73, 135, 137, 139, 140, 168, 184, 312, 315, 334
Boston Museum, 73, 170, 184
Boston Theatre, 138, 169; closed, 268
Boulogne, 28
Bowery Theatre, 50, 51, 52; destroyed by fire, 61
Braretta, Dr., 58
Brevitt, John, adventure with Richard, 16
Brignoli, Signor, 137
Broadway Theatre, 327
Brooklyn Academy of Music, 327
Brooklyn Theatre, panic and fire at, 294
Brown, Fanny, 177, 366
Brown, J. H., 271-272
Brown, John, revolt of, 155; hanging of, 155-156; compared with John Wilkes, 347-348
Brussels, 19, 20, 44, 54, 62
Brutus, 160
Brutus, 76, 87, 129, 275
Bryant, William L., 240-242·
Buckingham, J. E., 220
Buckstone, 163, 164
Buffalo, 72, 138, 316
Bull, Ole, 299
Burton, William E., 139
Butler, General Benjamin F., 161, 162, 179
Butler, M. P., arranges benefits for Edwin, 129-130
Byron, 45

Calais, 28
California Theatre, 288, 293, 294
Camilla's Husband, 182
Camille, 118
Camp Street Theatre, 45
Campbell Hospital, 204, 205, 206
Canito, Signor, 160
Canning, Matthew, owner of Columbus Theatre, 156; as John Wilkes' agent, 157-158; refuses John Wilkes, 194
Cape Hatteras, 35

INDEX

Capen, Nahum, letter from Edwin to, 341, 379
Carmelite Convent, 70-71
Carpenter, Harriet, theatrical expeditions of, 125; benefit for, 129
Carryl, Charles P., at Edwin's bedside, 331
Cary, Mrs. Richard F., 274
Chambers, Honorable Mrs., impressed by acting of Junius Brutus, 22; presents jewels to Mary Ann Holmes, 31
Chanfrau, Frank, 83
Chapman, Caroline, in Sacramento, 87; at San Francisco Theatre, 105-106; Edwin supports, 108; at Forrest Theatre, 119
Chapman, George, plays in San Francisco, 101
Chapman, Samuel, 20
Chapman, William B., 20, 84; makes San Francisco début, 83; in *Iron Chest*, 86; in Sacramento, 87
Charles II, or, The Days of the Merry Monarch, 117
Charleston, 33, 57, 136, 162
Charlestown, 155
Chester, Samuel Knapp, early acting of, 68; talks with John Wilkes, 194, 196; John Wilkes threatens, 199, 200
Chestnut Street Theatre, 41
Chicago, 137, 276, 293
Choate, Rufus, 91
Cincinnati, 91, 179
Ciocca, Madame, 77-78
City of Norfolk, 116
Clapp, C. C., 123
Clark, Professor, 182
Clarke, Asia Booth, letters belonging to, 7; insists parents were wed before leaving England, 31; birth of, 53; quoted, 337, 338, 345; books of, 301, 320, 337; death and burial of, 320; *see also* Asia Booth
Clarke, Creston, début of, 320; birth of, 369
Clarke, Edwin Booth, 320
Clarke, John Sleeper, and Edwin, 67, 68, 71; assists with Shakespearean reading in courthouse, 75-76; courts Asia, 112; marries Asia Booth, 142; helps John Wilkes, 149; success of, 149; at Winter Garden, 183, 191; hears of assassination, 267; arrested, 270-271, 372; in England, 273, 300; operates theatres, 274; at Booth's Theatre, 284; engages Marion, 291; affidavit of, 372-373
Clarke, Lillian, birth of, 369
Clemens, Samuel, in The Players, 310; *see also* Mark Twain
Cleveland, 175
Cleveland, Grover, at The Players, 330
Cleveland Academy of Music, 175
Cleveland *Leader*, 178
Cobb, Colonel C. F., meets John Wilkes, 217
Cobb, Sergeant Silas T., lets fugitives over bridge, 226; failure to question, 359
Coburg Theatre, 27
Codet, J. R., 74
Coghlan, Rose, 321
Cohasset, Mass., 327
Collyer, Reverend Robert, 307
Coloma, 127-128
Colombus Theatre, 156
Comedy of Errors, 118
Conger, Lieutenant Colonel E. J., pursues fugitives, 247-248; at Bowling Green, 253; at Garrett farm, 254-258; receives reward, 368
Conner, E. F., 128
Conner, T. L., arrested, 175
Cooke, George, 34
Cooper, John, 27
Cooper, Thomas, 33
Coquelin, 300
Corbett, Boston, at Garrett farm, 254; claims he shot John Wilkes, 257-258, 364-365; writes Edwin, 292-293; conversion of, 363; before Stanton, 365; receives reward, 368; in insane asylum, 377-378
Corday, Charlotte, 160
Corsican Brothers, The, 121-122
Cos Cob, 291, 296
Covent Garden Theatre, 18, 21-26
Coyle, Anna, 366
Coyle, John, 218
Cox, Samuel, in Confederate service, 231; aids fugitives to escape, 231-233; arrested, 361
Cushman, Charlotte, plays Romeo, 141; advises Mary Devlin, 142; acts with Edwin, 144; in Washington, 174; at Booth's Theatre, 285
Cuyler, 159
Cymbeline, 24

Daily Advertiser, 168
Daily Alta California, 86-87
Daily Crescent, 136-137

Daily National Intelligencer, 177
Daily Post, 157
Daly, Augustin, in The Players, 318; and The Players, 323; gives dinner for Edwin, 324-325
Daly, H. F., 86, 87
Daly, Joseph F., in The Players, 318; at Edwin's funeral 334
Daly's Fifth Avenue Theatre, 291
Damon and Pythias, 107
Damrosch, Walter, 321
Dante, 38
Davenport, E. L., manager for Edwin, 140; at Campbell Hospital, 205
Davenport, Jean, sails to Aspinwall, 113; in *Camille*, 118
Davis, Jefferson, leaves Richmond, 208
Dawison, Bogumil, 275
Dawson, Charles, identifies John Wilkes, 366
De Bar, Ben, manages St. Louis Theatre, 166, 175; hires John Wilkes, 176; manages St. Charles Theatre, 179; investigated, 373-375
De Bar, Blanche, 60, 142, 345
De Bar, Clementine, marries Junius, Jr., 60; prompt book of, 348; *see also* Clementine Booth
Debonay J. L., 219-220
Deery, John, 211-212
Delannoy, Adelaide, *see* Adelaide Booth
Delannoy, Madame, shelters Junius Booth, 20; and daughter's elopement, 20-21
Dennis, Sam, 96
Deptford, 19
Detroit, 138
Deveny, John, 222
Devlin, Mary, plays opposite Edwin, 136; courted by Edwin, 140, 141; marries Edwin, 142; *see also* Mary Booth
Diamond Springs, 127
Dielman, Louis H., 6
Dietrich, Louis, 327
Digger Indians, 127
Doherty, Lieutenant Edward P., searches for fugitives, 247-248; at Bowling Green, 253; at Garrett farm, 254-258; at steamer, 260; claims of, 363, 364; receives reward, 368
Dorchester, 169
Doster, W. E., defends Paine, 201
Douglas, Barton, 333
Dowling, James, 120
Doytt, John, arrested, 263
Drew, John, in The Players, 318

Drew, Mrs. John, 57
Drury Lane, 22, 23, 24, 25, 44
Dry Tortugas Island, 264, 316, 351, 354, 357, 359
Dugas, Louis, 71
Durant, Dr. G., cures Edwin of Black Tongue, 378
Dye, Sergeant Joseph, 220

Edwards, with John Wilkes in shooting gallery, 209
Edwards, Henry, at The Players, 318
Edwin, Sophie, at Forrest Theatre, 119
Elba, 19
Elder and the Younger Booth, The, 301
Eldridge, Louisa, quoted, 308
Elene, 289
Ellsler, John, 175, 178
Ellsler, Mrs. J., 263
English Theatre, 27
Era, London, 163, 164
Eradne, 47
Erskine, Lord, 22
Evening Post, 34
Everard, Marie, 294
Ewer, Ferdinand C., becomes Edwin's friend, 86; praises Edwin's acting, 104-105, 107; criticizes Collyer, 307

Fairchild, John, 82, 104
Fairclough, Boothroyd, 129
Faint Heart Never Won Fair Lady, 82
Farragut, David, 179
Fechter, Charles A., in *Hamlet*, 163, 284
Fenno, A. W., reports of West, 79; at Booth's Theatre, 278; goes West, 343
Ferguson, James P., John Wilkes exhibits his horse to, 218; witness of assassination, 356
Ferguson, W. J., witness of assassination, 356
Fifth Avenue Theatre, 312
Fletcher, John, 217; follows Atzerodt, 224; follows Herold, 225, 358-359
Florence, William, in *Hamlet*, 320-321
Flynn, Thomas, in Amsterdam, 27; as Booth's manager, 45-46; finds Booth on farm, 52; accompanies Booth on trip, 57
Folland, 96
Fool's Revenge, The, 182, 294
Forbes, Charles, statements of, 356
Ford, Harry, teases John Wilkes, 215
Ford, James, business manager, 354
Ford, John T., employs Gifford, 134; Mary Devlin under, 136; builds new theatre, 173; hires John Wilkes, 176;

arrested, 263; announces theatre to reopen, 264; regarding Junius, 270, 271; engages Marion 290; as Edwin's manager, 291-292
Ford's Richmond Theatre, 136
Ford's Theatre, 76; plot at, 216-219; Lincoln attends, 219-223; assassination at, 221-223; guarded, 263; becomes surgeon general's office, 264; tragedy at, 334
Forrest, Edwin, matrimonial troubles of, 105; at Niblo's Garden, 143, 169; rivalry with Edwin, 143-145, 169; rivalry with John Wilkes, 170, 172; at Ford's Theatre, 202; condemns the Booths, 272; declines Edwin's offer, 277; appointed trustee for Junius, Jr. and Rosalie, 338
Forrest Theatre, 119-123, 129
Forrnier, Mlle., 165
Fort Jefferson prison, 264, 351, 354
Fort McHenry, 167
Fort Sumter, 160, 162
Founder's Night, 323, 329, 330
Fox, Louis, H., 6
Freedley, George, 6
Freeman, Dr. Douglas S., 7
Freeman, Ned, 250; with John Wilkes' body, 259-260
Frisbie's Theatre, 128
Front Street Theatre, Lincoln renominated at, 184
Fulham, 165
Furness, Horace, 334

Gallagher, 282
Gallia, 308
Gamester, The, 150
Gardiner, George, 190
Gardiner, Polk, 226
Garfield, James A., assassination of, 306
Garrett, Joanna, 249
Garrett, John M., hears of Lincoln's assassination, 249; practices shooting with John Wilkes, 250; locks fugitives in barn, 252-253, 363; at barn, 255, 257; in Confederate uniform, 363
Garrett, Mrs., 250
Garrett, Richard H., fugitives at farm of, 246-247, 249-253; and officers, 254; Edwin replaces barn of, 364
Garrett, Robert, sees John Wilkes' weapons, 249; recalls burning of barn, 364
Garrett, William H., talks with John Wilkes, 249; practices shooting with John Wilkes, 250; and fugitives, 252-253, 363; in Confederate uniform, 363
Gates, D. V., 96
George III, 26
Germon, Effie, 366
Gettysburg, 184, 201
Gifford, James, architect for Booth, 76; duns Mary Ann, 134-135; alters stable for John Wilkes' horse, 198; carpenter at Ford's Theatre, 208
Gilbert, John, home at Singing Sands, 275; in *Hamlet*, 321
Gilfert, Charles, 32
Gillis, Mabel R., 7
Gladiator, The, 287
Gleason, Captain, 203
Globe Theatre, 294
Gobright, L. A., gives John Wilkes' pistol to police, 356; questions identity of assassin, 357
Golden Age, 130
Goldman, Mrs., 253
Goldsmith, 33
Goodale, Katherine, quoted, 317; and Edwin's superstitions, 333
Gooch, Walter, 299, 300, 302
Got, Edmond, alleges John Wilkes' visit, 351
Gould, Thomas R., 277
Graham, Lorrimer, and cast of Lincoln's hand, 332
Grant, Ulysses S., gives John Wilkes pass, 179; writes to Edwin, 182; takes command of army, 184; prohibits exchange of soldiers, 186, 350; plot against, 219; leaves Washington, 219, 355; Edwin writes to, 279-280
Grant, Mrs. Ulysses S., leaves Washington, 219, 355; social feud with Mary Lincoln, 355
Grass Valley, 97, 98
Grau, Maurice, takes over Booth's Theatre, 287
Gravesend, 20
Gray, Kate, goes to California, 79
Gray, Mark, attempts to kill Edwin, 296-297
Great Eastern, 165
Great Moral Drama, The, 123
Greenmount Cemetery, 282, 314, 320, 324, 340, 376
Green Street Gayety Theatre, 158, 159
Grey, Alice, 366
Grossman, Edwin Booth, 383
Grossman, Edwina, children of, 321, 383; death of, 383; *see also* Edwina Booth

INDEX

Grossman, Ignatius R., marries Edwina, 313; children of, 321
Grover, Leonard, 153
Grover's Theatre, 172, 173, 182, 190, 211, 217
Guardsman, The, 330
Guiteau, assassinates Garfield, 306

Hagar, 54, 55, 340
Hahn, Michael, 179
Hale, Bessie, fiancée of John Wilkes, 154, 209; letter concerning, 346-347; picture found on Wilkes' body, 366
Hall, Ann, 60; quoted, 64-65; welcomes Edwin home, 133
Hall, Joe, *see* Madagascan Joe
Hall, Joe Edwin, 338
Hall, Dr. Richard W., leases land to Junius Brutus, 37, 338
Hall, Thomas A., inspects Booth home, 367
Hamblin, manager of Junius Brutus, 49-51; manager of Junius, Jr., 61
Hamilton, Theodore, in Edwin's first company, 68, 69; at Booth's Theatre, 284
Hamlet, Junius Brutus in, 19; Edwin in, 104-105, 135, 143, 144, 170, 191-192, 274, 286, 300, 309, 316, 332; played by Edwin in Honolulu, 117; C. A. Fechter in, 163; Edwin's one hundredth consecutive appearance in, 206; Joseph Jefferson in, 320-321; Frank Mayo in, 321; Edwin's final appearance in, 327-328; Walker Whiteside in, 330
Hancock, Major General W. S., 243
Hanel, Blanch, 273
Harbin, Thomas, 240
Harper's Ferry, 155
Harris, Clara, at Ford's Theatre, 219, 355; at assassination, 222
Harrison, Susan B., 7
Harte, Bret, 127
Harvey and Marr, 280-281
Hawk, Harry; in *Our American Cousin*, 221; at assassination, 222; arrested, 263
Haymarket Theatre Royal, 163
Hayward, Nat, lives with Edwin, 103
Hazlett, 161
Henry V, 140
Hermitage, The, 41
Herold, David E., admirer of John Wilkes, 173; visits Surratt home,
201; plots against Lincoln, 202-208, 218-219; at White House, 210-211; at Deery's billiard room, 211-212; hires horse, 217; accompanies Paine, 224-225; escape of, 225-258; at Dr. Mudd's home, 227-230; aided by Jones and Cox, 232-237; at Port Royal Ferry, 243-245; at Bowling Green, 250; in Garrett barn, 255-256; surrender of, 256; returned to Washington, 259, 260; hanging and burial of, 264; body claimed, 281
Heron, Matilda, 108
Hess, C. D., sends note to Mrs. Lincoln, 211
Hide and Seek Theatre, 127
Hill, Barton, performs with Booths, 74; renews acquaintance with Edwin, 138; Forrest refuses, 277; takes Edwin west, 293; and Sydney Booth, 330
Holliday Street Theatre, 71, 76, 77, 135, 140, 151, 166, 276, 324
Holmes, Mary Ann, runs off with Booth, 27-31; birth of children, 33, 35, 37, 41, 44, 49, 53, 58, 59, 340; in Baltimore, 35; on Maryland farm, 36; visit to England, 43-44; marries Booth, 65; attitude toward Adelaide, 65; *see also* Mary Ann Booth
Holt, Judge, 261, 362
Honeymoon, The, 19, 106
Honolulu, 116-118
Hookstown, 186, 187
Hosmer, Belle Land, *see* Belle Land
Hough, Garry, 138
House, E. H., attends Edwin's play, 302; praises Edwin, 305
Houston, Sam, 41, 50, 52
Howard Athenaeum, 61, 140, 177
Howell, A. S., 203, 206
Howell, William A., shares room with John Wilkes, 161; talks with Joseph, 162
Hughes, Colonel John J., gives fugitives food, 238-239; admits seeing fugitives, 363
Hutton, Laurence, accompanies Edwin to Chicago, 307; on cruise with Edwin, 317; and Lincoln's death mask, 332
Hunchback, The, 83
Hyde, Charlotte, 326
Hyde, Susan, 71

Illinois, 84, 131
Independence, 89

INDEX

Iron Chest, The, 33, 74, 76, 86, 87, 125, 162, 182, 267
Irving, Henrietta, attempts to kill John Wilkes, 161
Irving, Henry, ignores Edwin, 299, 300; calls on Edwin, 301-302; plays with Edwin, 302-306; competes with Edwin, 312, 379; sends tribute to Edwin's funeral, 383

Jackson, Andrew, 41
Jackson, General Stonewall, 165
Jackson, T. B., manages Winter Garden, 169, 176
James, Macgill, 6
James, Rev. Fleming, at John Wilkes' funeral, 283; loses pastorate, 376
Janauschek, Mme., 275
Jarrett, Henry C., writes Edwin, 268; and Palmer, 287
Jefferson, Joseph, Mary Devlin lives with, 136; at Booth's Theatre, 286; in The Players, 318; in *Hamlet*, 320-321
Jenny Lind Theatre, building of, 80; opening of, 82; becomes burden, 83; turned into city hall, 86; closes, 87
Jett, Willie S., at Port Royal Ferry, 243-245; helps fugitives escape, 245-247; at Bowling Green, 250, 253; at Garrett farm, 254; arrested, 363; dies in asylum, 365
John Bull, 18
John S. Ide, 247, 259, 260
Johnson, Andrew, nominated for vice-president, 184; gets drunk, 210, 224; misses John Wilkes, 215-216, 217; plot against, 219; Edwin writes to, 280-281; releases John Wilkes' body, 281; pardons Arnold, 354; pardons Spangler, 357; pardons Mudd, 359
Johnson, Dr. Christopher, 276
Johnston, General Joseph E., 250
Jones, Avonia, 183
Jones, Thomas A., in Confederate service, 231; aids fugitives, 232-237; quoted, 361; arrested, 361; book of, 334, 384
Jonson, Ben, 45
Judah, Mrs., at Forrest Theatre, 119
Julius Caesar, 27, 167, 191, 286
Jumping Frog Jubilee, 127

Kamehameha IV, 117
Kane, George P., arrested, 167; upheld by John Wilkes, 168

Katherine and Petruchio, 105, 126, 182, 303
Kean, Edmund, rivalry with Booth, 21-23; causes disturbances, 24; in United States, 30, 34; at Park Theatre, 34; meets Booth in England, 43; pays Adelaide's passage to United States, 63
Keats, 38
Keene, Laura, blames Edwin for her failure, 108; experiences of, 108-110; in Australia, 115-116; in Honolulu, 117-118; in *Our American Cousin*, 215; at assassination, 222; arrested and released, 263
Keene, T. W., 294
Kellogg, Dr. A. O., in accident with Edwin, 291; visits Edwin, 296
Kellogg, Gertrude, in *Hamlet*, 321
Kelly, Old Aunt Mary, *see* Mary Swan
Kemble, Charles, 26, 34
Kemble, Fanny, 34
Kennedy, Robert C., confession of, 192
Kent, Will T., picks up pistol, 356
King, Charles A., 119
King John, 287, 289
King Lear, 26, 302
Knights of the Golden Circle, The, 158
Krupp, Isaac M., arrests Junius Jr., 270
Kunkel, George, hires John Wilkes, 151; deserted by John Wilkes, 156

Lady Jane, 117
Lady of Lyons, The, 115
Lafarge Hotel, fire in, 192
Lafferty, Samuel E., 6
Land, Agnes, arrives in California, 131-132; joins Booth company, 274; marries Junius, Jr., 275; *see also* Agnes Booth
Land, Belle, arrives in California; 131; takes care of Booth children, 289; buried at Rosedale Cemetery, 311; death of, 379
Lawrence, Joseph E., supports Edwin, 104
Lee, General Robert E., and John Brown's hanging, 156; daring exploits of, 165; rumors of success, 173; telegraphs Davis, 208
Leipzig, 310
Leman, W. M., at Forrest Theatre, 119
Le Roi S'Amuse, 182
Lewis, James, in The Players, 318; at Edwin's funeral, 334
Lincoln, Abraham, research on, 5; election of, 145; passes through Albany, 159; in *Evening Star* news, 172;

INDEX 413

attends Edwin's play, 182; renominated, 184; plots against, 186-190, 194, 195-211, 216-221; goes to Richmond, 209-210; at Ford's Theatre, 219; delayed at White House, 219, 354; assassination of, 221, 356; death of, 228; rejoicings over assassination of, 361
Lincoln, Mary Todd, attends Edwin's play, 182; at City Point, 207; at Ford's Theatre, 219; at Lincoln's assassination, 221-222; social feud with Mrs. Grant, 355
Lincoln, Robert, rescued by Edwin, 182
Lincoln, Tad, 207, 210
Little Barefoot, The, 60
Little Toddlekins, 123
Liverpool, 43, 164
Lloyd, John M., leases Mary Surratt's home, 194; joins in plot, 205-206; aids fugitives, 227; arrested, 355
London, 22, 24, 43-44, 55, 62, 163-165, 299-306, 308-309
Longstreet, Lieut.-Gen. James, 165
Love Chase, The, 108
Love's Sacrifice, 105, 106
Lucas, William, suggested by Stewart, 241; fugitives at home of, 242-243; arrested, 363
Lucretia Borgia, 149
Ludlow, Noah M., overcome by Booth's acting, 33; Booth's last engagement under his management, 89
Lutz, John, 68, 109, 263
Lyceum Theatre, 303-306, 330
Lyons, Joseph L., 6

Macbeth, 87, 172, 358
Mace, Harriet, in play with Junius, Jr., 61; affair with Junius, Jr., 62; in Sacramento, 81; sails to California, 79-81, 345; at Forrest Theatre, 129; *see also* Harriet Booth
Macready, W. C., 26, 143-144
Madagascan Joe marries, 38; lets John Wilkes ride nags, 66; posts programs, 76; children of, 338
Maddox, James, keeps John Wilkes' horse, 198; with John Wilkes, 218
Madeira, 29, 31
Mades, Chris, 210
Magonigle, J. H., representative of Booth's Theatre, 277; Edwin visits, 307; at Edwin's bedside, 331
Maguire, Thomas, owner of San Francisco theatre, 79; sends Junius Jr. to Sacramento, 80-81; attends *The School for Scandal,* 82; greets returning Booths, 85; builds San Francisco Hall, 101; opens Maguire Opera House, 131; rebuilds Jenny Lind Theatre, 343; former hoodlum, 343
Maguire Opera House, 131
Manassas, 165
Manchester, England, Booth's escapade in, 25; Edwin in, 164
Marble Heart, The, 121, 173, 182
Marie Victoria, 189
Mark of the Scalpel, The, 174, 366
Marshall, James, 127
Martin, in charge of John Wilkes' theatrical wardrobe, 189, 286
Martin, Martha, 7
Mary Ann Jones, 109
Maryland Booths, research on, 5-6; the mother of, 31, 311; Junius Brutus, founder of, 44; reunion of, 112-113; at John Wilkes' burial, 282-283; last to be buried in Greenmount Cemetery, 324
Marysville, 96, 100, 129
Masconomo House, 289-290, 311, 312, 380
Masconomo property, 275, 380
Massett, Stephen C., 103, 343
Mathews, Charles, ruins Booth's engagement, 36; in London, 163
Matrimony, 19
Matthews, Brander, in The Players, 318
Matthews, John, refuses part in plot, 198; receives note, 218
May, Dr. Frederick, quoted, 174; identifies John Wilkes, 261, 366
Mayo, Frank, at Nevada City, 128; in *Hamlet,* 321
Mazeppa, 61
McArdle, Joseph, 277
McCloskey, J. J., speaks of Edwin, 95-96; quoted, 103; gets drunk, 121-122
McConnell, Colonel H. L., 175
McCormack, Helen, 7
McCullough, John, rides with John Wilkes, 200; visits John Wilkes, 202; at Ford's Theatre, 203-204; at Booth's Theatre, 287; manages California Theatre, 288, 293, 294; in England, 300
McVicker, J. H., step-father of Mary, 137; offers John Wilkes rôle, 196
McVicker, Mary, joins Edwin, 276, 277; at Booth's Theatre, 278; marries Edwin, 278-279; *see also* Mary McVicker Booth
McVicker's Theatre, 166

INDEX

McVickers, the, in London, 304, 305-306; in New York, 306-307
Mears, Henry W., in charge of Booth graves, 376
Melbourne, 115
Menken, Helen, 7
Merchant of Venice, The, 19, 89, 115, 180, 275, 303
Methua-Scheller, Maria, 275
Micheau, Dr. Theodore, injures John Wilkes, 69; identifies John Wilkes, 282
Midsummer Night's Dream, A, 118
Mierke, George E., 6
Miles, John, 220
Miller, Joaquin, 127
Miller, Wynn, 308
Milton, 45
Missouri *Republican*, 166
Mitchell, Cora Elizabeth, marries Joseph, 324
Mitchell, Eliza, sells cakes and fruit, 60; marries William Ward, 60; parted from, 375
Mitchell, Jane, comes to United States, 56, death of, 60
Mitchell, Jimmy, bullies Booth, 55; comes to United States, 56; causes chaos, 58; leaves Maryland farm, 60
Mitchell, Maggie, in Petersburg, 153; at Booth's Theatre, 286
Mobile, 136
Modjeska, Helena, at Booth's Theatre, 310; in *Hamlet*, 321; tours with Edwin, 326; slander of, 382
Monstery, Colonel, 182
Montauk, 260, 261
Montez, Lola, 131
Montgomery, Commodore J. B., 260
Montplaisir Ballet Troupe, 108
Montreal, 188-189
Moore, Edward, 150
Morant, Fanny, 278
Morgan, Rhys, 320
Morning Courier and New York Inquirer, 50
Mother Lode, 96, 97, 125, 126
Moulton, Ben, adds Edwin to his company, 125-127; disasters on tour, 128-129, 344
Moulton, Harriet *see* Harriet Carpenter
Mount Auburn Cemetery, 171, 307, 334
Moxley, Basil, 377
Mozart Hall, 291
Much Ado About Nothing, 105, 116, 118, 119, 154

Mudd, Dr. Samuel A., helps John Wilkes purchase horse, 190; at National Hotel, 195-196; shelters fugitives, 227-230; imprisoned, 264; admits appointment with John Wilkes, 351; fate against, 359; on Dry Tortugas Island, 359; alibi of, 359-360
Mudd, Mrs. Samuel A., finds letter to John Wilkes, 191; kindness to John Wilkes, 229-230
Murdock, James E., stars opposite Mrs. Sinclair, 107; supported by Edwin, Metropolitan Theatre, 107; John Wilkes attempts to rival, 169
Murphy, Joseph, rescues Edwin, 119
Murty, Lizzy, 202, 351
Muzzy, Mrs., 221
Myers, Reverend B. F., 279

Napoleon, 19
National Hotel, 190, 195-196, 280
National Theatre, 76, 78, 153
Neptune, 57
Nevada City, 97-100, 128
New Orleans, 45, 89, 113, 136, 179-180
New Orleans *Times*, quoted, 180
Newport, 311
New Way to Pay Old Debts, A, 21, 89, 138, 140
New World, 130
New York, 44, 50, 51, 52, 60, 135, 137, 140, 143, 165, 167, 171, 191, 196, 291, 297-298, 312, 315; Booth's first sight of, 33; riots in, 175; plots in, 192; Booth's Theatre, 277
New York Academy of Music, 315, 316
New York *Clipper*, 6, 158, 349, 357
New York *Herald*, 192, 274, 348-349
Niagara Falls, 143
Niblo's Garden, 143, 169, 182
Nobles, Milton, quoted, 319
Norfolk, Virginia, 32
November Boughs, 91
Nunnikhuysen, Dr., 49

O'Beirne, Major James, 362, 377
Oberammergau, 300
Odeon Theatre, 72
Of Age To-morrow, 19
O'Flaherty, William, *see* William Stuart
O'Laughlin, Michael, plots with John Wilkes, 186-187; meets John Surratt, 199; plots against Lincoln, 203-208; misses Booth, 215; imprisoned, 264, 354; death of, 354
Old Capitol Prison, 263, 270, 363

INDEX 415

Olin, Stephen H., in The Players, 318
Oneida, 317
Orange, Prince of, 27
Osgood, Reverend, Samuel, marries Edwin and Mary Devlin, 142-143; Edwin calls on, 296
Ostend, 20
Othello, 18, 50, 184, 278, 302
Our American Cousin, 215, 216, 220

Pacific Theatre, 81
Paine, Lewis, plots against Lincoln, 201, 202-208, 218-219; deserts army, 201; attack on Seward, 224-225; hanging and burial of, 264, 281, 358; after Lincoln's assassination, 358
Pallen, Dr. M. A., 188
Palmer, Albert M., in The Players, 318; and Wallack benefit, 321; gives dinner for Edwin, 324-325
Panama City, 79, 84, 85, 130
Panic of 1873, 286
Paris, 309, 310
Park Theatre, 34, 50, 298
Parker, John, neglects post, 220; complaints against, 356
Parsons, H. S., 6
Parsons, Thomas W., 323
Passion Play, the, 300
Payne, John Howard, 76
Peacock, 29, 30, 32, 36, 40, 41, 44, 49
Peanut John, looks after John Wilkes' horse, 198; prepares theatre for presidential party, 216; with John Wilkes, 218; holds John Wilkes' horse, 220, 222
Penley and Jonas, 19
Pennsylvania House, 196
Pentonville, 54
Perry, Agnes Land, *see* Agnes Land *and* Agnes Booth
Perry, Harry, 132
Petersburg, 32, 153
Peyton, Sarah, 245-246
Philadelphia, 36, 41, 50, 62, 135, 142, 143, 150, 162, 169-170, 183, 194, 267, 297
Philadelphia Academy of Music, 144
Philadelphia Arch Street Theatre, 149, 170, 172
Phillips, Wendell, denounces Lincoln, 184
Picioli, Signor, 71
Pierce, Franklin, 86
Pink Dominoes, 291
Pitts, Edwin B., 6

Pittsburgh, 52, 137, 324
Pittsburgh Theatre, 52
Placerville, 126-127
Players, The, 317-318, 322-323, 334
Pope, General John, 165
Port Conway, fugitives at, 243; searching party at, 247-248
Porter, General Fitz-John, 165
Port Royal, fugitives at, 244-245; searching party at, 248; John Wilkes' body at, 259
Potter, Bishop, 334
Potter, John S., manages Forrest Theatre, 122-123
Powell, Lewis Paine, *see* Lewis Paine
Prince Charles, 309
Princess Theatre, 300-304
Princess Theatre Royal, 163
Proctor, Joseph, 275
Providence, 74, 327
Provost, Mary, manages Wallack Theatre, 167
Pumphrey, advises John Wilkes, 217

Queen, Dr., visited by John Wilkes, 190, 194
Queen's Husband, The, 107
Queen's Theatre, in Melbourne, 115
Quesenberry, Elizabeth, refuses Herold, 239-240; arrested and released, 361-362

Racine, 38
Rankin, George, 189
Rankin, McKee, 189, 286
Rathbone, Major, at Ford's Theatre, 219, 355; tries to stop John Wilkes, 221
Reade, Charles, attends Edwin's play, 302; praises Edwin, 303
Reignolds, Kate, quoted, 184
Richard II, Edwin in, 296-297
Richard III, Booth's favorite play, 18; Booth in, 19, 22, 24, 34, 36, 47, 48-49, 50, 52-53, 88-89; Junius, Jr., in, 52, 340; John Wilkes in, 134, 149, 151, 157, 158, 159, 166, 167, 168, 172, 173, 178, 180; Edwin in, 68-69, 73, 104, 117, 122, 123, 135, 139, 164, 171, 276
Richelieu, 82, 128, 135, 163, 164, 274, 285, 292, 301, 308, 327
Richmond, 49, 74, 153, 155, 156; surrender of, 208, 210
Richmond *Dispatch*, 156
Richmond Theatre, 32, 33, 140, 151
Rigoletto, 182
Rip Van Winkle, 286
Ristori, Mme., 275

INDEX

Ritterspaugh, Jacob, attends to John Wilkes' request, 218; at Lincoln's assassination, 222
River Queen, 210
Robbers, The, 137, 160, 167
Robertson, R. A., partner in Booth's Theatre, 277; ends partnership with Edwin, 285-286
Robey, Franklin A., takes charge of fugitives, 233; destroys horses, 361
Robinson, David G., 106
Robinson, Sergeant, 224-225
Robson, Stuart, in Edwin's first company, 68, 69
Rochester, 137, 325
Rogers, Elijah, 36
Rogers, Hughey, 70
Rogers, Mrs. Elijah, quoted, 49, 60, 140, 154, 282
Rollins, William, at Port Royal Ferry, 243, 245; guides searching party, 248; at Garrett farm, 254, 256
Romeo and Juliet, 136, 183, 288-289; opens Booth's Theatre, 278
Rookes, Mrs. Land, arrives from Australia, 131; *see also* Sarah Smeatham
Rosedale Cemetery, 290, 379
Rotterdam, 44
Rough and Ready, 97, 98, 100
Royal Hawaiian Theatre, 116, 117
Royal Victoria Theatre, 115
Royalty Theatre, 44
Ruggles, Mortimer B., at Port Royal Ferry, 243-245; helps fugitives escape, 246-247, 250-251; arrested, 363; believes John Wilkes shot himself, 365
Ruy Blas, 177
Ryer, George, 119, 169

Sacramento, 80, 81, 87, 100, 107, 125, 129; Edwin nearly drowns at, 119
Sacramento Theatre, success of, 121; Edwin at, 118, 123
Sage of Ossawatomie, 156
St. Charles Theatre, 89-90, 179, 180
St. Helen, John, impostor of John Wilkes, 377
St. Helena, 19
St. John's Wood, 273
St. Louis, 137, 166, 175
St. Mary's Church, 190, 195
Salvini, Tomasso, 313, 315
Sanborn, 53
San Francisco, 79-81, 95, 100-101, 114, 118, 123, 125, 162, 182, 293, 316; Bay City, 88, 99, 316

San Francisco Hall, building of, 83; description of, 101
San Francisco Theatre, complaints against, 106; reopening of, 107; enlargement of, 131
Saunders, George N., 188
Schoeffel, John B., marries Agnes Booth, 212
School for Scandal, The, 82, 106, 107
Scott, Clement, derides Edwin, 301; at Edwin's funeral, 383
Scott, John R., 77
Scott, Winfield, 86
Sedley, Henry, 121
Sefton, John, 74
Seward, Augustus, attack on, 225
Seward, Frederick, attack on, 224-225
Seward, William H., plot against, 219; attack on, 224-225
Seymour, May Davenport, 6
Seymour, William, 366
Shakespeare, 33, 38, 45
Shelley, 38
Sheridan, 33
Sherman, General William T., recollections of, 107; marches to sea, 184; in The Players, 318
Simpson, Edmund, at Park Theatre, 34
Simpson, James H., cares for Booth in last illness, 90-91
Sinclair, Catherine, in San Francisco, 105-108; offers jobs to Edwin and Anderson, 118; takes over Sacramento Theatre, 120; Forrest's attitude toward, 277
"Singing Sands," 275, 290
Singleton, General James W., delays Lincoln at White House, 219, 354
Slater, Mrs., sheltered by Surratts, 203; carries dispatches, 206
Smeatham, Sarah, cares for Booth children, 289; buried at Rosedale Cemetery, 379; *see also* Mrs. Land Rookes
Smith, Dr. St. Clair, goes to England with Booths, 308; attends Edwin, 331
Soldier's Home, 187, 204-205
Sonora, 114
Sothern, E. A., quoted, 169
Spangler, Edward, carpenter for Booth house, 76; cares for John Wilkes' horse, 198; at Ford's Theatre, 216-217; with John Wilkes, 218; holds John Wilkes' horse, 219, 220; imprisoned, 264; accusations against, 354, 355; pardoned, 357
Spear, George, Booth's drinking companion, 61; joins Booths on California trip, 84-85; on stage in California,

INDEX

86-87; in Willmarth Waller's troupe, 96; tells Edwin of father's death, 99-100; at Forrest Theatre, 119; gets drunk, 121-122; in *Our American Cousin*, 216; gets property from Ford's Theatre, 263-264; last days of, 368
Speare, W. R., 281
Spectre Bridegroom, The, 71
Stadt Theatre, 310
Stanton, Edwin, M., orders police marshal confined, 167; orders gun salute, 210; telegraphs Baker, 231; orders disposal of Booth's body, 261; closes Ford's Theatre, 264
Stanwix Hall, 159, 161
Stark, James, 82, 83
Stark, Mrs. James, 82, 83
Starr, Ella Turner, with John Wilkes, 186, 212; tries to end life, 263
Stedman, E. C., 303
Stephens, John L., 114
Stewart, J. B., and escape of John Wilkes, 222; denunciation of, 357-358
Stewart, Dr. Richard H., suggested by Dr. Mudd, 228; refuses to help fugitives, 240-242; John Wilkes writes note to, 243, 362; quoted, 359-360; arrested, 362
Still Water Runs Deep, 204, 352
Stoddard, Richard Henry, 170
Stout, George L., in Edwin's first company, 68-69; quoted, 197; identifies John Wilkes, 282
Stranger, The, 81, 87
Streets of New York, The, 298
Stuart, Henry, *see* Stuart Robson
Stuart, William, as Edwin's manager, 183, 274
Sumner, Dr. C. R., 325
Surratt, Anna, at mother's home, 195; quoted, 355
Surratt, Isaac, in Confederate army, 195
Surratt, John, plots against Lincoln, 195, 198, 202-208; meets Atzerodt, 198-199; talks to Wiechmann, 201-202; acquitted, 264, 354; flees from country, 354; responsible for cut telegraph wires, 357
Surratt, Mary, serenaded by David E. Herold, 174; runs boarding house, 195; capture of Richmond, 208; goes to Lloyd's tavern, 210, 353; visited by Booth, 216, 219, 355; hanging and burial of, 264; body claimed, 281
Surrattsville, 194, 216, 226, 227
Swan, Mary, story of, 360

Swan, Oswald, 231, 233
Sydney, 115

Tasso, 38
Taylor, John, marries Laura Keane, 108; in prison, 116
Taylor, Reverend, 80
Taylor, Tom, 182
Tennessee, 79
Tennyson, Alfred Lord, attends Edwin's play, 303
Terry, Ellen, quoted, 304
Thayer, Benjamin W., 275
Théâtre d'Orléans, 45
Theatre Royal, 309
Thompson, Jacob, 188
Thompson, John C., 190
Thompson, Launt, 170
Thorne, C. R., 80
Tilton, E. L., 167
Tilton, Mildred Booth, 383
Times, 144, 331
Toodles, 149
Townsend, George Alfred, quoted, 140, 157, 366
Townsend, Margaret, quoted, 295
Travelers Benighted, 19
Trent Affair, 165
Trial of John Surratt, 264
Tribune, 144, 269
Triplet Alley, 68
Tucker, Beverly, 188
Tudor Hall, building of, 76, 84; Mary Ann plans to move to, 100; Junius visits, 110; description of, 342
Twain, Mark, 127
Twelfth Night, 118
Two Brothers, 30

Ugolino, 41-42
Uncle Tom's Cabin, 119
Union Square Theatre, 330
Union Theatre, 109, 123
Urquhart, Dr., 258

Vandenhoff, Charles, 276
Van Tine, Mary J., 200
Vaux, Julia, 308
Venice Preserved, 87
Venua, Wesley, at Jenny Lind Theatre, 82; becomes treasurer of Sacramento Theatre, 120; prank played on, 121
Verdi, Dr., 224
Vernon, Ida, 333
Vestris, Madame, 108
Vicksburg, 179, 184

INDEX

Vienna, 310
Vigilantes, 81, 192, 269
Volkner, Widow, 210

Wagner, Henry C., 71
Wallack, Henry, Booth writes play for, 39, 41
Wallack, Mrs. Henry, Booth writes play for, 39, 41
Wallack, James W., in London, 27; in New York, 34
Wallack, Lester, benefit for, 320-321
Wallack Theatre, 167
Waller, Willmarth, engages Edwin, 95-96; at Booth's Theatre, 284
Waller, Mrs. Willmarth, 95-96
Walnut Street Theatre, 177, 183
Walters, Elizabeth, suit of, 15, 337
Walton, John, 235
Ward, William, 60, 375
Warde, Frederick, 292
Warning to Youth, A, 123
Washington, 136, 182; plottings at, 195-196
Washington *Evening Star*, 172
Washington Theatre, 174
Weaver, John H., 280-282
Wellington, Lord, 19
Wells, Colonel H. H., 264
Wells, William, suspects Jones, 234
Wells Fargo Company, 162, 347
Welten, Oscar, 309
Wemyss, Francis, 51-52
Wemyss, Mrs. Francis, 51
Westcott, J. D., 188
Western, Helen, 366
Wharton, 208
Wheeler, Frank, 107
Wheeling, 51, 137

Wheelock, Joseph, 289
Whistler, Elijah, attends school with John Wilkes Booth, 67
White, Stanford, 318, 322
Whiteside, Walker, in *Hamlet*, 330
Whitman, Walt, quoted, 91, 153; cheers soldiers, 173
Who's Got the Countess, 106
Whyte, Margery, 6
Wiechmann, Louis J., at National Hotel, 195-196; witness at trial, 196, 351; becomes inquisitive, 201-202, 203, 204, 206; goes to Lloyd's tavern, 210, 216
Wilkes, Elizabeth, marries John Booth, 16
Wilkes, John, and Richard's adventure, 16
Winter, Corporal John, guards Herold, 259
Winter, William, commends Edwin, 139; edits Edwin's prompt books, 296; Edwin writes to, 302-303; accompanies Edwin to Chicago, 307; quoted, 322-323; resigns from The Players, 381
Winter Garden, Edwin at, 140, 143, 169, 170, 183, 206; Booth brothers at, 191; burns, 275-276
Wirz, Captain Henry, 281, 375
Withers, Jr., William, 219
Woodland, Henry, 234, 236
Woodring, Honorable Harry H., 6
Wood's Theatre, 179
Wren, George, 158, 190
Wright, J. B., changes programs for Ford's Theatre, 354
Wroth, Reverend P., 315

Zachiah Swamp, Dr. Mudd points route through, 228; fugitives in, 230, 231

A CATALOGUE OF SELECTED DOVER BOOKS
IN ALL FIELDS OF INTEREST

A CATALOGUE OF SELECTED DOVER BOOKS
IN ALL FIELDS OF INTEREST

WHAT IS SCIENCE?, *N. Campbell*
The role of experiment and measurement, the function of mathematics, the nature of scientific laws, the difference between laws and theories, the limitations of science, and many similarly provocative topics are treated clearly and without technicalities by an eminent scientist. "Still an excellent introduction to scientific philosophy," H. Margenau in *Physics Today*. "A first-rate primer . . . deserves a wide audience," *Scientific American*. 192pp. 5⅜ x 8.
60043-2 Paperbound $1.25

THE NATURE OF LIGHT AND COLOUR IN THE OPEN AIR, *M. Minnaert*
Why are shadows sometimes blue, sometimes green, or other colors depending on the light and surroundings? What causes mirages? Why do multiple suns and moons appear in the sky? Professor Minnaert explains these unusual phenomena and hundreds of others in simple, easy-to-understand terms based on optical laws and the properties of light and color. No mathematics is required but artists, scientists, students, and everyone fascinated by these "tricks" of nature will find thousands of useful and amazing pieces of information. Hundreds of observational experiments are suggested which require no special equipment. 200 illustrations; 42 photos. xvi + 362pp. 5⅜ x 8.
20196-1 Paperbound $2.00

THE STRANGE STORY OF THE QUANTUM, AN ACCOUNT FOR THE GENERAL READER OF THE GROWTH OF IDEAS UNDERLYING OUR PRESENT ATOMIC KNOWLEDGE, *B. Hoffmann*
Presents lucidly and expertly, with barest amount of mathematics, the problems and theories which led to modern quantum physics. Dr. Hoffmann begins with the closing years of the 19th century, when certain trifling discrepancies were noticed, and with illuminating analogies and examples takes you through the brilliant concepts of Planck, Einstein, Pauli, Broglie, Bohr, Schroedinger, Heisenberg, Dirac, Sommerfeld, Feynman, etc. This edition includes a new, long postscript carrying the story through 1958. "Of the books attempting an account of the history and contents of our modern atomic physics which have come to my attention, this is the best," H. Margenau, Yale University, in *American Journal of Physics*. 32 tables and line illustrations. Index. 275pp. 5⅜ x 8.
20518-5 Paperbound $2.00

GREAT IDEAS OF MODERN MATHEMATICS: THEIR NATURE AND USE, *Jagjit Singh*
Reader with only high school math will understand main mathematical ideas of modern physics, astronomy, genetics, psychology, evolution, etc. better than many who use them as tools, but comprehend little of their basic structure. Author uses his wide knowledge of non-mathematical fields in brilliant exposition of differential equations, matrices, group theory, logic, statistics, problems of mathematical foundations, imaginary numbers, vectors, etc. Original publication. 2 appendixes. 2 indexes. 65 ills. 322pp. 5⅜ x 8.
20587-8 Paperbound $2.25

CATALOGUE OF DOVER BOOKS

THE MUSIC OF THE SPHERES: THE MATERIAL UNIVERSE — FROM ATOM TO QUASAR, SIMPLY EXPLAINED, Guy Murchie
Vast compendium of fact, modern concept and theory, observed and calculated data, historical background guides intelligent layman through the material universe. Brilliant exposition of earth's construction, explanations for moon's craters, atmospheric components of Venus and Mars (with data from recent fly-by's), sun spots, sequences of star birth and death, neighboring galaxies, contributions of Galileo, Tycho Brahe, Kepler, etc.; and (Vol. 2) construction of the atom (describing newly discovered sigma and xi subatomic particles), theories of sound, color and light, space and time, including relativity theory, quantum theory, wave theory, probability theory, work of Newton, Maxwell, Faraday, Einstein, de Broglie, etc. "Best presentation yet offered to the intelligent general reader," Saturday Review. Revised (1967). Index. 319 illustrations by the author. Total of xx + 644pp. 5⅜ x 8½.
21809-0, 21810-4 Two volume set, paperbound $5.00

FOUR LECTURES ON RELATIVITY AND SPACE, Charles Proteus Steinmetz
Lecture series, given by great mathematician and electrical engineer, generally considered one of the best popular-level expositions of special and general relativity theories and related questions. Steinmetz translates complex mathematical reasoning into language accessible to laymen through analogy, example and comparison. Among topics covered are relativity of motion, location, time; of mass; acceleration; 4-dimensional time-space; geometry of the gravitational field; curvature and bending of space; non-Euclidean geometry. Index. 40 illustrations. x + 142pp. 5⅜ x 8½. 61771-8 Paperbound $1.35

HOW TO KNOW THE WILD FLOWERS, Mrs. William Starr Dana
Classic nature book that has introduced thousands to wonders of American wild flowers. Color-season principle of organization is easy to use, even by those with no botanical training, and the genial, refreshing discussions of history, folklore, uses of over 1,000 native and escape flowers, foliage plants are informative as well as fun to read. Over 170 full-page plates, collected from several editions, may be colored in to make permanent records of finds. Revised to conform with 1950 edition of Gray's Manual of Botany. xlii + 438pp. 5⅜ x 8½. 20332-8 Paperbound $2.50

MANUAL OF THE TREES OF NORTH AMERICA, Charles Sprague Sargent
Still unsurpassed as most comprehensive, reliable study of North American tree characteristics, precise locations and distribution. By dean of American dendrologists. Every tree native to U.S., Canada, Alaska; 185 genera, 717 species, described in detail—leaves, flowers, fruit, winterbuds, bark, wood, growth habits, etc. plus discussion of varieties and local variants, immaturity variations. Over 100 keys, including unusual 11-page analytical key to genera, aid in identification. 783 clear illustrations of flowers, fruit, leaves. An unmatched permanent reference work for all nature lovers. Second enlarged (1926) edition. Synopsis of families. Analytical key to genera. Glossary of technical terms. Index. 783 illustrations, 1 map. Total of 982pp. 5⅜ x 8.
20277-1, 20278-X Two volume set, paperbound $6.00

CATALOGUE OF DOVER BOOKS

IT'S FUN TO MAKE THINGS FROM SCRAP MATERIALS,
Evelyn Glantz Hershoff
What use are empty spools, tin cans, bottle tops? What can be made from rubber bands, clothes pins, paper clips, and buttons? This book provides simply worded instructions and large diagrams showing you how to make cookie cutters, toy trucks, paper turkeys, Halloween masks, telephone sets, aprons, linoleum block- and spatter prints — in all 399 projects! Many are easy enough for young children to figure out for themselves; some challenging enough to entertain adults; all are remarkably ingenious ways to make things from materials that cost pennies or less! Formerly "Scrap Fun for Everyone." Index. 214 illustrations. 373pp. 5⅜ x 8½.   21251-3 Paperbound $1.75

SYMBOLIC LOGIC and THE GAME OF LOGIC, *Lewis Carroll*
"Symbolic Logic" is not concerned with modern symbolic logic, but is instead a collection of over 380 problems posed with charm and imagination, using the syllogism and a fascinating diagrammatic method of drawing conclusions. In "The Game of Logic" Carroll's whimsical imagination devises a logical game played with 2 diagrams and counters (included) to manipulate hundreds of tricky syllogisms. The final section, "Hit or Miss" is a lagniappe of 101 additional puzzles in the delightful Carroll manner. Until this reprint edition, both of these books were rarities costing up to $15 each. Symbolic Logic: Index. xxxi + 199pp. The Game of Logic: 96pp. 2 vols. bound as one. 5⅜ x 8.
20492-8 Paperbound $2.50

MATHEMATICAL PUZZLES OF SAM LOYD, PART I
selected and edited by M. Gardner
Choice puzzles by the greatest American puzzle creator and innovator. Selected from his famous collection, "Cyclopedia of Puzzles," they retain the unique style and historical flavor of the originals. There are posers based on arithmetic, algebra, probability, game theory, route tracing, topology, counter and sliding block, operations research, geometrical dissection. Includes the famous "14-15" puzzle which was a national craze, and his "Horse of a Different Color" which sold millions of copies. 117 of his most ingenious puzzles in all. 120 line drawings and diagrams. Solutions. Selected references. xx + 167pp. 5⅜ x 8.
20498-7 Paperbound $1.35

STRING FIGURES AND HOW TO MAKE THEM, *Caroline Furness Jayne*
107 string figures plus variations selected from the best primitive and modern examples developed by Navajo, Apache, pygmies of Africa, Eskimo, in Europe, Australia, China, etc. The most readily understandable, easy-to-follow book in English on perennially popular recreation. Crystal-clear exposition; step-by-step diagrams. Everyone from kindergarten children to adults looking for unusual diversion will be endlessly amused. Index. Bibliography. Introduction by A. C. Haddon. 17 full-page plates, 960 illustrations. xxiii + 401pp. 5⅜ x 8½.
20152-X Paperbound $2.25

PAPER FOLDING FOR BEGINNERS, *W. D. Murray and F. J. Rigney*
A delightful introduction to the varied and entertaining Japanese art of origami (paper folding), with a full, crystal-clear text that anticipates every difficulty; over 275 clearly labeled diagrams of all important stages in creation. You get results at each stage, since complex figures are logically developed from simpler ones. 43 different pieces are explained: sailboats, frogs, roosters, etc. 6 photographic plates. 279 diagrams. 95pp. 5⅜ x 8⅜.
20713-7 Paperbound $1.00

CATALOGUE OF DOVER BOOKS

PRINCIPLES OF ART HISTORY,
H. Wölfflin
Analyzing such terms as "baroque," "classic," "neoclassic," "primitive," "picturesque," and 164 different works by artists like Botticelli, van Cleve, Dürer, Hobbema, Holbein, Hals, Rembrandt, Titian, Brueghel, Vermeer, and many others, the author establishes the classifications of art history and style on a firm, concrete basis. This classic of art criticism shows what really occurred between the 14th-century primitives and the sophistication of the 18th century in terms of basic attitudes and philosophies. "A remarkable lesson in the art of seeing," *Sat. Rev. of Literature.* Translated from the 7th German edition. 150 illustrations. 254pp. 6⅛ x 9¼. 20276-3 Paperbound $2.25

PRIMITIVE ART,
Franz Boas
This authoritative and exhaustive work by a great American anthropologist covers the entire gamut of primitive art. Pottery, leatherwork, metal work, stone work, wood, basketry, are treated in detail. Theories of primitive art, historical depth in art history, technical virtuosity, unconscious levels of patterning, symbolism, styles, literature, music, dance, etc. A must book for the interested layman, the anthropologist, artist, handicrafter (hundreds of unusual motifs), and the historian. Over 900 illustrations (50 ceramic vessels, 12 totem poles, etc.). 376pp. 5⅜ x 8. 20025-6 Paperbound $2.50

THE GENTLEMAN AND CABINET MAKER'S DIRECTOR,
Thomas Chippendale
A reprint of the 1762 catalogue of furniture designs that went on to influence generations of English and Colonial and Early Republic American furniture makers. The 200 plates, most of them full-page sized, show Chippendale's designs for French (Louis XV), Gothic, and Chinese-manner chairs, sofas, canopy and dome beds, cornices, chamber organs, cabinets, shaving tables, commodes, picture frames, frets, candle stands, chimney pieces, decorations, etc. The drawings are all elegant and highly detailed; many include construction diagrams and elevations. A supplement of 24 photographs shows surviving pieces of original and Chippendale-style pieces of furniture. Brief biography of Chippendale by N. I. Bienenstock, editor of *Furniture World.* Reproduced from the 1762 edition. 200 plates, plus 19 photographic plates. vi + 249pp. 9⅛ x 12¼. 21601-2 Paperbound $3.50

AMERICAN ANTIQUE FURNITURE: A BOOK FOR AMATEURS,
Edgar G. Miller, Jr.
Standard introduction and practical guide to identification of valuable American antique furniture. 2115 illustrations, mostly photographs taken by the author in 148 private homes, are arranged in chronological order in extensive chapters on chairs, sofas, chests, desks, bedsteads, mirrors, tables, clocks, and other articles. Focus is on furniture accessible to the collector, including simpler pieces and a larger than usual coverage of Empire style. Introductory chapters identify structural elements, characteristics of various styles, how to avoid fakes, etc. "We are frequently asked to name some book on American furniture that will meet the requirements of the novice collector, the beginning dealer, and . . . the general public. . . . We believe Mr. Miller's two volumes more completely satisfy this specification than any other work," *Antiques.* Appendix. Index. Total of vi + 1106pp. 7⅞ x 10¾. 21599-7, 21600-4 Two volume set, paperbound $7.50

CATALOGUE OF DOVER BOOKS

THE BAD CHILD'S BOOK OF BEASTS, MORE BEASTS FOR WORSE CHILDREN, and A MORAL ALPHABET, *H. Belloc*
Hardly and anthology of humorous verse has appeared in the last 50 years without at least a couple of these famous nonsense verses. But one must see the entire volumes — with all the delightful original illustrations by Sir Basil Blackwood — to appreciate fully Belloc's charming and witty verses that play so subacidly on the platitudes of life and morals that beset his day — and ours. A great humor classic. Three books in one. Total of 157pp. 5⅜ x 8.
20749-8 Paperbound $1.00

THE DEVIL'S DICTIONARY, *Ambrose Bierce*
Sardonic and irreverent barbs puncturing the pomposities and absurdities of American politics, business, religion, literature, and arts, by the country's greatest satirist in the classic tradition. Epigrammatic as Shaw, piercing as Swift, American as Mark Twain, Will Rogers, and Fred Allen, Bierce will always remain the favorite of a small coterie of enthusiasts, and of writers and speakers whom he supplies with "some of the most gorgeous witticisms of the English language" (H. L. Mencken). Over 1000 entries in alphabetical order. 144pp. 5⅜ x 8. 20487-1 Paperbound $1.00

THE COMPLETE NONSENSE OF EDWARD LEAR.
This is the only complete edition of this master of gentle madness available at a popular price. *A Book of Nonsense, Nonsense Songs, More Nonsense Songs and Stories* in their entirety with all the old favorites that have delighted children and adults for years. The Dong With A Luminous Nose, The Jumblies, The Owl and the Pussycat, and hundreds of other bits of wonderful nonsense. 214 limericks, 3 sets of Nonsense Botany, 5 Nonsense Alphabets, 546 drawings by Lear himself, and much more. 320pp. 5⅜ x 8. 20167-8 Paperbound $1.75

THE WIT AND HUMOR OF OSCAR WILDE, *ed. by Alvin Redman*
Wilde at his most brilliant, in 1000 epigrams exposing weaknesses and hypocrisies of "civilized" society. Divided into 49 categories—sin, wealth, women, America, etc.—to aid writers, speakers. Includes excerpts from his trials, books, plays, criticism. Formerly "The Epigrams of Oscar Wilde." Introduction by Vyvyan Holland, Wilde's only living son. Introductory essay by editor. 260pp. 5⅜ x 8. 20602-5 Paperbound $1.50

A CHILD'S PRIMER OF NATURAL HISTORY, *Oliver Herford*
Scarcely an anthology of whimsy and humor has appeared in the last 50 years without a contribution from Oliver Herford. Yet the works from which these examples are drawn have been almost impossible to obtain! Here at last are Herford's improbable definitions of a menagerie of familiar and weird animals, each verse illustrated by the author's own drawings. 24 drawings in 2 colors; 24 additional drawings. vii + 95pp. 6½ x 6. 21647-0 Paperbound $1.00

THE BROWNIES: THEIR BOOK, *Palmer Cox*
The book that made the Brownies a household word. Generations of readers have enjoyed the antics, predicaments and adventures of these jovial sprites, who emerge from the forest at night to play or to come to the aid of a deserving human. Delightful illustrations by the author decorate nearly every page. 24 short verse tales with 266 illustrations. 155pp. 6⅝ x 9¼.
21265-3 Paperbound $1.50

CATALOGUE OF DOVER BOOKS

THE PRINCIPLES OF PSYCHOLOGY,
William James
The full long-course, unabridged, of one of the great classics of Western literature and science. Wonderfully lucid descriptions of human mental activity, the stream of thought, consciousness, time perception, memory, imagination, emotions, reason, abnormal phenomena, and similar topics. Original contributions are integrated with the work of such men as Berkeley, Binet, Mills, Darwin, Hume, Kant, Royce, Schopenhauer, Spinoza, Locke, Descartes, Galton, Wundt, Lotze, Herbart, Fechner, and scores of others. All contrasting interpretations of mental phenomena are examined in detail—introspective analysis, philosophical interpretation, and experimental research. "A classic," *Journal of Consulting Psychology.* "The main lines are as valid as ever," *Psychoanalytical Quarterly.* "Standard reading...a classic of interpretation," *Psychiatric Quarterly.* 94 illustrations. 1408pp. 5⅜ x 8.
20381-6, 20382-4 Two volume set, paperbound $6.00

VISUAL ILLUSIONS: THEIR CAUSES, CHARACTERISTICS AND APPLICATIONS,
M. Luckiesh
"Seeing is deceiving," asserts the author of this introduction to virtually every type of optical illusion known. The text both describes and explains the principles involved in color illusions, figure-ground, distance illusions, etc. 100 photographs, drawings and diagrams prove how easy it is to fool the sense: circles that aren't round, parallel lines that seem to bend, stationary figures that seem to move as you stare at them — illustration after illustration strains our credulity at what we see. Fascinating book from many points of view, from applications for artists, in camouflage, etc. to the psychology of vision. New introduction by William Ittleson, Dept. of Psychology, Queens College. Index. Bibliography. xxi + 252pp. 5⅜ x 8½. 21530-X Paperbound $1.50

FADS AND FALLACIES IN THE NAME OF SCIENCE,
Martin Gardner
This is the standard account of various cults, quack systems, and delusions which have masqueraded as science: hollow earth fanatics. Reich and orgone sex energy, dianetics, Atlantis, multiple moons, Forteanism, flying saucers, medical fallacies like iridiagnosis, zone therapy, etc. A new chapter has been added on Bridey Murphy, psionics, and other recent manifestations in this field. This is a fair, reasoned appraisal of eccentric theory which provides excellent inoculation against cleverly masked nonsense. "Should be read by everyone, scientist and non-scientist alike," R. T. Birge, Prof. Emeritus of Physics, Univ. of California; Former President, American Physical Society. Index. x + 365pp. 5⅜ x 8. 20394-8 Paperbound $2.00

ILLUSIONS AND DELUSIONS OF THE SUPERNATURAL AND THE OCCULT,
D. H. Rawcliffe
Holds up to rational examination hundreds of persistent delusions including crystal gazing, automatic writing, table turning, mediumistic trances, mental healing, stigmata, lycanthropy, live burial, the Indian Rope Trick, spiritualism, dowsing, telepathy, clairvoyance, ghosts, ESP, etc. The author explains and exposes the mental and physical deceptions involved, making this not only an exposé of supernatural phenomena, but a valuable exposition of characteristic types of abnormal psychology. Originally titled "The Psychology of the Occult." 14 illustrations. Index. 551pp. 5⅜ x 8. 20503-7 Paperbound $3.50

CATALOGUE OF DOVER BOOKS

FAIRY TALE COLLECTIONS, *edited by Andrew Lang*
Andrew Lang's fairy tale collections make up the richest shelf-full of traditional children's stories anywhere available. Lang supervised the translation of stories from all over the world—familiar European tales collected by Grimm, animal stories from Negro Africa, myths of primitive Australia, stories from Russia, Hungary, Iceland, Japan, and many other countries. Lang's selection of translations are unusually high; many authorities consider that the most familiar tales find their best versions in these volumes. All collections are richly decorated and illustrated by H. J. Ford and other artists.

THE BLUE FAIRY BOOK. 37 stories. 138 illustrations. ix + 390pp. 5⅜ x 8½.
21437-0 Paperbound $1.95

THE GREEN FAIRY BOOK. 42 stories. 100 illustrations. xiii + 366pp. 5⅜ x 8½.
21439-7 Paperbound $1.75

THE BROWN FAIRY BOOK. 32 stories. 50 illustrations, 8 in color. xii + 350pp. 5⅜ x 8½.
21438-9 Paperbound $1.95

THE BEST TALES OF HOFFMANN, *edited by E. F. Bleiler*
10 stories by E. T. A. Hoffmann, one of the greatest of all writers of fantasy. The tales include "The Golden Flower Pot," "Automata," "A New Year's Eve Adventure," "Nutcracker and the King of Mice," "Sand-Man," and others. Vigorous characterizations of highly eccentric personalities, remarkable imaginative situations, and intensely fast pacing has made these tales popular all over the world for 150 years. Editor's introduction. 7 drawings by Hoffmann. xxxiii + 419pp. 5⅜ x 8½. 21793-0 Paperbound $2.25

GHOST AND HORROR STORIES OF AMBROSE BIERCE,
edited by E. F. Bleiler
Morbid, eerie, horrifying tales of possessed poets, shabby aristocrats, revived corpses, and haunted malefactors. Widely acknowledged as the best of their kind between Poe and the moderns, reflecting their author's inner torment and bitter view of life. Includes "Damned Thing," "The Middle Toe of the Right Foot," "The Eyes of the Panther," "Visions of the Night," "Moxon's Master," and over a dozen others. Editor's introduction. xxii + 199pp. 5⅜ x 8½.
20767-6 Paperbound $1.50

THREE GOTHIC NOVELS, *edited by E. F. Bleiler*
Originators of the still popular Gothic novel form, influential in ushering in early 19th-century Romanticism. Horace Walpole's *Castle of Otranto*, William Beckford's *Vathek*, John Polidori's *The Vampyre*, and a *Fragment* by Lord Byron are enjoyable as exciting reading or as documents in the history of English literature. Editor's introduction. xi + 291pp. 5⅜ x 8½.
21232-7 Paperbound $2.00

BEST GHOST STORIES OF LEFANU, *edited by E. F. Bleiler*
Though admired by such critics as V. S. Pritchett, Charles Dickens and Henry James, ghost stories by the Irish novelist Joseph Sheridan LeFanu have never become as widely known as his detective fiction. About half of the 16 stories in this collection have never before been available in America. Collection includes "Carmilla" (perhaps the best vampire story ever written), "The Haunted Baronet," "The Fortunes of Sir Robert Ardagh," and the classic "Green Tea." Editor's introduction. 7 contemporary illustrations. Portrait of LeFanu. xii + 467pp. 5⅜ x 8. 20415-4 Paperbound $2.50

CATALOGUE OF DOVER BOOKS

EASY-TO-DO ENTERTAINMENTS AND DIVERSIONS WITH COINS, CARDS, STRING, PAPER AND MATCHES, *R. M. Abraham*
Over 300 tricks, games and puzzles will provide young readers with absorbing fun. Sections on card games; paper-folding; tricks with coins, matches and pieces of string; games for the agile; toy-making from common household objects; mathematical recreations; and 50 miscellaneous pastimes. Anyone in charge of groups of youngsters, including hard-pressed parents, and in need of suggestions on how to keep children sensibly amused and quietly content will find this book indispensable. Clear, simple text, copious number of delightful line drawings and illustrative diagrams. Originally titled "Winter Nights' Entertainments." Introduction by Lord Baden Powell. 329 illustrations. v + 186pp. 5⅜ x 8½. 20921-0 Paperbound $1.00

AN INTRODUCTION TO CHESS MOVES AND TACTICS SIMPLY EXPLAINED, *Leonard Barden*
Beginner's introduction to the royal game. Names, possible moves of the pieces, definitions of essential terms, how games are won, etc. explained in 30-odd pages. With this background you'll be able to sit right down and play. Balance of book teaches strategy — openings, middle game, typical endgame play, and suggestions for improving your game. A sample game is fully analyzed. True middle-level introduction, teaching you all the essentials without oversimplifying or losing you in a maze of detail. 58 figures. 102pp. 5⅜ x 8½. 21210-6 Paperbound $1.25

LASKER'S MANUAL OF CHESS, *Dr. Emanuel Lasker*
Probably the greatest chess player of modern times, Dr. Emanuel Lasker held the world championship 28 years, independent of passing schools or fashions. This unmatched study of the game, chiefly for intermediate to skilled players, analyzes basic methods, combinations, position play, the aesthetics of chess, dozens of different openings, etc., with constant reference to great modern games. Contains a brilliant exposition of Steinitz's important theories. Introduction by Fred Reinfeld. Tables of Lasker's tournament record. 3 indices. 308 diagrams. 1 photograph. xxx + 349pp. 5⅜ x 8. 20640-8 Paperbound $2.50

COMBINATIONS: THE HEART OF CHESS, *Irving Chernev*
Step-by-step from simple combinations to complex, this book, by a well-known chess writer, shows you the intricacies of pins, counter-pins, knight forks, and smothered mates. Other chapters show alternate lines of play to those taken in actual championship games; boomerang combinations; classic examples of brilliant combination play by Nimzovich, Rubinstein, Tarrasch, Botvinnik, Alekhine and Capablanca. Index. 356 diagrams. ix + 245pp. 5⅜ x 8½. 21744-2 Paperbound $2.00

HOW TO SOLVE CHESS PROBLEMS, *K. S. Howard*
Full of practical suggestions for the fan or the beginner — who knows only the moves of the chessmen. Contains preliminary section and 58 two-move, 46 three-move, and 8 four-move problems composed by 27 outstanding American problem creators in the last 30 years. Explanation of all terms and exhaustive index. "Just what is wanted for the student," Brian Harley. 112 problems, solutions. vi + 171pp. 5⅜ x 8. 20748-X Paperbound $1.50

CATALOGUE OF DOVER BOOKS

SOCIAL THOUGHT FROM LORE TO SCIENCE,
H. E. Barnes and H. Becker
An immense survey of sociological thought and ways of viewing, studying, planning, and reforming society from earliest times to the present. Includes thought on society of preliterate peoples, ancient non-Western cultures, and every great movement in Europe, America, and modern Japan. Analyzes hundreds of great thinkers: Plato, Augustine, Bodin, Vico, Montesquieu, Herder, Comte, Marx, etc. Weighs the contributions of utopians, sophists, fascists and communists; economists, jurists, philosophers, ecclesiastics, and every 19th and 20th century school of scientific sociology, anthropology, and social psychology throughout the world. Combines topical, chronological, and regional approaches, treating the evolution of social thought as a process rather than as a series of mere topics. "Impressive accuracy, competence, and discrimination . . . easily the best single survey," *Nation*. Thoroughly revised, with new material up to 1960. 2 indexes. Over 2200 bibliographical notes. Three volume set. Total of 1586pp. 5⅜ x 8.
20901-6, 20902-4, 20903-2 Three volume set, paperbound $9.00

A HISTORY OF HISTORICAL WRITING, *Harry Elmer Barnes*
Virtually the only adequate survey of the whole course of historical writing in a single volume. Surveys developments from the beginnings of historiography in the ancient Near East and the Classical World, up through the Cold War. Covers major historians in detail, shows interrelationship with cultural background, makes clear individual contributions, evaluates and estimates importance; also enormously rich upon minor authors and thinkers who are usually passed over. Packed with scholarship and learning, clear, easily written. Indispensable to every student of history. Revised and enlarged up to 1961. Index and bibliography. xv + 442pp. 5⅜ x 8½.
20104-X Paperbound $2.75

JOHANN SEBASTIAN BACH, *Philipp Spitta*
The complete and unabridged text of the definitive study of Bach. Written some 70 years ago, it is still unsurpassed for its coverage of nearly all aspects of Bach's life and work. There could hardly be a finer non-technical introduction to Bach's music than the detailed, lucid analyses which Spitta provides for hundreds of individual pieces. 26 solid pages are devoted to the B minor mass, for example, and 30 pages to the glorious St. Matthew Passion. This monumental set also includes a major analysis of the music of the 18th century: Buxtehude, Pachelbel, etc. "Unchallenged as the last word on one of the supreme geniuses of music," John Barkham, *Saturday Review Syndicate*. Total of 1819pp. Heavy cloth binding. 5⅜ x 8.
22278-0, 22279-9 Two volume set, clothbound $15.00

BEETHOVEN AND HIS NINE SYMPHONIES, *George Grove*
In this modern middle-level classic of musicology Grove not only analyzes all nine of Beethoven's symphonies very thoroughly in terms of their musical structure, but also discusses the circumstances under which they were written, Beethoven's stylistic development, and much other background material. This is an extremely rich book, yet very easily followed; it is highly recommended to anyone seriously interested in music. Over 250 musical passages. Index. viii + 407pp. 5⅜ x 8.
20334-4 Paperbound $2.25

CATALOGUE OF DOVER BOOKS

THREE SCIENCE FICTION NOVELS,
John Taine
Acknowledged by many as the best SF writer of the 1920's, Taine (under the name Eric Temple Bell) was also a Professor of Mathematics of considerable renown. Reprinted here are *The Time Stream*, generally considered Taine's best, *The Greatest Game*, a biological-fiction novel, and *The Purple Sapphire*, involving a supercivilization of the past. Taine's stories tie fantastic narratives to frameworks of original and logical scientific concepts. Speculation is often profound on such questions as the nature of time, concept of entropy, cyclical universes, etc. 4 contemporary illustrations. v + 532pp. 5⅜ x 8⅜.
21180-0 Paperbound $2.50

SEVEN SCIENCE FICTION NOVELS,
H. G. Wells
Full unabridged texts of 7 science-fiction novels of the master. Ranging from biology, physics, chemistry, astronomy, to sociology and other studies, Mr. Wells extrapolates whole worlds of strange and intriguing character. "One will have to go far to match this for entertainment, excitement, and sheer pleasure . . ."*New York Times*. Contents: The Time Machine, The Island of Dr. Moreau, The First Men in the Moon, The Invisible Man, The War of the Worlds, The Food of the Gods, In The Days of the Comet. 1015pp. 5⅜ x 8.
20264-X Clothbound $5.00

28 SCIENCE FICTION STORIES OF H. G. WELLS.
Two full, unabridged novels, *Men Like Gods* and *Star Begotten*, plus 26 short stories by the master science-fiction writer of all time! Stories of space, time, invention, exploration, futuristic adventure. Partial contents: *The Country of the Blind, In the Abyss, The Crystal Egg, The Man Who Could Work Miracles, A Story of Days to Come, The Empire of the Ants, The Magic Shop, The Valley of the Spiders, A Story of the Stone Age, Under the Knife, Sea Raiders,* etc. An indispensable collection for the library of anyone interested in science fiction adventure. 928pp. 5⅜ x 8. 20265-8 Clothbound $5.00

THREE MARTIAN NOVELS,
Edgar Rice Burroughs
Complete, unabridged reprinting, in one volume, of Thuvia, Maid of Mars; Chessmen of Mars; The Master Mind of Mars. Hours of science-fiction adventure by a modern master storyteller. Reset in large clear type for easy reading. 16 illustrations by J. Allen St. John. vi + 490pp. 5⅜ x 8½.
20039-6 Paperbound $2.50

AN INTELLECTUAL AND CULTURAL HISTORY OF THE WESTERN WORLD,
Harry Elmer Barnes
Monumental 3-volume survey of intellectual development of Europe from primitive cultures to the present day. Every significant product of human intellect traced through history: art, literature, mathematics, physical sciences, medicine, music, technology, social sciences, religions, jurisprudence, education, etc. Presentation is lucid and specific, analyzing in detail specific discoveries, theories, literary works, and so on. Revised (1965) by recognized scholars in specialized fields under the direction of Prof. Barnes. Revised bibliography. Indexes. 24 illustrations. Total of xxix + 1318pp.
21275-0, 21276-9, 21277-7 Three volume set, paperbound $8.25

CATALOGUE OF DOVER BOOKS

HEAR ME TALKIN' TO YA, *edited by Nat Shapiro and Nat Hentoff*
In their own words, Louis Armstrong, King Oliver, Fletcher Henderson, Bunk Johnson, Bix Beiderbecke, Billy Holiday, Fats Waller, Jelly Roll Morton, Duke Ellington, and many others comment on the origins of jazz in New Orleans and its growth in Chicago's South Side, Kansas City's jam sessions, Depression Harlem, and the modernism of the West Coast schools. Taken from taped conversations, letters, magazine articles, other first-hand sources. Editors' introduction. xvi + 429pp. 5⅜ x 8½.   21726-4 Paperbound $2.00

THE JOURNAL OF HENRY D. THOREAU
A 25-year record by the great American observer and critic, as complete a record of a great man's inner life as is anywhere available. Thoreau's Journals served him as raw material for his formal pieces, as a place where he could develop his ideas, as an outlet for his interests in wild life and plants, in writing as an art, in classics of literature, Walt Whitman and other contemporaries, in politics, slavery, individual's relation to the State, etc. The Journals present a portrait of a remarkable man, and are an observant social history. Unabridged republication of 1906 edition, Bradford Torrey and Francis H. Allen, editors. Illustrations. Total of 1888pp. 8⅜ x 12¼.
20312-3, 20313-1 Two volume set, clothbound $30.00

A SHAKESPEARIAN GRAMMAR, *E. A. Abbott*
Basic reference to Shakespeare and his contemporaries, explaining through thousands of quotations from Shakespeare, Jonson, Beaumont and Fletcher, North's *Plutarch* and other sources the grammatical usage differing from the modern. First published in 1870 and written by a scholar who spent much of his life isolating principles of Elizabethan language, the book is unlikely ever to be superseded. Indexes. xxiv + 511pp. 5⅜ x 8½. 21582-2 Paperbound $3.00

FOLK-LORE OF SHAKESPEARE, *T. F. Thistelton Dyer*
Classic study, drawing from Shakespeare a large body of references to supernatural beliefs, terminology of falconry and hunting, games and sports, good luck charms, marriage customs, folk medicines, superstitions about plants, animals, birds, argot of the underworld, sexual slang of London, proverbs, drinking customs, weather lore, and much else. From full compilation comes a mirror of the 17th-century popular mind. Index. ix + 526pp. 5⅜ x 8½.
21614-4 Paperbound $2.75

THE NEW VARIORUM SHAKESPEARE, *edited by H. H. Furness*
By far the richest editions of the plays ever produced in any country or language. Each volume contains complete text (usually First Folio) of the play, all variants in Quarto and other Folio texts, editorial changes by every major editor to Furness's own time (1900), footnotes to obscure references or language, extensive quotes from literature of Shakespearian criticism, essays on plot sources (often reprinting sources in full), and much more.

HAMLET, *edited by H. H. Furness*
Total of xxvi + 905pp. 5⅜ x 8½.
21004-9, 21005-7 Two volume set, paperbound $5.25

TWELFTH NIGHT, *edited by H. H. Furness*
Index. xxii + 434pp. 5⅜ x 8½.   21189-4 Paperbound $2.75

CATALOGUE OF DOVER BOOKS

LA BOHEME BY GIACOMO PUCCINI,
translated and introduced by Ellen H. Bleiler
Complete handbook for the operagoer, with everything needed for full enjoyment except the musical score itself. Complete Italian libretto, with new, modern English line-by-line translation—the only libretto printing all repeats; biography of Puccini; the librettists; background to the opera, Murger's La Boheme, etc.; circumstances of composition and performances; plot summary; and pictorial section of 73 illustrations showing Puccini, famous singers and performances, etc. Large clear type for easy reading. 124pp. 5⅜ x 8½.
20404-9 Paperbound $1.25

ANTONIO STRADIVARI: HIS LIFE AND WORK (1644-1737),
W. Henry Hill, Arthur F. Hill, and Alfred E. Hill
Still the only book that really delves into life and art of the incomparable Italian craftsman, maker of the finest musical instruments in the world today. The authors, expert violin-makers themselves, discuss Stradivari's ancestry, his construction and finishing techniques, distinguished characteristics of many of his instruments and their locations. Included, too, is story of introduction of his instruments into France, England, first revelation of their supreme merit, and information on his labels, number of instruments made, prices, mystery of ingredients of his varnish, tone of pre-1684 Stradivari violin and changes between 1684 and 1690. An extremely interesting, informative account for all music lovers, from craftsman to concert-goer. Republication of original (1902) edition. New introduction by Sydney Beck, Head of Rare Book and Manuscript Collections, Music Division, New York Public Library. Analytical index by Rembert Wurlitzer. Appendixes. 68 illustrations. 30 full-page plates. 4 in color. xxvi + 315pp. 5⅜ x 8½.
20425-1 Paperbound $2.25

MUSICAL AUTOGRAPHS FROM MONTEVERDI TO HINDEMITH,
Emanuel Winternitz
For beauty, for intrinsic interest, for perspective on the composer's personality, for subtleties of phrasing, shading, emphasis indicated in the autograph but suppressed in the printed score, the mss. of musical composition are fascinating documents which repay close study in many different ways. This 2-volume work reprints facsimiles of mss. by virtually every major composer, and many minor figures—196 examples in all. A full text points out what can be learned from mss., analyzes each sample. Index. Bibliography. 18 figures. 196 plates. Total of 170pp. of text. 7⅞ x 10¾.
21312-9, 21313-7 Two volume set, paperbound $5.00

J. S. BACH,
Albert Schweitzer
One of the few great full-length studies of Bach's life and work, and the study upon which Schweitzer's renown as a musicologist rests. On first appearance (1911), revolutionized Bach performance. The only writer on Bach to be musicologist, performing musician, and student of history, theology and philosophy, Schweitzer contributes particularly full sections on history of German Protestant church music, theories on motivic pictorial representations in vocal music, and practical suggestions for performance. Translated by Ernest Newman. Indexes. 5 illustrations. 650 musical examples. Total of xix + 928pp. 5⅜ x 8½. 21631-4, 21632-2 Two volume set, paperbound $4.50

CATALOGUE OF DOVER BOOKS

THE METHODS OF ETHICS, *Henry Sidgwick*
Propounding no organized system of its own, study subjects every major methodological approach to ethics to rigorous, objective analysis. Study discusses and relates ethical thought of Plato, Aristotle, Bentham, Clarke, Butler, Hobbes, Hume, Mill, Spencer, Kant, and dozens of others. Sidgwick retains conclusions from each system which follow from ethical premises, rejecting the faulty. Considered by many in the field to be among the most important treatises on ethical philosophy. Appendix. Index. xlvii + 528pp. 5⅜ x 8½.
21608-X Paperbound $2.50

TEUTONIC MYTHOLOGY, *Jakob Grimm*
A milestone in Western culture; the work which established on a modern basis the study of history of religions and comparative religions. 4-volume work assembles and interprets everything available on religious and folkloristic beliefs of Germanic people (including Scandinavians, Anglo-Saxons, etc.). Assembling material from such sources as Tacitus, surviving Old Norse and Icelandic texts, archeological remains, folktales, surviving superstitions, comparative traditions, linguistic analysis, etc. Grimm explores pagan deities, heroes, folklore of nature, religious practices, and every other area of pagan German belief. To this day, the unrivaled, definitive, exhaustive study. Translated by J. S. Stallybrass from 4th (1883) German edition. Indexes. Total of lxxvii + 1887pp. 5⅜ x 8½.
21602-0, 21603-9, 21604-7, 21605-5 Four volume set, paperbound $11.00

THE I CHING, *translated by James Legge*
Called "The Book of Changes" in English, this is one of the Five Classics edited by Confucius, basic and central to Chinese thought. Explains perhaps the most complex system of divination known, founded on the theory that all things happening at any one time have characteristic features which can be isolated and related. Significant in Oriental studies, in history of religions and philosophy, and also to Jungian psychoanalysis and other areas of modern European thought. Index. Appendixes. 6 plates. xxi + 448pp. 5⅜ x 8½.
21062-6 Paperbound $2.75

HISTORY OF ANCIENT PHILOSOPHY, *W. Windelband*
One of the clearest, most accurate comprehensive surveys of Greek and Roman philosophy. Discusses ancient philosophy in general, intellectual life in Greece in the 7th and 6th centuries B.C., Thales, Anaximander, Anaximenes, Heraclitus, the Eleatics, Empedocles, Anaxagoras, Leucippus, the Pythagoreans, the Sophists, Socrates, Democritus (20 pages), Plato (50 pages), Aristotle (70 pages), the Peripatetics, Stoics, Epicureans, Sceptics, Neo-platonists, Christian Apologists, etc. 2nd German edition translated by H. E. Cushman. xv + 393pp. 5⅜ x 8.
20357-3 Paperbound $2.25

THE PALACE OF PLEASURE, *William Painter*
Elizabethan versions of Italian and French novels from *The Decameron*, Cinthio, Straparola, Queen Margaret of Navarre, and other continental sources — the very work that provided Shakespeare and dozens of his contemporaries with many of their plots and sub-plots and, therefore, justly considered one of the most influential books in all English literature. It is also a book that any reader will still enjoy. Total of cviii + 1,224pp.
21691-8, 21692-6, 21693-4 Three volume set, paperbound $6.75

CATALOGUE OF DOVER

The Wonderful Wizard of Oz, L. F. Baum

All the original W. W. Denslow illustrations in full color—as much a part of "The Wizard" as Tenniel's drawings are of "Alice in Wonderland." "The Wizard" is still America's best-loved fairy tale, in which, as the author expresses it, "The wonderment and joy are retained and the heartaches and nightmares left out." Now today's young readers can enjoy every word and wonderful picture of the original book. New introduction by Martin Gardner. A Baum bibliography. 23 full-page color plates. viii + 268pp. 5⅜ x 8.

20691-2 Paperbound $1.95

The Marvelous Land of Oz, L. F. Baum

This is the equally enchanting sequel to the "Wizard," continuing the adventures of the Scarecrow and the Tin Woodman. The hero this time is a little boy named Tip, and all the delightful Oz magic is still present. This is the Oz book with the Animated Saw-Horse, the Woggle-Bug, and Jack Pumpkinhead. All the original John R. Neill illustrations, 10 in full color. 287pp. 5⅜ x 8.

20692-0 Paperbound $1.75

Alice's Adventures Under Ground, Lewis Carroll

The original *Alice in Wonderland*, hand-lettered and illustrated by Carroll himself, and originally presented as a Christmas gift to a child-friend. Adults as well as children will enjoy this charming volume, reproduced faithfully in this Dover edition. While the story is essentially the same, there are slight changes, and Carroll's spritely drawings present an intriguing alternative to the famous Tenniel illustrations. One of the most popular books in Dover's catalogue. Introduction by Martin Gardner. 38 illustrations. 128pp. 5⅜ x 8½.

21482-6 Paperbound $1.00

The Nursery "Alice," Lewis Carroll

While most of us consider *Alice in Wonderland* a story for children of all ages, Carroll himself felt it was beyond younger children. He therefore provided this simplified version, illustrated with the famous Tenniel drawings enlarged and colored in delicate tints, for children aged "from Nought to Five." Dover's edition of this now rare classic is a faithful copy of the 1889 printing, including 20 illustrations by Tenniel, and front and back covers reproduced in full color. Introduction by Martin Gardner. xxiii + 67pp. 6⅛ x 9¼.

21610-1 Paperbound $1.75

The Story of King Arthur and His Knights, Howard Pyle

A fast-paced, exciting retelling of the best known Arthurian legends for young readers by one of America's best story tellers and illustrators. The sword Excalibur, wooing of Guinevere, Merlin and his downfall, adventures of Sir Pellias and Gawaine, and others. The pen and ink illustrations are vividly imagined and wonderfully drawn. 41 illustrations. xviii + 313pp. 6⅛ x 9¼.

21445-1 Paperbound $2.00

Prices subject to change without notice.

Available at your book dealer or write for free catalogue to Dept. Adsci, Dover Publications, Inc., 180 Varick St., N.Y., N.Y. 10014. Dover publishes more than 150 books each year on science, elementary and advanced mathematics, biology, music, art, literary history, social sciences and other areas.

DATE DUE

MR 8
AP 16

MONTGOMERY COLLEGE LIBRARIES
tako, circ   PN 2285.K45 1970
The mad Booth
0 0000 00104745 5

2 7 3 1 9 1 8 6
P N 2 2 8 5 . K 4 5   1 9 7 0
K I M M E L   S T A N L E Y   P R E S
M A D   B O O T H S   O F
M A R Y L A N D

MONTGOMERY COLLEGE LIBRARY
TAKOMA PARK, MARYLAND